POCKET

PCRef

by

Thomas J. Glover
Millie M. Young

Seventh Edition

Sequoia Publishing, Inc.
Littleton, Colorado   U.S.A.

This PCRef belongs to:
NAME:
HOME ADDRESS:
HOME PHONE:
WORK PHONE:
BUSINESS ADDRESS:
In case of accident or serious illness, please notify: Name: Phone Number:

ISBN 1-885071-13-2

Products by Sequoia Publishing, Inc.

Pocket Ref, 2nd Edition
    by Thomas J. Glover
    1989-1997, 544p, ISBN 1-885071-00-0

DeskRef, 2nd Edition
    by Thomas J. Glover
    6"x 9" version of *Pocket Ref*
    1995-1997, 544p, ISBN 0-885071-06-X

MegaRef, Version 2
    IBM PC and compatibles software version of
    the book *Pocket Ref.*

Pocket PC DIRectory, 1998 Edition
    by Thomas J. Glover
    November 1997, ISBN 1-885071-14-0

TechRef, 2nd Edition
    by Thomas J. Glover & Millie M. Young
    5"x 7.5" combined version of *Pocket PCRef*
    and the *Pocket PC DIRectory*
    November 1997, ISBN 1-885071-12-4

Send your Name and Address to:

> Mailing List Group
> Sequoia Publishing, Inc
> P.O. Box 620820
> Littleton, CO   80162-0820

World Wide Web Site
http://www.sequoiapub.com/

Preface

Sequoia Publishing, Inc. has made a serious effort to provide accurate information in this book. However, the probability exists that there are errors and misprints. Sequoia Publishing, Inc. and the authors do not represent the information as being exact and make no warranty of any kind with regard to the content of Pocket PCRef. Sequoia Publishing, Inc. and the authors shall not be held liable for any errors contained in Pocket PCRef or for incidental or consequential damages in connection with any use of the material herein.

The publishers would appreciate being notified of any errors, omissions, or misprints which may occur in this book. *__Your suggestions for future editions would also be greatly appreciated.__*

The information in this manual was collected from numerous sources and if not properly acknowledged, Sequoia Publishing, Inc. and the authors would like to express their appreciation for those contributions. See page 6 for specific trade name, trade mark, and credit information.

Sequoia Publishing, Inc.
Department 101
P.O. Box 620820
Littleton, Colorado 80162–0820
(303) 972-4167
Web address http://www.sequoiapub.com/

Acknowledgements

POCKET PCRef would not have been possible without the efforts and endless patience of our families and many co-workers. Our deepest love and thanks to all of you.

Our deepest gratitude to Dave Derby, co-owner of Sequoia Publishing, for his technical editing, suggestions, and effort in tracking down the true meaning of Keyboard Scan Codes (a task no less difficult than tracking down the true meaning of life!).

Many thanks to Richard Young for his relentless pursuit of the perfect DOS Chapter. (Richard knows the true meaning of life and he has assured us that it has nothing to do with DOS!). Thanks to Liz Young, Trish Glover, Laurie Vendryes, Bob and Carrie Olson and Becky Tennessen for their help in compiling and verifying the Phone Book. Many thanks to Donna Baumgarten for her efforts in the never ending task of updating the hard and floppy drive sections.

Thank you never seems to be enough when you're saying it to the ones you care about the most! My family, Mary, Trish and Carrie, have supported and loved me through the whole monumental process of writing and publishing a book . . . Thank you and I love you. A very special thank you to my dear friend and co-author Millie, who has taught me the true meanings of courage, dedication and perseverance. *Thomas*

It is amazing to me, what one person can accomplish when that accomplishment is based on the faith another person has in you. I share only in a small part of this book, the DOS Commands section, and though that may seem insignificant to some, it is a major accomplishment to this novice in the computer world. To the man I love, my gentle and patient husband Richard and our understanding offspring, Elizabeth, Christopher, and Stephanie, none of this would have been possible without you. And, especially to my mentor and friend Thomas, who doesn't know the meaning of limitations. To all of you who have had great faith in me and have allowed *this humble sparrow to soar as an eagle*, I give my sincerest thanks. *Millie*

REFERENCES, TRADE NAMES and TRADE MARKS

The following are Registered Trademarks or Trade names:
ASCII – American Standard Code for Information Interchange
Commodore 64 – Commodore Computers
Diablo 630 – Xerox Corporation
Epson, FX–80 – Epson America Inc
Hayes – Hayes Microcomputer Products, Inc.
HP, HP-IB, Hewlett-Packard, Laserjet – Hewlett–Packard Company
IBM , AT, XT, PC, PS/2, PC Convertible, PC Jr., PC-DOS - International Business Machines Corporation
ISO – International Organization for Standardization
Macintosh, Apple IIc, Apple – Apple Computer, Inc.
Microsoft, MS–DOS, and Microsoft Windows – Microsoft Corporation
NEC, Pinwriter – NEC Corporation

The following books were used as references during the writing of Pocket PCRef. (They are all excellent references and should be added to any good reference library):

DOS Power Users Guide by Kris Jamsa
    McGraw Hill, 1988, ISBN 0-07-881310-7
Hard Disk Handbook by Alfred Glossbrenner and Nick Anis
    Osborne McGraw Hill, 1989, ISBN 0-07-881604-1
The Hard Disk Technical Guide by Douglas T. Anderson
    PCS Publications, 1991
The Micro House Hard Drive Encyclopedia, Edited by Douglas
    T. Anderson, Micro House, 1992, 1993, 1994, 1995
Inside the IBM PC by Peter Norton
    Brady Books, 1986, ISBN0-89303-583-1
PC Magazine DOS Power Tools by Paul Somerson
    Bantam Computer Books, 1988, ISBN 0-553-34526-5
Que's Computer User's Dictionary by Bryan Pfaffenberger
    Que Corporation, 1990, ISBN 0-88022-540-8
Que's Upgrading & Repairing PCs by Scott Mueller
    Que Corporation, 1994, ISBN 1-56529-736-9
MSDOS User's Guide and Reference, Ver 2.11, 3.0, 3.1, 3.2, 3.3,
    4.01, 5.0, 6.0, & 6.2 by Microsoft Corporation.
Pocket Ref by Thomas J. Glover
    Sequoia Publishing, Inc, 1989, ISBN 0-9622359-0-3
Supercharging MSDOS by Van Wolverton
    Microsoft Press, 1986, ISBN 0-914845-95-0
The Winn Rosch Hardware Bible by Winn L. Rosch
    Brady Books, 1989, ISBN 0-13-160979-3
PocketPOST by Data Depot
    Clearwater, Florida (813) 446-3402
PC DOS Command Reference and Error Messages, Ver.6.0 and
    6.3, by IBM Corporation.
Microsoft Windows User's Guide, Ver. 3.1, by Microsoft Corp.

NOTE: There are many more references, most of which are referenced on specific pages in Pocket PCRef. If we have omitted a reference, we apologize, please let us know and we will include it in the next printing of Pocket PCRef. See page 430 for additional hard drive references.

TABLE OF CONTENTS

NOTE: The ***Printer Control Codes*** chapter will no longer be included in Pocket PCRef. It will continue to be included in Sequoias publication TechRef.

NOTES

Chapter 1

ASCII and Numerics

COMPUTER ASCII CODES

The following ASCII (**A**merican **S**tandard **C**ode for Information Interchange) tables are used by most of the microcomputer industry. The codes occur in two sets: the "low–bit" set, from Dec 0 to Dec 127, and the "high–bit" set, from Dec 128 to Dec 255. The "low–bit" set is standard for almost all microcomputers but the "high–bit" set varies between the different computer brands. For instance, in the case of Apple computers and Epson printers, the "high–bit" set repeats the "low–bit" set except that the alphameric characters are italic. In the case of IBM and many other MSDOS systems, the "high–bit" set is composed of foreign language and box drawing characters and mathematic symbols.

Hex	Dec	Description	Abbr	Character	Control
00	0	Null	Null		Control @
01	1	Start Heading	SOH	☺	Control A
02	2	Start of Text	STX	☻	Control B
03	3	End of Text	ETX	♥	Control C
04	4	End Transmit	EOT	♦	Control D
05	5	Enquiry	ENQ	♣	Control E
06	6	Acknowledge	ACK	♠	Control F
07	7	Beep	BEL	•	Control G
08	8	Back space	BS	◘	Control H
09	9	Horizontal Tab	HT	○	Control I
0A	10	Line Feed	LF	◙	Control J
0B	11	Vertical Tab	VT	♂	Control K
0C	12	Form Feed	FF	♀	Control L
0D	13	Carriage Ret.	CR	♪	Control M
0E	14	Shift Out	SO	♫	Control N
0F	15	Shift In	SI	☼	Control O
10	16	Device Link Esc	DLE	►	Control P
11	17	Dev Cont 1 X-ON	DC1	◄	Control Q
12	18	Dev Control 2	DC2	↕	Control R
13	19	Dev Cont 3 X-OFF	DC3	‼	Control S
14	20	Dev Control 4	DC4	¶	Control T
15	21	Negative Ack	NAK	§	Control U
16	22	Synchronous Idle	SYN	▬	Control V
17	23	End Trans Block	ETB	↨	Control W
18	24	Cancel	CAN	↑	Control X
19	25	End Medium	EM	↓	Control Y
1A	26	Substitute	SUB	→	Control Z
1B	27	Escape	ESC	←	Control [

COMPUTER ASCII CODES

Hex	Dec	Description	Abbr	Character	Control
1C	28	Cursor Right	FS	└	Control \
1D	29	Cursor Left	GS	↔	Control]
1E	30	Cursor Up	RS	▲	Control ^
1F	31	Cursor Down	US	▼	Control _

Hex	Dec	Character	Description
20	32		Space (SP)
21	33	!	Exclamation Point
22	34	"	Double Quote
23	35	#	Number sign
24	36	$	Dollar sign
25	37	%	Percent
26	38	&	Ampersand
27	39	'	Apostrophe
28	40	(	Left parenthesis
29	41	)	Right parenthesis
2A	42	*	Asterisk
2B	43	+	Plus sign
2C	44	,	Comma
2D	45	–	Minus sign
2E	46	.	Period
2F	47	/	Right or Front slash
30	48	0	Zero
31	49	1	One
32	50	2	Two
33	51	3	Three
34	52	4	Four
35	53	5	Five
36	54	6	Six
37	55	7	Seven
38	56	8	Eight
39	57	9	Nine
3A	58	:	Colon
3B	59	;	Semicolon
3C	60	<	Less than
3D	61	=	Equal sign
3E	62	>	Greater than
3F	63	?	Question mark
40	64	@	"at" symbol

COMPUTER ASCII CODES

Hex	Dec	Character	Description
41	65	A	Uppercase A
42	66	B	Uppercase B
43	67	C	Uppercase C
44	68	D	Uppercase D
45	69	E	Uppercase E
46	70	F	Uppercase F
47	71	G	Uppercase G
48	72	H	Uppercase H
49	73	I	Uppercase I
4A	74	J	Uppercase J
4B	75	K	Uppercase K
4C	76	L	Uppercase L
4D	77	M	Uppercase M
4E	78	N	Uppercase N
4F	79	O	Uppercase O
50	80	P	Uppercase P
51	81	Q	Uppercase Q
52	82	R	Uppercase R
53	83	S	Uppercase S
54	84	T	Uppercase T
55	85	U	Uppercase U
56	86	V	Uppercase V
57	87	W	Uppercase W
58	88	X	Uppercase X
59	89	Y	Uppercase Y
5A	90	Z	Uppercase Z
5B	91	[	Left bracket
5C	92	\	Left or Back Slash
5D	93	]	Right bracket
5E	94	^	Caret
5F	95	_	Underline
60	96	`	Accent
61	97	a	Lowercase a
62	98	b	Lowercase b
63	99	c	Lowercase c
64	100	d	Lowercase d
65	101	e	Lowercase e
66	102	f	Lowercase f
67	103	g	Lowercase g

COMPUTER ASCII CODES

Hex	Dec	Standard Character	Description
68	104	h	Lowercase h
69	105	i	Lowercase i
6A	106	j	Lowercase j
6B	107	k	Lowercase k
6C	108	l	Lowercase l
6D	109	m	Lowercase m
6E	110	n	Lowercase n
6F	111	o	Lowercase o
70	112	p	Lowercase p
71	113	q	Lowercase q
72	114	r	Lowercase r
73	115	s	Lowercase s
74	116	t	Lowercase t
75	117	u	Lowercase u
76	118	v	Lowercase v
77	119	w	Lowercase w
78	120	x	Lowercase x
79	121	y	Lowercase y
7A	122	z	Lowercase z
7B	123	{	Left brace
7C	124	l	Vertical line
7D	125	}	Right brace
7E	126	~	Tilde
7F	127	DEL	Delete

Hex	Dec	Standard Character	IBM Set	Standard Description
80	128	Null	Ç	Null
81	129	SOH	ü	Start Heading
82	130	STX	é	Start of Text
83	131	ETX	â	End of Text
84	132	EOT	ä	End Transmit
85	133	ENQ	à	Enquiry
86	134	ACK	å	Acknowledge
87	135	BEL	ç	Beep
88	136	BS	ê	Back Space
89	137	HT	ë	Horiz Tab
8A	138	LF	è	Line Feed

ASCII and Numerics   13

COMPUTER ASCII CODES

Hex	Dec	Standard Character	IBM Set	Standard Description
8B	139	VT	ï	Vertical Tab
8C	140	FF	î	Form Feed
8D	141	CR	ì	Carriage Return
8E	142	SO	Ä	Shift Out
8F	143	SI	Å	Shift In
90	144	DLE	É	Device Link Esc
91	145	DC1	æ	Device Cont 1 X–ON
92	146	DC2	Æ	Device Control 2
93	147	DC3	ô	Device Cont 3 X–OFF
94	148	DC4	ö	Device Control 4
95	149	NAK	ò	Negative Ack
96	150	SYN	û	Synchronous Idle
97	151	ETB	ù	End Transmit Block
98	152	CAN	ÿ	Cancel
99	153	EM	Ö	End Medium
9A	154	SUB	Ü	Substitute
9B	155	ESC	¢	Escape
9C	156	FS	£	Cursor Right
9D	157	GS	¥	Cursor Left
9E	158	RS	Pt	Cursor Up
9F	159	US	ƒ	Cursor Down
A0	160	Space	á	Space
A1	161	!	í	Italic Exclamation point
A2	162	"	ó	Italic Double quote
A3	163	#	ú	Italic Number sign
A4	164	$	ñ	Italic Dollar sign
A5	165	%	Ñ	Italic Percent
A6	166	&	ª	Italic Ampersand
A7	167	'	º	Italic Apostrophe
A8	168	(	¿	Italic Left parenthesis
A9	169	)	⌐	Italic Right parenthesis
AA	170	*	¬	Italic asterisk
AB	171	+	½	Italic plus sign
AC	172	,	¼	Italic comma
AD	173	–	¡	Italic minus sign
AE	174	.	«	Italic period
AF	175	/	»	Italic right slash
B0	176	0		Italic Zero
B1	177	1		Italic One

COMPUTER ASCII CODES

Hex	Dec	Standard Character	IBM Set	Standard Description
B2	178	2		Italic Two
B3	179	3			Italic Three
B4	180	4	┤	Italic Four
B5	181	5	╡	Italic Five
B6	182	6	╢	Italic Six
B7	183	7	╖	Italic Seven
B8	184	8	╕	Italic Eight
B9	185	9	╣	Italic Nine
BA	186	:	║	Italic colon
BB	187	;	╗	Italic semicolon
BC	188	<	╝	Italic less than
BD	189	=	╜	Italic equal
BE	190	>	╛	Italic greater than
BF	191	?	┐	Italic question mark
C0	192	@	└	Italic "at" symbol
C1	193	A	┴	Italic A
C2	194	B	┬	Italic B
C3	195	C	├	Italic C
C4	196	D	─	Italic D
C5	197	E	┼	Italic E
C6	198	F	╞	Italic F
C7	199	G	╟	Italic G
C8	200	H	╚	Italic H
C9	201	I	╔	Italic I
CA	202	J	╩	Italic J
CB	203	K	╦	Italic K
CC	204	L	╠	Italic L
CD	205	M	═	Italic M
CE	206	N	╬	Italic N
CF	207	O	╧	Italic O
D0	208	P	╨	Italic P
D1	209	Q	╤	Italic Q
D2	210	R	╥	Italic R
D3	211	S	╙	Italic S
D4	212	T	╘	Italic T
D5	213	U	╒	Italic U
D6	214	V	╓	Italic V
D7	215	W	╫	Italic W
D8	216	X	╪	Italic X

COMPUTER ASCII CODES

Hex	Dec	Standard Character	IBM Set	Description
D9	217	Y	⌐	Italic Y
DA	218	Z		Italic Z
DB	219	$[$	■ ⌐	Italic left bracket
DC	220	\	■	Italic left or back slash
DD	221	$]$	▌	Italic right bracket
DE	222	^	▐	Italic caret
DF	223	'	■	Italic underline
E0	224	,	α	Italic accent / alpha
E1	225	a	β	Italic a / beta
E2	226	b	Γ	Italic b / gamma
E3	227	c	π	Italic c / pi
E4	228	d	Σ	Italic d / sigma
E5	229	e	σ	Italic e / sigma
E6	230	f	μ	Italic f / mu
E7	231	g	γ	Italic g / gamma
E8	232	h	Φ	Italic h / phi
E9	233	i	θ	Italic i / theta
EA	234	j	Ω	Italic j / omega
EB	235	k	δ	Italic k / delta
EC	236	l	∞	Italic l / infinity
ED	237	m	$\varnothing$	Italic m / slashed zero
EE	238	n	$\in$	Italic n
EF	239	o	$\cap$	Italic o
F0	240	p	$\equiv$	Italic p
F1	241	q	$\pm$	Italic q
F2	242	r	$\geq$	Italic r
F3	243	s	$\leq$	Italic s
F4	244	t	$\int$	Italic t
F5	245	u	$\int$	Italic u
F6	246	v	$\div$	Italic v
F7	247	w	$\approx$	Italic w
F8	248	x	$\circ$	Italic x
F9	249	y	$\bullet$	Italic y
FA	250	z	$\cdot$	Italic z
FB	251	$\{$	$\sqrt{}$	Italic left bracket
FC	252	$|$	^{n}	Italic vertical line
FD	253	$\}$	$_2$	Italic right bracket
FE	254	~	■	Italic tilde
FF	255	Blank	Blank	Blank

NUMERIC PREFIXES

Prefix	Abbreviation	Pronounce	Multiplier
yocto	y	yok-to	10^{-24}
zepto	z	zep-to	10^{-21}
atto	a	at-to	10^{-18}
femto	f	fem-to	10^{-15}
pico	p	pe-ko	10^{-12}
nano	n	nan-o	10^{-9}
micro	μ	mi-kro	10^{-6}
milli	m	mil-l	10^{-3}
centi	c	sent-ti	10^{-2}
deci	d	des-l	10^{-1}
deka	da	dek-a	10^{1}
hecto	h	hek-to	10^{2}
kilo	k	kil-o	10^{3}
mega	M	meg-a	10^{6}
giga	G	gig-a	10^{9}
tera	T	ter-a	10^{12}
peta	P	pe-ta	10^{15}
exa	E	ex-a	10^{18}
zetta	Z	za-ta	10^{21}
yotta	Y	yot-ta	10^{24}
		octillion	10^{27}
		nonillion	10^{30}

MEGABYTES AND KILOBYTES

1 kilobyte = 2^{10} bytes = exactly 1,024 bytes
1 megabyte = 2^{20} bytes = exactly 1,048,576 bytes
1 gigabyte = 2^{30} bytes = 1 billion bytes
1 terabyte = 2^{40} bytes = 1 trillion bytes
1 petabyte = 2^{50} bytes = 1 quadrillion bytes
1 byte = 8 bits (bit is short for binary digit)
8 bit computers (such as the 8088)
    move data in 1 byte chunks
16 bit computers (such as the 80286 and 80386SX)
    move data in 2 byte chunks
32 bit computers (80386DX,80486,Pentium, Power PC)
    move data in 4 byte chunks
64 bit computers (such as the Alpha AXP)
    move data in 8 byte chunks

POWERS OF 2

n	2^n	Hexadecimal
0	1	1
1	2	2
2	4	4
3	8	8
4	16	10
5	32	20
6	64	40
7	128	80
8	256	100
9	512	200
10	1024	400
11	2048	800
12	4096	1000
13	8192	2000
14	16384	4000
15	32768	8000
16	65536	10000
17	131072	20000
18	262144	40000
19	524288	80000
20	1048576	100000
21	2097152	200000
22	4194304	400000
23	8388608	800000
24	16777216	1000000
25	33554432	2000000
26	67108864	4000000
27	134217728	8000000
28	268435456	10000000
29	536870912	20000000
30	1073741824	40000000
31	2147483648	80000000
32	4294967296	100000000

HEX to DECIMAL CONVERSION

↓Hex→	8	9	A	B	C	D	E	F
94	2376	2377	2378	2379	2380	2381	2382	2383
95	2392	2393	2394	2395	2396	2397	2398	2399
96	2408	2409	2410	2411	2412	2413	2414	2415
97	2424	2425	2426	2427	2428	2429	2430	2431
98	2440	2441	2442	2443	2444	2445	2446	2447
99	2456	2457	2458	2459	2460	2461	2462	2463
9A	2472	2473	2474	2475	2476	2477	2478	2479
9B	2488	2489	2490	2491	2492	2493	2494	2495
9C	2504	2505	2506	2507	2508	2509	2510	2511
9D	2520	2521	2522	2523	2524	2525	2526	2527
9E	2536	2537	2538	2539	2540	2541	2542	2543
9F	2552	2553	2554	2555	2556	2557	2558	2559
A0	2568	2569	2570	2571	2572	2573	2574	2575
A1	2584	2585	2586	2587	2588	2589	2590	2591
A2	2600	2601	2602	2603	2604	2605	2606	2607
A3	2616	2617	2618	2619	2620	2621	2622	2623
A4	2632	2633	2634	2635	2636	2637	2638	2639
A5	2648	2649	2650	2651	2652	2653	2654	2655
A6	2664	2665	2666	2667	2668	2669	2670	2671
A7	2680	2681	2682	2683	2684	2685	2686	2687
A8	2696	2697	2698	2699	2700	2701	2702	2703
A9	2712	2713	2714	2715	2716	2717	2718	2719
AA	2728	2729	2730	2731	2732	2733	2734	2735
AB	2744	2745	2746	2747	2748	2749	2750	2751
AC	2760	2761	2762	2763	2764	2765	2766	2767
AD	2776	2777	2778	2779	2780	2781	2782	2783
AE	2792	2793	2794	2795	2796	2797	2798	2799
AF	2808	2809	2810	2811	2812	2813	2814	2815
B0	2824	2825	2826	2827	2828	2829	2830	2831
B1	2840	2841	2842	2843	2844	2845	2846	2847
B2	2856	2857	2858	2859	2860	2861	2862	2863
B3	2872	2873	2874	2875	2876	2877	2878	2879
B4	2888	2889	2890	2891	2892	2893	2894	2895
B5	2904	2905	2906	2907	2908	2909	2910	2911
B6	2920	2921	2922	2923	2924	2925	2926	2927
B7	2936	2937	2938	2939	2940	2941	2942	2943
B8	2952	2953	2954	2955	2956	2957	2958	2959
B9	2968	2969	2970	2971	2972	2973	2974	2975
BA	2984	2985	2986	2987	2988	2989	2990	2991
BB	3000	3001	3002	3003	3004	3005	3006	3007
BC	3016	3017	3018	3019	3020	3021	3022	3023
BD	3032	3033	3034	3035	3036	3037	3038	3039
BE	3048	3049	3050	3051	3052	3053	3054	3055
BF	3064	3065	3066	3067	3068	3069	3070	3071
C0	3080	3081	3082	3083	3084	3085	3086	3087
C1	3096	3097	3098	3099	3100	3101	3102	3103
C2	3112	3113	3114	3115	3116	3117	3118	3119
C3	3128	3129	3130	3131	3132	3133	3134	3135
C4	3144	3145	3146	3147	3148	3149	3150	3151
C5	3160	3161	3162	3163	3164	3165	3166	3167
C6	3176	3177	3178	3179	3180	3181	3182	3183
C7	3192	3193	3194	3195	3196	3197	3198	3199
C8	3208	3209	3210	3211	3212	3213	3214	3215
C9	3224	3225	3226	3227	3228	3229	3230	3231
CA	3240	3241	3242	3243	3244	3245	3246	3247

HEX to DECIMAL CONVERSION

↓ Hex→0	1	2	3	4	5	6	7
CB	3248	3249	3250	3251	3252	3253	3254	3255
CC	3264	3265	3266	3267	3268	3269	3270	3271
CD	3280	3281	3282	3283	3284	3285	3286	3287
CE	3296	3297	3298	3299	3300	3301	3302	3303
CF	3312	3313	3314	3315	3316	3317	3318	3319
D0	3328	3329	3330	3331	3332	3333	3334	3335
D1	3344	3345	3346	3347	3348	3349	3350	3351
D2	3360	3361	3362	3363	3364	3365	3366	3367
D3	3376	3377	3378	3379	3380	3381	3382	3383
D4	3392	3393	3394	3395	3396	3397	3398	3399
D5	3408	3409	3410	3411	3412	3413	3414	3415
D6	3424	3425	3426	3427	3428	3429	3430	3431
D7	3440	3441	3442	3443	3444	3445	3446	3447
D8	3456	3457	3458	3459	3460	3461	3462	3463
D9	3472	3473	3474	3475	3476	3477	3478	3479
DA	3488	3489	3490	3491	3492	3493	3494	3495
DB	3504	3505	3506	3507	3508	3509	3510	3511
DC	3520	3521	3522	3523	3524	3525	3526	3527
DD	3536	3537	3538	3539	3540	3541	3542	3543
DE	3552	3553	3554	3555	3556	3557	3558	3559
DF	3568	3569	3570	3571	3572	3573	3574	3575
E0	3584	3585	3586	3587	3588	3589	3590	3591
E1	3600	3601	3602	3603	3604	3605	3606	3607
E2	3616	3617	3618	3619	3620	3621	3622	3623
E3	3632	3633	3634	3635	3636	3637	3638	3639
E4	3648	3649	3650	3651	3652	3653	3654	3655
E5	3664	3665	3666	3667	3668	3669	3670	3671
E6	3680	3681	3682	3683	3684	3685	3686	3687
E7	3696	3697	3698	3699	3700	3701	3702	3703
E8	3712	3713	3714	3715	3716	3717	3718	3719
E9	3728	3729	3730	3731	3732	3733	3734	3735
EA	3744	3745	3746	3747	3748	3749	3750	3751
EB	3760	3761	3762	3763	3764	3765	3766	3767
EC	3776	3777	3778	3779	3780	3781	3782	3783
ED	3792	3793	3794	3795	3796	3797	3798	3799
EE	3808	3809	3810	3811	3812	3813	3814	3815
EF	3824	3825	3826	3827	3828	3829	3830	3831
F0	3840	3841	3842	3843	3844	3845	3846	3847
F1	3856	3857	3858	3859	3860	3861	3862	3863
F2	3872	3873	3874	3875	3876	3877	3878	3879
F3	3888	3889	3890	3891	3892	3893	3894	3895
F4	3904	3905	3906	3907	3908	3909	3910	3911
F5	3920	3921	3922	3923	3924	3925	3926	3927
F6	3936	3937	3938	3939	3940	3941	3942	3943
F7	3952	3953	3954	3955	3956	3957	3958	3959
F8	3968	3969	3970	3971	3972	3973	3974	3975
F9	3984	3985	3986	3987	3988	3989	3990	3991
FA	4000	4001	4002	4003	4004	4005	4006	4007
FB	4016	4017	4018	4019	4020	4021	4022	4023
FC	4032	4033	4034	4035	4036	4037	4038	4039
FD	4048	4049	4050	4051	4052	4053	4054	4055
FE	4064	4065	4066	4067	4068	4069	4070	4071
FF	4080	4081	4082	4083	4084	4085	4086	4087

HEX to DECIMAL CONVERSION

↓ Hex→	8	9	A	B	C	D	E	F
CB	3256	3257	3258	3259	3260	3261	3262	3263
CC	3272	3273	3274	3275	3276	3277	3278	3279
CD	3288	3289	3290	3291	3292	3293	3294	3295
CE	3304	3305	3306	3307	3308	3309	3310	3311
CF	3320	3321	3322	3323	3324	3325	3326	3327
D0	3336	3337	3338	3339	3340	3341	3342	3343
D1	3352	3353	3354	3355	3356	3357	3358	3359
D2	3368	3369	3370	3371	3372	3373	3374	3375
D3	3384	3385	3386	3387	3388	3389	3390	3391
D4	3400	3401	3402	3403	3404	3405	3406	3407
D5	3416	3417	3418	3419	3420	3421	3422	3423
D6	3432	3433	3434	3435	3436	3437	3438	3439
D7	3448	3449	3450	3451	3452	3453	3454	3455
D8	3464	3465	3466	3467	3468	3469	3470	3471
D9	3480	3481	3482	3483	3484	3485	3486	3487
DA	3496	3497	3498	3499	3500	3501	3502	3503
DB	3512	3513	3514	3515	3516	3517	3518	3519
DC	3528	3529	3530	3531	3532	3533	3534	3535
DD	3544	3545	3546	3547	3548	3549	3550	3551
DE	3560	3561	3562	3563	3564	3565	3566	3567
DF	3576	3577	3578	3579	3580	3581	3582	3583
E0	3592	3593	3594	3595	3596	3597	3598	3599
E1	3608	3609	3610	3611	3612	3613	3614	3615
E2	3624	3625	3626	3627	3628	3629	3630	3631
E3	3640	3641	3642	3643	3644	3645	3646	3647
E4	3656	3657	3658	3659	3660	3661	3662	3663
E5	3672	3673	3674	3675	3676	3677	3678	3679
E6	3688	3689	3690	3691	3692	3693	3694	3695
E7	3704	3705	3706	3707	3708	3709	3710	3711
E8	3720	3721	3722	3723	3724	3725	3726	3727
E9	3736	3737	3738	3739	3740	3741	3742	3743
EA	3752	3753	3754	3755	3756	3757	3758	3759
EB	3768	3769	3770	3771	3772	3773	3774	3775
EC	3784	3785	3786	3787	3788	3789	3790	3791
ED	3800	3801	3802	3803	3804	3805	3806	3807
EE	3816	3817	3818	3819	3820	3821	3822	3823
EF	3832	3833	3834	3835	3836	3837	3838	3839
F0	3848	3849	3850	3851	3852	3853	3854	3855
F1	3864	3865	3866	3867	3868	3869	3870	3871
F2	3880	3881	3882	3883	3884	3885	3886	3887
F3	3896	3897	3898	3899	3900	3901	3902	3903
F4	3912	3913	3914	3915	3916	3917	3918	3919
F5	3928	3929	3930	3931	3932	3933	3934	3935
F6	3944	3945	3946	3947	3948	3949	3950	3951
F7	3960	3961	3962	3963	3964	3965	3966	3967
F8	3976	3977	3978	3979	3980	3981	3982	3983
F9	3992	3993	3994	3995	3996	3997	3998	3999
FA	4008	4009	4010	4011	4012	4013	4014	4015
FB	4024	4025	4026	4027	4028	4029	4030	4031
FC	4040	4041	4042	4043	4044	4045	4046	4047
FD	4056	4057	4058	4059	4060	4061	4062	4063
FE	4072	4073	4074	4075	4076	4077	4078	4079
FF	4088	4089	4090	4091	4092	4093	4094	4095

ALPHABET-DEC-HEX-EBCDIC

Hex	Dec	Alph	EBCDIC	Hex	Dec	Alph	EBCDIC
00	0	Null	00	3F	63	?	6F
01	1	SOH	01	40	64	@	7C
02	2	STX	02	41	65	A	C1
03	3	ETX	03	42	66	B	C2
04	4	EOT	37	43	67	C	C3
05	5	ENQ	2D	44	68	D	C4
06	6	ACK	2E	45	69	E	C5
07	7	BEL	2F	46	70	F	C6
08	8	BS	16	47	71	G	C7
09	9	HT	05	48	72	H	C8
0A	10	LF	25	49	73	I	C9
0B	11	VT	0B	4A	74	J	D1
0C	12	FF	0C	4B	75	K	D2
0D	13	CR	0D	4C	76	L	D3
0E	14	SO	0E	4D	77	M	D4
0F	15	SI	0F	4E	78	N	D5
10	16	DLE	10	4F	79	O	D6
11	17	DC1	11	50	80	P	D7
12	18	DC2	12	51	81	Q	D8
13	19	DC3	13	52	82	R	D9
14	20	DC4	3C	53	83	S	E2
15	21	NAK	3D	54	84	T	E3
16	22	SYN	32	55	85	U	E4
17	23	ETB	26	56	86	V	E5
18	24	CAN	18	57	87	W	E6
19	25	EM	19	58	88	X	E7
1A	26	SUB	3F	59	89	Y	E8
1B	27	ESC	27	5A	90	Z	E9
1C	28	FS	22	5B	91	[	—
1D	29	GS	—	5C	92	\	E0
1E	30	RS	35	5D	93	]	—
1F	31	US	—	5E	94	^	—
20	32	space	40	5F	95	_	6D
21	33	!	5A	60	96	`	—
22	34	"	7F	61	97	a	81
23	35	#	7B	62	98	b	82
24	36	$	5B	63	99	c	83
25	37	%	6C	64	100	d	84
26	38	&	50	65	101	e	85
27	39	'	7D	66	102	f	86
28	40	(	4D	67	103	g	87
29	41	)	5D	68	104	h	88
2A	42	*	5C	69	105	i	89
2B	43	+	4E	6A	106	j	91
2C	44	,	6B	6B	107	k	92
2D	45	-	60	6C	108	l	93
2E	46	.	4B	6D	109	m	94
2F	47	/	61	6E	110	n	95
30	48	0	F0	6F	111	o	96
31	49	1	F1	70	112	p	97
32	50	2	F2	71	113	q	98
33	51	3	F3	72	114	r	99
34	52	4	F4	73	115	s	A2
35	53	5	F5	74	116	t	A3
36	54	6	F6	75	117	u	A4
37	55	7	F7	76	118	v	A5
38	56	8	F8	77	119	w	A6
39	57	9	F9	78	120	x	A7
3A	58	:	7A	79	121	y	A8
3B	59	;	5E	7A	122	z	A9
3C	60	<	4C	7B	123	{	C0
3D	61	=	7E	7C	124	|	6A
3E	62	>	6E	7D	125	}	D0
				7E	126	~	A1
				7F	127	DEL	07

Chapter 2

PC Hardware

VIDEO STANDARDS

Video Standard (year)	Mode	Horz x Vert Resolution (pixels)	Simultaneous Colors	Vert Freq Hz	Horz Freq kHz	Band Width MHz
MDA (1981)	Text	720x350	1	50Hz	18.43	16.257
HGC	Text	640x400	1	50	18.43	16.257
	Graph	720x348	1	50	"	"
CGA (1981)	Text	320x200	16	60	15.75	14.318
	Text	640x200	16	60	"	"
	Graph	320x200	4	60	"	"
	Graph	640x200	2	60	"	"
EGA Color (1985)	Text	640x350	16	60	15.75	14.318
	Graph	640x350	16	60	to	to
	Graph	320x200	16	60	21.85	16.257
	Graph	640x350	64	60	"	"
EGA Mono	Graph	640x350	1	50	"	"
MCGA (1987)	Text	320x400	16	70	31.50	25.175
	Text	640x400	16	70	"	"
	Graph	640x480	2	60	"	"
	Graph	320x200	256	70	"	"
VGA (1987)	Text	360x400	16	70	31.50	25.175
	Text	720x400	16	70	"	to
	Graph	640x350	16	70	"	28.322
	Graph	640x480	16	60	"	"
	Graph	640x480	2	60	"	"
	Graph	320x200	256	70	"	"
Super VGA (1989)	Graph	800x600	16	50,60	35,37	
	Graph	800x600	256	and	and	
	Graph	1024x768	16	72	60,80	
8514-A (1987)	Graph	1024x768	16	43.48	35.52	44.897
	Graph	640x480	256	60	31.5	"
	Graph	1024x768	256	43.48	35.52	"
XGA (1990)	Graph	640x480	256	43.48	35.52	
	Graph	1024x768	256	43.48	"	
	Graph	640x480	65536	60	31.5	
	Text	1056x400	16	70	"	

Note: Most video cards built around the standards listed above are downward compatible and will function in the modes of the earlier standards. For example, most VGA cards will operate in all of the MDA, CGA, and EGA modes.

VIDEO STANDARDS

Abbreviations for the graphics standards defined on the previous page are as follows:

MDA.	Monochrome Display Adapter
HGC.	Hercules Graphics Card
CGA.	Color Graphics Adapter
EGA.	Enhanced Graphics Adapter
PGA.	Professional Graphics Adapter
MCGA	Multi Color Graphics Array
VGA.	Video Graphics Array - digital
8514-A. . . .	Video Graphics Array - analog
Super VGA	Super Video Graphics Array, VESA
XGA.	Extended Graphics Array

Pixels are coded by assigning bits to the colors. 1 bit/pixel boards can only display 1 color, monochrome (the bit is either on or off). 2 bits/pixel boards can display 4 colors (CGA for example). 8 bits/pixel can display 256 colors (VGA for example). 24 bits/pixel can display 16,777,216 simultaneous colors. Video board memory limits the number of colors that a graphics adapter can store; for example, a 1024x768 adapter requires 786,432 bytes of memory in order to display 256 colors. Needless to say, future video memory requirements will continue to grow. Consider that a 4096x4096 image with 24 bit/pixel color will require nearly 50 Mb of video RAM.

KEYBOARD SCAN CODES

Generally, expanded PC/XT, AT and PS/2 keyboard scan codes are converted to PC/XT standard scan codes prior to ROM BIOS ASCII Code conversion. Notable exceptions are the F11 and F12 keys, which generate new scan codes (see table below). Extended ASCII characters and some special "characters" are achieved by combining 2 or more key presses.

Shaded areas in the table represent keys and scan codes of the standard 84 key PC/XT keyboard, however, the "Key #" listed in column 1 of the table is not the correct Key # for the XT class keyboard. See your computer's keyboard documentation for verification of the correct Key # to Key Name assignments. AT Scan Codes are only relevant to AT class (Models 50 and above) computers.

Key # for 101 Keybd	Key Name	XT scan codes Down • Up	AT hardware scan codes Down • Up
1	Esc	01 • 81	76 • F0 76
2	F1	3B • BB	05 • F0 05
3	F2	3C • BC	06 • F0 06
4	F3	3D • BD	04 • F0 04
5	F4	3E • BE	0C • F0 0C
6	F5	3F • BF	03 • F0 03
7	F6	40 • C0	0B • F0 0B
8	F7	41 • C1	83 • F0 83
9	F8	42 • C2	0A • F0 0A
10	F9	43 • C3	01 • F0 01
11	F10	44 • C4	09 • F0 09
12	F11	57 • D7	78 • F0 78
13	F12	58 • D8	07 • F0 07

Special Keys (expanded keyboards only)

Key #	Key Name	XT scan codes Down • Up	AT hardware scan codes Down • Up
14	*PrtScn / SysReq*		
14	–PRINT SCRN	E0 2A E0 37 •	E0 12 E0 7C •
14		E0 B7 E0 AA	E0 F0 7C E0 F0 12
14	–Sys Req (+ CTRL)	E0 37 • E0 B7	E0 7C • E0 F0 7C
14	–Sys Req (+ ALT)	54 • D4	84 • F0 84
15	ScrollLock	46 • C6	7E • F0 7E
16	*Pause / Break*		
16	–PAUSE (key alone)	E1 1D 45 E1 9D C5 •	E1 14 77 E1 F0 14 F0 77 •
16	(No Auto Repeat)	No Up Code	No Up Code
16	–BREAK (+ CTRL)	E0 46 E0 C6 •	E0 7E E0 F0 7E •
16	(No Auto Repeat)	No Up Code	No Up Code
31	*Insert Key*	E0 52 • E0 D2	E0 70 • F0 70
31	–LEFT SHIFT case	E0 AA E0 52 •	E0 F0 12 E0 70 •
31		E0 D2 E0 2A	E0 F0 70 E0 12
31	–RIGHT SHIFT case	E0 B6 E0 52 •	E0 F0 59 E0 70 •
31		E0 D2 E0 36	E0 F0 70 E0 59
31	–NUM LOCK ON case	E0 2A E0 52 •	E0 12 E0 70 •
31		E0 D2 E0 AA	E0 F0 70 E0 F0 12

KEYBOARD SCAN CODES (cont.)

Key # for 101 Keybd	Key Name	XT scan codes Down • Up	AT hardware scan codes Down • Up
32	**Home**	E0 47 • E0 C7	E0 6C • E0 F0 6C
32	–LEFT SHIFT case	E0 AA E0 47 •	E0 F0 12 E0 6C •
32		E0 C7 E0 2A	E0 F0 6C E0 12
32	–RIGHT SHIFT case	E0 B6 E0 47 •	E0 F0 59 E0 6C •
32		E0 C7 E0 36	E0 F0 6C E0 59
32	–NUM LOCK ON case	E0 2A E0 47 •	E0 12 E0 6C •
32		E0 C7 E0 AA	E0 F0 6C E0 F0 12
33	**PageUp**	E0 49 • E0 C9	E0 7D • E0 F0 7D
33	–LEFT SHIFT case	E0 AA E0 49 •	E0 F0 12 E0 7D •
33		E0 C9 E0 2A	E0 F0 7D E0 12
33	–RIGHT SHIFT case	E0 B6 E0 49 •	E0 F0 59 E0 7D •
33		E0 C9 E0 36	E0 F0 7D E0 59
33	–NUM LOCK ON case	E0 2A E0 49 •	E0 12 E0 7D •
33		E0 C9 E0 AA	E0 F0 7D E0 F0 12
52	**Delete**	E0 53 • E0 D3	E0 71 • E0 F0 71
52	–LEFT SHIFT case	E0 AA E0 53 •	E0 F0 12 E0 71 •
52		E0 D3 E0 2A	E0 F0 71 E0 12
52	–RIGHT SHIFT case	E0 B6 E0 53 •	E0 F0 59 E0 71 •
52		E0 D3 E0 36	E0 F0 71 E0 59
52	–NUM LOCK ON case	E0 2A E0 53 •	E0 12 E0 71 •
52		E0 D3 E0 AA	E0 F0 71 E0 F0 12
53	**End**	E0 4F • E0 CF	E0 69 • E0 F0 69
53	–LEFT SHIFT case	E0 AA E0 4F •	E0 F0 12 E0 69 •
53		E0 CF E0 2A	E0 F0 69 E0 12
53	–RIGHT SHIFT case	E0 B6 E0 4F •	E0 F0 59 E0 69 •
53		E0 CF E0 36	E0 F0 69 E0 59
53	–NUM LOCK ON case	E0 2A E0 4F •	E0 12 E0 69 •
53		E0 CF E0 AA	E0 F0 69 E0 F0 12
54	**PageDown**	E0 51 • E0 D1	E0 7A • E0 F0 7A
54	–LEFT SHIFT case	E0 AA E0 51 •	E0 F0 12 E0 7A •
54		E0 D1 E0 2A	E0 F0 7A E0 12
54	–RIGHT SHIFT case	E0 B6 E0 51 •	E0 F0 59 E0 7A •
54		E0 D1 E0 36	E0 F0 7A E0 59
54	–NUM LOCK ON case	E0 2A E0 51 •	E0 12 E0 7A •
54		E0 D1 E0 AA	E0 F0 7A E0 F0 12
87	**UpArrow**	E0 48 • E0 C8	E0 75 • E0 F0 75
87	–LEFT SHIFT case	E0 AA E0 48 •	E0 F0 12 E0 75 •
87		E0 C8 E0 2A	E0 F0 75 E0 12
87	–RIGHT SHIFT case	E0 B6 E0 48 •	E0 F0 59 E0 75 •
87		E0 C8 E0 36	E0 F0 75 E0 59
87	–NUM LOCK ON case	E0 2A E0 48 •	E0 12 E0 75 •
87		E0 C8 E0 AA	E0 F0 75 E0 F0 12
97	**LeftArrow**	E0 4B • E0 CB	E0 6B • E0 F0 6B
97	–LEFT SHIFT case	E0 AA E0 4B •	E0 F0 12 E0 6B •
97		E0 CB E0 2A	E0 F0 6B E0 12
97	–RIGHT SHIFT case	E0 B6 E0 4B •	E0 F0 59 E0 6B •
97		E0 CB E0 36	E0 F0 6B E0 59
97	–NUM LOCK ON case	E0 2A E0 4B •	E0 12 E0 6B •
97		E0 CB E0 AA	E0 F0 6B E0 F0 12

Key # for 101 Keybd	Key Name	XT scan codes Down • Up	AT hardware scan codes Down • Up
98	*DownArrow*	E0 50 • E0 D0	E0 72 • E0 F0 72
98	–LEFT SHIFT case	E0 AA E0 50 •	E0 F0 12 E0 72 •
98		E0 D0 E0 2A	E0 F0 72 E0 12
98	–RIGHT SHIFT case	E0 B6 E0 50 •	E0 F0 59 E0 72 •
98		E0 D0 E0 36	E0 F0 72 E0 59
98	–NUM LOCK ON case	E0 2A E0 50 •	E0 12 E0 72 •
98		E0 D0 E0 AA	E0 F0 72 E0 F0 12
99	*RightArrow*	E0 4D • E0 CD	E0 74 • E0 F0 74
99	–LEFT SHIFT case	E0 AA E0 4D •	E0 F0 12 E0 74 •
99		E0 CD E0 2A	E0 F0 74 E0 12
99	–RIGHT SHIFT case	E0 B6 E0 4D •	E0 F0 59 E0 74 •
99		E0 CD E0 36	E0 F0 74 E0 59
99	–NUM LOCK ON case	E0 2A E0 4D •	E0 12 E0 74 •
99		E0 CD E0 AA	E0 F0 74 E0 F0 12

Alpha–Numeric Primary Keyboard Keys
(includes expanded keys)

17	` ~ (accent, tilde)	29 • A9	0E • F0 0E
18	1 !	02 • 82	16 • F0 16
19	2 @	03 • 83	1E • F0 1E
20	3 #	04 • 84	26 • F0 26
21	4 $	05 • 85	25 • F0 25
22	5 %	06 • 86	2E • F0 2E
23	6 ^ (6, caret)	07 • 87	36 • F0 36
24	7 &	08 • 88	3D • F0 3D
25	8 * (8, asterisk)	09 • 89	3E • F0 3E
26	9 (	0A • 8A	46 • F0 46
27	0)	0B • 8B	45 • F0 45
28	– _ (dash, underline)	0C • 8C	4E • F0 4E
29	= + (equal, plus)	0D • 8D	55 • F0 55
30	Bkspace	0E • 8E	66 • F0 66
38	Tab	0F • 8F	0D • F0 0D
39	q Q	10 • 90	15 • F0 15
40	w W	11 • 91	1D • F0 1D
41	e E	12 • 92	24 • F0 24
42	r R	13 • 93	2D • F0 2D
43	t T	14 • 94	2C • F0 2C
44	y Y	15 • 95	35 • F0 35
45	u U	16 • 96	3C • F0 3C
46	i I	17 • 97	43 • F0 43
47	o O	18 • 98	44 • F0 44
48	p P	19 • 99	4D • F0 4D
49	[{	1A • 9A	54 • F0 54
50	] }	1B • 9B	5B • F0 5B
51	\ | (backslash, bar)	2B • AB	5D • F0 5D
59	CapsLock	3A • BA	58 • F0 58
60	a A	1E • 9E	1C • F0 1C
61	s S	1F • 9F	1B • F0 1B
62	d D	20 • A0	23 • F0 23
63	f F	21 • A1	2B • F0 2B
64	g G	22 • A2	34 • F0 34

Key # for 101 Keybd	Key Name	XT scan codes Down • Up	AT hardware scan codes Down • Up
65	h H	23 • A3	33 • F0 33
66	j J	24 • A4	3B • F0 3B
67	k K	25 • A5	42 • F0 42
68	l L	26 • A6	4B • F0 4B
69	; : (semicolon,colon)	27 • A7	4C • F0 4C
70	' " (single quote,double)	28 • A8	52 • F0 52
71	Enter	1C • 9C	5A • F0 5A
75	Shift(left)	2A • AA	12 • F0 12
76	z Z	2C • AC	1A • F0 1A
77	x X	2D • AD	22 • F0 22
78	c C	2E • AE	21 • F0 21
79	v V	2F • AF	2A • F0 2A
80	b B	30 • B0	32 • F0 32
81	n N	31 • B1	31 • F0 31
82	m M	32 • B2	3A • F0 3A
83	, < (comma,less than)	33 • B3	41 • F0 41
84	. > (period,greater than)	34 • B4	49 • F0 49
85	/ ? (forward slash, ?)	35 • B5	4A • F0 4A
86	Shift(right)	36 • B6	59 • F0 59
92	Ctrl(left)	1D • 9D	14 • F0 14
93	Alt(left)	38 • B8	11 • F0 11
94	Space	39 • B9	29 • F0 29
95	Alt(right)	E0 38 • E0 B8	E0 11 • E0 F0 11
96	Ctrl(right)	E0 1D • E0 9D	E0 14 • E0 F0 14

Keypad keys
(Includes expanded keyboard layout)

34	NumLock	45 • C5	77 • F0 77
35	/	E0 35 • E0 B5	E0 4A • E0 F0 4A
35	–LEFT SHIFT case	E0 AA E0 35 •	E0 F0 12 E0 4A •
35		E0 B5 E0 2A	E0 4A • E0 F0 4A
35	–RIGHT SHIFT case	E0 B6 E0 35 •	E0 F0 59 E0 4A •
35		E0 B5 E0 36	E0 4A • E0 F0 59
36	* (PrtSc 84 key)	37 • B7	7C • F0 7C
37	–	4A • C4	7B • F0 7B
55	Home 7	47 • C7	6C • F0 6C
56	UpArrow 8	48 • C8	75 • F0 75
57	PageUp 9	49 • C9	7D • F0 7D
58	+	4E • CE	79 • F0 79
72	LeftArrow 4	4B • CB	6B • F0 6B
73	5	4C • CC	73 • F0 73
74	RightArrow 6	4D • CD	74 • F0 74
88	End 1	4F • CF	69 • F0 69
89	DownArrow 2	50 • D0	72 • F0 72
90	PageDown 3	51 • D1	7A • F0 7A
91	Enter	E0 1C • E0 9C	E0 5A • E0 F0 5A
100	Ins 0	52 • D2	70 • F0 70
101	Del .	53 • D3	71 • F0 71

IBM HARDWARE RELEASES

Date	Code	Hardware Release	Date	Code	Hardware Release
04-24-81	FF	PC (the original!)	01-29-88 to		
10-19-81	FF	PC (fixed bugs)	02-20-89	F8	PS/2 Model 70 - 386
10-27-82	FF	PC hard drive	08-25-88	FC	PS/2 Model 30 - 286
		support & 640k	11-02-88	F8	PS/2 Model 55 - SX
11-08-82	FE	PC-XT	01-18-89	F8	PS/2 Model P70 - 386
06-01-83	FD	PC jr	06-28-89	FC	PS/2 Model 25 - 286
01-10-84	FC	AT	06-28-89	FC	PS/2 Model 30 - 286
06-10-85	FC	AT revision 1	09-29-89 to		
09-13-85	F9	PC Convertible	12-01-89	F8	PS/2 Model 70 - 486
11-15-85	FC	AT w/speed control	11-21-89	F8	PS/2 Model 80 - 386-25
		(30 meg HD)	12-01-89	FC	PS/1 Model
01-10-86	FB	XT revision 1	02-08-90	F8	PS/2 Model 65 - SX
04-21-86	FC	XT-286 model 2	10-05-90	F8	PS/2 Model P75 - 486
05-09-86 to			02-27-91	F8	PS/2 Model L40 - SX
02-05-87	FB	XT revision 2	03-15-91 to		
09-02-86	FA	PS/2 Model 30	04-09-91	F8	PS/2 Model 35 - SX
02-13-87 to			03-15-91 to		
05-09-87	FC	PS/2 Model 50 model 4	04-09-91	F8	PS/2 Model 40 - SX
02-13-87	FC	PS/2 Model 60 model 5	07-03-91	F8	PS/2 Model 57 - SX
03-30-87	F8	PS/2 Model 80 16 MHz	?	F8	PS/2 Model 90 - XP 486
06-26-87	FA	PS/2 Model 25	?	F8	PS/2 Model 95 - XP 486
10-07-87	F8	PS/2 Model 80 20 MHz			
01-28-88 to					
04-18-88	FC	PS/2 Model 50Z			

IBM® PC/XT MOTHERBOARD
SWITCH 1 SETTINGS

Switch #	On/Off	Function
1	Off	Always off
2	On	Coprocessor NOT present in system
2	Off	Coprocessor present in system

		Switch 3,4 System motherboard memory
3,4	3 On, 4 On	PC=16K XT=64K
3,4	3 Off, 4 On	PC=32K XT=128K
3,4	3 On, 4 Off	PC=48K XT=192K
3,4	3 Off, 4 Off	PC=64K XT=256K
5,6	5 On, 6 On	EGA/VGA video adapter present
5,6	5 Off, 6 Off	Monochrome video adapter present
5,6	5 On, 6 Off	CGA video adapter present, 80x25 mode
5,6	5 Off, 6 On	CGA video adapter present, 40x25 mode
7,8	7 On, 8 On	One floppy disk drive present
7,8	7 Off, 8 On	Two floppy disk drives present
7,8	7 On, 8 Off	Three floppy disk drives present
7,8	7 Off, 8 Off	Four floppy disk drives present

IBM® PC MOTHERBOARD
SWITCH 2 SETTINGS (MEMORY)

System Memory Size	sw2-1	sw2-2	sw2-3	sw2-4	256K board sw2-5	64K board sw2-5
64K	On	On	On	On	On	Off
96K	Off	On	On	On	On	Off
128K	On	Off	On	On	On	Off
160K	Off	Off	On	On	On	Off
192K	On	On	Off	On	On	Off
224K	Off	On	Off	On	On	Off
256K	On	Off	Off	On	On	Off
288K	Off	Off	Off	On	On	Off
320K	On	On	On	Off	On	Off
352K	Off	On	On	Off	On	Off
384K	On	Off	On	Off	On	Off
416K	Off	Off	On	Off	On	Off
448K	On	On	Off	Off	On	Off
480K	Off	On	Off	Off	On	Off
512K	On	Off	Off	Off	On	Off
544K	Off	Off	Off	Off	On	Off
576K	On	On	On	On	Off	N/A
608K	Off	On	On	On	Off	N/A
640K	On	Off	On	On	Off	N/A
704K	On	On	Off	On	Off	N/A

Notes:
1. Switch 2 listed on this page is <u>not</u> used on an IBM® XT.

2. The 256K board listed at the head of column 6 is the PC2 motherboard. The 64K board at the head of column 7 is the PC1 motherboard.

3. Switch 1-3 and 1-4 on the previous page must both be OFF if the motherboard is fully populated with memory chips on either the 64K or 256K motherboard.

4. Switch 1 on the IBM® AT, is a single switch that selects whether the installed video adapter is color or monochrome.

RESISTOR COLOR CODES

Color	1st Digit(A)	2nd Digit(B)	Multiplier(C)	Tolerance(D)
Black	0	0	1	
Brown	1	1	10	1%
Red	2	2	100	2%
Orange	3	3	1,000	3%
Yellow	4	4	10,000	4%
Green	5	5	100,000	
Blue	6	6	1,000,000	
Violet	7	7	10,000,000	
Gray	8	8	100,000,000	
White	9	9	10^9	
Gold			0.1 (EIA)	5%
Silver			0.01 (EIA)	10%
No Color				20%

Example: Red–Red–Orange = 22,000 ohms, 20%

Additional information concerning the Axial Lead resistor can be obtained if Band A is a wide band. Case 1: If only Band A is wide, it indicates that the resistor is wirewound. Case 2: If Band A is wide and there is also a blue fifth band to the right of Band D on the Axial Lead Resistor, it indicates the resistor is wirewound and flame proof.

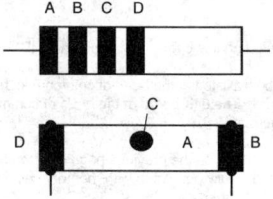

Axial Lead Resistor

Radial Lead Resistor

PAPER SIZES

Paper Size	Standard	Millimeters	Inches
Eight Crown	IMP	1461 x 1060	57-1/2 x 41-3/4
Antiquarian	IMP	1346 x 533	53 x 21
Quad Demy	IMP	1118 x 826	44 x 32-1/2
Double Princess	IMP	1118 x 711	44 x 28
Quad Crown	IMP	1016 x 762	40 x 30
Double Elephant	IMP	1016 x 686	40 x 27
B0	ISO	1000 x 1414	39.37 x 55.67
Arch-E	USA	914 x 1219	36 x 48
Double Demy	IMP	889 x 572	35 x 22-1/2
– E	ANSI	864 x 1118	34 x 44
A0	ISO	841 x 1189	33.11 x 46.81
Imperial	IMP	762 x 559	30 x 22
Princess	IMP	711 x 546	28 x 21-1/2
B1	ISO	707 x 1000	27.83 x 39.37
Arch-D	USA	610 x 914	24 x 36
A1	ISO	594 x 841	23.39 x 33.11
Demy	IMP	584 x 470	23 x 18-1/2
– D	ANSI	559 x 864	22 x 34
B2	ISO	500 x 707	19.68 x 27.83
Arch-C	USA	457 x 610	18 x 24
– C	ANSI	432 x 559	17 x 22
A2	ISO	420 x 594	16.54 x 23.39
B3	ISO	353 x 500	13.90 x 19.68
Brief	IMP	333 x 470	13-1/8 x 18-1/2
Foolscap folio	IMP	333 x 210	13-1/8 x 8-1/4
Arch-B	USA	305 x 457	12 x 18
A3	ISO	297 x 420	11.69 x 16.54
– B	ANSI	279 x 432	11 x 17
Demy quarto	IMP	273 x 216	10-3/4 x 8-1/2
B4	ISO	250 x 353	9.84 x 13.90
Crown quarto	IMP	241 x 184	9-1/2 x 7-1/4
Royal octavo	IMP	241 x 152	9-1/2 x 6
Arch-A	USA	229 x 305	9 x 12
Demy octavo	IMP	222 x 137	8-3/4 X 5-3/8
– A	ANSI	216 x 279	8.5 x 11
A4	ISO	210 x 297	8.27 x 11.69
Foolscap quarto	IMP	206 x 165	8-1/8 x 6-1/2
Crown Octavo	IMP	181 x 121	7-1/8 x 4-3/4
B5	ISO	176 x 250	6.93 x 9.84
A5	ISO	148 x 210	5.83 x 8.27
	USA	140 x 216	5.5 x 8.5
	USA	127 x 178	5 x 7
A6	ISO	105 x 148	4.13 x 5.83
	USA	102 x 127	4 x 5
	USA	76 x 102	3 x 5
A7	ISO	74 x 105	2.91 x 4.13
A8	ISO	52 x 74	2.05 x 2.91
A9	ISO	37 x 52	1.46 x 2.05
A10	ISO	26 x 37	1.02 x 1.46

Abbreviations for the above table are:

ISO	International Organization for Standardization
ANSI	American National Standards Institute
USA	United States
IMP	Imperial paper and plan sizes
Arch	United States architectural standards

PARALLEL PRINTER INTERFACE

Printer Pin Number	Signal Description	Function	Signal Direction At Printer
1	STROBE	Reads in the data	Input
2	DATA Bit 0	Data line	Input
3	DATA Bit 1	Data line	Input
4	DATA Bit 2	Data line	Input
5	DATA Bit 3	Data line	Input
6	DATA Bit 4	Data line	Input
7	DATA Bit 5	Data line	Input
8	DATA Bit 6	Data line	Input
9	DATA Bit 7	Data line	Input
10	ACKNLG	Acknowledge receipt of data	Output
11	Busy	Printer is busy	Output
12	Paper Empty	Printer out of paper	Output
13	SLCT	Online mode indicator	Output
14	Auto Feed XT		Input
15	Not Used	Not Used	
16	Signal ground	Signal ground	
17	Frame ground	Frame ground	
18	+5 volts	+5 volts	
19-30	Ground	Return signals of pins 1–12, twisted pairs.	
31	Input Prime or INIT	Resets printer, clears buffer & initializes	Input
32	Fault or Error	Indicates offline mode	Output
33	Signal ground	External ground	
34	Not Used	Not Used	
35	+5 Volts	+5 Volts (3.3 K-ohm)	
36	SLCT IN	TTL high level	Input

The above pinout is at the printer plug, computer side pinouts are on the next page. The "Parallel" or "Centronics" configuration for printer data transmission has become the de facto standard in the personal computer industry. This configuration was developed by a printer manufacturer (Centronics) as an alternative to serial data transmission. High data transfer rates are the main advantage of parallel and are attained by simultaneous transmission of all bits of a binary "word" (normally an ASCII code). Disadvantages of the parallel transfer are the requirement for 8 separate data lines and computer to printer cable lengths of less than 12 feet.

PARALLEL PINOUTS @ COMPUTER

DB25 Systems

Computer Pin Number	Signal Description	Function	Signal Direction At Computer
1	STROBE	Reads in the data	Output
2	DATA Bit 0	Data line	Output
3	DATA Bit 1	Data line	Output
4	DATA Bit 2	Data line	Output
5	DATA Bit 3	Data line	Output
6	DATA Bit 4	Data line	Output
7	DATA Bit 5	Data line	Output
8	DATA Bit 6	Data line	Output
9	DATA Bit 7	Data line	Output
10	ACKNLG	Acknowledge receipt of data	Input
11	Busy	Printer is busy	Input
12	Paper Empty	Printer out of paper	Input
13	SLCT	Online mode indicator	Input
14	Auto Feed XT		Input
15	Fault or Error	Indicates offline mode	Input
16	Input Prime or INIT	Resets printer, clears buffer & initializes	Output
17	SLCT IN	TTL high level	Output
18-25	Ground	Return signals of pins 1–12, twisted pairs.	

LOOPBACK DIAGNOSTIC PLUGS

Parallel-IBM DB25	Parallel-Other DB25	Serial-IBM DB25	Serial-Other DB25
1 to 13	2 to 15	1 to 7	2 to 3
2 to 15	3 to 13	2 to 3	4 to 5
10 to 16	4 to 12	4 to 5 to 8	6 to 8 to 20 to 22
11 to 17	5 to 10	6 to 11 to 20 to 22	
12 to 14	6 to 11	15 to 17 to 23	
		18 to 25	

Loopback plugs work in conjunction with various software diagnostics programs and are used to determine whether or not a parallel or serial port is functioning correctly. The plugs labeled "IBM" will work with the IBM Corporation Advanced Diagnostics software and those labeled as "Other" will work with a variety of other programs such as Norton Diagnostics.

SERIAL I/O INTERFACES (RS232C)

Standard DB25 Pin Connector

Serial Pin Number	Signal Description	Function	Signal Direction At Device
1	FG	Frame ground	
2	TD	Transmit Data	Output
3	RD	Receive Data	Input
4	RTS	Request to Send	Output
5	CTS	Clear to Send	Input
6	DSR	Data Set Ready	Input
7	SG	Signal Ground	
8	DCD	Data Carrier Detect	Input
9	+V	+DC test voltage	Input
10	– V	– DC test voltage	Input
11	QM	Equalizer Mode	Input
12	(S)DCD	2nd Data Carrier Detect	Input
13	(S)CTS	2nd Clear to Send	Input
14	(S)TD	2nd Transmitted Data	Output
15	TC	Transmitter Clock	Input
16	(S)RD	2nd Received Data	Input
17	RC	Receiver Clock	Input
18	Not used	Not used	
19	(S)RTS	2nd Request to Send	Output
20	DTR	Data Terminal Ready	Output
21	SQ	Signal Quality Detect	Input
22	RI	Ring Indicator	Input
23		Data Rate Selector	Output
24	(TC)	External Transmitter Clk	Output
25	Not used	Not used	

IBM® Standard DB9 Pin Connector

Serial Pin Number	Signal Description	Function	Signal Direction At Device
1	DCD	Data Carrier Detect	Input
2	RD	Receive Data	Input
3	SD	Transmit Data	Output
4	DTR	Data Terminal Ready	Output
5	SG	Signal Ground	
6	DSR	Data Set Ready	Input
7	RTS	Request to Send	Output
8	CTS	Clear to Send	Input
9	RI	Ring Indicator	Input

NOTES ON SERIAL INTERFACING

Printers and asynchronous modems are relatively unsophisticated pieces of electronic equipment. Although all 25 pins of the Standard DB25 serial connector are listed 1 page back, only a few of the pins are needed for normal applications. The following list gives the necessary pins for each of the indicated applications.

1. "Dumb Terminals" – 1,2,3, & 7
2. Printers and asynchronous modems –   1,2,3,4,5,6,7,8, & 20
3. "Smart" and synchronous modems –   1,2,3,4,5,6,7,8,13,14,
   15,17,20,22, & 24

Cable requirements also differ, depending on the particular hardware being used. The asynchronous modems normally use the 9 pin or 25 pin cables and are wired 1 to 1 (ie, pin 1 on one end of the cable goes to pin 1 on the other end of the cable.)   Serial printers, however, have several wires switched in order to accommodate "handshaking" between computer and printer. The rewired junction is called a "Modem Eliminator". In the case of Standard DB25 the following are typical rewires:

DB25 @ Computer Standard	DB25 @ Printer IBM PC
1	1
3	2
2	3
8	4
4	8
5 & 6	20
20	5 & 6
7	7

DB25 @ Computer Second Standard	DB25 @ Printer PC
1	1
3	2
2	3
20	5, 6 & 8
7	7
5, 6 & 8	20

PC to Terminal	
1	1
2	3
3	2
4	5
5	4
6 & 8	20
20	6 & 8
7	7

Std Hewlett-Packard	
1	1
2	3
3	2
4 & 5	8
8	4 & 5
6	20
7 & 22	7 & 22
17	15
11	12
12	11
15 & 24	17
20	6

GPIB I/O INTERFACE (IEEE-488)

The HPIB/GPIB/IEEE–488 standard is a very powerful interface developed originally by Hewlett–Packard (HP–IB). The interface has been adopted by a variety of groups, such as IEEE, and is known by names such as HP–IB, GPIB, IEEE–488 and IEC Standard 625–1 (outside the US). Worldwide use of this standard has come about due to its ease of use, handshaking protocol, and precisely defined function.

Information management is handled by three device types: Talkers, Listeners, and Controllers. Talkers send information, Listeners receive data, and Controllers manage the interactions. Up to 15 devices can be interconnected, but are usually located within 20 feet of the computer. Additional extenders can be used to access more than 15 devices.

GPIB 24 Line Bus

Pin Number	Signal Description	Function
1	DATA I/O 1	Data line I/O bus
2	DATA I/O 2	Data line I/O bus
3	DATA I/O 3	Data line I/O bus
4	DATA I/O 4	Data line I/O bus
5	EIO	End or Identify
6	DAV	Data valid
7	NRFD	Not Ready For Data
8	NDAC	Data Not Accepted
9	SRQ	Service Request
10	IFC	Interface Clear
11	ATN	Attention
12	Shield	or wire ground
13	DATA I/O 5	Data line I/O bus
14	DATA I/O 6	Data line I/O bus
15	DATA I/O 7	Data line I/O bus
16	DATA I/O 8	Data line I/O bus
17	REN	Remote Enable
18	Ground	Ground
19	Ground	Ground
20	Ground	Ground
21	Ground	Ground
22	Ground	Ground
23	Ground	Ground
24	Logic Ground	Logic Ground

Devices can be set up in star, linear or other combinations and are easily set up using male/female stackable connectors.

VIDEO CARD PINOUTS

Pin Number	Description

Monochrome Display Adapter (MDA and HGC)

1 & 2	Ground
3, 4, & 5	Not Used
6	+ Intensity
7	+ Video
8	+ Horizontal Drive
9	– Vertical Drive

Color Graphics Display Adapter (CGA)

1 & 2	Ground
3	Red
4	Green
5	Blue
6	+ Intensity
7	Reserved
8	+ Horizontal Drive
9	– Vertical Drive

CGA Composite Video (RCA phono jack)

1 (pin)	1.5 volt DC video signal
2 (shell)	Ground

Enhanced Graphics Adapter (EGA)

1	Ground
2	Secondary Red
3	Red
4	Green
5	Blue
6	Secondary Green / Intensity
7	Secondary Blue / Monochrome
8	Horizontal Drive
9	Vertical Drive

Video Graphics Array (VGA)

Color VGA	Monochrome VGA
1. . . . Red (Output)	1 . . . Not Used
2. . . . Green (Output)	2 . . . Monochrome Video
3. . . . Blue (Output)	3 . . . Not Used
4. . . . Reserved	4 . . . Not Used
5. . . . Digital Ground	5 . . . Ground
6. . . . Red Return (Input)	6 . . . Key
7. . . . Green Return (Input)	7 . . . Monochrome Ground
8. . . . Blue Return (Input)	8 . . . Not Used
9. . . . Plug	9 . . . No Connection
10. . . Digital Ground	10 . . Horizontal Sync Ground
11. . . Reserved	11 . . Not Used
12. . . Reserved	12 . . Vertical Sync Ground
13. . . Horizontal Sync (Output)	13 . . Horizontal Sync
14. . . Vertical Sync (Output)	14 . . Vertical Sync
15. . . Reserved	15 . . No Connection

KEYBOARD PLUG - 5 Pin Din

Pin #	Description
1	Clock (TTL signal)
2	Data (TTL signal)
3	Not used
4	Ground
5	Power (+5 volt)

KEYBOARD PLUG - 6 Pin MiniDin

Pin #	Description
1	Data (TTL signal)
2	Not used
3	Ground
4	Power (+5 volt)
5	Clock (TTL signal)
6	Not used

KEYBOARD PLUG - 6 Pin SDL

Pin #	Description
A	Not used
B	Data (TTL signal)
C	Ground
D	Clock (TTL signal)
E	Power (+5 volt)
F	Not used

MOUSE 9 Pin D-Shell

Pin #	Description
1	Not Used
2	Data
3	Clock
4	+5 Volt
5	Ground
6	Not Used
7	Enable Mouse
8	Mouse Ready
9	Not Used

MOUSE 6 Pin Mini DIN

Pin #	Description
1	Data
2	Not Used
3	Signal Ground
4	+5 Volt
5	Clock
6	Not Used
Shell	Shield Ground

MOUSE 9 Pin Microsoft Inport

Pin #	Description
1	+5 Volt
2	XA
3	XB
4	YA
5	YB
6	Switch 1
7	Switch 2
8	Switch 3
9	Signal Ground
Shell	Shield Ground

LIGHT PEN INTERFACE

Pin #	Description
1	– Light Pen Input
2	No connection
3	– Light Pen Switch
4	Chassis Ground
5	+5 Volts
6	+12 Volts

GAME CONTROL CABLE

Joystick Pin Number	Signal Description	Function	Signal Direction At Joystk
1	+5 Volts	Supply voltage	Input
2	Button 1	Push Button 1	Output
3	Position 0	X Coordinate	Output
4	Ground	Ground	
5	Ground	Ground	
6	Position 1	Y Coordinate	Output
7	Button 2	Push Button 2	Output
8	+5 Volts	Supply voltage	Input
9	+5 Volts	Supply voltage	Input
10	Button 3	Push Button 3	Output
11	Position 2	X Coordinate	Output
12	Ground	Ground	
13	Position 3	Y Coordinate	Output
14	Button 4	Push Button 4	Output
15	+5 Volts	Supply voltage	Input

286/386/486 BATTERY CONNECTOR

Pin #	Description
1	Ground
2	Not used
3	Not used, or alignment key
4	+6 volt

SPEAKER CONNECTOR

1	Audio
2	Alignment key
3	Ground
4	+5 volt

KEYBOARD LOCKOUT / POWER LED CONNECTOR-MOTHERBOARD

Pin #	Description
1	LED Power, +5 Volt
2	Alignment Key
3	Ground
4	Keyboard Lockout
5	Ground

PS-8 and 9 POWER CONNECTOR

Pin #	PS-8 (XT)	PS-8 (AT)	PS-9 (XT & AT)
1	Power ground	Power good	Ground
2	Align Key	+5 volt	Ground
3	+12 volt	+12 volt	−5 volt
4	−12 volt	−12 volt	+5 volt
5	Ground	Ground	+5 volt
6	Ground	Ground	+5 volt

DISK DRIVE POWER CONNECTOR

Pin #	Description (4 pin molex)	Wire Color
1	+12 volt	Yellow
2	Ground	Black
3	Ground	Black
4	+5 volt	Red

UNIVERSAL SERIAL BUS CONNECTOR

Pin #	Description
1	+5 volt
2	Data −
3	Data +
4	Ground
5	No Connection
6	+5 volt
7	Data −
8	Data +
9	Ground
10	No Connection

CPU PROCESSOR TYPES

CPU Type	Date	MaxMem Phys/Virt	Bus Int/Ext	Number of Transistors	Speeds MHz
Advanced Micro Devices					
AM386SX	7-91	4Gb	32/16	161k	25,33,40
AM386DX	3-91	4Gb	32/32	161k	25,33,40
AM486SX (doubler)	7-93	4Gb/64Tb	32/32	900k	33,40,25/50
AM486SXLV (3.3V)	7-93	4Gb/64Tb	32/32	900k	33
AM486DX	?	4Gb/64Tb	32/32	1,300k	33, 40
AM486DX2 (doubler)	?	4Gb/64Tb	32/32	1,300k	25/50,33/66,40/80
AM486DX4 (doubler, 3.3V)	?	4Gb/64Tb	32/32	1,300k	100
AM486DXLV (3.3V)	?	4Gb/64Tb	32/32	1,300k	33
AM486DXL2 (doubler)	?	4Gb/64Tb	32/32	1,300k	25/50,33/66,40/80
AM486DXL4 (doubler)	?	4Gb/64Tb	32/32	1,300k	50/100
AMD5x86 (3.3V)	12-95	4Gb/64Tb	32/32	1,300k	75
AMD-K5 (3.5V)	3-96	?/?	64/64	4,300k	75, 90, 100, 117
AMD-K6 (3.5V)	11-96	?/?	64/64	8,800k	180
AMD-K6 MMX (3.5V)	4-97	?/?	64/64	8,800k	166, 200, 233
Advanced Micro Devices - Upgrade Chips					
AM186EM	9-94	?/?	16/16	?	25, 33, 40
AM386EM	9-94	?/?	32/32	?	25, 33
AM486SE (3 or 5V)	9-94	?/?	?/?	?	25, 33
Centaur Technology					
IDT-C6 (3.3V)	10-97	?/?	?/?	5,400k	150, 180, 200
Cyrix Corporation					
CX486SLC (3 or 5V)	4-92	16Mb	32/16	600k	20, 25, 33
CX486DLC	6-92	4Gb/64Tb	32/32	600k	25, 33, 40
CX486S	2-93	4Gb/64Tb	32/32	?	33, 40
CX486DX	9-93	4Gb/64Tb	32/32	?	33, 40, 50
CX486DX2 (doubler)	9-93	4Gb/64Tb	32/32	?	25/50, 33/66
CX486SLC2 (doubler)	10-93	4Gb/64Tb	32/16	?	25/50
CX486DXV (3V)	?	4Gb/64Tb	32/32	?	33
CX486DX2V (doubler, 3V)	?	4Gb/64Tb	32/32	?	25/50,33/66,40/80
5x86 (3.3V)	7-95	?/?	32/64	2,000k	100, 120
6x86 (3.3V)	10-95	?/?	32/64	3,000k	100, 110, 120, 133, 150
6x86MX (3.3V)	5-97	?/?	32/64	6,000k	150, 166, 188, 200,250
M3	Q2-98				
MediaGX (3.3V)	2-97	?/?	64/64	2,400k	120, 133, 150, 166, 180, 200
(Multimedia accelerator chip)					
Cyrix Corporation - Upgrade Chips					
CX486DRX2 (doubler)	8-93	4Gb/64Tb	32/32	?	16/32,20/40, 25/50,33/66
CX486SRX2 (doubler)	10-93	4Gb/64Tb	32/16	?	20/40, 25/50
Digital Equipment Corporation					
Alpha 21064 (3.3V)	1992	16Gb/?	64/64	1,680k	150, 300
Alpha 21064A (3.3V)	10-93	16Gb/?	64/64	2,800k	200,233,275,300
Alpha 21066 (3.3V)	?	16Gb/?	64/64	1,750k	166
Alpha 21066A (3.3V)	1-95	16Gb/?	64/64	1,750k	100, 233

CPU PROCESSOR TYPES

CPU Type	Date	MaxMem Phys/Virt	Bus Int/Ext	Number of Transistors	Speeds MHz
Digital Equipment Corporation (cont.)					
Alpha 21164 (3.3V)	1994	1Tb/8Tb.	64/64	9,300k	266, 300, 333, 366,433,500,600
Alpha 21164A (3.3V)	?	? / ?	? / ?	9,000k	417
Alpha 21164PC (3.3V)	3-97	? / ?	64/64	3,400k	300, 366, 433, 500, 533, 600
EV6 (Alpha 21264)	H2-97	? / ?	64/64	15,200k	500
EV67 (Alpha 21264a)	1999	? / ?		15,200k	500
EV7 (Alpha 21364)	2000			100,000k	500 to 750
EV78 (Alpha 21364a)	2002			100,000k	750
EV8 (Alpha 21464)	2003			250,000k	750 to 1,000
Evergreen Technologies Inc. - Upgrade Chips					
Rev To 486	?	? / ?	? / ?	?	25/50, 25/75
Rev To DX4	9-94	? / ?	? / ?	?	75/25,33/100,50/100
Evergreen 586	?	? / ?	64/64	4,300k	133
Evergreen PR166	?	? / ?	64/64	3,000k	150
Evergreen MxPro	9-97	? / ?	64/64	8,800k	233
Exponential Technology, Inc.					
Exponential-X740	1998	? / ?	64/32	2,700k	410
(Out of business 5/97 after Apple declined use of the X740 in its Power Mac line)					
Fujitsu Microelectronics, Inc.					
TurboSPARC (3.3V)	9-96	? / ?	32/32	3,000k	160, 170
Hewlett-Packard Company					
PA-7100LC (3.3V)	1994	4Gb/ ?	32/32	800k	60, 80, 100
PA-7150 (3.3V)	12-93	? / ?	32/32	850k	125
PA-7200 (3.3V)	1-95	? / ?	32/32	1,260k	120
PA-7300LC (3.3V)	10-95	? / ?	32/32	9,200k	160
PA-8000 (3.3V)	3-96	? / ?	64/64	?	180
PA-8200 (3.3V)	3-97	? / ?	64/64	3,800k	220
PA-8500 (3.3V)	10-98		64/64	120,000k	
Merced (with Intel)	1999				
Hitachi America, Ltd.					
SH7702 (3.3V)	?	4Gb/ ?	? / ?	?	45
SH7708 (3.3V)	?	4Gb/ ?	? / ?	?	60
Intel Corporation					
8080	4-74	64Kb.	8/8	6k	2
8086	6-78	1Mb.	16/16	29k	5, 8, 10
8088	6-79	1Mb.	16/8	29k	5, 8
80286	2-82	16Mb/1 Gb.	16/16	134k	6, 10, 12
80386DX	10-85	4Gb/64Tb.	32/32	275k	16, 20, 25, 33
80386SX	6-88	4Gb/64Tb.	32/16	275k	16, 20, 25, 33
80486DX (3.3 or 5V)	4-89	4Gb/64Tb.	32/32	1,200k	25, 33, 50
80386SL (3.3 or 5V)	10-90	4Gb/64Tb.	32/16	855k	20, 25
80486SX (3.3 or 5V)	4-91	4Gb/64Tb.	32/32	1,185k	16, 20, 25, 33
80486DX2(doubler,3.3or5V)	3-92	4Gb/64Tb.	32/32	1,200k	25/50, 33/66
80486SL (3.3 or 5V)	9-92	64Mb/64Tb.	32/32	1,400k	20, 25, 33
Pentium (3.3 or 5V)	3-93	4Gb/64Tb.	32/64	3,100k	60, 66
80486DX4 (3.3 or 5V)	3-94	4Gb/64Tb.	32/32	1,600k	75, 100

CPU PROCESSOR TYPES

CPU Type	Date	MaxMem Phys/Virt	Bus Int/Ext	Number of Transistors	Speeds MHz
Intel Corporation (cont.)					
Pentium SL (3.3 or 5V)	3-94	4Gb/64Tb	32/64	3,300k	75, 100, 120, 133, 150, 166, 200
Pentium (3.3 or 5V)	10-94	4Gb/64Tb	32/64	3,200k	75, 90, 100, 120
Pentium (3.3 or 5V)	6-95	4Gb/64Tb	32/64	3,300k	133,150,166,200
Pentium Pro (3.3V)	1-95	64Gb/64Tb	64/64	5,500k	150,166,180,200
Pent. w/ MMX (3.3 or 5V)	1-97	4Gb/64Tb	32/64	4,500k	166, 200, 233
Pentium II	5-97	64Gb/64Tb	64/64	7,500k	233, 266, 300
P6 (Deschutes)	1998				
P7 (Merced w/ HP)	1999				
Intel Corporation - Upgrade Chips					
SX2Overdrive (3.3 or 5V)	?	4Gb/64Tb	32/32	?	50
DX2Overdrive	?	4Gb/64Tb	32/32	900k	40, 50, 66
DX4Overdrive	10-94	4Gb/64Tb	32/32	1,600k	63, 83
Pentium Overdrive	?	4Gb/64Tb	32/32	3,300k	120, 133
Pent. Over. w/ MMX (3.3V)	?	? / ?	? / ?	?	125, 150, 166
International Business Machines Corporation					
80386SLC	12-91	16Mb/ ?	32/16	800k	16, 20, 25
80486SLC2 (doubler)	9-92	16Mb/ ?	32/16	1,425k	20/40,25/50,33/66
80486SLC3 (tripler)	?	16Mb/ ?	32/16	1,425k	25/75
BL486DX (doubler)	?	4Gb/64Tb	32/32	~1,400k	25/50, 33/66, 40/80, 50/100
BL486DX2 (doubler)	?	4Gb/64Tb	32/32	~1,400k	25/50, 33/66, 40/80
BL486DXV (3.3V)	?	4Gb/64Tb	32/32	~1,400k	33, 40
BL486DX2V (3.3V)	?	4Gb/64Tb	32/32	~1,400k	25/50, 33/66, 40/80
6x86 (3.3V)	?	? / ?	32/32	?	120, 133, 150
PowerPC 603 (3.3V)	?	? / ?	32/32	1,600k	66, 80
PowerPC 603 (3.3V)	?	? / ?	32/32	2,500k	100
PowerPC 604 (3.3V)	10-94	? / ?	32/32	3,600k	100, 120, 133, 150, 166, 180
PowerPC 603e (3.3V)	10-95	? / ?	32/32	2,600k	150,160,166, 180, 200,225,233,240,250
6x86MX (3.3V)	5-97	? / ?	32/32	?	150, 165, 188
PowerPC 604e (3.3V)	6-97	? / ?	32/32	5,100k	160, 180, 200, 225,233,240,250
International Meta Systems, Inc.					
Meta 6000	1-98	? / ?	? / ?	?	225
Meta Expresso	1-98	? / ?	? / ?	?	150 to 200
Meta 6500	7-98	? / ?	? / ?	?	450
Meta 7000/BiFrost	1-99	? / ?	? / ?	?	700
Kingston Technology Company - Upgrade Chips					
SLC/Now!-20 (386SLC-20)	?	? / ?	32/32	?	20
SLC/Now!-25 (386SLC-25)	?	? / ?	32/32	?	25
SLC/Now!-50 (486SLC-50)	?	? / ?	32/32	?	50
486/Now! (486/25CS3 or /33CD3)	?	? / ?	? / ?	?	25, 33
(486/25PS3 or /33PS3)	?	? / ?	? / ?	?	25, 33
Lightning 486 (486/BL66 or /CLN66)	?	? / ?	? / ?	?	66

CPU PROCESSOR TYPES

CPU Type	Date	MaxMem Phys/Virt	Bus Int/Ext	Number of Transistors	Speeds MHz
Kingston Technology Company - Upgrade Chips (cont.)					
MCMaster					
(MC50PD or MC66PD)	?	? / ?	? / ?	?	50, 66
TurboChip 486					
(TC486/100 or / 75)	?	? / ?	? / ?	?	75, 100
TurboChip 133 (TC5x86/133)	?	? / ?	? / ?	?	133
MIPS Technologies, Inc.					
R2000	1986	? / ?	32/32	110k	8
R3000 (5V)	1988	? / ?	32/32	?	40
R6000	1991	? / ?	32/32	?	66.7
R4000	1992	? / ?	64/64	1,100k	100
R4400 (3.3V)	1992	64Gb/ ?	64/64	2,300k	150, 200, 250
R4200 (3.3V)	1993	? / ?	64/64	1,400k	80
R4600 (3.3V)	1994	? / ?	64/64	1,850k	133, 150
R8000 (3.3V)	1994	? / ?	64/64	3,430k	75, 90
R4300i (3.3V)	1995	? / ?	64/64	1,700k	100, 133
R4700 (3.3V)	1995	? / ?	64/64	1,800k	175
R5000 (3.3V)	1996	? / ?	64/64	3,600k	180, 200, 250
R10000 (3.3V)	1996	? / ?	64/64	6,800k	150,175,200,275
R5000A (3.3V)	1997	? / ?	64/64	3,600k	
RM7000	1997	? / ?	64/64	?	300
R12000 (3.3V)	1998		64/64		300
H1 Series	1999		64/64		
H2 Series	2000		64/64		
Motorola Communications and Electronics, Inc.					
68020 (5V)	1985	? / ?	? / ?	?	25
68030 (5V)	?	? / ?	? / ?	270k	50
68040 (5V)	1989	? / ?	? / ?	1,200k	25
68060 (3.3V)	1993	? / ?	? / ?	2,400k	50
PowerPC 601 (3.6V)	1993	? / ?	32/64	2,800k	66, 80, 100
PowerPC 603 (3.3V)	1994	4Gb/4Pb.	32/64	1,600k	50, 66, 80
PowerPC 604 (3.3V)	1994	4Gb/4Pb.	32/64	3,600k	100, 133, 180
PowerPC 602 (3.3V)	1995	4Gb/4Pb.	32/64	1,000k	66
PowerPC 603e (3.3V)	1995	4Gb/4Pb.	32/64	2,600k	100,120,133,166, 180,200,250,275,300
PowerPC 620 (3.3V)	1995	1Tb/1Hb.	64/64	7,000k	133, 200
PowerPC 604e (3.3V)	1996	4Gb/4Pb.	32/64	5,100k	180,200,225,233, 250, 300, 350
PowerPC 630 (3.3V)	1997				600
PowerPC 740					
(3.3V, G3 Series)	1998	4Gb/ ?.	32/64	6,350k	200, 233, 266
PowerPC 750					
(3.3V, G3 Series)	1998	4Gb/ ?.	32/64	6,350k	200, 233, 266
PowerPC 604r					
(Mach 5, 3.3V)	1999				
PowerPC 770 (G3 Series)	1999			~30,000k	
G4 Series	2000			~50,000k	
NEC America, Inc.					
V3.	3-84	1Mb.	16/16	63k	8, 10
V20.	3-84	1Mb.	16/8	63k	8, 10
VR4100 (3.3V)	?	? / ?	64/64	?	40

CPU PROCESSOR TYPES

CPU Type	Date	MaxMem Phys/Virt	Bus Int/Ext	Number of Transistors	Speeds MHz
NEC America, Inc. (cont.)					
VR4101 (3.3V)	?	? / ?	64/64	?	33
VR4300 (3.3V)	?	? / ?	64/64	?	100, 133
VR4400 (3.3V)	?	? / ?	64/64	?	200, 250
VR4400MC (3.3V)	?	? / ?	64/64	?	200
VR5000 (3.3V)	?	? / ?	64/64	?	150, 180, 200
VR10000 (3.3V)	?	? / ?	64/64	?	200
NexGen, Inc.					
Nx586	?	? / ?	32/32	3,500k	70, 75, 84, 93
(Company acquired by Advanced Micro Devices in 1995.)					
Philips Semiconductor					
TriMedia TM-1000	7-97	? / ?	? / ?...	5,500k	100, 133, 166
(Multimedia accelerator chip)					
Ross Technology, Inc. - Upgrade Chips					
hyperSPARC (5V)	1994	? / ?	32/32	1,500k	90, 100, 125, 142, 150, 180
SGS-Thomson Microelectronics					
ST486DX (5V)	?	4Gb/ ?	32/32	?	33, 40, 50
ST486DX2 (5V, doubler)	?	4Gb/ ?	32/32	?	50, 66, 80
ST6x86 (3.3V)	?	? / ?	64/32	?	80, 100, 110, 120, 133, 150
MPact R (3.3V)	4-97	? / ?	32	?	75
(Multimedia co-processor developed with Chromatic Research, Inc.)					
Sun Microsystems, Inc.					
Thunder I (5V)	1993	? / ?	32/32	6,000k	50
microSPARC-II	1994	? / ?	32/32	2,300k	85, 100
SuperSPARC-II (5V)	1995	? / ?	32/32	3,100k	75, 90
UltraSPARC-I (3.3V)	10-95	? / ?	64/64	5,200k	143,167,182,200
UltraSPARC-II (3.3V)	10-95	? / ?	64/64	5,400k	250, 300, 330
UltraSPARC-IIi (3.3V)	10-96	? / ?	64/64	?	266, 300
microSPARC-IIep (3.3V)	?	? / ?	32/32	?	100 to 125
Texas Instruments, Inc.					
TI486SXLC (3.3V)	?	16Mb/ ?	32/16	?	25, 33
TX486SXLC (5V)	?	16Mb/ ?	32/16	?	33
TX486SXLC2 (5V, doubler)	?	16Mb/ ?	32/16	?	25/50
TX486SL (3.3V)	?	4Gb/ ?	32/32	?	33
TX486SL (5V)	?	4Gb/ ?	32/32	?	40
TX486SXL2 (3.3V, doubler)	?	4Gb/ ?	32/32	?	20/40
TX486SXL2 (5V, doubler)	?	4Gb/ ?	32/32	?	25/50
Texas Instruments, Inc. - Upgrade Chips					
TI486SLC/E (5V)	?	16Mb/ ?	32/16	?	25, 33
TI486SLC/E-V (3.3V)	?	16Mb/ ?	32/16	?	25
TI486DLC/E (5V)	?	4Gb/ ?	32/32	?	33, 40
TI486DLC/E-V (3.3V)	?	4Gb/ ?	32/32	?	25, 33

MATH CoPROCESSOR TYPES

CPU Type	CoProcessor
8086,8088,V20 & V30	8087
80286	80287XL
80386SX & SL	80387SX
80386DX	80387DX
80486SX	80487SX
80486DX	Built In
Pentium - all versions	Built In

PC MEMORY MAP

Address Range	Size	Description
00000-003FF	1K	Interrupt Vectors
00400-7FFFF	512K	Bios, DOS, 512K RAM Expansion
80000-9FFFF	128K	128K RAM Expansion (Top of 640K)
A0000-AFFFF	64K	EGA Video Buffer
B0000-B7FFF	32K	Monochrome & other screen buffers
B8000-BFFFF	32K	CGA and EGA Buffers
AT LIM Expanded Memory 64K page is between 768K and 896K		
C0000-C3FFF	16K	EGA Video Bios
C4000-C7FFF	16K	ROM Expansion Area
XT LIM Expanded Memory 64K page is between 800K and 960K		
C8000-CCFFF	20K	XT Hard Disk Controller Bios
CD000-CFFFF	12K	User PROM, Memory mapped I/O
D0000-DFFFF	64K	User PROM, normal LIM Location for Expanded Memory
E0000-EFFFF	64K	ROM expansion, I/O for XT
F0000-FDFFF	56K	ROM BASIC
FE000-FFFD9	8K	BIOS
FFFF0-FFFF4	4	1st Code run after system power on
FFFF5-FFFFC	8	BIOS Release Date
FFFFE-FFFFF	2	Machine ID (Top of 1 Meg RAM)
100000-FFFFFF	15Meg	AT Extended Memory

PC HARDWARE INTERRUPTS

NMI . . . . Non-Maskable Interrupt (Parity)

Interrupt Controller 1:

IRQ0	Timer Output
IRQ1	Keyboard controller
IRQ2	XT – Available
	AT – Route to Interrupt Controller 2, IRQ8 to 15
IRQ3	Serial Port COM2: or SDLC (see page 58)
IRQ4	Serial Port COM1: or SDLC (see page 58)
IRQ5	XT – Hard Disk Controller
	AT – Parallel Printer Port 2
IRQ6	Floppy Disk Controller
IRQ7	Parallel Printer Port LPT1:

Interrupt Controller 2 (AT Only):

IRQ8	Real Time Clock
IRQ9	Software redirect to IRQ2 (Int 0A Hex)
IRQ10	Reserved
IRQ11	Reserved
IRQ12	Reserved
IRQ13	80287 Math Coprocessor
IRQ14	Hard Disk Controller
IRQ15	Some hard drive and SCSI controllers

DMA CHANNELS

XT 8 bit ISA Bus

Channel	Function
0	Dynamic memory refresh
1	Unassigned or SDLC
2	Floppy disk controller
3	Hard disk controller

16 bit ISA, EISA, and MCA Bus

Channel	Function
DMA Controller #1	
0	Dynamic memory refresh
1	Unassigned or SDLC
2	Floppy disk controller
3	Unassigned
DMA Controller #2	
4	First DMA Controller
5	Unassigned
6	Unassigned
7	Unassigned

SERIAL/COM: PORTS

Com: Port	PC / ISA IRQ / Address	PS2 / MCA IRQ / Address
1	4 / 03F8h	4 / 03F8h
2	3 / 02F8h	3 / 02F8h
3	4 / 03E8h*	3 / 3220h
4	3 / 02E8h*	3 / 3228h
5	not available	3 / 4220h
6	not available	3 / 4228h
7	not available	3 / 5220h
8	not available	3 / 5228h

* Note that some software and hardware products do not support
the COM3: and COM4: addresses and interrupts

PC HARDWARE I/O MAP

8088 Class Systems

Address	Function
000–00F	DMA Controller (8237A)
020–021	Interrupt controller (8259A)
040–043	Timer (8253)
060–063	PPI (8255A)
080–083	DMA page register (74LS612)
0A0–0AF	NMI – Non Maskable Interrupt
200–20F	Game Port Joystick controller
210–217	Expansion Unit
2E8–2EF	COM4: Serial Port (see page 58)
2F8–2FF	COM2: Serial Port
300–31F	Prototype Card
320–32F	Hard Disk
378–37F	Parallel Printer Port 1
380–38F	SDLC
3B0–3BF	MDA – Monochrome Adapter and printer
3D0–3D7	CGA – Color Graphics Adapter
3E8–3EF	COM3: Serial Port (see page 58)
3F0–3F7	Floppy Diskette Controller
3F8–3FF	COM1: Serial Port

80286 /386/486 Class Systems

Address	Function
000–01F	DMA Controller #1 (8237A–5)
020–03F	Interrupt controller #1 (8259A)
040–05F	Timer (8254)
060–06F	Keyboard (8042)
070–07F	NMI – Non Maskable Interrupt & CMOS RAM
080–09F	DMA page register (74LS612)
0A0–0BF	Interrupt controller #2 (8259A)
0C0–0DF	DMA Controller #2 (8237A)
0F0–0FF	80287 Math Coprocessor
1F0–1F8	Hard Disk
200–20F	Game Port Joystick controller
258–25F	Intel Above Board
278–27F	Parallel Printer Port 2
2E8–2EF	COM4: Serial Port (see page 58)
2F8–2FF	COM2: Serial Port
300–31F	Prototype Card
378–37F	Parallel Printer Port 1
380–38F	SDLC or Bisynchronous Comm Port 2
3A0–3AF	Bisynchronous Comm Port 1
3B0–3BF	MDA – Monochrome Adapter
3BC–3BE	Parallel Printer on Monochrome Adapter
3C0–3CF	EGA – Reserved
3D0–3D7	CGA – Color Graphics Adapter
3E8–3EF	COM3: Serial Port (see page 58)
3F0–3F7	Floppy Diskette Controller
3F8–3FF	COM1: Serial Port

PC SOFTWARE INTERRUPTS

Address	Int #	Interrupt Name
000–003	0	Divide by zero
004–007	1	Single Step IRET
008–00B	2	NMI Non Maskable Interrupt
00C–00F	3	Breakpoint
010–013	4	Overflow IRET
014–017	5	Print Screen
018–01F	6	Reserved 018–01B and 01C–01F
020–023	8	Time of Day Ticker IRQ0
024–027	9	Keyboard IRQ1
028–02B	A	XT Reserved, AT IRQ2 direct to IRQ9
02C–02F	B	COM2 communications, IRQ3
030–033	C	COM1 communications, IRQ4
034–037	D	XT Hard disk, AT Parallel Printer, IRQ5
038–03B	E	Floppy Diskette, IRQ6
03C–03F	F	Parallel Printer 1, IRQ7, slave 8259, IRET
040–043	10	ROM Handler – Video
044–047	11	ROM Handler – Equipment Check
048–04B	12	ROM Handler – Memory Check
04C–04F	13	ROM Handler – Diskette I/O
050–053	14	ROM Handler – COMM I/O
054–057	15	XT Cassette, AT ROM Catchall Handlers
058–05B	16	ROM Handler – Keyboard I/O
05C–05F	17	ROM Handler – Printer I/O
060–063	18	ROM Handler – Basic Startup
064–067	19	ROM Handler – Bootstrap
068–06B	1A	ROM Handler – Time of Day
06C–06F	1B	ROM Handler – Keyboard Break
070–073	1C	ROM Handler – User Ticker
074–077	1D	ROM Pointer, Video Initialization
078–07B	1E	ROM Pointer, Diskette Parameters
07C–07F	1F	ROM Pointer, Graphics Characters Set 2
080–083	20	DOS – Terminate Program
084–087	21	DOS – Function Call
088–08B	22	DOS – Program's Terminate Address
08C–08F	23	DOS – Program's Control–Break Address
090–093	24	DOS – Critical Error Handler
094–097	25	DOS – Absolute Disk Read
098–09B	26	DOS – Absolute Disk Write
09C–09F	27	DOS – TSR Terminate & Stay Ready
0A0–0FF	28–3F	DOS – Idle Loop, IRET
100–103	40	Hard Disk Pointer – Original Floppy Handler
104–107	41	ROM Pointer, XT Hard Disk Parameters
108–10B	42–45	Reserved
10C–10F	46	ROM Pointer, AT Hard Disk Parameters
110–17F	47–5F	Reserved
180–19F	60–67	Reserved for User (67 is Expanded Mem)
1A0–1BF	68–6F	Not Used
1C0–1C3	70	AT Real Time Clock, IRQ8
1C4–1C7	71	AT Redirect to IRQ2, IRQ9, LAN Adapter 1
1C8–1CB	72	AT Reserved, IRQ10
1CC–1CF	73	AT Reserved, IRQ11
1D0–1D3	74	AT Reserved, IRQ12
1D4–1D7	75	AT 80287 Error to NMI, IRQ13
1D8–1DB	76	AT Hard Disk, IRQ14
1DC–1DF	77	AT Reserved, IRQ15
1E0–1FF	78–7F	Not Used
200–217	80–85	Reserved for BASIC
218–21B	86	NetBIOS, Relocated Interrupt 18H
218–3C3	87–F0	Reserved for BASIC Interpreter
3C4–3FF	F1–FF	Not Used

AUDIO ERROR CODES

A variety of tests are executed automatically when computers are first turned on. Initially, the "Power-On Self Test" (POST) is run. It provides error or warning messages whenever a faulty component is encountered. Typically, two types of messages are issued: **Audio Beep Codes** and **Display Error Messages.**

Audio Beep Codes consist of a series of beeps that identify a faulty component. In the case of an IBM computer, if it is functioning normally, you will hear one short beep when the system is turned on. However, if a problem is detected, a series of beeps or no beeps will occur. The type and number of beeps define the problem. Audio Beep Codes for some of the major BIOS manufacturers are included below.

If the system has problems but completes the POST process, then additional errors may be reported in the form of **Display Error Messages.** The list of **Display Error Messages** is quite extensive and only the IBM PC/XT/PS2 messages are included in Pocket PCRef.

American Megatrends Bios (AMI)

Beeps	Error Description
Fatal Errors	
1	DRAM refresh failed
2	Parity circuit failed
3	Base 64K or CMOS RAM failed
4	System timer failed
5	Processor failed
6	Keyboard controller or gate A20 error
7	Virtual mode exception error
8	Display memory write/read test failed
9	ROM BIOS checksum failed
10	CMOS RAM shutdown register failed
11	Cache memory bad, do not enable cache
Nonfatal errors	
1 long, 3 short	Conventional/extended memory failed
1 long, 8 short	Display and retrace failed

Dell Computer Corporation Bios

Beeps	Error Description
1-3	Video memory test failure
1-1-2	Testing CPU register
1-1-3	CMOS write/read test failed
1-1-4	ROM BIOS checksum bad
1-2-1	Programmable interval timer failed
1-2-2	DMA initialization failed
1-2-3	DMA page register write/read bad
1-3-1	RAM refresh verification failed

Dell Computer Corporation Bios (cont.)

Beeps	Error Description
1-3-2	Testing first 64K RAM
1-3-3	First 64K RAM chip or data line bad, multi-bit
1-3-4	First 64K RAM odd/even logic bad
1-4-1	Address line fault in first 64K RAM
1-4-2	Parity error detected in first 64K RAM
2-1-1	Bit 0 fault in first 64K RAM
2-1-2	Bit 1 fault in first 64K RAM
2-1-3	Bit 2 fault in first 64K RAM
2-1-4	Bit 3 fault in first 64K RAM
2-2-1	Bit 4 fault in first 64K RAM
2-2-2	Bit 5 fault in first 64K RAM
2-2-3	Bit 6 fault in first 64K RAM
2-2-4	Bit 7 fault in first 64K RAM
2-3-1	Bit 8 fault in first 64K RAM
2-3-2	Bit 9 fault in first 64K RAM
2-3-3	Bit 10 fault in first 64K RAM
2-3-4	Bit 11 fault in first 64K RAM
2-4-1	Bit 12 fault in first 64K RAM
2-4-2	Bit 13 fault in first 64K RAM
2-4-3	Bit 14 fault in first 64K RAM
2-4-4	Bit 15 fault in first 64K RAM
3-1-1	Slave DMA register bad
3-1-2	Master DMA register bad
3-1-3	Master interrupt mask register bad
3-1-4	Slave interrupt mask register bad
3-2-2	Interrupt vector loading in progress
3-2-4	Keyboard controller test failed
3-3-1	CMOS RAM power bad; calculating checksum
3-3-2	CMOS configuration validation in progress
3-3-4	Video memory test failed
3-4-1	Video initialization failed
3-4-2	Video retrace failure
3-4-3	Search for video ROM in progress
none	Screen operable, running with video ROM
none	Monochrome monitor operable
none	Color monitor (40 column) operable
none	Color monitor (80 column) operable
4-2-1	Timer tick interrupt test in progress or bad
4-2-2	Shutdown test in progress or bad
4-2-3	Gate A20 bad
4-2-4	Unexpected interrupt in protected mode
4-3-1	RAM test in progress or high address line bad FFFF
4-3-3	Interval timer channel 2 test or bad
4-3-4	Time-of-Day clock test or bad
4-4-1	Serial port test or bad

Dell Computer Corporation Bios (cont.)

Beeps	Error Description
4-4-2	Parallel port test or bad
4-4-3	Math coprocessor test or bad
4-4-4	Cache test failure
5-1-2	BIOS update error; no RAM in system
5-1-3	BIOS update error; external video card detected
5-1-4	BIOS execution error
6-1-2	I/O controller failure
6-1-3	Keyboard controller failure
6-1-4	CMOS register test failure
6-2-1	BIOS shadowing failure
6-2-2	Pentium speed determination failure
6-2-3	No SIMM installed

IBM Corporation Bios

Beeps	Error Description
1 short	Successful Post, no errors
2 short	Initialization error - serial, parallel, floppy, ROM, or DMA
1 long, 1 short	System Board
1 long, 2 short	Video adapter or video memory failed
1 long, 3 short	Video adapter failed, EGA
3 long	3270 keyboard card failure
None	Power supply or system board
Continuous	Power supply or system board
Repeating short	Power supply or system board

Mylex and Eurosoft Bios

Beeps	Error Description
1	Always present to indicate start of beep coding
2	Video adapter bad or not detected
3	Keyboard controller error
4	Keyboard error
5	8259 Programmable Interrupt Controller (PIC) 1 Er
6	8259 PIC 2 error
7	DMA page register failure
8	RAM refresh error
9	RAM data test failed
10	RAM parity error occurred
11	8237 DMA controller 2 failed
12	CMOS RAM failure
13	8237 DMA controller 2 failed
14	CMOS RAM battery failure
15	CMOS RAM checksum error
16	RIOS ROM checksum error

Phoenix Bios

Beeps	Error Description
none/1-1-2	CPU reguster test in progress
1-1-3	CMOS write/read test failed
1-1-4	ROM BIOS checksum bad
1-2-1	Programmable interval timer failed
1-2-2	DMA initialization failed
1-2-3	DMA page register write/read bad
1-3-1	RAM refresh verification failed
none/1-3-2	Testing first 64K RAM
1-3-3	First 64K RAM chip or data line fault, multi-bit
1-3-4	First 64K RAM odd/even logic bad
1-4-1	Address line bad first 64K RAM
1-4-2	Parity error detected in first 64K RAM
1-4-3	EISA fail-safe timer test in progress
1-4-4	EISA s/w NMI port 462 test in progress
2-1-1	Bit 0 fault in first 64K RAM
2-1-2	Bit 1 fault in first 64K RAM
2-1-3	Bit 2 fault in first 64K RAM
2-1-4	Bit 3 fault in first 64K RAM
2-2-1	Bit 4 fault in first 64K RAM
2-2-2	Bit 5 fault in first 64K RAM
2-2-3	Bit 6 fault in first 64K RAM
2-2-4	Bit 7 fault in first 64K RAM
2-3-1	Bit 8 fault in first 64K RAM
2-3-2	Bit 9 fault in first 64K RAM
2-3-3	Bit 10 fault in first 64K RAM
2-3-4	Bit 11 fault in first 64K RAM
2-4-1	Bit 12 fault in first 64K RAM
2-4-2	Bit 13 fault in first 64K RAM
2-4-3	Bit 14 fault in first 64K RAM
2-4-4	Bit 15 fault in first 64K RAM
3-1-1	Slave DMA register bad
3-1-2	Master DMA register bad
3-1-3	Master interrupt mask register bad
3-1-4	Slave interrupt mask register bad
none/3-2-2	Interrupt vector loading in progress
3-2-4	Keyboard controller test failed
none/3-3-1	CMOS RAM power bad; calculating checksum
none/3-3-2	CMOS configuration validation in progress
3-3-4	Video memory test failed
3-4-1	Video initialization failed
3-4-2	Video retrace failure
none/3-4-3	Search for video ROM in progress
none	DDNIL bit scan failed
none	Screen operable, running with video ROM
none	Monochrome monitor operable

Phoenix Bios (cont.)

Beeps	Error Description
none	Color monitor (40 column) operable
none	Color monitor (80 column) operable
4-2-1	Timer tick interrupt test in progress or bad
4-2-2	Shutdown test in progress or bad
4-2-3	Gate A20 bad
4-2-4	Unexpected interrupt in protected mode
4-3-1	RAM test in progress or high address line bad FFFF
4-3-3	Interval timer channel 2 test or bad
4-3-4	Time-of-Day clock test or bad
4-4-1	Serial port test or bad
4-4-2	Parallel port test or bad
4-4-3	Math coprocessor test or bad
4-4-4	Cache test failure (Dell)
low-1-1-2	System board select bad (MCA only)
low-1-1-3	Extended CMOS RAM bad (MCA only)

Quadtel Bios

Beeps	Error Description
1 beep	POST ran okay and detected no error. System will now boot.
2 beeps.	POST detected a configuration error, or a CMOS RAM change since the last time you ran Setup. Check the CMOS battery and rerun Setup.
1 long, 2 short . .	Faulty video configuration (no or bad video card installed), or bad ROM on a peripheral controller card (address range C0000 through FFFF)
1 long, 3+shorts	Faulty peripheral controller, such as VGA. Usually, the display shows a descriptive message. Check the setup of peripheral controllers.

Tandon Bios

Beeps	Error Description
long-short-long-short . .	8254 counter timer failure
short-long-short	RAM refresh failure
long-long-long	System RAM failure
short-short-short.	BIOS RAM checksum failure
long-long.	No video adapter is installed
long-long-long-long . . .	Video adapter failure

IBM XT/AT CLASS ERROR CODES

Code	Description
01x	Undetermined problem errors
02x	Power supply errors
1xx	**System board error**
101	Interrupt failure
102	Timer failure
103	Timer interrupt failure
104	Protected mode failure
105	Last 8042 command not accepted
106	Converting logic test
107	Hot NMI test
108	Timer bus test
109	Direct memory access test error
121	Unexpected hardware interrupts occurred
131	Cassette wrap test failed
152	System board error: defective battery
161	System Options Error-(Run SETUP) [Battery failure]
162	System options not set correctly-(Run SETUP)
163	Time and date not set-(Run SETUP)
164	Memory size error-(Run SETUP)
199	User indicated configuration not correct
2xx	**Memory (RAM) errors**
201	Memory test failed
202	Memory address error
203	Memory address error
3xx	**Keyboard errors**
301	Keyboard did not respond to software reset correctly or a stuck key failure was detected. If a stuck key was detected, the scan code for the key is displayed in hexadecimal. For example, the error code 49 301 indicates that key 73, the PgUp key has failed (49 Hex = 73 decimal)
302	User indicated error from the keyboard test or AT system unit keylock is locked
303	Keyboard or system unit error
304	Keyboard or system unit error; CMOS does not match system
4xx	**Monochrome monitor errors**
401	Monochrome memory test, horizontal sync frequency test, or video test failed
408	User indicated display attributes failure
416	User indicated character set failure
424	User indicated 80X25 mode failure
432	Parallel port test failed (monochrome adapter)
5xx	**Color monitor errors**
501	Color memory test failed, horizontal sync frequency test, or video test failed
508	User indicated display attribute failure
516	User indicated character set failure
524	User indicated 80X25 mode failure
532	User indicated 40X25 mode failure
540	User indicated 320X200 graphics mode failure
548	User indicated 640X200 graphics mode failure
6xx	**Diskette drive errors**

IBM XT/AT CLASS ERROR CODES

Code	Description
601	Diskette power on diagnostics test failed
602	Diskette test failed; boot record is not valid
606	Diskette verify function failed
607	Write protected diskette
608	Bad command diskette status returned
610	Diskette initialization failed
611	Time-out - diskette status returned
612	Bad NEC - diskette status returned
613	Bad DMA - diskette status returned
621	Bad seek - diskette status returned
622	Bad CRC - diskette status returned
623	Record not found - diskette status returned
624	Bad address mark - diskette status returned
625	Bad NEC seek - diskette status returned
626	Diskette data compare error
7xx	**8087 or 80287 math coprocessor errors**
9xx	**Parallel printer adapter errors**
901	Parallel printer adapter test failed
10xx	**Reserved for parallel printer adapter**
11xx	**Asynchronous communications adapter errors**
1101	Async communications adapter test failed
12xx	**Alternate asynchronous communications adapter errors**
1201	Alternate asynchronous communications adapter test failed
13xx	**Game control adapter errors**
1301	Game control adapter test failed
1302	Joystick test failed
14xx	**Printer errors**
1401	Printer test failed
1404	Matrix printer failed
15xx	**Synchronous data link control (SDLC) comm adapter errors**
1510	8255 port B failure
1511	8255 port A failure
1512	8255 port C failure
1513	8253 timer 1 did not reach terminal count
1514	8253 timer 1 stuck on
1515	8253 timer 0 did not reach terminal count
1516	8253 timer 0 stuck on
1517	8253 timer 2 did not reach terminal count
1518	8253 timer 2 stuck on
1519	8273 port B error
1520	8273 port A error
1521	8273 command/read time-out
1522	Interrupt level 4 failure
1523	Ring Indicate stuck on
1524	Receive clock stuck on
1525	Transmit clock stuck on
1526	Test indicate stuck on
1527	Ring indicate not on
1528	Receive clock not on
1529	Transmit clock not on
1530	Test indicate not on
1531	Data set ready not on

IBM XT/AT CLASS ERROR CODES

Code	Description
1532	Carrier detect not on
1533	Clear to send not on
1534	Data set ready stuck on
1536	Clear to send stuck on
1537	Level 3 interrupt failure
1538	Receive interrupt results error
1539	Wrap data mis-compare
1540	DMA channel 1 error
1541	DMA channel 1 error
1542	Error in 8273 error checking or status reporting
1547	Stray interrupt level 4
1548	Stray interrupt level 3
1549	Interrupt presentation sequence time-out
16xx	**Display emulation errors (327x, 5520, 525x)**
17xx	**Fixed disk errors**
1701	Fixed disk POST error
1702	Fixed disk adapter error
1703	Fixed disk drive error
1704	Fixed disk adapter or drive error
1780	Fixed disk 0 failure
1781	Fixed disk 1 failure
1782	Fixed disk controller failure
1790	Fixed disk 0 error
1791	Fixed disk 1 error
18xx	**I/O expansion unit errors**
1801	I/O expansion unit POST error
1810	Enable/Disable failure
1811	Extender card wrap test failed (disabled)
1812	High order address lines failure (disabled)
1813	Wait state failure (disabled)
1814	Enable/Disable could not be set on
1815	Wait state failure (disabled)
1816	Extender card wrap test failed (enabled)
1817	High order address lines failure (enabled)
1818	Disable not functioning
1819	Wait request switch not set correctly
1820	Receiver card wrap test failure
1821	Receiver high order address lines failure
19xx	**3270 PC attachment card errors**
20xx	**Binary synchronous communications (BSC) adapter errors**
2010	8255 port A failure
2011	8255 port B failure
2012	8255 port C failure
2013	8253 timer 1 did not reach terminal count
2014	8253 timer 1 stuck on
2016	8253 timer 2 did not reach terminal count or timer 2 stuck on
2017	8251 Data set ready failed to come on
2018	8251 Clear to send not sensed
2019	8251 Data set ready stuck on
2020	8251 Clear to send stuck on
2021	8251 hardware reset failed
2022	8251 software reset failed
2023	8251 software "error reset" failed

Code	Description
2024	8251 transmit ready did not come on
2025	8251 receive ready did not come on
2026	8251 could not force "overrun" error status
2027	Interrupt failure - no timer interrupt
2028	Interrupt failure - transmit, replace card or planar
2029	Interrupt failure - transmit, replace card
2030	Interrupt failure - receive, replace card or planar
2031	Interrupt failure - receive, replace card
2033	Ring indicate stuck on
2034	Receive clock stuck on
2035	Transmit clock stuck on
2036	Test indicate stuck on
2037	Ring indicate stuck on
2038	Receive clock not on
2039	Transmit clock not on
2040	Test indicate not on
2041	Data set ready not on
2042	Carrier detect not on
2043	Clear to send not on
2044	Data set ready stuck on
2045	Carrier detect stuck on
2046	Clear to send stuck on
2047	Unexpected transmit interrupt
2048	Unexpected receive interrupt
2049	Transmit data did not equal receive data
2050	8251 detected overrun error
2051	Lost data set ready during data wrap
2052	Receive time-out during data wrap
21xx	**Alternate binary synchronous communications adapter errors**
2110	8255 port A failure
2111	8255 port B failure
2112	8255 port C failure
2113	8253 timer 1 did not reach terminal count
2114	8253 timer 1 stuck on
2115	8253 timer 2 did not reach terminal count or timer 2 stuck on
2116	8251 Data set ready failed to come on
2117	8251 Clear to send not sensed
2118	8251 Data set ready stuck on
2119	8251 Clear to send stuck on
2120	8251 hardware reset failed
2121	8251 software reset failed
2122	8251 software "error reset" failed
2123	8251 transmit ready did not come on
2124	8251 receive ready did not come on
2125	8251 could not force "overrun" error status
2126	Interrupt failure - no timer interrupt
2128	Interrupt failure - transmit, replace card or planar
2129	Interrupt failure - transmit, replace card
2130	Interrupt failure - receive, replace card or planar
2131	Interrupt failure - receive, replace card
2133	Ring indicate stuck on
2134	Receive clock stuck on
2135	Transmit clock stuck on

IBM XT/AT CLASS ERROR CODES

Code	Description
2136	Test indicate stuck on
2137	Ring indicate stuck on
2138	Receive clock not on
2139	Transmit clock not on
2140	Test indicate not on
2141	Data set ready not on
2142	Carrier detect not on
2143	Clear to send not on
2144	Data set ready stuck on
2145	Carrier detect stuck on
2146	Clear to send stuck on
2147	Unexpected transmit interrupt
2148	Unexpected receive interrupt
2149	Transmit data did not equal receive data
2150	8251 detected overrun error
2151	Lost data set ready during data wrap
2152	Receive time-out during data wrap
22xx	**Cluster adapter errors**
24xx	**Enhanced graphics adapter errors**
29xx	**Color matrix printer errors**
2901	
2902	
2904	
33xx	**Compact printer errors**

IBM is a registered trademark of the International Business Machine Corporation.

PC Hardware

Chapter 3

Modems

*See page 58 for information on
Serial/COM: port addresses and interrupts.*

MODEM STANDARDS

V.xx Standards are international data communication standards defined by CCITT (Consultative Committee for International Telephone and Telegraph).

Standard	Description
V.13	Simulated half-duplex for synchronous networks.
V.21	300 bps, compatible with Bell 103.
V.22	1200 bps, compatible with Bell 212A; full duplex; sync or async.
V.22bis	2400 bps with fall back to 1200 bps, compatible with Bell 212A and V.22; full duplex; sync or async.
V.23	1200 bps with 75 bps back channel for use in the United Kingdom.
V.25	Provides autodialing capabilities to sync or async dialup lines. Parallel interface.
V.25bis	Provides autodialing capabilities to sync or async dialup lines. Serial interface.
V.32	4800 and 9600 bps with fall back to 4800; full duplex, sync or async. The first universal standard for 9600 bps modems.
V.32bis	14,400 bps with fall back to 12000, 9600 , 7200 and 4800 bps. Sync or async; full duplex. V.32bis incorporates "fastrain" in which it can automatically increase or decrease modem speed during operation.
V.33	14,400 or 12,000 bps sync transmission over 4 wire leased lines. Used in very high speed super computer environments. V.32bis provides the same capability but over 2 wire dialup lines.
V.34	28,800 bps Standard approved in June 1994 and is the state-of-the-art protocol for high speed modem communications. It includes a 4-dimension 64 state trellis coding not found in the V.FC modems and also includes a V.8 high speed startup sequence.
V.42	LAP-M (Link Access Protocol) Error Correction and support for MNP levels 1 to 4; falls back to MNP 1-4 if LAP-M is not available.
V.42bis	V.42 with intelligent data compression and support for MNP5; compression up to 4:1.
V.FC or V.Fast	A class of modems incorporating some of the V.34 standards.

Bell Standards are USA data communication standards defined by Bell Labs and AT&T.

Standard	Description
Bell 103	300 bps, async, full duplex over 2 wire dialup or leased lines. Comparable to V.21.
Bell 201B	2400 bps, sync, full duplex over 4 wire, half duplex over 2 wire dialup lines. Comparable to V.26.

Bell 201C	Same as 201B but dialup lines only.
Bell 208A	4800 bps, sync, full duplex over 4 wire leased line or half duplex over 2 wire leased line. Comparable to V.27
Bell 208B	Same as 208A but 2 wire dialup lines only
Bell 212A	1200 bps, sync or async, full duplex over 2 wire leased or dialup lines. Comparable to V.22.

MNP (Microcom Networking Protocol) Error Correction and Data Compression. In order to use MNP, the modems at both ends of the phone line must have the same MNP capability.

Standard	Description
MNP Level 1-4	Error correcting routines used to filter out line noise. It also reduces the size of data transferred by up to 20%, thereby speeding up transfers.
MNP Level 5	Conventional data compression of up to 2:1; useful for ASCII type files only not binary files like ZIP and ARC files. MNP 5 effectively doubles the baud rate of the transfer.

UART SERIAL CHIPS

The UART (Universal Asynchronous Receiver-Transmitter) is the heart of a computer's serial port and it provides a parallel to serial and serial to parallel translation link between computer and modem. The chips listed below are made by Intel (INS) and National Semiconductor (NS).

INS8250

The original UART used in IBM's first PC serial port. It has slow access cycle delays and requires extra NOPS between CPU read-write cycles. Several bugs (one of which was an interrupt enable problem) are present in the chip but are not serious. The 8250 was replaced by the 8250A. Chip will not work properly at 9600 bps.

INS8250A and INS82C50A

This chip is an upgrade to the original 8250 and fixes some of the original bugs. The "A" series chip was designed to correct the bugs in conjunction with the PC and XT BIOS and is therefore not compatible with many software packages and other computer's. Avoid using this chip! Chip will not work properly at 9600 bps.

INS8250B

The final upgrade of the 8250 chip series in which the bugs of the first two versions have been repaired. This chip will work in PC and XT class systems, however, it may or may not function correctly in 80286 and higher systems. Chip will not work properly at 9600 bps.

NS16450 and NS16C450

A higher speed version of the 8250 chip. It was designed for 80286 and higher systems and may or may not work correctly in PC and XT class computer's. A scratch register (#7) has been included. The OS2 operating system requires the 16450 or higher in serial ports. Maximum data rate is 38,400 bps.

NS16550

This chip is an upgrade to the 16450. It provides higher baud rates and a DMA interface. It does not support FIFO (first in - first out). It works well in 80286 and higher systems and the maximum data rate is 115,200 bps.

NS16550A

A higher speed version of the 16550 chip. It was designed for 80286 and higher systems. It allows multiple DMA access and has a built-in 16 character transmit and receive FIFO (first in - first out) buffer. The 16550A is currently the recommended UART for high speed data communications. Maximum data rate is 115,200 bps.

HAYES COMPATIBLE MODEM COMMAND SETTINGS

Command	Function
	>>>>>Note: all commands are _not_ available on all modems!<<<<<
+++	Default escape code, wait for modem to return state
A	Force answer mode; Immediate answer on ring
A /	Repeat last command line (Replaces AT)
AT	Attention code
Cn	n=Ø is Transmitter off, n=1 is on, (1=default)
Bn	n=Ø is CCITT answer tone, n=1 is US/Canada Tone
Dn	Dial telephone number
	n=Ø to 9 for phone numbers
	n=T is Touch Tone Dial, P is Pulse Dial
	n=R is Originate Only, n= , is Pause
	n=! is xfer call to following extension
	n=" is dial letters that follow
	n=@ is Dial, Wait for answer, & continue
	n= ; is Return to command mode after dialing
En	n=Ø is no character echo in command state
	n=1 is echo all characters in command state
Fn	n=Ø is Half Duplex: n=1 if Full Duplex
Hn	n=Ø is On Hook (Hang Up), n=1 is Off Hook
	n=2 is Special Off Hook
In	n=Ø is Display product code, n=1 show Check Sum
	n=2 is show RAM test, n=3 is show call time length
	n=4 is show current modem settings
Kn	n=Ø at AT13 show last call length, n=1 show time
Ln	Speaker volume control: n=Ø or 1 is low volume
	n=2 is medium volume; n=3 is high volume.
Mn	n=Ø is Speaker always off, n=2 is always on
	n=1 is Speaker on until carrier detected (default)
	n=3 is Speaker on during CONNECT sequence only.
Nn	Auto data standard/speed adjust; n=Ø is connect at S37,
	n=1 is auto data standard and speed adjust to match
On	n=Ø is return to on-line; n=1 is return to on-line & retain
Qn	n=Ø is send Result Codes; n=1 is do not send code
	n=2 is send result code only when originating call.
SØ=n	n=Ø to 255 rings before answer (see switch 5)
S1=n	Counts rings from Ø to 255
S2=n	Set escape code character, n=Ø to 127, 43 default
S3=n	Set carriage return character, n=Ø to 127, 13 default
S4=n	Set line feed character, n=Ø to 127, 10 default
S5=n	Set backspace character, n=Ø to 127, 8 default
S6=n	Wait time for dial tone, n=2 to 255 seconds
S7=n	Wait time for carrier, n=2 to 255 seconds
S8=n	Set duration of "," pause character, n=Ø to 255 sec.
S9=n	Carrier detect response time, n=1 to 255 1/10 secs.
S10=n	Delay time carrier loss to hang-up, n=1 to 255 1/10 s.
S11=n	Duration & space of Touch Tones, n=50 to 255 ms.
S12=n	Escape code guard time, n=50 to 255 1/50 seconds
S13=n	UART Status Register Bit Mapped (reserved)
S14=n	Option Register, Product code returned by AT1Ø
S15=n	Flag Register (reserved)

Command	Function
S16=n	Self test mode. n=Ø is data mode (default), n=1 is Analog Loopback, n=2 is dial test, n=4 is Test Pattern, n=5 is Analog Loopback and Test Pattern.
S18=n	Test timer for modem diagnostic tests
S37=n	Set line speed. Used in conjunction with Nn. n=Ø Attempt at speed of last AT command; n=1 to 3 attempt at 300bps; n=4 reserved; n=5 attempt 1200bps; n=6 attempt 2400bps; n=7 reserved; n=8 use 4800bps; n=9 use 9600; =10-12200bps; =11-14400bps; =12-7200
Sn ?	Send contents of Register n (Ø to 16) to Computer
Vn	n=Ø is send result codes as digits, n=1 is words
Wn	Protocol negotiation progress report; n=Ø is progress is not reported; n=1 is reported but CONNECT XXXX message reports DCE speed
Xn	Send normal or extended result codes: n=Ø send basic set/blind dial; n=1 extended/blind dial; n=2 extended/dial tone; n=3 extended/blind & busy; n=4 extended/dial tone, busy.
Yn	Long space disconnect: n=Ø is disabled; n=1 is enabled.
Zn	Modem reset: n=Ø is power on; =1 to 3 user; =4 is factory
&Cn	n=Ø is DCD always active; =1 active during connect
&Dn	n=Ø is DTR always ignored, =1 DTR causes return to command, =2 DTR disconnects, =3 disconnect/reset
&F	Get Factory Configuration
&Gn	n=Ø is Disable Guard Tone, =1 is 550hz, =2 is 1800hz
&Kn	DTE: n=Ø is disable flow control; n=3 Enable RTS/CTS flow control; n=4 enable XON/XOFF flow control; n=5 enable transparent XON/XOFF flow control.
&Ln	n=Ø or 1 Speaker Volume Low, =2 medium, =3 high
&Mn	Communications mode (same as &Qn).
&Pn	n=Ø Pulse Make/Break Ratio USA 39% / 61% n=1 Pulse Make/Break Ratio UK 33% / 67%
&Qn	Communication mode: n=Ø is Async, Direct mode; n=4 modem issues OK result code; n=5 Error correction mode; n=6 Async, Normal mode; n=8 MNP; n=9 V.42 and V.42bis modes.
&Rn	n=Ø is CTS tracks RTS, n=1 CTS always active
&Sn	n=Ø is DSR always active, n=1 DSR active at connect
&Tn	Test Commands: n=Ø end test, =1 local analog loopback, =3 local digital loopback, =4 enable Rmt digital loopback, =5 disable digital loopback, =6 request Rmt digital loop, =7 request Rmt dig loop & enter self test, =8 local analog loop & self test
&Vn	View current configuration
&W	Write Configuration to Memory
&Yn	n=Ø is Default is user configuration at NVRAM Ø ; n=1 default is user configuration at NVRAM location 1.
&Zn=x	Store Phone Number "x" at location "n". n=0,1,2, or 3

Chapter 4

DOS COMMANDS

Through MS-DOS® Version 6.22

This chapter is a concise general reference of DOS commands, <u>listed in alphabetic order regardless of command type!</u> In order to assist you in using the reference more effectively, a guide to conventions used in this chapter has been provided on page 78. A list of all DOS commands, grouped by command type, is located on page 80.

Editors Note: We strongly recommend that you upgrade your operating system with an official copy of MS-DOS 6.2x. Numerous functions and features that were not included in previous versions are now available and for the most part are bug free. The MS-DOS Users Guide and Technical Reference (order direct from Microsoft) are well written and are excellent resources. See page 6 for additional references. *If you are using Version 6.0, it is strongly recommended that you do not use DBLSPACE or SMARTDRV. Both of these programs caused a variety of problems with hard drives and are considered not safe to use.* MS-DOS 6.2x and several aftermarket programs are available which can safely provide the same features.

Command descriptions in this chapter are based on the following notations and syntax:

COMMAND NAME

Short Description: Long description

Syntax (shaded is optional):

COMMAND   Drive: \Path   /switches parameters

(Shaded areas indicate optional paramaters and switches)

> Examples: Samples of the syntax and command layout

Syntax Options:

Drive:\Path . . .	Drive & Directory containing command.
/switches	*Switches* modify the way a command performs its particular function.
parameters . . .	Data (usually numeric) passed to the command when it's started.

Command Type and Version:

External command	DOS commands stored as files on a disk. All externals end in .EXE, .COM or .SYS.
Internal command	DOS commands contained in COMMAND.COM. These are loaded into the system on startup.
Batch command	A script (text) file containing a sequence of commands to be run. The file always ends in .BAT
Config.sys command . . .	Script (text) file containing start-up system configuration information and device drivers.
Network command	Will function on a network.
Introduced with Ver X.XX	The DOS version in which a command became available.

	New commands Version 6.0
	New commands Version 6.2
Danger V6.0	Dangerous Command Version 6.0
Removed V6.2	Command Removed Version 6.2

MS-DOS vs. PC-DOS

The following files contain the **D**isc **O**perating **S**ystem (DOS).

MS-DOS systems (most clones)

MSDOS.SYS
IO.SYS
COMMAND.COM

PC-DOS systems (IBM)

IBMBIO.COM
IBMDOS.COM
COMMAND.COM

These files (except COMMAND.COM) have attributes of "read only", "system" and "hidden" and are located in the root directory of the system's boot drive (hard drive or floppy drive). If any of these files are missing, the system will not start!

Despite the differences in these "operating system" files, most of the other commands prior to Version 6.0 have the same file names, e.g. both MS and PC use the FORMAT and FDISK programs to prepare a hard drive.

Due to space limitations, Sequoia Publishing is unable to provide information on commands for **PC**-DOS Versions 6.0, 6.1, and 6.3. Beginning with Version 6.0, Microsoft and IBM have taken radically different approaches to the commands supplied on the system disks, particularly the utility programs used for procedures such as disk repair and compression. We regret not being able to include these new PC-DOS commands, but we simply can't include the additional 100+ pages it would require. See page 81 for a list of the commands not covered.

MSDOS COMMANDS, DRIVERS & UTILITIES

External		Internal	
Ados.com	Keyb.com	CD (Chdir)	Fastopen.exe
Append.exe	Keybxx.com	Chcp	FCBS
Assign.com	Label.exe	Chdir (CD)	Files
Attrib.exe	Link.exe	Cls	Himem.sys
Backinfo.exe	Loadfix.com	Copy	Include
Backup.exe	Mem.exe	Ctty	Install
Basic.exe	Memmaker.exe	Date	Interlnk.exe
Basica.exe	Mirror.com	Del (Erase)	Kbdbuf.sys
Chkdsk.exe	Mode.com	Dir	Keyb.com/
Chkstate.sys	More.com	Echo	Keyboard.sys
Command.com	Move.exe	Erase (Del)	Lastdrive
Comp.exe	Msav/Mwav.exe	Exit	Menucolor
Country.sys	Msbackup/	For	Menudefault
CV.com	Mwbackup.exe	LH(load high)	Menuitem
Dblboot.bat	Mscdex.exe	Loadhigh	Nlsfunc.exe
Dblspace.exe	Msd.com &.exe	MD (Mkdir)	Numlock
Debug.exe	Msherc.com	Mkdir (MD)	Power.exe
Defrag.exe	Nlsfunc.exe	Path	Printer.sys
Deloldos.exe	Power.exe	Prompt	Ramdrive.sys/
Deltree.exe	Print.exe	RD (Rmdir)	Vdisk.sys
Diskcomp.com	Printfix.com	Rem	Rem
Diskcopy.com	Qbasic.exe	Ren (Rename)	Setver.exe
Doskey.com	Recover.exe	Rename (Ren)	Share.exe
Dosshell.com	Replace.exe	Rmdir (RD)	Shell
Dosshell.exe	Restore.exe	Set	Smartdrv.exe
Drvboot.bat	Scandisk.exe	Time	Smartdrv.sys
Drvspace.exe	Select.exe	Type	Stacks
Dvorak.sys	Setup/	Ver	Submenu
Edit.com	Busetup.exe	Verify	Switchar
Edlin.exe	Setver.exe	Vol	Switches
Emm386.exe	Share.exe		
Exe2bin.exe	Sizer.exe	**Config.sys**	**Batch**
Expand.exe	Smartdrv.exe	Ansi.sys	@
Fasthelp.exe	Smartmon.exe	Break	Break
Fastopen.exe	Sort.exe	Buffers	Call
FC.exe	Spatch.bat	Command.com	Choice.com
Fdisk.exe	Subst.exe	Country.sys	Echo
Find.exe	Sys.com	Dblspace.sys	For
Format.com	Tree.com	Device	Goto
Graftabl.com	Truename.exe	Devicehigh	IF
Graphics.com	Undelete/	Display.sys	Pause
GW-Basic.exe	Mwundel.exe	DOS	Rem
Help.com	Unformat.com	Driver.sys	Shift
Help.exe	Uninstal.exe	Drivparm	
Interlnk.exe	Vsafe.exe	Drvspace.sys	
Intersvr.exe	Wina20.386	EGA.sys	
Join.exe	Xcopy.exe	Emm386.exe	

MS-DOS vs. PC-DOS

DOS COMMANDS, DRIVERS AND UTILITIES

Operating System
See also p. 79

Microsoft
  MSDOS files:
  Command.com
  Io.sys
  Msdos.sys

IBM
  PCDOS files:
  Command.com
  Ibmbio.com
  Ibmdos.com

Can Not Use on a Network
Chkdsk
Diskcomp
Diskcopy
Fastopen
Fdisk
Format
Join
Label
Recover
Scandisk
Subst
Sys
Unformat

Can Not Use While Running Windows
Append
Defrag
Emm386
Fastopen
Memmaker
Mscdex
Nlsfunc
Smartdrv
Subst
Vsafe

The Following PC-DOS Version 6.0, 6.1, and 6.3 Files are Not Described in this Edition of Pocket PCRef
See page 79
Cmosclk.sys
Cpbackup
Cpbdir
Cpsched
Datamon
Drvlock
E
Eject
Ibmavd
Ibmavw
Ibmavsp
Installhigh
Meutoini
Mouse
Pcformat
Pcmata
Pcmcs.sys
Pcmcs.exe
Pcmfdd
Pcmfdd.exe
Pcinfo
Pcmmtd
Pcmmtd.exe
Pcmscd.exe
Pcmscd
Pcmvcd.386
Pendos
Pendev.sys
Qconfig
Ramboost.exe
Ramsetup
Schedule
Setup
Umbcga.sys
Umbems.sys
Umbherc.sys
Umbmono.sys
Wnbackup
Wnschedl

DOS History

		System File Sizes			
DOS Type	Release Date	Command. COM	io and ibmbio	msdos & ibmdos	Loaded System (if High)
PC 1.0 MS 1.0	8-4-81	3,231	1,920	6,400	13,312
PC 1.1 MS 1.25	5-7-82	4,959	1,920	6,400	14,336
Zenith		4,986	1,713	6,138	
PC 2.0 MS 2.0	3-8-83	17,792	4,608	17,152	40,960
Wang 2.01	12-22-83	15,877	30,482(Bios)	17,521	
PC 2.1 MS 2.11	10-20-83	17,792	4,736	17,024	40,960
?mfg PC 2.11	11-17-83 11-17-83	15,957	6,836	17,176	25,680
PC 2.11	5-30-84	18,272	5,120	17,408	
PCAT&T 2.11	6-5-85	15,957	6,917	17,176	
MSSanyo2.11 MS 2.25	9-83-84	16,117	5,164	17,019	
PC 3.0 MS 3.0	8-14-84	22,042	8,964	27,920	60,416
PC 3.1 MS 3.1	3-7-85	23,210	9,564	27,760	62,464
PC 3.2	12-30-85	23,791	16,369	28,477	69,632
MS 3.2	7-7-86	23,612	16,138	28,480	55,568
MS 3.21 ZenithMS 3.21	5-1-87 9-28-87	23,948	18,501	28,480	
PC 3.3	3-17-87	25,307	22,100	30,159	78,848
MS 3.3	7-24-87	25,276	22,357	30,128	55,440
MS 3.3a	2-2-88	25,308	22,398	30,128	
MS 4.0	10-6-88				
PC 4.01	3-89				
MS 4.01	11-30-88				
MS 4.01a	4-7-89	37,557	33,337	37,376	73,232
PC 5.0	5-9-91	47,987	33,430	37,378	
MS 5.0	4-9-91	33,430	37,394	47,845	62,576 (21,776)
PC 5.00.1a	2-28-92	48,006	33,446	37,378	
PC 5.02	9-1-92	47,990	33,718	37,362	

System File Sizes

DOS Type	Release Date	Command. COM	io and ibmbio	msdos & ibmdos	Loaded System (if High)
MS 6.0	3-10-93	52,925	40,470	38,138	63,065 (17,197)
IBM 6.1	6-29-93	52,589	40,964	38,138	
PC 6.1	9-30-93	52,797	40,964	38,138	
MS 6.2R0	9-30-93	54,619	40,566	38,138	63,085 (22,093)
MS 6.22	5-31-94	54,645	40,774	38,138	63,085 (25,037)
PC 6.3	12-31-93	54,654	40,758	37,174	

NOTE: *According to Microsoft, there were no official versions of MS-DOS prior to version 3.2. Prior to version 3.2, only OEM versions were sold with computers by the computer manufacturers. Slight variations in the sizes do occur, so use these as a general reference only. If you have one of the OEM versions listed above, for which there is no data, we would appreciate hearing from you so we can fill in the gaps. See page 4 for a contact address and phone number.*

ADOS.COM `New V6.0`

Starts AccessDOS: AccessDOS contains a set of public domain MS-DOS extensions developed for persons with motion and hearing disabilities by the University of Wisconsin.

Syntax (shaded is optional):

ADOS /a /c /L /m /x

> Examples: ados /c

Syntax options:

/a	Starts installation of AccessDOS.
/c	Runs in color mode.
/ L	Runs in LCD mode.
/m	Runs in monochrome mode.
/x	Runs in minimal mode.

Command Type and Version:

External command, Introduced with Ver 6.0.

Available in the MS-DOS 6.0, 6.21, and 6.22 Supplemental disks.

Notes:

1. See the ADOS.TXT and AREADME.TXT files in the Supplemental disks for user information.

ANSI.SYS

A device driver loaded through CONFIG.SYS that allows the user to control the computer's display and keyboard. Once the ANSI.SYS driver has been loaded, ANSI escape code sequences can be used to customize both the display and keyboard. This was developed by the American National Standards Institute (ANSI).

Syntax (shaded is optional):

DEVICE = Drive:\Path\ANSI.SYS `/x /k /r`

> Examples: device=c:\dos\ansi.sys /x
>
> If ANSI.SYS is loaded, try the following example for some enhancement of a color display:
> PROMPT $e[35;44;1m$pge[33;44;1m

Syntax Options:

Drive:	Letter of drive containing \Path.
\Path	Directory containing ANSI.SYS.
/x	Remaps 101-key keyboards so that the extended keys operate independently.
/k	Extended keys on the 101-key keyboards will be ignored. This is particularly important on systems that do not accurately handle extended keyboard functions. Added in Version 5.0
/r 6.2	Used with screen-reading programs to adjust rate of line scrolling for easier reading.

Command Type and Version:

CONFIG.SYS command; Introduced with Ver 2.0

Notes:

1. The user has a lot of control over screen colors at the DOS level when the ANSI.SYS driver is loaded. See also PROMPT, p. 227.

2. The .SYS extension must be used in the syntax.

3. Using the Escape Code sequences is sometimes not an easy task. See PC Magazines book *DOS Power Tools, page 420,* for an example of how to write simple programs to send these codes.

ANSI escape sequences are a series of characters beginning with the ESCAPE (character 27) key, followed by open left bracket ([ ), followed by parameters sometimes, and ending with a letter or number. Note that the ending letter must be used in the correct upper or lower case format.

Parameters used in the escape sequences are as follows:

pl	. . . .	Line number (decimal value)
pc	. . . .	Column number (decimal value)
pn	. . . .	Specifies parameter is numeric.
ps	. . . .	Specific decimal number for a function. Multiple *ps* functions are separated with a **;**

ANSI escape sequences:

ESC [*pl* ; *pc* H . .	Moves cursor to a specific line (*pl* parameter) and column (*pc* parameter). If no *pl* or *pc* is specified, the cursor goes to the Home position.
ESC [*pl* ; *pc* f	Functions same as **ESC [*pl* ; *pc* H.**
ESC [*pn* A	Moves Cursor Up *pn* number of lines. If cursor is on top line, ANSI.SYS ignores sequence.
ESC [*pn* B	Moves Cursor Down *pn* number of lines. If the cursor is on the bottom line, ANSI.SYS ignores this sequence.
ESC [*pn* C	Moves Cursor Forward *pn* number of columns. If the cursor is at the farthermost right column, ANSI.SYS ignores this sequence.
ESC [*pn* D	Moves Cursor Backward *pn* number of lines. If the cursor is at the farthermost left column, ANSI.SYS ignores this sequence.
ESC [6n	Reports status of selected device.
ESC [s	Save Cursor Position. The cursor may be moved to the saved position by using the Restore Cursor sequence.
ESC [u	Restore Cursor Position. Moves the cursor to the Save Cursor Position.
ESC [2 J	Erase Display. Erases the screen and returns the cursor to the home position.
ESC [K	Erase Line. Erases all characters from the cursor to the end of the line.
ESC [*ps* ; .. ; *ps* m	Sets graphics functions (text attributes and foreground and background colors). Note: These functions stay active until a new set of parameters is issued with this command.

Text Attributes:	All Attributes Off. . . . 0	
	Bold On 1	
	Faint On 2	
	Italic On 3	
	Underscore 4	(Mono adapter only)
	Blink On. 5	
	Rapid Blink On . . . 6	
	Reverse Video On. . 7	
	Concealed On 8	

Colors	Foreground	Background
Black	30	40
Red	31	41
Green	32	42
Yellow	33	43
Blue	34	44
Magenta	35	45
Cyan	36	46
White	37	47

Example: Try using the following PROMPT command if you have a color monitor and ANSI.SYS has been loaded in CONFIG.SYS.

    PROMPT $e[35;44;1m$pge[33;44;1m

ESC [= **ps** h ..... Set Mode function. The active screen width and graphics mode type is changed with this sequence using the following values: ("mono" means monochrome.)

Mode		Mode	
ps	**(Graphics unless noted)**	**ps**	**(Graphics unless noted)**
0	40 x 25 mono (text)	13	320 x 200 color
1	40 x 25 color (text)	14	640 x 200 color (16 color)
2	80 x 25 mono (text)	15	640 x 350 mono (2 color)
3	80 x 25 color (text)	16	640 x 350 color (16 color)
4	320 x 200 (4-color)	17	640 x 480 mono (2 color)
5	320 x 200 mono	18	640 x 480 (16 color)
6	640 x 200 mono	19	320 x 200 color (256 color)
7	Enables line wrapping		

ESC [= **ps** l (l in the sequence to the left is a lower case **L**)
This sequence resets the Mode sequence described above. The *ps* parameter uses the same values as those shown in the Set Mode sequence above.

ESC [*code* ; *string* ;...**P** Redefine a specific keyboard key with a specific string of characters. *code* is one of the values in the ASCII Key Code table, on the next three pages, that represent keyboard keys or combinations of keys. Gray keys or codes shown in ( ) in the table may not function on some keyboards (try using the /x switch on the ANSI.SYS command line. *string* is either the decimal ASCII code for a single character (76 is the letter "C") or a string of characters in quotes ("<"). For example:

    ESC ["<" ; "+" p ESC ["+" ; "<" p
    ESC [60 ; 43 p ESC [43 ; 60 p

Both of the above sequences do the same task, they exchange the < and + keys.
Note that it is not possible to alter the ALT and Caps Lock keys.

ANSI.SYS   87

NOTE: Some values listed in the ASCII Key Codes table below may not be valid for all computers! If in doubt, be sure to check the computer's documentation for verification.

ASCII Key Codes for ANSI.SYS

Key	K means Key ➡ K Code	SHIFT+K Code	CTRL+K Code	ALT+K Code
F1	0;59	0;84	0;94	0;104
F2	0;60	0;85	0;95	0;105
F3	0;61	0;86	0;96	0;106
F4	0;62	0;87	0;97	0;107
F5	0;63	0;88	0;98	0;108
F6	0;64	0;89	0;99	0;109
F7	0;65	0;90	0;100	0;110
F8	0;66	0;91	0;101	0;111
F9	0;67	0;92	0;102	0;112
F10	0;68	0;93	0;103	0;113
F11	0;133	0;135	0;137	0;139
F12	0;134	0;136	0;138	0;140
Home	0;71	55	0;119	—
Up Arrow	0;72	56	(0;141)	—
Page Up	0;73	57	0;132	—
Left Arrow	0;75	52	0;115	—
Right Arrow	0;77	54	0;116	—
End	0;79	49	0;117	—
Down Arrow	0;80	50	(0;145)	—
Page Down	0;81	51	0;118	—
Insert	0;82	48	(0;146)	—
Delete	0;83	46	(0;147)	—
Home (gray key) . . .	224;71	224;71	224;119	224;151
Up Arrow (gray key)	224;72	224;72	224;141	224;152
Page Up (gray key)	224;73	224;73	224;132	224;153
Left Arrow (gray key)	224;75	224;75	224;115	224;155
Right Arrow (gray K)	224;77	224;77	224;116	224;157
End (gray key).	224;79	224;79	224;117	224;159
Down Arrow (gray key)	224;80	224;80	224;145	224;154
Page Down (gray key)	224;81	224;81	224;118	224;161
Insert (gray key) . . .	224;82	224;82	224;146	224;162
Delete (gray key). . .	224;83	224;83	224;147	224;163
Print Screen	—	—	0;114	—
Pause/Break	—	—	0;0	—
Backspace	8	8	127	(0)

Key	K means Key ➡ K Code	SHIFT+K Code	CTRL+K Code	ALT+K Code
Tab	9	0;15	(0;148)	(0;165)
Null	0;3	—	—	—
A	97	65	1	0;30
B	98	66	2	0;48
C	99	66	3	0;46
D	100	68	4	0;32
Enter	13	—	10	(0;28)
E	101	69	5	0;18
F	102	70	6	0;33
G	103	71	7	0;34
H	104	72	8	0;35
I	105	73	9	0;36
J	106	74	10	0;36
K	107	75	11	0;37
L	108	76	12	0;38
M	109	77	13	0;50
N	110	78	14	0;49
O	111	79	15	0;24
P	112	80	16	0;25
Q	113	81	17	0;16
R	114	82	18	0;19
S	115	83	19	0;31
T	116	84	20	0;20
U	117	85	21	0;22
V	118	86	22	0;47
W	119	87	23	0;17
X	120	88	24	0;45
Y	121	89	25	0;21
Z	122	90	26	0;44
1	49	33	—	0;120
2	50	64	0	0;121
3	51	35	—	0;122
4	52	36	—	0;123
5	53	37	—	0;124
6	54	94	30	0;125
7	55	38	—	0;126
8	56	42	—	0;127
9	57	40	—	0;128
0	48	41	—	0;129
– (minus sign)	45	95	31	0;130
= (equal sign)	61	43	—	0;131

ASCII Key Codes for ANSI.SYS (cont.)

Key	K means Key ➡ K Code	SHIFT+K Code	CTRL+K Code	ALT+K Code
[(left bracket)	91	123	27	0;26
] (right bracket)	93	125	29	0;27
\ (back slash).	92	124	28	0;43
; (semi-colon)	59	58	—	0;39
' (apostrophe)	39	34	—	0;40
, (comma)	44	60	—	0;51
. (period)	46	62	—	0;52
/ (forward slash) . . .	47	63	—	0;53
' (accent)	96	126	—	(0;41)
ENTER (on keypad)	13	—	10	(0;166)
/ (on keypad).	47	47	(0;142)	(0;74)
* (on keypad).	42	(0;144)	(0;78)	—
– (on keypad)	45	45	(0;149)	(0;164)
+ (on keypad)	43	43	(0;150)	(0;55)
5 (on keypad)	(0;76)	53	(0;143)	—

APPEND.EXE

Sets directory search order : Searchs specified directories on specified drives to locate files outside of the current directory that have extensions other than .COM, .EXE, or .BAT. *Use Caution!*

Syntax (shaded is optional):

APPEND Drive: \Path /X /E /Path:on or off ;

Examples: APPEND /X /E
APPEND C:\WORDDATA; D:\PFS
APPEND ;

Syntax Options:

Drive:. . . . . Letter of drive to be searched.
\Path . . . . Directory searched for data files.

/X :on or :off . .	Extends the DOS search path for specified files when executing programs. Processes SEARCH FIRST, FIND FIRST, and EXEC functions. :ON and :OFF, new to Version 5.0, toggles this switch on and off.
/Path :on or :off	If path is already included for a program file, :on tells program to also search in appended directories. Default= :on; added in DOS Ver 5.0
/E	Causes the appended path to be stored in the DOS environment and searched for there.
;	Use ";" to separate multiple Drive:\Path statements on one line. APPEND ; by itself will cancel the APPEND list.

Command Type and Version:

External command; Network; Introduced with Ver 3.2

Notes:

1. /X and /E switchs can only be used the first time you use Append. The line following the APPEND /X /E line contains the Drive:\Path.

2. You can not use any paths on the same command line as /X & /E.

3. :ON and :OFF switchs are valid for Ver 5.0 and later.

4. Do not use APPEND with Windows.

ASSIGN.COM `Removed V6.0`

Assign disk drive: Instructs DOS to redirect disk operations on one drive to a different drive.

Syntax (shaded is optional):

ASSIGN Source = Target /status

Examples: ASSIGN A = B   or   ASSIGN A: = B;
ASSIGN A = B B = C   ❺
ASSIGN
ASSIGN /status

Syntax Options:

ASSIGN . . . . . ASSIGN with no switch cancels redirected drive assignments and sets them back to their origional drives.

Source. . . . . . . Letter(s) of source drive(s).

Target . . . . Letter(s) of target drive(s). Starting with Version 5.0, a colon can be used with each assigned drive letter. For example; ASSIGN A: = B:

/Status . . . . . . Lists current drive assignments. Ver 5.0.

Command Type and Version:

External command; Network; Introduced with Ver 2.0 Removed from Version 6.0, considered too dangerous. Available in the MS-DOS 6.0, 6.21, 6.22 Supplemental Disks.

Notes:

1. DO NOT use a colon after a drive letter in versions prior to 5.0.
2. FORMAT, DISKCOPY, DISKCOMP, BACKUP, JOIN, LABEL, RESTORE, PRINT and SUBST cannot be used on ASSIGNed drives.
3. Be careful to reassign drives back to their original designations before running other programs.
4. If ASSIGN and APPEND are both used, the APPEND command must be used first.
5. See also the SUBST command.

ATTRIB.EXE Removed V6.0

Changes or displays file attributes: Sets, displays or clears a files read-only, archive, system, and hidden attributes.

Syntax (shaded is optional):

ATTRIB +r-r +a-a +s-s +h-h Drive:\Path\Filename /s

> Examples: ATTRIB wordfile.doc
> ATTRIB +r wordfile.doc
> ATTRIB +r d:\worddata*.* /s

Syntax Options:

Drive:........	Letter of drive containing \path\filename.
\Path	Directory containing filename.
Filename	Filename(s) of which attributes are to be displayed or changed. Wildcards (? and *) can be used for groups of files.
+r	Sets file to read-only.
−r	Removes read-only attribute.
+a	Sets the archive file attribute.
−a	Removes the archive file attribute.
+s	Sets file as a system file. Ver. 5
−s	Removes system file attribute. Ver 5
+h	Sets file as a hidden file. Ver 5
−h	Removes the hidden file attribute. Ver 5
/s	ATTRIB command processes files in the current directory and its subdirectories.

Command Type and Version:

External command; Network; Introduced with Ver 3.0

Notes:

1. When the system or hidden attribute is set , the read-only and archive attributes cannot be changed.

2. The archive attribute is used by the DOS BACKUP, RESTORE, and XCOPY commands when their /m switch is used and also the XCOPY command when the /a switch is used.

@ (at)

Turns off the command echo function: In a batch file, placing the @ symbol at the start of a command line surpresses the echoed display of the command on the screen.

Syntax (shaded is optional):

@ command

Examples: @xcopy a:*.* b:

@ECHO off

Syntax Options:

command. . . . Any DOS command.

Command Type and Version:

Batch command; Introduced with Ver 3.3

Notes:

1. Useful in preventing the words ECHO OFF from displaying on the screen when ECHO OFF is used in a Batch file. This command is useful if all screen echos need to be turned off in a Batch file.

2. See also ECHO.

BACKINFO.EXE Removed V6.0

MS-DOS utility: Allows viewing of files on a backup disk created by the DOS Version 3.3, 3.31, 4.0, 4.01, and 5.0 BACKUP command.

Syntax (shaded area optional):

BACKINFO drive1:

Example: backinfo b:

Syntax options:

drive1: . . . . Drive containing the BACKUP disk.

Command Type and Version:

External command, Introduced with Ver 3.3.
Removed from Ver 6.0

BACKUP.EXE `Removed V6.0`

Back up files: Backs up files from one drive to another drive. Source and target drives may be either hard disks or floppy disks. DOSV6 use MSBACKUP.

Syntax (shaded is optional):

BACKUP Source:\Path\Filename Target: /s /m
/a /d:date /t:time /f:size /L:LogDrive\Path\Log

> Examples: BACKUP C:*.* B: /s
> BACKUP C:\DATA*.* B: /s /L:C:\LOG

Syntax Options:

Source:\Path . .	Source drive & directory to be backed up.
Filename	Filename (s) to be backed up. Use of Wild cards (? and *) is allowed.
Target:	Target drive for backed up files.
/s	Backs up all files in Source:\Path and subdirectories under Source:\Path
/m	Backs up all files that have changed since the last backup (backup looks at the files archive attribute) and then turns off the files archive attribute.
/a	Adds new backup files to the existing backup disk (existing files are not deleted.) If a backup was made with DOS 3.2 or earlier, the /a switch is ignored.
/d:date	Only files created or modified after date are backed up. The way date is written depends on COUNTRY.SYS settings.

/t:time	Only files created or modified after *time* are backed up. The way *time* is written depends on COUNTRY.SYS settings. Always use the /d:date switch when /t:time is used.
/f:size	Format backup disk to the following *size*: (*size* can also be with k or kb, e.g. 160 can be 160k or 160kb; or 1200 can be 1200k, 1200kb, 1.2, 1.2m or 1.2mb, etc)

size	Disk size and type
160. . . .	160k single sided DD 5.25" disk
180. . . .	180k single sided DD 5.25" disk
320. . . .	320k double sided DD 5.25" disk
360. . . .	360k double sided DD 5.25" disk
720. . . .	720k double sided DD, 3.5" disk
1200. . . .	1.2meg double sided HD, 5.25"
1440. . . .	1.44meg double sided HD, 3.5"
2880. . . .	2.88meg double sided, 3.5" disk
	(DD=Double Density, HD=High Density)

/L:	Creates a log file during a specific backup operation.
Logdrive:\Path .	Drive & Directory where backup *Log* is to be sent.
Log	Text file log of a backup operation.

Command Type and Version:

External command; Network; Introduced with Ver 2.0
Removed from Version 6.0, replaced with MSBACKUP.
Available in the MS-DOS 6.0 and 6.22 Supplemental Disks.

Notes:

1. See also RESTORE, COPY, XCOPY, DISKCOPY, IF
2. The sequence number of a backup disk can be checked by doing a DIR of the backup disk (Valid for version after DOS 3.3)
3. BACKUP does not backup the 3 system files, COMMAND.COM, MSDOS.SYS (or IBMDOS.SYS) , and IO.SYS (or IBMBIO.SYS).
4. BACKUP/RESTORE commands are not very compatible between pre DOS 5.0 version. DOS 5.0 will restore previous versions.
5. Do not use BACKUP when the ASSIGN, JOIN, or SUBST commands have been used.
6. When the IF ERRORLEVEL functions are used, BACKUP Exit Codes can be used to show why a backup failed (see IF):

Exit Code	Code Meaning
0	Successful backup
1	No files found to be backed up
2	File-sharing conflict, some files not backed up
3	BACKUP terminated by user with CTRL–C
4	Error terminated BACKUP procedure

7. Backup floppies are not readable by DOS, a special file format is used.

BASIC®.EXE and BASICA®.EXE

BASIC Computer Language: Depending on the system in use and version of DOS, it will run one of the BASIC interpreters (BASIC, BASICA, GW-BASIC, or QBASIC) and provide an environment for programming in the BASIC language. BASIC and BASICA are versions that were shipped with IBM® systems and were simply entry programs that started BASIC from the system's ROM. GW-BASIC is Microsoft's own version of BASIC that is shipped with MS-DOS versions through 4.01. For specifics on DOS 5.0/6.0 QBASIC, refer to page 228.

Syntax (shaded is optional):

BASIC Filename

> Examples: BASIC Test.bas
> BASICA

Syntax Options:

BASIC . . . .   BASIC without a filename just starts the BASIC Interpreter.

Filename . . . . .   A program written in BASIC that is loaded and run when the BASIC interpreter starts. The files normally end with .BAS

Command Type and Version:

External command; Network; Introduced with Ver 1.0

Notes:

1. See also QBASIC and GW-BASIC.

BREAK

Turns on/off the DOS check for Control-C or Control-Break: Determines when DOS looks for a Ctrl-C or Ctrl-Break more frequently in order to stop a program.

Syntax (shaded is optional):

BREAK on off

> Examples: BREAK
> BREAK = ON (syntax for CONFIG.SYS)
> BREAK ON (syntax at DOS prompt)

Syntax Options:

BREAK . . . . BREAK, with no switches or options, displays the current setting of BREAK.

ON. . . . . Tells DOS to check for Ctrl-C or Ctrl-Break from the keyboard, during disk reads and writes, and during screen and printer writes.

OFF. . . . . Tells DOS to check for Ctrl-C or Ctrl-Break from the keyboard only during screen and printer writes.

Command Type and Version:

Internal command; CONFIG.SYS and Batch command; Introduced with Ver 2.0

Notes:

1. If BREAK is ON, your system will run slightly slower.
2. The default setting is BREAK=OFF.

BUFFERS

Sets number of disk buffers in memory: A disk buffer is a block of RAM memory that DOS uses to hold data while reading and writing data to a disk.

Syntax (shaded is optional):

BUFFERS = X ,Y

Examples: BUFFERS = 35
BUFFERS = 35,8

Syntax Options:

X . . . . The number of disk buffers allocated. The total may range from 1 to 99 for versions Ver 4.0 to 6.2x. Versions prior to 4.0 can be in the range from 2 to 255. Default values are as follows:

Buffers Drive Configuration

2 . . . <128K RAM & 360k drive only
3 . . . <128K RAM & Disks over 360K
5 . . . 128K to 255K RAM
10 . . . 256K to 511K RAM
15 . . . 512K or more RAM

Y . . . . The number of secondary cache buffers. The total may range from 1 to 8, the default is 1.

Command Type and Version:

CONFIG.SYS command; Introduced with Ver 2.0

Notes:

1. Each buffer takes up approximately 532 bytes of RAM.
2. Standard buffer sizes should range from 20 to 30, unless more are required by a specific application (such as Dbase III Plus®).
3. If a disk cache program, such as SMARTDRV.SYS is used, the number of buffers can be set at 8 to 15 (sometimes lower).
4. In Ver 5.0, if DOS is in high memory, buffers are also in high mem.
5. The number of buffers (up to 35) significantly affects system speed; over 35, speed still increases but at much slower rate.
6. /X switch from earlier DOS versions is no longer available.

CALL

Calls a batch program: Starts one batch program from inside another batch program, without causing the initial batch program to stop.

Syntax (shaded is optional):

CALL Drive:\Path\ Filename Parameters

      Examples: CALL C:\TEST %1

Syntax Options:

Drive:. . . . . Letter of drive containing path.

\Path . . . . Path containing filename.

Filename . . . . . Filename specifies name of the batch program to be called. *Filename* must have a .BAT extension.

Parameters . . . Specifies command-line information required by the batch program, including switches, filenames, pass through parameters such as %1, and variables.

Command Type and Version:

Internal command; Batch; Introduced with Ver 3.3

Notes:

1. Any information that can be passed to a batch program can be contained in the *Batch-parameters*, including switches, filenames, replaceable parameters %1 through %9, and variables such as % Parity %

2. Pipes and redirection symbols cannot be used with CALL.

3. If a recursive call (a program that calls itself) is created, an exit condition must be provided or the two batch programs will loop endlessly.

CD or CHDIR

Change directory: Changes (moves) to another directory or shows the name of the current directory path.

Syntax (shaded is optional):

CD Drive:\Path

> Examples: CD (displays current drive and directory)
> CD D:\PFS (change to PFS directory on D: drive)
> CD\ (changes to root directory)

Syntax Options:

Drive: . . . . Drive containing the subdirectory to be changed. CD does not move to Drive:, it remains on the current drive.

\Path . . . . Directory path name to be made current, if *Drive:* is the current drive. If *Drive:* is not the current drive, *\Path* is simply the active path on *Drive:* and the current drive and directory remain unchanged. Pathname can be no longer than 63 characters and (\) is to be used as the path's first character to move to the root directory.

Command Type and Version:

Internal command; Network; Introduced with Ver 2.0

Notes:

1. When a drive letter is not specified, the current drive is assumed.
2. **CD ..** specifies move up one directory level.

CHCP

Change code page: Displays or changes the number of the active code page for the command processor COMMAND.COM.

Syntax (shaded is optional):

CHCP ccc

Examples: CHCP   (reports current *ccc* setting)
CHCP 863

Syntax Options:

ccc. . . . . These are the numbers that represent the prepared system code pages defined by the COUNTRY.SYS command in the CONFIG.SYS file. Valid code page numbers are as follows:

437. . . . United States
850. . . . Multilingual (Latin I)
852. . . . Slavic (Latin II)
860. . . . Portuguese
863. . . . Canadian-French
865. . . . Nordic

Command Type and Version:

Internal command; Network; Introduced with Ver 3.3

Notes:

1. Once a specified code page has been selected, all programs that are started will use that new code page.
2. NLSFUNC (national language support functions) must be installed before a code page can be switched with CHCP.
3. MODE SELECT can also be used to change code pages.
4. See also DOS commands COUNTRY.SYS, NLSFUNC, DEVICE, and MODE.

CHKDSK.EXE

Checks disk: Scans the disk and reports size, disk memory available, RAM available and checks for and corrects logical errors. A status report is displayed on screen.

Syntax (shaded is optional):

CHKDSK Drive:\Path\Filename /f /v

Examples: CHKDSK C: / f
(If no Drive: is specified, the current drive is used.)

Syntax Options:

Drive:. . . . . Drive letter of the disk to be checked.

\Path . . . . Directory path containing file to be checked.

Filename . . . . . Name of file to be checked by CHKDSK for fragmentation. Wildcards * & ? are allowed.

/ f. . . . . Fixes logical errors on the disk.

/ v . . . . Verbose switch. Displays CHKDSK progress by listing each file in every directory as it is being checked.

Command Type and Version:

External command; Can NOT check a Network drive; Introduced with Ver 1.0

Notes:

1. CHKDSK analyzes a disk's File Allocation Table (FAT) and file system. / f must be specified in order to fix errors. If / f is not used, CHKDSK reports the error, but does not fix the error, even if you answer yes to fixing the error at the CHKDSK prompt.
2. When CHKDSK / f finds an error, it asks if you want to covert the "lost clusters" to files. If you answer Yes, files in the form FILE0001.CHK are created and the lost areas dumped into those files. You must then determine if any valuable info is in that file. If they don't contain useful information, delete them.
3. Do not use CHKDSK from inside any other program, especially Windows.
4. Only logical errors are repaired by CHKDSK, not physical errors.
5. CHKDSK will not work when SUBST, JOIN or ASSIGN has been used.

CHKSTATE.SYS New V6.2

CHKSTATE is used only by MemMaker to track the memory optimization process: During the memory optimization process, MemMaker adds CHKSTATE.SYS to the beginning of the CONFIG.SYS file. When the memory optimization process is complete, MemMaker automatically removes CHKSTATE.SYS.

CHOICE.COM New V6.0

Pauses the system and prompts the user to make a choice in a batch file: This command can only be used in batch programs.

Syntax (shaded is optional):

CHOICE /C:keys /N /S /T:c,nn text

Syntax Options:

/C:keys ...... Defines which keys are allowed in the prompt. The : is optional. Displayed keys are separated by commas and will be enclosed in [ ] brackets. Multiple keystroke characters are allowed. Default is [YN] (yes/no).

/ N .... Prevents display of prompt, but the specified keys are still valid.

/ S .... Specifies that CHOICE is case sensitive.

/ T:c,nn ...... Forces CHOICE to pause for *nn* seconds before defaulting to a specified key *(c)*. nn can range from 0 to 99. The *c* key specified must be included in the */C:keys* definition.

text	Defines what text is displayed before the prompt. Quotation marks ("") must be used if a "/" character is included in the prompt. Default for CHOICE is no text displayed.

Command Type and Version:

Internal Batch command; Network; Introduced with Ver 6.0

Notes:

1. ERRORLEVEL 0 is returned if Control-C or Control-Break is pressed.

CLS

Clears or Erases Screen: All information is cleared from the DOS screen and the prompt and cursor is returned to the upper left corner of the screen.

Syntax (shaded is optional):

CLS

Examples: CLS

Syntax Options:

None

Command Type and Version:

Internal command; Network; Introduced with Ver 2.0

Notes:

1. Screen colors set by ANSI.SYS will remain set.

2. If more than one video display is attached to the system, only the active display is cleared.

3. If ANSI.SYS is not loaded on the system, CLS will clear the screen to gray (or amber on an amber monitor, etc) on black.

COMMAND.COM

Start a new DOS command processor: The command processor is responsible for displaying the prompt on the computer's display and contains all of the Internal DOS commands. It is also used to set variables such as environment size. Use the EXIT command to stop the new processor.

Syntax (shaded is optional):

COMMAND Drive:\Path\Device / e:xxxx / y / c text / k

In CONFIG.SYS use the following:
SHELL = Drive:\Path\   COMMAND.COM / e:xxxx / p / msg

    Examples: COMMAND /e:1024
    (use the following in CONFIG.SYS with SHELL)
    SHELL = Drive:\Path\COMMAND.COM /e:512 /p

Syntax Options:

Drive:\Path . . .   Drive and \Path of the command device. Must be included if COMMAND.COM is not located in the root directory.

\Device . . . . . .   Device for command input or outpur (see the CTTY command on page 112).

/ e:xxxx . . . . . .   Set environment size in bytes (xxxx). Default for Ver 5.0,6.0, and 6.2x = 256 bytes; default for versions before 5.0 is 160 bytes. Range is 160 to 32768 bytes.

/p	Makes the new command processor the permanent processor. Used only with SHELL command.
/c text.	Forces the command processor to perform the commands specified by *text*. On completion, it returns to the primary command processor. Must be last switch on command line.
/msg	Causes error messages to be stored in memory. The /p switch must also be used when /msg is used.
/k ❻	Execute a command, but after the command is executed, do not terminate the second COMMAND.COM that is running. Must be last switch on command line
/y 62.	Tells COMAND.COM to step through files specified by the /c text or /k switches

Command Type and Version:

External command;
CONFIG.SYS command when used with SHELL;
Introduced with Ver 1.0

Notes:

1. See also CTTY, EXIT and SHELL
2. Default environment sizes are commonly not large enough. Try setting the environment to 512 or 1024.
3. In Version 6.0, if DOS is unable to find COMMAND.COM, a warning message is issued that allows the user to "Enter correct name of Command Interpreter (e.g., C:\COMMAND.COM). This is a much improved error handling function and allows the system to complete the booting process.
4. Exercise caution when you are "messing around" with COMMAND.COM. It can get the user into some dangerous situations!
5. The SHELL command in CONFIG.SYS is the preferred method of increasing the environment size with the /e:xxxx switch.

Compare files: Compares the contents of two sets of disk files to see if they are the same or different. The comparison is made on a byte by byte basis. COMP displays filenames, locations and the differences found during the compare process .

Syntax (shaded is optional):

COMP   Drive1:\Path1\File1   Drive2:\Path2\File2
/d /a /L /n=xx /c

Examples: COMP   (prompts for file locations)
            COMP   C:\File1   D:\File2   /a

Syntax Options:

Drive1: Drive2:	Letters of drives containing the file (s) to be compared.
\Path1 \Path2 .	Paths of files to be compared.
File1 File2	Filenames to be compared. The names may be the same if they are in different locations. Wild cards (*?) are allowed.
/d	Displays file differences in decimal format, the default format is hexadecimal. Ver 5
/a	File differences displayed as characters. Ver 5.0
/L	Display Line numbers with different data instead of byte offsets. Ver 5.0
/n=xx	Compares the first number of lines (xx) in each file, even if files are different sizes. Ver 5.0
/c	Upper and lower case is ignored. Ver 5.0

Command Type and Version:

External command; Network; Introduced with Ver 1.0
Removed from Ver 6.0, replaced by FC.
Available on the MS-DOS 6.0, 6.21, and 6.22 Supplimental Disks.

Notes:

1. If the drive, path and filename information is not specific enough, COMP will prompt for the correct information

2. If more than 10 mismatches are found, COMP ends the compare.

3. See also DISKCOMP (for floppy disk comparisons) and FC.

COPY

Copies file(s) from one location to another: Files can also be combined (concatenated) using COPY.

Syntax (shaded is optional):

COPY /y / -y /a /b Source /a /b+Source /a /b +. . .
         Target /a /b /v

Examples: COPY C:\Test*.* D:\Test2
           COPY Test1.txt + Text2.txt Test3.txt /a

Syntax Options:

Source. . . . . . . Source Drive, Directory, and File(s) or Devices to be copied **from**.

Target . . . . Destination Drive, Directory, and File(s) or Devices being copied **to**.

/ a . . . . Denotes an ASCII text file. If /a preceeds a filename, that file and all following files are treated as ASCII files until a /b switch is encountered, then files that follow are considered to be binary files. If /a follows a filename, it applies to all files before and after the /a until a /b switch is encountered, then files that follow are considered to be binary files.

/ b . . . . Denotes a Binary file. If /b preceeds a filename, that file and all following files are treated as binary files until a /a switch is encountered, then files that follow are considered to be ASCII files. If

---

	/b follows a filename, it applies to all files before and after the /b until a /a switch is encountered, then files that follow are considered to be ASCII files. /b forces copy to read exactly the number of bytes allocated to the file's size in the directory.
/v	Verifies files were copied correctly.
/y 6.2	Directs COPY to replace existing file without confirmation prompt. Confirmation prompt is default.
/-y 6.2	Directs COPY to ask for confirmation prior to replacing existing files.

Command Type and Version:

Internal command; Network; Introduced with Ver 1.0

Notes:

1. COPY will only copy the contents of 1 directory. If a directory and its subdirectories need to be copied, use the XCOPY command.

2. COPY will not copy files 0 bytes in length, use XCOPY instead.

3. Both *Source* and *Destination* can be a device such as COM1: or LPT1:, however, when sending to *Destination*, if the /b switch is used, all characters, including control codes, are sent to the device as data. If no switch is used, the data transfers as ASCII data and the transmitted control codes may perform their special function on the device. For example, if a Ctrl + L code is sent to a printer on LPT1:, the printer will form feed.

4. If Destination Filename is not specified, COPY will create a file with the same name and date and time of creation in the current directory (*Target*). If a file with the same name as *Filename* exists in the current directory, DOS will not copy the file and display an error message that says "File cannot be copied onto itself. 0 Files Copied".

5. If the + function is used to combine files, it is assumed that the files are ASCII files. Normally you should NOT combine binary files since the internal format of binary files may be different.

6. /v slows down the copy process. If a verify error occurs, the message is displayed on the screen.

7. In order to change the date and time of a file during the copy process, use the following syntax:
   COPY /b Source + , ,

8. See also DISKCOPY and XCOPY.

COUNTRY and COUNTRY.SYS

Country dependent information: Enables DOS to use international time, date, currency, and case conversions.

Syntax (shaded is optional):

COUNTRY= ccc ppp Drive:\Path \Filename

    Examples: COUNTRY = 002

Syntax Options:

ccc . . . . Country code number. Default 001, USA
ppp . . . . Code page number.
Drive:\Path . . . Drive & subdirectory containing *Filename*..
Filename . . . . . File containing country information.

Command Type and Version:

CONFIG.SYS; Introduced with Ver 3.0

Notes:

1. COUNTRY is put in CONFIG.SYS . If the *Drive:\Path\Filename* option is not used to specify which file contains country information, COUNTRY.SYS must be in the root directory of the system's boot drive so that COUNTRY can retrieve the country data.

Country Code	Country or Language	Code Page	Time Format	Date Format
001	United States	437, 850	2:35:00.00p	06-30-1991
002	Canadian-French	863, 850	14:35:00,00	1991-06-30
003	Latin America	850, 437	2:35:00.00p	30/06/1991
031	Netherlands	850, 437	14:35:00,00	30-06-1991
032	Belgium	850, 437	14:35:00,00	30/06/1991
033	France	850, 437	14:35:00,00	30.06.1991
034	Spain	850, 437	14:35:00,00	30/06/1991
036	Hungary	852, 850	14:35:00,00	1991-06-30
038	Croatia\Slovenia\ Yugoslavia\Serbia	852, 850	14:35:00,00	1991-06-30
039	Italy	850, 437	14:35:00,00	30/06/1991
041	Switzerland	850, 437	14,35,00,00	30.06.1991
042	Czech Rep\Slovakia	852, 850	14:35:00,00	1991-06-30
044	United Kingdom	437, 850	14:35:00,00	30/06/1991
045	Denmark	850, 865	14.35.00,00	30-06-1991
046	Sweden	850, 437	14.35.00,00	1991-06-30
047	Norway	850, 865	14:35:00,00	30.06.1991
048	Poland	852, 850	14:35:00,00	1991-06-30
049	Germany	850, 437	14:35:00,00	30.06.1991
055	Brazil	850, 437	14:35:00,00	30/06/1991

CTTY

Change to a remote console: Allows you to choose the device from which you issue commands. USE WITH CAUTION, you could loose control of your system!

Syntax (shaded is optional):

CTTY   Device

> Examples: CTTY aux
> CTTY com1
> CTTY con

Syntax Options:

Device . . . .   Any valid DOS device for issuing commands. Examples include com1, com2, com3, com4, con, aux, prn (rare).

Command Type and Version:

Internal command; Network; Introduced with Ver 2.0

Notes:

1. *Device* refers to a character-oriented remote unit, or secondary terminal, that will be used for command input and *output*. This device name must be a valid MS/PC-DOS name, specifically, AUX, COM1, COM2, COM3, COM4, CON. The use of a colon after the device name is optional.

2. *ctty con* moves the input and output back to the main terminal (the local console screen and keyboard).

3. *When redirected, some programs that are designed to work with the video display's control codes may not function correctly.*

4. Other redirected IO or piping is not affected by CTTY.

5. CAUTION: the command CTTY NUL will disconnect the screen and keyboard !!!! Do not use unless the CTTY CON command is executed under some type of program control, such as a batch file.

CV.COM and CV.EXE Removed V6.2

CV starts the CodeView program: CodeView is a debugging utility for programs written in C.

Command Type and Version:

External command, Introduced with Ver 5.0.

Removed Ver. 6.2.

Available in the MS-DOS 6.0, 6.21, and 6.22 Supplemental Disks.

Notes:

1. CAUTION- Using CodeView CV.EXE Versions 3.0 to 3.13 with a 80386 memory manager such as EMM386 may cause loss of data. This problem has been fixed in Version 3.14 of CodeView. To start CodeView Versions 3.0 to 3.13 safely, use CV.COM.

2. Use HIMEM.SYS Version 2.77 or later with CodeView.

DATE

Date: Change and /or display the system date. (Note: This does not reset the computer's battery powered clock if DOS 3.21 or earlier is used.)

Syntax (shaded is optional):

DATE   month-day-year

> Examples: **date mm-dd-yy** (for North America)
> Note: If COUNTRY in config.sys is set for a country other than a North American country, then the following syntax is used:
> > **DATE dd-mm-yy**   for Europe
> > DATE yy-mm-dd   for Far East

Syntax Description and Options:

month . . . . . . One or two digit number (1 to 12)

day.	One or two digit number (1 to 31). DOS knows the correct number of days in each month (28, 29, 30 or 31).
year	Two or four digit number (80 to 99 – The 19 is assumed for 1980 to 1999).

Command Type and Version:

Internal command; Network; Introduced with Ver 1.0

Notes:

1. You may separate the day, month and the year by the use of hyphens, periods or slashes.

2. If a system does not have an AUTOEXEC.BAT file in the root directory of the boot drive, the date and time functions are activated automatically when the system starts and the user is prompted for change or confirmation.

3. DOS has been programmed to change the year, month and day and adjusts the number of days in a month accordingly. DOS also knows which months have 28, 29, 30, or 31 days. DOS will issue errors if valid dates are not used.

4. Beginning with DOS 3.3, DATE and TIME both set the system's CMOS (battery powered) calendar (except in XT class systems).

5. See also TIME

DBLBOOT.BAT Removed V6.22

Creates a bootable DBLSPACE floppy disk:

Syntax (shaded is optional):

DBLBOOT drive1:

    Example: dblboot a:

Syntax options:

drive1: . . . . Drive containing floppy disk to be compressed.

Command Type and Version:

External command, Introduced with MS-DOS Ver 6.0.

Available in the MS-DOS 6.0, 6.21, and 6.22 Supplemental Disks; Removed in version 6.22.

Notes:
1. DBLBOOT works only on high-density floppy disks (1.44 or 1.2 MB).
2. DBLSPACE must be installed prior to using DBLBOOT.

DBLSPACE.EXE

`New V6.0` `Danger V6.0` `Removed V6.22`

Utility to compress both hard and floppy disk drives so that there is more available storage space on the drive: Once the .EXE program has been run, DBLSPACE.SYS must be included in CONFIG.SYS. *Many problems have been reported with the DOS 6.0 version of this program. USE WITH CAUTION or not at all, you could lose data on your drive!*

Syntax (shaded is optional):

DBLSPACE /Automount /Chkdsk /Compress /Convstac /Create /Defragment /Delete /Format /Info /List /Mount /Ratio /Size /Unmount

Syntax Options:

/Automount . . .	Automatically mount a compressed disk.
/ Chkdsk	Check the validity of a compressed disk's directory and FAT and report the status of the drive.
/ Compress . . .	Start the compression process on a drive.

/ Convstac	**Removed V6.2** Converts a Stacker compressed drive to a DBLSPACE compressed drive.
/ Create	Creates a new compressed drive in the free space of an existing drive.
/ Defragment . .	Defragment the files on an existing drive.
/ Delete	Remove a compressed drive.
/ *Format*	Format a compressed drive.
/ Info	Display detailed information on a compressed drive.
/ List.	Display a list of both compressed and uncompressed drives on a system. It does not report network drives.
/ Mount	Mount a compressed drive.
/ Ratio	Display and change the estimated compression ratio of a compressed drive.
/ Size	Change the size of a compressed drive.
/ Uncompress **6.2**	Uncompresses a drive compressed by DBLSPACE.
/ Unmount	Unmount a compressed drive.

Command Type and Version:

External command; Introduced with Ver 6.0

Removed with Ver. 6.2, revision 2, and replaced by DRVSPACE.

Notes:

1. DBLSPACE can be run as a menu driven utility or with the command line switches listed under Syntax Options.
2. The maximum size of a DBLSPACE volume is 512 MB.
3. Default cluster size of a compressed volume is 8k.
4. When DBLSPACE.EXE is run, DBLSPACE.SYS is automatically placed in CONFIG.SYS as part of the installation process.
5. See Also DBLSPACE.SYS

DBLSPACE.SYS

Device driver that activates a compressed drive: DBLSPACE.SYS determines the final memory location of DBLSPACE.BIN, which provides access to the compressed drives *Many problems have been reported with the DOS 6.0 version of this program. USE WITH CAUTION or not at all, you could lose data on your drive!*

Syntax (shaded is optional):

DEVICE = Drive:\Path\ DBLSPACE.SYS
/ Move / Nohma

Examples: DEVICE = C:\DBLSPACE.SYS

It may also be loaded high using:
DEVICEHIGH = C:\DBLSPACE.SYS / Move

Syntax Options:

Drive:\ *Path*\ . . Drive and Path of the DBLSPACE.SYS

/ Move . . . . Moves the DBLSPACE.BIN file to a different location in memory. By default it is loaded at the top of conventional memory. /Move moves it to the bottom of conventional memory. Note that if DEVICEHIGH is used, it can be moved to upper memory, thereby freeing up conventional memory.

/ Nohma . . . . . Tells DBLSPACE.SYS not to move DBLSPACE.BIN into high memory.

Command Type and Version:

CONFIG.SYS command; Introduced with Ver 6.0
Removed with Ver. 6.2, revision2, and replaced by DRVSPACE

Notes:

1. DBLSPACE can be run as a menu driven utility or with the command line switches listed under Syntax Options.
2. DBLSPACE.SYS is automatically inserted into CONFIG.SYS when the DBLSPACE.EXE installation program is run.
3. See also DBLSPACE.EXE and DEVICEHIGH.

DEBUG.EXE

Starts a debugging program: Debug is a program that provides a testing environment for binary and executable programs, i.e. all programs that have .EXE or .COM extensions . It is also commonly used to run executable programs that are in memory, such as a hard drive's setup program stored in ROM on a hard drive controller. The full use of DEBUG is beyond the scope of this book. Refer to books such as Microsoft's *DOS Manuals* or PC Magazine's *DOS Power Tools*.

Syntax (shaded is optional):

There are two methods of starting DEBUG.
Method 1:
    DEBUG Drive:\Path\ Filename Parameter
Method 2:
    DEBUG

    Examples:
    Method 1: DEBUG   C:\test.exe
    Method 2: DEBUG   (run in command line mode)

Syntax Options:

Method 1:

Drive:\Path . . . Drive and Path of the executable
                Filename to be tested.

Filename . . . . . Name of executable file to be tested.

| Parameter .... | Command line information needed by *Filename*. |

Method 2:

| Debug .... | Starts DEBUG in the command line mode where debug commands are given at the DEBUG hyphen prompt (–). |

Command Type and Version:

External command; Introduced with Ver 1.0

Debug Commands for Method 2:

Case makes no difference; *address* and *range* is in hex

?	Display list of all DEBUG commands.
A address.....	Assemble 8086/8087/8088 mnemonics directly into memory at *address* (hex).
C range address	Compares contents of two memory blocks. *range* is the starting and ending address or starting address and length of Block 1 and *address* is the starting address of Block 2.
D range	Dump (display) contents of memory with starting and ending addresses of *range*.
E address data	Enter data into memory starting at *address*. *data* is entered into successive bytes of memory.
F range data ..	Fill memory with *data* (hex or ASCII) in starting and ending addresses or starting address & length defined by *range*.
G=address bkp.	Run program in memory starting at *address*. *bkp* defines 1 to 10 temporary breakpoints.
H hex1 hex2 ..	Does hexadecimal math on *hex1* & *hex2*. Two results are returned, first the sum of *hex1* and *hex2*; second, *hex1* minus *hex2*.
I port........	Read (input) & display 1 byte from *port*.
L address drive:start number	Load a file or specific drive sectors into memory. *address* is the memory location you want to load to. *drive* contains the sectors to be

---

read. *start* is the hex value of the first sector to be read. *number* is the number of consecutive sectors to load.

M range address Copies memory contents from the starting and ending address or starting address and length of *range*. *address* is the starting address of the destination.

N d:\path\file parameters .... Name the *drive:\path\filename* of an executable file for Debug *L* or *W*. Also used to specify *parameters* for the executable file. *N* by itself clears the current specification.

O port data ... Output *data* to a *port* (by address).

P=address value Run a loop, string instruction, subroutine, or software interrupt starting at *address* and for *value* number of instructions.

Q .... Stop DEBUG without saving the file being tested. Returns to DOS.

R register ..... Display or alter CPU (central processing units) *register*. *R* by itself displays contents of all registers.

S range data .. Search for *data* at the beginning and ending address of *range*.

T=address value Trace instructions starting at *address* and for *value* number of instructions.

U range ...... Unassemble code at the start & end address or start address & length of *range*.

W address drive:start number .... Write a file or specific drive sectors into memory. *address* is the memory location you want to write to. *drive* contains the sectors to be written. *start* is the hex value of the first sector to be written. *number* is the number of consecutive sectors to write.

XA count. ..... Allocate count number of 16k expanded memory pages.

XD handle .... Deallocate a handle to expanded memory

XM Lpage Ppage handle   Map a *Lpage* logical
                                   page of expanded memory belonging
                                   to *handle*, to a *Ppage* physical page of
                                   expanded memory.

XS . . . . Display status information of expanded
                                   memory.

DEBUG ERROR MESSAGES: BF=Bad Flag;
BP=Too many breakpoints; BR=Bad Register;
DF=Double Flag

DEFRAG.EXE   New V6.0

Reorganizes or defragments a disk in order to opti-
mize disk drive performance.

Syntax (shaded is optional):

DEFRAG Drive: /F /U /S:order /B /Skiphigh
/LCD /BW /GØ /A /H

    Examples: DEFRAG C: /U /B

Syntax Options:

Drive:.	Drive letter to be defragmented.
/ F	Insures that no empty disk space remains between files.
/ U	Leaves empty space, if any, between files.
/ S:order . .	Sort files in a specific sort *"order"*.

        N . . In alphabetic order by name
        -N . In reverse alphabetic name order
        E . . In alphabetic order by extension
        -E . In reverse alphabetic order by extension
        D . . By date & time, earliest first
        -D . By date & time, latest first
        S . . By size, smallest first
        -S . By size, largest first

/ B . . . . Reboot system after DEFRAG is done.

/ Skiphigh .	Load DEFRAG into conventional memory, instead of the default upper memory
/ LCD	Start DEFRAG in LCD color scheme mode.
/ BW	Start DEFRAG in black & white color mode.
/ GØ	Disable graphics mouse and character set.
/ A	Start DEFRAG in Automatic mode.
/ H	Moves hidden files.

Command Type and Version:

External command; Network; Introduced with Ver 6.0

Notes:

1. Do not use DEFRAG while Windows is running.
2. DEFRAG exit codes (ERRORLEVEL parameter) are:

0	Successful deframentation.
1	Internal error.
2	No free clusters, DEFRAG needs at least 1 free cluster.
3	Process aborted with CTRL+C by user.
4	General error.
5	Error occurred while reading a cluster.
6	Error occurred while writing a cluster.
7	Allocation error, correct using SCANDISK.
8	Memory error.
9	Insufficient memory for defragmentation.

DEL or ERASE

Delete or Erase: Deletes specified files from a directory.

Syntax (shaded is optional):

DEL Drive:\Path\ **Filename** /p

Examples: DEL *.*
DEL *.exe
DEL C:\budget\1990 /p
ERASE C:\Bin*.dbf

Syntax Options:

Drive:	Drive letter containing *Path*
Path	Subdirectory containing *Filename*
Filename	Filename(s) to be deleted.
/P.	Screen prompts user for confirmation of the file(s) to be deleted.

Command Type and Version:

Internal command; Network; Introduced with Ver 1.0

Notes:

1. Use of wildcards * and ? is allowed. Use DEL *.* with caution, it will delete all files in the current directory. If you happen to be in the root directory of your boot drive when DEL *.* is used, COMMAND.COM, AUTOEXEC.BAT, CONFIG.SYS, etc will be deleted and the system will probably not start.

2. Files may be UNDELETED in DOS Versions 5.0, 6.0, and 6.2x..

3. See also RMDIR, MIRROR, and UNDELETE.

DELOLDOS.EXE Removed V6.2

Directs DOS to delete the OLD_DOS directory: During setup (installation) DOS moves any previous DOS version files to a directory called OLD_DOS. The DELOLDOS command deletes the OLD_DOS directory and all contained files.

Syntax (Shaded is optional):

DELOLDOS

Examples: deloldos

Syntax options: None

Command Type and Version:

External command, Introduced Ver 6.0. Removed 6.2

Notes:

1. Deloldos should be the last step in the installation process for DOS Ver 6.0. When finished, DELOLDOS also deletes itself!

DELTREE.EXE `New V6.0`

Deletes a directory and all the files and subdirectories that are in it: Exercise caution when using this command.

Syntax (shaded is optional):

DELTREE / Y Drive:\Path\Filename

Examples: DELTREE / Y A:*.*
DELTREE / Y C:\DATA

Syntax Options:

Drive: . . . . Drive letter containing *Path*
\\ *Path* . . . . Subdirectory containing *Filename*
\\ *Filename* . . . . Filename(s) to be deleted.
/ Y . . . . Completes DELTREE without first prompting for confirmation of the deletion. Don't use this switch if you can avoid it.

Command Type and Version:

External command; Network; Introduced with Ver 6.0

Notes:

1. If a filename is not specified, all files and subdirectories in the Drive:\Path are deleted.
2. Wild card are supported in the filenames.
3. Attributes such as read only, system and hidden are ignored when a filename is specified.
4. See also DEL and RMDIR.

DEVICE

Loads a device driver into memory: Device drivers are loaded by way of CONFIG.SYS.

Syntax (shaded is optional):

DEVICE = Drive:\Path\ Filename Parameters

Examples: DEVICE = C:\Dos\Himem.sys
DEVICE = Smartdrv.sys 1024 512

Syntax Options:

Drive:\Path . . . Drive and directory(s) containing *Filename*.

\Filename . . . . Driver to be loaded.

Parameters . . . Switches and/or parameters needed by the device driver.

Command Type and Version:

CONFIG.SYS command; Introduced with Ver 2.0

Notes:

1. Standard installable device drivers are: ANSI.SYS, DISPLAY.SYS, DRIVER.SYS, EGA.SYS, PRINTER.SYS, RAMDRIVE.SYS, EMM386.EXE, HIMEM.SYS, and SMARTDRV.SYS. SMARTDRV.SYS is in DOS 5.0 only, SMARTDRV.EXE replaced it first in Windows and then in DOS 6. Other device drivers, such as SETVER and DBLSPACE or DRVSPACE may also be loaded.

2. COUNTRY.SYS and KEYBOARD.SYS are files, not device drivers. Do not try to load either of these files using the DEVICE command or your system will lock up and DOS will not be able to restart.

3. When new devices are purchased, such as a mouse or scanner, you will usually receive device driver software. Use DEVICE to install these drivers, making certain that the device driver is in the specified directory.

4. Install third party console drivers before DISPLAY.SYS.

5. See also DEVICEHIGH.

DEVICEHIGH

Load a device driver into upper memory: After
DOS=umb and HIMEM.SYS have been loaded in
CONFIG.SYS, DEVICEHIGH makes it possible to
load device drivers into the upper memory area.
Loading devices high will free up conventional
memory for other programs.

Syntax (shaded is optional):

DEVICEHIGH = Drive:\Path\ Filename dswitch
or
DEVICEHIGH SIZE=hexsize Drive:\Path
                          \Filename dswitch

DEVICEHIGH /L:(see below) / S Drive:\Path
         ❻   \Filename dswitch

    Examples: DEVICEHIGH = C:\Filename.sys
               DEVICEHIGH SIZE=FF C:\Filename.sys

Syntax Options:

Drive:\Path . . .   Drive and Path of driver to be loaded high.

Filename . . . . .   Device driver to be loaded high.

dswitch . . . . . .   Command line switches required by the
                    device driver being loaded.

SIZE= *hexsize*   Minimum number of bytes (in hex) that
                    must be available for DEVICEHIGH to
                    try to load a driver in high memory. Ver 5

/ L:region1[,minsize1][;region2[,minsize2] ❻ . . .
                    This switch specfies one or more mem-
                    ory regions into which to load a device
                    driver. Normally, DOS loads the driver
                    into the largest free UMB. / L allows a
                    specific region to be selected. See
                    your DOS manual for detailed informa-
                    tion on using this switch.

/ S **6** . . . . *Use / S only in conjunction with / L.*
/ S shrinks the UMB to its minimum
size while a driver is loading and there-
fore makes the most efficient use of
memory.

Command Type and Version:

CONFIG.SYS command; Introduced with Ver 5.0
Updated with different switches in Ver 6.0

Notes:

1. DOS=umb and HIMEM.SYS must be loaded before DEVICE-
   HIGH in order to function. The following is typical in CONFIG.SYS:

   DEVICE = C:\HIMEM.SYS
   DOS = umb
   DEVICE = C:\DOS\EMM386.EXE
   DEVICEHIGH = C:\Filename.sys

   As the example shows, EMM386.EXE or a comparable third-party
   product must be loaded before DEVICEHIGH will work. See DOS
   for more information.

2. If the driver being loaded high requires more high memory than is
   available, the system may lock-up. Use SIZE= to specify the
   memory required by the driver, after determining how much
   memory the driver normally takes by using MEM /DEBUG.

3. See also DOS, LOADHIGH, HIMEM.SYS and EMM386.

4. In MS-DOS Ver 6.0, see also MEMMAKER.

DIR

Directory: Displays the list of files and subdirectories within the current or a designated directory.

Syntax (shaded is optional):

DIR Drive:\Path\Filename /p /w /a:attrib
/ o:sort /s /b /L /c (hd)

Examples: DIR or DIR *.* (wild cards are allowed)
DIR *.exe /p

Syntax Options:

Drive:*Path* . . .   Drive and subdirectory to be listed
Filename . . . .   File name(s) and/or extension to display.

/p	Displays one screen of information, then pauses until any key is pressed.
/w	Displays a wide screen list of files and subdirectories, but the file creation date & time, file size, and <DIR> subdirectory indicator are not shown.
/a : attrib	Displays only files with *attrib* attributes: h=hidden, –h=not hidden, s=system, –s=not system, d=directories, –d=files, a=files ready for archive, –a=files not changed, r=read only, –r=not read only. Introduced with Ver 5.0
/o : sort	Displays by *sort* order: n=alphabetic by name, –n=reverse alphabetic, e=alphabetic by extension, –e=reverse extension alphabetic, d=earliest date/time 1st, –d=latest date/time 1st, s=smallest first, –s=largest 1st, g=group directories before files, –g=group directories after. Introduced with Ver 5.0
	❻ c=compression ratio (least compressed first), -c=compression ratio (most compressed first)
/s	Show all occurrences in both the current directory and all subdirectories below it. Introduced with Ver 5.0
/b	Displays directory 1 line at a time. Ver 5
/L	Displays unsorted names in lowercase. Introduced with Ver 5.0
/c (hd) **❻** . . .	Displays compression ratio. The optional (hd) switch displays compression ratio of DBLSPACE files based on cluster size of host drive. If /w or /b switches are used, /c (hd) is ignored.

Command Type and Version:

Internal command; Network; Introduced with Ver 1.0

Notes:

1. The date and time formats displayed by the *DIR* command will vary, depending on which COUNTRY code is in CONFIG.SYS.

DISKCOMP.COM

Compares Disks: Compares the contents of the floppy disk in the Source drive to the contents of the floppy disk in the Target drive.

Syntax (shaded is optional):

DISKCOMP Source: Target: /1 /8

> Examples:
> DISKCOMP (first floppy disk drive is used)
> DISKCOMP A: B: /1

Syntax Options:

Source:	Source drive containing one of the floppy disks to be compared.
Target:	Target drive containing the other disk to be compared.
/1	Compares only the first side of disks.
/8	Compares first 8 sectors per track.

Command Type and Version:

External command; Not for network. Introduced with Ver 1.0

Notes:

1. DISKCOMP must be used with identical size floppy disks. It cannot be used with a hard drive.

2. If a target drive is not specified, DISKCOMP uses the current drive.

3. DISKCOMP prompts you when to swap disks as necessary.

4. DISKCOMP cannot compare double-sided disk with single-sided disk, or double-density disk with high-density disk.

5. Do not use DISKCOMP on a drive that is affected by the ASSIGN, JOIN, or SUBST commands or DISKCOMP will display an error message. Do not use DISKCOMP on a network drive.

6. When using DISKCOMP to compare a disk made with the COPY comand, although it is duplicate information, COPY may not put the information in the same location on the target disk and DISKCOMP will display an error message.

7. DISKCOMP exit codes are:

0	Disks are the same.
1	Disks are different.
2	Process aborted with CTRL+C by user.
3	Critical error.
4	Initialization error.

DISKCOPY.COM

Copies disks: Copies entire contents of the disk (including the DOS system files) in the source drive onto the disk in the target drive.

Syntax (shaded is optional):

DISKCOPY Source: Target: /1 / v /m

Examples:
DISKCOPY   (current drive must be A: or B:)
DISKCOPY A: B: /1
DISKCOPY A: A: (prompts to change disks)

Syntax Options:

Source:	The floppy disk to be copied.
Target:	The floppy disk to be copied to.
/1	Copies one side of disk.
/ v	Verifies that information is correctly copied. Introduced with Ver 5.0
/ m 62	Forces the use of only conventional memory for interim storage.

Command Type and Version:

External command; Not for networks; Introduced Ver 1.0

Notes:

1. DISKCOPY must be used with identical size floppy disks only. It will not work with a hard disk.

2. If you do not enter a target drive, DOS uses the default drive as the target drive and DISKCOPY will overwrite all information that is on the target disk.

3. DISKCOPY will duplicate disk fragmentation from the source disk. Using the COPY command or the XCOPY command will give you a new disk that will be in sequential order and will not be fragmented.

4. DISKCOPY works only with removable (i.e. floppy) uncompressed disks.

5. DISKCOPY exit codes (ERRORLEVEL parameter) are:

0	Successful copy.
1	Nonfatal read/write error.
2	Process aborted with CTRL+C by user.
3	Critical error.
4	Initialization error.

DISPLAY.SYS

Driver that supports code page switching for the display: Supported types include Mono, CGA, EGA (includes VGA), and LCD.

Syntax (shaded is optional):

DEVICE = Drive:\Path\ DISPLAY.SYS
CON:= (type, hwcp, (n,m))

    Examples:
      DEVICE = DISPLAY.SYS con:=(ega,437,2)

Syntax Options:

Drive:\Path . . .	Drive & directory containing DISPLAY.SYS
type	Type of display adapter,
hwcp	The number assigned to a particular code page. Choices are as follows:

        437. . . . United States
        850. . . . Multilingual (Latin I)
        852. . . . Slavic (Latin II)
        860. . . . Portuguese
        863. . . . Canadian-French
        865. . . . Nordic

n	Number of code pages supported by the hardware: Range is 0 through 6, max for EGA is 6, LCD is 1.
m	Number of subfonts supported by the hardware. Default=2 for EGA, 1 if LCD. If the *m* option is omitted, the parentheses around *n,m* can be omitted.

Command Type and Version:

CONFIG.SYS command; Introduced with Ver 3.3

Notes:

1. Code-page switching has no effect with monochrome and CGA display adapters.
2. If 3rd party console drivers are installed, make sure they are installed <u>before</u> DISPLAY.SYS.

DOS

Forces DOS to keep a link with the upper memory area or to load itself into high memory: HIMEM.SYS must be loaded before DOS= can be used. DOS is useful in that it is part of the program set that frees up conventional memory.

Syntax (shaded is optional):

DOS = high or low , umb or noumb

or

DOS = high or low, umb or noumb

Examples: DOS = high
DOS = umb
DOS = high, umb or DOS = umb, high

Syntax Options:

high	Loads a portion of DOS into high memory.
low	Forces DOS to stay in conventional mem.

| umb . . . . | Forces DOS to maintain a link between high (upper) memory and conventional memory. |
| noumb . . . . | Breaks the link between upper memory and conventional memory. |

Command Type and Version:

CONFIG.SYS command: Introduced with Ver 5.0

Notes:

1. See also DEVICEHIGH and LOADHIGH.
2. UMB must be used in order to load either DOS or drivers into upper memory. EMM386.EXE or a comparable third party product must be loaded and configured in order to provide upper memory blocks from extended memory for DOS=UMB to work.
3. DOS can be placed anywhere in the CONFIG.SYS file.
4. UMB or NOUMB can be combined with HIGH or LOW in the same DOS = command line, see the example above.

DOSKEY.COM

Starts the DOSKEY program, which allows the user to edit command lines, create macros, and recall DOS commands:

Syntax (shaded is optional):

DOSKEY /reinstall /bufsize=nnn /macros /history /insert /overstrike /macroname=text

Examples: DOSKEY   (start DOSKEY with defaults)
DOSKEY / history > special.bat

Syntax Options:

/ reinstall	Installs DOSKEY again. If DOSKEY is currently running, this command clears the buffer.
/ bufsize=nnn . .	Sets the size of the buffer where DOS-KEY store commands. Default=512 bytes, minimum=256 bytes.
/ macros or /m .	Displays the current list of DOSKEY macros.

/ history or /h . .	Displays a list of all commands that were stored in memory.
/ insert	Sets typing to insert mode (text is not overwritten as typing occurs)
/ overstrike. . . .	Sets typing to overstrike mode (text <u>is</u> overwritten as typing occurs)
/ macroname=.	Name of file created to hold *text* macro.
text	The commands and text to be recorded in the file named *macroname*.

Command Type and Version:

External command; Network; Introduced with Ver 5.0

Notes:

1. */macros* and */history* can be used with DOS redirection to a file.
   e.g. DOSKEY */macros* > Macro.txt creates a text file list of macros.
2. DOSKEY is a very powerful program, see the Microsoft **Users Guide and Reference** for detailed comments and examples.

When DOSKEY is on, the following can be used to recall/edit commands from its command buffer:

Up Arrow	Recall command issued before currently displayed command.
Down Arrow . .	Recall command issued after the currently displayed command.
Page Up	Recall oldest command in current session.
Page Down . . .	Recall most recent command in current session.
Left Arrow	Moves cursor left one character.
Right Arrow . . .	Moves cursor right one character.
Ctrl+Left Arrow	Moves cursor left one word.
Ctrl+Rght Arrow	Moves cursor right one word.
Home	Moves cursor to start of line.
End	Moves cursor to end of line.
Esc	Clears the display command line.
F1	Copy one character from last command buffer to the command line.

Key	Description
F2	Look forward for the next key typed after pressing F2.
F3	Copies the remainder of the current template line at the current cursor position to the command line.
F4	Delete all characters of the current template line, up to but not including the character pressed after F4 is pressed
F5	Copy current line to template and clear command line
F6	Put Ctrl+Z (end of line marker) at the end of the current line.
F7	Displays all commands and numbers, beginning with the oldest, currently stored in the command buffer.
Alt+F7	Delete all commands in command buffer.
F8	Locate the most recently used command in the buffer that begins with a specific character(s). At the DOS prompt, simply type those beginning characters and then press F8.
F9	Display the command associated with a specific command line number in buffer.
Alt+F10	Delete all macros.

The following are special codes that can be used in creating macros. Code letters shown can be used in either upper or lower case.

Code	Description
$G	Redirect output (same as >) to a device other than the screen. e.g. a printer.
GG	Append output data (same as >>) to the end of a file instead of overwriting file.
$L	Redirect input (same as <) to read from a device other than the keyboard.
$B	Send output from macro to another command (same as I).
$T	Used to separate commands in either a macro or at the DOSKEY command line.
$$	Used to specify the $ character

$1 to $9..... Batch parameters (similar to %1) for passing command line info to the macro when it's run.

$ * .... A replaceable parameter similar to $1 to $9, except that everything that is typed on the command line after *macroname* is substituted for the $ * in the macro.

Macros are run by simply typing the *macroname* at the DOS prompt, followed by any parameter info such as $1 or $*. If a macro is created that has the same name as a normal DOS command, the DOS command is started by typing a space and then the command name, whereas with the macro, simply type the *macroname* without a space preceeding it.

DOSSHELL.COM & EXE

Starts the DOS graphical user interface shell:

Syntax (shaded is optional):

DOSSHELL /t or /g :Res n /b

Examples: DOSSHELL / t
DOSSHELL / g:m
DOSSHELL / g /b

Syntax Options:

/ t............ Directs DOSSHELL to start in text mode.
/ g .... Directs DOSSHELL to start in graphics mode.
:Res......... Screen resolution class. *l* (lowercase L) for Low, *m* for medium and *h* for high resolution.

n	If there is more than one resolution available in the *Res* category, n provides additional information concerning which category to use. n is hardware dependent.
/b	Starts DOSSHELL in black & white mode or the state /t or /g is in.

Command Type and Version:

External command; Network; Introduced with Ver 4.0

Notes:

1. If DOSSHELL has already been started, the screen resolution can be changed from the options menu.
2. DOSSHELL is very useful for such tasks as renaming subdirectories.

DRIVER.SYS

Defines a logical drive from an existing physical drive: A logical drive is simply a drive letter used to point to the actual physical drive. The new drive letter established by DRIVER.SYS is the next highest drive letter above the system's highest current drive.

Syntax (shaded is optional):

DEVICE = Drive:\Path\ DRIVER.SYS /d:number /c / f:factor /h:heads /s:sectors / t:tracks

Examples:
DEVICE=C:\dos\driver.sys /d:1 /f:2 /h:2 /s:9 /t:80
(above configures a 3.5" 720k floppy drive, if the last hard drive was drive E:, then the 3.5 inch would be designated as drive F:)

Syntax Options:

Drive:.	Drive letter containig *\Path*
\Path	Subdirectory containing *DRIVER.SYS*

/d: number	Specifies physical drive number. Values must be in the range of 0 to 127. Normally, Drive A=0, Drive B=1, etc.
/c	Specifies that the driver will be able to tell that the floppy disk drive door is open.
/f: factor	Specifies type of drive. Default value= 2

Factor .	Description
0	160kb/180kb or 320kb/360kb
1	1.2 megabyte (Mb)
2	720kb (3.5 in. disk)
7	1.44Mb (3.5 in. disk)
9	2.88Mb (3.5 in.disk)

/h: heads	Specifies max. number of heads. Value for **heads** must be in the 1 to 99 range.
/s: sectors	Number of sectors per track, ranging in value from 1 to 99. The default varies according to the /f factor selected above. Normal values are 360kb and 720kb = 9 sectors, 1.44 meg = 18 sectors, 1.2 meg = 15 sectors and 2.8 meg = 36 sectors.
/t: tracks	Number of tracks per side on the block device, ranging from 1 to 999. Default values vary according to the /f factor selected above. Normal values are 360kb = 40 tracks, 720kb, 1.44 meg, and 1.2 meg = 80 tracks.

Command Type and Version:

CONFIG.SYS command; Introduced with Ver 3.2

Notes:

1. DRIVER.SYS is commonly used to set up a 3.5 inch floppy drive on a system that does not support 3.5 inch drives directly. Setting up external 3.5 inch drives is also common.

2. See also the DRIVEPARM command, it is used to modify existing parameters of a physical device.

3. DRIVER.SYS can not be used to define hard drives. If hard drive logical drive assignments need to be changed, see the SUBST command.

4. If two DRIVER.SYS command lines are used for the same physical drive, then two logical drive letters will be assigned to the single physical drive.

5. XT class systems, with standard floppy controllers, will still need either a special driver or special controller in order to recognize a 1.44 or 2.8 Mb 3.5 inch floppy or 1.2 Mb 5-1/4 inch floppy.

DRIVPARM

Defines block device parameters: DRIVPARM allows the default or original device driver settings to be overridden when DOS is started.

Syntax (shaded is optional):

DRIVPARM=/d:number /c / f:factor /h:heads
/ i / n /s:sectors / t:tracks

Examples: DRIVPARM=/d:1 /c /f:2 /h:2 /s:9 /t:80
(above configures a 3.5" 720k floppy drive)

Syntax Options:

/d: number	Specifies physical drive number. Numbers must be in the range of 0 to 255. Normally, Drive A=0, Drive B=1, etc.
/c	Specifies that the driver will be able to tell that the floppy disk drive door is open.
/ f: factor	Specifies type of drive. Default value= 2

Factor .	Description
0	160K/180K or 320K/360
1	1.2 megabyte (MB)
2	720K (3.5 in. disk)
5	Hard disk
6	Tape
7	1.44MB (3.5 in. disk)
8	Read/write optical disk
9	2.88MB (3.5 in.disk)

/ h: heads	Specifies max. number of heads. Value for **heads** must be in the 1 to 99 range.

/i ④	. . . . .	Specifies an electronically-compatible 3.5 in. floppy disk drive. Use the / i switch if the ROM BIOS does not support 3.5 in. floppy disk drives.
/n	. . . .	Non-removable block device.
/s: sectors	. . . .	Number of sectors per track, ranging in value from 1 to 99. The default varies according to the /f factor selected above. Normal values are 360kb and 720kb = 9 sectors, 1.44 Mb = 18 sectors, 1.2 Mb = 15 sectors and 2.8 Mb = 36 sectors.
/t: tracks	. . . . .	Number of tracks per side on the block device, ranging from 1 to 999. Default values vary according to the /f factor selected above. Normal values are 360kb = 40 tracks, 720kb, 1.44 Mb, and 1.2 Mb = 80 tracks.

Command Type and Version:

CONFIG.SYS command; Introduced with Ver 3.2

Notes:

1. DRIVPARM is particularly useful in configuring 3.5 inch floppy drives.
2. Settings in DRIVPARM will override any settings specified for a device prior to the DRIVPARM command line.
3. Although DRIVPARM is listed as an option in DOS Ver 3.3, the command will not function in that version.
4. DRIVPARM does not create new logical drives, it can only modify existing physical drive parameters.
5. See also DRIVER.SYS

DRVBOOT.BAT New Ver 6.22

Creates a bootable DRVSPACE floppy disk:

Syntax (shaded area optional):

DRVBOOT drive1:

Example: drvboot a:

Syntax options:

drive1: . . . .   Drive containing floppy disk to be
                         compressed.

Command Type and Version:

External command, Introduced with Ver 6.22.
Available in the MS-DOS 6.22 Supplemental Disks.

Notes:

1. DRVBOOT works only on high-density floppy disks (1.44 or 1.2
   MB).
2. DRVSPACE must be installed prior to using DRVBOOT.

DRVSPACE.EXE   New Ver 6.22

Directs DOS to compress hard drives or floppy
disks or configure compressed files:

Syntax (Shaded is optional):

DRVSPACE (starts the interactive DriveSpace
             program)

    Examples: DRVSPACE
                  or
             DRVSPACE /task (executes task com-
             mand without starting the DriveSpace
             program)
    Example: DRVSPACE /create c: /newdrive=d:
             /reserve=50

Syntax for Task Command Options:

**/compress drive1: /newdrive=drive2 /re-
serve=size /f**

Directs DOS to compress files on an existing disk
(hard drive, floppy, or other removable media).

---

drive1: .... Specifies existing drive to compress.

/compress or /com ...... Compresses the floppy disk or hard drive specified by drive1:.

/newdrive=drive2: or /new ...Identifies the drive letter for the uncompressed drive. After compression, the drive will contain an existing compressed drive (drive1:) and a new uncompressed drive (newdrive).

/reserve=size or /res ... Size, in megabytes, of space to leave uncompressed. Space will be located on drive2:.

/f .... Suppresses display of the final DriveSpace screen and returns to command prompt.

/create drive1: /newdrive=drive2 /reserve=size /size=size

Directs DOS to create a new compressed drive in free space on an uncompressed drive. The new compressed drive will provide more storage space than the amount of uncompressed storage it uses.

drive1: .... Specifies uncompressed existing drive containing space to create new drive.

/create .... or /cr Creates a new compressed drive in free space on the uncompressed drive specified by drive1:.

/newdrive=drive2: or /n ....Identifies the drive letter for the new compressed drive.

/reserve=size or /re ..... Size, in megabytes, of space to leave uncompressed. Space will be located n drive2:. Can not use with /size=size.

/size=size or /si ....Total size, in megabytes, of the compressed .volume file. Can not use with /reserve=size.

/defragement /f drive1:

Directs DOS to defragment the specified compressed drive.

drive1: .... Specifies existing compressed drive to defragment.

/defragment or def ...... Defragments specified compressed drive.

/f .... Specifies full defragmentation of specified drive.

/delete drive1:

Directs DOS to delete selected compressed drive and erase associated volume file.

drive1: .... Specifies drive to be deleted. Will not allow deletion of drive c:.

/delete or del .... Deletes the specified drive.

/format drive1:

Directs DOS to format selected compressed drive. Caution-A compressed drive can not be unformatted after formatting using DRVSPACE /FORMAT.

drive1: .... Specifies drive to be formated. Will not allow formatting of drive c:.

/format or /f... Formats the specified drive.

/info drive1:

Directs DOS to display information about selected compressed drive. Information includes free and un-used space, name of compressed volume file, and estimated and actual compression ratios. Command may be used while Windows is running.

drive1: .... Specifies drive for which information is desired.

/format or /f... Displays information for the specified drive.

/list

Directs DOS to list and describe, in brief terms, all available drives, except network and CD-ROM drives.

/list or /li .... Displays a list of all system drives, except CD-ROM or network drives.

/mount=nnn drive1: /newdrive=drive2

Directs DOS to create a reference between a compressed volume file (CVF) and a drive letter. DRVSPACE normally mounts compressed volume files automatically.

drive1: .... Specifies an existing drive containing the compressed volume file to be mounted. A drive must be specified.

/mount=ext or /mo=ext ......Directs DOS to mount the compressed volume file with the filename extension specified by ext.

/newdrive=drive2: or /new ...Identifies the drive letter for the new drive.

/ratio=r.r drive1: /all

Directs DOS to change the estimated compression ratio of the specified compressed drive. DOS uses the ratio to estimate the amount of free space the drive contains.

drive1: .... Specifies existing compressed drive to defragment.

/ratio=r.r or /ra=r.r .... Changes the ratio of specified compressed drive. Ratios are allowed in the range from 1.0 to 16.0. If not specified, DOS sets the ratio to the average compression ratio for all compressed files on the drive.

/all................ Specifies a change of all mounted compressed drives. Do not use if a drive is specified using drive1.

/size=size1 /reserve=size2 drive1:

Directs DOS to enlarge or reduce the current size of a compressed drive. The command is used to free-up space on a drive or enlarge a compressed drive if ample free space is available.

drive1: .... Specifies the drive containing to be resized.

/size=size1 or /si=size1 ....Changes the size of the drive specified by drive1: to size1 in megabytes. Can not be used with /reserve=size2.If neither switch is used, DOS will makes the compressed drive as small as possible.

/reserve=size2 or /res=size2 ......Size, in megabytes, of space to leave uncompressed. Can not use with /size=size1.

/uncompress drive1:

Directs DOS to uncompress files on an existing disk (hard drive, floppy, or other removable media). Uncompressing the last mounted drive also removes DRVSPACE.BIN from memory.

drive1: .... Specifies drive to uncompress.

/uncompress ....Uncompresses the floppy disk or hard drive specified by drive1:

/unmount drive1:

Directs DOS to eliminate a previous reference between a compressed volume file (CVF) and the specified drive. The unmounted drive is unavailable until again mounted. Drive c: can not be unmounted.

drive1: .... Specifies the drive to be unmounted. If no drive is specified DRVSPACE unmounts the current drive.

/unmount ...... Directs DOS to unmount the specified drive.

Command Type and Version:

External command, Interactive
Introduced in MS-DOS Version 6.2, Revision 2.

Notes:

1. DRVSPACE is the Microsoft DOS Ver 6.2, Revision 2, replacement for DBLSPACE.
2. DRVSPACE requires 33Kb of memory to install.
3. DRVSPACE may slow down the speed of a system with a slow CPU.

DRVSPACE.SYS New Ver 6.22

Device driver which directs DOS to move DRVSPACE.BIN to its final memory location: DRVSPACE.BIN provides DOS with access to compressed files. When the computer is started, DOS loads DRVSPACE.BIN at the top of conventional memory at the same time it loads other operating system functions; that is, prior to executing the CONFIG.SYS and AUTOEXEC.BAT files. After processing the CONFIG.SYS file, DOS moves DRVSPACE.BIN to the bottom of conventional memory. Running DRVSPACE.SETUP adds a command for DRVSPACE.SYS to the CONFIG.SYS file.

Syntax (shaded is optional):

DEVICE = DRVSPACE.SYS /move /nohma
or
DEVICEHIGH = DRVSPACE.SYS /move /nohma

Examples: DEVICE = DRVSPACE.SYS /move

Syntax Options:

/move . . . . Directs DOS to move DRVSPACE.BIN
to its final memory location.

/nohma . . . . Tells DRVSPACE.SYS not to move
DRVSPACE.BIN into high memory.

Command Type and Version:

External command, Introduced in Ver 6.2, revision 2.

DVORAK.SYS `New V6.0`

Used with KEYB to provide an alternative to the standard QWERTY keyboard layout:

Syntax (shaded area optional):

KEYB nn,,drive1:\directory \DVORAK.SYS

Example: KEYB rh,,d:\dos\dvorak.sys

Syntax Options:

drive1: . . . . Drive containing DVORAK.SYS.

\directory . . . . . Directory containing DVORAK.SYS.

nn . . . . Designates keyboard configuration.

. . . . dv = two-handed layout

. . . . rh = right-handed layout

. . . . lh = left-handed layout.

Command Type and Version:

External command, Introduced with MS-DOS Ver 6.0.

Available in the MS-DOS 6.0, 6.21, and 6.22 Supplemental Disks.

Notes:
1. To return to the U. S. standard keyboard press CTRL+ALT+F1.
2. To return to the Dvorak keyboard layout press CTRL+ALT+F2.

ECHO

Display a message or turn command echo feature on or off: When batch files are run, DOS usually displays (echos) the name of the program being run to the display. This feature can be turned on or off with the ECHO command.

Syntax (shaded is optional):

ECHO Message | on | off

Examples: ECHO off
ECHO Enter program name to be run!
ECHO on

Syntax Options:
Message: . . . . Text to be displayed on screen.
on . . . . Turn display echo on.
off . . . . Turn display echo off.

Command Type and Version:
Internal and Batch command; Introduced with Ver 2.0

Notes:
1. Use the @ symbol in front of a batch file command in order to turn the screen echo function off.
2. NOTE: in DOS 6.0, ECHO. (with the period) on a command line will output a blank line. ECHO by itself displays ECHO status.

EDIT.COM

Starts MS-DOS Editor: EDIT is a full-screen text editor which can create, save, edit and print ASCII text files.

Syntax (shaded is optional):

EDIT Drive:\Path \Filename /b /g /h /nohi

Examples: EDIT C:\Autoexec.bat
EDIT D:\Bin\Test.bat /h

Syntax Options:

Drive: \Path . . .	Location of *Filename*.
\Filename	Name of ASCII text file to be edited.
/b	Editor displayed in black and white.
/g	Provides CGA monitors with the fastest screen update.
/h	Allows monitor to display maximum number of lines on the screen.
/nohi	Normally, DOS uses a 16 color mode for monitors. This switch enables the use of 8 color monitors.

Command Type and Version:

External command; Network; Introduced with Ver 5.0

Notes:

1. QBASIC.EXE must be in the same directory as EDIT or included in the DOS path. If it is not, EDIT will not function.

2. Shortcut keys that are shown on the bottom line of the screen may not display properly. If this occurs, use the /b and /nohi switches.

EDLIN.EXE Removed V6.0

Line oriented text editor: Edlin is an editor used to
insert, change, copy, move and delete lines of text
in an ASCII file. If a full screen editor is required,
use EDIT (page 149). 24 lines of text can be displayed on the screen at one time.

Syntax (shaded is optional):

EDLIN Drive:\Path\ Filename / b

      Examples: EDLIN Test
                     EDLIN C:\Autoexec.bat

Syntax Options:

Drive:*Path* . . . Drive and directory containg the file to
                 be edited.

Filename . . . . . File to be edited. If Edlin cannot find the
                 file named *Filename*, it will automat-
                 ically create the file in the specified
                 Drive:\Path location.

/ b . . . . Causes EDLIN to ignore Ctrl–Z (end of
                 file character).

Command Type and Version:

External command; Network; Introduced with Ver 1.0
Removed from DOS Ver 6.0, use the EDIT command.

Available In the MS-DOS 6.0, 6.21, and 6.22 Supplemental Disks.

Notes:

1. Edlin can handle a maximum of 253 characters per line.

2. A full description of EDLIN is beyond the scope of this book. See
   a full DOS manual for additional details and instructions.

3. EDLIN uses an asterisk * prompt on a line by itself to ask for a
   command. If the * occurs after a line number, it indicates that that
   line number is the current line.

EDLIN Commands:(case doesn't matter)

  ? . . . . Displays the list of EDLIN commands.

Line	Just typing a number, at the prompt, displays the text contained in that line #.
Ctrl–C	Exits user out of the insert (I) mode.
n A	Append *n* number of lines into memory from disk. Edlin will load till 75% of available memory is full.
L1,L2,L3,count C . . .	Copy a block of lines. *L1*=first line to copy, *L2*=last line to copy, *L3*=line before which EDLIN is to insert the block, *count*=number of times to copy.
L1, L2 D	Delete from line *L1* to line *L2*.
E	Write current file to disk and stop EDLIN.
L1 I	Insert lines before line *L1*. Ctrl-C stops.
L1, L2 L	List (display) lines between *L1* and *L2*.
L1, L2, L3 M . .	Move a block of lines. *L1*=first line to
or *L1,+n,L3 M*.	move, *L2*=last line to move, *L3*=line before which EDLIN is to move the block, *+n*=include the next *n* lines.
L1, L2 P	Display all or part of the file one full screen of text at a time. *L1*=first line and *L2*=last line.
Q	Quit EDLIN without saving the current file to disk. Return to DOS.
L1,L2 ? R S1 S2 S3 . . .	Replace a block of lines with a string. *L1*=first line to replace, *L2*=last line to replace, *?*=prompt user to confirm replacement, *S1*=string to be replaced, *S2*=Ctrl-Z separator, *S3*=string to replace S1.
L1,L2 ? S S1 .	Search between *L1* first line and *L2* last line for string *S1*. *?*=prompt user when string *S1* is located.
L1 T D:\Path\Filename . . .	Transfer (merge) contents of a second file from disk into the current edited file. *L1*=line in current file before which user wants inserted file to be placed. *D:\Path\Filename*=name and directory location of file to be inserted into current file.

n W.	Write *n* number of lines, starting at the first line, to disk.

EGA.SYS

When using Task Swapper with an EGA monitor, the EGA.SYS command saves and restores the display.

Syntax (shaded is optional):

DEVICE = Drive\path\ EGA.SYS

Examples: DEVICE=C:\Dos\EGA.SYS

Syntax Options:

Drive:\ *Path* . . . Specifies the location of the EGA.SYS file.

Command Type and Version:

CONFIG.SYS command; Introduced with Ver 5.0

Notes:

1. To save memory when using a mouse on a system, install EGA.SYS before installing the mouse driver.

EMM386.EXE

Activates or deactivates expanded memory emulator for 80386 and higher systems: EMM386 is both a device driver loaded through CONFIG.SYS and an External command. It also enables or disables support of the Weitek coprocessor.

Syntax (shaded is optional):

To load EMM386 initially in CONFIG.SYS:
Device= Drive:\Path\ EMM386.EXE on *or* off *or*
auto memory min=size w=on *or* w=off mx *or*
frame = address *or* /pmmm pn=address
x=mm-nn
i=mm-nn b=address L=minXMS a=altregs
h=handles d=nnn ram=mm-nn noems novcpi
highscan verbose win=mm-nn nohi rom=mm-nn
nomovexbda altboot

To use EMM386 as an External command:
EMM386 on *or* off *or* auto w=on *or* w=off /?

Examples: Device=C:\EMM386.EXE noems
           EMM386 on   (at DOS prompt)
           EMM386   (at DOS prompt to show status)

Syntax Options:

Drive:\Path . . .	Drive and directory containing EMM386
EMM386	At the DOS prompt this displays the current status of EMM386.
on	Activates EMM386 driver. (default)
off	Deactivates EMM386 driver.
auto	Places EMM386 driver in auto mode, where expanded memory support is turned on when a program needs expanded memory.
memory	kbytes of memory allocated to EMM386. Default:256, Range:16 to 32768, use multiples of 16. This memory is in addition to low-memory backfilling.
w=on	Enable Weitek coprocessor support.
w=off	Disable Weitek coprocessor support.
mx	Address of page frame. Values for *x* can be 1 to 14 below. On systems with only 512k of memory, only 10 to 14 can be used.

1=C000 hex	8=DC00 hex
2=C400 hex	9=E000 hex
3=C800 hex	10=8000 hex

	4=CC00 hex	11=8400 hex
	5=D000 hex	12=8800 hex
	6=D400 hex	13=8C00 hex
	7=D800 hex	14=9000 hex

frame=*address* Specific page-frame segment address for base page. *address* can be C000h to E000h and 8000h to 9000h, in increments of 400h.

/p*mmm* ...... Address of page frame. *mmm* can range from C000h to E000h and 8000h to 9000h, in increments of 400h.

p*n*=*mmm* ..... Specific segment address (*mmm*) of a specific page *n*. *n* can range from 0 to 255. *mmm* can range from 8000h to 9C00h and C000h to EC00h, in increments of 400h.

x=*mm–nn* .... Excludes a range of segment addresses from EMS page use. *mm* and *nn* can both range from A000h to FFFFh, and are rounded off to the nearest 4k. x overrides i when two ranges overlap.

i=*mm–nn* ..... Includes a range of segment addresses for EMS page or RAM use. *mm* and *nn* can both range from A000h to FFFFh, and are rounded off to the nearest 4k. x overrides i when two ranges overlap.

b=*address* .... Lowest segment address that can be used for bank swapping of 16k EMS pages. Default=4000h, range=1000h to 4000h.

L=*minXMS* ... Specifies that *minXMS* kbytes of extended memory will remain after EMM386 has been loaded. Default=0

a=*altregs* ..... *altregs* number of fast alternate register sets are allocated to EMM386. Default= 7, range=0 to 254. Each register uses an additional 400 bytes of memory.

h=*handles* .... Number of handles EMM386 can have. Default=64, range=2 to 255.

---

d=*nnn*	Kbytes of memory reserved for buffered DMA (direct memory access). Default= 16, range=16 to 256.
ram	Upper memory and expanded memory access is provided.
noems	Upper memory access provided but not to expanded memory.
novcpi **6.2**	Disables VCPI application support. Used with /noems.
highscan **6.2** ..	Directs EMM386 to check availability of upper memory for UMB or EMS windows.
verbose or v **6.2**	Directs EMM386 to display error and/or status messages while loading.
Win=*mm-nn* **6.2**	Directs EMM386 to reserve the specified range of segment addresses for Windows. Values of mm and nn are in the range A000h through FFFh, rounded down to the nearest 4 Kb boundary. The /x switch takes precedence over /win if overlap occurs. The /win switch takes precedence over /ram, /rom, or /i switches if overlap occurs.
nohi **6.2**	Forces EMM386 to load into conventional memory thus increasing upper memory available for UMBs.
rom=*mm-nn*.**6.2**	Directs EMM386 to reserve the specified range of segment addresses for shadow RAM. Values of mm and nn are in the range A000h through FFFh, rounded down to the nearest 4 Kb boundary.
nomovexbda **6.2**	Directs EMM386 to keep extended BIOS data in conventional memory.
altboot **❻**	Provides an alternate boot sequence for some computers with compatibility problems. Used if computer doesn't recognize Ctrl-Alt-Del.
/ ?	Help with command line switches.

Command Type and Version:

External and CONFIG.SYS command;
Introduced with Ver 4.0

Notes:

1. HIMEM.SYS must be loaded before EMM386.EXE is loaded.
2. The .EXE extension of EMM386 must be used to load the driver.
3. The order of switches and parameters is not important.
4. Device=EMM386.EXE must preceed DEVICEHIGH commands.
5. If enough memory is not available to set up a 64k page frame, the "Unable to set base address" error message will display.
6. DOS=umb must be used in CONFIG.SYS to provide access to the upper memory block.
7. See also DOS, HIMEM.SYS, DEVICEHIGH, and LOADHIGH.
8. Using EMM386.EXE and the Note 7 commands is a very complicated task. It is strongly recommended that the user spend a great deal of time with Microsoft's *MS-DOS 5.0 User's Guide and Reference* learning about memory management and system optimization.

EXE2BIN.EXE Removed V6.0

Converts an executable file to a binary file: Converting executable files (.EXE extension) to files with a binary format, is only useful to software developers and is of no value to general users.

Syntax (shaded is optional):

EXE2BIN   Drive1:\Path1\   INfile
          Drive2:\Path2\   OUTfile

Examples: EXE2BIN C:\Test.exe C:\test.bin

Syntax Options:

Drive1:\Path1 . Drive and directory of input .EXE file.
Drive2:\Path2 . Drive and directory of output binary file.
INfile . . . . Input .EXE file to be converted.
OUTfile . . . . . . Output binary file.

Command Type and Version:

External command; Introduced with Ver 1.0
Removed from DOS Ver 6.0
Available in the MS-DOS 6.0, 6.21, and 6.22 Supplemental Disks.

Notes:

1. EXE2BIN is not for the general computer user, only programmers.
2. Default extensions for INfile is .EXE and for OUTfile is .BIN.
3. INfile must have been produced by LINK and must not be a packed file.
4. See also LINK

EXIT

Exits a secondary command processor and returns to the primary processor if one exists.

Syntax (shaded is optional):

EXIT

   Examples: EXIT

Syntax Options:

No options

Command Type and Version:

Internal; Network; Command processor function;
Introduced with Ver 2.0

Notes:

1. If a secondary command processor is not loaded (or /P is used with COMMAND.COM) , the EXIT command will have no effect.
2. See Also COMMAND

EXPAND.EXE

Expands a compressed DOS file: Compressed files are not usable unless exanded. Use EXPAND to retrieve files from DOS installation or update disks.

Syntax (shaded is optional):

EXPAND `Drive:\Path\` Filename Destination

Examples:
EXPAND B:\Dos\FIND.EX_ C:\Dos\FIND.EXE

Syntax Options:

Drive: \Path . . .　Specifies location and name of a compressed file to be expanded.

Filename . . . . .　File to be expanded.

Destination . . .　Target location where expanded files are to be placed. Destination can be a drive letter and colon, a filename, a directory name or a combinaton. A destination filename can only be used if a single compressed Filename is used.

Command Type and Version:

External command; Network; Introduced with Ver 5.0

Notes:

1. Wildcards (* and ?) **cannot** be used.

2. Compressed files, such as installation or update files, have a file extension which ends with an underscore character (_)

3. Although EXPAND is normally used by the DOS 5.0 Upgrade program to install all DOS 5.0 files, you can copy a single compressed file, such as FIND.EX_ , from an upgrade disk to the hard drive and EXPAND it for full use. A complete list of all files and what disk they are on is included in the file named PACKING.LST on upgrade disk 1 or 2.

4. One or more source filenames may be specified. Destination may include a filename only if a single source filename is specified. If no destination is specified, EXPAND prompts for it.

FASTHELP.EXE `New V6.0`

Displays a list and gives a brief description of all DOS 6.0 commands: This command is a direct replacement for the DOS Ver 5.0 HELP.
/? can be used in conjunction with other DOS commands to display the same help as FASTHELP would display for the same command.

Syntax (shaded is optional):

FASTHELP   command

> Examples: FASTHELP   Chkdsk
> FASTHELP
> DISKCOPY /?

Syntax Options:

command . . . .   The particular DOS command that you want help about.

Command Type and Version:

External command; Network; Introduced with Ver 6.0

Notes:

1. FASTHELP without a command displays a list and brief description of all DOS 6.0 commands contained in the DOSHELP.HLP file.
2. Detailed information on DOS commands is available with the HELP command.
3. FASTHELP is a direct replacement for the DOS Ver 5.0 HELP command.

FASTOPEN.EXE

Fast opening of files: Decreases the amount of time to open frequently used files by keeping directory information in memory. FASTOPEN can be started at the DOS prompt or in either a Batch file or CONFIG.SYS. *DOS V4 is different, see manual.*

Syntax (shaded is optional):

To start in a Batch file or at the DOS Prompt:
    FASTOPEN Drive1: = nnn Drive2:= nnn ... /x
To start in CONFIG.SYS use the following:
    Install=Drive:\Path\FASTOPEN.EXE
                    Drive1: = nnn Drive2:=nnn ... /x

    Examples: FASTOPEN C:=97 /x
               Install=C:\DOS\FASTOPEN C:=97

Syntax Options:

Drive1: Drive2: One or more drives FASTOPEN tracks.

nnn . . . . Number of files FASTOPEN can work
                 with at the same time. The valid values
                 are 10 through 999. 48 is the default.

/x . . . . Creates the *name cache* in expanded
                 memory rather than conventional mem-
                 ory. *name cache* is a buffer where
                 names and locations of open files are
                 stored.

Drive:*Path* . . . Drive and directory containing FASTOPEN.

Command Type and Version:

External and CONFIG.SYS command; NOT for Network
Introduced with Ver 3.3

Notes:
1. When placed in CONFIG.SYS, FASTOPEN.EXE must be used, not FASTOPEN without the extension.
2. FASTOPEN uses approximately 48 bytes of memory for each file that it tracks.
3. Deactivate FASTOPEN **BEFORE** disk compaction is used!!!!!

4. FASTOPEN works with hard drives only, not floppy drives.

FC.EXE

Compare two files and report the differences: FC reports the differences it finds between two files and displays them on screen. The comparison can be of ASCII or binary files.

Syntax (shaded is optional):

FC /a /c /L /Lbx /n /t /w /nnn
    Drive1:\Path\ File1 Drive2:\Path\ File2
or
FC /b Drive1:\Path\ File1 Drive2:\Path\ File2

> Examples: FC /a C:\DATA\Test.txt D:\Master.txt

Syntax Options:

Drive1:\Path . .	Drive and directory of first file *(File1)*.
Drive2:\Path . .	Drive and directory of second file *(File2)*.
File1 & File2 . .	The two files to be compared.
/ a	Abbreviate ASCII comparison output, will only display first and last line of different block.
/ c	Ignore upper/ lower case.
/ L	Files comparred in ASCII mode.
/ Lbx	Set *x* lines of internal line buffer.
/ n	During ASCII compare, displays line #s.
/ t	Do not expand tabs to spaces. Default is to treat tabs as spaces with stops at every 8th position.
/ w	During comparison, tabs and spaces are compressed. Also causes FC to ignore space that occurs at the beginning and end of lines.

| / nnn . . . . | Set the number of consecutively matching lines before files are resynchronized. |
| /b . . . . | Files compared in binary mode. This is the default for all files ending in .EXE, .COM, .SYS, .OBJ, .LIB and .BIN. |

Command Type and Version:

External command; Network;
Introduced with Version 2.1

Notes:

1. See also COMP and DISKCOMP.
2. Use of wild cards (* or ?) is allowed.
3. For ASCII comparisons, the *File1* name is displayed, then the lines from *File1* that are different are displayed, then the first line to match in both files, then the *File2* name is displayed, then the lines from *File2* that are different, and finally, the first line to match in *File2*. FC uses a 100 line buffer to hold the lines being compared, if there are more than 100 lines of differences, FC cannot complete the comparison and issues a Resynch Failed error message.
4. For binary comparisons, the differences are reported on a single line as xxxxxxxx: **yy zz**, where xxxxxxxx is the hex address from the beginning of the file where the difference occurs. yy is the byte that is different in *File1* and zz is the byte that is different in *File2*. FC uses the same line buffer as Note 4 for binary comparisons, however if it runs out of memory, it will overlay portions of the memory until the comparison is completed.
5. FC is only available with MS-DOS®, not PC-DOS.

FCBS

Sets number of file control blocks that DOS can have open at the same time:

Syntax (shaded is optional):

FCBS = x

Examples: FCBS = 10

Syntax Options:

x . . . . File control blocks that DOS can have
open at one time. Default = 4. Values
can range from 1 through 255.

Command Type and Version:

CONFIG.SYS command; Introduced with Ver 3.0

Notes:

1. Normally, this command should only be used if a program
   specifically requires that FCBS be set to a specific value.
2. DOS may close a file opened earlier if there are not enough
   FCBs set aside.
3. The **,y** Syntax Option available in DOS Versions 4.01 and
   earlier, is no longer a valid option.

FDISK.EXE

Configures hard disk: After the low level format of
a hard drive, FDISK is used to partition the drive
for DOS. A series of menus are displayed to assist in the partitioning process. *Caution:* When a
partition is deleted, all of the data stored on that
partition is also deleted.

Syntax (shaded is optional):

FDISK / status

Examples: FDISK

Syntax Options:

/ status ❻ . . . . Display partition table info for hard
drives installed in the system.
/ mbr . . . . Master boot record. Undocumented

Command Type and Version:

External command; Network, introduced with Ver 2.0

Notes:

1. Before DOS 3.3, FDISK did not create extended partitions or logical drives in the partitions. There could be only one DOS partition per drive. Until DOS 3.31 & 4.0, max size was 32Mb.

2. Using the FDISK command, you can accomplish the following:
   Create a primary DOS partition on a hard drive.
   Create an extended DOS partition on a hard drive.
   Delete a partition on a hard drive.
   Change the active partition on a hard drive.
   Displays partition data for a hard drive.
   Selects a different hard disk for partitioning.

3. Maximum partition size is 2 gigabytes.

4. In order to change the size of a partition, the partition must be deleted first, and a new partition created.

5. Drives formed by ASSIGN, SUBST, or JOIN cannot be partictioned with FDISK.

6. USE WITH CAUTION, backup hard drive data files before changing or deleting a partition.

7. The formatting of a hard drive for use by DOS is a three step process: Low level format, FDISK, then FORMAT. Note that IDE hard drives have been low level formatted at the factory, do not re-low level format these drives, only use FDISK then FORMAT.

8. See also FORMAT.

FILES

Sets the number of open files DOS can access.

Syntax (shaded is optional):

FILES = nnn

    Examples: FILES=20

Syntax Options:

nnn . . . . Number of files DOS can access, at one time, with valid values ranging from 8-255. The Default is 8.

Command Type and Version:

CONFIG.SYS command; Introduced with Ver 2.0

Notes:

1. The standard value for files is FILES=20, however, many software packages, such as database managers, will require values in the range of 35 to 40. See the documentation for each program you

wish to run and verify that your FILES= statement is not smaller than that required by the program. It is all right if FILES= is larger than a program requires.

FIND.EXE

Looks for a text string in a file(s): Once the text string is located that FIND is searching for, it displays those lines of text containing the text string.

Syntax (shaded is optional):

FIND /v /c /n /i text Drive:\Path\ Filename

Examples: FIND /v /i "Dear Sir" C:\Test.doc
FIND "Dear Sir" Test.doc
FIND "Dear Sir" "Sincerely" "Help" C:\Test.doc

Syntax Options:

Drive:*Path* . . . Drive and directory containing *Filename*.
Filename . . . . . File being searched for *Text*.
text . . . . Text string being searched for.
/ v . . . . Display lines that do not contain *Text*.
/ c . . . . Display line count of lines containing *Text*.
/ n . . . . File's line number containing *Text*.
/ i . . . . Ignore upper/lower case during search.
Ver 5.0

Command Type and Version:

External command; Network; Introduced with Ver 2.0

Notes:

1. Wild cards (* and ?) cannot be used in filenames being searched for by FIND. See the FOR command for help in this area.
2. FIND ignores carriage returns, so *Text* must be a string that does not contain any carriage returns.
3. If /c and /n are used together, the /n is disregarded.
4. If Filename is not specified, FIND will act as a filter for any standard device (keyboard, file, pipe, etc) and display those lines containing *Text*.
5. DOS provides three filter commands, FIND, MORE, and SORT.

6. /c /v used together will return a count of lines that do not contain *Text*.

FOR

A logical batch command that runs a specific command for each file in a group: FOR can be run from inside a batch file or at the DOS prompt.

Syntax (shaded is optional):

If used in a batch file, use the following:
FOR %%variable IN (set) DO command `cpar`
If used at the DOS prompt, use the following:
FOR %variable IN (set) DO command `cpar`

> Examples:
> FOR %T IN (*.doc, *.asc) DO DEL %T
> (deletes all .doc and .asc files in current directory)

Syntax Options:

%variable . . . . Replaceable variable for use at the DOS prompt. The *variable* name can be any character(s) except the numbers 0 to 9. FOR replaces *variable* with each text string contained in *(set)* and runs *command* over and over until all are processed.

%%variable . . . Same as %*variable*, except for use in batch files only.

(set) . . . . One or more files or text strings on which *command* is to operate. ( ) is required

command . . . . Any DOS command to be run on each item listed in *(set)*.

cpar . . . . Parameters for *command*.

Command Type and Version:

Batch and Internal command; Introduced with Ver 2.0

Notes:

1. FOR..IN..DO commands cannot be nested on a single command line.
2. Wild cards (* and ?) are allowed in *(set)*.
3. Multiple %variable names are allowed.

FORMAT.EXE

Format a floppy or hard disk: A disk must be formatted before DOS can recognize it.

Syntax (shaded is optional):

There are 4 different syntax choices:

FORMAT Drive: /v:name /q /u /f:size /b /s /c
FORMAT Drive: /v:name /q /u /t:trak /n:sect /b /s /c
FORMAT Drive: /v:name /q /u /1 /4 /b /s /c
FORMAT Drive: /q /u /1 /4 /8 /b /s /c /autotest

Examples: FORMAT A: / s /autotest
FORMAT B: / f:720k / s

Syntax Options:

Drive:. . . . . Drive to be formatted. If no switches are used, the drive is formatted according to its system drive type.

/ v:name . . . . . Assign the disk the volume label *name*. *name* can be up to 11 characters long. If /v is not used, DOS will automatically prompt the user for a volume name when the format process is finished. /v is not compatible with /8. See also the VOL, DIR, and LABEL commands.

/ q . . . . Quick format a disk by deleting the FAT (File Allocation Table) and root directory. Only use this on disks that have already been formatted. You can not use /q with /autotest. Ver 5.0

/ u	Unconditional format. Destroys all data and UNFORMAT will not work. Use if read or write errors occur with this disk or when a new disk is to be formatted. Ver. 5.0
/ 1	Format 1 side of floppy only.
/ 4	Formats a DSDD (double-sided double-density) 5-1/4 inch, 360k floppy in a 1.2 m floppy drive. Warning: some 1.2m drives can not reliably do this format!
/ 8	Formats a 5-1/4 disk with 8 sectors per track. 8 sectors per track are necessary for use with pre DOS 2.0 operating systems.
/ f:size	Floppy disk size. Use instead of /t and /n switches if possible:

160, 160k or 160kb	160k SSDD, 5-1/4"
180, 180k or 180kb	180k SSDD, 5-1/4"
320, 320k or 320kb	320k DSDD, 5-1/4"
360, 360k or 360kb	360k DSDD, 5-1/4"
720, 720k, or 720kb	720k DSDD, 3.5"
1200, k, kb, 1.2, 1.2m, 1.2mb	1.2m DSHD, 5-1/4"
1440, k, kb, 1.44, 1.44m, 1.44mb	1.44m DSHD, 3.5"
2880, k, kb, 2.88, 2.88m, 2.88mb	2.88m DSEHD, 3.5"

/ b	Obsolete switch used to reserve space for the system files. No longer generally used, retained for compatibility only.
/ s	Copies all 3 system files, [IO.SYS and MSDOS.SYS] or [IBMBIO.COM and IBMDOS.COM] and COMMAND.COM to the disk after formatting has finished. The DBLSPACE.BIN file is also copied to the target drive (if you are not using the DBLSPACE program, you can remove the hidden, system, read-only attributes from DBLSPACE.BIN on the target disk and then delete it.)
/ t:trak	Number of tracks on disk, must be used with the /n switch. Use / f:size switch if possible.
/ n:sect	Number of sectors on disk, must be used with the / t switch. Use / f:size switch if possible.

| / autotest **6** .. | Bypasses prompts during formatting. Note that this is an undocumented command. Will not work with /q. |
| /c **6.2** .... | Retests for bad cluster |

Command Type and Version:

External command; Introduced with Ver 1.0

Notes:

1. New floppy disks need only be formatted in order to make the disk useable by DOS. Hard drives, however, require a 2 or 3 step format process which includes a low level format (Not on IDE drives), then partitioning with FDISK, and finally FORMAT.

2. If the / U switch is **not** used, UNFORMAT can unformat the disk. See also UNFORMAT

3. Format issues a warning when a hard drive is to be formatted.

4. Do not format Network drives or drives that have had ASSIGN, JOIN or SUBST used on the drive.

5. FORMAT / S and the DOS "SYS" command both copy the DBLSPACE.BIN file to the Target Disk.

6. FORMAT Exit codes are:
0	Successful FORMAT
3	Aborted with Ctrl+C by user
4	Fatal error other than 0,3, or 5
5	No response to Proceed?

GOTO

***Directs DOS to process commands starting
with the line after a specified label:*** Within a
Batch program, when DOS finds the specified label, it processes the commands beginning with
the next line after that label.

Syntax (shaded is optional):

GOTO Label
:Label

        Examples: GOTO Start
                       Test.bat   (bypassed by GOTO)
                       :Start   (must begin with :)

Syntax Options:

Label . . . .   Directs DOS to a specific line in a batch
                     file. Valid values for *Label* can include
                     spaces but cannot include other separa-
                     tors, such as equal signs and
                     semicolons. GOTO will recognize only
                     the first 8 characters of the *Label*
                     name. *Label,* on the GOTO command
                     line, does not begin with a colon and it
                     must have a matching *Label* line in the
                     batch program. The *Label* line in the
                     batch program must begin with a colon.
                     You can also substitute an environment
                     variable enclosed in percent signs, e.g.
                     %RETURN%, for *Label.*

Command Type and Version:

Internal command; only used in a Batch program;
Introduced with Ver 2.0

Notes:

1. A batch-program line beginning with a colon (:) is a label line,
and will not be processed as a command. When the line begins
with a (:) colon, DOS ignores any commands on that line.

GRAFTABL.COM `Removed V6.0`

Allows a display to show extended characters in graphics mode from a specific code page:
This command is required when a monitor is not able to display extended characters in graphics mode. (Most monitors do not need GRAFTABL.)

Syntax (shaded is optional):

GRAFTABL nnn
  or
GRAFTABL /status

     Examples:
       GRAFTABL 860   (Portuguese code page)

Syntax Options:

nnn	Code page used to define extended characters.

437	United States
850	Multilingual
852	Slavic
860	Portuguese
863	Canadian-French
865	Nordic

/status	Identifies current country code page.

Command Type and Version:

External command; Network; Introduced with Ver 3.0 Beginning with MS-DOS Ver 6.0, GRAFTABL is only available on Microsoft's DOS Supplemental Disks.

Notes:

1. The active code page is not changed when GRAFTABL is run.
2. GRAFTABL uses approximately 1K of RAM.
3. GRAFTABL exit codes are as follows:

0	Successful load of character set.
1	Current character set replaced by new table.
2	File error has occurred.
3	Incorrect parameter, new table not loaded.
4	Incorrect DOS version, 5.0 required.

GRAPHICS.COM

Configures DOS so that Print Screen (Shift+Print Scrn) can print a graphics screen to a printer. GRAPHICS supports CGA, EGA, and VGA display modes:

Syntax (shaded is optional):

GRAPHICS Type Drive:\Path\ Filename /r /b
/Lcd /pb:std or /pb:Lcd

Examples: GRAPHICS color4 /b

Syntax Options:

Type	Printer type (HP=Hewlett-Packard)
color1	IBM Color Printer with black ribbon
color4	IBM Color Printer with RGB ribbon
color8	IBM Color Printer with CMY ribbon
hpdefault	Any HP PCL printer
deskjet	HP DeskJet printer
graphics	IBM Graphics, Proprinter or Quietwriter
graphicswide . .	IBM Graphics Printer with 11inch carriage
laserjet	HP LaserJet printer
laserjetii	HP LaserJet II printer
paintjet	HP PaintJet printer
quietjet	HP QuietJet printer
quietjetplus . . .	HP QuietJet Plus printer
ruggedwriter . . .	HP Rugged Writer printer
ruggedwriterwide	HP Rugged Writerwide printer
thermal	IBM PC-convertible Thermal Printer
thinkjet	HP ThinkJet printer
Drive:\Path . . .	Drive and directory containing *Filename*.
Filename	Printer profile where graphics screen is to be printed to. Default is GRAPHICS.PRO.
/r	Prints the image as white characters on a black background (black characters on a white background is the Default).

/ b	Prints the background in color. (only color4 and color8 types are valid)
/ Lcd	Prints image using an LCD screen aspect ratio instead of a CGA screen aspect ratio.
/ pb:std . . . . . . or / pb:Lcd . .	Sets printbox size. If this switch is used, you must check the GRAPHICS.PRO file and change each printbox line to *std* or *Lcd* so that it matches what you selected for */pb* :

Command Type and Version:

External command; Network; Introduced with Ver 2.0

Notes:

1. The GRAPHICS command does use a limited amout of conventional RAM when it is loaded.

2. Four shades of gray are printed if *color1* or *graphics* is in effect and the screen is in the 320x200 mode.

3. If a printer profile such as GRAPHICS.PRO is already loaded, and you wish to load a different .PRO file, the new .PRO must be smaller than the currently loaded .PRO. If it is larger, your system must be re-booted first in order for the larger profile to be loaded.

4. Use the Graphics or Graphicswide printer types if the printer you are using is an Epson.

5. Supported displays include EGA and VGA.

6. See also PRINT

7. Do not use the / b switch in conjunction with the / r switch or with a black and white printer.

GW-BASIC®.EXE

BASIC language intrepreter: GW-BASIC® is Microsoft's own version of BASIC that shipped with MS–DOS versions prior to Ver 5.0. Starting with Ver 5.0, QBASIC is shipped with DOS.

Syntax (shaded is optional):

GWBASIC Drive:\Path\Filename < Input
>> Output /f:n /i /s:n /c:n /m:n,n /d

Examples: GWBASIC (starts BASIC)
GWBASIC C:\BAS\test.bas /f:4 /d

Syntax Options:

Drive:\Path . . .	Drive and directory containing *Filename*.
Filename	The BASIC program file to be run. The default file extension is **.BAS**
< *Input*	Standard input is read from *Input* file.
> *Output*	Output is redirected to *Output* file or a device (screen, printer, etc)
>>	Causes *Output* to be appended.
/f:n	Max number *n* of simultaneously open files while a BASIC program is running. Default is 3. */i* must be used at the same time. Size requirement includes 194 bytes (File Control Block) plus 128 bytes (data buffer).
/i	Forces static allocation of memory for file operations.
/s:nn	Max record length *nn* for a file. Default is 128 bytes, maximum is 32,767 bytes.
/c:nn	Allocates *nn* bytes of Receive buffer and 128 bytes of Transmit buffer for RS-232 (serial) communications. */c:0* disables support. Defaults are 256 byte receive buffer and 128 byte transmit buffer for each RS-232 card.
/m:x,y	Sets the highest memory location *x* and the maximum block size *y* in bytes. Block size is in multiples of 16.
/d	Activates double-precision for the following functions: ATN, COS, EXP, LOG, SIN, SQR and TAN.

Command Type and Version:

External command; Network; Introduced with Ver 1.0

Notes:

1. See also BASIC, BASICA, and QBASIC.

2. Variables n, nn, x, and y listed above are all given in decimal values. If you wish to use hexadecimal values, preceed the value with &H. If you wish to use octal values, preceed the value with &O (O is the letter O, not zero).

3. A complete discussion of GW-BASIC is beyond the scope of this book. If you need information on GW-BASIC commands and how to program in BASIC, refer to Microsoft's manual on GW-BASIC or other texts on BASIC.

4. Different versions of GWBASIC were released and each needs to be run with its correct version of DOS.

5. Programs written in BASIC (IBM's version) may require small adjustments in order to run correctly under GW-BASIC

HELP.EXE - Version 5.0 only

Online information about MS-DOS version 5.0 commands:

Syntax (shaded is optional):

HELP `command`

> Examples: HELP (brief description of commands)
> HELP chkdsk
> DISKCOPY / ? (see Note: 1 below)

Syntax Options:

Command . . . . Any specific DOS version 5.0 command on which more information is desired.

Command Type and Version:

External command; Network; Introduced with Ver 5.0
FASTHELP in Ver 6.0 is the same as HELP in Ver 5.0

Notes:

1. You can get online HELP in two ways. Either specify the name of the command on the HELP command line or type the command name and the /? switch at the command prompt.

HELP - Version 6.0 and 6.2x New V6.0

***Online information about MS-DOS Version 6.0
and 6.2x commands and a list of all DOS commands:*** The Ver 6.0 AND 6.2 information for
HELP is much more detailed than FASTHELP or
DOS Ver 5.0 HELP.

Syntax (shaded is optional):

HELP command /B /G /H /nohi

    Examples: HELP   (List of commands)
                  HELP chkdsk
                  DISKCOPY / ?   (see Note: 1 below)

Syntax Options:

Command	Any specific DOS version 6.0 command on which more information is desired.
/B.	Display in black-and-white mode.
/G	Display in CGA color mode.
/H.	Display HELP with the maximum number of lines that the display supports.
/nohi	Turn high-intensity display off.

Command Type and Version:

External command; Network; Introduced with Ver 6.0
FASTHELP in Ver 6.0 and 6.2x is the same as HELP in
Ver 5.0

Notes:

1. You can get online HELP in two ways. Either specify the name
of the command on the HELP command line or type the command
name and the /? switch at the command prompt.

HIMEM.SYS

Extended memory and HMA (high memory area) manager: HIMEM.SYS prevents programs from using the same memory locations at the same time.

Syntax (shaded is optional):

Device= Drive:\Path\ HIMEM.SYS /hmamin=m
/numhandles=n /int15=xxx /machine:xxx
/a20control:on or off /shadowram:on or off
/cpuclock:on or off /EISA /verbose
/test:on or off

Examples: Device=C:\Dos\HIMEM.SYS /test:off

Syntax Options:

Drive:\Path . . .	Drive and directory containing HIMEM.
/hmamin=m . . .	Minimum *m* kilobytes of memory a program must use before it can use the HMA. Default=0, Range=0 to 63. The most efficient use of HMA is accomplished by setting m to the amount of memory required by the program that uses the most HMA.
/numhandles=n	Maximum number (*n*) of EMB (extended memory block) handles that can be used at the same time. Each handle uses 6 bytes of RAM. Default=32, Range=1 to 128.
/int15=xxx	*xxx* kilobytes of memory are assigned to the Interrupt 15h interface. Programs must recognize VDisk headers in order to use this switch.
/machine:xxx . .	Defines a specific A20 handler *xxx* to be used. Normally, HIMEM automatically detects which A20 is to be used. Default=1. If the required handler is not

listed in the following table, see the README.TXT file in your DOS directory for additional information.

Number	Code	A20 handler
1	at	IBM PC/AT, Compuadd 386 JDR 386/33
2	ps2	IBM PS/2, Datamedia 386/486, Unisys PowerPort
3	ptlcascade	Phoenix Cascade Bios
4	hpvectra	HP Vectra, A and A+
5	att6300plus	AT&T 6300 Plus
6	acer1100	Acer 1100
7	toshiba	Toshiba 1600, 1200XE and 5100
8	wyse	Wyse 12.5 MHz 286, Intel 361Z or 302, Hitachi HL500C, Compuadd 386
9	tulip	Tulip SX
10	zenith	Zenith ZBIOS
11	at1	IBM PC/AT
12	at2	IBM PC/AT (alt. delay)
12	css	CSS Labs
13	at3	IBM PC/AT (alt. delay)
13	philips	Philips
14	fasthp	HP Vectra
15 🄶	ibm7552	IBM 7552 Industrial Comp.
16 🄶	bullmicral	Bull Micral 60
17 🄶	dell	Dell XBIOS

/a20control:on
or /a20control:off — Off allows HIMEM.SYS to take control of the A20 line only if A20 was off when HIMEM.SYS was loaded. Default=:on

/shadowram:on
or /shadowram:off — If your system has Shadow RAM, :off switches the Shadow RAM off and returns control of that RAM to HIMEM. Default=:off if your system has less than 2 megabytes of RAM.

/cpuclock:on	If your system slows down when HIMEM.SYS is loaded, specifying *:on* might correct the problem. *:on* will slow down HIMEM.SYS.
/ EISA ❻	*Used only on EISA systems to specify that HIMEM allocates all available extended memory.*
/ verbose or / v ❻	HIMEM displays status and error messages while loading. Hold ALT key down during system startup to disable /verbose.
/ test:on or :off	Turns the HIMEM.SYS testing of all extended memory *:on* or *:off* during system startup.

Command Type and Version:

Config.sys command; Introduced with Ver 5.0

Notes:

1. Only one program at a time can use the high memory area.
2. HIMEM.SYS, or another XMS driver such as 386MAX or QEMM must be loaded before DOS can be loaded into HMA with the DOS=high command.
3. In most cases, command line switches do not need to be used. since the defaults are designed to work with most computer hardware.

IF

Performs a command based on the result of a condition in batch programs: If a conditional statement is true, DOS executes the command, if the condition is false, DOS ignores the command.

Syntax (shaded is optional):

Three syntax formats are valid:

IF `not` errorlevel nnn *command*
IF `not` string1==string2 *command*
IF `not` exist filename *command*

Examples: IF errorlevel 3 goto end

Syntax Options:

not . . . . The command is to be carried out only if the statement is false.

errorlevel nnn . True only if the previous program executed by COMMAND.COM had an exit code equal to or greater than *nnn*.

command . . . . The specified command that DOS is to perform if the preceding condition is met.

string1==string2 True, only if *string1* and *string2* are the same. The values of *string1* and *string2* can be literal strings or batch variables. Strings may not contain separators, such as commas, semicolons, spaces, etc.

exist filename . True condition if *filename* exists.

Command Type and Version:

Internal command but only used in Batch programs; Introduced with Ver 2.0

Notes:

1. The *errorlevel* parameter allows you to use exit codes as conditions. An exit code is returned to DOS whenever a program stops.
2. Use " " quotes around strings when comparing, it's safer.

INCLUDE

Includes the contents of one configuration block within another configuration block: This is one of five special CONFIG.SYS commands used to define multiple configurations.

Syntax (shaded is optional):

INCLUDE=blockname

Syntax Options:

blockname. . . .   The name of the configuration block to be included.

Command Type and Version:

CONFIG.SYS command; Introduced with Ver 6.0

Notes:

1. See also MENUITEM, MENUDEFAULT, MENUCOLOR, and SUBMENU. These are the other four special CONFIG.SYS commands used to define multiple configurations

2. Refer to your DOS 6.0 manual for more information on setting up the special multiple configuration menus.

INSTALL

Loads a memory-resident program when DOS is started: Use the INSTALL command to load FASTOPEN, KEYB, NLSFUNC, or SHARE in CONFIG.SYS.

Syntax (shaded is optional):

INSTALL = `Drive: \Path\` Filename `parameters`

Examples: INSTALL = C:\Dos\NLSFUNC

Syntax Options:

Drive:\Path . . . Drive and directory containing *Filename*.

\Filename . . . . Name of memory-resident program that you want to run.

Parameters . . . Command parameters, if any, required by *Filename*.

Command Type and Version:

Config.sys command; Network; Introduced with Ver 4.0

Notes:

1. Less memory is used when you load a program with INSTALL instead of loading from the AUTOEXEC.BAT file since an environment for a program is not created by INSTALL .

2. Do not use INSTALL to load programs that use shortcut keys, environment variables, or require COMMAND.COM for error handling.

3. Not all programs will function properly if loaded with INSTALL.

4. See also FASTOPEN, KEYB, NLSFUNC, SHARE, CONFIG.SYS.

INTERLNK `New V6.0`

Link computers to share resources:

INTERLNK.EXE must be installed as a device driver in the CONFIG.SYS file before the INTERLNK and INTERSVR commands can be run.

Syntax (shaded is optional):

INTERLNK `client :` = `server :`

Examples: INTERLNK C: = F:

Syntax Options:

client : . . . . *The drive letter of the client drive that is redirected to a drive on the server.*

server : . . . . . . The drive letter on the server that will be redirected. If a letter is not specified, the client drive will no longer be redirected.

Command Type and Version:

External command; Network; Introduced with Ver 6.0

Notes:

1. See also INTERLNK.EXE and INTERSVR.
2. Note, the LASTDRIVE command may need to be used if drive letters greater than E are used.

INTERLNK.EXE   `New V6.0`

Link computers to share resources:

INTERLNK.EXE must be installed as a device driver in the CONFIG.SYS file before the INTERLNK and INTERSVR commands can be run.

Syntax (shaded is optional):

Device= Drive: \Path\ INTERLNK.EXE /drives:n /noprinter /com:nladdress /lpt:nladdress /auto /noscan /low /baud:rate /v

Examples: Device=C:\ INTERLNK.EXE /drives:4

Syntax Options:

Drive:\Path . . . Drive and directory containing the INTERLNK.EXE program.

/drives:n. . . . . . The number of redirected drives. Default is n=3. If n=0, only the printers are redirected.

/ noprinter	No printers are to be redirected. Default is INTERLNK redirects all ports.
/ com:nladdress	Specifies that serial port *n* be used to transfer data. If *n* or the address is omitted, INTERLNK scans for the first available port. Default is INTERLNK redirects all ports.
/ lpt:nladdress .	Specifies that parallel port n be used to transfer data. If *n* or the address is omitted, INTERLNK scans for the first available port. Default is INTERLNK redirects all ports.
/ auto	INTERLNK.EXE is installed in memory only if *client* can make a connection when the *server* starts up. Default is INTERLNK is installed whether or not *server* is there.
/ noscan......	INTERLNK.EXE driver is installed, but a connection between *client* and *server* is prevented.
/ low.........	INTERLNK.EXE forces driver to be loaded into conventional memory. Default is driver loaded into upper memory if it is available.
/ baud:rate....	Sets baud rate for com serial ports. Default=115200. Valid values are 9600, 19200, 38400, 57600, & 115200.
/ v	Used to resolve problems and conflicts between *com* and *lpt* ports and the computer's timer.

Command Type and Version:

CONFIG.SYS command; Network; Introduced Ver 6.0

Notes:

1. See also INTERSVR and INTERLNK the command.

INTERSVR.EXE   New V6.0

Starts the INTERLNK server so that resources can be shared between linked computers:
INTERLNK.EXE must be installed as a device driver in the CONFIG.SYS file before the INTERLNK and INTERSVR commands can be run.

Syntax (shaded is optional):

> INTERSVR drive: /X=drive /lpt:nladdress
> /com:nladdress /baud:rate /b /v /rcopy

    Examples: INTERSVR / rcopy

Syntax Options:

/ X=drive	Specifies those drives that will not be redirected. Default is all drives are redirected.
/ lpt:nladdress .	Specifies that serial port n be used to transfer data. If n or the address is omitted, INTERLNK scans for the first available port. Default is INTERSVR scans all ports.
/ com:nladdress	Specifies that serial port n be used to transfer data. If n or the address is omitted, INTERLNK scans for the first available port. Default is INTERSVR scans all ports.
/ baud:rate	Sets baud rate for com serial ports. Default=115200. Valid values are 9600, 19200, 38400, 57600, & 115200.
/ b	Display stat screen in black-and-white.
/ v	Used to resolve problems and conflicts between *com* and *lpt* ports and the computer's timer.

/ rcopy	Copies all INTERLNK files from one computer to another. Note that a full 7 wire null-modem serial cable must be installed on the *com* port and the DOS MODE command must be available.

Command Type and Version:

External command; Network; Introduced with Ver 6.0

Notes:

1. See also INTERLNK.EXE and INTERLNK.
2. If port numbers for com and lpt are not specified, INTERLNK will scan and select the first port it finds.

JOIN.EXE   Removed V6.0

Joins a disk drive to a specific directory on another disk drive: Once joined, DOS treats the directories and files of the first drive as the contents of the second drive and path.

Syntax (shaded is optional):

Two syntax formats are valid:
JOIN Drive1: Drive2:\Path
JOIN Drive: /d

    Examples: JOIN C: D:\Notes
              JOIN C: D:\Notes\Bin   (valid for DOS 5.0 only)

Syntax Options:

Drive1:	Drive to be joined to *Drive2:\Path*.
Drive2:\Path . .	Drive and Path to which you want to
. . . .	JOIN *Drive1:*. *Drive2:\Path* must be empty and other than the root directory. With DOS Ver 5.0, you can JOIN to a subdirectory also, e.g. C:\Notes\Bin
Drive:	Drive on which JOIN is to be canceled.
/ d	Cancels the JOIN command.

Command Type and Version:

External command; Introduced with Ver 3.0

Removed from MS DOS Version 6.0, however, it is available on Microsoft's MS-DOS 6.0 and 6.2x Supplemental Disks.

Considered too dangerous to use.

Notes:

1. Once you use the JOIN command, Drive1: becomes invalid.
2. If a specified path already exists before using JOIN, that directory cannot be used while JOIN is in effect. The specified directory must be empty or the JOIN operation will be incomplete and an error message will be displayed.
3. Commands that do not work with drives formed by JOIN are: ASSIGN, BACKUP, CHKDSK, DISKCOMP, DISKCOPY, FDISK, FORMAT, LABEL, MIRROR, RECOVER, RESTORE, SYS.
4. Use JOIN without parameters to show a list of the currently joined drives.

KBDBUF.SYS   New V6.0

A device driver that sets the number of keystrokes stored in the keyboard buffer.

Syntax (shaded is optional):

DEVICE = KBDBUF.SYS   xxxx

Example: DEVICE = KBDBUF.SYS 200

Syntax Options (shaded is optional):

xxxx . . . . Designates the number of keystrokes held in the buffer. This number can range from 16 to 1024.

Command Type and Version:

CONFIG.SYS command

Introduced with MS-DOS Ver. 6.0

Available only on Microsoft's Supplemental Disks for MS-DOS Versions 6.0, 6.21 and 6.22.

KEYB.COM and KEYBOARD.SYS

Configures a keyboard for use with a specific language (installs alternate keyboard layout):

Syntax (shaded is optional):

If started in a batch file or at the DOS prompt:
  KEYB xx,yyy,Drive:\Path\Filename /e / id:nn

If started in CONFIG.SYS:
  install = Drive1:\Path1\KEYB.COM xx, yyy, Drive:\Path\Filename /e / id:nn

  Examples: KEYB fr,850,437,C:\Dos\Keyboard.sys
  install = C:\KEYB.COM fr , , C:\Dos\Keyboard.sys

Syntax Options:

xx	Keyboard code. See table on next page.
yyy	Code page. See table on next page.
Drive:\Path . . .	Drive and directory containing *Filename*.
Filename	Keyboard definition file. Default=KEYBOARD.SYS
/e	Enhanced keyboard is being used. Ver5
/id:nn	Defines which keyboard is in use. See table on next page.
Drive1:\Path1 .	Drive and directory containing KEYB.COM

Command Type and Version:

External command; Network; Introduced with Ver 3.3

Notes:

1. When KEYB is installed through CONFIG.SYS, KEYB.COM with the .COM must be used. See also the CHCP command.
2. The Code Page specified with yyy must already be loaded on your system before KEYB is used.
3. You can switch from the default keyboard configuration to the KEYB configuration by pressing Ctrl+Alt+F2. To switch to the default keyboard configuration, press Ctrl+Alt+F1
4. The following are KEYB exit codes:
     0 . . . . KEYB definition file loaded successfully.
     1 . . . . Invalid Keyboard Code, Code Page, or syntax.

```
2 . . . . . . . Bad or missing keyboard definition file.
4 . . . . . . . Communication error with CON device.
5 . . . . . . . Requested Code Page has not been prepared.
```

The following table lists xx, yyy, and nnn values for different countries and languages.

Country or language	Keyboard Code xx	Code Page yyy	Keyboard ID nnn
Belgium	be	850,437	
Brazil	br	850,437	
Canadian-French	cf	850,863	
Czeck Republic	cz	852,850	
Denmark	dk	850,865	
Finland	su	850,437	
France	fr	850,437	120,189
Germany	gr	850,437	
Hungary	hu	852,850	
Italy	it	850,437	141,142
Latin America	la	850,437	
Netherlands	nl	850,437	
Norway	no	850,865	
Poland	pl	852,850	
Portugal	po	850,860	
Slovakia	sl	852,850	
Spain	sp	850,437	
Sweden	sv	850,437	
Switzerland (French)	sf	850,437	
Switzerland (German)	sg	850,437	
United Kingdom	uk	850,437	166,168
United States	us	850,437	
Yugoslavia	yu	852,850	

KEYBxx.COM

Loads a keyboard program for a specific country or keyboard type:

Syntax (shaded is optional):

KEYBxx

    Examples: KEYBGR
                KEYBUK

Syntax Options:

xx. . . . .   Code for a specific keyboard type:

    KEYBdv . . . . Dvorak keyboard
    KEYBfr. . . . . France
    KEYBgr . . . . Germany
    KEYBit. . . . . Italy
    KEYBsp. . . . Spain
    KEYBuk. . . . United Kingdom

Command Type and Version:

External command; Network; Introduced with Ver 3.0

Notes:

1. KEYBxx was discontinued after DOS version 3.2 and was replaced by KEYB.
2. Only one keyboard program can be loaded at a time.
3. You can switch from the default keyboard configuration to the KEYBxx configuration by pressing Ctrl+Alt+F2. To switch to the default keyboard configuration, press Ctrl+Alt+F1.
4. If you need to change from one keyboard type to another, restart the system after the changes have been made.

LABEL.EXE

***Creates, changes or deletes the name or
volume label of a disk:*** DOS displays the volume
label and serial number, if it exists, as part of the
directory listing.

Syntax (shaded is optional):

LABEL Drive: Label

    Examples: LABEL
                 LABEL A: datadisc

Syntax Options:

Drive:. . . . . Drive or diskette to be named.
Label . . . . New volume label, up to 11 characters.
                     A colon (:) must be included between
                     the drive letter and label, but <u>NO</u> space.

Command Type and Version:

External command; Introduced with Ver 3.0

Notes:

1. Using the LABEL command without a label displays the following:
                . Volume in Drive A is nnnnnnnnnn
                . Volume Serial Number is nnnn-nnnn
                . Volume Label (11 characters, ENTER for none)?
2. The Volume label cannot include tabs. Spaces are allowed, but
   consecutive spaces may be treated as a single space.
3. **Do not** use the following characters in a volume label:

                * ? / \ | . , ; : + = [ ] ( ) & ^ < > "

4. LABEL is not case sensitive. (lower case is automatically
   converted to upper case.)
5. LABEL does not work on a drive created by ASSIGN, JOIN or
   SUBST.

LASTDRIVE

Number of drives installed: By default, the last drive is the one *after* the last drive used by your computer. DOS 4 and earlier it was E:

Syntax (shaded is optional):

LASTDRIVE = parameter

   Examples: LASTDRIVE = F

Syntax Options:

parameter . . . .   A drive letter in the range of A through Z
                     to correspond to the number of logical
                     drives installed. Default is the drive af-
                     ter the last one used by the computer.

Command Type and Version:

   CONFIG.SYS command; Introduced with Ver 3.0

Notes:

1. Memory is allocated by DOS for each drive specified by
   LASTDRIVE, therefore, don't specify more drives than are
   necessary.

LINK.EXE   Removed V5.0

8086 Object Linker that creates executable pro-grams from Microsoft Macro Assembler (MASM) object files: LINK is for the experienced programmer and is not used by the general user.

Syntax (shaded is optional):

LINK   (LINK prompts for file names, etc)
LINK object , execute , map , library options ;

   Examples: LINK file /se:192 , , ;

Syntax Options:

object........	Object files to be linked together.
execute......	Name for created executable file.
map.........	Map listing file.
library.......	Name(s) of library files to LINK.
options.......	Options for the LINK program
;............	Terminates command line.

Command Type and Version:

External command; Introduced with Ver 1.0
Removed from Ver 5.0

Notes:

1. Further discussion of LINK is beyond the scope of POCKET PCRef.

LOADFIX.COM

Forces a program to load above the first 64k of conventional memory and then runs the program.

Syntax (shaded is optional):

LOADFIX Drive: \Path\ Filename parameters

Examples: LOADFIX C:\TEST.EXE

Syntax Options:

Drive:\Path...	Drive and directory containing *Filename*.
Filename.....	Name of program that you want to run.
Parameters...	Command parameters, if any, required by *Filename*.

Command Type and Version:

External command; Introduced with Ver 5.0

Notes:

1. Use LOADFIX when the error message "Packed file corrupt" is reported during the execution of a program.

LOADHIGH or LH

Loads programs into upper memory: Loading programs into upper memory frees up conventional memory for other programs. An upper memory manager such as EMM386 must be loaded first in order for LOADHIGH to function. LH and LOADHIGH are equivalent commands.

Syntax (shaded is optional):

LOADHIGH Drive:\Path\ Filename /L:region /s parameters

> Examples: LOADHIGH C:\Dos\doskey.com
> LH C:\Dos\doskey.com

Syntax Options:

Drive:\Path . . . Drive and directory containing *Filename*.

\Filename . . . . Program to be loaded into high memory.

/L:region . . . . . Load the device driver into a specific upper memory region.

/s 6.2 . . . . Shrinks the upper-memory block (UMB) to minimum size while loading program. Used only with the */L:region* switch. Typically used only by MEMMAKER.

parameters . . . Command line parameters required by *Filename*.

Command Type and Version:

Internal command; Network; Introduced with Ver 5.0

Notes:

1. DOS=umb must be included in your CONFIG.SYS in order for LOADHIGH to function.
2. HIMEM.SYS and EMM386.EXE must be loaded in CONFIG.SYS on a 386/486 system in order to provide upper memory management for 386/486 systems. (Programs such as 386MAX and QEMM will provide the same capabilities.)
3. If there is not enough upper memory to load a program, DOS will load the program into conventional memory (no notice is given).
4. See also DEVICEHIGH, DOS, HIMEM.SYS, and EMM386.

5. When LOADHIGH is used, it is typically placed in the AUTOEXEC.BAT file.
6. Use MEM /c to see where programs are loaded.
7. Running MEMMAKER will automatically add all necessary LOADHIGH commands to AUTOEXEC.BAT

MD or MKDIR

Makes a Directory: Creates a new subdirectory under the current directory (if no Drive:\Path is specified). A new subdirectory on a different drive or under a different path can also be created. MD and MKDIR are equivalent commands.

Syntax (shaded is optional):

MD Drive:\Path\ subdirectory

Examples: MD contract
MKDIR contract
MD C:\contract\bin

Syntax Options:

Drive: . . . . Letter of drive for *subdirectory*.
Path . . . . Path where subdirectory is to be made. If no path is specified, e.g. C:\ only, the new directory is made a subdirectory under the root directory.
subdirectory . . . Name of the *subdirectory* being created.

Command Type and Version:

Internal command; Network; Introduced with Ver 2.0

Notes:

1. DOS will always assume that the MD command is on the current directory if no path is specified.
2. The maximum length of any path to the final subdirectory is 63 characters, including backslashes.

MEM.EXE

***Display information about used and free
system memory:*** Options are available that will
display items such as which programs are loaded,
the order of loaded programs, free memory, etc.

Syntax (shaded is optional):

MEM /program /page /a /c /d /f /m progname

      Examples: MEM
                      MEM /classify

Syntax Options:

MEM	Without any switches, the status of used and free memory is displayed.
/ *program* or / *p*	**DOS Version 4/5 only**: Displays the status of programs currently loaded into memory. This switch can not be used at the same time as /*debug* and /*classify*.
/ *page* or / *p* ⑥	**DOS Version 6 only.** Pauses display output after each screen.
/a ⑥.②	Adds a line to the display stating the amount of memory available in HMA (High Memory Area)
/c or / *classify*	Displays the status of all programs and drivers currently loaded into conventional and upper memory. Other info, such as memory use and largest memory blocks available are also displayed. This switch can not be used at the same time as /*program* and /*debug*. Version 5.0
/ d or / *debug* .	Displays the status of programs and drivers currently loaded into memory. This switch can not be used at the same time as /*program* and /*classify*.
/ f or / *free*	Lists free regions in upper memory. / *free* can not be used with other switches, except /*module*.

/m progname or */module progname* . . . Display info on a
particular program loaded in memory.
This switch can not be used with any
other switches except */ page*.

Command Type and Version:

External command; Network; Introduced with Ver 4.0

Notes:

1. Extended memory usage is displayed only if the installed system
   memory is 1 meg or greater. Only LIM 4.0 expanded memory use
   is displayed.
2. Total conventional memory=first 640k of RAM. Extended = mem-
   above 1 meg. Expanded = bank switched LIM 4.0 memory.
3. If information is needed on hard drive available space, see the
   CHKDSK command.

MEMMAKER.EXE   New V6.0

*Optimizes computer memory by moving de-
vice drivers and memory-resident programs
(TSR's) into upper memory:* The system must
be either a 386 or 486 and have extended memory available.

Syntax (shaded is optional):

MEMMAKER /b /batch /session /swap:drive
/T /undo /w:size1,size2

Examples: MEMMAKER
MEMMAKER /undo

Syntax Options:

/b . . . . Display in black-and-white mode. Use
if there are problems with your mono-
chrome monitor.

/ batch . . . . Run MEMMAKER in unattended mode.
This forces acceptance of defaults at
all prompts. If an error occurs during
the process, MEMMAKER restores the

	original AUTOEXEC.BAT, CONFIG.SYS, and Windows SYSTEM.INI. Status messages and errors are reported in the MEMMAKER.STS file.
/ session	This switch is only used by MEMMAKER during the optimizing process.
/ swap:drive...	Specifies the drive letter of the system startup drive, if it has changed since the system started up. (encountered with some disk swapping programs)
/ T	If problems are encountered between MEMMAKER and an IBM Token Ring network, use this switch. It disables the Token-Ring detection function.
/ undo	Forces MEMMAKER to undo the most recent changes it has made to the system. This switch is normally used if problems are encountered after MEMMAKER has been run and you wish the system to be returned to its original confituration.
/ w:size1,size2.	Sets the upper memory size reserved for Windows translation buffers. Windows needs two separate areas of upper memory for the buffers. size1 is the size of the first area, size2 is the size of the second area. The default is no buffers are created (/ w:0,0).

Command Type and Version:

External command; Introduced with Ver 6.0

Notes:

1. See also DEVICEHIGH and LOADHIGH.
2. **WARNING: Do not run this program if Windows is running!**
3. CHKSTATE.SYS is a CONFIG.SYS command line that is automatically created by MEMMAKER during the optimization process. At the end of the process, it is automatically removed from CONFIG.SYS.

Command line to set text and background colors for the DOS startup menu in the CONFIG.SYS file: The startup menu is a list of system configuration choices that appear when your system is started. Each menu item is a set of CONFIG.SYS commands and is called a "configuration block". See your DOS manual for details of setting up and using the startup menu.

Syntax (shaded is optional):

MENUCOLOR = X ,Y

Examples: MENUCOLOR 7, 9

Syntax Options:

X . . . . Sets menu text color. Valid values are 0 to 15.

, Y . . . . Sets screen background color. Valid values are 0 to 15. Default=0 (black).

Color Values . .

0=Black	8=Gray
1=Blue .	9=Bright blue
2=Green	10=Bright green
3=Cyan	11=Bright cyan
4=Red .	12=Bright red
5=Magenta	13=Bright magenta
6=Brown	14=Yellow
7=White	15=Bright white

Note: colors 8 to 15 blink on some displays.

Command Type and Version:

CONFIG.SYS command; Network; Introduced with Ver 6.0

Notes:

1. See also MENUDEFAULT, MENUITEM, NUMLOCK, INCLUDE and SUBMENU. All are used by the startup menu.
2. Don't make X and Y the same number, text won't show!

Command line to set the default menu item for the DOS startup menu in CONFIG.SYS: The startup menu is a list of system configuration choices that appear when your system is started. Each menu item is a set of CONFIG.SYS commands and is called a "configuration block". See your DOS manual for details of setting up and using the startup menu.

Syntax (shaded is optional):

MENUDEFAULT = blockname , timeout

Examples: MENUDEFAULT = NET, 20

Syntax Options:

blockname. . . . Sets the default menu item. If no default is specified, item 1 is selected.

, timeout . . . . . The number of seconds DOS waits before starting your computer with a default configuration.

Command Type and Version:

CONFIG.SYS command; Network; Introduced with Ver 6.0

Notes:
1. See also MENUCOLOR, MENUITEM, NUMLOCK, INCLUDE and SUBMENU. All are used by the startup menu.

MENUITEM   New V6.0

Command line to define a menu item for the DOS startup menu in CONFIG.SYS: The startup menu is a list of system configuration choices that appear when your system is started. Each menu item is a set of CONFIG.SYS commands and is called a "configuration block". See your DOS manual for details of setting up and using the startup menu.

Syntax (shaded is optional):

MENUITEM   blockname , menutext

Examples: MENUITEM   NET, Start your Network

Syntax Options:

blockname. . . .   Defines a menu item on the startup menu. It is usable only within a menu block and there can be a maximum of nine menu items per menu. If DOS cannot find a specified name, the item will not appear on the startup menu. blockname can be up to 70 characters long but you cannot use spaces, \ (backslashes), / (forward slashes), commas, semicolons, equal signs or square brackets.

, menutext . . . .   Up to 70 characters of text to display for the menu item. If no text is given, DOS displays *blockname* as the menu item.

Command Type and Version:

CONFIG.SYS command; Network; Introduced with Ver 6.0

Notes:

1. See also MENUCOLOR, MENUDEFAULT, NUMLOCK, INCLUDE and SUBMENU. All are used by the startup menu.

Records information about 1 or more disks for use by UNFORMAT and UNDELETE commands:

Syntax (shaded is optional):

Three syntax formats are valid:

MIRROR Drives: /1 /Tdrive – entries . . .
MIRROR /u
MIRROR /partn

Examples: MIRROR /u
MIRROR C: /Ta /Tc

Syntax Options:

Drives:	The drive or drives to be MIRRORed.
/ 1	Instructs MIRROR to retain only the latest information about a disk. The default causes MIRROR to make a backup of existing information before new information is recorded.
/T *drive – entries*	Loads a deletion–tracking program that maintains information so that the UNDELETE command can recover files. *drive* is required and is the drive to be MIRRORed. *entries* is optional and is the maximum number of entries in PCTRACKR.DEL (the deletion tracking file). *entries* can range from 1 to 999 and the *entries* defaults are as follows:

Disk Size	Default Entry	File Size
360k	25	5k
720k	50	9k
1.2 meg	75	14k
1.44 meg	75	14k
20 meg	101	18k
32 meg	202	36k
>32 meg . . .	303	55k

/u	Unload and disable the deletion tracking program. If other memory resident programs have been loaded after MIRROR, the /u switch will not function.
/partn	Save partitioning information for the UNFORMAT command. The information is saved on a floppy disk for use at a later time if partitions need to be rebuilt by UNFORMAT. The default drive to save the information to is A:, although a different drive can be specified at the prompt.

Command Type and Version:

External command; Network; Introduced with Ver 5.0 Removed from DOS Ver 6.0, functionally replaced by the UNDELETE / T command.

MIRROR is available on Microsoft's MS-DOS Ver. 6.0, 6.21, and 6.22 Supplemental Disks.

Notes:

1. If MIRROR is used without any switches, it saves information about the disk in the current drive.

2. Do not use MIRROR on any drive that has been redirected using the JOIN or SUBST commands. If ASSIGN is used, it must be used before MIRROR.

3. MIRROR saves a copy of a drive's FAT (file allocation table) and a copy of the drive's root directory. Since this information may change regularly, it is recommended that you use MIRROR regularly in order to maintain current information for UNFORMAT to use. It is recommended that MIRROR be placed in your AUTOEXEC.BAT file so that current information is saved every time your system is turned on or re-booted.

4. See also UNFORMAT and UNDELETE.

5. **DOS 6.0 Note:** MIRROR is still available from Microsoft as a supplemental disk, call them for details.

MODE.COM

Controls system devices such as display, serial ports, printer ports, and system settings:
NOTE: Since there are many functions that MODE addresses, they will each be treated separately in the following pages.

Command Type and Version:

External command; Network; Introduced with Ver 1.0

MODE to Display Device Status

Syntax (shaded is optional):

MODE device /status

> Examples:
> MODE   (Display status of all system devices)
> MODE con   (Display console status)
> MODE lpt1 /status

Syntax Options:

device . . . .   Device for which status is requested.
/status or */sta*. .   Displays status of redirected parallel printers.

Notes:

None

MODE to Configure Printer

Configures parallel port printers: Ports that can be addressed include PRN, LPT1, LPT2, and LPT3. Printer types that can be configured are IBM compatibles and Epson compatibles.

Syntax (shaded is optional):

```
MODE Lptn : c , L , r
MODE Lptn : cols=c lines=L retry=r
```

> Examples: MODE Lpt2:132,6
> MODE Lpt1 cols=132 lines=8

Syntax Options:

Lptn . . . . Parallel port to be configured. Valid numbers for *n* are 1, 2, and 3.

c or cols=. . . . . Number of character columns per line. Default=80, Values=80 or 132.

L or lines= . . . . Number of vertical lines per inch. Default=6, Values=6 or 8.

r or retry= . . . . Type of retry if time-out error occurs. This option leaves a memory resident piece of MODE in RAM. Valid *r*'s are:

　e . . . . Return busy port error from status check.
　b . . . . Return busy port "Busy" from status check.
　p . . . . Continue retry until printer accepts data.
　r. . . . . Return "Ready" from busy port status check.
　n . . . . Disable retry (Default). "none" is also valid.

Notes:

1. *retry=b* is equivalent to the "p" parameter in earlier DOS versions.
2. Ctrl+C will break out of a time-out loop.
3. PRN and LPT1 can be used interchangeably.
4. Do not use any *retry* options over a network.
5. The colon (:) with Lptn is optional.

MODE to Configure Serial Port

Configures a serial communications port:
Ports that can be addressed include COM1,
COM2, COM3, and COM4.

Syntax (shaded is optional):

```
MODE  COMn : b , p , d , s , r
MODE  COMn : baud=b parity=p data=d
                    stop=s  retry=r
```

Examples: MODE COM1:24,N,8,1

Syntax Options:

COM*n*	Asynchronous serial port to be configured. Valid values are 1, 2, 3, and 4.
b or *baud=*	Transmission rate in bits per second. Only the first 2 digits are required. Valid values are 11=110 baud, 15=150, 30=300, 60=600, 12=1200, 24=2400, 48=4800, 96=9600, & 19=19,200 baud.
p or *parity=* . . .	Parity check. N=none, E=even, O=odd, M=mark, S=space. Default=E
d or *data=*	Number of data bits in a character. Valid values are 5, 6, 7, 8. Default=7
s or *stop=*	Number of stop bits for end of character. Valid values are 1, 1.5 or 2. Default=1 (Default at 110 baud=2)
r or *retry=*	Type of retry if time-out error occurs. This option leaves a memory resident piece of MODE in RAM. Valid *r*'s are:
	e . . . . Return busy port error from status check.
	b . . . . Return busy port "Busy" from status check.
	p . . . . Continue retry until printer accepts data.
	r . . . . Return "Ready" from busy port status check.
	n . . . . Disable retry (Default). "none" is also valid.

Notes:

1. If any parameters are omitted in the MODE statement, the most recent setting is used.
2. Do not use *retry* values over a network.
3. *retry=b* is equivalent to the "p" parameter in earlier DOS versions.

MODE to Redirect Printing

***Redirects output from a parallel port to a
serial port:***

Syntax (shaded is optional):

MODE Lpt*m* : = COM*r* :

    Examples: MODE Lpt1: = COM1:
                MODE Lpt1 = COM2

Syntax Options:

Lpt*m* . . . . The parallel port to be redirected.
                     Valid *m* values are 1, 2, and 3.

COM*n* . . . . The serial port to be redirected to.
                     Valid *n* values are 1, 2, 3, and 4

Notes:

1. Following a redirection, the original output direction can be restored by typing MODE lptm where m is the original printer port.

MODE to Set Device Code Pages

***Selects, refreshes, prepares, or displays code
page numbers for parallel printers and the
console:***

Syntax (shaded is optional):

MODE device codepage prepare= yyy
                          Drive:\Path\Filename
MODE device codepage select=yyy
MODE device codepage refresh
MODE device codepage /status

    Examples:
      MODE CON codepage prepare = 860
      MODE LPT1 codepage /status

Syntax Options:

device . . . . Device to be affected. Valid values are CON, LPT1, LPT2, and LPT3.

codepage prepare or *cp prep*.. . . . Prepares the code page for the specific *device*. Use *codepage select* after this command.

Drive:\Path\Filename Drive, directory and file containing code page information (.CPI files) needed to prepare a code page.

EGA.CPI . . . . . Enhanced graphics adapter or PS2

EGA2.CPI . . . . Similar to EGA.CPI, but with more code pages.

4201.CPI . . . . . IBM Proprinters II and III, Model 4201
                IBM Proprinters II & III, Model 4202

4208.CPI . . . . . IBM Proprinter X24E Model 4207
                IBM Proprinter XL24E Model 4208

5202.CPI . . . . . IBM Quietwriter III Printer

LCD.CPI . . . . . IBM PC Convertible Liquid Crystal Disp.

ISO.CPI . . . . . Complies with Part 3 of ISO 9241 specification.

codepage select or *cp sel* Selects a code page for a specific device. *cp prep* above must be run first.

codepage refresh or *cp ref* If a code page is lost, this command reinstates it.

codepage . . . . When used alone, codepage displays the numbers of the code pages that have been prepared for a specific device.

/status or */sta*. . Displays the current code page numbers

Notes:

1. See also NLSFUNC and CHCP.
2. EGA.CPI and EGA2.CPI are shipped with DOS. All others are supplied on Microsoft's MS-DOS Supplemental Disks.

MODE to Set Display Mode

Reconfigure or select active display adapter:

Syntax (shaded is optional):

```
MODE adapter , shift , t
MODE adapter , n
MODE CON : cols=c lines=n
```

Examples: MODE co80,r
           MODE CON:cols=40 lines=43

Syntax Options:

adapter	Display adapter category as follows:
40 or 80	Number of characters/line.
bw40 or bw80	CGA (color graphics with color disabled. Characters per line = 40 or 80
co40 or co80	Color display with color enabled. Characters per line = 40 or 80.
mono	Monochrome display with 80 characters per line.
shift	Shift CGA screen left or right. Valid values are L for left, R for right.
t	Starts a test pattern for screen alignment.
n	Vertical lines per screen. Valid values are 25, 43, and 50. ANSI.SYS must be loaded in CONFIG.SYS for this to work.
cols=	Characters or columns per line. Valid values are 40 and 80.
lines=	Vertical lines per screen. Valid values are 25, 43, and 50. ANSI.SYS must be loaded in CONFIG.SYS for this to work.

Notes:

1. Some monitors do not support 43 and 50 vertical lines per screen.

MODE to Set Typematic Rate

Set the rate at which DOS repeats a character when a keyboard key is held down: Some keyboards do not recognize this command.

Syntax (shaded is optional):

MODE con : rate= r delay= d

Examples: MODE con : rate=20 delay=2

Syntax Options:

con or con: ... Keyboard

rate=*r*. . . . . . . The rate that a character is repeated on the display when a key is held down. *r* Default=20 for AT keyboards, Default=21 for PS2 keyboards. *r* Range = 1 to 32, which is equivalent to the following: rate 1 = 2 characters per second (cps), 10 = 4.3 cps, 20 = 10 cps, 30 = 24 cps and 32 = 30 cps.

delay=*d* . . . . . . The amount of time, after a key is held down, before the repeat function activates. *d* Default=2, *d* valid values are 1, 2, 3 and 4 (equivalent to 0.25, 0.50,0.75, and 1 second respectively). If a delay is specified, rate must also be specified.

Notes:

1. The keyboard must be an AT or PS/2 class or higher keyboard in order for this command to work.

MORE.COM

Displays output one screen at a time: MORE reads standard input from a pipe or redirected file and is typically used to view lengthy files. Each screen of information ends with the prompt -More- and you can press any key to view the next screen.

Syntax (shaded is optional):

MORE < Drive: \Path\ Filename
                 or
command | MORE

> Examples: MORE < C:\Data.txt
> DIR | MORE

Syntax Options:

Drive:\Path . . . Drive and directory containing *Filename*.

Filename . . . . . Name of file that supplies data to be displayed.

command . . . . Name of command that supplies data to be displayed, for example, DIR

Command Type and Version:

External command; Network; Introduced with Ver 2.0

Notes:

1. When using the pipe (|) for redirection, you are able to use DOS commands, such as DIR, SORT, and TYPE with MORE, but the TEMP environment variable in AUTOEXEC.BAT file should be set first.

2. MORE saves input information in a temporary file on disk until the data is ready to be displayed. If there is no room on the disk, MORE will not work. Also, if the current drive is a write-protected drive, MORE will return an error.

Move files from one drive or directory to an-other: You can also move and rename complete directories, along with their files and subdirectories, to other drives or directories. **Warning:** DOS does not warn you if it is about to overwrite files with the same name.

Syntax (shaded is optional):

```
MOVE   / Y / -Y Drive: \Path\    Filename
       , Drive: \Path\ . . . Filename  Destination
```

Examples: M

Syntax Options:

/ Y ⑥②	Directs MOVE to replace existing files without a confirmation prompt.
/ -Y ⑥②	Directs MOVE to ask for confirmation prior to replacing an existing file.(Default)
Drive:\Path . . .	Drive and directory containing *Filename*.
Filename	Name of file(s) that you want to move.
Destination . . .	The new location of the file(s) being moved. This can be a drive, subdirectory, or combination of the two.

Command Type and Version:

External command; Network; Introduced with Ver 6.0

Notes:

1. If more than one file is being moved, the Destination must be a drive and subdirectory.

Microsoft Anti-Virus scanners for DOS (MSAV) and Windows (MWAV).

Syntax (shaded is optional):

MSAV Drive: /S /C /R /A /L /N /P /F /ss
/video /IN /BW /mono /LCD /FF /BF /NF
/BT /NGM /LE /PS2

Examples: MSAV C: /A /N /F

Syntax Options:

Drive:	Drive to be scanned. The Default is the current drive.
/ S	Scan but do not remove viruses.
/ C	Scan and remove viruses.
/ R	Create a MSAV.RPT report that lists the number of files scaned, the number of viruses found, and the number of viruses removed. Default=no report.
/ A	Scan all drives except A and B.
/ L	Scan all logical drives except networks.
/ N	Run in command mode, not graphical. Also, display contents of a MSAV.TXT file if it's present.
/ P	Run in command line mode w/ switches.
/ F	Do not display file names during scan.
/ ss	Set screen display size: /25=25 lines, this is the default /28=28 lines, use with VGA /43=43 lines, use with EGA or VGA /50=50 lines, use with VGA /60=60 lines, use with VGA and Video7
/ video	Display list of valid video screen switches.
/ IN	Run MSAV using a color scheme.
/ BW	Run MSAV in black-and-white mode.
/ mono	Run MSAV in monochrome mode.

/LCD	Run MSAV in LCD mode.
/FF	Run MSAV in fast screen mode for CGA monitors. Screen quality is worse.
/BF	Use computer BIOS to display video.
/NF	Disable use of alternate screen fonts.
/BT	Enable graphics mouse in Windows.
/NGM	Use default mouse character instead of the graphics character.
/LE	Switch left and right mouse buttons.
/PS2	Reset mouse if the mouse cursor locks up or disappears.

Command Type and Version:

External command; Network; Introduced with Ver 6.0

Notes:

1. MSAV is actually Central Point Software's Anti-Virus program which has been licensed to Microsoft.

MSBACKUP-MWBACKUP.EXE

New V6.0

Microsoft's menu driven program to backup and restore one or more files from one disk to another disk: This program is a replacement for BACKUP and RESTORE used in previous DOS versions. MSBACKUP is for DOS and MWBACKUP is for Windows.

Syntax (shaded is optional):

MSBACKUP setup_file /BW /LCD /MDA

    Examples: MSBACKUP /BW

Syntax Options:

setup_file.	Predefined setup that specifies which files to backup and the type of backup to be performed. MSBACKUP automatically creates this file if "save program settings". During the "save program" function, if no file name is specified, the file name DEFAULT.SET is used.
/BW	Run screen in black-and-white mode.
/LCD.	Run screen in LCD mode.
/MDA	Run screen in monochrome mode.

Command Type and Version:

External command; Network; Introduced with Ver 6.0

Notes:

1. MSBACKUP does not support the use of tape backups.
2. Backups and catalog files are compatible between MSBACKUP and MWBACKUP.

MSCDEX.EXE New V6.0

Microsoft's CD-ROM Extensions : MSCDEX is used in conjunction with the CD-ROM device driver that was shipped with the drive. It is normally executed in the AUTOEXEC.BAT file.

Syntax (shaded is optional):

MSCDEX /D:driver   /D:driver2 . . . /E /K /S /V /L:letter /M:number

Examples: MSCDEX /D:1

Syntax Options:

/D:driver.	Drive signature for the first CD-ROM drive. Typically this is MSCD0000. The drive signature must match that of the CD-ROM driver in CONFIG.SYS.
/D:driver2.	Drive signature of the second CD-ROM drive. Typically this is MSCD0001.
/E	CD-ROM drive can use expanded memory, if available, to store sector buffers.
/K	Provide Kanji support for CD-ROM.
/S	Share CD-ROM on MS-NET network or Windows for workgroup servers.
/V	Display MSCDEX memory stats when the program starts.
/L:letter.	Specifies drive letter for first CD-ROM. If more than one CD-ROM, DOS assigns the subsequent drive letters.
/M:number . . .	Specifies the number of sector buffers.

Command Type and Version:

External command; Network; Introduced with Ver 6.0

Notes:

1. Do not start MSCDEX after Windows has been started.

MSD.COM & .EXE New V6.0

Microsoft's menu driven system diagnostics:
This program provides detailed technical information about your system.

Syntax (shaded is optional):

MSD /I /B [/F drive:\path\filename]
    [/P drive:\path\filename]
    [/S drive:\path\filename]

    Examples: MSD
              MSD / B / I

Syntax Options:

/I . . . . Forces MSD to not initially detect hardware when it starts. This may be necessary if MSD is not running properly or locks up.

/B . . . . Run MSD in black-and-white mode.

drive:\path . . . . Drive and path where a MSD report file is to be written.

/F *drive:\path\filename*. . Prompts for a company, address, & phone to be written on the MSD report named *filename*.

/P *drive:\path\filename* . Writes a complete MSD report to a file named *filename*.

/S *drive:\path\filename* . Writes a summary MSD report to a file named *filename*.

Command Type and Version:

External command; Network; Introduced with Ver 6.0

Notes:

1. MSD has shipped with Windows for quite some time and is an excellent diagnostics tool.

MSHERC.COM

Installs support for Qbasic graphics programs using the Hercules graphics card:

Syntax (shaded is optional):

MSHERC   / half

    Examples: MSHERC / half

Syntax Options:

/ half . . . .   Use this switch if a color adapter card
                   is also installed in the system.

Command Type and Version:

External command; Network; Introduced with Ver 5.0

NLSFUNC.EXE

National language support function, which loads country-specific information and code-page switching: Use NLSFUNC from either the command line or through **CONFIG.SYS.**

Syntax (shaded is optional):

At the DOS prompt:
  NLSFUNC   Drive:\Path\ Filename
If loaded through CONFIG.SYS:
INSTALL= Drive1:\Path1\   NLSFUNC.EXE
          country

    Examples: NLSFUNC C:\Bin\Newcode.sys

Syntax Options:

Drive:\Path . . .   Drive and directory containing *Filename.*
Filename . . . . .   File containing country-specific information.
Drive1:\Path1 .   Drive and directory containing NSLFUNC.
country . . . . . .   Same as *Filename.*

Command Type and Version:

External & CONFIG.SYS command; Network; Introduced with Ver 3.3

Notes:

1. The COUNTRY command in CONFIG.SYS defines the default value for Drive:\Path \Filename. If there is no COUNTRY command in CONFIG.SYS, NLSFUNC looks for COUNTRY.SYS in the root directory of the start up drive.

2. See also CHCP and MODE.

NUMLOCK   New V6.0

Command line to set the NUM LOCK key to ON or OFF for the DOS startup menu in the CONFIG.SYS file: The startup menu is a list of system configuration choices that appear when your system is started. Each menu item is a set of CONFIG.SYS commands and is called a "configuration block". See your DOS manual for details of setting up and using the startup menu.

Syntax (shaded is optional):

NUMLOCK = ON or OFF

Examples: NUMLOCK = ON

Syntax Options:

ON. . . . . Turns NUM LOCK key on.
OFF. . . . . Turns NUM LOCK key off.

Command Type and Version:

CONFIG.SYS command; Network; Introduced with Ver 6.0

Notes:

1. See also MENUDEFAULT, MENUITEM, MENUCOLOR, INCLUDE and SUBMENU. All are used by the startup menu.

PATH

Sets a directory search path: DOS uses the path command to search for executable files in specified directories. The default is the current working directory.

Syntax (shaded is optional):

PATH Drive1: \Path1; Drive2: \Path2;...

Examples: PATH C:\ ;D:\ ;D:\Dos;D:\Utility\test
PATH   (displays the current search path)
PATH ;   (clears search-path settings other than default setting (current directory).

Syntax Options:

Drive1: Drive2: Specifies drive letters to be included in the search path

\Path1 \Path 2 Specifies directory (s) in the search path where DOS should look for files.

; . . . . Must be used to separate multiple *Drive:\Path* locations or if used as *Path ;* it clears search-path settings other than the default setting.

Command Type and Version:

Internal command; Network; Introduced with Ver 2.0

Notes:

1. The maximum number of characters allowed in the PATH statement is 127. See SUBST for ways to get around this limit. Also see the SET Path statement.

2. If files have the same name but different extensions, DOS searches for files in the following order: .COM, .EXE, .BAT.

3. If identical file names occur in different directories, DOS looks in the current directory first, then in locations specified in PATH in the order they are listed in the PATH statement.

4. A PATH command is usually included in the AUTOEXEC.BAT file so that it is issued at the time the system starts.

PAUSE

Pauses the processing of a batch file: Suspends processing of a batch file and prompts the user to press any key to continue.

Syntax (shaded is optional):

PAUSE
   Examples: PAUSE

Syntax Options:
   None

Command Type and Version:
   Internal command; Only used in Batch Programs;
   Introduced with Ver 1.0

Notes:
1. Earlier versions of PAUSE indicated that a text comment could be inserted after PAUSE and the message would display when PAUSE ran, for example "PAUSE This is a test". This message function is not functional.
2. Ctrl+C or Ctrl Break will stop a Batch program while running or at pause

POWER　New V6.0

Reduces power consumption in a computer when applications and devices are idle: Once the POWER.EXE driver is loaded through the CONFIG.SYS file, POWER at the command line turns power on/off, reports status and sets conservation levels.

Syntax (shaded is optional):

POWER
   ADV[:MAX or REG or MIN] or STD or OFF

   Examples: POWER (displays current settings)
              POWER OFF

Syntax Options:

ADV[:MAX or REG or MIN] . . . Conserves power when
devices are idle. MAX=maximum
power conservation, REG=default, bal-
ance conservation with device performance, MIN=higher device performance
is needed.

STD. . . . . If the computer supports APM, STD
conserves power. If not supported, it
turns off the power.

OFF. . . . . Turns off power management.

Command Type and Version:

External command;
Network; Introduced with Ver 6.0

Notes:

1. See also POWER.EXE.
2. If the computer does not support APM, using STD will disable the
   power completely.

POWER.EXE   New V6.0

Reduces power consumption in a computer when applications and devices are idle:
This driver conforms to the Advanced Power Man-
agement (APM) specifications and is loaded
through the CONFIG.SYS file.

Syntax (shaded is optional):

Device = Drive:\Path\   POWER.EXE
ADV[:MAX or REG or MIN] or STD or OFF /low

Examples: Device = POWER.EXE

Syntax Options:

Drive1\Path . . Specifies the location of POWER.EXE
ADV[:MAX or REG or MIN] . . . Conserves power when
devices are idle. MAX=maximum
power conservation, REG=default, bal-

ance conservation with device performance, MIN=higher device performance is needed.

STD.........	If the computer supports APM, STD conserves power. If not supported, it turns off the power.
OFF.........	Turns off power management.
/ low	Loads driver into conventional memory, even if upper memory is available. The default is load into upper memory.

Command Type and Version:

CONFIG.SYS command; Network; Introduced with Ver 6.0

Notes:

1. See also POWER.
2. If the computer does not support APM, using STD will disable the power completely.

PRINT.EXE

Prints a text file to a line printer, in the background. Other DOS commands can be executed at the same time PRINT is running:

Syntax (shaded is optional):

PRINT /d:device /b:size /u:ticks1 /m:ticks2 /s:ticks3 /q:qsize /t
Drive\Path\ Filename ... /c /p

Examples: PRINT C:\Test.txt /c C:\test2.txt /p
PRINT /d:Lpt1 /u:25

Syntax Options:

/d:device ..... Name of printer device.
Parallel Ports: Lpt1, Lpt2, Lpt3.
Serial Ports: com1,com2, com3, com4.

	PRN and Lpt1 refer to the same parallel port. Default=PRN
	/d must precede Filename.
/b:size	Sets size (in bytes) of internal buffer. Default=512, Range=512 to 16384.
/u:ticks1	Maximum number of clock ticks PRINT is to wait for a printer to become available. Default=1, Value Range=1 to 255.
/m:ticks2	Maximum number of clock ticks PRINT can take to print a character on printer. Default=2, Value Range=1 to 255.
/s:ticks3	Maximum number of clock ticks allocated for background printing. Default=8, Value Range=1 to 255.
/q:qsize	Max number of files allowed in print queue. Default=10 Value Range=4 to 32.
/t	Removes files from the print queue.
Drive:\Path\Filename . .	.Location & Filename of file to be printed.
/c	Removes files from the print queue. Both the /c and /p switches can be used on the same command line. When the /c **precedes** the Filenames on the command line, it applies to all the files that follow until PRINT comes to a /p, in which case the /p switch applies to the file preceding the /p. When the /c switch **follows** the Filenames, it applies to the file that precedes the /c and all files that follow until PRINT comes to a /p switch.
/p	Adds files to the print queue. Both the /c and /p switches can be used on the same command line. When the /p **precedes** the Filenames on the command line, it applies to all the files that follow until PRINT comes to a /c, in which case the /c switch applies to the file preceding the /c. When the /p switch **follows** the Filenames, it applies to the file that precedes the /p and all files that follow until PRINT comes to a /c switch.

Command Type and Version:

External command; Introduced with Ver 2.0

Notes:

1. You can use the /d,/b,/u,/m,/s and /q switches only the first time you use PRINT. DOS must be restarted to use them again.
2. Use a program's own PRINT command to print files created with that program. PRINT only functions correctly with ASCII text.
3. Each queue entry includes a drive, directory and subdirectory and must not exceed 64 characters per entry.

PRINTER.SYS Removed V6.0

Installable device driver that supports code-page switching for parallel ports PRN, LPT1, LPT2, AND LPT3:

Syntax (shaded is optional):

DEVICE = Drive:\Path\ PRINTER.SYS
LPTn = (type , hwcp , n)

Examples:
DEVICE=C:\Dos\PRINTER.SYS LPT1:=(4201,437,2)

Syntax Options:

Drive:\Path . . .	Drive and directory containing PRINTER.SYS
LPT*n*	LPT1, LPT2, or LPT3
type	Type of printer in use. Valid values for *type* and the printer represented by each value are as follows:
	4201. . . IBM Proprinters II and III M.4201
	IBM Proprinters II and III XL M.4202
	4208. . . IBM Proprinters X24E M.4207
	IBM Proprinters XL24E M.4208
	5202. . . IBM Quietwriter III M.5202
hwcp	Code-page supported by your hardware. DOS supports the following code pages:
	437. . . . United States

850. . . .	Multilingual (Latin I)
852. . . .	Slavic (Latin II)
860. . . .	Portuguese
863. . . .	Canadian-French
865. . . .	Nordic
n	Number of additional code-pages.

Command Type and Version:

CONFIG.SYS command; Introduced with Ver 3.3

Removed in Ver. 6.0, however it is available from Microsoft on the MS-DOS 6.0, 6.21, and 6.22 Supplemental Disks

PRINTFIX.COM New V6.0

Stops MS-DOS from Checking the status of the printer attached to the system:

Syntax (shaded is optional):

PRINTFIX
  Example: printfix

Syntax Options:

None

Command Type and Version:

External command, Introduced with Ver. 6.0

Available from Microsoft on the MS-DOS 6.0, 6.21, and 6.22 Supplemental Disks.

Notes:

1. Use only if printing problems occurred while installing MS-DOS 6.0, 6.21, or 6.22.

PROMPT

Change Prompt: Customizing prompt to display text or information and change color. Example: time or date, current directory or default drive.

Syntax (shaded is optional):

PROMPT Text $Characters

> Examples: PROMPT pg (Most commonly used)
> If ANSI.SYS is loaded and you have a color monitor, try the following for colors at the DOS level:
> PROMPT $e[35;44;1m$pge[33;44;1m

Syntax Options:

PROMPT.....	PROMPT by itself resets to default prompt.
Text	*Text* can be any typed message.
$Characters...	Type in special characters from the table below to create special prompts.

Typed character	displayed prompt
$q	The = character
$$	The $ sign
$t	Current time
$d	Current date
$p	Current drive and path
$v	DOS version number
$n	Current drive
$g	>Greater-than symbol
$l	<Less-than symbol
$b	(I) vertical bar
$_	Enter, first position of next line
$e	ASCII escape code (code 27)
$h	Backspace (deletes a **prompts** command line character)

Command Type and Version:

Internal command; Network; Introduced with Ver 2.0

Notes:

1. See also ANSI.SYS
2. The PROMPT command is typically inserted in AUTOEXEC.BAT

QBASIC®.EXE

Basic computer language: A program that reads instructions and interprets those instructions into executable computer code. A complete environment for programming in the Basic language is provided by the QBASIC program.

Syntax (shaded is optional):

QBASIC /b /editor /g /h /mbf /nohi /run
Drive:\Path \Filename

Examples: QBASIC
QBASIC C:\Qb\Bin\Test

Syntax Options:

Drive:\Path . . .	Drive and directory containing *Filename*.
\Filename	Name of file to load when QBASIC starts.
/b.	QBASIC is displayed in black and white.
/editor	Invokes EDIT, DOS full-screen text Editor.
/g	Fastest screen update of a CGA monitor.
/h.	Displays max. number of display lines.
/mbf.	Converts the resident functions MKS$, MKD$, CVS, and CVD to MKSMBF$, MKDMBF$, CVSMBF, and CVDMBF.
/nohi	Allows use of monitor without high-intensity video support. COMPAQ laptop computers cannot use this switch.
/run	The specified BASIC program is run before being displayed.

Command Type and Version:

External command; Network; Introduced with Ver 5.0

Notes:

1. QBASIC.EXE must be in the current directory, search path, or in same directory as EDIT.COM in order to use the DOS Editor.
2. Consecutive Basic programs can be run from a Batch file if the Basic system command and the /run switch is used.
3. If GW-BASIC programs need to be converted to QBASIC, read REMLINE.BAS in QBASIC's subdirectory.
4. If a monitor does not support shortcut keys, use /b and /nohi.

RAMDRIVE.SYS or VDISK.SYS

Creates a simulated hard disk from the system's RAM memory: RAM disks are much faster than hard disks but they are temporary (if the system shuts down, the data is lost).

Syntax (shaded is optional):

Device=Drive:\Path\ RAMDRIVE.SYS disksize sectorsize numentry / e / a

Examples:
Device=C:\Dos\RAMDRIVE.SYS 4096 /a

Syntax Options:

Drive:\Path . . .	Drive & directory containing RAMDRIVE.SYS
disksize	Sets size of RAM disk in kilobytes. Valid sizes range from 4 to 32767. Default=64.
sectorsize	Sets sector size in bytes. Valid sizes are 128, 256, and 512. Default=512. Do not change default if possible.
numentry	Sets the number of files and directories that the RAM disk's root directory can hold. Default=64, range=2 to 1024. If this parameter is used, *disksize* and *sectorsize* must also be set.
/e	RAM disk uses extended memory. 4Kb minimum extended memory is needed. Default=uses conventional memory.
/a	RAM disk uses expanded memory. 4Kb minimum extended memory is needed. Default= uses conventional memory.

Command Type and Version:

CONFIG.SYS command; Introduced with Ver 3.1(Vdisk=3.0)

Notes:

1. Multiple RAM disks are allowed.
2. Always try to use /e or /a so that conventional RAM is not used.
3. A memory manager like HIMEM.SYS must be used if /e is used.
4. An expanded memory manager must be installed if /a is used.

RD or RMDIR

Removes a directory: You cannot delete a directory without first deleting its files and subdirectories. The directory must be empty except for the "." and ". ." symbols which represent the directory itself and the parent directory. RD and RMDIR are equivalent commands.

Syntax (shaded is optional):

RD Drive: \Path

    Examples: RD \Data
                      RD \Data\Smith

Syntax Options:

Drive . . . . Drive containing *Path*.
Path . . . . Directory to be deleted.

Command Type and Version:

Internal command; Network; Introduced with Ver 2.0

Notes:

1. Use DIR to list hidden and system files and ATTRIB to remove hidden and system file attributes in order to empty directory.

2. When a backslash (\) is used before the first directory name in *Path*, DOS treats the directory as a subdirectory of the root directory. Omit the backslash (\) before the first directory name and DOS treats the directory as a subdirectory of the current directory.

3. The directory being deleted cannot be the current directory and must be an empty directory.

RECOVER.EXE Removed V6.0

Recovers readable information from a disk containing bad sectors: When CHKDSK reports bad sectors on a disk, use the RECOVER command to read a file, sector by sector, and recover data from the good sectors.

Syntax (shaded is optional):

RECOVER `Drive:\Path\` Filename

Examples: RECOVER A:

Syntax Options:

Drive:\Path . . . Drive and directory containing *Filename*.

\Filename . . . . *Filename* to be recovered. If no *Filename*
or *Path* is specified, the entire drive is
recovered.

Command Type and Version:

External command; Introduced with Ver 2.0
Removed from Ver 6.0, deemed too dangerous.

Notes:

1. Wildcards (* and ?) cannot be used with the RECOVER command.

2. When an entire disk is recovered, each file is placed in the root
   directory in a FILEnnnn.REC file. The 4 digit numbering sequence
   on each recovered file is as follows: FILE0001.REC, FILE0002, etc.

3. Since all data in bad sectors is lost when you recover a file, it is
   best to recover files one at a time, allowing you to edit each file
   and re-enter missing information.

4. If a drive was formed by the ASSIGN, JOIN or SUBST command,
   the RECOVER command will not work. It will not work with the
   BACKUP or RESTORE command since you must use RESTORE
   with backup files that you created with the BACKUP command.

5. RECOVER cannot recover files on a network drive.

6. If an entire drive is recovered, it is possible that some files will be
   lost, since the recovered files are written to the root directory and
   a limited number of files will fit in the root directory.

7. See also CHKDSK

REM

***Allows use of remarks (comments) in a Batch
file or in CONFIG.SYS. :*** Any BATCH command
or CONFIG.SYS line beginning with REM is ignored by DOS.

Syntax (shaded is optional):

REM Comment

    Examples: REM begin files here

Syntax Options:

Comment .... Line of text that you want to include as
          a comment.

Command Type and Version:

Internal command;
   Batch command; Introduced with Ver 1.0
   CONFIG.SYS command; Introduced with Ver 4.0

Notes:

1. ECHO ON must be used in the Batch or CONFIG.SYS file for a
   comment to be displayed.
2. REM can be used without a comment to add vertical spacing to
   a Batch file, but you can also use blank lines. Blank lines are
   ignored by DOS.
3. Do not use redirection characters (>or <) or pipe (I) in a Batch
   file comment.
4. a ";" can be used in place of REM in the WIN.INI file.

REN or RENAME

Renames a file(s): Changes the name(s) on all
files matching a specified Filename. REN and RE-
NAME are equivalent commands.

Syntax (shaded is optional):

REN `Drive:\Path\` Filename1 Filename2

   Examples: REN C:\ data*.dbf *.db2

Syntax Options:

Drive:\Path . . . Drive and directory containing *Filename*.
Filename1 . . . . File(s) to be renamed.
Filename2 . . . . New name for file(s). You cannot rename
                   Drive or Path.

Command Type and Version:

Internal command; Network; Introduced with Ver 1.0

Notes:

1. The use of Wildcards (* and ?) are allowed.
2. You cannot duplicate a *Filename*.
3. See also LABEL, COPY and XCOPY.

REPLACE.EXE

*Replaces files in the target drive with files
from the source drive when the filenames are
the same:* If same name files are not on the target
drive, the new files will be added to the target drive.

Syntax (shaded is optional):

REPLACE `Source:\Path1\` Filename
        `Target:\Path2 /a /p /r /w`

REPLACE `Source:\Path1\` Filename
        `Target:\Path2 /p /r /s /w /u`

   Examples: REPLACE A:*.* C:\Test /a /s

Syntax Options:

Source:\Path1 . Source drive and directory containing *File-
                  name*.

Filename	Name of source file.
Target:\Path2 .	Location of the destination file(s).
/a	Adds, instead of replacing, new files to the destination file. This switch **cannot** be used with /s or /u.
/p	Prompts for confirmation before adding a source file or replacing the destination file.
/r	Replaces read-only and unprotected files.
/s	Searches subdirectories of the destination directory and replaces files matching files with the source file. The /s switch **cannot** be used with /a.
/w	Waits for a disk to be inserted before REPLACE starts copying. If /w is not specified, REPLACE begins immediately.
/u	Updates or replaces files in the destination directory that are older than files in the source directory.

Command Type and Version:

External command; Network; Introduced with Ver 3.2

Notes:

1. REPLACE issues a message concerning the number of files that have been added or replaced when the operation is complete.
2. Use /w if you need to change disks during REPLACE.
3. REPLACE does not function on system or hidden files.
4. REPLACE returns the following exit codes: (see IF errorlevel)

0	Files successfully added or replaced
2	Source files could not be found
3	Source or destination path could not be found
5	User does not have access to files being replaced
8	Insufficient system memory to complete command
11	Wrong command line syntax

RESTORE.EXE

Restores files that were backed up using the BACKUP command: The "backed up" and "restored to" disk types do not have to be identical. In Ver 6.0, RESTORE will only restore backups made with previous versions of DOS. It will **NOT** restore backups made with the Ver 6.0 or 6.2x MSBACKUP program!

Syntax (shaded is optional):

RESTORE Drive1: Drive2: \Path\ Filename /s /p /b:date /a:date /e:time /L:time /m /n /d

    Examples: RESTORE A: C:*.* /s
               RESTORE B: D:\Data*.dbf /s / m

Syntax Options:

Drive1:	Drive on which backed-up files are stored.
Drive2:\Path . .	Drive and directory to which backed-up files will be restored.
Filename	Name(s) of backed-up file(s) to be restored.
/ s	Restores all subdirectories.
/ p	Prompts for permission to restore files that are read-only or files that have changed since last backup.
/ b:date	Restores files changed or modified on or before a specified *date*.
/ a :date	Restores files changed or modified on or after a specified *date*.
/ e:time	Restores files changed or modified at or earlier than a specified *time*.
/ L :time	Restores files changed or modified at or later than a specified *time*.
/ m	Restores only files changed or modified since the last backup.
/ n	Restores files that no longer exist on the destination disk. (Drive2)

/d . . . . Without restoring, /d displays a list of files
on the backup disk that match names
specified in *Filename*. Version 5.0

Command Type and Version:

External command; Network; Introduced with Ver 2.0

Notes:

1. RESTORE does not restore the system files (IO.SYS and
   MSDOS.SYS or IBMBIO.COM and IBMDOS.COM).
2. RESTORE will not function on drives that have been redirected
   with ASSIGN, JOIN, or SUBST.
3. MS-DOS RESTORE Version 5.0 will restore backups made with
   all previous versions of BACKUP.
4. RESTORE returns the following exit codes: (see IF errorlevel)

   0 . . . . Files successfully restored
   1 . . . . Files to be restored could not be found
   3 . . . . RESTORE stopped by user Ctrl+C
   4 . . . . RESTORE ended in error.
5. BACKUP is not included in DOS Ver 6.0, see the MSBACKUP
   utility program.

SCANDISK.EXE   New V6.2

*MS-DOS utility program to analyze and recover
lost chains and lost clusters on hard or floppy
disks to make more space available on these
devices.* SCANDISK also checks the surface of
the disk for errors. Lost chains or lost clusters recovered by SCANDISK are saved in the root directory as files with a .CHK extension. The contents
of each file can be examined using the MORE
command or any text editor. The files can then be
saved or deleted as needed. SCANDISK is an interactive program that steps the user through a series of options in order to scan and repair each
selected drive.

Syntax (shaded is optional):

SCANDISK   Drive1: Drive2: Volume_Name
Drive:\Path\Filename /all /autofix
/checkonly /custom /fragment
/mono /nosave /nosummary
/surface /undo Undo_Drive

Examples: SCANDISK C: /autofix
SCANDISK /all
SCANDISK /fragment C:\TEST\data

Syntax Options:

Drive:	Identifies drive (disk) to scan.
Drive:\Path\Filename	Identifies drive (disk), directory, and file to be checked for fragmentation
/all	Scan and repair all local drives.
/autofix	Scan and repair without prompts.
/checkonly	Only scans the selected drives, no repairs are made. Can not be used with */custom* or */autofix*.
/custom	Scan and repair according to parameters set in SCANDISK.INI file. Can not be used with */autofix* or */checkonly*.
/fragment	Check for fragmentation of files on selected drives. Individual directories and files may be indicated and wildcards may be used.
/mono	Execute in monochrome mode.
/nosave	Scans automatically and deletes any lost chain or cluster. Can be used only with */autofix*. If */nosave* is left off, all lost chains and clusters will automatically be saved as .CHK files in the root directory of the drive being scanned.
/nosummary . .	Disables full-screen summary display. Full-screen summary display is the default setting for SCANDISK.
/surface	Scans for physical errors on disk.

Volume_Name	Name of unmounted compressed volume (compressed using either DRVSPACE or DBLSPACE) to be scanned and repaired.
/undo	Undo any repairs made by SCANDISK. Use a blank disk as the undo disk.
Undo_Drive . . .	Drive containing the current undo disk.

Command Type and Version:

External command, Interactive, NOT for Network; Introduced with Version 6.2

Notes:
1. Do not use SCANDISK on CD-ROM drives, network drives, or drives created using ASSIGN, SUBST, JOIN, or INTERLNK.
2. Do not use SCANDISK on drives compressed using PC-DOS Ver 6.1.
3. All applications (including Windows) must be stopped before running SCANDISK or data may be lost.
4. Memory resident programs may need to be disabled in the AUTOEXEC.BAT and CONFIG.SYS files prior to running SCANDISK.
5. SCANDISK.INI file is a text file containing settings which determine how SCANDISK operates on start-up. Sections such as Environment and Custom contain the required settings. For more information see comments in the file.
6. SCANDISK is similar to CHKDSK but is more comprehensive in its analysis of a drive.
7. SCANDISK sets ERRORLEVEL to one of the following values upon return to the DOS prompt:
   0 - No problems detected.
   1 - Syntax error.
   2 - Unexpected termination due to an internal error or an out-of-memory error.
   3 - User exit prior to completion.
   4 - User exit during surface scan.
   254 - Disk problems found and all corrected.
   255 - Disk problems found but not all corrected.

SELECT.EXE `Removed V5.0`

Installs DOS on a new disk along with country specific information such as time and date formats and collating sequences: Select also formats the target disk, creates CONFIG.SYS and AUTOEXEC.BAT on a new disk and copies the source disk to the target disk.

Syntax (shaded is optional):

SELECT Source Target\Path yyy xx

    Examples: SELECT B: A: 045 dk

Syntax Options:

Source	Drive containing Information to be copied.
Target	Drive containing disk onto which DOS is to be copied.
\Path	Name of directory containing information to be copied.
yyy	Country code. See COUNTRY Command.
nn	Keyboard code. See KEYB Command.

Command Type and Version:

External command; Introduced with Ver 3.0
Removed from Version 5.0

Notes:

1. WARNING: SELECT is used to install DOS for the first time. Everything on the *target* disk is erased. SELECT is not available for use on Version 5.0 and should be used with caution in earlier versions.

2. The *Source Drive* can be either Drive A: or Drive B:.

3. If a hard disk is used in the Target Drive, DOS will prompt for the correct internal label for that disk. If the wrong label is typed in, SELECT ends.

Sets, removes or displays environment variables: SET is normally used in the AUTOEXEC.BAT file to set environment variables when the system starts.   With DOS Ver 6.0, SET can be used in CONFIG.SYS. **❻**

Syntax (shaded is optional):

SET variable = string

    Examples:
    SET   (displays current environment settings)
    SET TEMP=E:\Windows\Temp
    SET variable =
       (above clears *string* associated with *variable*)

Syntax Options:

variable . . . . . .   The *variable* to be set or modified.

string . . . .   Text *string* to be associated with *variable*.

Command Type and Version:

Internal command; Network; Introduced with Ver 2.0

Notes:

1. If SET is used to define values for both *variable* and *string*, DOS adds *variable* to the environment and associates *string* with it. If *variable* already existed, the new *variable* replaces the old one.

2. In a Batch file, SET can be used to create variables that can be used in the same way as %1 through %9. In order to use the new variable, it must be enclosed with %, e.g. %variable%

3. The SET command uses memory from the environment space. If the environment space is too small, DOS will issue the error message "Out of Environment Space". See the SHELL command and COMMAND.COM for ways to increase environment space.

4. See also PATH, PROMPT, SHELL and DIR for additional information on environment variables.

SETUP and BUSETUP.EXE

Programs which initially install MS-DOS.

Syntax(shaded is optional):

Initial installation from command prompt:

drive1:SETUP
    Example: a:setup

Installation of certain utilities after initial installation from command line:

drive1:SETUP /e /f /u /i
    Example: a:setup /e

Installation of certain utilities after initial installation by insertion of Setup disk and restart of computer:

drive1:BUSETUP /e /u
    Example: a:busetup /e

Syntax options:

drive1:	Drive containing the SETUP program.
/f	If the system drive A is not compatible with the Setup disk, this switch makes a minimal installation of DOS by copying essential command files on a floppy disk which is compatible with drive A.
/u	Used when installing MS-DOS 6 with certain third-party disk-partitioning software.
/e	Used to install Anti-Virus, Backup, or Undelete after initial installation.
/i	Causes Setup to skip automatic hardware detection.

Command Type and Version:

External command, Introduced with Version 5.0.

Notes:

1. See the README.TXT files with MS-DOS Versions 5.0, 5 Upgrade, 6.0, and 6.2 for more information.
2. Press F3 twice to exit Setup.

SETVER.EXE

Sets the DOS version number that is reported to a program by MS-DOS® 5.0: If a program will not run under Ver 5.0 and issues the error "Incorrect DOS Version", adding the program to the SETVER file may allow the program to run.

Syntax (shaded is optional):

To initially load the SETVER table in CON-
FIG.SYS Drive:\Path\

Device =   SETVER.EXE

At DOS p Drive:\Path\ tch file:

SETVER Drive:\Path Filename v.vv

SETVER Drive:\Path Filename /delete /d /quiet

SETVER

    Examples: Device=C:\DOS\SETVER.EXE

    SETVER C:\DOS   (Displays current ver. table)
    SETVER C:\DOS TEST.EXE 3.30
    (above adds TEST.EXE to the version table)
    SETVER C:\DOS TEST.EXE /delete

Syntax Options:

Drive:\Path . . .	Drive and directory containing SETVER.
Filename	Program file to be added to version table. Must be a .EXE or .COM file. Wild cards are not allowed.
v.vv	The DOS version number that should be reported to the program when it is run.
/delete or */ d* . .	Delete the version table entry for the *Filename* program.

/quiet . . . . Hides the message normally displayed during the deletion process.

Command Type and Version:

External and CONFIG.SYS command;
Network; Introduced with Ver 5.0

Notes:

1. When loaded in CONFIG.SYS, the .EXE extension with SETVER.EXE must be used.

2. In order for SETVER to function at the DOS prompt or in a Batch file, it must first be loaded through CONFIG.SYS. SETVER is automatically added to CONFIG.SYS by the MS-DOS 5.0 setup program.

3. If you set a version number for your MS-DOS 5.0 COMMAND.COM, your system may not start.

4. If changes or additions or deletions are made to the SETVER table, your system must be restarted in order for the changes to take effect.

5. If a program starts correctly after it has been added to the SETVER table, the program may still not run correctly under Ver 5.0 if a compatibility problem exists.

6. If a program is added to the SETVER table and the program name is already in the table, the new entry and version number will replace the existing entry.

7. The following SETVER exit codes can be used in conjunction with the IF errorlevel command to report completion and error codes:

   0 . . . . SETVER function completed successfully
   1 . . . . Invalid command switch.
   2 . . . . Invalid *Filename.*
   3 . . . . Insufficient system memory to complete command.
   4 . . . . Invalid version number (*v.vv*) format specified.
   5 . . . . Specified entry not currently in version table.
   6 . . . . SETVER could not find the SETVER.EXE file.
   7 . . . . Invalid drive specified.
   8 . . . . Too many command line parameters specified by user.
   9 . . . . Missing command line parameter.
   10 . . . . . . Error whie reading SETVER.EXE file.
   11 . . . . . . Corrupt SETVER.EXE file.
   12 . . . . . . Specified SETVER.EXE file does not support a version table.
   13 . . . . . . Insufficient space in version table to add a new entry.
   14 . . . . . . Error detected while writing to the SETVER.EXE file.

SHARE.EXE

Program that installs file-sharing and locking capabilities on hard disk: The share command is installed through AUTOEXEC.BAT or CONFIG.SYS and is used by networking, multi-tasking under Windows, DOSSHELL, and others.

Syntax (shaded is optional):

In a Batch file or at the DOS prompt:
SHARE /f:space /L:locks
In CONFIG.SYS:
INSTALL= Drive:\Path\ SHARE.EXE
/ f:space /L:locks

Examples: SHARE / f:4096 /L:40
INSTALL=C:\Dos\SHARE.EXE

Syntax Options:

Drive:\Path . . .	Drive and directory containing the SHARE.EXE file.
/f:space	File space allocated in bytes for the DOS storage area used to record file-sharing information. Default=2048
/L:locks	Number of files that are to be locked. Default=20

Command Type and Version:

External command; Network; Introduced with Ver 3.0

Notes:

1. In CONFIG.SYS, the .EXE extension must be included with SHARE.EXE
2. SHARE allows DOS to check and verify all read and write requests from programs.
3. The average length of a file name and its Path is 20 bytes. Use that value when calculating the /f:space switch.
4. Beginning with Ver 5.0, SHARE is no longer required to support drive partitions >32mb.

SHELL

Specifies the name and location of a command interpreter, other than COMMAND.COM:
Include the SHELL command to CONFIG.SYS to add a different Command Interpreter.

Syntax (shaded is optional):

SHELL = Drive:\Path\ Filename parameters

> Examples:
> SHELL=C:\COMMAND.COM /e:1024 /p

Syntax Options:

Drive:Path . . . . Drive and directory containing *Filename*.
\Filename . . . . Command Interpreter to be used.
Parameters . . . Command-line parameters or switches to be used with Command Interpreter.

Command Type and Version:

CONFIG.SYS command; Introduced with Ver 2.0

Notes:

1. The SHELL command does not use or accept any switches, only the Command Interpreter uses switches .
2. The default Command Interpreter is COMMAND.COM.
3. SHELL must be used if the Command Interpreter is in a location other than the Root directory or if you need to change the environment size of COMMAND.COM.
4. **DOSSWAP** is the DOS Task Swapper and is used internally by the SHELL command. There are no switches for DOSSWAP and it should not be run from the DOS command line.

SHIFT

Allows a change in the position of replaceable command line parameters in a Batch file: Specifically, SHIFT copies the value of each replaceable parameter to the next lowest parameter (for example, %1 is copied to %0, %2 is copied to %1, etc).

Syntax (shaded is optional):

SHIFT

Examples: SHIFT

Syntax Options:

None

Command Type and Version:

Internal command only used in Batch programs; Introduced with Ver 2.0

Notes:

1. Batch files, usually limited to ten parameters (%0 through %9) on the command line, can now use more than 10. This is made possible because if more than 10 parameters are used, those appearing after the 10th will be shifted one at a time into %9.

2. Once the parameters are shifted, they cannot be shifted back.

SIZER.EXE

SIZER is used only by MEMMAKER during the memory optimizing process. It is used to determine the size, in memory, of device drivers and memory resident programs. It is added automatically to AUTOEXEC.BAT or CONFIG.SYS in order to determine the memory size, and when MEMMAKER is finished, SIZER is automatically removed.

SMARTDRV.EXE New V6.0

Directs DOS to create a disk cache in extended memory or conventional memory: The cache effectively increases the speed of all disk functions. The SMARTDRV command allows management of the cache created by SMARTDRV.EXE.

Syntax (shaded is optional):

SMARTDRV /x Drive: + or - /b:buffer_size /c /e:element_size /f /initcachesize[wincachesize] / l /n /q /r /s /u /v

> Example: SMARTDRV C-
> SMARTDRV / r

DEVICE = SMARTDRV.EXE /x Drive: + or - /b:buffer_size /e:element_size /f /initcachesize[wincachesize] / l /n /q /r /s /u / v

> Example: DEVICE = SMARTDRV.EXE C 1024 512
> DEVICE = SMARTDRV.EXE /q

DEVICE = SMARTDRV.EXE /Double_buffer

Syntax options:

Drive:	Identifies the drive (disk) that will use the cache. No specification allows all drives to use the cache. Ver 6.2 allows the caching of CD_ROM drives.
+ or -	Cache-type (read or write) is enabled or disabled for identified drive. With Ver 6.0, "+" allows both read and write caching for the disk, "-" allows no caching, no specification for a floppy disk allows only read caching, and no specification for a hard drive allows both read and write caching. With Ver 6.2, "+" allows

	both read and write caching for the disk, "-" allows no caching, no specification for a floppy disk, CD-ROM drive, or drives created using INTERLINK allows only read caching, and no specification for a hard drive allows both read and write caching
/b:buffer_size. .	States the size of the read-ahead buffer. The buffer size can be set to any multiple of the element_size. The default size is 16 384 bytes (16K) which is twice the maximum (default) element_size of 8192 bytes (8K).
/c	Directs SMARTDRV to clear the buffer by writing all data in the cache to the cached disk. Use this switch before turning off the computer to save the cached data to the disk.
/e: element_size	States the size of cache that SMARTDRV moves at one time. Element_ size(bytes) can be one of the following: 1024, 2048, 4096, or 8192 (default).
/f 6.2	Directs SMARTDRV to write data in the cache to the disk after completion of each command. This is the default setting.
/initcachesize. .	States size, in kilobytes, of the initial cache when SMARTDRV starts and Windows is not active. If not specified SMARTDRV sets initcachesize according to the amount of extended memory available as follows:

Extended Memory	Initcachesize
below 1MB	All extended
1MB to 2MB	1MB
2MB to 4MB	1MB
4MB to 6MB	2MB
above 6MB	2MB

/L	Limits SMARTDRV to only conventional (low) memory, even if extended memory (Upper Memory Blocks, UMB) is available.

/n (6.2)	Directs SMARTDRV to write data in the cache to the disk only when the system is idle.
/q	Directs SMARTDRV to load in the quiet mode with no messages on status or errors. Switch can not be used with /v.
/r	Restarts SMARTDRV after clearing all data from the current cache to the cached disk.
/s	Status of SMARTDRV is displayed.
/u (6.2)	Disables the loading of CD-ROM caching.
/v	Directs SMARTDRV to display messages on status or errors when loading. Default is to <u>not</u> display messages unless error conditions are encountered. Switch can not be used with /q.
/ wincachesize .	States, in kilobytes, the amount of cache that SMARTDRV will remove from init-cachesize prior to starting Windows. If not specified SMARTDRV sets win-cachesize according to the amount of extended memory available as follows:

Extended Memory	Wincachesize
below 1MB	0 (no cache)
from 1MB to 2MB	256KB
from 2MB to 4MB	512KB
from 4MB to 6MB	1MB
above 6MB	2MB

/ x (6.2)	Directs SMARTDRV to disable write-behind caching for all drives.
/ Double_buffer	Directs SMARTDRV to perform double buffering which is needed for compatibility with some hard-disk controllers.

Command Type and Version:

External Command or Device Driver
Introduced with Ver 6.0, and some Windows before that.

Notes:

1. Do not start or load SMARTDRV while Windows is running.

2. For a CD-ROM drive to be cached SMARTDRV must load after MSCDEX.

3. MS-DOS LOADHIGH (LH) command can be used to load SMARTDRV high.

4. If the hard drive requires use of the double_buffer switch to perform properly, the double_buffer component of SMARTDRV must be loaded in conventional memory and the DEVICE command line for SMARTDRV must appear in the CONFIG.SYS file before the DEVICE command line for EMM386.

5. CONFIG.SYS must contain a DEVICE command which loads HIMEM.SYS or some other memory manager in order for SMARTDRV to use extended memory.

6. SMARTDRV is not an interactive program which steps the user through a series of screens.

7. If SMARTDRV is run without parameters being set, DOS will set up a disk cache using default parameters.

SMARTDRV.SYS   Removed V6.0

Creates a disk cache in extended or expanded memory: A disk cache can significantly increase the speed of any disk operations.

Syntax (shaded is optional):

DEVICE = Drive:\Path\ SMARTDRV.SYS initsize minsize /a

Examples:
DEVICE=C:\DOS\SMARTDRV.SYS 1024 512

Syntax Options:

Drive:\Path . . .	Drive and directory containing SMARTDRV.SYS.
initsize	Initial size of disk cache in kilobytes. Default=256; Range=128 to 8192. Size is rounded off to 16k blocks.
minsize	Minimum size of disk cache in kilobytes. Default=no minimum size. This option is important to programs such as Windows, which can reduce the cache size as required for its own use.

| /a . . . . | Specifies that the disk cache is to be set up in expanded memory. The Default places the cache in extended memory. |

Command Type and Version:

CONFIG.SYS command; Introduced with Ver 4.0

Removed from MS-DOS Ver 6.0

Notes:

1. If no sizes are specified with SMARTDRV, then all available extended or expanded memory is allocated to the cache.

2. In order to use extended memory, HIMEM.SYS or another extended memory manager must be installed. HIMEM.SYS must precede SMARTDRV in CONFIG.SYS.

3. On 80286 / 386 / 486 systems, extended memory is probably the best choice for SMARTDRV.

4. Do not use disk compaction programs while SMARTDRV is loaded.

SMARTMON.EXE New V6.0

Monitors SMARTDRV cache performance under Windows. Removed from DOS 6.2

Command Type and Version:

External command, Introduced with MS-DOS Ver 6.0. Removed from DOS 6.2

SORT.EXE

A filtering program that reads the input, sorts the data and then writes the results to a screen, file or another device: The SORT command alphabetizes a file, rearranges in ascending or descending order by using a collating table based on Country Code and Code Page settings.

Syntax (shaded is optional):

SORT /r /+n < Drive1:\ Path1\   Filename1 >
                Drive2:\ Path2\ Filename2
command | SORT /r /+n > Drive2:\ Path2\
                Filename2

Examples: SORT < C:\Data\Text.txt
            DIR | SORT > C:\Sortdata.txt

Syntax Options:

Drive1:\Path1 .   Drive and directory containing *Filename*.

Filename1 . . . .   File containing data to be sorted.

\Drive2:\Path2   Drive and directory containing *Filename2*.

Filename2 . . . .   File in which to store sorted data.

Command . . . .   Specific command whose output is data
                    to be sorted.

/r . . . .   Reverses sorting order: Z to A and 9 to 0.

/+n . . . .   Sorts according to character in column *n*.

Command Type and Version:

External command; Network; Introduced with Ver 2.0

Notes:

1. Use the pipe (|) or the less-than (<) to direct data through SORT
   from a command or filename. Before using a pipe for redirection,
   set the TEMP environment variable in AUTOEXEC.BAT.

2. Specify the MORE command to display information one screen
   at a time. You are prompted to continue after one screen is shown.

3. SORT is not case sensitive.

4. Files as large as 64K can be accommodated by SORT.

5. ASCII characters with codes higher than 127 are sorted based on
   the system's configuration with CONTRY.SYS.

Batch file needed to maintain compatibility between MS-DOS 6.0, 6.21, or 6.22 and the permanent swap file established by Windows Ver 3.0.

Command Type and Version:

External command, Introduced with MS-DOS Ver 6.0. Available on the MS-DOS 6.0, 6.21, and 6.22 Supplemental Disks.

STACKS

Supports the dynamic use of data stacks: The STACKS command is used in CONFIG.SYS.

Syntax (shaded is optional):

STACKS = n,s
    Examples: STACKS = 8, 512

Syntax Options:

n	Defines the number of STACKS. Valid values for n are 0 and numbers in the range 8 to 64.
s	Defines STACK size in bytes. Valid values for s are 0 and numbers in the range 32 to 512.

Command Type and Version:

CONFIG.SYS; Introduced with Ver 3.2

Notes:

1. Default setting for the STACKS command are as follows:

COMPUTER	STACKS
IBM PC, IBM PC/XT	0,0
IBM PC-PORTABLE	0,0
OTHER	9, 128

2. When the values for n and s are specified at 0, DOS allocates no stacks. If your computer does not seem to function properly when STACKS are set to 0, return to the default values.

Command line to setup an item to display another set of choices for the DOS startup menu in CONFIG.SYS: The startup menu is a list of system configuration choices that appear when your system is started. Each menu item is a set of CONFIG.SYS commands and is called a "configuration block". See your DOS manual for details of setting up and using the startup menu.

Syntax (shaded is optional):

SUBMENU = blockname , menutext

Examples: SUBMENU = NET, Network Choices

Syntax Options:

blockname. . . . Sets the name of the associated menu block. The menu block must be defined somewhere else in the CONFIG.SYS file and can contain other menu definition commands. *Blockname* can be up to 70 characters but without spaces, backslashes, forward slashes, commas, semicolons, equal signs and square brackets.

, menutext . . . . Text to be displayed for the menu item. If no text is defined, DOS displays the *blockname* as the menu item. menutext can be up to 70 characters long.

Command Type and Version:

CONFIG.SYS command; Network; Introduced with Ver 6.0

Notes:

1. See also MENUCOLOR, MENUITEM, NUMLOCK, INCLUDE and MENUDEFAULT. All are used by the startup menu.

SUBST.EXE

Substitutes a path with a drive letter: The
SUBST command lets you use a drive letter (also
known as a virtual drive) in commands as though
it represents a physical drive.

Syntax (shaded is optional):

```
SUBST   (Lists the virtual drives in effect)
SUBST   Drive1: Drive2:\ Path
SUBST   Drive1: /d (deletes virtual drive)
```

>   Examples: SUBST
>   SUBST R: B: \Data\Text.txt

Syntax Options:

Drive1:	Virtual drive to which a path is assigned.
Drive2:	Physical drive that contains the specified path.
\Path	Path to be assigned to the virtual drive named *Drive1:*
/d	Deletes the *Drive1:* virtual drive.

Command Type and Version:

External command; Introduced with Ver 3.1

Notes:

1. Commands that do not work on drives where SUBST has been
   used are as follows:

ASSIGN	DISKCOPY	RECOVER
BACKUP	FDISK	RESTORE
CHKDSK	FORMAT	SYS
DEFRAG	LABEL	UNDELETE /s
DISKCOMP	MIRROR	

2. A virtual drive letter must be included in the LASTDRIVE
   command in CONFIG.SYS.

3. Use SUBST rather than ASSIGN to ensure compatibility with
   future DOS versions.

4. If using drive letters higher than E, the LASTDRIVE command
   must also be used.

5. Do not use SUBST while Windows is running!

SWITCHAR

Changes the switch character: The forward slash, " / " is the standard switch character. SWITCHAR allows the user to choose another switch character.

Syntax (shaded is optional):
SWITCHAR= cc

Example: switchar = *

Syntax Options:
cc. . . . .   New switch character.

Command Type and Version:
CONFIG.SYS command, Introduced with Ver 2.0. Removed Version 3.0.

SWITCHES

Forces enhanced keyboard to function like a conventional keyboard: This command is used in the CONFIG.SYS file.

Syntax (shaded is optional):
SWITCHES = /W /K /N /F

Examples: SWITCHES = / k

Syntax Options:
/ W. . . . .   If Windows 3.0 is used in enhanced mode and you have moved the WINA20.386 file, use this switch to tell DOS that the file has been moved.

/K **6**	Ignores extended keys on 101-key keyboards. It forces COMMAND.COM to use an older BIOS call to read the keyboard , making it possible to use certain older TSRs that depend on the older call. Actually, this switch was introduced in DOS V4.0, but was undocumented.
/N **6**	Disables the F5 and F8 keys so that you cannot bypass startup commands.
/F **6**	Skips the 2 second system delay after "Starting MS-DOS . . ." is displayed during startup.

Command Type and Version:

CONFIG.SYS command; Introduced with Ver 4.0

Notes:

1. Use the SWITCHES command when there is a program that does not properly interpret input from an enhanced keyboard. This command enables the enhanced keyboard to use conventional keyboard functions.

2. If SWITCHES=/k is used in a system that uses ANSI.SYS, be sure to also use the /k switch on the ANSI.SYS command.

SYS.COM

Copies the DOS system files (IO.SYS and MSDOS.SYS on MS-DOS systems or IBMBIO.COM and IBMDOS.COM on PC-DOS systems) and the Command Interpreter from one disk drive to another disk drive.

Syntax (shaded is optional):

SYS Drive1:\Path Drive2

       Examples: SYS A: (current drive to drive A:)
                    SYS D:\ A: (copy from disk in D: to A:)

Syntax Options:

Drive1:\Path . .   Drive and directory where system files are located. If a path is not specified, DOS searches the root directory. If a drive is not specified, DOS uses the current drive as the system files source drive.

Drive2: . . . .   Drive to which system files are to be copied. These files can be copied to a root directory only.

Command Type and Version:

External command; Introduced with Ver 1.0

Notes:

1. The order in which the SYS command files are copied is as follows: IO:SYS, MSDOS.SYS and COMMAND.COM.
2. The two system files no longer need to be "contiguous" in Ver 5.0. In simple terms, this means that pre DOS 3.3 disks do not need to be reformatted in order to install the Ver 5.0 operating system.
3. The SYS command will not work on drives redirected by ASSIGN, JOIN or SUBST.
4. The SYS command does not work on Network drives.
5. See also DISKCOPY, which duplicated disks of the same size (including transfer of the operating system). See also COPY and XCOPY for information on copying all files except system and hidden files.
6. ❻ With **DOS 6.0**, DBLSPACE.BIN is also copied to the target drive.
7. Pre DOS 5.0 can only be SYS Drive1:

TIME

Enter or change current system time: DOS
uses the internal clock to update the directory with
date and time when a file is created or changed.

Syntax (shaded is optional):

TIME Hours: Minutes: Seconds: Hundredths
a *or* p

Examples: TIME
TIME 13:45 or TIME 1:45 p
TIME 11:28p

Syntax Options:

Hours: . . . . Specifies the hour. One or two digit
number with valid values from 0-23.

Minutes: . . . . . . Specifies the minute. One or two digit
number with valid values from 0-59.

Seconds: . . . . . Specifies the seconds. One or two digit
number with valid values from 0-59.

Hundredths: . . . Specifies hundredths of a second. One
or two digit number with valid values
from 0-99.

a or *p* . . . . When a 12 hour time format is used instead of the 24 hour format, use **a** or **p**
to specify A.M. or P.M. When a valid
12 hour time is entered and a parameter is not entered, *time* uses **a** (A.M.).

Command Type and Version:

Internal command; Network; Introduced with Ver 1.0

Notes:

1 Using *time* without parameters will display the current time and
prompt you for a time change.

2 Use a colon (:) to separate hours, minutes, (seconds and hundredths of a second are optional), if as defined in COUNTRY, dependent
information file for the United States.

3 With all versions of DOS 3.3 and later, the TIME command will
update the system's battery powered clock (except XT-type
systems).

TREE.COM

Displays the directory structure of a path on a specific drive. See also DIR.

Syntax (shaded is optional):

TREE Drive:\ Path /f /a

Examples: TREE (all directories and subdirectories)
TREE \ (names of all subdirectories)
TREE D:\ /f | MORE
TREE D:\ /f > PRN

Syntax Options:

Drive:\Path . . . Drive and directory containing disk for display of directory structure.

/f . . . . Displays file names in each directory.

/a ❹ . . . . . . Text characters used for linking lines, instead of graphic characters. /a is used with code pages that do not support graphic characters and to send output to printers that do not properly interpret graphic characters.

Command Type and Version:

External command; Network; Introduced with Ver 2.0

Notes:

1. The path structure displayed by the TREE command will depend upon the specified parameters on the command line.
2. The TREE command in MS-DOS 5.0 has been greatly enhanced.

TRUENAME

Displays the TRUENAME of directories and logical drives created with ASSIGN, JOIN, and SUBST.

Syntax (shaded if optional):

TRUENAME drive1: \ path \filename
Example: truename f:

Syntax options:

drive1:. . . . . . . Drive created by ASSIGN, JOIN, or
SUBST.

\ *path\ filename* Path and filename created by ASSIGN,
JOIN, or SUBST.

Command Type and Version:

Internal command, Introduced with Ver 4.0.

TYPE

Screen display of a text file's contents: The
TYPE command is used to view a text file without
modifying it.

Syntax (shaded is optional):

TYPE   Drive:\ Path\   Filename

> Examples: TYPE C:\Act\Receivbl.dat
> TYPE C:\Act\Receivbl.dat | MORE

Syntax Options:

Drive:\Path . . . Drive and directory containing Filename.

\Filename . . . . Name of text file to be viewed.

Command Type and Version:

Internal command; Network; Introduced with Ver 1.0

Notes:

1. Avoid using the TYPE command to display binary files or files
   created using a program as you may see strange characters on
   the screen which represent control codes used in binary files.
2. Use DIR to find the name of a file and EDLIN or EDIT to change
   its contents.
3. When using the pipe (|) for redirection, set the TEMP environ-
   ment variable in AUTOEXEC.BAT.
4. See also DIR and MORE.

UNDELETE / MWUNDEL.EXE

Recovers files that have been deleted with the
DEL command: UNDELETE is the DOS version
and MWUNDEL is the Windows version.

Syntax (shaded is optional):

UNDELETE Drive:\Path\ Filename /List or /all
/purge:drive /status /load [/dos or /dt or /ds]
/sentry:drive /tracker:drive-entries /unload

Examples: UNDELETE /all
UNDELETE C:\Data*.*

Syntax Options:

Drive:\Path ... Drive and directory containing *Filename*.

Filename ..... File to be undeleted. By default, all files
in the current directory will be undeleted.
Wild cards * and ? are allowed.

/ List .... Lists all deleted files in the *Drive:\Path*
that can be undeleted, but does not un-
delete them.

/ all .... Recovers all deleted files without a confirmation prompt. If the deletion tracking
file is present, it is used, otherwise deleted file information is taken from the
DOS directory. See Note: 3.

/ purge:drive **❻** Deletes all files in the sentry directory on
the specified *drive*.

/ status **❻** .... Displays the current UNDELETE protection level that is enabled.

/ load **❻** ..... Load UNDELETE as memory resident, in
order to track deleted files.

/ unload **❻** ... Unload the resident portion of the
UNDELETE delete tracker.

/ dos .... Causes UNDELETE to ignore the deletion
tracking file and recover only those files
listed as deleted by DOS. A confirmation
prompt occurs with each undelete.

/ dt	Causes UNDELETE to ignore the files listed as deleted by DOS and only recover those files listed in the deletion tracking file. A confirmation prompt occurs with each undelete.
/ ds ❻	UNDELETE only the files in the /Sentry directory.
/ Sentry:drive ❻	Specify the drive to be used for delete sentry files.
/ Tracker:drive-entries ❻ . . .	Specify the drive to track deleted files on. The maximum number of deleted files to track can range from 1 to 999.

Command Type and Version:

External command; Introduced with Ver 5.0

Notes:

1. For best results, use MIRROR and the deletion tracking system.

2. When a file is recovered, it is assigned a # for the first character of its name, if a duplicate exists, another letter is selected, in order from the following list, until a unique filename is possible: #%&−1234567890ABCDEFGHIJKLMNOPQRSTUVWXYZ

3. If a switch is not specified with UNDELETE, the deletion tracking file is automatically used. If the deletion tracking file is not present, the DOS directory information is used. The deletion tracking system is much more accurate.

4. UNDELETE cannot undelete a directory.

5. UNDELETE cannot undelete a file if its directory has been deleted. A possible exception to this rule exists if the deleted directory was a main directory under the root directory and not a subdirectory of some other directory. If this is the case, see the UNFORMAT command. It is possible the directory and file can be saved. Use extreme caution with UNFORMAT and understand exactly what you are doing!!! If not used correctly, UNFORMAT can lose data and you might be worse off than when you started!

6. UNDELETE may not be able to recover a deleted file if data of any kind has been written to the disk since the file was deleted. If you accidentally delete a file, stop what you are doing immediately and run the UNDELETE program.

7. Some MIRROR commands from DOS 5.0 are included in the DOS 6.0 UNDELETE command.

8. See also the UNFORMAT command.

UNFORMAT.COM

Restores a disk that has been reformatted or restructured by the RECOVER command:
UNFORMAT can also rebuild disk partition tables that have been corrupted. Do not use UNFORMAT on a network drive.

Syntax (shaded is optional):

UNFORMAT Drive: /J

UNFORMAT Drive: /U /L /test /P

UNFORMAT /partn /L

Examples: UNFORMAT C: /J
UNFORMAT A: /test

Syntax Options:

Drive: . . . . Drive containing disk to be unformatted.

/J . . . . Check the file created by MIRROR for
Removed V6.0   use with UNFORMAT to make sure it agrees with the system information. Use this switch only by itself.

/U . . . . UNFORMAT a disk without using the
Removed V6.0   MIRROR file.

/L . . . . If /partn is not used, /L lists every file and directory found by UNFORMAT. Use if the MIRROR file is to be ignored. If /partn is used also, /L displays the complete partition table of the drive. Standard 512 byte sectors are assumed when the partition table size is displayed. ***Description for Version 5 ONLY.***

/L . . . . Lists every file and subdirectory found by UNFORMAT. Default is to list only subdirectories and files that are fragmented. ***Description for Version 6.x ONLY.***

/test . . . . Displays how UNFORMAT would rebuild information on the disk, but it does NOT unformat the disk. Use this switch only

	if you want UNFORMAT to ignore the MIRROR file. ***Description for Version 5 ONLY.***
/ test	Displays how UNFORMAT would rebuild information on the disk, but it does NOT unformat the disk. ***Description for Version 6 ONLY.***
/ P	Outputs messages to the LPT1 printer.
/ partn . . . . **Removed V6.0**	Rebuilds and restores a corrupted partition table of a hard drive. This switch will only work if MIRROR was run previously and the PARTNSAV.FIL file is available to UNFORMAT.

Command Type and Version:

External command; Introduced with Ver 5.0

Notes:

1. Although UNFORMAT is a very powerful tool, it can also do a lot of damage if not used correctly. BE CAREFUL!

2. UNFORMAT normally restores a disk based on MIRROR information. If disk information has changed since MIRROR was run, UNFORMAT may not be able to recover it. Use MIRROR frequently in order to assure an accurate restoration of the disk.

3. If FORMAT with its /u switch was used, UNFORMAT cannot restore the disk.

4. Per Microsoft's Ver 5.0 User's Guide: "The only case in which you would want to use a prior mirror file is the following: you use the MIRROR command, then the disk is corrupted, then you use the FORMAT command. If you use the MIRROR command and the FORMAT command after the disk is corrupted, the UNFORMAT command will not work. UNFORMAT searches the disk for the MIRROR file. Because UNFORMAT searches the disk directly, the disk does not have to be "readable" by MS-DOS for UNFORMAT to work. Do not use the FDISK command before using UNFORMAT; doing so can destroy information not saved by the MIRROR program."

5. If UNFORMAT does not use the MIRROR file, the restore will take much longer and be less reliable.

6. Without a MIRROR file, UNFORMAT cannot recover a file that is fragmented. It will recover what it can, then prompt for truncation of the file or delete the file.

7. If DOS displays the message "Invalid drive specification", the problem might be a corrupted disk partition table, which UNFORMAT can probably repair. In order to recover the disk partition table, the MIRROR file must be available.

---

8. When the /partn switch is used, you are prompted to insert a system disk in drive A: and press ENTER to restart. The restart will allow DOS to read the new partition table data. Once the system has been restarted, use UNFORMAT without the /partn switch to recover directories and the FAT (file allocation table).

9. See also UNDELETE, MIRROR, FORMAT, and FDISK.

10. In DOS Ver 5.0, the /p switch is not compatible with the /u switch.

UNINSTALL.EXE   New V6.0

Restores the previous version of DOS after the MS-DOS 6 is installed: Used in conjunction with the Uninstall Disk to protect files while MS-DOS 6 is installed. If problems occurs during installation, UNINSTALL can be used to restore the previous version of DOS.

Command Type and Version:

External command, Introduced with Version 6.0.

VER

Displays DOS version number: Type **ver** and the version number will display on the screen.

Syntax (shaded is optional):

VER /R

Examples: VER

Syntax Options:

/R ❻ . . . . Provides a more detailed report.

Command Type and Version:

Internal command; Network; Introduced with Ver 2.0

VERIFY

Disk verification: Verifies that the files are written correctly to a disk.

Syntax (shaded is optional):

VERIFY `on / off`

      Examples: VERIFY on

Syntax Options:

Verify	**Verify** without an option will state whether verification is turned on or off.
on	Forces DOS to confirm that information is being written correctly. The verify command will function until the system is rebooted or **verify off** is used.
off	Turns verification off once it is on.

Command Type and Version:

Internal command; Network; Introduced with Ver 2.0

Notes:

1. When the VERIFY command is used, DOS verifies data as it is written to a disk. This will slow writing speed slightly.
2. COPY / V or XCOPY / V can also be used to verify that files are being copied correctly but on a case by case basis.
3. Verify does not perform a physical disk to disk comparison.

VOL

Displays disk Volume label: The VOL command displays the name of volume label given to a disk when it was formatted. DOS Version 4.0 and greater will also display a volume serial number.

Syntax (shaded is optional):

VOL `Drive:`

> Examples: VOL A:
> VOL

Syntax Options:

VOL. . . . . VOL, without options, displays the volume label and volume serial number of the disk in current drive.

Drive:. . . . . Specifies the drive that contains the disk whose label is to be displayed.

Command Type and Version:

Internal command; Network; Introduced with Ver 2.0
Volume serial numbers introduced with DOS Ver 4.0

Notes:

1. See also FORMAT and LABEL.

Continuously monitors a system for viruses and displays a warning if it finds one:

VSAFE is a memory resident program that uses approximately 22k of memory. See Windows Note below.

Syntax (shaded is optional):

VSAFE   /option + or - /NE /NX /A# /C# /N /D /U

Example: VSAFE / 2+ /NE /AV

Syntax Options:

/ option + or -..   Specifies how VSAFE looks for viruses. The + or - is used to either turn on or turn off the option. Options are as follows:

1 - Warn of a formatting request. Default=On

2 - Warn if a program tries to stay resident. Default=Off

3 - Disable all disk writes. Default=Off

4 - Check executable files that DOS opens. Default=On

5 - Check for boot sector viruses. Default=On

6 - Warns if a program tries to write to the boot sector or partition table of a hard disk. Default=On

7 - Warns if a program tries to write to the boot sector of a floppy disk. Default=Off

8 - Warns if an attempt is made to modify an executable file. Default=Off

/ NE . . . .   Prevents VSAFE from loading into expanded memory.

/ NX . . . .   Prevents VSAFE from loading into extended memory.

/ A# . . . .   Sets the VSAFE hot key as Alt plus the key specified by #.

/ C# . . . .   Sets the VSAFE hot key as Ctrl plus the key specified by #.

/ N . . . .   Enable network drive monitoring.

| /D .... | Disable CRC checksumming. |
| /U .... | Unloads VSAFE from memory. |

Command Type and Version:

External command; Network; Introduced with Ver 6.0

Notes:

1. If VSAFE is to be used when Windows 3.1 is running, you must include " load=MWAVTSR.EXE" in the WIN.INI file.

WINA20.386

The WINA20.386 file must be located in the root directory in order for Microsoft Windows Ver. 3.0 to run in enhanced mode. It is automatically placed in the root directory by MS-DOS during the installation process:

If the file is not in the root directory, you will receive the message "You must have the file WINA20.386 in the root of your boot drive to run Windows in Enhanced Mode."

WINA20.386 must remain in the root directory unless the SWITCHES /W command is used to tell DOS that it has been moved. You must also add a DEVICE command under the [386Enh] section of your Windows SYSTEM.INI file, which specifies where WINA20.386 is now located.

Command Type and Version:

External command; Introduced with Ver 5.0

XCOPY.EXE

Copies files, directories, and subdirectories from one location to another location: XCOPY will not copy system or hidden files.

Syntax (shaded is optional):

XCOPY Source Destination /a /d:date /e /m /p /s /v /w /y /-y

Examples: XCOPY C:\Dos*.* D:\Dos2\ /s

Syntax Options:

Source.	Location and names of files to be copied.
Destination . . .	Destination of the files to be copied.
/a	Copies *Source* files that have their archive file attributes set **without** modifying it.
/d:date	Copies *Source* files that have been modified on or after a specific date.
/e	Copies subdirectories even if empty.
/m.	Copies *Source* files that have their archive file attributes set and turns them off.
/p	Prompts whether you want to create each destination file.
/s	Copies directories and subdirectories, unless they are empty.
/v	Verifies each file, as it is written, to confirm that the destination and source files are identical.
/w.	Displays "Press any key to begin copying file (s)", and waits for response before starting to copy files.
/y 6.2	Directs XCOPY to replace existing files without a confirmation prompt.
/-y 6.2	Directs XCOPY to ask for confirmation prior to replacing an existing file. Default

Command Type and Version:

External command; Network; Introduced with Ver 3.2

Notes:

1. The default *Destination* is the current directory.

2. If the *Destination* subdirectory does not end with a " \ ", DOS will prompt you to find out if the subdirectory is a subdirectory or a file.

3. XCOPY will not copy system or hidden files.

4. When a file is copied to *Destination*, the archive attribute is turned on, regardless of the file attribute in *Source*.

5. In order to copy between disks that are different formats, use XCOPY, not DISKCOPY, but remember that XCOPY does not copy the hidden or system files.

6. XCOPY exit codes are as follows: (see IF errorlevel)

   0 . . . . Files copied successfully
   1 . . . . Source files not found
   2 . . . . XCOPY stopped by user Ctrl+C
   4 . . . . One of the following errors occurred:
   - a. Initialization error
   - b. Not enough disk space
   - c. Insufficient memory available
   - d. Invalid drive name
   - e. Invalid syntax was used.
   5 . . . . Disk write error occurred.

7. When a files size is larger than 64k, use XCOPY instead of the COPY command.

Chapter 5

Microsoft
Windows 3.1
Shortcut Keys

General Windows 3.1

ALT	In an open Application: Use to activate the Menu Bar, same as F10.
ALT + BACKSPACE	In a Text Box or Window: Use to undo last editing command, same as CTRL + Z.
ALT + DOWN ARROW	In a Dialog Box: Use to close or open a selected List.
ALT + ENTER	In 386 enhanced Mode: Moves an MS-DOS Application from a window to full screen and back.
ALT + ESC	Moves immediately to the next open Application.
ALT + F4	(1) Use to exit Windows (2) In a Dialog Box: Use to cancel the Dialog Box (3) In any open Application: Use to Quit that Application.
ALT + HYPHEN	In an open Application: Use to open Control Menu.
ALT + HYPHEN + N	In an open Application: Use to miNimize a second (or child) window.
ALT + HYPHEN + X	In an open Application: Use to maXimize a second (or child) window.
ALT + PRINT SCREEN	In an open Application: Copies an image of the active window to the Clipboard.
ALT + SHIFT + ESC	Moves immediately to the previous open Application.
ALT + SPACEBAR	In an open Application: Use to open Control Menu.
ALT + SPACEBAR + N	In an open Application: Use to miNimize a window.
ALT + SPACEBAR + M	In an open Application: Use to Move a window.
ALT + SPACEBAR + X	In an open Application: Use to maXimize a window.
ALT + TAB	Displays and scrolls forward through a list of open Applications. Releasing the TAB key opens the selected Application.
ALT + TAB + TAB	Displays only the Title Bar of open Applications and scrolls through the open Applications. Releasing the TAB key opens the selected Application.

General Windows 3.1 (cont.)

ALT + Underlined Character .... (1) In an open Application: (a) Menu bar: Open Menu with Underlined Character (b) Menu: Select Menu Item with Underlined Character from Menu (2) In a Dialog Box: Use to move to a Dialog Box item with Underlined Character.

ARROW KEYS .... Move between Menu commands, characters in a text box, or items in a list.

BACKSPACE .... In a Text Box or Window: Use to delete character to the left of the cursor.

CTRL + ALT + Character .... In 386 enhanced Mode: Use to assign Character as an Application Shortcut Key, Character is user selected and can be any letter, numeral, or special key.

CTRL + ALT + SHIFT + Character .... In 386 enhanced Mode: Use to assign Character as an Application Shortcut Key, Character is user selected and can be any letter, numeral, or special key.

CTRL + BACK SLASH (\) ... In a Dialog Box: Use to cancel all selected items from a list except the current item.

CTRL + C .... In a Text Box or Window: Use to copy selected text to the Clipboard, same as CTRL + INSERT.

CTRL + END .... In a Document: Use to move to end of document.

CTRL + ESC .... Opens the Task List window.

CTRL + F4 .... In an open Application: Use to close an active document or window.

CTRL + FORWARD SLASH (/) .... In a Dialog Box: Use to select all items from a list.

CTRL + HOME .... In a Document: Use to move to the beginning of the document.

CTRL + INSERT .... In a Text Box or Window: Use to copy selected text to the Clipboard, same as CTRL + C.

CTRL + LEFT ARROW .... In a Dialog Box: Use to move left one word in a text box.

CTRL + RIGHT ARROW .... In a Dialog Box: Use to move right one word in a text box.

CTRL + SHIFT + Character	In 386 enhanced Mode: Use to assign Character as an Application Shortcut Key, Character is user selected and can be any letter, numeral, or special key.
CTRL + SHIFT + ALT + Character	In 386 enhanced Mode: Use to assign Character as an Application Shortcut Key, Character is user selected and can be any letter, numeral, or special key.
CTRL + V	In a Text Box or Window: Use to paste selected text from the Clipboard, same as SHIFT + INSERT.
CTRL + X	In a Text Box or Window: Use to move selected text on to the Clipboard, same as SHIFT + DELETE.
CTRL + Z	In a Text Box or Window: Use to undo last editing command, same as ALT + BACKSPACE.
DELETE	(1) Use to delete a group or program item (2) In a Text Box or Window: Use to delete character to the right of the cursor.
END	Move to the end of a line, screen, or list.
ENTER	In a Dialog Box: Use to close Dialog Box and initiate all highlighted commands.
ESC	In a Dialog Box: Use to cancel the Dialog Box.
F1	Starts the Help Program from within an open Application.
F10	In an open Application: Use to activate the Menu Bar, same as ALT.
HOME	Move to beginning of a line, screen, or list.
PAGE DOWN	Use to move down one screen.
PAGE UP	Use to move up one screen.
PRINT SCREEN	Use to copy an entire screen to the Clipboard.
SHIFT + ALT + ESC	Moves immediately to the previous open application.
SHIFT + ALT + TAB	Displays and scrolls backward through a list of open applications. Releasing the TAB key opens the selected Application.
SHIFT + CTRL + END	In a Document: Use to move to end of document.
SHIFT + CTRL + HOME	In a Document: Use to move to beginning of document.

General Windows 3.1 (cont.)

SHIFT + CTRL + LEFT ARROW .... In a Document: Use to move to previous word in document.

SHIFT + CTRL + RIGHT ARROW .... In a Document: Use to move to next word in document.

SHIFT + DELETE .... In a Text Box or Window: Use to move selected text to the Clipboard, same as CTRL + X.

SHIFT + DOWN ARROW ... In a Document: Use to select whole line below the cursor location.

SHIFT + END .... In a Document: Use to move to end of a line.

SHIFT + F8 .... In a Dialog Box: Use to select nonconsecutive items from a list.

SHIFT + HOME .... In a Document: Use to move to beginning of a line.

SHIFT + INSERT .... In a Text Box or Window: Use to paste selected text from the Clipboard, same as CTRL + V.

SHIFT + LEFT ARROW ...... In a Document: Use to move one letter left in document.

SHIFT + RIGHT ARROW ... In a Document: Use to move one letter right in document.

SHIFT + TAB .... In a Dialog Box: Moves to previous command in the Dialog Box.

SHIFT + UP ARROW .... In a Document: Use to select whole line above the cursor location.

SPACEBAR .... In a Dialog Box: Use to choose a selected Command.

TAB .... In a Dialog Box: Moves to next command in the Dialog Box.

Calendar Win 3.1

CTRL + END .... In Day View: Use to move to 12 entries after the starting time.

CTRL + HOME .... In Day View: Use to move the starting time.

CTRL + INSERT .... In Day View: Use to move selection to the Clipboard.

CTRL + PAGE DOWN .... In Day View: Use to move to next day.

CTRL + PAGE UP .... In Day View: Use to move to previous day.

DOWN ARROW (1) .... In Month View: Use to move to next month (2) In Day View: Use to move to next time, same as ENTER.

ENTER .... (1) In Month View: Use to change day (2) In Day View: Use to move to next time, same as DOWN ARROW.

Calendar Win 3.1 (cont.)

PAGE DOWN .... (1) In Month View: Use to move to next month (2) In Day View: Use to move to next screen.

PAGE UP .... (1) In Month View: Use to move to previous month (2) In Day View: Use to move to previous screen.

SHIFT + DELETE .... In Day View: Use to move a selection to the Clipboard.

SHIFT + INSERT .... In Day View: Use to paste a selection from the Clipboard to the appointment area or scratch pad.

TAB .... (1) In Month View: Use to move between date and scratch pad (2) In Day View: Use to move between appointment and scratch pad.

UP ARROW .... (1) In Month View: Use to move to previous week (2) In Day View: Use to move to previous time.

Cardfile Win 3.1

CTRL + END .... Use to display the last card.

CTRL + HOME .... Use to display first card.

DOWN ARROW .... Use to scroll forward one card in list.

PAGE DOWN .... Use to scroll forward one card.

PAGE UP .... Use to scroll backward one card.

SHIFT + CTRL + Character .... Use to display first card beginning with Character.

UP ARROW .... Use to scroll backward one card in list.

Clipboard Viewer Win 3.1

DELETE .... Clear the contents of the Clipboard.

File Manager Win 3.1

ALT + ENTER .... Use to display properties of a file or directory.

ALT + F + N .... Use to rename a file.

ALT + F + U .... Use to undelete a file (MS-DOS 6.0 and 6.2 only).

ALT + V + A .... Use to display a file's date, file attributes, and size.

ALT + V + S .... Use to sort files by filename.

Character .... Go to directory or file where directory name or filename starts with Character.

File Manager Win 3.1 (cont.)

CTRL + Drive Letter	Use to changed displayed drive.
CTRL + *	Use to expand all directories and subdirectories.
DELETE	Use to delete a directory or file
ENTER	Use to display or hide a displayed directory's subdirectories, start an application, or open a file.
F2	Use to display drive list.
F5	Use to update the displayed file or directory.
F6	Use to scroll between the displayed drive, directory, and file, same as TAB.
F7	Use to move a displayed file or directory.
F8	Use to copy a displayed file or directory.
SHIFT + ENTER	Use to open a new window and display contents of a directory.
TAB	Use to scroll between the displayed drive, directory, and file, same as F6.
+	Use to expand displayed directories one level to show subdirectories.
*	Use to expand displayed subdirectory.
-	Use to collapse displayed subdirectory.

Help Program Win 3.1

ALT + F4	Use to quit the Help Program.
ALT + PRINT SCREEN	Use to copy Help Screen to Clipboard.
CTRL + TAB	Highlights all key words on a Help Screen.
SHIFT + TAB	Use to move to previous Help Item.
TAB	Use to move to next Help Item.

Object Packager Win 3.1

TAB	Use to move between Content and Appearance windows.

Paintbrush Win 3.1

ARROW KEYS	Use to move the cursor.
CTRL + S	Use to save file.
CTRL + Z	Use to undo everything drawn since selecting a tool.

Paintbrush Win 3.1 (cont.)

DELETE	Use to simulate clicking the right mouse button.
END	Use to move to the bottom of the drawing area.
F9 + INSERT	Use to simulate double-clicking the left mouse button.
HOME	Use to move to the top of the drawing area.
INSERT	Use to simulate clicking the left mouse button.
INSERT + ARROW KEYS	Use to simulate dragging the cursor.
PAGE DOWN	Use to move down one screen.
PAGE UP	Use to move up one screen.
SHIFT + DOWN ARROW	Use to move down one line.
SHIFT + END	Use to move to the right side of the drawing area.
SHIFT + HOME	Use to move to the left side of the drawing area.
SHIFT + LEFT ARROW	Use to move left one space.
SHIFT + PAGE DOWN	Use to move right one screen.
SHIFT + PAGE UP	Use to move left one screen.
SHIFT + RIGHT ARROW	Use to move right one space.
SHIFT + TAB	Use to move among drawing area, palette, linesize box, and toolbox; same as TAB.
SHIFT + UP ARROW	Use to move up one line.
TAB	Use to move among drawing area, palette, linesize box, and toolbox; same as SHIFT + TAB.

Print Manager Win 3.1

CTRL + DOWN ARROW	Use to move selected document down in the queue.
CTRL + UP ARROW	Use to move selected document up in the queue.
DOWN ARROW	Use to move between queues or documents in a queue.
UP ARROW	Use to move between queues or documents in a queue.

Program Manager Win 3.1 (cont.)

ALT + W	Use to move between groups, same as CTRL + TAB or CTRL + F6.
ARROW KEYS	Use to move between items in a group window.
CTRL + F4	Use to close an active group window.
CTRL + F6	Use to move between groups, same as CTRL + TAB or ALT + W.
CTRL + TAB	Use to move between groups, same as CTRL + F6 or ALT + W.
DELETE	Use to delete a program item.
ENTER	Use to open a selected Application.
SHIFT + F4	Use to tile the group windows.
SHIFT + F5	Use to cascade the group windows.

Sound Recorder and Media Player Win 3.1

END	Use to move to the end of the sound when scroll bar is selected.
HOME	Use to move to the beginning of the sound when scroll bar is selected.
LEFT ARROW	Use to move backward when scroll bar is selected.
PAGE DOWN	Use to move forward 1 second when scroll bar is selected.
PAGE UP	Use to move backward 1 second when scroll bar is selected.
RIGHT ARROW	Use to move forward when scroll bar is selected

Write Win 3.1

ALT + BACKSPACE	Use to undo last editing action.
ALT + F6	Use to switch between the document and the find/replace Dialog Box.
ARROW KEYS	Use to move the picture size cursor.
CTRL + ENTER	Use to insert manual page break.
CTRL + SHIFT + HYPHEN	Use to insert an invisible hyphen.
CTRL + Z	Use to undo last typing action.
DOWN ARROW	Use to select an object or picture, cursor must be above upper-left corner of object or picture
5 + DOWN ARROW	Use to move to next paragraph, 5 is on the numeric key pad with the NUM LOCK key turned OFF.

Write Win 3.1 (cont.)

5 + LEFT ARROW	Use to move to next sentence, 5 is on the numeric key pad with the NUM LOCK key turned OFF.
5 + PAGE DOWN	Use to move to next page, 5 is on the numeric key pad with the NUM LOCK key turned OFF.
5 + PAGE UP	Use to move to previous page, 5 is on the numeric key pad with the NUM LOCK key turned OFF.
5 + RIGHT ARROW	Use to move to previous sentence, 5 is on the numeric key pad with the NUM LOCK key turned OFF.
5 + UP ARROW	Use to move to previous paragraph, 5 is on the numeric key pad with the NUM LOCK key turned OFF.

Chapter 6

Microsoft Windows 95 Shortcut Keys

General Windows 95 Shortcuts

ALT	Activate Menu bar, same as F10
ALT+F4	Quit an application
ALT+S	Display Start Menu when no windows are open or applications selected on desktop. Use arrow keys to select menu commands.
ALT+TAB	Switch to previous window
CTRL+C	Copy
CTRL+ESC	Open Start Menu
CTRL+ESC, then ALT+M	Minimize all windows, return to desktop
CTRL+TAB	Tab through pages in a properties dialog box
CTRL+V	Paste
CTRL+X	Cut
CTRL+Z	Undo last action
DELETE	Remove selected item
F1	Help
F10	Activate menu bar, same as ALT
SHIFT while inserting CD ROM	Bypass AutoPlay when inserting a compact disc
SHIFT+F10	View shortcut menu for a selected item, same as right mouse click

Shortcuts For the 95 Desktop, My Computer and Windows Explorer

ALT+ENTER or ALT + DOUBLE CLICK	View item properties (same as right click, select "Properties")
CTRL+SHIFT while dragging file	Pull up menu to move, copy, or create shortcut.
CTRL while dragging file	Copy file
F2	Rename an object (some objects cannot be renamed)
F3	Find a folder or file
SHIFT+DELETE	Delete an item immediately without placing it in the Recycle Bin.

Shortcuts For My Computer and Windows Explorer

BACKSPACE	View the folder one level up
CTRL+A	Select All
F5	Refresh a window
SHIFT while clicking the Close (X) button	Close the selected folder and all its parent folders

Shortcuts for Windows 95 Explorer Only

ALT+ENTER	Display properties of a selected item
ALT+F+M	Rename a selected file
ALT+F+S	Create a shortcut to selected file
BACKSPACE	Go to parent folder
CTRL+Arrow Key	Scroll without changing the selected file
CTRL+G	Go to
F6	Switch between panes
LEFT ARROW	Collapse current selection if expanded; otherwise select parent folder
NUMLOCK + MINUS SIGN (– on numeric keypad)	Collapse the selected folder
NUMLOCK + PLUS SIGN (+ on numeric keypad)	Expand the selected folder
NUMLOCK + ASTERISK (* on numeric keypad)	Expand all subfolders under the selected folder
RIGHT ARROW	Expand current selection if collapsed; otherwise select first subfolder
* on numeric keypad	Expand everything under the selection
+ on numeric keypad	Expand the selected item
— on numeric keypad	Collapse the selected item

Shortcuts for Win 95 "Open" and "Save As" Dialogue Boxes

BACKSPACE	Open folder one level up, if a folder is selected.
CTRL+SHIFT+TAB	Move backward through category tabs
CTRL+TAB	Move forward through category tabs
F4	Open the "Save In" or "Look In" List
F5	Refresh

Shortcuts for Accessibility Options

To use Accessibility Options shortcut keys, the shortcut keys must be enabled.

LEFT ALT+ LEFT SHIFT+
    NUMLOCK.........................Toggle MouseKeys on and off
LEFT ALT+LEFT SHIFT +
    PRINT SCREEN..............Toggle High Contrast on and off
NUMLOCK for 5 seconds ....Toggle ToggleKeys on and off
RIGHT SHIFT for 8 seconds ..Toggle FilterKeys on and off
SHIFT 5 times ....Toggle StickyKeys on and off

Shortcuts Within an Open Win 95 Application

ALT...Activate Menu Bar, same as F10
ALT+BACKSPACE ....Undo last editing command, same as CTRL+Z.
ALT+ESC.................................Open Start Menu, same as clicking on start button.
ALT+F4....................................Exit the application
ALT+HYPHEN ....Bring up Window sizing menu
ALT+HYPHEN +N ....Minimize a second (Child) window
ALT+PRINT SCREEN ....Copy an image of the active window to the clipboard
ALT+SHIFT+ESC ....Switch directly from one open application to another open application
ALT+SPACEBAR.....................Open window sizing menu, same as ALT+HYPHEN.
ALT+SPACEBAR+N ....Minimize the current window
ALT+SPACEBAR+M ....Move a window
ALT+TAB ....Display open applications. Holding down tab key scrolls through the list; repeatedly pressing the TAB key displays open applications one at a time. Releasing the ALT key opens the selected application.
ALT + Underlined Character...ALT activates the menu bar; underlined character pulls down corresponding menu. Within a menu, typing underlined character selects corresponding command. Within a dialogue box, typing underlined character moves cursor to corresponding field.
ARROW KEYS...........................Move between menu items, characters in a text box, or items in a list.

Within Open Win 95 Application (cont.)

BACKSPACE	Delete character to left of cursor
CTRL+C	Copy text to Clipboard
CTRL+END	Move to end of document
CTRL+ESC	Open Start Menu
CTRL+F4	Close an open application
CTRL+HOME	Move to beginning of document
CTRL+LEFT ARROW	Move cursor 1 item or word to the left
CTRL+RIGHT ARROW	Move cursor 1 item or word to the right
CTRL+V	Paste
CTRL+X	Cut (moves object to clipboard)
CTRL+Z	Undo last editing command
DELETE	Delete character to the right of the cursor.
END	Move to the end of a line
ENTER	In a dialog box, close the box and initiate all selected commands.
ESC	Cancel a dialog box
F1	Access Help for the current application
F10	Activate Menu Bar, same as ALT.
HOME	Move to beginning of current line
PAGE DOWN	Move down one screen
PAGE UP	Move up one screen
PRINT SCREEN	Copy an entire screen to the clipboard
SHIFT+ALT+ESC	Toggle to previous open application
SHIFT+ALT+TAB	Bring up box to allow to to select an open application. Releasing tab key selects application
SHIFT+CTRL+END	Select all text from cursor to end of document and moves cursor toend.
SHIFT+CTRL+HOME	Select all text from cursor back to beginning of document and moves cursor to beginning
SHIFT+CTRL+LEFT ARROW	Select word immediately left of cursor
SHIFT+CTRL+RIGHT ARROW	Select word immediately right of cursor
SHIFT+DELETE	Cut (moves text to clipboard, same as CTRL+X)
SHIFT+DOWN ARROW	Select one line of text just below or right of the cursor
SHIFT+END	Select text from cursor to end of line
SHIFT+HOME	Select text from the cursor back to the beginning of line
SHIFT+INSERT	Paste text from clipboard at location of cursor

Within Open Win 95 Application (cont.)

SHIFT+LEFT ARROW	Select one character immediately left of cursor
SHIFT+RIGHT ARROW	Select one character immediately right of cursor
SHIFT+TAB	Move one space backward (or left) in a dialog box
SHIFT+UP ARROW	Select one whole line above the cursor
TAB	Move one space forward (right) in a dialog box

Win 95 Calculator Shortcut Keys
Standard Calculator

CTRL+C	Copy
CTRL+V	Paste
BACKSPACE	Delete last digit displayed, same as "back" button.
DELETE	Clear displayed number, same as "CE" button.
ESC	Clear current calculation, same as "C" button.
CTRL+L	Clear memory, same as "MC" button.
CTRL+M	Store displayed number in memory, same as "MS" button
CTRL+P	Add displayed # to memory, same as "M+" button.
CTRL+R	Recall number stored in memory, same as "MR" button.

Shortcuts for Win 95 Scientific Calculator

Same as Standard Calculator above,
Plus the Following Shortcuts

F9	+/-	Change sign of displayed number.
r	1/x	Calculate reciprocal of displayed number.
ENTER	=	Calculate last 2 numbers.
&	And	Calculate bitwise AND.
CTRL+A	Ave	Mean of numbers in Statistics Box.
BACKSPACE	Back	Delete last digit of displayed number.
F8	Bin	Convert to binary number system.
F4	Byte	Display lower 8 bits of number
o	cos	Calculate cosine of displayed number
INSERT	Dat	Enter number in Statistics Box.
F6	Dec	Convert to decimal number system.
F2	Deg	Set trigonometric input for degrees.

Shortcuts for Win 95 Scientific Calculator (cont.)

m	dms	Set degrees to degree-minute-second fmt.
F2	Dword	Show 32-bit representation of number.
x	exp	Set to scientific notation.
v	F-E	Toggle scientific notation on/off.
F4	Grad	Set trigonometric input for gradient.
F5	Hex	Convert to hexadecimal number system.
h	hyp	Enable hyperbolic function.
n	ln	Calculate base e logarithm.
;	Int	Show integer portion of a decimal value.
i	Inv	Enable inverse function.
L	Log	Calculate base 10 logarithm.
<	Lsh	Shift left, specify number of positions.
%	Mod	Display remainder of x/y.
!	n!	Compute factorial of displayed number.
~	Not	Calculate binary inverse.
F7	Oct	Convert to octal number system.
l(vertical bar)	Or	Calculate bitwise OR.
p	PI	Show value of pi (3.1415...)
F3	Rad	Set trigonometric input for radians.
CTRL+D	s	Standard deviation when Population=n-1.
s	sin	Compute sine of displayed number.
i+@	sqrt (inv+x^2)	Find square root of displayed number.
CTRL+S	Sta	Turn on statistics mode, open Statistics Box.
CTRL+T	Sum	Add values in Statistics Box.
t	tan	Compute tangent of displayed number.
F3	Word	Show lower 16 bits of current number.
^	Xor	Calculate bitwise exclusive OR.
@	x^2	Square the displayed number.
#	x^3	Cube the displayed number.
y	x^y	Compute x to the yth power.

Shortcuts for Win 95 Control Panel/Printers

CTRL+A	Select All
CTRL+C	Copy
CTRL+V	Paste
CTRL+X	Cut
CTRL+Z	Undo

Win 95 Note Pad Shortcuts

CTRL+C	Copy
CTRL+V	Paste

Win 95 Note Pad Shortcuts (cont.)

CTRL+X	Cut
CTRL+Z	Undo
F1	Help
F3	Find Next
F5	Time/Date

Win 95 Paint Shortcuts

ALT+F4	Exit application
CTRL+A	View Color Box
CTRL+C	Copy
CTRL+E	Image Attributes
CTRL+F	View bitmap
CTRL+I	Invert Colors
CTRL+L	Select All
CTRL+N	Start new file
CTRL+O	Open existing file
CTRL+P	Print
CTRL+R	Flip/Rotate image
CTRL+S	Save
CTRL+T	View Tool Box
CTRL+V	Paste
CTRL+W	Stretch or Skew image
CTRL+X	Cut
CTRL+Z	Undo
CTRL+SHIFT+N	Clear Image
F4	Repeat last edit

Shortcuts for Win 95 WordPad

ALT+BACKSPACE	Undo last edit, same as CTRL+Z
ALT+ENTER	Object Properties
ALT+F6	Toggle between document and Find/Replace dialog box.
CTRL+A	Select All
CTRL+C	Copy
CTRL+F	Find
CTRL+H	Replace
CTRL+N	Create New file
CTRL+O	Open file
CTRL+P	Print
CTRL+S	Save
CTRL+V	Paste
CTRL+X	Cut
CTRL+Z	Undo
F3	Find Next

Chapter 7

Hard Drive
Specifications

STD 286/386/486 HARD DISK TYPES

Drive Type	# of Cylinders	# of Heads	Write Precomp	Land Zone	Size in Megabytes
1	306	4	128	305	10
2	615	4	300	615	21
3	615	6	300	615	31
4	940	8	512	940	63
5	940	6	512	940	47
6	615	4	65535	615	21
7	462	8	256	511	31
8	733	5	65535	733	31
9	900	15	65535	901	112
10	820	3	65535	820	21
11	855	5	65535	855	36
12	855	7	65535	855	50
13	306	8	128	319	21
14	733	7	65535	733	43
15	0	0	0	0	0
16	612	4	0	663	21
17	977	5	300	977	41
18	977	7	65535	977	57
19	1024	7	512	1023	60
20	733	5	300	732	31
21	733	7	300	732	43
22	733	5	300	733	31
23	306	4	0	336	10
24	698	7	300	732	42
25	615	4	0	615	21
26	1024	4	65535	1023	34
27	1024	5	65535	1023	43
28	1024	8	65535	1023	68
29	512	8	256	512	34
30	615	2	615	615	10
31	732	7	300	732	44
32	1023	5	65535	1023	44
33	306	4	0	340	10
34	976	5	488	977	42
35	1024	9	1024	1024	77
36	1024	5	512	1024	43
37	830	10	65535	830	69
38	823	10	256	824	68
39	615	4	128	664	21
40	615	8	128	664	41
41	917	15	65535	918	114
42	1023	15	65535	1024	127
43	823	10	512	823	68
44	820	6	65535	820	41
45	1024	8	65535	1024	68
46	925	9	65535	925	69
47	699	7	256	700	41

Note: Drive types over #24 vary between computer manufacturers

Hard Drive Table Syntax and Notations

See page 430 for comments on the hard drive data included in this chapter and a hard drive resource list. The following are descriptions of the information contained in the hard drive tables.

Telephone and BBS numbers for hard drive manufacturers are listed in the Phone Book (Chapter 9) of this Pocket PCRef.

1. Format Size MB   Formatted drive size in megabytes (Mb).
2. Heads ....   Number of data heads
3. Cyl ....   Number of cylinders
4. Sect/Trac .....   Number of sectors per track, V=Variable
5. Translate .....   Head-Cyl-Sector/Track Translation. *UNIV is a Universal Translation where any drive setup can be used as long as the total translated sectors is less than total drive sectors (Total drive sectors=physical heads x physical cylinders x physical sectors per track)
6. RWC ....   Start Reduced Write Current cylinder
7. WPC ....   Start Write Precompensation cylinder
8. Land zone ....   Safe cylinder for parking drive heads
9. Seek Time ....   Avg. drive head access time, milliseconds
10. Interface .....   Type of drive interface used
                         ST412/506, ESDI, SCSI, IDE AT, IDE XT, EIDE
11. Encode ......   Data encoding method used on drive
                         MFM, 2,7RLL, 1,7 RLL, RLL ZBR, ERLL
12. Form Factor ..   Physical diameter and height of drive
                         5.25HH, 3.5HH, 3.5/3H, 2.5
13. Cache ....   Read ahead cache/buffer, in kilobytes (kb)
14. mtbf.........   Mean time between failures in kilohours (kh)
15. RPM ....   Drive motor Revolutions Per Minute
16. Obs Y ....   Is the drive obsolete? Y=Yes

PLEASE NOTE: The density of information in the hard drive table has made it necessary to conserve space by abbreviating kilobytes "kb" as "k" and kilohours "kh" as "k".

Hard Drive Manufacturers Directory

The following table is a general summary of companies that have manufactured and/or are still manufacturing hard drives. The number of models shown is based on data contained in the Pocket PCRef Hard Drive Specifications table and Sequoia Publishing does not represent this summary as being exact. If you have information concerning the status of any of these companies, such as "XYZ Company went bankrupt in August, 1990" or "XYZ Company was bought by Q Company", please let us know so we can keep this section current. If a phone number is listed in the Status column, the company is in business.

Manufacturer	Number of Models	Status
Alps America	8	800-449-2577; No longer make hard drives.
Ampex	4	415-367-2685; No longer make hard drives.
Areal Technology, Inc	17	Out of Business; No longer make hard drives as of 9-96.
Atasi Technology, Inc	17	Out Of Business; Lipsig & Assoc provide support 408-733-1844
Aura Associates	8	408-364-6700; No longer make hard drives.
BASF	5	201-426-2600
Brand Technologies	17	Out of Business
Bull	4	508-294-6000; No longer makes hard drives.
C.itoh Electronics, Inc	1	800-347-2484; Doing business as Itochu Tech; sold hard drive division to Y-E Data.
Cardiff	5	760-752-5200; No longer make hard drives.
CDC	214	408-438-6550; See Seagate
Century Data	18	919-821-5696; Not a manufacturer.
CMI	21	Out of Business
CMS Enhancements, Inc	50	954-967-2397; Not a manufacturer. Ameriquest parent company
Cogito	5	Out of Business
Compaq	27	281-370-0670
Comport	3	Unknown
Conner Peripherals, Inc.	171	800-468-3472; Merged with Seagate Technology 2-5-96.
Core International	58	561-997-6033 Stopped Manufacturing hard drives August

Manufacturer	Number of Models	Status
		1995. Split into 2 companies-Iowa Data Product Services (561-997-6033-old drive support) and Core Engineering (561-998-3800).
Digital Equipment Corp.	33	800-344-4825; Sold Storage Division to Quantum 1st Quarter 1995. Sold Direct Sales Division To PC Complete; OEM Hard Drives from Quantum & Seagate.
Disc Tec	9	407-671-5500; Maker of removable-hard drives.
Disctron (Otari)	12	Out Of Business
DMA	1	Out of Business
Eloch	2	Unknown
Epson	10	800-922-8911; No longer make hard drives.
Fuji	18	510-438-9700; Do not manufacture hard drives in US.
Fujitsu America, Inc.	198	800-626-4686
Hewlett-Packard Co	109	Corporate: 415-857-1501; Most drives are OEM.
Hitachi America	62	800-448-2244
Hyosung	3	Unknown
IBM	101	408-256-1600
IBM Corp. (Storage Sys Div)	218	408-256-1600
IMI	7	Unknown
Integral Peripherals	8	303-449-8009
JCT	7	Unknown
JTS	12	888-587-0945
JVC Companies Of America	22	714-816-6500; No longer manufacture hard drives.
Kalok Corporation	20	Out of Business; see JTS at 888-587-0945.
Kyocera Electronics, Inc.	7	908-563-4300; No longer manufacture hard drives.
Lanstor	4	Unknown
Lapine	17	Unknown
Maxtor Corporation	197	408-432-1700; Sold XT product line to Sequel in 1992.
Mega Drive Systems	16	310-247-0006
Memorex	8	972-444-3500; No longer a manufacturer.
Micropolis Corp	224	800-847-8153

Manufacturer	Number of Models	Status
Microscience International Corp	57	Out of Business
Miniscribe Corporation	90	Out Of Business, Portions Bought By Maxtor Corporation
Mitsubishi Electronics	13	800-843-2515
Mitsumi Electronics Corp.	2	973-550-7300; No longer manufacture hard drives.
MMI	9	Unknown
NCL America	1	408-737-2496; No longer manufacture hard drives.
NCR Corp	9	800-531-2222; No longer manufacture hard drives; call AT&T Global Info.
NEC Technologies Inc	64	508-264-8000
NEI	4	Unknown
Newbury Data	16	Unknown
NPL	13	Unknown
Okidata	2	609-235-2600
Olivetti	9	509-927-5600; No longer make or support drives.
Optima Technology Corp	26	714-476-0515
Orca Technology Corp	6	Unknown
Otari	1	Out of Business
Pacific Magtron	11	408-733-1188; No longer make hard drives.
Panasonic	2	201-348-7000
Plus Development	27	408-894-4000; Bought Out By Quantum
Prairietek Corp	9	Unknown
Priam Corporation	62	Out Of Business; Lipsig & Assoc provide support 408-733-1844
Procom Technology	123	714-852-1000; Does Not manufacture drives, they Bundle
PTI (Peripheral Technology)	23	510-724-1486
Quantum Corporation	192	408-894-4000
Ricoh	5	800-955-3453; No longer manufacture drives.
RMS	4	212-840-8666; They say they have never manufactured drives.
Rodime Systems, Inc	92	Out of Business
Samsung	49	800-726-7864
Seagate Technologies	512	408-438-6550
Sequel, Inc	30	408-987-1000; Purchased XT model lines from Maxtor.

Manufacturer	Number of Models	Status
Shugart	12	520-294-0898
Siemens	12	Out of Business
Sony	3	408-432-1600
Storage Dimensions	41	408-954-0710; Do not manufacture hard drives, they bundle.
Syquest Technology	28	510-226-4000
Tandon Computer Corporation	34	213-726-0303; Filed Chapter 11 Bankruptcy March 1993.
Tandy Corp	3	817-390-3011; No longer manufacture hard drives.
Teac America, Inc.	22	213-726-0303
Texas Instruments	4	800-848-3927
Toshiba America, Inc.	119	714-583-3000
Tulin	7	408-432-9025; Not a manufacturer.
Vertex (see Priam)	1	Out Of Business; Lipsig & Assoc provide support 408-733-1844
Western Digital	116	714-932-5000
Xebec	4	Out of Business
Y-E Data America, Inc	13	847-855-0890; No longer manufacture drives, they make heads.
Zentec	10	Unknown

Total Number of Drives 3870

Drive Model	Format Size MB	Head	Cyl	Sect/ Trac	Translate H/C/S	RWC/ WPC	Land Zone
ALPS AMERICA							
DR311C	106	2	2108	V		NA/NA	AUTO
DR311D	106	2	2108	V		NA/NA	AUTO
DR312C	212	4	2108	V		NA/NA	AUTO
DR312D	212	4	2108	V		NA/NA	AUTO
DRND-10A	11	2	615	17		616/616	AUTO
DRND-20A	21	4	615	17		616/616	AUTO
DRPO-20A	16	2	615	26		616/616	AUTO
DRPO-20D	16	2	615	26		616/616	
AMPEX							
PYXIS-13	11	4	320	17		132/132	
PYXIS-20	17	6	320	17		132/132	
PYXIS-27	22	8	320	17		132/132	
PYXIS-7	6	2	320	17		132/132	
AREAL TECHNOLOGY, INC							
A120	132	4	1070	63	10/535/50	NA/NA	NONE
A130	130	4	1438	V	5/856/60	---/---	
A180	183	4	1430	62	10/715/50	NA/NA	NONE
A260	260	4	1438	V	10/856/60	---/---	
A340	350	4	2120	V	12/950/60	---/---	
A520	526	6	2120	V	16/1020/63	---/---	
A85	86	2	1344	V		AUTO/AUTO	NA
A90	92	2	1430	62	10/715/25	NA/NA	NONE
BP100 (never made)	105	2	1720	V		NA/NA	AUTO
BP200 (never made)						---/---	
BP500 (never made)						---/---	
MD2050 (never made)	49	2	819	V		---/---	
MD2060	62	2	1024	59	7/1024/17	NA/NA	NONE
MD2065	62	2	1024			---/---	
MD2080	81	2	1330	59	14/665/17	NA/NA	NONE
MD2085	86	2	1410	59	14/705/17	NA/NA	NONE
MD2100 (never made)	100	2	1638	V		---/---	
ATASI TECHNOLOGY, INC							
3020	17	3	645	17		320/320	
3033	28	5	645	17		320/320	
3046	39	7	645	17		320/320	644
3051	43	7	704	17		---/352	703
3051+	44	7	733	17		---/368	732
3053	44	7	733	17		350/368	
3075	67	8	1024	17		1025/1025	
3085	72	8	1024	17		---/512	1023
3128	128	8	1024	26		---/---	1023
519	159	15	1224	17		NA/NA	
519R	244	15	1224	26		NA/NA	
6120	1051	15	1925	71		NA/NA	AUTO
638	338	15	1225	36		NA/NA	AUTO
676	676	15	1632	54		NA/NA	AUTO
7120	1034	15	1919	71		NA/NA	AUTO
738	336	15	1225	36		NA/NA	AUTO
776	668	15	1632	54		NA/NA	AUTO
AURA ASSOCIATES							
AU126	125	4				---/---	
AU211	211					NA/NA	AUTO
AU211S	211					NA/NA	AUTO
AU245	245					NA/NA	AUTO
AU245S	245					NA/NA	AUTO
AU43	42	2				---/---	

Drive Model	Seek Time	Interface	Encode	Form Factor	cache kb	mtbf	RPM	Obsolete? ⇩
ALPS AMERICA								
DR311C	13	IDE AT	1,7 RLL	3.5 3H		150k		Y
DR311D	13	SCSI-2	1,7 RLL	3.5 3H		150k		Y
DR312C	13	IDE AT	1,7 RLL	3.5 3H		150k		Y
DR312D	13	SCSI-2	1,7 RLL	3.5 3H		150k		Y
DRND-10A	60	ST412/506	MFM	3.5 HH				Y
DRND-20A	60	ST412/506	MFM	3.5 HH				Y
DRPO-20A	60	ST412/506	2,7 RLL	3.5 HH				Y
DRPO-20D	60	ST412/506	2,7 RLL	3.5 HH				Y
AMPEX								
PYXIS-13	90	ST412/506	MFM	5.25 FH				Y
PYXIS-20	90	ST412/506	MFM	5.25 FH				Y
PYXIS-27	90	ST412/506	MFM	5.25 FH				Y
PYXIS-7	90	ST412/506	MFM	5.25 FH				Y
AREAL TECHNOLOGY, INC								
A120	15	IDE AT	2,7-1,7RLL	2.5 4H	32k	100k	2981	
A130		IDE AT	1,7 RLL	2.5 4H		150k	2981	
A180	17	IDE XT-AT	2,7 RLL	2.5 4H	32k	100k	2981	
A260		IDE AT	1,7 RLL	2.5 4H		150k	2981	
A340	13	IDE AT	1,7 RLL	2.5 4H		150k		
A520	13	IDE AT	1,7 RLL	2.5 4H		150k		
A85	15	IDE	2,7 RLL	2.5 4H		100k		
A90	15	IDE XT-AT	2,7 RLL	2.5 4H	32k	100k	2981	
BP100 (never made)	27	SCSI		2.5 4H				Y
BP200 (never made)								Y
BP50 (never made)								Y
MD2050 (never made)			2,7 RLL	2.5 4H				Y
MD2060	19	IDE AT	2,7 RLL	2.5 4H	32k	45k	1565	
MD2065		IDE AT	RLL	2.5 4H		100k	2504	
MD2080	19	IDE AT	2,7 RLL	2.5 4H	32k	100k	1565	
MD2085	19	IDE AT	2,7 RLL	2.5 4H	32k	100k	1565	
MD2100 (never made)	29	SCSI	2,7 RLL	2.5 4H	32k	100k	2504	
ATASI TECHNOLOGY, INC								
3020		ST412/506	MFM	5.25 FH				Y
3033	30	ST412/506	MFM	5.25 FH				Y
3046	30	ST412/506	MFM	5.25 FH				
3051	33	ST412/506	MFM	5.25 FH				
3051+		ST412/506	MFM	5.25 FH				
3053	27	ST412/506	MFM	5.25 FH				
3075	27	ST412/506	MFM	5.25 FH				Y
3085	27	ST412/506	MFM	5.25 FH				Y
3128		ST412/506	2,7 RLL	5.25 FH				
519	22	ST412/506	MFM	5.25 FH		40k		
519R	22	ST412/506	2,7 RLL	5.25 FH		40k		
6120	14	ESDI		5.25 FH		150k	3600	
638	18	ESDI		5.25 FH		40k	3600	
676	16	ESDI	2,7 RLL	5.25 FH		150k	3600	
7120	14	SCSI	2,7 RLL	5.25 FH		150k	3600	
738	18	SCSI		5.25 FH		40k	3600	
776	16	SCSI		5.25 FH		150k	3600	
AURA ASSOCIATES								
AU126	17	PCMCIA-ATA	1,7 RLL	1.8 4H	32k	100k	5400	Y
AU211	13	ATA		1.8 4H	128k		3448	Y
AU211S	13	SCSI-2		1.8 4H	128k		3448	Y
AU245	13	ATA		1.8 4H	128k		3448	Y
AU245S	13	SCSI-2		1.8 4H	128k		3448	Y
AU43	17	IDE AT	1,7 RLL	1.8 4H	32k	100k	5400	Y

Drive Model	Format Size MB	Head	Cyl	Sect/ Trac	Translate H/C/S	RWC/ WPC	Land Zone
AU63	42	2				---/---	
AU85	85	4				---/---	

BASF

Drive Model	Format Size MB	Head	Cyl	Sect/ Trac	Translate H/C/S	RWC/ WPC	Land Zone
6185	23	6	440	17		220/220	
6186	15	4	440	17		220/220	
6187	8	2	440	17		220/220	
6188-R1	10	2	612	17		---/---	
6188-R3	21	4	612	17		---/---	

BRAND TECHNOLOGIES

Drive Model	Format Size MB	Head	Cyl	Sect/ Trac	Translate H/C/S	RWC/ WPC	Land Zone
9121A (never made)	107	5	1166	36	10/583/36	NA/NA	AUTO
9121E (never made)	107	5	1166	36		NA/NA	AUTO
9121S (never made)	107	5	1166	36		NA/NA	AUTO
9170A	150	7	1165	36	14/583/36	NA/NA	AUTO
9170E	150	7	1166	36		NA/NA	AUTO
9170S	150	7	1166	36		NA/NA	AUTO
9220A	200	9	1209	36	16/401/61	NA/NA	AUTO
9220E	200	9	1210	36		NA/NA	AUTO
9220S	200	9	1210	36		NA/NA	AUTO
BT8085	71	8	1024	17		NA/NA	AUTO
BT8128	109	8	1024	26		NA/NA	AUTO
BT8170E	142	8	1024	34		NA/NA	AUTO
BT8170S	142	8	1024	34		NA/NA	AUTO
BT9400A (never made)	400	6	1800	36		NA/NA	AUTO
BT9400S (never made)	400	6	1800	36	16/801/61	NA/NA	AUTO
BT9650A (never made)	650	10	1800	36	16/1024/63	NA/NA	AUTO
BT9650S (never made)	650	10	1800	36		NA/NA	AUTO

BULL

Drive Model	Format Size MB	Head	Cyl	Sect/ Trac	Translate H/C/S	RWC/ WPC	Land Zone
D530	25	3	987	17		988/988	
D550	43	5	987	17		988/988	
D570	60	7	987	17		988/988	
D585	71	7	1166	17		1166/1166	

C.ITOH ELECTRONICS, INC

Drive Model	Format Size MB	Head	Cyl	Sect/ Trac	Translate H/C/S	RWC/ WPC	Land Zone
SEE YE-DATA						---/---	

CARDIFF

Drive Model	Format Size MB	Head	Cyl	Sect/ Trac	Translate H/C/S	RWC/ WPC	Land Zone
F3053	44	5	1024	17		---/---	
F3080E	68	5	1024	26		NA/NA	
F3080S	68	5	1024	26		NA/NA	
F3127E	109	5	1024	35		NA/NA	
F3127S	109	5	1024	35		NA/NA	

CDC

Drive Model	Format Size MB	Head	Cyl	Sect/ Trac	Translate H/C/S	RWC/ WPC	Land Zone
94151-25 WREN II	25	3	921	19		---/---	
94151-27 WREN II	26	3	921	19		---/---	
94151-42 WREN II	42	5	921	19		---/---	
94151-44 WREN II	44	5	921	19		---/---	
94151-59 WREN II	59	7	921	19		---/---	
94151-62 WREN II	62	7	921	19		---/---	
94151-76 WREN II	76	9	921	19		---/---	
94151-80 WREN II	80	9	921	19		---/---	
94151-80SA WREN II	72	9	921	17		---/---	
94151-80SC WREN II	70	9	921	17		---/---	
94151-86 WREN II	72	9	925	17		925/925	
94155-021 WREN I	18	3	697	17		697/697	
94155-025 WREN I	24	4	697	17		697/128	
94155-028 WREN I	24	3	697	17		698/128	

Drive Model	Seek Time	Interface	Encode	Form Factor	cache kb	mtbf	RPM	Obsolete? ⇓
AU63	17	PCMCIA-ATA	1,7 RLL	1.8 4H	32k	100k	5400	Y
AU85	17	IDE AT	1,7 RLL	1.8 4H	32k	100k	5400	Y

BASF

6185	150/70?	ST412/506	MFM	5.25 FH				
6186	70	ST412/506	MFM	5.25 FH				
6187	70	ST412/506	MFM	5.25 FH				
6188-R1	70	ST412/506	MFM	5.25 FH				
6188-R3	70	ST412/506	MFM	5.25 FH				

BRAND TECHNOLOGIES

9121A (never made)	16.5	IDE AT	2,7 RLL	3.5 HH		50k		
9121E	16.5	SCSI	2,7 RLL	3.5 HH		50k		Y
9121S	16.5	SCSI	2,7 RLL	3.5 HH		50k		Y
9170A	16.5	IDE AT	2,7 RLL	3.5 HH		50k		Y
9170E	16.5	ESDI	2,7 RLL	3.5 HH	64k	50k	3565	Y
9170S	16.5	SCSI	2,7 RLL	3.5 HH		50k		Y
9220A	16.5	IDE AT	2,7 RLL	3.5 HH	64k	50k		Y
9220E	16.5	ESDI	2,7 RLL	3.5 HH	64k	50k	3565	Y
9220S	16.5	SCSI	2,7 RLL	3.5 HH	64k	50k		Y
BT8085	25	ST412/506	MFM	5.25 FH		50k		Y
BT8128	25	ST412/506	2,7 RLL	5.25 FH		50k		Y
BT8170E	25	ESDI	2,7 RLL	5.25 FH		50k		Y
BT8170S	25	SCSI	2,7 RLL	5.25 FH		50k		Y
BT9400A (never made)	12	IDE AT	1,7 RLL	5.25 FH				Y
BT9400S (never made)	12	SCSI-2	1,7 RLL	5.25 FH				Y
BT9650A (never made)	12	IDE AT	1,7 RLL	5.25 FH				Y
BT9650S (never made)	12	SCSI-2	1,7 RLL	5.25 FH				Y

BULL

D530		ST412/506	MFM	5.25 FH				Y
D550		ST412/506	MFM	5.25 FH				Y
D570		ST412/506	MFM	5.25 FH				Y
D585		ST412/506	2,7 RLL	5.25 FH				Y

C.ITOH ELECTRONICS, INC

SEE YE-DATA

CARDIFF

F3053	20	ST412/506	MFM	3.5 HH				Y
F3080E	20	ESDI	2,7 RLL	3.5 HH				Y
F3080S	20	SCSI	2,7 RLL	3.5 HH				Y
F3127E	20	ESDI	2,7 RLL	3.5 HH				Y
F3127S	20	SCSI	2,7 RLL	3.5 HH				Y

CDC

94151-25 WREN II				5.25 FH				Y
94151-27 WREN II				5.25 FH				Y
94151-42 WREN II				5.25 FH				Y
94151-44 WREN II				5.25 FH				Y
94151-59 WREN II				5.25 FH				Y
94151-62 WREN II				5.25 FH				Y
94151-76 WREN II				5.25 FH				Y
94151-80 WREN II				5.25 FH				Y
94151-80SA WREN II	38	SCSI		5.25 FH				Y
94151-80SC WREN II	38	SCSI		5.25 FH				Y
94151-86 WREN II	38	ST412/506	MFM	5.25 FH				Y
94155-021 WREN I		ST412/506	MFM	5.25 FH				Y
94155-025 WREN I		ST412/506	MFM	5.25 FH				Y
94155-028 WREN I	28	ST412/506	MFM	5.25 FH				Y

Drive Model	Format Size MB	Head	Cyl	Sect/ Trac	Translate H/C/S	RWC/ WPC	Land Zone
94155-029 WREN I	25	3	925	17		---/---	
94155-036 WREN I	31	5	733	17		697/128	
94155-037 WREN I	32	4	925	17		---/---	
94155-038 WREN I	31	5	733	17		734/0	
94155-048 WREN II	40	5	925	17		926/128	
94155-051 WREN II	43	5	989	17		990/128	
94155-057 WREN II	48	6	925	17		926/128	AUTO
94155-057P WREN II	48	6	925	17		926/128	
94155-067 WREN II	56	7	925	17		926/128	AUTO
94155-067P WREN II	56	7	925	17		926/128	
94155-077 WREN II	64	8	925	17		926/128	AUTO
94155-085 WREN II	71	8	1024	17		1025/128	AUTO
94155-085P WREN II	71	8	1024	17		1025/128	AUTO
94155-086 WREN II	72	9	925	17		926/128	AUTO
94155-087 WREN II	72	9	925	17		---/---	
94155-092 WREN II	77	9	989	17		---/-1.0	
94155-092P WREN II	77	9	989	17		---/128	

Conversion Chart: Part I			
Old CDC/Imprimis model # to new Seagate model #			
CDC/Imprimis ➡	Seagate	Seagate ➡	CDC/Imprimis
94155-135	ST4135R	ST1090A	94354-090
94155-85	ST4085	ST1090N	94351-090
94155-86	ST4086	ST1100	94355-100
94155-96	ST4097	ST1111A	94354-111
94161-182	ST4182N	ST1111E	94356-111
94166-182	ST4182E	ST1111N	94351-111
94171-350	ST4350N	ST1126A	94354-126
94171-376	ST4376N	ST1126N	94351-126
94181-385H	ST4385N	ST1133A	94354-133
94181-702	ST4702N	ST1133NS	94351-133S
94186-383	ST4383E	ST1150R	94355-150
94186-383H	ST4384E	ST1156A	94354-155
94186-442	ST4442E	ST1156E	94356-155
94191-766	ST4766N	ST1156N	94351-155
94196-766	ST4766E	ST1156NS	94351-155S
94204-65	ST274A	ST1162A	94354-160
94204-71	ST280A	ST1162N	94351-160
94204-74	ST274A	ST1186A	94354-186
94204-81	ST280A	ST1186NS	94351-186S
94205-51	ST253	ST1201A	94354-200
94205-77	ST279R	ST1201E	94356-200
94211-106	ST2106N	ST1201N	94351-200
94216-106	ST2106E	ST1201NS	94351-200S
94221-125	ST2125N	ST1239A	94354-239
94241-502	ST2502N	ST1239NS	94351-230S
94244-274	ST2274A	ST2106E	94216-106
94244-383	ST2383A	ST2106N	94211-106
94246-182	ST2182E	ST2125N	94221-125
94246-383	ST2383E	ST2182E	94246-182
94351-090	ST1090N	ST2274A	94244-274
94351-111	ST1111N	ST2383A	94244-383
94351-126	ST1126N	ST2383E	94246-383
94351-133S	ST1133NS	ST2502N	94241-502
94351-155	ST1156N	ST253	94205-51
94351-155S	ST1156NS	ST274A	94204-74
94351-160	ST1162N	ST274A	94204-65
94351-186S	ST1186NS	ST279R	94205-77
94351-200	ST1201N	ST280A	94204-81
94351-200S	ST1201NS	ST280A	94204-71
94351-230S	ST1239NS	ST4085	94155-85
94354-090	ST1090A	ST4086	94155-86

Drive Model	Seek Time	Interface	Encode	Form Factor	cache kb	mtbf	Obsolete? RPM ⇓
94155-029 WREN I	28	ST412/506	MFM	5.25 FH			Y
94155-036 WREN I		ST412/506	MFM	5.25 FH			Y
94155-037 WREN I	28	ST412/506	MFM	5.25 FH			Y
94155-038 WREN I	28	ST412/506	MFM	5.25 FH			Y
94155-048 WREN II	28	ST412/506	MFM	5.25 FH			Y
94155-057 WREN II	28	ST412/506	MFM	5.25 FH			Y
94155-057P WREN II	28	ST412/506	MFM	5.25 FH		40k	Y
94155-067 WREN II	28	ST412/506	MFM	5.25 FH			Y
94155-067P WREN II	28	ST412/506	MFM	5.25 FH		40k	Y
94155-077 WREN II	38	ST412/506	MFM	5.25 FH			Y
94155-085 WREN II	28	ST412/506	MFM	5.25 FH		40k	Y
94155-085P WREN II	28	ST412/506	MFM	5.25 FH		40k	Y
94155-086 WREN II	28	ST412/506	MFM	5.25 FH		40k	Y
94155-087 WREN II	38	ESDI		5.25 FH			Y
94155-092 WREN II	38	ST412/506	MFM	5.25 FH			Y
94155-092P WREN II	38	ST412/506	MFM	5.25 FH			Y

Conversion Chart: Part II
Old CDC/Imprimis model # to new Seagate model

CDC/Imprimis ➡	Seagate	Seagate ➡	CDC/Imprimis
94354-111	ST1111A	ST4097	94155-96
94354-126	ST1126A	ST41200N	94601-12G/M
94354-133	ST1133A	ST41201J	97100-12G
94354-155	ST1156A	ST41201K	97509-12G
94354-160	ST1162A	ST4135R	94155-135
94354-186	ST1186A	ST41520N	97501-12G
94354-200	ST1201A	ST4182E	94166-182
94354-239	ST1239A	ST4182N	94161-182
94355-100	ST1100	ST4350N	94171-350
94355-150	ST1150R	ST4376N	94171-376
94356-111	ST1111E	ST4383E	94186-383
94356-155	ST1156E	ST4384E	94186-383H
94356-200	ST1201E	ST4385N	94181-385H
94601-12G/M	ST41200N	ST4442E	94186-442
94601-767H	ST4767N	ST4702N	94181-702
97100-80	ST683J	ST4766E	94196-766
97150-160	ST6165J	ST4766N	94191-766
97150-300	ST6315J	ST4767N	94601-767H
97150-340	ST6344J	ST6165J	97150-160
97150-500	ST6516J	ST6315J	97150-300
97200-1130	ST81123J	ST6344J	97150-340
97200-12G	ST81236J	ST6516J	97150-500
97200-23G	ST82272K	ST683J	97100-80
97200-25G	ST82500J	ST81123J	97200-1130
97200-368	ST8368J	ST81154K	97229-1150
97200-500	ST8500J	ST81236J	97200-12G
97200-736	ST8741J	ST81236K	97209-12G
97200-850	ST8851J	ST81236N	97201-12G
97201-12G	ST81236N	ST82105K	97289-21G
97201-25G	ST82500N	ST82272K	97200-23G
97201-368	ST8368N	ST82368K	97299-23G
97201-500	ST8500N	ST82500J	97200-25G
97201-736	ST8741N	ST82500N	97209-25G
97201-850	ST8851N	ST82500N	97201-25G
97209-12G	ST81236K	ST8368J	97200-368
97209-25G	ST82500K	ST8368N	97201-368
97229-1150	ST81154K	ST8500J	97200-500
97289-21G	ST82105K	ST8500N	97201-500
97299-23G	ST82368K	ST8741J	97200-736
97500-12G	ST41201J	ST8741N	97201-736
97501-12G	ST41520N	ST8851J	97200-850
97509-12G	ST41201K	ST8851N	97201-850

Drive Model	Format Size MB	Head	Cyl	Sect/ Trac	Translate H/C/S	RWC/ WPC	Land Zone
94155-096 WREN II	80	9	1024	17		---/---	AUTO
94155-120 WREN II	120	8	960	26		961/128	AUTO
94155-130 WREN II	122	9	1024	26		---/128	
94155-135 WREN II	115	9	960	26		961/128	AUTO
94156-048 WREN II	40	5	925	17		926/128	AUTO
94156-067 WREN II	56	7	925	17		926/128	AUTO
94156-086 WREN II	72	9	925	17		926/128	AUTO
94156-48 WREN II	40					---/---	
94156-67 WREN II	56					---/---	
94156-86 WREN II	72					---/---	
94161-086 WREN III	86	5	969	35		NA/NA	AUTO
94161-101 WREN III	84	5	969	34		NA/NA	AUTO
94161-103 WREN III	104	6	969	35		NA/NA	AUTO
94161-121 WREN III	121	7	969	35		NA/NA	AUTO
94161-138 WREN III	138	8	969	35		NA/NA	AUTO
94161-141 WREN III	118	7	969	35		NA/NA	AUTO
94161-151 WREN III	151	9	969	34		NA/NA	AUTO
94161-155 WREN III	132	9	969	35		---/-1.0	
94161-156 WREN III	132	9	969	36		---/-1.0	
94161-160 WREN III	160		969			---/---	
94161-182 WREN III	156	9	969	35		NA/NA	AUTO
94161-182M WREN III	160	9	969			---/---	
94166-086 WREN III	86	5	969	35		---/-1.0	
94166-101 WREN III	86	5	969	35		NA/NA	AUTO
94166-103 WREN III	104	6	969	35		---/-1.0	
94166-121 WREN III	107	6	969	36		NA/NA	AUTO
94166-138 WREN III	138	8	969	35		---/-1.0	
94166-141 WREN III	125	7	969	36		NA/NA	AUTO
94166-161 COMPAQ	160	9	969	36		NA/NA	AUTO
94166-161 WREN III	142	8	969	36		NA/NA	AUTO
94166-182 WREN III	161	9	969	36		NA/NA	AUTO
94171-300 WREN IV	300	9	1412			NA/NA	AUTO
94171-307 WREN IV	300	9	1412			NA/NA	AUTO
94171-327 WREN IV	300	9	1412			NA/NA	AUTO
94171-330 WREN IV	330					---/---	
94171-344 WREN IV	323	9	1549	V		NA/NA	AUTO
94171-350 WREN IV	307	9	1412	V		NA/NA	AUTO
94171-375 WREN IV	330	9	1549	V		NA/NA	AUTO
94171-376 WREN IV	330	9	1546	V		NA/NA	AUTO
94171-376D WREN IV	323	9	1549	V		NA/NA	AUTO
94181-383 WREN IV	330	15	1224			---/---	
94181-385D WREN V	337	15	791	V		NA/NA	AUTO
94181-385H WREN V	337	15	791	V		NA/NA	AUTO
94181-574 WREN V	574	15	1549	V		NA/NA	AUTO
94181-702 WREN V	613	15	1546	V		NA/NA	AUTO
94181-702D WREN V	601	15	1546	V		---/---	
94181-702M WREN V	613	15	1549			---/---	
94186-265 WREN V	234	9	1412	36		NA/NA	AUTO
94186-324 WREN V	278	11	1412	35		NA/NA	AUTO
94186-383 WREN V	338	7	1747	35		NA/NA	AUTO
94186-383H WREN V	338	7	1747	35		NA/NA	AUTO
94186-383S WREN V	338	13	1412	36		NA/NA	AUTO
94186-442 WREN V	380	15	1412	35		NA/NA	AUTO
94186-442S WREN V	390	15	1412	36		NA/NA	AUTO
94191-766 WREN VI	677	15	1632	54		NA/NA	AUTO
94191-766D WREN VI	677	15	1632	54		NA/NA	AUTO
94196-383 WREN VI	338	7	1747	54		NA/NA	AUTO
94196-766 WREN VI	677	15	1632	54		NA/NA	AUTO
94204-051 WREN II	43	5	989	26		NA/NA	AUTO
94204-065 WREN II	63	5	948	26		NA/NA	AUTO
94204-071 WREN II	63	5	1032	27		NA/NA	AUTO
94204-074 WREN II	63	5	948	26		NA/NA	AUTO
94204-081 WREN II	71	5	1032	27		NA/NA	AUTO

Drive Model	Seek Time	Interface	Encode	Form Factor	cache kb	mtbf	RPM	Obsolete?
94155-096 WREN II	28	ST412/506	MFM	5.25 FH		40k		Y
94155-120 WREN II	28	ST412/506	2,7 RLL	5.25 FH		40k		Y
94155-130 WREN II	28	ST412/506	RLL	5.25 FH				Y
94155-135 WREN II	28	ST412/506	2,7 RLL	5.25 FH		40k		Y
94156-048 WREN II	28	ESDI	MFM	5.25 FH		40k		Y
94156-067 WREN II	28	ESDI	MFM	5.25 FH		40k		Y
94156-086 WREN II	28	ESDI	MFM	5.25 FH		40k		Y
94156-48 WREN II		ESDI	ST412/506	5.25 FH				Y
94156-67 WREN II		ESDI	ST412/506	5.25 FH				Y
94156-86 WREN II		ESDI	ST412/506	5.25 FH				Y
94161-086 WREN III	16.5	SCSI	2,7 RLL	5.25 FH				Y
94161-101 WREN III	16.5	SCSI	2,7 RLL	5.25 FH		100k		Y
94161-103 WREN III	16.5	SCSI	2,7 RLL	5.25 FH		100k		Y
94161-121 WREN III	16.5	SCSI	2,7 RLL	5.25 FH		100k		Y
94161-138 WREN III	16.5	SCSI	2,7 RLL	5.25 FH		100k		Y
94161-141 WREN III	16.5	SCSI	2,7 RLL	5.25 FH		100k		Y
94161-151 WREN III	16.5	SCSI	2,7 RLL	5.25 FH		100k		Y
94161-155 WREN III	17	SCSI	RLL	5.25 FH				Y
94161-156 WREN III	17	SCSI	RLL	5.25 FH				Y
94161-160 WREN III		SCSI	2,7 RLL	5.25 FH				Y
94161-182 WREN III	16.5	SCSI	2,7 RLL	5.25 FH		100k		Y
94161-182M WREN III	17	SCSI	ZBR	5.25 FH				Y
94166-086 WREN III	25	ESDI	RLL	5.25 FH				Y
94166-101 WREN III	16.5	ESDI	2,7 RLL	5.25 FH		100k		Y
94166-103 WREN III	25	ESDI	RLL	5.25 FH				Y
94166-121 WREN III	16.5	ESDI	2,7 RLL	5.25 FH		100k		Y
94166-138 WREN III	25	ESDI	RLL	5.25 FH				Y
94166-141 WREN III	16.5	ESDI	2,7 RLL	5.25 FH		100k		Y
94166-161 COMPAQ		ESDI	2,7 RLL	5.25 FH		100k		Y
94166-161 WREN III		ESDI	2,7 RLL	5.25 FH		100k		Y
94166-182 WREN III	16.5	ESDI (10)	2,7 RLL	5.25 FH		100k		Y
94171-300 WREN IV	17	SCSI	RLL ZBR	5.25 FH				
94171-307 WREN IV	17	SCSI	RLL ZBR	5.25 FH				
94171-327 WREN IV	17	SCSI	RLL ZBR	5.25 FH				
94171-344 WREN IV		SCSI	RLL ZBR	5.25 FH				
94171-350 WREN IV	16.5	SCSI	RLL ZBR	5.25 FH		100k		
94171-375 WREN IV	16	SCSI	RLL ZBR	5.25 FH				
94171-376 WREN IV	17.5	SCSI	RLL ZBR	5.25 FH		100k		
94171-376D WREN IV		SCSI	RLL ZBR	5.25 HH		100k		
94181-382 WREN IV	18	SCSI	ZBR	5.25 FH				
94181-385D WREN IV		SCSI	RLL ZBR	5.25 FH		100k		
94181-385H WREN V	10.7	SCSI	RLL ZBR	5.25 FH		100k		
94181-574 WREN V	16	SCSI	RLL ZBR	5.25 FH		100k		
94181-702 WREN V	16.5	SCSI	RLL ZBR	5.25 FH		100k		
94181-702D WREN V		SCSI	RLL ZBR	5.25 FH		100k		
94181-702M WREN V	17	SCSI	ZBR	5.25 FH				
94186-265 WREN V		ESDI (10)	2,7 RLL	5.25 FH		100k		
94186-324 WREN V		ESDI (10)	2,7 RLL	5.25 FH				
94186-383 WREN V		ESDI (10)	2,7 RLL	5.25 FH		100k		
94186-383H WREN V		ESDI (10)	2,7 RLL	5.25 FH		100k		
94186-383S WREN V	19	SCSI	2,7 RLL	5.25 FH		100k		
94186-442 WREN V		ESDI (10)	2,7 RLL	5.25 FH		100k		
94186-442S WREN V	15	SCSI	2,7 RLL	5.25 FH				
94191-766 WREN VI	15.5	SCSI	2,7 RLL	5.25 FH		100k		
94191-766D WREN VI		SCSI	2,7 RLL	5.25 FH		100k		
94196-383 WREN V		ESDI (15)	2,7 RLL	5.25 FH		100k		
94196-766 WREN V		ESDI (15)	2,7 RLL	5.25 FH		100k		
94204-051 WREN II		IDE AT	2,7 RLL	5.25 HH		40k		Y
94204-065 WREN II		IDE AT	2,7 RLL	5.25 HH		40k		Y
94204-071 WREN II		IDE AT	2,7 RLL	5.25 HH		40k		Y
94204-074 WREN II	28	IDE AT	2,7 RLL	5.25 HH		40k		Y
94204-081 WREN II	28	IDE AT	2,7 RLL	5.25 HH		40k		Y

Hard Drives

Drive Model	Format Size MB	Head	Cyl	Sect/ Trac	Translate H/C/S	RWC/ WPC	Land Zone
94205-030 WREN II	26	3	989	17		989/---	AUTO
94205-041 WREN II	43	4	989	17		990/128	AUTO
94205-051 WREN II	43	5	989	17		990/128	AUTO
94205-053 WREN II	43	5	1024	17		990/128	AUTO
94205-071 WREN II	43	5	989	26		990/128	AUTO
94205-075 WREN II	62	5	966	25		966/128	AUTO
94205-077 WREN II	66	5	989	26		---/---	AUTO
94208-062 WREN II	60	5	989	17		---/---	
94208-075 WREN II	66	5	989	26		NA/NA	AUTO
94208-106 WREN II	91		989			---/---	
94208-51 WRENII	43		989			---/---	
94208-91 WRENII	80		989			---/---	
94208-951 WREN II	42	5	989	17		990/128	
94211-086 WREN III	72	5	1024			---/---	
94211-091 WREN III	77	5	1024	17		970/970	
94211-106 WREN III	92	5	1024	35		NA/NA	AUTO
94211-106M WREN III	94	5	1024			1025/1025	
94211-209 WREN III	183	15	1547			1548/1548	
94216-106 WREN III	90	5	1024	34		NA/NA	AUTO
94221-125 WREN V	110	3	1544	V		NA/NA	AUTO
94221-169 WREN V	159	5	1310	V		NA/NA	AUTO
94221-190 WREN V	190	5	1547	V		NA/NA	AUTO
94221-209 WREN V	183	5	1544	V		NA/NA	AUTO
94241-383 WREN VI	338	7	1400	V		NA/NA	AUTO
94241-502 WREN VI		7	1765	V		NA/NA	AUTO
94241-502M WREN VI		7	1765	V		NA/NA	AUTO
94244-219 WREN VI	186	4	1747	54		1748/-1.0	
94244-274 WREN VI	233	5	1747	52		NA/NA	AUTO
94244-383 WREN VI	338	7	1747	54		NA/NA	AUTO
94246-182 WREN VI	161	4	1453	54		NA/NA	AUTO
94246-383 WREN VI	338	7	1747			NA/NA	
94311-136 SWIFT SL	120	5				NA/NA	AUTO
94311-136S SWIFT SL	120	5	1247	36		NA/NA	AUTO
94314-136 SWIFT SL	120	5				NA/NA	AUTO
94316-111 SWIFT	98	5		36		NA/NA	AUTO
94316-136 SWIFT SL	120	5		36		NA/NA	AUTO
94316-155 SWIFT	138	7	1072	36		NA/NA	AUTO
94316-200 SWIFT	177	5		36		NA/NA	AUTO
94335-055 SWIFT SL	46	5				---/---	
94335-100 SWIFT	85	9	1072	17		---/---	
94335-150 SWIFT	128	5		26		---/---	
94351-090 SWIFT	80	5	1068			NA/NA	AUTO
94351-111 SWIFT	98	5	1068			NA/NA	AUTO
94351-128 SWIFT	111	7	1068	29		NA/NA	AUTO
94351-133S SWIFT	117	5	1268	36		NA/NA	AUTO
94351-134 SWIFT	120	7	1268			---/---	
94351-135 SWIFT	121	6	1068				
94351-155 SWIFT	138	7	1068	36		NA/NA	AUTO
94351-155S SWIFT	138	5	1268	36		NA/NA	AUTO
94351-160 SWIFT	143	9	1068	29		NA/NA	AUTO
94351-172 SWIFT	177	9	1068	36		NA/NA	AUTO
94351-186S SWIFT	164	7	1268	36		NA/NA	AUTO
94351-200 SWIFT	178	7	1068	36		NA/NA	AUTO
94351-200S SWIFT	177	9	1068	36		NA/NA	AUTO
94351-230 SWIFT	210	9	1268	36		NA/NA	AUTO
94351-230S SWIFT	210	9	1268	36		NA/NA	AUTO
94354-090 SWIFT	80	5	102	29		---/-1.0	
94354-111 SWIFT	99	5	1072	36		NA/NA	AUTO
94354-126 SWIFT	111	7	1072	29		NA/NA	AUTO
94354-133 SWIFT	117	5	1272	36		NA/NA	AUTO
94354-155 SWIFT	138	7	1072	36		NA/NA	AUTO
94354-160 SWIFT	143	9	1072	29		NA/NA	AUTO

Drive Model	Seek Time	Interface	Encode	Form Factor	cache kb	Obsolete? mtbf	RPM
94205-030 WREN II		ST412/506	MFM	5.25 FH		40k	Y
94205-041 WREN II		ST412/506	MFM	5.25 HH		40k	Y
94205-051 WREN II	28	ST412/506	MFM	5.25 HH		40k	Y
94205-053 WREN II		ST412/506	MFM	5.25 HH		40k	Y
94205-071 WREN II		ST412/506	RLL	5.25 HH		40k	Y
94205-075 WREN II	28	ST412/506	RLL	5.25 HH		40k	Y
94205-077 WREN II	28	ST412/506	2,7 RLL	5.25 HH		40k	Y
94208-062 WREN II		COMPAQ	MFM	5.25 HH			Y
94208-075 WREN II	30	IDE AT	2,7 RLL	5.25 HH			Y
94208-106 WREN II		IDE AT		5.25 HH			Y
94208-51 WRENII		IDE AT		5.25 HH			Y
94208-91 WRENIII		IDE AT		5.25 HH			Y
94208-951 WREN II	28	COMPAQ	MFM	5.25 FH			Y
94211-086 WREN III	18	SCSI	RLL	5.25 HH			Y
94211-091 WREN III	18	SCSI	MFM	5.25 HH			Y
94211-106 WREN III	18	SCSI	2,7 RLL	5.25 HH	100k		Y
94211-106M WREN III	18	SCSI	ZBR	5.25 FH			
94211-209 WREN III	18	SCSI	ZBR	3.5 HH			Y
94216-106 WREN III	18	ESDI (10)	2,7 RLL	5.25 HH	100k		Y
94221-125 WREN V	18	SCSI	RLL ZBR	5.25 HH	100k		Y
94221-169 WREN V	18	SCSI	RLL ZBR	5.25 HH	100k		Y
94221-190 WREN V	18	SCSI	RLL ZBR	5.25 HH	100k		Y
94221-209 WREN V	18	SCSI	RLL ZBR	5.25 HH	100k		Y
94241-383 WREN VI	14	SCSI	RLL ZBR	5.25 HH	100k		
94241-502 WREN VI		SCSI	RLL ZBR	5.25 HH	100k		
94241-502M WREN VI	16	SCSI(MAC)	RLL ZBR	5.25 HH	100k		Y
94244-219 WREN VI	16	AT	RLL	5.25 HH			Y
94244-274 WREN VI	16	IDE AT	2,7 RLL	5.25 HH	100k		
94244-383 WREN VI	16	IDE AT	2,7 RLL	5.25 HH	100k		
94246-182 WREN VI	16	ESDI (20)	2,7 RLL	5.25 HH	100k		
94246-383 WREN VI	16	SCSI (20)	2,7 RLL	5.25 HH	100k		
94311-136 SWIFT SL	15	SCSI	2,7 RLL	3.5 3H	70k		Y
94311-136S SWIFT SL	15	SCSI-2	2,7 RLL	3.5 3H	70k		Y
94314-136 SWIFT SL	15	IDE AT	2,7 RLL	3.5 3H	70k		Y
94316-111 SWIFT	23	ESDI	2,7 RLL	3.5 HH	70k		Y
94316-136 SWIFT SL	15	ESDI	2,7 RLL	3.5 HH	70k		Y
94316-155 SWIFT	15	ESDI	2,7 RLL	3.5 HH	70k		Y
94316-200 SWIFT	15	ESDI	2,7 RLL	3.5 HH	70k		Y
94335-085 SWIFT SL		RLL		3.5 HH			Y
94335-100 SWIFT	25	ST412/506	MFM	3.5 HH			Y
94335-150 SWIFT	25	ST412/506	RLL	3.5 HH			Y
94351-090 SWIFT	15	SCSI	RLL	3.5 HH			Y
94351-111 SWIFT	15	SCSI	2,7 RLL	3.5 HH	70k		Y
94351-126 SWIFT	15	SCSI	2,7 RLL	3.5 HH	70k		Y
94351-128 SWIFT	15	SCSI	2,7 RLL	3.5 HH	70k		Y
94351-133S SWIFT	15	SCSI-2	2,7 RLL	3.5 HH	70k		Y
94351-134 SWIFT	15	SCSI	RLL	3.5 HH			Y
94351-135 SWIFT	15	SCSI	RLL	3.5 HH			Y
94351-155 SWIFT	15	SCSI	2,7 RLL	3.5 HH	70k		Y
94351-155S SWIFT	15	SCSI-2	2,7 RLL	3.5 HH	70k		Y
94351-160 SWIFT	15	SCSI	2,7 RLL	3.5 HH	150k		Y
94351-172 SWIFT	15	SCSI	2,7 RLL	3.5 HH	150k		Y
94351-186S SWIFT	15	SCSI-2	2,7 RLL	3.5 HH	150k		Y
94351-200 SWIFT	15	SCSI	2,7 RLL	3.5 HH	150k		Y
94351-200S SWIFT	15	SCSI-2	2,7 RLL	3.5 HH	150k		Y
94351-230 SWIFT	15	SCSI		3.5 HH	70k		Y
94351-230S SWIFT	15	SCSI-2	2,7 RLL	3.5 HH	70k		Y
94354-090 SWIFT	15	AT	RLL	3.5 HH			Y
94354-111 SWIFT	15	IDE AT	2,7 RLL	3.5 HH	70k		Y
94354-126 SWIFT	15	IDE AT	2,7 RLL	3.5 HH	150k		Y
94354-133 SWIFT	15	IDE AT	2,7 RLL	3.5 HH	70k		Y
94354-155 SWIFT	15	IDE AT	2,7 RLL	3.5 HH	70k		Y
94354-160 SWIFT	15	IDE AT	2,7 RLL	3.5 HH	150k		Y

Drive Model	Format Size MB	Head	Cyl	Sect/ Trac	Translate H/C/S	RWC/ WPC	Land Zone
94354-186 SWIFT	164	7	1272	36		NA/NA	AUTO
94354-200 SWIFT	178	9	1072	36		NA/NA	AUTO
94354-230 SWIFT	204					---/---	AUTO
94354-239 SWIFT	211	9	1272	36		NA/NA	AUTO
94355-055 SWIFT II	46	5		17		---/---	AUTO
94355-100 SWIFT	84	9	1072	17		1073/300	AUTO
94355-150 SWIFT	128	9	1072	26		1073/300	AUTO
94355-55 SWIFT	46					---/---	AUTO
94356-111 SWIFT	99	5	1072	36		NA/NA	AUTO
94356-155 SWIFT	138	7	1072	36		NA/NA	AUTO
94356-200 SWIFT	178	9	1072	36		NA/NA	AUTO
94601-12D WREN VII	1035	15	1931	V		NA/NA	AUTO
94601-12G WREN VII	1037	15	1937	V		NA/NA	AUTO
94601-12GM WREN VII	1037	15	1937	V		NA/NA	AUTO
94601-767H WREN VII	676	15	1356	V		NA/NA	AUTO
97155-036	30			17		---/---	AUTO
9720-1123 SABRE	964	19				---/---	AUTO
9720-1130 SABRE	1050	15	1635			---/---	AUTO
9720-2270 SABRE	1948	19				---/---	AUTO
9720-2500 SABRE	2145	19				---/---	AUTO
9720-368 SABRE	368		1635			1218/1218	AUTO
9720-500 SABRE	500	10	1217			1218/1218	AUTO
9720-736 SABRE	736	15	1635			1636/1636	AUTO
9720-850 SABRE	727	15	1381			1382/1382	AUTO
97229-1150 WREN V	990	19				---/---	AUTO
97501-15G ELITE	1500	17				NA/NA	AUTO
97509-12G ELITE	1050	17				---/---	AUTO
BJ7D5A/77731600	18	3	697	17		---/128	
BJ7D5A/77731601	18	3	697	17		---/128	
BJ7D5A/77731602	30	5	697	17		---/128	
BJ7D5A/77731603	30	5	697	17		---/128	
BJ7D5A/77731604	36	5	697			---/128	
BJ7D5A/77731605	30	5	697	17		---/128	
BJ7D5A/77731606	27			17		---/128	
BJ7D5A/77731607	18	3	697	17		---/128	
BJ7D5A/77731608	29	5	670	17		---/128	
BJ7D5A/77731609	30	5	697	17		---/128	
BJ7D5A/77731610	18	3	697	17		---/128	
BJ7D5A/77731611	30	5	697	17		---/128	
BJ7D5A/77731612	24	4	697	17		---/128	
BJ7D5A/77731613	31	5	733	17		---/128	
BJ7D5A/77731614	23	4	670	17		---/128	
BJ7D5A/77731615	24	4	697	17		---/128	
BJ7D5A/77731616	31	5	733	17		---/128	
BJ7D5A/77731617	30	5	697	17		---/128	
BJ7D5A/77731618	30	5	697	17		---/128	
BJ7D5A/77731619	30	5	697	17		---/128	
BJ7D5A/77731620	30	5	697	17		---/128	
SABRE 1123	964	19				---/---	AUTO
SABRE 1150	990	19				---/---	AUTO
SABRE 1230	1050	15	1635			---/---	AUTO
SABRE 2270	1948	19				---/---	AUTO
SABRE 2500	2145	19				---/---	AUTO
SABRE 368	368	10	1635			---/---	AUTO
SABRE 500	500	10	1217			---/---	AUTO
SABRE 736	741	15	1217			---/---	AUTO
SABRE 850	851	15	1635			---/---	AUTO

CENTURY DATA

Drive Model	Format Size MB	Head	Cyl	Sect/ Trac	Translate H/C/S	RWC/ WPC	Land Zone
CAST-10203E	55	3	1050	35		NA/NA	AUTO
CAST-10203S	55	3	1050	35		NA/NA	AUTO
CAST-10304E	75	4	1050	35		NA/NA	AUTO
CAST-10304S	75	4	1050	35		NA/NA	AUTO

Drive Model	Seek Time	Interface	Encode	Form Factor	cache kb	mtbf	Obsolete? RPM
94354-186 SWIFT	15	IDE AT	2,7 RLL	3.5 HH		150k	Y
94354-200 SWIFT	15	IDE AT	2,7 RLL	3.5 HH		150k	Y
94354-230 SWIFT	15	IDE AT	2,7 RLL	3.5 HH			Y
94354-239 SWIFT	15	IDE AT	2,7 RLL	3.5 HH			Y
94355-055 SWIFT II	25	ST412/506	MFM	3.5 HH		70k	Y
94355-100 SWIFT	15	ST412/506	MFM	3.5 HH		70k	Y
94355-150 SWIFT	15	ST412/506	2,7 RLL	3.5 HH		150k	Y
94355-55 SWIFT			MFM	3.5 HH			Y
94356-111 SWIFT	15	ESDI (10)	2,7 RLL	3.5 HH		150k	Y
94356-155 SWIFT	15	ESDI (10)	2,7 RLL	3.5 HH		70k	Y
94356-200 SWIFT	15	ESDI (10)	2,7 RLL	3.5 HH		70k	Y
94601-12D WREN VII	15	SCSI	2,7 RLL	5.25 FH		150k	
94601-12G WREN VII	15	SCSI	RLL ZBR	5.25 FH		150k	
94601-12GM WREN VII	15	SCSI(MAC)	RLL ZBR	5.25 FH		150k	
94601-767H WREN VII	15	SCSI(MAC)	RLL ZBR	5.25 FH		100k	
97155-036		ST412/506	MFM	8.0 FH		70k	Y
9720-1123 SABRE	15	SMD	2,7 RLL	8.0 FH		70k	
9720-1130 SABRE	15	SMD/SCSI	2,7 RLL	8.0 FH		100k	
9720-2270 SABRE	12	SMD	2,7 RLL	8.0 FH		100k	
9720-2500 SABRE	15	SMD/SCSI	2,7 RLL	8.0 FH		100k	
9720-368 SABRE	18	SMD/SCSI	2,7 RLL	8.0 FH		30k	
9720-500 SABRE	18	SMD/SCSI	2,7 RLL	8.0 FH		30k	
9720-736 SABRE	15	SMD/SCSI	2,7 RLL	8.0 FH		50k	
9720-850 SABRE	15	SMD/SCSI	2,7 RLL	8.0 FH		50k	
97229-1150 WREN V	15	IPI-2		8.0 FH		100k	
97501-15G ELITE	12	SCSI-2	RLL	5.25 FH		100k	
97509-12G ELITE	12	IPI-2		5.25 FH		100k	
BJ7D5A/77731600		ST412/506	MFM	5.25 FH			Y
BJ7D5A/77731601		ST412/506	MFM	5.25 FH			Y
BJ7D5A/77731602		ST412/506	MFM	5.25 FH			Y
BJ7D5A/77731603		ST412/506	MFM	5.25 FH			Y
BJ7D5A/77731604		ST412/506	MFM	5.25 FH			Y
BJ7D5A/77731605		ST412/506	MFM	5.25 FH			Y
BJ7D5A/77731606		ST412/506	MFM	5.25 FH			Y
BJ7D5A/77731607		ST412/506	MFM	5.25 FH			Y
BJ7D5A/77731608		ST412/506	MFM	5.25 FH			Y
BJ7D5A/77731609		ST412/506	MFM	5.25 FH			Y
BJ7D5A/77731610		ST412/506	MFM	5.25 FH			Y
BJ7D5A/77731611		ST412/506	MFM	5.25 FH			Y
BJ7D5A/77731612		ST412/506	MFM	5.25 FH			Y
BJ7D5A/77731613		ST412/506	MFM	5.25 FH			Y
BJ7D5A/77731614		ST412/506	MFM	5.25 FH			Y
BJ7D5A/77731615		ST412/506	MFM	5.25 FH			Y
BJ7D5A/77731616		ST412/506	MFM	5.25 FH			Y
BJ7D5A/77731617		ST412/506	MFM	5.25 FH			Y
BJ7D5A/77731618		ST412/506	MFM	5.25 FH			Y
BJ7D5A/77731619		ST412/506	MFM	5.25 FH			Y
BJ7D5A/77731620		ST412/506	MFM	5.25 FH			Y
SABRE 1123	15				100k		
SABRE 1150	15				100k		
SABRE 1230	15				100k		
SABRE 2270	12				100k		
SABRE 2500	12				100k		
SABRE 368	18				30k		
SABRE 500	18				30k		
SABRE 736	15				50k		
SABRE 850	15				50k		

CENTURY DATA

CAST-10203E	28	ESDI	2,7 RLL	5.25 FH			
CAST-10203S	28	SCSI	2,7 RLL	5.25 FH			
CAST-10304E	28	ESDI	2,7 RLL	5.25 FH			
CAST-10304S	28	SCSI	2,7 RLL	5.25 FH			

Drive Model	Format Size MB	Head	Cyl	Sect/ Trac	Translate H/C/S	RWC/ WPC	Land Zone
CAST-10305E	94	5	1050	35		NA/NA	AUTO
CAST-10305S	94	5	1050	35		NA/NA	AUTO
CAST-14404E	114	4	1590	35		NA/NA	AUTO
CAST-14404S	114	4	1590	35		NA/NA	AUTO
CAST-14405E	140	5	1590	35		NA/NA	AUTO
CAST-14405S	140	5	1590	35		NA/NA	AUTO
CAST-14406E	170	6	1590	35		NA/NA	AUTO
CAST-14406S	170	6	1590	35		NA/NA	AUTO
CAST-24509E	258	9	1599	35		NA/NA	AUTO
CAST-24509S	258	9	1599	35		NA/NA	AUTO
CAST-24611E	315	11	1599	35		NA/NA	AUTO
CAST-24611S	315	11	1599	35		NA/NA	AUTO
CAST-24713E	372	13	1599	35		NA/NA	AUTO
CAST-24713S	372	13	1599	35		NA/NA	AUTO

CMI

Drive Model	Format Size MB	Head	Cyl	Sect/ Trac	Translate H/C/S	RWC/ WPC	Land Zone
CM3412	10	4	306	17		306/256	
CM3426	20	4	615	17		616/256	
CM5018H	15	2		17		---/---	
CM5205	4	2	256	17		128/128	
CM5206	5	2	306	17		307/128	
CM5410	8	4	256	17		128/128	
CM5412	10	4	306	17		307/128	
CM5616	14	6	256	17		257/257	
CM5619	16	6	306	17		307/128	
CM5826	20	8	306	17		---/---	
CM6213	11	2	640	17		641/256	
CM6426	22	4	615	17		---/300	615
CM6426S	22	4	615	17		256/300	615
CM6640	33	6	615	17		616/300	615
CM7000	44	7	733	17		733/512	
CM7030	25	4	733	17		733/512	
CM7038	31	5	733	17		733/512	
CM7053	44	7	733	17		733/512	
CM7085	71	8	1024	17		1024/512	
CM7660	50	6	960	17		961/450	
CM7880	67	8	960	17		961/450	

CMS ENHANCEMENTS, INC

Drive Model	Format Size MB	Head	Cyl	Sect/ Trac	Translate H/C/S	RWC/ WPC	Land Zone
B1.0A1-U1	1281				16/2100/63	NA/NA	AUTO
B340A4-U1	340				12/1010/55	NA/NA	AUTO
B420A4-U1	425				16/1010/51	NA/NA	AUTO
B540A4-U1	541				16/1023/63	NA/NA	AUTO
B730A4-U1	731				16/1416/63	NA/NA	AUTO
D20XT-OK	21	4	615	17		---/---	
D30XT-OK	32	4	615	26		---/---	
D40XT-OK	42	5	977	17		---/---	
F115ESD1-T	115	7	915	35		---/---	AUTO
F150AT-CA	150	9	969	34		---/---	
F150AT-WCA	151	9	969	34		---/---	AUTO
F150EQ-WCA	151	9	969	34		---/---	AUTO
F320AT-CA	320	15	1224	34		---/---	AUTO
F70ESDI-T	73	7	583	35		---/---	AUTO
H100286D-P	105	8	776	34		---/---	
H100386S-P	105	8	776	34		---/---	
H330E1 (PS Express)	330	7	1780	54		---/---	AUTO
H340E1 (PS Express)	340	7	1780	54		---/---	AUTO
H40M50-P	42	5	977	17		---/---	
H60286D-P	64	7	948	27		---/---	
H60SCSI-S	65	6	628	34		---/---	
H65M50-P	65	9	1024	17		---/---	
H80AT	84	9	1072	17		---/---	

Drive Model	Seek Time	Interface	Encode	Form Factor	cache kb	Obsolete? mtbf	RPM ↓
CAST-10305E	28	ESDI	2,7 RLL	5.25 FH			
CAST-10305S	28	SCSI	2,7 RLL	5.25 HH			
CAST-14404E	25	ESDI	2,7 RLL	5.25 HH			
CAST-14404S	25	SCSI	2,7 RLL	5.25 HH			
CAST-14405E	25	ESDI	2,7 RLL	5.25 HH			
CAST-14405S	25	SCSI	2,7 RLL	5.25 HH			
CAST-14406E	25	ESDI	2,7 RLL	5.25 HH			
CAST-14406S	25	SCSI	2,7 RLL	5.25 HH			
CAST-24509E	18	ESDI	2,7 RLL	5.25 FH			
CAST-24509S	18	SCSI	2,7 RLL	5.25 FH			
CAST-24611E	18	ESDI	2,7 RLL	5.25 FH			
CAST-24611S	18	SCSI	2,7 RLL	5.25 FH			
CAST-24713E	18	ESDI	2,7 RLL	5.25 FH			
CAST-24713S	18	SCSI	2,7 RLL	5.25 FH			

CMI

Drive Model	Seek Time	Interface	Encode	Form Factor	cache kb	Obsolete? mtbf	RPM
CM3412		ST412/506	MFM	5.25 FH			Y
CM3426	85	ST412/506	MFM	5.25 FH			Y
CM5018H	85	ST412/506	MFM	5.25 FH			Y
CM5205		ST412/506	MFM	5.25 FH			Y
CM5206	102	ST412/506	MFM	5.25 FH			Y
CM5410	102	ST412/506	MFM	5.25 FH			Y
CM5412	85	ST412/506	MFM	5.25 FH			Y
CM5616	102	ST412/506	MFM	5.25 FH			Y
CM5619	85	ST412/506	MFM	5.25 FH			Y
CM5826	102	ST412/506	MFM	5.25 FH			Y
CM6213	48	ST412/506	MFM	5.25 FH			Y
CM6426	39	ST412/506	MFM	5.25 FH			Y
CM6426S	39	ST412/506	MFM	5.25 FH			Y
CM6640	39	ST412/506	MFM	5.25 FH			Y
CM7000	42	ST412/506	MFM	5.25 FH			Y
CM7030	42	ST412/506	MFM	5.25 FH			Y
CM7038	42	ST412/506	MFM	5.25 FH			Y
CM7053	42	ST412/506	MFM	5.25 FH			Y
CM7085	42	ST412/506	MFM	5.25 FH			Y
CM7660	28	ST412/506	MFM	5.25 FH			Y
CM7880	28	ST412/506	MFM	5.25 FH			Y

CMS ENHANCEMENTS, INC

Drive Model	Seek Time	Interface	Encode	Form Factor	cache kb	mtbf	Obsolete? RPM
B1.0A1-U1	10	IDE AT		3.5 3H	250k	4500	Y
B340A4-U1	13	IDE AT		3.5 3H	250k	3600	
B420A4-U1	13	IDE AT		3.5 3H	250k	3300	
B540A4-U1	14	IDE AT		3.5 3H	300k	3600	
B730A4-U1	11	IDE AT		3.5 3H	300k	4500	
D20XT-OK	62	ST412/506	MFM	3.5 HH			Y
D30XT-OK	62	ST412/506	2,7 RLL	3.5 HH			Y
D40XT-OK	24	ST412/506	MFM	3.5 HH			Y
F115ESD1-T	30	ESDI	2,7 RLL	5.25 FH	25k		Y
F150AT-CA	17	ESDI	2,7 RLL	5.25 FH	40k		Y
F150AT-WCA	17	ESDI	2,7 RLL	5.25 FH	40k		Y
F150EQ-WCA	17	ESDI	2,7 RLL	5.25 FH	40k		Y
F320AT-CA	18	ESDI	2,7 RLL	5.25 FH	40k		Y
F70ESDI-T	30	ESDI	2,7 RLL	5.25 FH	25k		Y
H100286D-P	25	IDE AT		5.25 HH	20k		Y
H100386S-P	25	IDE AT		5.25 HH	20k		Y
H330E1 (PS Express)	14	ESDI		5.25 HH	150k		
H340E1 (PS Express)	14	ESDI	2,7 RLL	5.25 HH	150k		
H40M50-P	24	ST412/506	MFM	3.5 HH	45k		Y
H60286D-P	29	IDE AT		5.25 HH	40k		Y
H60SCSI-S	28	SCSI		5.25 HH	40k		Y
H65M50-P	15	ST412/506	MFM	3.5 HH	30k		Y
H80AT	15	SCSI		5.25 HH	30k		Y

Drive Model	Format Size MB	Head	Cyl	Sect/ Trac	Translate H/C/S	RWC/ WPC	Land Zone
H80SCSI-S	85	6	820	34		---/---	
HD20AT-S	21	4	615	17		---/---	
HD30AT-S	32	6	615	17		---/---	
HD40AT-S1	43	6	820	17		---/---	
K120M50Z-70P	125	8	925	33		---/---	
K20M25-WS	21	2	636	34		---/---	
K20M25/30-OK	21	4	615	17		---/---	
K20M25/30-WS	21	4	615	17		---/---	
K30M25/30-OK	32	6	615	17		---/---	
K30M25/30-WS	32	6	615	17		---/---	
K30M30E-P	31	4	615	25		---/---	
K40M25/30-WS	42	5	977	17		---/---	
K45M30286-ZS	48	6	615	26		---/---	
K50M50Z/70P	63	6	767	27		---/---	
K60M30286-ZS	61	5	921	26		---/---	
K80M25Z/30	84	9	1072	17		---/---	
K80M30286-WS	84	7	906	26		---/---	
LDSNECMS-20	20	4	575	32		---/---	
LDZE386-100	100	8	776	34		---/---	
PB340	340					NA/NA	AUTO
PB520	520					NA/NA	AUTO
PSEXPRESS 150	150					---/---	AUTO
PSEXPRESS 320	320					---/---	AUTO
SENTRY 180	180	5	1546			---/---	
SENTRY 300	290	9	1546			---/---	
SENTRY 600	600	15	1546			---/---	
SENTRY 90	90	5	1024			---/---	

COGITO

Drive Model	Format Size MB	Head	Cyl	Sect/ Trac	Translate H/C/S	RWC/ WPC	Land Zone
CG906	5	2	306	17		128/128	
CG912	10	4	306	17		128/128	
CG925	21	4	612	17		307/307	
PT912	11	2	612	17		307/307	
PT925	21	4	612	17		307/307	

COMPAQ

Drive Model	Format Size MB	Head	Cyl	Sect/ Trac	Translate H/C/S	RWC/ WPC	Land Zone
113640-001	43	2	1053	40		NA/NA	AUTO
113641-001	112	8	832	33		NA/NA	AUTO
115145-001	84	6	832	33		NA/NA	AUTO
115147-001	325	7	1744	52		NA/NA	AUTO
115158-001	651	15	1631	52		NA/NA	AUTO
115627-001	112	8	832	33		NA/NA	AUTO
115830-001	318	15	1220	34		NA/NA	AUTO
116562-001	123	4	1552	39		NA/NA	AUTO
116565-001	207	8	1336	38		NA/NA	AUTO
122136-001	60	2	1520	39		NA/NA	AUTO
131067-001	510	12	1806	46		NA/NA	AUTO
131362-001	325	7	1744	52		NA/NA	AUTO
142018-001	1049	13	1974	56-96		---/---	
142021-001	2097	18	262668-108			---/---	
146742-001	2097	18	262668-108			---/---	
146742-003	1049	13	1974	56-96		---/---	
146742-005	4293	21	360682-135			---/---	
146742-006	4293	21	360682-135			---/---	
146742-007	2097	11	351186-135			---/---	
172492-002	421	4	251955-104		16/1010/51	---/---	
172493-001	1083	6	381161-117		16/2100/63	---/---	
172678-002	730	4	365864-128		16/1416/63	---/---	
172874-001	541	4	285358-118		9/1926/61	---/---	
196408-002	270	2	285358-118		14/944/40	---/---	
199580-001	4293	21	360682-135			---/---	
199597-001	4293	21	360682-135			---/---	

Drive Model	Seek Time	Interface	Encode	Form Factor	cache kb	mtbf	RPM	Obsolete?
H80SCSI-S	28	SCSI		5.25 HH		45k		Y
HD20AT-S	65	ST412/506	MFM	5.25 HH		50k		Y
HD30AT-S	40	ST412/506	MFM	5.25 HH		50k		Y
HD40AT-S1	28	ST412/506	MFM	5.25 HH		50k		Y
K120M50Z-70P	23	MCA	2,7 RLL	3.5 HH				Y
K20M25-WS	27	IDE AT		3.5 HH		20k		Y
K20M25/30-OK	62	ST412/506	MFM	3.5 HH		20k		Y
K20M25/30-WS	40	ST412/506	MFM	3.5 HH		20k		Y
K30M25/30-OK	62	ST412/506	MFM	3.5 HH		50k		Y
K30M25/30-WS	40	ST412/506	MFM	3.5 HH		50k		Y
K30M30E-P	39	IDE AT		3.5 HH		25k		Y
K40M25/30-WS	28	ST412/506	MFM	3.5 HH		45k		Y
K45M30286-ZS	28	SCSI		3.5 HH		45k		Y
K50M50Z/70P	27	MCA	2,7 RLL	3.5 HH				Y
K60M30286-ZS	24	SCSI		3.5 HH		40k		Y
K80M25Z/30	15	ST412/506	MFM	3.5 HH				Y
K80M30286-WS	24	SCSI		3.5 HH		40k		Y
LDSNECMS-20	28	IDE AT	2,7 RLL	3.5 HH		20k		Y
LDZE386-100	25	IDE AT		3.5 HH		20k		Y
PB340	12	SCSI-2	1,6 RLL		128k	150k	4200	
PB520	17	SCSI-2	1,7 RLL		128k	350k	4500	
PSEXPRESS 150	17	ESDI	2,7 RLL	5.25 FH		40k		
PSEXPRESS 320	17	ESDI	2,7 RLL	5.25 FH		40k		
SENTRY 180	18	SCSI		5.25 FH		40k		
SENTRY 300	16.5	SCSI		5.25 FH		40k		Y
SENTRY 600	16	SCSI		5.25 FH		30k		Y
SENTRY 90	18	SCSI		5.25 FH		30k		Y

COGITO

Drive Model	Seek Time	Interface	Encode	Form Factor	cache kb	mtbf	RPM	Obsolete?
CG906	93	ST412/506	MFM	5.25 HH				Y
CG912	93	ST412/506	MFM	5.25 HH				Y
CG925	93	ST412/506	MFM	5.25 HH				Y
PT912	93	ST412/506	MFM	5.25 HH				Y
PT925	93	ST412/506	MFM	5.25 HH				Y

COMPAQ

Drive Model	Seek Time	Interface	Encode	Form Factor	cache kb	mtbf	RPM	Obsolete?
113640-001	29			3.5 HH		40k		
113641-001	25			3.5 HH		40k		
115145-001	25			3.5 HH		40k		
115147-001	19	ESDI		5.25 HH		60k		
115158-001	19	ESDI		5.25 FH		40k		
115627-001	25			3.5 HH		40k		
115830-001	18	ESDI		5.25 FH		40k		
116562-001	19			3.5 HH		40k		
116565-001	19			3.5 HH		40k		
122136-001	19			3.5 HH		40k		
131067-001	2			3.5 HH		150k		
131362-001	18	ESDI		5.25 HH		60k		
142018-001	10	SCSI-2 FAST		3.5 HH			5400	
142216-001	9	SCSI-2 FAST		3.5 HH			6400	
146742-001	9	SCSI-2 FAST		3.5 HH			6400	
146742-003	10	SCSI-2 FAST		3.5 HH			5400	
146742-005	9	SCSI-2 FSTW		3.5 HH			7200	
146742-006	9	SCSI-2 FSTW		3.5 HH			7200	
172492-002	14	IDE AT		3.5 3H	96k		3600	
172493-001	14	IDE AT		3.5 3H	128k		4495	
172678-002	11	IDE AT		3.5 3H	96k		4500	
172874-001	14	IDE AT		3.5 3H	96k		3600	
196408-002	14	IDE AT		3.5 3H	96k		3600	Y
199580-001	9	SCSI-2 FAST		3.5 HH			7200	
199597-001	9	SCSI-2 FSTW		3.5 HH			7200	

Drive Model	Format Size MB	Head	Cyl	Sect/Trac	Translate H/C/S	RWC/WPC	Land Zone
199642-001	2097	11	351186-135			---/---	

COMPORT

2040	44	4	820	26		---/---	
2041	44	4	820	26		---/---	
2082	86	6	820	34		---/---	

CONNER PERIPHERALS, INC.

Drive Model	Format Size MB	Head	Cyl	Sect/Trac	Translate H/C/S	RWC/WPC	Land Zone
CFA1080A	1080	8		72-114		---/---	
CFA1080S	1080	8		72-114		---/---	
CFA1275A	1278	6			16/2479/63	---/---	
CFA1275S	1278	6				---/---	
CFA170A	172	2	2111	V		AUTO/AUTO	NA
CFA170S	172	2	2111	67-91		---/---	
CFA2161A	2110	16	4095	63		---/---	
CFA270A	270	2		72-114		---/---	
CFA270S	270	2		72-114		---/---	
CFA340A	343	4		67-91		NA/NA	AUTO
CFA340S	343	4		67-91		NA/NA	AUTO
CFA540A	541	4		72-114		---/---	
CFA540S	541	4		72-114		---/---	
CFA810A	810	6		72-114		---/---	
CFA810S	810	6		72-114		---/---	
CFA850A	852	4				---/---	
CFA850S	852	4				---/---	
CFL350A	350	4	2225		12/905/63	---/---	
CFL420A	422	4	2393	V	16/818/63	---/---	
CFN170A	168	4		47-72		---/---	
CFN170S	168	4		47-72		---/---	
CFN250A	252	6		47-72		16/489/63	
CFN250S	252	6		47-72		---/---	
CFN340A	344	6		53-89		16/667/63	
CFN340S	344	6		53-89		---/---	
CFP1060D	1062	8				---/---	
CFP1060E	1062	8				---/---	
CFP1060S	1062	8				---/---	
CFP1060W	1062	8				---/---	
CFP1080E	1080	6		365866-120		---/---	
CFP1080S	1080	6		365866-120		---/---	
CFP2105E	2147	10		394867-139		---/---	
CFP2105S	2147	10		394867-139		---/---	
CFP2105W	2147	10		394867-139		---/---	
CFP2107E	2147	10		401669-124		---/---	
CFP2107S	2147	10		401669-124		---/---	
CFP2107W	2147	10		401669-124		---/---	
CFP4207E	4294	20		401669-124		---/---	
CFP4207S	4294	20		401669-124		---/---	
CFP4207W	4294	20		401669-124		---/---	
CFP4217C (FILEPRO)	4294		6028			NA/NA	AUTO
CFP4217E (FILEPRO)	4294		6028			NA/NA	AUTO
CFP4217S (FILEPRO)	4294		6028			NA/NA	AUTO
CFP4217W (FILEPRO)	4294		6028			NA/NA	AUTO
CFP4217WD (FILEPRO)	4294		6028			NA/NA	AUTO
CFP9117C (FILEPRO)	9100		6028			NA/NA	AUTO
CFP9117E (FILEPRO)	9100		6028			NA/NA	AUTO
CFP9117S (FILEPRO)	9100		6028			NA/NA	AUTO
CFP9117W (FILEPRO)	9100		6028			NA/NA	AUTO
CFP9117WD (FILEPRO)	9100		6028			NA/NA	AUTO
CFS1060A	1060	16	2064	63		---/---	
CFS1081A	1080	4	3930			---/---	
CFS1275A	1275	6	3640		16/2479/63	---/---	
CFS1276A	1275		4893			NA/NA	AUTO

Drive Model	Seek Time	Interface	Encode	Form Factor	cache kb	mtbf	Obsolete? RPM
199642-001	9	SCSI-2 FSTW		3.5 HH			7200

COMPORT

2040	35	ST412/506	2,7 RLL	5.25 HH		30k	
2041	29	IDE AT		5.25 HH		30k	
2082	29	SCSI		5.25 HH		30k	

CONNER PERIPHERALS, INC.

Drive Model	Seek Time	Interface	Encode	Form Factor	cache kb	mtbf	RPM	Obsolete?
CFA1080A	12	IDE AT	1,7 RLL	3.5 3H	256k	300k	4500	
CFA1080S	12	SCSI-2 FAST	1,7 RLL	3.5 3H	256k	300k	4500	
CFA1275A	12	EIDE	1,7 RLL	3.5 3H	256k	300k	4500	
CFA1275S	12	SCSI-2	1,7 RLL	3.5 3H	256k	300k	4500	
CFA170A	13	IDE	1,7 RLL	3.5 3H	64k	250k		Y
CFA170S	13	IDE AT	1,7 RLL	3.5 3H	64k	250k	4011	Y
CFA2161A		IDE AT		3.5 3H				
CFA270A	12	IDE AT	1,7 RLL	3.5 3H	256k	250k	4500	Y
CFA270S	12	SCSI-2	1,7 RLL	3.5 3H	256k	250k	4500	Y
CFA340A	13	IDE AT	1,7 RLL	3.5 3H	64k	300k	4011	Y
CFA340S	13	SCSI-2	1,7 RLL	3.5 3H	64k	300k	4011	Y
CFA540A	12	IDE AT	1,7 RLL	3.5 3H	256k	300k	4500	
CFA540S	12	SCSI-2 FAST	1,7 RLL	3.5 3H	256k	300k	4500	
CFA810A	12	IDE AT	1,7 RLL	3.5 3H	256k	300k	4500	
CFA810S	12	SCSI-2 FAST	1,7 RLL	3.5 3H	256k	300k	4500	Y
CFA850A	12	IDE AT	1,7 RLL	3.5 3H	256k	300k	4500	Y
CFA850S	12	SCSI-2	1,7 RLL	3.5 3H	256k	300k	4500	Y
CFL350A	12	IDE AT	1,7 RLL	2.5 4H	32k	300k	3750	
CFL420A	12	IDE AT	1,7 RLL	2.5 4H	64k	300k	3600	Y
CFN170A	12	IDE AT	1,7 RLL	2.5 4H	32k	150k	4500	Y
CFN170S	12	SCSI	1,7 RLL	2.5 4H	32k	150k	4500	Y
CFN250A	12	IDE AT	1,7 RLL	2.5 4H	32k	150k	4500	
CFN250S	12	SCSI	1,7 RLL	2.5 4H	32k	150k	4500	
CFN340A	13	IDE AT	1,7 RLL	2.5 4H	32k	150k	4000	
CFN340S	13	SCSI	1,7 RLL	2.5 4H	32k	150k	4000	
CFP1060D	9	SCSI-2 FAST	1,7 RLL	3.5 3H	512k	500k	5400	
CFP1060E	9	SCSI	1,7 RLL	3.5 3H	512k	500k	5400	
CFP1060S	9	SCSI-2 FAST	1,7 RLL	3.5 3H	512k	500k	5400	
CFP1060W	9	SCSI-2 FSTW	1,7 RLL	3.5 3H	512k	500k	5400	
CFP1080E	11	SCSI-2 FSTW	1,7 RLL	3.5 3H	512k	1000k	5400	
CFP1080S	11	SCSI-2 FSTW	1,7 RLL	3.5 3H	256k	1000k	5400	
CFP2105E	9	SCSI-2 FSTW	1,7 RLL	3.5 3H	512k	1000k	5400	
CFP2105S	9	SCSI-2 FSTW	1,7 RLL	3.5 3H	512k	1000k	5400	
CFP2105W	9	SCSI-2 FSTW	1,7 RLL	3.5 3H	512k	1000k	5400	
CFP2107E	9	SCSI-2 FSTW	1,7 RLL	3.5 3H	512k	1000k	7200	
CFP2107S	9	SCSI-2 FSTW	1,7 RLL	3.5 3H	512k	1000k	7200	
CFP2107W	9	SCSI-2 FSTW	1,7 RLL	3.5 3H	512k	1000k	7200	
CFP4207E	9.5	SCSI-2 FAST	1,7 RLL	3.5 HH	512k	1000k	7200	
CFP4207S	9.5	SCSI-2 FAST	1,7 RLL	3.5 HH	512k	1000k	7200	
CFP4207W	9.5	SCSI-2 FSTW	1,7 RLL	3.5 HH	512k	1000k	7200	
CFP4217C (FILEPRO)	9	SSA		3.5 HH	512k	999k	7200	
CFP4217E (FILEPRO)	9	SCA		3.5 HH	512k	999k	7200	
CFP4217S (FILEPRO)	9	SCSI-3		3.5 HH	512k	999k	7200	
CFP4217W (FILEPRO)	9	SCSI-3Wide		3.5 HH	512k	999k	7200	
CFP4217WD (FILEPRO)	9	SCSI-3Wide		3.5 HH	512k	999k	7200	
CFP9117C (FILEPRO)	9	SSA	RLL 8,9	3.5 HH	512k	999k	7200	
CFP9117E (FILEPRO)	9	SCA	RLL 8,9	3.5 HH	512k	999k	7200	
CFP9117S (FILEPRO)	9	SCSI-3	RLL 8,9	3.5 HH	512k	999k	7200	
CFP9117W (FILEPRO)	9	SCSI-3Wide	RLL 8,9	3.5 HH	512k	999k	7200	
CFP9117WD (FILEPRO)	9	SCSI-3Wide	RLL 8,9	3.5 HH	512k	999k	7200	
CFS1060A		IDE AT		3.5 3H				
CFS1081A	14	IDE AT	1,7 RLL	3.5 3H	64k	300k	3600	
CFS1275A	14	IDE	1,7 RLL	3.5 3H	64k	250k	3600	
CFS1276A	14	ATA-2	1,7 RLL	3.5 3H	64k	300k	4500	

Drive Model	Format Size MB	Head	Cyl	Sect/ Trac	Translate H/C/S	RWC/ WPC	Land Zone
CFS1621A	1620	6	3930			--/--	
CFS2105S	2147	10	3948			--/--	
CFS210A	213	2		68-107		--/--	
CFS270A	270	2	2595		16/525/63	--/--	
CFS420A	426	4		68-107		--/--	
CFS425A	425	2	3687		16/826/63	--/--	
CFS540A	540	4	3517		16/1050/63	--/--	
CFS541A	540	2	3924			--/--	
CFS635A	635	3	3640			--/--	
CFS636A	635	2	4893			--/--	
CFS850A	850	4	3640		16/1652/63	--/--	
CP1044 (DERRINGER)	42.6	2				NA/NA	AUTO
CP2020 (KATO)	21	2	653	32		NA/NA	AUTO
CP2022	20	2	653	32	4/615/17	NA/NA	AUTO
CP2024 (KATO)	21	2	653	32	4/615/17	NA/NA	AUTO
CP2027	20	2				NA/NA	
CP2031	30	2			4/411/38	NA/NA	AUTO
CP2034 (PANCHO)	32	2	823	38	4/615/17	NA/NA	AUTO
CP2040	43	4	548	38		NA/NA	AUTO
CP2044 (PANCHO)	42	4	552	38	5/977/17	NA/NA	AUTO
CP2045	40	2				NA/NA	
CP2048 (PANCHO)					4/548/38	NA/NA	AUTO
CP2060	64	4	823	38		NA/NA	AUTO
CP2061	60	2				--/--	
CP2064 (PANCHO)	64	4	823	38	4/615/17	NA/NA	AUTO
CP2067	60	2				--/--	
CP2081	80	2				--/--	
CP2084 (PANCHO)	85	4	1096	38	8/548/38	NA/NA	AUTO
CP2088	85	4		38	8/548/38	NA/NA	AUTO
CP2124 (PANCHO)	120	4	1123	53	*UNIV T	NA/NA	AUTO
CP2250	253					NA/NA	
CP2254 (TRIGGER)	253					NA/NA	
CP2304	209	8	1348	39	*UNIV T	NA/NA	AUTO
CP3000	42	2	1045	40	5/980/17	NA/NA	AUTO
CP30060	60	2	1524	39		NA/NA	AUTO
CP30061	60					--/--	
CP30064 (HOPI)	60	2	1524	39	4/762/39	NA/NA	AUTO
CP30064H (HOPI)	60	2	1524	39	4/762/39	NA/NA	AUTO
CP30069 (HOPI)	60	2	1524	39		NA/NA	AUTO
CP30080 (HOPI)	84	4	1053	39		NA/NA	AUTO
CP30080E (JAGUAR)	85	2	1806	46		NA/NA	AUTO
CP30081	85	4	1058	39	8/526/39	NA/NA	AUTO
CP30084 (HOPI)	84	4	1053	39	8/526/39	NA/NA	AUTO
CP30084E (JAGUAR)	85	2	1806	46	4/903/46	NA/NA	AUTO
CP30100 (HOPI)	120	4	1522	39		NA/NA	AUTO
CP30101	122	4	1524	9	8/762/39	--/--	761
CP30101 (HOPI)	121	8	761	39	*UNIV T	NA/NA	AUTO
CP30101G	122	4	1524	9	8/762/39	--/--	761
CP30104 (HOPI)	121	4	1524	39	8/762/39	NA/NA	AUTO
CP30104H (HOPI)	121	4	1524	39	8/762/39	NA/NA	AUTO
CP30109 (HOPI)	120	4	1522	39		NA/NA	AUTO
CP30124	126	2		62	5/895/55	--/--	
CP30170	172	4	2111	67-91		--/--	
CP30170E (JAGUAR)	170	4	1806	46		NA/NA	AUTO
CP30174	172	4	2111	67-91		--/--	
CP30174E (JAGUAR)	170	4	1806	46	8/903/46	NA/NA	AUTO
CP3020	21	2	636	33		NA/NA	AUTO
CP30200 (COUGAR)	212	4	2124	49		NA/NA	AUTO
CP30201	212					--/--	
CP30204 (COUGAR)	212	4		49	16/683/38	NA/NA	
CP3022	21	2	636	33	4/615/17	NA/NA	AUTO
CP3023	21	2				--/--	
CP3024	22	2	636	33	4/615/17	NA/NA	AUTO

Drive Model	Seek Time	Interface	Encode	Form Factor	cache kb	mtbf	RPM	Obsolete?
CFS1621A	14	IDE AT	1,7 RLL	3.5 3H	64k	300k	3600	
CFS2105S	9	SCSI-2 FAST	1,7 RLL	3.5 3H	512k	1000k	5400	
CFS210A	14	IDE AT	1,7 RLL	3.5 3H	32k	250k	3600	Y
CFS270A	14	IDE	1,7 RLL	3.5 3H	32k	250k	3400	Y
CFS420A	14	IDE AT	1,7 RLL	3.5 3H	32k	250k	3600	
CFS425A	14	IDE	1,7 RLL	3.5 3H	64k	250k	3600	
CFS540A	14	IDE	1,7 RLL	3.5 3H	64k	250k	3600	
CFS541A	14	IDE AT	1,7 RLL	3.5 3H	64k	300k	3600	
CFS635A	14	IDE AT	1,7 RLL	3.5 3H	64k	300k	3600	
CFS636A	14	ATA-2	1,7 RLL	3.5 3H	64k	300k	4500	
CFS850A	14	IDE	1,7 RLL	3.5 3H	64k	250k	3600	
CP1044 (DERRINGER)	19			2.5 4H	32k			Y
CP2020 (KATO)	23	SCSI	2,7 RLL	2.5 4H	8k	100k		Y
CP2022	23	IDE AT	2,7 RLL	3.5 HH				Y
CP2024 (KATO)	23	IDE AT	2,7 RLL	2.5 4H	8k	100k	3433	Y
CP2027		IDE AT	2,7 RLL	2.5 4H				Y
CP2031	19	ATA	2,7 RLL	2.5 4H	32k	100k		Y
CP2034 (PANCHO)	19	IDE AT	2,7 RLL	2.5 4H	32k	100k	3433	Y
CP2040	17	SCSI	2,7 RLL	2.5 4H	32k	50k	3486	Y
CP2044 (PANCHO)	19	IDE AT	2,7 RLL	2.5 4H	32k	100k	3486	Y
CP2045		SCSI	2,7 RLL	2.5 4H				Y
CP2048 (PANCHO)	19	ATA	2,7 RLL	2.5 4H	32k	100k	3486	Y
CP2060	19	SCSI	2,7 RLL	2.5 4H	32k	50k	3486	Y
CP2061		IDE AT	2,7 RLL	2.5 4H				Y
CP2064 (PANCHO)	19	IDE AT	2,7 RLL	2.5 4H	32k	100k	3486	Y
CP2067		IDE AT	2,7 RLL	2.5 4H				Y
CP2081		IDE AT	2,7 RLL	2.5 4H				Y
CP2084 (PANCHO)	19	IDE AT	1,7 RLL	2.5 4H	32k	150k	3486	Y
CP2088	19	IDE AT	1,7 RLL	2.5 4H	32k	150k	3486	Y
CP2124 (PANCHO)	26	IDE AT	1,7 RLL	2.5 4H	32k	100k		Y
CP2250	12	SCSI		2.5 4H	32k			Y
CP2254 (TRIGGER)	12	ATA		2.5 4H	32k			Y
CP2304	19	IDE AT	RLL	3.5 HH				Y
CP3000	28	IDE AT	2,7 RLL	3.5 3H	8k	150k	3557	Y
CP30060	19	SCSI	1,7 RLL	3.5 3H		150k		Y
CP30061		IDE AT	1,7 RLL	3.5 3H				Y
CP30064 (HOPI)	19	IDE AT	1,7 RLL	3.5 3H	64k	100k	3400	Y
CP30064H (HOPI)	19	IDE AT	1,7 RLL	3.5 3H	32k	150k	3400	Y
CP30069 (HOPI)	19	MCA	1,7 RLL	3.5 3H	64k	100k	3399	Y
CP30080 (HOPI)	19	SCSI	1,7 RLL	3.5 3H	64k	100k	3400	Y
CP30080E (JAGUAR)	17	SCSI	1,7 RLL	3.5 3H	32k	150k	3822	Y
CP30081		IDE AT	2,7 RLL	3.5 4H		150k		Y
CP30084 (HOPI)	19	IDE AT	1,7 RLL	3.5 3H	64k	100k	3400	Y
CP30084E (JAGUAR)	17	IDE AT	1,7 RLL	3.5 3H	32k	150k	3822	Y
CP30100 (HOPI)	19	SCSI	2,7 RLL	3.5 3H	64k	150k	3400	Y
CP30101	19	IDE AT	2,7 RLL	3.5 3H				Y
CP30101 (HOPI)	10	IDE AT	2,7 RLL	3.5 3H				Y
CP30101G		IDE AT	2,7 RLL	3.5 3H				Y
CP30104 (HOPI)	19	IDE AT	1,7 RLL	3.5 3H	32k	100k	3400	Y
CP30104H (HOPI)	19	IDE AT	1,7 RLL	3.5 3H	32k	150k	3400	Y
CP30109 (HOPI)	19	MCA	2,7 RLL	3.5 3H	64k	150k	3400	Y
CP30124	14	IDE AT	1,7 RLL	3.5 3H	32k	250k	4542	Y
CP30170	13	SCSI-2	1,7 RLL	3.5 3H	64k	250k	4011	Y
CP30170E (JAGUAR)	17	SCSI	1,7 RLL	3.5 3H	32k	150k	3833	Y
CP30174	13	IDE AT	1,7 RLL	3.5 3H	64k	250k	4011	Y
CP30174E (JAGUAR)	17	IDE AT	1,7 RLL	3.5 3H	32k	150k	3833	Y
CP3020	27	SCSI	2,7 RLL	3.5 3H	8k	50k	3575	Y
CP30200 (COUGAR)	12	SCSI-2	2,7 RLL	3.5 3H	256k	150k	4500	Y
CP30201		IDE AT	2,7 RLL	3.5 3H				Y
CP30204 (COUGAR)	12	IDE AT	2,7 RLL	3.5 3H	256k	150k	4500	Y
CP3022	27	IDE AT	2,7 RLL	3.5 3H		50k		Y
CP3023		IDE AT	2,7 RLL	3.5 3H				Y
CP3024	27	IDE AT	2,7 RLL	3.5 3H	8k	50k	3575	Y

Drive Model	Format Size MB	Head	Cyl	Sect/ Trac	Translate H/C/S	RWC/ WPC	Land Zone
CP30254	252	4	1985	62	10/895/55	NA/NA	AUTO
CP30340	343	4		67-91		NA/NA	AUTO
CP30344	343	4			16/665/63	NA/NA	AUTO
CP3040	40	2	1026	40		NA/NA	AUTO
CP3041	42	2	1047	40	5/977/17	NA/NA	AUTO
CP3044	42	2	1047	40	5/977/17	NA/NA	AUTO
CP3045	40					---/---	
CP30540	545	6	2243			---/---	
CP30544	545	6	2243		16/989/63	---/---	
CP3100	104	8	776	33		NA/NA	AUTO
CP3101	104					---/---	
CP3102	104	8	776	33	*UNIV T	NA/NA	AUTO
CP3104	104	8	776	33	13/925/17	NA/NA	AUTO
CP3106	104					---/---	
CP3111	107	8	832	33	*UNIV T	NA/NA	AUTO
CP3114	107	8	832	33	8/832/33	NA/NA	AUTO
CP31370	1372	14	2386			---/---	
CP31374 BAJA	1372	14				NA/NA	AUTO
CP3150	52	4	776	33		NA/NA	AUTO
CP3180	84	6	832	33		NA/NA	AUTO
CP3181	84	6	832	33		NA/NA	AUTO
CP3184	84	6	832	33	9/1024/17	NA/NA	AUTO
CP320	20	2	752	26		NA/NA	AUTO
CP3200	209	8	1366	38		NA/NA	AUTO
CP3200F	212	8	1366	38		NA/NA	AUTO
CP3201I	215	8	1348	39	*UNIV T	NA/NA	AUTO
CP3204	209	8	1366	38	16/683/38	NA/NA	AUTO
CP3204F	212	8	1366	38	16/683/38	NA/NA	AUTO
CP3209F	212	8	1366	38	*UNIV T	NA/NA	AUTO
CP321	20	2	752	26	4/615/17	NA/NA	AUTO
CP323	20	2	752	26	4/615/17	NA/NA	AUTO
CP324	20	2	752	26	4/615/17	NA/NA	AUTO
CP3304 (SUMMIT)	340	8	1806	46	16/659/63	NA/NA	AUTO
CP3360 (SUMMIT)	362	8	1807	49		NA/NA	AUTO
CP3364 (SUMMIT)	362	8	1808	49	16/702/63	NA/NA	AUTO
CP340	42	4	788	26		NA/NA	AUTO
CP341	42	4	805	26	5/977/17	NA/NA	AUTO
CP341I	42	4	805	26	5/977/17	NA/NA	AUTO
CP342	40	4	805	26	4/805/26	NA/NA	AUTO
CP343 (ZENITH)	43	4	805		5/977/17	NA/NA	AUTO
CP344	43	4	805	26	5/977/17	NA/NA	AUTO
CP346	42					---/---	
CP3500 (SUMMIT)	510	12	1806	49		NA/NA	AUTO
CP3501	510	12	1806	46	AUTO/AUTO		NA
CP3504 (SUMMIT)	510	12		48	16/987/63	NA/NA	AUTO
CP3505	510	12	1806	46		NA/NA	AUTO
CP3540 (SUMMIT)	543	12	1807	49		NA/NA	AUTO
CP3544 (SUMMIT)	544	12	1808	49	16/1023/63	NA/NA	AUTO
CP4021	20					---/---	
CP4024 (STUBBY)	21	2	627	34	4/615/17	NA/NA	AUTO
CP4041	42					---/---	
CP4044 (STUBBY)	43	2	1097	38	5/977/17	NA/NA	AUTO
CP4084 (GATOR)	85	2	1806	46		NA/NA	AUTO
CP5500	510	20	2034	50		NA/NA	AUTO

CORE INTERNATIONAL

Drive Model	Format Size MB	Head	Cyl	Sect/ Trac	Translate H/C/S	RWC/ WPC	Land Zone
3SHC230	230	5	1511	V		NA/NA	AUTO
AT115	115	7	968	35		---/---	AUTO
AT145	58	7	968			---/---	
AT150	156	9	968	35		---/---	AUTO
AT20	20	4	615	17		---/---	
AT26	26	3	988	17		---/---	
AT260	260	12	1212	35		---/---	AUTO

Drive Model	Seek Time	Interface	Encode	Form Factor	cache kb	mtbf	RPM	Obsolete?
CP30254	14	IDE AT	1,7 RLL	3.5 3H	64k	250k	4542	Y
CP30340	13	SCSI-2	1,7 RLL	3.5 3H	64k	300k	4011	Y
CP30344	13	ATA		3.5 3H	64k	250k	4500	Y
CP3040	25	SCSI	2,7 RLL	3.5 3H	8k	50k	3557	Y
CP3041	25	IDE AT	2,7 RLL	3.5 3H		50k		Y
CP3044	25	IDE AT	2,7 RLL	3.5 3H	8k	50k	3557	Y
CP3045		IDE AT	2,7 RLL	3.5 3H				Y
CP30540	10	SCSI-2 FAST	1,7 RLL	3.5 3H	256k	250k	5400	
CP30544	10	IDE AT	1,7 RLL	3.5 3H	256k	250k	5400	
CP3100	25	SCSI	2,7 RLL	3.5 HH	32k	50k	3575	Y
CP3101		IDE AT	2,7 RLL	3.5 HH				Y
CP3102	25	IDE AT	2,7 RLL	3.5 HH	16k	50k		Y
CP3104	25	IDE AT	2,7 RLL	3.5 HH	16k	30k	3575	Y
CP3106		IDE AT	2,7 RLL	3.5 HH				Y
CP3111	25	IDE AT	2,7 RLL	3.5 HH	16k	50k		Y
CP3114	25	IDE AT	2,7 RLL	3.5 HH				Y
CP31370	10	SCSI-2 FAST	1,7 RLL	3.5 HH	256k	250k	5400	
CP31374 BAJA	11	ATA		3.5 HH	256k			
CP3150	25	SCSI	2,7 RLL	3.5 HH		50k		Y
CP3180	25	SCSI	2,7 RLL	3.5 HH	32k	50k	3575	Y
CP3181	25	IDE AT	2,7 RLL	3.5 HH		50k		Y
CP3184	25	IDE AT	2,7 RLL	3.5 HH	32k	50k	3575	Y
CP320		SCSI	2,7 RLL	3.5 3H				Y
CP3200	16	SCSI	2,7 RLL	3.5 HH	64k	50k	3485	Y
CP3200F	16	SCSI	2,7 RLL	3.5 HH	64k	50k	3485	Y
CP3201I	19	IDE AT	2,7 RLL	3.5 HH		150k		Y
CP3204	19	IDE AT	2,7 RLL	3.5 HH	64k	50k	3485	Y
CP3204F	16	SCSI	2,7 RLL	3.5 HH	64k	50k	3485	Y
CP3209F	16	IDE AT	2,7 RLL	3.5 HH		50k		Y
CP321		IDE AT	2,7 RLL	3.5 3H				Y
CP323		ZENITH	2,7 RLL	3.5 3H				Y
CP324		IDE AT	2,7 RLL	3.5 3H				Y
CP3304 (SUMMIT)		IDE AT	1,7 RLL	3.5 HH		150k		Y
CP3360 (SUMMIT)	12	SCSI-2	2,7 RLL	3.5 HH	256k	150k	4500	Y
CP3364 (SUMMIT)	12	IDE AT	2,7 RLL	3.5 HH	256k	150k	4498	Y
CP340	29	SCSI	2,7 RLL	3.5 HH	1k	20k	3600	Y
CP341	29	IDE AT	2,7 RLL	3.5 HH				Y
CP341I	29	IDE AT	2,7 RLL	3.5 HH				Y
CP342	29	IDE AT		3.5 HH				Y
CP343 (ZENITH)	29	ZENITH		3.5 HH				Y
CP344	29	IDE AT	2,7 RLL	3.5 HH	8k	20k	3600	Y
CP346		IDE AT	2,7 RLL	3.5 HH				Y
CP3500 (SUMMIT)	12	SCSI	2,7 RLL	3.5 HH	256k	100k	3609	Y
CP3501	12	IDE AT	2,7 RLL	3.5 HH		150k		
CP3504 (SUMMIT)	12	IDE AT	2,7 RLL	3.5 HH	256k	150k	3828	
CP3505	12	IDE AT	2,7 RLL	3.5 HH		150k		
CP3540 (SUMMIT)	12	SCSI-2	2,7 RLL	3.5 HH	256k	150k	4500	Y
CP3544 (SUMMIT)	12	IDE AT	2,7 RLL	3.5 HH	256k	150k	4498	
CP4021		IDE AT	2,7 RLL	3.5 4H				Y
CP4024 (STUBBY)		IDE AT	2,7 RLL	3.5 4H	8k	40k	2913	Y
CP4041		IDE AT	2,7 RLL	3.5 4H				Y
CP4044 (STUBBY)		IDE AT	2,7 RLL	3.5 4H	8k	50k		Y
CP4084 (GATOR)	19	IDE AT	2,7 RLL	3.5 4H				Y
CP5500	12	SCSI-2	RLL		512k	150k	4498	

CORE INTERNATIONAL

Drive Model	Seek Time	Interface	Encode	Form Factor	cache kb	mtbf	RPM	Obsolete?
3SHC230	13	SCSI		3.5 HH		150k		Y
AT115	16	ESDI		5.25 FH		33k	3597	Y
AT145	17	ST412/506	MFM	5.25 FH				Y
AT150	16	ESDI	2,7 RLL	5.25 FH		33k	3597	Y
AT20	20	ST412/506	MFM	5.25 FH		25k		Y
AT26	26	ST412/506	MFM	5.25 HH		25k		Y
AT260	25	ESDI		5.25 FH	32k	25k	3524	Y

Drive Model	Format Size MB	Head	Cyl	Sect/ Trac	Translate H/C/S	RWC/ WPC	Land Zone
AT30	32	5	733	17		---/---	
AT30R	49	5	733	26		---/---	
AT32	32	5	733	17		---/---	
AT32R	49	5	733	26		---/---	
AT40	40	5	924	17		---/---	
AT40F	40	4	564	35		---/---	AUTO
AT40R	62	5	924	26		---/---	
ATPLUS20	21	4	615	17		---/---	
ATPLUS43	43	5	988	17		---/---	
ATPLUS43R	66	5	988	26		---/---	
ATPLUS44	44	7	733	17		---/---	
ATPLUS44R	68	7	733	26		---/---	
ATPLUS56	56	7	924	17		---/---	
ATPLUS63	42	5	988	17		---/---	
ATPLUS63R	65	65	988	26		---/---	
ATPLUS72	73	9	924	17		---/---	
ATPLUS72R	107	9	924	26		---/---	
ATPLUS80	80	9	1024			---/---	
ATPLUS80R	132	9	1024			---/---	
ATPLUS82	82	5	968	35		---/---	AUTO
HC100	101	15	379	35		---/---	AUTO
HC1000	1056	15	1787	77		NA/NA	AUTO
HC1000-20	1056	15	1787	77		---/---	AUTO
HC1000S	1005	16	1918	64		---/---	AUTO
HC150	150	7	1250	35		---/---	AUTO
HC150FH	151	9	969	34		NA/NA	AUTO
HC150S	155	9	969	35		---/---	AUTO
HC175	177	9	1072	35		---/---	AUTO
HC200	200	8			12/986/33	---/---	
HC230	230	5				NA/NA	AUTO
HC25	250					---/---	AUTO
HC260	260	12	1212	35		NA/NA	
HC310	325	7	1747	52		NA/NA	AUTO
HC310S	330	8	1447	56		---/---	AUTO
HC315-20	340	8	1447	57		---/---	AUTO
HC380	376	15	1412	35		---/---	AUTO
HC40	40	4	564	35		NA/NA	AUTO
HC650	658	15	1661	53		---/---	AUTO
HC650S	663	16	1447	56		---/---	AUTO
HC655-20	680	16	1447	57		---/---	AUTO
HC90	91	5	969	35		NA/NA	
MC120	120	8	920	32		NA/NA	AUTO
MC60	60	4	928	32		NA/NA	AUTO
OPTIMA 30	31	5	733	17		---/---	
OPTIMA 30R	48	5	733	26		---/---	
OPTIMA 40	41	5	963	17		---/---	
OPTIMA 40R	64	5	963	26		---/---	
OPTIMA 70	71	9	918	17		---/---	
OPTIMA 70R	109	9	918	17		---/---	
OPTIMA 80	80	9	1024	17		---/---	
OPTIMA 80R	132	9	1024	26		---/---	

DIGITAL EQUIPMENT CORP.

Drive Model	Format Size MB	Head	Cyl	Sect/ Trac	Translate H/C/S	RWC/ WPC	Land Zone
CAPELLA 3055	550					NA/NA	AUTO
CAPELLA 3110	1100					NA/NA	AUTO
CAPELLA 3221	2200					NA/NA	AUTO
DSP2022A	220	5				---/---	
DSP2022S	220	5				---/---	
DSP3053L	535	4	3117			NA/NA	AUTO
DSP3080	852					NA/NA	AUTO
DSP3085	852	14		57		---/---	
DSP3105	1050	14		57		---/---	
DSP3107L	1070	8	3117			NA/NA	AUTO

Drive Model	Seek Time	Interface	Encode	Form Factor	cache kb	mtbf	RPM	Obsolete?
AT30	21	ST412/506	MFM	5.25 FH		50k		Y
AT30R	21	ST412/506	2,7 RLL	5.25 HH		50		Y
AT32	21	ST412/506	MFM	5.25 HH		50k		Y
AT32R	21	ST412/506	2,7 RLL	5.25 HH		50k		Y
AT40	26	ST412/506	MFM	5.25 FH		50k		Y
AT40F	10	ESDI		5.25 FH		33k	3597	Y
AT40R	26	ST412/506	2,7 RLL	5.25 FH		50k		Y
ATPLUS20	26	ST412/506	MFM	5.25 FH		50k		Y
ATPLUS43	26	ST412/506	MFM	5.25 FH		50k		Y
ATPLUS43R	26	ST412/506	2,7 RLL	5.25 FH		50k		Y
ATPLUS44	26	ST412/506	MFM	3.5 HH		50k		Y
ATPLUS44R	26	ST412/506	2,7 RLL	3.5 HH		50k		Y
ATPLUS56	26	ST412/506	MFM	5.25 FH		33k		Y
ATPLUS63	26	ST412/506	MFM	5.25 FH		50k		Y
ATPLUS63R	26	ST412/506	2,7 RLL	5.25 FH		50k		Y
ATPLUS72	26	ST412/506	MFM	5.25 FH		50k		Y
ATPLUS72R	26	ST412/506	2,7 RLL	5.25 FH		50k		Y
ATPLUS80	15	ST412/506	MFM	3.5 HH		50k		Y
ATPLUS80R	15	ST412/506	2,7 RLL	3.5 HH		50k		Y
ATPLUS82	16	ESDI		5.25 FH		33k	3597	Y
HC100	9	ESDI		5.25 FH		50k		Y
HC1000	14	ESDI (24)	2,7 RLL	5.25 FH		150k		Y
HC1000-20	14	ESDI	2,7 RLL	5.25 FH		150k	3600	Y
HC1000S	15	SCSI	2,7 RLL	5.25 FH		150k	4002	Y
HC150	17	ESDI	2,7 RLL	5.25 HH		100k	3600	Y
HC150FH	16	ESDI (10)	2,7 RLL	5.25 FH		100k		Y
HC150S	16.5	SCSI	2,7 RLL	5.25 HH		150k	3597	Y
HC175	14	ESDI	2,7 RLL	5.25 FH		50k		Y
HC200	16	IDE AT		5.25 FH		150k		Y
HC230	13	SCSI		3.5 FH		150k		Y
HC25		ESDI		5.25 FH				Y
HC260	25	ESDI	2,7 RLL	5.25 FH				Y
HC310	18	ESDI	2,7 RLL	5.25 FH		100k	3600	Y
HC310S	16.5	SCSI	2,7 RLL	5.25 FH		150k	4002	Y
HC315-20	17	ESDI	2,7 RLL	5.25 FH		150k	4002	Y
HC380	16	ESDI	2,7 RLL	5.25 FH		50k		Y
HC40	9	ESDI	2,7 RLL	5.25 FH		50		Y
HC650	17	ESDI	2,7 RLL	5.25 FH		100k	3600	Y
HC650S	16.5	SCSI	2,7 RLL	5.25 FH		150k	4002	Y
HC655-20	17	ESDI	2,7 RLL	5.25 FH		150k	4002	Y
HC90	16	ESDI	2,7 RLL	5.25 FH		50k		Y
MC120	23	MCA		3.5 HH		45k	3600	Y
MC60	23	MCA		3.5 HH		45k	3600	Y
OPTIMA 30	21	ST412/506	MFM	5.25 FH				Y
OPTIMA 30R	21	ST412/506	2,7 RLL	5.25 FH				Y
OPTIMA 40	26	ST412/506	MFM	5.25 FH		35k		Y
OPTIMA 40R	26	ST412/506	2,7 RLL	5.25 FH		35k		Y
OPTIMA 70	26	ST412/506	MFM	5.25 FH		35k		Y
OPTIMA 70R	26	ST412/506	2,7 RLL	5.25 FH		35k		Y
OPTIMA 80	15	ST412/506	MFM	3.5 HH		35k		Y
OPTIMA 80R	15	ST412/506	2,7 RLL	3.5 HH		35k		Y

DIGITAL EQUIPMENT CORP.

Drive Model	Seek Time	Interface	Encode	Form Factor	cache kb	mtbf	RPM	Obsolete?
CAPELLA 3055	9	SCSI-2Fast		3H		700k	5400	
CAPELLA 3110	9	SCSI-2Fast		3H		700k	5400	
CAPELLA 3221	9	SCSI-2Fast		3H		700k	5400	
DSP2022A		IDE AT	1,7 RLL	2.5 4H	512k	250k	5400	
DSP2022S		SCSI-2 FAST	1,7 RLL	2.5 4H	512k	250k	5400	
DSP3053L	9.5	SCSI-2 FAST	1,7 RLL	3.5 3H	512k	500k	5400	
DSP3080	10	SCSI-2		3H	512k		5400	
DSP3085	9	SCSI-2 FAST	1,7 RLL	3.5 3H	512k	250k	5400	
DSP3105	9	SCSI-2 FAST	1,7 RLL	3.5 3H	512k	250k	5400	
DSP3107L	9.5	SCSI-2Diff	1,7 RLL	3.5 3H	512	500k	5400	

Drive Model	Format Size MB	Head	Cyl	Sect/ Trac	Translate H/C/S	RWC/ WPC	Land Zone
DSP3133L	1337	10	3117			NA/NA	AUTO
DSP3160	1600	16				---/---	
DSP3210	2148	16				NA/NA	AUTO
DSP5200	2000	21				---/---	
DSP5300	3000	21				NA/NA	AUTO
DSP5350	3572	25				---/---	
DSP5400	4000	26				NA/NA	AUTO
DSRZ1BB-VW	2100					---/---	
DSRZ1CB-VW	4300					---/---	
DSRZ1DB-VW	9100					---/---	
DSRZ26N-VZ	1050					---/---	
DSRZ28L-VA	2100					---/---	
DSRZ28M-VZ	2100					---/---	
DSRZ29L-VA	4300					---/---	
DSRZ40-VA	9100					---/---	
RZ26N-VA	1050					---/---	
RZ26N-VW	1050					---/---	
RZ28D-VA	2100					---/---	
RZ28D-VW	2100					---/---	
RZ28M-VA	2100					---/---	
RZ28M-VW	2100					---/---	
RZ29B-VA	4300					---/---	
RZ29B-VW	4300					---/---	

DISC TEC

Drive Model	Format Size MB	Head	Cyl	Sect/ Trac	Translate H/C/S	RWC/ WPC	Land Zone
RHD 260	260					---/---	
RHD 340	340					---/---	
RHD 520	520					---/---	
RHD-120	130					NA/NA	AUTO
RHD-180	183					NA/NA	AUTO
RHD-20 (Removable)	21	2	615	34		NA/NA	AUTO
RHD-210	210					NA/NA	AUTO
RHD-60	62	2	1024	60		NA/NA	AUTO
RHD-80	81					NA/NA	AUTO

DISCTRON (OTARI)

Drive Model	Format Size MB	Head	Cyl	Sect/ Trac	Translate H/C/S	RWC/ WPC	Land Zone
D214	11	4	306	17		128/128	
D503	3	2	153	17		---/---	
D504	4	2	215	17		---/---	
D506	5	4	153	17		---/---	
D507	5	2	306	17		128/128	
D509	8	4	215	17		128/128	
D512	11	8	153	17		---/---	
D513	11	6	215	17		128/128	
D514	11	4	306	17		128/128	
D518	15	8	215	17		128/128	
D519	16	6	306	17		128/128	
D526	21	8	306	17		128/128	

DMA

Drive Model	Format Size MB	Head	Cyl	Sect/ Trac	Translate H/C/S	RWC/ WPC	Land Zone
306	11	2	612	17		612/400	

ELOCH

Drive Model	Format Size MB	Head	Cyl	Sect/ Trac	Translate H/C/S	RWC/ WPC	Land Zone
DISCACHE10	10	4	320	17		321/321	
DISCACHE20	20	8	320	17		321/321	

EPSON

Drive Model	Format Size MB	Head	Cyl	Sect/ Trac	Translate H/C/S	RWC/ WPC	Land Zone
HD560	21	4	615	17		615/300	
HD830	10	2	612	17		---/---	
HD850	10	4	306	17		---/---	
HD860	21	4	612	17		---/---	

Drive Model	Seek Time	Interface	Encode	Form Factor	cache kb	mtbf	Obsolete? RPM
DSP3133L	9.5	SCSI-2 FAST	1,7 RLL	3.5 3H	512k	500k	5400
DSP3160	9.7	SCSI-2 FAST	1,7 RLL	3.5 HH	512k	350k	5400
DSP3210	9.5	SCSI-2 FAST	1,7 RLL	3.5 HH	1024k	500k	5400
DSP5200	12	SCSI-2 FAST	1,7 RLL	5.25 FH	512k	250k	3600
DSP5300	12	SCSI-2 FAST	1,7 RLL	5.25 FH	512k	300k	5400
DSP5350	12	SCSI-2 FAST	1,7 RLL	5.25 FH	512k	300k	5400
DSP5400	12	SCSI-2 FAST	1,7 RLL	5.25 FH	1024k	300k	5400
DSRZ1BB-VW	9	SCSI-2FstWd		3.5 FH	512k		7200
DSRZ1CB-VW	9	Ultra SCSI		3.5 FH	512k		7200
DSRZ1DB-VW	9	Ultra SCSI		3.5 FH	512k		7200
DSRZ26N-VZ	10	Ultra SCSI		3.5 FH	480k		5400
DSRZ28L-VA	9	Ultra SCSI		3.5 FH	512k		7200
DSRZ28M-VZ	10	Ultra SCSI		3.5 FH	480k		5400
DSRZ29L-VA	9	Ultra SCSI		3.5 FH	512k		7200
DSRZ40-VA	9	SCSI-2		3.5 FH	512k		7200
RZ26N-VA	14.5	SCSI-2Fast		3.5 FH	480k		5400
RZ26N-VW	14.5	SCSI-2fstWd		3.5 FH	480k		5400 Y
RZ28D-VA	12.2	SCSI-2Fast		3.5 FH	480k		7200 Y
RZ28D-VW	12.2	SCSI-2fstWd		3.5 FH	480k		7200 Y
RZ28M-VA	14.5	SCSI-2Fast		3.5 FH	480k		5400 Y
RZ28M-VW	14.5	SCSI-2fstWd		3.5 FH	480k		5400 Y
RZ29B-VA	12.2	SCSI-2Fast		3.5 FH	1000k		7200 Y
RZ29B-VW	12.2	SCSI-2fstWd		3.5 FH	1000k		7200 Y

DISC TEC

Drive Model	Seek Time	Interface	Encode	Form Factor	cache kb	mtbf	Obsolete? RPM
RHD 260	14	IDE AT	RLL	3.5 3H		100k	
RHD 340	14	IDE AT	RLL	3.5 3H		100k	
RHD 520	14	IDE AT	RLL	3.5 3H		100k	
RHD-120	17	IDE AT	RLL	3.5 3H		100k	Y
RHD-180	15	IDE AT	RLL	3.5 3H		100k	Y
RHD-20 (Removable)	23	IDE AT	RLL	3.5 3H		20k	Y
RHD-210	19	IDE AT	RLL	3.5 3H		150k	Y
RHD-60	22	IDE AT	RLL	3.5 3H		45k	Y
RHD-80	16	IDE AT	RLL	3.5 3H		150k	Y

DISCTRON (OTARI)

Drive Model	Seek Time	Interface	Encode	Form Factor	cache kb	mtbf	Obsolete? RPM
D214		ST412/506	MFM	5.25 FH			Y
D503		ST412/506	MFM	5.25 FH			Y
D504		ST412/506	MFM	5.25 FH			Y
D506		ST412/506	MFM	5.25 FH			Y
D507		ST412/506	MFM	5.25 FH			Y
D509		ST412/506	MFM	5.25 FH			Y
D512		ST412/506	MFM	5.25 FH			Y
D513		ST412/506	MFM	5.25 FH			Y
D514		ST412/506	MFM	5.25 FH			Y
D518		ST412/506	MFM	5.25 FH			Y
D519		ST412/506	MFM	5.25 FH			Y
D526		ST412/506	MFM	5.25 FH			Y

DMA

Drive Model	Seek Time	Interface	Encode	Form Factor	cache kb	mtbf	Obsolete? RPM
306	170?	ST412/506	MFM	5.25 HH			Y

ELOCH

Drive Model	Seek Time	Interface	Encode	Form Factor	cache kb	mtbf	Obsolete? RPM
DISCACHE10	65?	ST412/506	MFM	5.25 FH			
DISCACHE20	65?	ST412/506	MFM	5.25 FH			

EPSON

Drive Model	Seek Time	Interface	Encode	Form Factor	cache kb	mtbf	Obsolete? RPM
HD560	78	ST412/506	MFM	5.25 HH			Y
HD830	93	ST412/506	MFM	5.25 HH			Y
HD850		ST412/506	MFM	5.25 HH			Y
HD860		ST412/506	MFM	5.25 HH			Y

Hard Drives 323

Drive Model	Format Size MB	Head	Cyl	Sect/ Trac	Translate H/C/S	RWC/ WPC	Land Zone
HMD710	10	2	615	17		---/---	
HMD720	21	4	615	17		---/---	
HMD726A	21	4	615	32		---/---	AUTO
HMD755	21	2	615	34		---/---	
HMD765	42	4	615	34		---/---	
HMD976	69						

FUJI

Drive Model	Format Size MB	Head	Cyl	Sect/ Trac	Translate H/C/S	RWC/ WPC	Land Zone
FK301-1	10					---/---	
FK301-13	10	4	306	17		307/128	
FK302	20					---/---	
FK302-13	10	2	612	17		613/307	
FK302-26	21	4	612	17		613/307	
FK302-39	32	6	612	17		613/307	
FK303-52	40	8	615	17		---/616	
FK305-26	21	4	615	17		---/616	
FK305-26R	21		615	26		---/---	
FK305-39	32	6	615	17		---/616	
FK305-39R	32	4	615	26		---/616	
FK305-58	32	6	615	17		---/---	
FK305-58R	49	6	615	26		---/616	
FK308S-39R	45	6	615			---/---	
FK308S-58R	32	4	615	26		---/616	
FK309-26	21	4	615	17		---/616	
FK309-39R	32	4	615	26		---/616	
FK309S-50R	41	4	615			---/---	

FUJITSU AMERICA, INC.

Drive Model	Format Size MB	Head	Cyl	Sect/ Trac	Translate H/C/S	RWC/ WPC	Land Zone
M1603 SAU	540	3				---/---	
M1603 TAU	540	4				---/---	
M1606 SAU	1080	6	3457	94		---/---	
M1606 TAU	1080	6				---/---	
M1612 TAU	545	2	4133	85-153		---/---	
M1614 TAU	1090	4	4133	85-153		---/---	
M1623 TAU	1700	3				---/---	
M1624 TAU	2100	4				---/---	
M1636 TAU	1200	2				---/---	
M1638 TAU	2500	4				---/---	
M2225D	40	4	615	17		---/---	
M2225D2	20	4	615	17		---/---	
M2225DR	32	4	615	17		---/---	
M2226D	60	6	615	17		---/---	
M2226D2	30	6	615	17		---/---	
M2226DR	49	6	615	26		---/---	
M2227D	80	8	615	17		---/---	
M2227D2	42	8	615	17		---/---	
M2227DR	65	8	615	26		---/---	
M2230	5	2	320	17		320/180	
M2230AS	5	2	320	17		320/320	
M2230AT	5	2	320	17		320/320	
M2231	5	2	306	17		---/---	
M2233	10	4	320	17		320/128	
M2233AS	10	4	320	17		320/320	
M2233AT	10	4	320	17		320/320	
M2234	15	6	320	17		320/128	
M2234AS	15	6	306	17		320/320	
M2235	21	8	320	17		320/128	
M2235AS	20	8	306	17		320/320	
M2241AS	26	4	754	17		---/375	754
M2241AS2	24	4	754	32		---/375	AUTO
M2242AS	45	7	754	17		754/375	AUTO
M2242AS2	43	7	754	17		---/---	AUTO

Drive Model	Seek Time	Interface	Encode	Form Factor	cache kb	Obsolete? mtbf	RPM ⇓
HMD710	78	ST412/506	MFM	5.25 HH			Y
HMD720	78	ST412/506	MFM	5.25 HH			Y
HMD726A	80	SCSI	2,7 RLL	3.5 HH		20k	Y
HMD755	80	ST412/506	2,7 RLL	5.25 HH		20k	Y
HMD765	80	ST412/506	2,7 RLL	5.25 HH		20k	Y
HMD976		SCSI		3.5 HH			Y

FUJI

Drive Model	Seek Time	Interface	Encode	Form Factor	cache kb	Obsolete? mtbf	RPM ⇓
FK301-1		ST412/506	MFM	3.5 HH			Y
FK301-13	65	ST412/506	MFM	3.5 HH		45k	Y
FK302		ST412/506	MFM	3.5 HH			Y
FK302-13	65	ST412/506	MFM	3.5 HH			Y
FK302-26	65	ST412/506	MFM	3.5 HH			Y
FK302-39	65	ST412/506	MFM	3.5 HH			Y
FK303-52	65?	ST412/506	MFM	3.5 HH		20k	Y
FK305-26	65	ST412/506	MFM	3.5 HH		20k 3350	Y
FK305-26R	65	ST412/506	2,7 RLL	3.5 HH		20k	Y
FK305-39	65	ST412/506	MFM	3.5 HH		20k	Y
FK305-39R	65	ST412/506	2,7 RLL	3.5 HH		20k 3350	Y
FK305-58	65	ST412/506	MFM	3.5 HH		20k	Y
FK305-58R	65	ST412/506	2,7 RLL	3.5 HH		20k 3350	Y
FK308S-39R	65	SCSI	2,7 RLL	3.5 HH		20k	Y
FK308S-58R	65	ST412/506	2,7 RLL	3.5 HH			Y
FK309-26	65	ST412/506	MFM	3.5 HH		20k	Y
FK309-39R	65	ST412/506	2,7 RLL	3.5 HH		20k	Y
FK309S-50R	45	SCSI	2,7 RLL	3.5 HH		20k	Y

FUJITSU AMERICA, INC.

Drive Model	Seek Time	Interface	Encode	Form Factor	cache kb	Obsolete? mtbf	RPM ⇓
M1603 SAU	10	SCSI-2 FAST	1,7 RLL	3.5 3H	512k	800k	5400
M1603 TAU	10	ATA-2	1,7 RLL	3.5 3H	256k	500k	5400
M1606 SAU	10	SCSI-2 FAST	1,7 RLL	3.5 3H	512k	800k	5400
M1606 TAU	10	ATA-2	1,7 RLL	3.5 3H	256k	300k	5400
M1612 TAU	11	ATA-2	PRML8,9	3.5 3H	64k	300k	4500
M1614 TAU	11	ATA-2	PRML8,9	3.5 3H	64k	300k	4500
M1623 TAU	10	ATA-2	PRML	3.5 3H	128k	500k	5400
M1624 TAU	10	ATA-2	PRML	3.5 3H	128k	500k	5400
M1636 TAU	10	ATA-2	PRML	3.5 3H	128k	500k	5400
M1638 TAU	10	ATA-2	PRML	3.5 3H	128k	500k	5400
M2225D	40	ST412/506	MFM	3.5 HH		30k	Y
M2225D2	35	ST412/506	MFM	3.5 HH			Y
M2225DR	35	ST412/506	2,7 RLL	3.5 HH			Y
M2226D	40	ST412/506	MFM	3.5 HH		30k	Y
M2226D2	35	ST412/506	MFM	3.5 HH			Y
M2226DR	35	ST412/506	2,7 RLL	3.5 HH			Y
M2227D	40	ST412/506	MFM	3.5 HH		30k	Y
M2227D2	35	ST412/506	MFM	3.5 HH			Y
M2227DR	35	ST412/506	2,7 RLL	3.5 HH			Y
M2230	85	ST412/506	MFM	5.25 FH			Y
M2230AS	27	ST412/506	MFM	5.25 FH		3600	
M2230AT	8	ST412/506	MFM	5.25 FH		3600	
M2231	85	ST412/506	MFM	5.25 FH			Y
M2233	80	ST412/506	MFM	5.25 FH			Y
M2233AS	27	ST412/506	MFM	5.25 FH		3600	Y
M2233AT	8	ST412/506	MFM	5.25 FH		3600	Y
M2234	8	ST412/506	MFM	5.25 FH		3600	Y
M2234AS	27	ST412/506	MFM	5.25 FH		3600	Y
M2235	85	ST412/506	MFM	5.25 FH		3600	Y
M2235AS	27	ST412/506	MFM	5.25 FH		3600	Y
M2241AS		ST412/506	MFM	5.25 FH			Y
M2241AS2	30	ST412/506	MFM	5.25 FH		20k	Y
M2242AS	30	ST412/506	MFM	5.25 FH		30k	Y
M2242AS2	30	ST412/506	MFM	5.25 FH			Y

Drive Model	Format Size MB	Head	Cyl	Sect/ Trac	Translate H/C/S	RWC/ WPC	Land Zone
M2243AS	72	11	754	17		754/375	AUTO
M2243AS2	67	11	754	17		---/---	AUTO
M2243R	110	7	1186	26		---/---	AUTO
M2243T	68	7	1186	17		---/---	AUTO
M2244E	73	5	823	35		NA/NA	AUTO
M2244S	85U	5	823	65		NA/NA	AUTO
M2244SA	85U	5	823	35		NA/NA	AUTO
M2244SB	85U	5	823	19		NA/NA	AUTO
M2245E	120	7	823	35		NA/NA	AUTO
M2245S	120U	7	823	65		NA/NA	AUTO
M2245SA	120U	7	823	35		NA/NA	AUTO
M2245SB	120U	7	823	19		NA/NA	AUTO
M2246E	138	10	823	35		NA/NA	AUTO
M2246S	171U	10	823	65		NA/NA	AUTO
M2246SA	171U	10	823	35		NA/NA	AUTO
M2246SB	171U	10	823	19		NA/NA	AUTO
M2247E	285	7	1243			NA/NA	AUTO
M2247S	289	7	1243	65		NA/NA	AUTO
M2247SA	160	7	1243	36		NA/NA	AUTO
M2247SB	169	7	1243			NA/NA	AUTO
M2248E	266	11	1243			NA/NA	AUTO
M2248S	227	11	1243			NA/NA	AUTO
M2248SA	252	11	1243	36		NA/NA	AUTO
M2248SB	266	11	1243			NA/NA	AUTO
M2249E	334	15	1243	35		NA/NA	AUTO
M2249S	334	15	1243	35		NA/NA	AUTO
M2249SA	334	15	1243	35		NA/NA	AUTO
M2249SB	362	15	1243			NA/NA	AUTO
M2261E	321	8	1658			NA/NA	AUTO
M2261HA	357	8	1658	53		NA/NA	AUTO
M2261S	321	8	1658			NA/NA	AUTO
M2261SA	415U	8	1658	53		NA/NA	AUTO
M2262E	448	11	1658			NA/NA	AUTO
M2262HA	476	11	1658	51		NA/NA	AUTO
M2262SA	476	11	1658	51		NA/NA	AUTO
M2263E	688	15	1658	53		NA/NA	AUTO
M2263HA	672	15	1658	53		NA/NA	AUTO
M2263S	650	15	1658	53		NA/NA	AUTO
M2266E	674	15	1658	53		NA/NA	AUTO
M2266H	953	15	1658			NA/NA	AUTO
M2266HA	1079	15	1658			NA/NA	AUTO
M2266HB	1140	15	1658			NA/NA	AUTO
M2266S	953	15	1658			NA/NA	AUTO
M2266SA	1079	15	1658	65		NA/NA	AUTO
M2266SB	1140	15	1658			NA/NA	AUTO
M2344KS	690	27	624	NA		NA/NA	AUTO
M2372K	823	27	745			---/---	
M2372KS	823	27	745			---/---	
M2382K	10000	27	745			---/---	
M2382P	1000	27	745			---/---	
M2392K	2020	21	1916			---/---	
M2511A	128	1	9952	25		---/---	
M2611H	46	2	1334	34		NA/NA	AUTO
M2611S	46	2	1334	68		NA/NA	AUTO
M2611SA	46	2	1334	34		NA/NA	AUTO
M2611SB	46	2	1334	17		NA/NA	AUTO
M2611T	45	2	1334	33	4/667/33	NA/NA	AUTO
M2612ES	90	4	1334			NA/NA	AUTO
M2612ESA	90	4	1334	34		NA/NA	AUTO
M2612ESB	90	4	1334			NA/NA	AUTO
M2612ET	90	4	1334	34	8/667/33	NA/NA	AUTO
M2612S	92	4	1334	34		NA/NA	AUTO
M2612SA	91	4	1334	33		NA/NA	AUTO

Drive Model	Seek Time	Interface	Encode	Form Factor	cache kb	mtbf	RPM	Obsolete?
M2243AS	30	ST412/506	MFM	5.25 FH		30k		Y
M2243AS2	30	ST412/506	MFM	5.25 FH		30k		Y
M2243R	25	ST412/506	2,7 RLL	5.25 FH				Y
M2243T	25	ST412/506	MFM	5.25 HH				Y
M2244E	25	ESDI	2,7 RLL	5.25 FH				Y
M2244S	25	SCSI	2,7 RLL	5.25 FH		35k	3600	Y
M2244SA	25	SCSI	2,7 RLL	5.25 FH		35k	3600	Y
M2244SB	25	SCSI	2,7 RLL	5.25 FH		35k	3600	Y
M2245E	25	ESDI	2,7 RLL	5.25 FH				Y
M2245S	25	SCSI	2,7 RLL	5.25 FH			3600	Y
M2245SA	25	SCSI	2,7 RLL	5.25 FH			3600	Y
M2245SB	25	SCSI	2,7 RLL	5.25 FH			3600	Y
M2246E	25	ESDI	2,7 RLL	5.25 FH		30k		Y
M2246S	25	SCSI	2,7 RLL	5.25 FH		30k	3600	Y
M2246SA	25	SCSI	2,7 RLL	5.25 FH		30k	3600	Y
M2246SB	25	SCSI	2,7 RLL	5.25 FH		30k	3600	Y
M2247E	18	ESDI	1,7 RLL	5.25 FH		30k		Y
M2247S	18	SCSI	1,7 RLL	5.25 FH		30k		Y
M2247SA	18	SCSI	1,7 RLL	5.25 FH		30k		Y
M2247SB	18	SCSI	1,7 RLL	5.25 FH		30k		Y
M2248E	18	ESDI	1,7 RLL	5.25 FH		130k		Y
M2248S	18	SCSI	1,7 RLL	5.25 FH		130k		Y
M2248SA	18	SCSI	1,7 RLL	5.25 FH		130k		Y
M2248SB	18	SCSI	1,7 RLL	5.25 FH		130k		Y
M2249E	18	ESDI	1,7 RLL	5.25 FH		30k		Y
M2249S	18	SCSI	1,7 RLL	5.25 FH		30k		Y
M2249SA	18	SCSI	1,7 RLL	5.25 FH		30k		Y
M2249SB	18	SCSI	1,7 RLL	5.25 FH		30k		Y
M2261E	16	ESDI	1,7 RLL	5.25 FH		200k		Y
M2261HA	16	SCSI	1,7 RLL	5.25 FH		200k		Y
M2261S	16	SCSI	2,7 RLL	5.25 FH		200k		Y
M2261SA		SCSI		5.25 FH				Y
M2262E	16	ESDI	1,7 RLL	5.25 FH		200k		Y
M2262HA	16	SCSI	1,7 RLL	5.25 FH		200k		Y
M2262SA	16	SCSI	1,7 RLL	5.25 FH		200k		Y
M2263E	16	ESDI	1,7 RLL	5.25 FH		30k	3600	
M2263HA	16	SCSI	1,7 RLL	5.25 FH		200k		
M2263S	16	SCSI	1,7 RLL	5.25 FH		30k		
M2266E	16	ESDI	1,7 RLL	5.25 FH		200k		
M2266H	14.5	SCSI	1,7 RLL	5.25 FH		200k	3600	
M2266HA	14.5	SCSI	1,7 RLL	5.25 FH		200k	3600	
M2266HB	14.5	SCSI	1,7 RLL	5.25 FH		200k	3600	
M2266S	14.5	SCSI	1,7 RLL	5.25 FH		200k	3600	
M2266SA	14.5	SCSI	1,7 RLL	5.25 FH		200k	3600	
M2266SB	14.5	SCSI	1,7 RLL	5.25 FH	256k	200k	3600	
M2344KS	16	SCSI/SMD	RLL	8 FH		200k		
M2372K	16	HSMD	2,7 RLL					
M2372KS	16	SCSI	2,7 RLL					
M2382K	16	ESMD	1,7 RLL					
M2382P	16	IPI	1,7 RLL					
M2392K	12	ESMD	1,7 RLL					
M2511A	30	SCSI-2	1,7 RLL	3.5 3H	256k	30k	3600	Y
M2611H	25	SCSI	1,7 RLL	3.5 HH		50k		Y
M2611S	25	SCSI	1,7 RLL	3.5 HH		50k		Y
M2611SA	25	SCSI	1,7 RLL	3.5 HH	24k	50k	3490	Y
M2611SB	25	SCSI	1,7 RLL	3.5 HH		50k	3490	Y
M2611T	25	IDE AT	1,7 RLL	3.5 HH	64k	50k	3490	Y
M2612ES	20	SCSI	1,7 RLL	3.5 HH		50k		Y
M2612ESA	20	SCSI	1,7 RLL	3.5 HH	24k	50k	3490	Y
M2612ESB	20	SCSI	1,7 RLL	3.5 HH		50k	3490	Y
M2612ET	20	IDE AT	1,7 RLL	3.5 HH	64k	50k	3490	Y
M2612S	20	SCSI	1,7 RLL	3.5 HH		50k	3490	Y
M2612SA	25	SCSI	1,7 RLL	3.5 HH	24k	30k	3490	Y

Drive Model	Format Size MB	Head	Cyl	Sect/Trac	Translate H/C/S	RWC/WPC	Land Zone
M2612T	90	4	1334	33	8/667/33	NA/NA	AUTO
M2613ES	139	6	1334			NA/NA	AUTO
M2613ESA	137	6	1334	34		NA/NA	AUTO
M2613ESB	139	6	1334			NA/NA	AUTO
M2613ET	137	6	1334	34	12/667/33	NA/NA	AUTO
M2613S	139	6	1334	34		NA/NA	AUTO
M2613SA	137	6	1334	34		NA/NA	AUTO
M2613SB	139	6	1334	17		NA/NA	AUTO
M2613T	137	6	1334	34	12/667/33	NA/NA	AUTO
M2614ES	185	8	1334			NA/NA	AUTO
M2614ESA	182	8	1334	34		NA/NA	AUTO
M2614ESB	185	8	1334			NA/NA	AUTO
M2614ET	180	8	1334	34	16/667/33	NA/NA	AUTO
M2614S	185	8	1334	34		NA/NA	AUTO
M2614SA	182	8	1334	34		NA/NA	AUTO
M2614SB	186	8	1334	17		NA/NA	AUTO
M2614T	180	8	1334	34	16/667/33	NA/NA	AUTO
M2616ESA	105	4	1542	34		NA/NA	AUTO
M2616ET	105	4	1542	34	8/771/33	NA/NA	AUTO
M2616SA	105	4	1542			NA/NA	AUTO
M2616T	105	4	1542		8/771/33	NA/NA	AUTO
M2621S	235	5	1435			NA/NA	
M2622FA	293	7	1435			---/---	
M2622F	330	7	1435			---/---	
M2622S	330	7	1153	80		NA/NA	AUTO
M2622SA	329	7	1429	56-70		NA/NA	AUTO
M2622T	326	7	1435		10/1013/63	NA/NA	AUTO
M2623F	377	9	1435	V		NA/NA	AUTO
M2623FA	498	9	1435			---/---	
M2623S	425	9	1153	80		NA/NA	AUTO
M2623SA	425	9	1429	64		NA/NA	AUTO
M2623T	420	9	1435		13/002/63	NA/NA	AUTO
M2624F	461	6	1435			---/---	
M2624FA	520	11	1435			---/---	
M2624S	520	11	1463	63		NA/NA	AUTO
M2624SA	520	11	1429	64		NA/NA	AUTO
M2624T	513	11	1429	63	16/995/63	NA/NA	AUTO
M2635S	160	4	1569			---/---	
M2635T	160	4	1569		8/620/63	---/---	
M2637S	240	6	1574	49		---/---	
M2637SA	240	6	1574			---/---	
M2637T	240	6	1569		8/930/63	---/---	
M2651SA	1400	16	1944	88		---/---	
M2652H	1628	20	1893	84		NA/NA	AUTO
M2652HA	1600	20	1944			NA/NA	AUTO
M2652HD	1628	20	1893	84		NA/NA	AUTO
M2652P	1600	20	1893			NA/NA	AUTO
M2652S	1628	20	1893	84		NA/NA	AUTO
M2652SA	1750	20	1944	88		NA/NA	AUTO
M2653	1400	15	2078	88		---/---	
M2654HA	2000	21	2179			NA/NA	AUTO
M2654SA	2061	21	2179	88		---/---	
M2671P	2640	15	2671			---/---	
M2681SAU	264	3	2379			---/---	
M2681TAU	264	3	2379		11/977/48	---/---	
M2682SAU	350	4	2379	64-90		---/---	
M2682TAU	352	4	2378	64-90	11/992/63	---/---	
M2684SAU	525	6	2379	74		---/---	
M2684TAU	525	6	2379		16/1024/63	---/---	
M2691EHA	645	9	1818	V		NA/NA	AUTO
M2691EQ	756U	9	1831			---/---	
M2691ER	756U	9	1831			---/---	
M2691ESA	645	9	1818	V		NA/NA	AUTO

Drive Model	Seek Time	Interface	Encode	Form Factor	cache kb	mtbf	RPM	Obsolete?
M2612T	25	IDE AT	1,7 RLL	3.5 HH	64k	50k	3490	Y
M2613ES	20	SCSI	1,7 RLL	3.5 HH		50k	3490	Y
M2613ESA	20	SCSI	1,7 RLL	3.5 HH	24k	30k	3490	Y
M2613ESB	20	SCSI	1,7 RLL	3.5 HH				Y
M2613ET	20	IDE AT	1,7 RLL	3.5 HH	64k	50k	3490	Y
M2613S	20	SCSI	1,7 RLL	3.5 HH		50k		Y
M2613SA	25	SCSI	1,7 RLL	3.5 HH	24k	30k	3490	Y
M2613SB	20	SCSI	1,7 RLL	3.5 HH		50k		Y
M2613T	25	IDE AT	1,7 RLL	3.5 HH	64k	50k	3490	Y
M2614ES	20	SCSI	1,7 RLL	3.5 HH				Y
M2614ESA	20	SCSI	1,7 RLL	3.5 HH	24k	30k	3490	Y
M2614ESB	20	SCSI	1,7 RLL	3.5 HH				Y
M2614ET	20	IDE AT	1,7 RLL	3.5 HH		50k		Y
M2614S	25	SCSI	1,7 RLL	3.5 HH	24k	50k	3490	Y
M2614SA	25	SCSI	1,7 RLL	3.5 HH	24k	30k	3490	Y
M2614SB	20	SCSI	1,7 RLL	3.5 HH		50k		Y
M2614T	20	IDE AT	1,7 RLL	3.5 HH	64k	50k	3490	Y
M2616ESA	20	SCSI	1,7 RLL	3.5 HH	64k	50k	3490	Y
M2616ET	20	IDE AT	1,7 RLL	3.5 HH		30k	3490	Y
M2616T	20	SCSI	1,7 RLL	3.5 HH	24k	64k	50k 3490	Y
M2621S	12	SCSI-2	1,7 RLL	3.5 HH				
M2622F	12	SCSI	1,7 RLL	3.5 HH			4400	
M2622FA	12	SCSI-1/2	1,7 RLL	3.5 HH	240k	200k	4400	
M2622S	12	SCSI-2	1,7 RLL	3.5 HH			4400	
M2622SA	12	SCSI-2	1,7 RLL	3.5 HH	240k	200k	4400	
M2622T	12	IDE AT	1,7 RLL	3.5 HH	240k	200k	4400	
M2623F	12	SCSI 1/2	1,7 RLL	3.5 HH		200k	4400	
M2623FA	12	SCSI-1/2	1,7 RLL	3.5 HH	240k	200k	4400	
M2623S	12	SCSI-2	1,7 RLL	3.5 HH	240k	200k	4400	
M2623SA	12	SCSI-2	1,7 RLL	3.5 HH	240k	200k	4400	
M2623T	12	IDE AT	1,7 RLL	3.5 HH	240k	200k	4400	
M2624F	12	SCSI	1,7 RLL	3.5 HH			4400	
M2624FA	12	SCSI-1/2	1,7 RLL	3.5 HH	240k	200k	4400	
M2624S	12	SCSI-2	1,7 RLL	3.5 HH	240k	200k	4400	
M2624SA	12	SCSI-2	1,7 RLL	3.5 HH	240k	200k	4400	
M2624T	12	IDE AT	1,7 RLL	3.5 HH	240k	200k	4400	
M2635S	14	SCSI-2	1,7 RLL	2.5 4H	256k	150k	4500	
M2635T	14	IDE AT	1,7 RLL	2.5 4H	256k	150k	4500	
M2637S	14	SCSI-2	1,7 RLL	2.5 4H	256	150k	4500	
M2637SA	14.5	SCSI-2	1,7 RLL	FH	256k		4500	Y
M2637T	14	IDE AT	1,7 RLL	2.5 4H	256k	150k	4500	
M2651SA	12	SCSI-2	1,7 RLL	5.25 FH	256k	300k	5400	
M2652H	11	SCSI-2	1,7 RLL	5.25 HH		200k	5400	
M2652HA	11	SCSI-2Diff	1,7 RLL	FH		200k	5400	
M2652HD	11	SCSI-2	1,7 RLL	5.25 FH		200k	5400	
M2652P	11	IPI-2	1,7 RLL	FH		300k	5400	
M2652S	11	SCSI-2	1,7 RLL	5.25 FH		200k	5400	
M2652SA	11	SCSI-2	1,7 RLL	5.25			5400	
M2653	12	SCSI-2 DIFF	1,7 RLL	5.25	256k		5400	Y
M2654HA	12	SCSI-2Diff	1,7 RLL	FH		300k	5400	
M2654SA	12	SCSI-2	1,7 RLL	5.25 FH	256k	300k	5400	
M2671P	12	IPI-2	1,7 RLL	8 FH		200k	4340	
M2681SAU	12	SCSI-2	1,7 RLL	3.5 3H	256k	250k	4500	
M2681TAU	12	IDE AT	1,7 RLL	3.5 3H	256k	250k	4500	
M2682SAU	12	SCSI-2	1,7 RLL	3.5 3H	256k	250k	4500	
M2682TAU	12	IDE AT	1,7 RLL	3.5 3H	256k	250k	4500	
M2684SAU	12	SCSI-2	1,7 RLL	3.5 3H	256k	250k	4500	
M2684TAU	12	IDE AT	1,7 RLL	3.5 3H	256k	250k	4500	
M2691EHA	10	SCSI-2	1,7 RLL	3.5 HH	256k	300k	5400	
M2691EQ	10	SCSI	1,7 RLL	3.5 HH	512k		5400	
M2691ER	10	SCSI-2 DIFF	1,7 RLL	3.5 HH	512k		5400	
M2691ESA	10	SCSI-2	1,7 RLL	3.5 HH	256k	300k	5400	

Drive Model	Format Size MB	Head	Cyl	Sect/ Trac	Translate H/C/S	RWC/ WPC	Land Zone
M2692EQ	925U	11	1831			---/---	
M2692ER	925U	11	1831			---/---	
M2693EQ	1093U	13	1831			---/---	
M2693ER	1093U	13	1831			---/---	
M2694EHA	1080	15	1818	V		NA/NA	AUTO
M2694EQ	1261U	15	1831			---/---	
M2694ER	1261U	15	1831			---/---	
M2694ESA	1080	15	1818	V		NA/NA	AUTO
M2703S	260	3	2305			---/---	
M2703T	260	3	2305			---/---	
M2704	260	3				---/---	
M2704S	350	4	2305			---/---	
M2704T	350	4	2305			---/---	
M2705	350	4				---/---	
M2706	530	6				---/---	
M2706S	530	6	2305			---/---	
M2706T	530	6	2305			---/---	
M2712TAM	540	1				---/---	
M2713TAM	1080	2				---/---	
M2714TAM	1080	2				---/---	
M2723	1200	3				---/---	
M2724	1600	4				---/---	
M2903	2100	14	3139			---/---	
M2909	3100	20	3139			---/---	
M2914	2100	7				---/---	
M2915	2100	16	3012			---/---	
M2927	1100	4				---/---	
M2932	2170	10	3422			---/---	
M2934	4350	19	3422			---/---	
M2948S	8800	18	5751			---/---	
M2949S	9100	18	5772			---/---	
M2952S	2200	5	5565			---/---	
M2954S	4400	9	5565			---/---	
MPA3017A	1750	2	8713132-25			---/---	
MPA3026AT	2620	3	8713132-25			---/---	
MPA3035AT	3500	4	8713132-25			---/---	
MPA3043AT	4370	5	8713132-25			---/---	
MPA3052AT	5250	6	8713132-25			---/---	

HEWLETT-PACKARD CO

Drive Model	Format Size MB	Head	Cyl	Sect/ Trac	Translate H/C/S	RWC/ WPC	Land Zone
HP97501A	10	2	698	28	8/142/17	---/---	
HP97501B	20	2	1400	28	8/288/17	---/---	
HP97530E	136	4				NA/NA	AUTO
HP97530S	204	6				NA/NA	AUTO
HP97532D	215	4	1643	64*V		NA/NA	AUTO
HP97532E	215	4	1643	64		NA/NA	AUTO
HP97532S	215	4	1643	64		NA/NA	AUTO
HP97532T	215	4	1643	64		NA/NA	AUTO
HP97533D	323	6	1643	64		NA/NA	AUTO
HP97533E	323	6	1643	64		NA/NA	AUTO
HP97533S	323	6	1643	64		NA/NA	AUTO
HP97533T	323	6	1643	64		NA/NA	AUTO
HP97536D	646	12	1643	64		NA/NA	AUTO
HP97536E	646	12	1643	64		NA/NA	AUTO
HP97536S	646	12	1643	64		NA/NA	AUTO
HP97536SP	320					---/---	
HP97536SX	322					---/---	
HP97536T	646	12	1643	64		NA/NA	AUTO
HP97536TA	320					---/---	
HP97544D	331	8	1447	56		NA/NA	AUTO
HP97544E	337	8	1447	56		NA/NA	AUTO
HP97544P	331	8	1447	56		NA/NA	AUTO
HP97544S	331	8	1447	56		NA/NA	AUTO

| Drive | Seek | | | Form | cache | | Obsolete? |
Model	Time	Interface	Encode	Factor	kb	mtbf	RPM ⇓
M2692EQ	10	SCSI	1,7 RLL	3.5 HH	512k		5400
M2692ER	10	SCSI-2 DIFF	1,7 RLL	3.5 HH	512k		5400
M2693EQ	10	SCSI	1,7 RLL	3.5 HH	512k		5400
M2693ER	10	SCSI-2 DIFF	1,7 RLL	3.5 HH	512k		5400
M2694EHA	10	SCSI-2 DIFF	1,7 RLL	3.5 HH	256k	300k	5400
M2694EQ	10	SCSI	1,7 RLL	3.5 HH	512k		5400
M2694ER	10	SCSI-2 DIFF	1,7 RLL	3.5 HH	512k		5400
M2694ESA	10	SCSI	1,7 RLL	3.5 HH	512k		5400
M2703S	12	SCSI-2 FAST		2.5 4H	512k	300k	5400 Y
M2703T	12	ATA-2	RLL	2.5 4H	256k	300k	5400 Y
M2704	12	SCSI		2.5 4H	256	250k	5400 Y
M2704S	12	SCSI-2 FAST	RLL	2.5 4H	512k	300k	5400 Y
M2704T	12	ATA-2	RLL	2.5 4H	512k	300k	5400 Y
M2705	12	SCSI		2.5 4H	256	250k	5400 Y
M2706	12	SCSI		2.5 4H	512k	300k	5400
M2706S	12	SCSI-2 FAST	RLL	2.5 4H	512k	300k	5400
M2706T	12	ATA-2	RLL	2.5 4H	256k	300k	5400
M2712TAM	12	ATA	PRML8,9	2.5 4H	128k	300k	3634
M2713TAM	12	ATA	PRML8,9	2.5 4H	128k	300k	3634
M2714TAM	12	ATA	PRML8,9	2.5 4H	128k	300k	3634
M2723	12	ATA-3	PRML	3.5 3H	128k	300k	4000
M2724	12	ATA-3	PRML	3.5 3H	128k	300k	4000
M2903	10.5	SCSI-2 FSTW	RLL	3.5 HH	512k	500k	5400
M2909	10.5	SCSI-2 FSTW	RLL	3.5 HH	512k	500k	5400
M2914	9	SCSI-2 FSTW		3.5 HH	512k	500k	7200
M2915	9.8	SCSI-2 FSTW		3.5 HH	512k	500k	7200
M2927	10.5	SCSI-2 FSTW		3.5 HH	512k	500k	5400
M2932	11	SCSI-2 FAST	RLL	3.5 HH	510k	800k	5400
M2934	11	SCSI-2 FAST	RLL	3.5 HH	510k	800k	7200
M2948S	10	SCSI-2FstWd	PR4ML	3.5 HH	512k	1000k	7200
M2949S	10	SCSI-2FstWd	RLL 0,4,4	3.5 HH	512k	1000k	7200
M2952S	8	SCSI-2FstWd	RLL 8,9	3.5 3H	512k	1000k	7200
M2954S	8	SCSI-2FstWd	RLL 8,9	3.5 3H	512k	1000k	7200
MPA3017A	10	ATA-3	PRML8,9	3.5 3H	128k	500k	5400
MPA3026AT	10	ATA-3	PRML8,9	3.5 3H	128k	500k	5400
MPA3035AT	10	ATA-3	PRML8,9	3.5 3H	128k	500k	5400
MPA3043AT	10	ATA-3	PRML8,9	3.5 3H	128k	500k	5400
MPA3052AT	10	ATA-3	PRML8,9	3.5 3H	128k	500k	5400

HEWLETT-PACKARD CO

Drive Model	Seek Time	Interface	Encode	Form Factor	cache kb	mtbf	RPM	Obsolete?
HP97501A	75		MFM	3.5 HH				Y
HP97501B			MFM	3.5 HH				Y
HP97530E	18	ESDI	2,7 RLL	5.25 FH				Y
HP97530S	18	SCSI	2,7 RLL	5.25 FH				Y
HP97532D	17	SCSI	2,7 RLL	5.25 FH	16k	99k	3348	Y
HP97532E	17	ESDI (10)	2,7 RLL	5.25 FH	16k	99k	3348	Y
HP97532S	17	SCSI	2,7 RLL	5.25 FH	16k	99k	3348	Y
HP97532T	17	SCSI	2,7 RLL	5.25 FH	16k	99k	3348	Y
HP97533D	17	SCSI	2,7 RLL	5.25 FH	16k	99k	3348	Y
HP97533E	17	ESDI	2,7 RLL	5.25 FH	16k	99k	3348	Y
HP97533S	17	SCSI	2,7 RLL	5.25 FH	16k	99k	3348	Y
HP97533T	17	SCSI	2,7 RLL	5.25 FH	16k	99k	3348	Y
HP97536D	17	SCSI	2,7 RLL	5.25 FH	16k	99k	3348	Y
HP97536E	17	ESDI	2,7 RLL	5.25 FH	16k	99k	3348	
HP97536S	17	SCSI	2,7 RLL	5.25 FH	16k	99k	3348	
HP97536SP		SCSI	2,7 RLL	5.25 FH				Y
HP97536SX		SCSI	2,7 RLL	5.25 FH				Y
HP97536T	17	SCSI	2,7 RLL	5.25 FH	16k	99k	3348	
HP97536TA		SCSI	2,7 RLL	5.25 FH				Y
HP97544D	16	SCSI	2,7 RLL	5.25 HH	64k	150k	4002	Y
HP97544E	17	ESDI	2,7 RLL	5.25 FH	64k	150k	4002	Y
HP97544P	17	SCSI-2	2,7 RLL	5.25 FH	64k	150k	4002	Y
HP97544S	16	SCSI	2,7 RLL	5.25 FH	64k	150k	4002	Y

Drive Model	Format Size MB	Head	Cyl	Sect/Trac	Translate H/C/S	RWC/WPC	Land Zone
HP97544SA	331					---/---	
HP97544T	331	8	1447	56		NA/NA	AUTO
HP97548D	663	16	1447	56		NA/NA	AUTO
HP97548E	675	16	1447	56		NA/NA	AUTO
HP97548P	663	16	1447	56		NA/NA	AUTO
HP97548S	663	16	1447	56		NA/NA	AUTO
HP97548SZ	663					---/---	
HP97548T	663	16	1447	56		NA/NA	AUTO
HP97549D	1001	16	1911	64		NA/NA	AUTO
HP97549T	1001	16	1911	69		NA/NA	AUTO
HP97556	786					---/---	
HP97556E	688	11	1697	72		NA/NA	AUTO
HP97556P	677	11	1670	72		NA/NA	AUTO
HP97556T	677	11	1670	72		NA/NA	AUTO
HP97558E	1084	15	1962	72		NA/NA	AUTO
HP97558P	1069	15	1935	72		NA/NA	AUTO
HP97558T	1069	15	1935	72		NA/NA	AUTO
HP97560	1300					---/---	
HP97560E	1374	19	1962	72		NA/NA	AUTO
HP97560P	1355	19	1935	72		NA/NA	AUTO
HP97560T	1355	19	1935	72		NA/NA	AUTO
HPC2233 ATA	238	5	1546	V	16/462/63	NA/NA	AUTO
HPC2233S	234	5	1546	V		NA/NA	AUTO
HPC2234 ATA	334	7	1546	V	16/647/63	NA/NA	AUTO
HPC2234S	328	7	1546	V		NA/NA	AUTO
HPC2235A	429					NA/NA	AUTO
HPC2235S	422	9	1546	V		NA/NA	AUTO
HPC2244	566	7	2051	79		---/---	
HPC2245	728	9	2051	79		---/---	
HPC2246	890	11	2051	79		---/---	
HPC2247	1052	13	1981	56-96		NA/NA	AUTO
HPC2247D	1052	13	1981	56-96		NA/NA	AUTO
HPC2247SE	1052	13	1981	56-96		NA/NA	AUTO
HPC2247W	1052	13	1981	56-96		NA/NA	AUTO
HPC2270S	320					---/---	
HPC2271S	663					---/---	
HPC2490D	2100	18	258268-108			---/---	
HPC2490SE	2100	18	258268-108			---/---	
HPC2490W	2100	18	258268-108			---/---	
HPC3007	1370		2255			NA/NA	AUTO
HPC3009	1792		2255			NA/NA	AUTO
HPC3010	2003					---/---	
HPC3013A	21	3	700		4/615/17	---/---	
HPC3014A	42	4	786			---/---	
HPC3031A	21	3				---/---	
HPC3323D	1050	7	291072-120			NA/NA	AUTO
HPC3323SE	1050	7	291072-120			NA/NA	AUTO
HPC3323W	1050	7	291072-120			NA/NA	AUTO
HPC3324	1050	9	3703	100		---/---	
HPC3325A	2170	9	3610100-14			---/---	
HPC3335 ATA	429	9	1546	V		NA/NA	AUTO
HPC3550	2000					---/---	
HPC3555	1000					---/---	
HPC3653A	8700	20	5371124-17			---/---	
HPC3724D	1200	9	3610100-14			NA/NA	AUTO
HPC3724S	1200	9	3610100-14			NA/NA	AUTO
HPC3724W	1200	9	3610100-14			NA/NA	AUTO
HPC3725D	2170	9	3610100-14			---/---	
HPC3725S	2170	9	3610100-14			---/---	
HPC3725W	2170	9	3610100-14			---/---	
HPC5270A	1084	4	91-155			---/---	
HPC5271A	1626	6	91-155			---/---	
HPC5272A	1336	4	94-162			---/---	

Drive Model	Seek Time	Interface	Encode	Form Factor	cache kb	mtbf	RPM	Obsolete?
HP97544SA		SCSI	2,7 RLL	5.25 FH				Y
HP97544T	17	SCSI-2	2,7 RLL	5.25 FH				Y
HP97548D	16	SCSI-2	2,7 RLL	5.25 FH	64k	150k	4002	Y
HP97548E	17	ESDI	2,7 RLL	5.25 FH	64k	150k	4002	Y
HP97548P	17	SCSI-2	2,7 RLL	5.25 FH	64k	150k	4002	Y
HP97548S	16	SCSI	2,7 RLL	5.25 FH	64k	150k	4002	Y
HP97548SZ		SCSI	2,7 RLL	5.25 FH				
HP97548T	17	SCSI-2	2,7 RLL	5.25 FH				
HP97549P	17	SCSI-2	2,7 RLL	5.25 FH	64k	150k	4002	
HP97549T	17	SCSI-2	2,7 RLL	5.25 FH	128k	150k	4002	
HP97556			2,7 RLL	5.25 FH				Y
HP97556E	14	ESDI	2,7 RLL	5.25 FH	128k	150k	4002	
HP97556P	14	SCSI-2	2,7 RLL	5.25 FH	128k	150k	4002	
HP97556T	14	SCSI-2	2,7 RLL	5.25 FH	128k	150k	4002	
HP97558E	14	ESDI	2,7 RLL	5.25 FH	128k	150k	4002	
HP97558P	14	SCSI-2	2,7 RLL	5.25 FH	128k	150k	4002	
HP97558T	14	SCSI-2	2,7 RLL	5.25 FH	128k	150k	4002	
HP97560		SCSI-2	2,7 RLL	5.25 FH		150k		
HP97560E	14	ESDI	2,7 RLL	5.25 FH	128k	150k	4002	
HP97560P	14	SCSI-2	2,7 RLL	5.25 FH	128k	150k	4002	
HP97560T	14	SCSI-2	2,7 RLL	5.25 FH	128k	150k	4002	
HPC2233 ATA	12.6	IDE AT	2,7 RLL	3.5 HH	64k	150k	3600	Y
HPC2233S	12	SCSI-2	2,7 RLL	3.5 HH	64k	150k	3600	Y
HPC2234 ATA	12.6	IDE AT	2,7 RLL	3.5 HH	64k	150k	3600	Y
HPC2234S	12	SCSI-2	2,7 RLL	3.5 HH	64k	150k	3600	Y
HPC2235A	13	ATA		FH			150k	
HPC2235S	12	SCSI-2	2,7 RLL	3.5 HH	64k	150k	3600	Y
HPC2244	10	SCSI-2	1,7 RLL	3.5 HH	256k	300k	5400	Y
HPC2245	10	SCSI-2	1,7 RLL	3.5 HH	256k	300	5400	Y
HPC2246	10	SCSI-2	1,7 RLL	3.5 HH	256k	300	5400	Y
HPC2247	10	SCSI-2	1,7 RLL	3.5 HH	256k	300k	5400	Y
HPC2247D	10	SCSI-2 DIFF	1,7 RLL	3.5 HH	256k	300k	5400	Y
HPC2247SE	10	SCSI-2	1,7 RLL	3.5 HH	256k	300k	5400	Y
HPC2247W	10	SCSI-2 FSTW	1,7 RLL	3.5 HH	256k	300k	5400	Y
HPC2270S		SCSI		5.25 FH				Y
HPC2271S		SCSI		5.25 FH				Y
HPC2490D	9	SCSI-2 DIFF		3.5 HH		500k	6400	Y
HPC2490SE	9	SCSI-2		3.5 HH		500k	6400	Y
HPC2490W	9	SCSI-2 FSTW		3.5 HH		500k	6400	Y
HPC3007	12	SCSI-2		FH	256k	300k	5400	
HPC3009	12	SCSI-2		FH	256k	300k	5400	
HPC3010	12	SCSI-2		FH	256k	300k	5400	
HPC3013A	15	IDE AT	1,7 RLL	1.3 4H		300k		
HPC3014A	18	IDE		1.3 4H		300k	5310	
HPC3031A	18	IDE		1.3 4H		300k	5310	
HPC3323D	9.5	SCSI-2 DIFF		3.5 3H	512k	500k	5400	Y
HPC3323SE	9.5	SCSI-2		3.5 3H	512k	500k	5400	Y
HPC3323W	9.5	SCSI-2 DIFF		3.5 3H	512k	500k	5400	Y
HPC3324	9.5	SCSI-2	1,7 RLL	3.5 3H	512k	500	5400	
HPC3325A	10.5	SCSI-2	PRML	3.5 3H	512k		5400	
HPC3335 ATA	12.6	IDE AT	2,7 RLL	3.5 HH	64k	150k	3600	
HPC3550		SCSI-2 FSTW		3.5 HH				
HPC3555		SCSI-2 FSTW		3.5 HH				
HPC3653A	9	SE SCSI	PRML	3.5 HH	512k		7200	
HPC3724D	9.5	SCSI-2 DIFF		3.5 3H		800k	5400	
HPC3724S	9.5	SCSI-2		3.5 3H		800k	5400	
HPC3724W	9.5	SCSI-2 FSTW		3.5 3H		800k	5400	
HPC3725D	9.5	SCSI-2 DIFF		3.5 3H		800k	5400	
HPC3725S	9.5	SCSI-2		3.5 3H		800k	5400	
HPC3725W	9.5	SCSI-2 DIFF		3.5 3H		800k	5400	
HPC5270A		EIDE/ATA-2		3.5 HH	128k	300k	4480	
HPC5271A		EIDE/ATA-2		3.5 HH	128k	300k	4480	
HPC5272A		EIDE/AT	1,7 RLL	3.5 3H	64k	300k	4480	

Drive Model	Format Size MB	Head	Cyl	Sect/ Trac	Translate H/C/S	RWC/ WPC	Land Zone
HPC5273A	2004	6		94-162		---/---	
HPC5273AK	1336	4		94-162		---/---	
HPC5280A	1084	4		91-155		---/---	
HPC5281A	1626	6		91-155		---/---	
HPC5283A	2004	6		94-162		---/---	
HPC5421SK	8700	20	5371124-17			---/---	
HPC5421TK	8700	20	5371124-17			---/---	
HPC5435A	1336	4		94-162		---/---	
HPC5435AK	1300					---/---	
HPC5436AK	2004	6		94-162		---/---	
HPD1296A	21	4	615	17		0/300	670
HPD1297A	42	6	820	17		---/---	
HPD1660A	340	8	1457	57		NA/NA	AUTO
HPD1661A	680	16	1457	57		NA/NA	AUTO
HPD1674A	108	6	820	40		---/---	
HPD1675A	155	6	820	40		---/---	
HPD1676A	310	6	820	40		---/---	
HPD1697A	240	4	1800		8/930/63	---/---	
HPD2076B	1050					---/---	
HPD2077A	2100					---/---	
HPD2389A	540					---/---	
HPD3340A	2100					---/---	
HPD3341A	4200					---/---	

HITACHI AMERICA

Drive Model	Format Size MB	Head	Cyl	Sect/ Trac	Translate H/C/S	RWC/ WPC	Land Zone
						NA/NA	AUTO
DK211A-51	510	6				NA/NA	AUTO
DK211A-54	540	16	1047	63	16/1047/63	NA/NA	AUTO
DK211A-68	680				16/1384/60	---/---	
DK211C-11	510	6				NA/NA	AUTO
DK212A-10	1080	8				---/---	
DK212A-81	810	8				---/---	
DK213A-13	1350	10	2605			---/---	
DK213A-18	1800				16/3491/63	---/---	
DK221A-34	340	4				NA/NA	AUTO
DK222A-54	540	4				---/---	
DK223A-11	1080				16/2095/63	---/---	
DK223A-81	810	6	2605			---/---	
DK224A-14	1440				16/2792/63	---/---	
DK225A-21	2160				16/4188/63	---/---	
DK226A-32	3240				16/6282/63	---/---	
DK301-1	10	4	306	17		---/---	
DK301-2	15	6	306	17		---/---	
DK312C-20	209	9	1076	38		---/---	
DK312C-25	251	11	1076	38		---/---	
DK314C-41	419	14		17		---/---	
DK315C-10	1000	11				NA/NA	AUTO
DK315C-11	1100	15				NA/NA	AUTO
DK315C-14	1400	15				NA/NA	AUTO
DK318H-91	9100	20				---/---	
DK325C-57	573	6	2458	75		NA/NA	AUTO
DK326C-10	1050	8				NA/NA	AUTO
DK326C-10WD	1050	7				NA/NA	AUTO
DK326C-6	601	4				NA/NA	AUTO
DK326C-6WD	601	4				NA/NA	AUTO
DK328C-10	1050	3				---/---	
DK328C-21	2100	5				---/---	
DK328C-43	4300	10				---/---	
DK328H-43	4370	10				---/---	
DK503-2	10					---/---	
DK505-2	21	4	615	17		---/---	
DK511-3	29	5	699	17		---/300	699
DK511-5	41	7	699	17		---/300	699
DK511-8	67	10	823	17		---/400	822

Drive Model	Seek Time	Interface	Encode	Form Factor	cache kb	mtbf	RPM	Obsolete?
HPC5273A		EIDE/AT	1,7 RLL	3.5 3H	128k	300k 4480		
HPC5273AK		EIDE/ATA-2		3.5 3H	128k	300k 4480		
HPC5280A		EIDE		3.5 3H	128k	300k 4480		
HPC5281A		EIDE		3.5 3H	128k	300k 4480		
HPC5283A		EIDE/AT	1,7 RLL	3.5 3H	128k	300k 4480		
HPC5421SK	8.7	SE SCSI	PRML	3.5 HH	512k	7200		
HPC5421TK	8.7	SE SCSI-2W	PRML	3.5 HH	512k	7200		
HPC5435A		EIDE/AT	1,7 RLL	3.5 3H	128k	300k 4480		
HPC5435AK		EIDE	1,7 RLL	3.5 3H	128k	300k 4480		
HPC5436AK		EIDE/AT	1,7 RLL	3.5 3H	128k	300k 4480		
HPD1296A	65	ST412/506	MFM	5.25 HH		100k		Y
HPD1297A	40	ST412/506	MFM	5.25 HH		100k		Y
HPD1660A	16	ESDI (15)	2,7 RLL	5.25 HH	64k	150k		Y
HPD1661A	16	ESDI (15)	2,7 RLL	5.25 HH	64k	150k		Y
HPD1674A	40	ST412/506	MFM	5.25 FH		100k		Y
HPD1675A	40	ESDI (15)	2,7 RLL	5.25 FH		100k		Y
HPD1676A	40	ESDI (15)	2,7 RLL	5.25 FH		100k		Y
HPD1697A	17	IDE AT	1,7 RLL	3.5 3H		100k		Y
HPD2076B	10.5	SCSI-2 FAST			256k	500k 5400		
HPD2077A	10.5	SCSI-2 FAST			256k	500k 5400		
HPD2389A	14	IDE AT		3.5		300k 3600		
HPD3340A	8.4	SCSI-2			512k	1000k 5400		
HPD3341A	8.4	SCSI-2			512k	1000k 5400		

HITACHI AMERICA

Drive Model	Seek Time	Interface	Encode	Form Factor	cache kb	mtbf	RPM	Obsolete?
DK211A-51	12.6	IDE AT		2.5 4H	64k	300k 4464		
DK211A-54	12	ATA		2.5 4H	64k	4464		
DK211A-68	12	IDE AT		2.5 4H	64k	4464		Y
DK211C-51	12.6	SCSI-2 FAST		2.5 4H	512k	300k		
DK212A-10	12	EIDE/ATA-2	PRML8,9	2.5 4H	64k	300k 4464		
DK212A-81	12	EIDE/ATA-2	PRML8,9	2.5 4H	64k	4464		
DK213A-13	12	ATA-2	PRML8,9	2.5 4H	128k	300k 4464		
DK213A-18	12	ATA-2		2.5 4H	128k	4464		
DK221A-34	12.6	IDE AT		2.5 4H	64k	300k 4464		
DK222A-54	12	EIDE/ATA-2	PRML8,9	2.5 4H	64k	300k 4464		
DK223A-11	12	ATA-2		2.5 4H	128k	4464		
DK223A-81	12	ATA-2	PRML8,9	2.5 4H	128k	300k 4464		
DK224A-14	12	ATA-2		2.5 4H	128k	4464		
DK225A-21	12	ATA-2 Fast		2.5 4H	128k	4464		
DK226A-32	12	ATA-3		2.5 4H	128k	4000		
DK301-1	85	ST412/506	MFM	3.5 HH				Y
DK301-2	85	ST412/506	MFM	3.5 HH				Y
DK312C-20	17	SCSI	2,7 RLL	3.5 HH		40k		Y
DK312C-25	17	SCSI	2,7 RLL	3.5 HH		40k		Y
DK314C-41	17	SCSI	2,7 RLL	3.5 HH	64k	150k		Y
DK315C-10	11.8	SCSI-2 FAST		3.5 HH	256k	400k		Y
DK315C-11	11	SCSI-2		3.5 HH	256k	150k		Y
DK315C-14	11	SCSI-2 FAST		3.5 HH	256k	400k		Y
DK318H-91		SCSI		3.5 HH				
DK325C-57	9	Ultra SCSI		3.5 HH	512k	7200		
DK326C-10	12	SCSI-2	1,7 RLL	5.25 HH		200k 4500		
DK326C-10	9.8	SCSI-2 FAST		3.5 3H	448k	400k 6300		
DK326C-10WD	9.8	SCSI-2 FSTW		3.5 3H	448k	400k 6300		
DK326C-6		SCSI-2 FAST		3.5 3H	448k	400k		Y
DK326C-6WD		SCSI-2 FSTW		3.5 3H	448k	400k		Y
DK328C-10		SCSI-2		3.5 3H	448k	400k		
DK328C-21	9.8	SE SCSI-2F		3.5 3H	512k	800k 5400		
DK328C-43	9.8	SE SCSI-2D		3.5 3H	512k	800k 5400		
DK328H-43	9.8	SE SCSI-2F		3.5 3H	512k	800k 5400		
DK503-2		Ultra SCSI		3.5 3H	512k	7200		
DK505-2	85	ST412/506	MFM	5.25 HH				Y
DK511-3	30	ST412/506	MFM	5.25 HH				Y
DK511-5	26	ST412/506	MFM	5.25 FH				Y
DK511-8	23	ST412/506	MFM	5.25 FH				Y

Drive Model	Format Size MB	Head	Cyl	Sect/ Trac	Translate H/C/S	RWC/ WPC	Land Zone
DK512-12	94	7	823			NA/NA	
DK512-17	134	10	823			NA/NA	
DK512-8	67	5	823			NA/NA	AUTO
DK512C-12	94	7	823			---/---	
DK512C-17	134	10	819	35		---/---	
DK512C-8	67	5	823			---/---	
DK512S-17	143					---/---	
DK514-38	330	14	903	51		NA/NA	
DK514C-38	322	14	898	50		---/---	
DK514S-38	332					---/---	
DK515-12	1229	15		69		NA/NA	AUTO
DK515-78	673	14	1361	69		---/---	
DK515C-78	670	14	1356	69		---/---	
DK515C-78D	673	14	1361	69		NA/NA	AUTO
DK515S-78	673	14				---/---	
DK516-12	1230					NA/NA	AUTO
DK516-15	1320	15				---/---	
DK516C-16	1340	15				NA/NA	AUTO
DK517C-26	2000	14				NA/NA	AUTO
DK517C-37	2900	21				NA/NA	AUTO
DK521-5	51	6	823	17		---/NONE	822
DK522-10	91	6	823	36		NA/NA	
DK522C-10	87	6	819	35		---/---	
DK524C-20	169	6	1105	51		---/---	

HYOSUNG

Drive Model	Format Size MB	Head	Cyl	Sect/ Trac	Translate H/C/S	RWC/ WPC	Land Zone
HC8085	71	8	1024	17		NA/NA	AUTO
HC8128	109	8	1024	26		NA/NA	AUTO
HC8170E	150	8	1024	36		NA/NA	AUTO

IBM

Drive Model	Format Size MB	Head	Cyl	Sect/ Trac	Translate H/C/S	RWC/ WPC	Land Zone
06H3370	2250					---/---	
06H3372	2250					---/---	
06H5709	4510					---/---	
06H5710	5318					---/---	
06H6111	1080	2				---/---	
06H6740	2255					---/---	
06H6741	4510					---/---	
06H6742	4512					---/---	
06H6749	5318					---/---	
06H6750	5318					---/---	
06H7141	540					---/---	
06H7142	540					---/---	
06H8558	540					---/---	
06H8724	1700	2				---/---	
06H8891	1080					---/---	
07H0386	125	3				---/---	
07H0387	2250	5				---/---	
07H0834	4510	10				---/---	
07H1124	2160	3				---/---	
07H1128	2160	3				---/---	
32G3796	2000					---/---	
32G4194	245					---/---	
32G4195	340					---/---	
32G4196	527					---/---	
32G4198	1000					---/---	
32G4199	105					---/---	
32G4336	2000					---/---	
32G4338	2880					---/---	
3513364	364					---/---	
3513527	527					---/---	
70G7164	1000					---/---	

Drive Model	Seek Time	Interface	Encode	Form Factor	cache kb	mtbf	RPM	Obsolete?
DK512-12	23	ESDI	2,7 RLL	5.25 FH		20k	3482	Y
DK512-17	23	ESDI	2,7 RLL	5.25 FH		20k	3482	Y
DK512-8	23	ESDI	2,7 RLL	5.25 FH		20k	3482	Y
DK512C-12	23	SCSI	2,7 RLL	5.25 FH				Y
DK512C-17	23	SCSI	2,7 RLL	5.25 FH				Y
DK512C-8	23	SCSI	2,7 RLL	5.25 FH				Y
DK512S-17		SMD-E		5.25 FH				Y
DK514-38	16	ESDI	2,7 RLL	5.25 HH		30k	3600	Y
DK514C-38	16	SCSI	2,7 RLL	5.25 FH		30k		Y
DK514S-38		SMD-E		5.25 FH				Y
DK515-12	14	ESDI	2,7 RLL	5.25 FH		150k		
DK515-78	16	ESDI	2,7 RLL	5.25 FH		150k		
DK515C-78	16	SCSI	2,7 RLL	5.25 FH		150k		
DK515S-78D	16	E-SMD		5.25 FH		150k		
DK516-12	14	ESDI		5.25 FH		150k		
DK516-15	14	ESDI		5.25 FH		100k		
DK516C-16	14	SCSI	2,7 RLL	5.25 FH		150k		
DK517C-26	12	SCSI-2		5.25 FH		150k		
DK517C-37	12	SCSI-2 FAST		5.25 FH	512k	400k		Y
DK521-5	25	ST412/506	MFM	5.25 HH				Y
DK522-10	25	ESDI	2,7 RLL	5.25 HH		30k		Y
DK522C-10	25	SCSI	2,7 RLL	5.25 HH		30k		Y
DK524C-20	25	SCSI-2	2,7 RLL	5.25 HH		40k	3600	Y

HYOSUNG

Drive Model	Seek Time	Interface	Encode	Form Factor	cache kb	mtbf	RPM	Obsolete?
HC8085	25	ST412/506		5.25 FH		28k		
HC8128	25	ST412/506		5.25 FH		28k		
HC8170E	25	ESDI		5.25 FH		28k		

IBM

Drive Model	Seek Time	Interface	Encode	Form Factor	cache kb	mtbf	RPM	Obsolete?
06H3370	7.5	SCSI-2 FAST		3.5 3H	512k	1000k	7200	
06H3372	7.5	SCSI-2 FSTW		3.5 3H	512k	1000k	7200	
06H5709	8	SCSI-2 FSTW		3.5 HH	512k		7200	
06H5710	8	SCSI-2 FSTW		3.5 HH	512k	1000k	5400	
06H6111	10.5	ATA-2		3.5 HH	512k	500k	5400	
06H6740	7.5	SCSI-2 DIFF		3H		1000k	7200	
06H6741	8	SCSI-2 FAST		3.5 HH	512k		7200	
06H6742	8	SCSI-2 DIFF		3.5 HH		1000k	7200	
06H6749	8	SCSI-2 DIFF		3.5 HH		1000k	5400	
06H6750	8	SCSI-2 DIFF		3.5 HH		1000k	5400	
06H7141	12	ATA-2		3.5 3H	128k	350k	4500	
06H7142	12	ATA-2		3.5 3H	128k	350k	4500	
06H8558	12	SCSI-2 FAST		3.5 3H	128k	300k	4500	
06H8724	12	ATA-2		3.5 3H	128k	350k	4500	
06H8891	10.5	SCSI-2 FAST		3.5 3H	512k	500k	5400	
07H0386	8.5	SCSI-2-FstWd		3.5 3H		800k	7200	
07H0387	8.5	SCSI-2-FstWd		3.5 3H		800k	7200	
07H0834	8.5	SCSI-2-FstWd		3.5 HH		800k	7200	
07H1124	8.5	SCSI-2Fast		3.5 3H	512k	800k	5400	
07H1128	8.5	Ultra SCSIW		3.5 3H	512k	800k	5400	
32G3796	9.5	SCSI-2 FSTW		3.5 HH	512k	750k	7200	
32G4194	15	IDE AT		3.5 3H				
32G4195	14	IDE AT		3.5 3H				
32G4196	9	IDE AT		3.5 3H				
32G4198	8.6	SCSI-2 FAST		3.5 3H	512k	800k	5400	
32G4199	15	PCMCIA		FH				
32G4336	9.5	SCSI-2 FAST		3.5 HH	512k	750k	5400	
32G4338	94	AT BUS		3.5 3H				
3513364	12	PCMCIA		HH		200k		
3513527	12	PCMCIA		HH		200k		
70G7164	8.6	SCSI-2 FAST		3.5 3H	512k	800k	5400	

Drive Model	Format Size MB	Head	Cyl	Sect/ Trac	Translate H/C/S	RWC/ WPC	Land Zone
70G7424	170	2	2233			---/---	
70G8480	170	2	2111			---/---	
70G8481	340	4	2111			---/---	
70G8486	527					---/---	
70G8487	270					---/---	
70G8488	364					---/---	
70G8491	540	7	2466			---/---	
70G8492	1052	6				---/---	
70G8493	2014	16				---/---	
70G8494	2014	16				---/---	
70G8495	40					---/---	
70G8499	1440					---/---	
70G8500	1440					---/---	
70G8511	728	4	3875			---/---	
70G8512	1000	5				---/---	
70G8847	270					---/---	
70G8848	364					---/---	
70G8849	527					---/---	
70G8850	728					---/---	
70G9743	1000					---/---	
71G0666	1000	5				---/---	
71G6550	170	2	2111			---/---	
82G5926	270					---/---	
82G5927	364					---/---	
82G5928	540					---/---	
82G5929	1000	5				---/---	
82G5930	270					---/---	
82G5931	364					---/---	
82G5932	540					---/---	
82G5933	728					---/---	
82G6106	527					---/---	
92F0428	1052	6				---/---	
92F0440	2014	16				---/---	
94G2413	1052	6				---/---	
94G2439	270					---/---	
94G2440	364					---/---	
94G2441	540					---/---	
94G2442	728					---/---	
94G2644	270					---/---	
94G2645	364					---/---	
94G2646	540					---/---	
94G2647	728					---/---	
94G2649	1120					---/---	
94G2650	2250					---/---	
94G2651	4510					---/---	
94G3052	1120					---/---	
94G3054	2250					---/---	
94G3055	2250					---/---	
94G3056	2255					---/---	
94G3057	4510					---/---	
94G3059	5318					---/---	
94G3183	1080	2				---/---	
94G3184	1080	2				---/---	
94G3186	1080	2				---/---	
94G3187	1080	2				---/---	
94G3192	2250					---/---	
94G3193	2250					---/---	
94G3195	4510					---/---	
94G3196	4510					---/---	
94G3197	5318					---/---	
94G3198	4510					---/---	
94G3199	2255					---/---	
94G3200	4512					---/---	

Drive Model	Seek Time	Interface	Encode	Form Factor	cache kb	Obsolete? mtbf	RPM
70G7424	14	IDE AT		3.5 3H	96k	250k	3322
70G8480	13	SCSI-2 FAST		3.5 3H	64k	250k	4011
70G8481	13	SCSI-2		3.5 3H	64k	250k	4011
70G8486	12	IDE AT		3.5 3H	96k	300k	4500
70G8487	12	IDE AT		3.5 3H	96k	300k	4500
70G8488	12	IDE AT		3.5 3H	96k	300k	4500
70G8491	8.5	SCSI-2 FAST		3.5 3H	256k	300k	6300
70G8492	8.6	SCSI-2 FAST		3.5 3H	512k	800k	5400
70G8493	9.5	SCSI-2 FAST		3.5 HH	512k	750k	5400
70G8494	9.5	SCSI-2 FSTW		3.5 HH	512k	750k	5400
70G8495	18	PCMCIA		FH			
70G8499	94	IDE AT		3.5 3H			
70G8500	94	IDE AT		5.25 HH			
70G8511	12	IDE AT		3.5 3H	96k	300k	4500
70G8512	8.5	IDE AT		3.5 3H	512k	800k	5400
70G8847	12	IDE AT		3.5 3H	96k	300k	4500
70G8848	12	IDE AT		3.5 3H	96k	300k	4500
70G8849	12	IDE AT		3.5 3H	96k	300k	4500
70G8850	12	IDE AT		3.5 3H	96k	300k	4500
70G9743	8	SCSI-2 FSTW		3.5 3H	512k	800k	5400
71G0666	8.5	IDE AT		3.5 3H	512k	800k	5400
71G6550	13	SCSI-2 FAST		3.5 3H	64k	250k	4011
82G5926	12	IDE AT		3.5 3H	96k	300k	4500
82G5927	12	IDE AT		3.5 3H	96k	300k	4500
82G5928	12	ATA-2		3.5 3H	128k	350k	4500
82G5929	8.5	SCSI-2 FAST		3.5 3H	512k	800k	5400
82G5930	12	SCSI-2 FAST		3.5 3H	96k	300k	4500
82G5931	12	SCSI-2 FAST		3.5 3H	96k	300k	4500
82G5932	12	SCSI-2 FAST		3.5 3H	96k	300k	4500
82G5933	12	SCSI-2 FAST		3.5 3H	96k	300k	4500
82G6106	12	IDE AT		3.5 3H	96k	300k	4500
92F0428	8.6	SCSI-2 FAST		3.5 3H	512k	800k	5400
92F0440	9.5	SCSI-2 FAST		3.5 HH	512k	750k	5400
94G2413	8.6	SCSI-2 FAST		3.5 3H	512k	800k	5400
94G2439	12	SCSI-2 FAST		3.5 3H	96k	300k	4500
94G2440	12	SCSI-2 FAST		3.5 3H	96k	300k	4500
94G2441	12	SCSI-2 FAST		3.5 3H	96k	300k	4500
94G2442	12	SCSI-2 FAST		3.5 3H	96k	300k	4500
94G2644	12	SCSI-2 FAST		3.5 3H	96k	300k	4500
94G2645	12	SCSI-2 FAST		3.5 3H	96k	300k	4500
94G2646	12	SCSI-2 FAST		3.5 3H	96k	300k	4500
94G2647	12	SCSI-2 FAST		3.5 3H	96k	300k	4500
94G2649	6	SCSI-2 FSTW		3.5 3H	512k	1000k	7200
94G2650	7	SCSI-2 FSTW		3.5 3H	512k	1000k	7200
94G2651	8	SCSI-2 FSTW		3.5 HH	512k	1000k	7200
94G3052	6.9	SCSI-2 FSTW		3.5 3H	512k	1000k	7200
94G3054	7.5	SCSI-2 FAST		3.5 3H	512k	1000k	7200
94G3055	7.5	SCSI-2 FSTW		3.5 3H	512k	1000k	7200
94G3056	7.5	SCSI-2 FSTW		3.5 3H	512k	1000k	7200
94G3057	8	SCSI-2 FSTW		3.5 HH	512k	1000k	7200
94G3059	8	SCSI-2 FSTW		3.5 HH	512k	1000k	5400
94G3183	10.5	ATA-2		3.5 3H	512k	500k	5400
94G3184	10.5	SCSI-2 FAST		3.5 3H	512k	500k	5400
94G3186	10.5	ATA-2		3.5 3H	512k	500k	5400
94G3187	10.5	SCSI-2 FAST		3.5 3H	512k	500k	5400
94G3192	7.5	SCSI-2 FAST		3.5 3H	512k	1000k	7200
94G3195	7.5	SCSI-2 FSTW		3.5 3H	512k	1000k	7200
94G3196	8	SCSI-2 FAST		3.5 HH	512k	1000k	7200
94G3197	8	SCSI-2 FSTW		3.5 HH	512k	1000k	5400
94G3198	8	SCSI-2 FAST		3.5 HH	512k	1000k	7200
94G3199	7.5	SCSI-2 DIFF		3H	512k	1000k	7200
94G3200	8	SCSI-2 DIFF		3.5 HH	512k	1000k	7200

Drive Model	Format Size MB	Head	Cyl	Sect/ Trac	Translate H/C/S	RWC/ WPC	Land Zone
94G3201	5318					---/---	
94G3203	2255					---/---	
94G3204	4512					---/---	
94G3205	5318					---/---	
94G3787	5318					---/---	
94G3794	5318					---/---	
94G4196	527					---/---	

IBM CORP. (STORAGE SYS DIV)

Drive Model	Format Size MB	Head	Cyl	Sect/ Trac	Translate H/C/S	RWC/ WPC	Land Zone
0661-371	326	14	949	48		NA/NA	AUTO
0661-371	325	14	949	48		---/---	
0661-437	467					---/---	
0661-467	412	14	1199	48		NA/NA	AUTO
0661-467	406	14	1199	48		---/---	
0661-467R	400	14	1199	48		---/---	
0662-A10	1052	6				---/---	
0662-S12	1062	6				---/---	
0662-S1D	1052					NA/NA	AUTO
0662-SW1	1062	6				---/---	
0662-SWD	1062	6				---/---	
0663-E12	1044	14				---/---	
0663-E15	1206	16				---/---	
0663-E15R	1206	15	2463	66		---/---	
0663-H11	868	13	2051	66		---/---	
0663-H12	1004	15	2051	66		NA/NA	AUTO
0663-L08	623	9	2051	66		NA/NA	AUTO
0663-L11	868	13	2051	66		NA/NA	AUTO
0663-L12R	1004	15	2051	66		NA/NA	AUTO
0663-W2H	2412	15				---/---	
0664-CSH	4027	38	2328	211		---/---	
0664-DSH	4027	32				---/---	
0664-ESH	4027	38	2328	211		---/---	
0664-FSH	4027	32				---/---	
0664-M1H	2013	16				---/---	
0664-N1H	2013	16				---/---	
0664-P1S	1741	16	2304			---/---	
0665-30	25					---/---	
0665-38	31	5	733	17		NA/NA	AUTO
0665-53	44	7	733	17		NA/NA	AUTO
0667-61	52	5	582	35		NA/NA	AUTO
0667-85	73	7	582	35		NA/NA	AUTO
0669-133	133					---/---	
0671-315/S	315					---/---	
0671-S11	234	11	1224	34		NA/NA	AUTO
0671-S15	319	15	1224	34		NA/NA	AUTO
0681-1000	865	20	1458	58		NA/NA	AUTO
0681-500	476	11	1458	58		NA/NA	AUTO
115MB	118	7	915	36		---/---	AUTO
120MB	120	8	920	32		---/---	
120MB	120	8	920	32		---/---	
1430	21	4	615	17		320/128	307
1431	31	5	733	17		733/733	
1470	31	5	733	17		733/733	
1471	31	5	733	17		733/733	
20MB	21	4	612	17		---/306	663
20MB PS/2	21	4	612	17		---/---	128
245MB	245					---/---	
30MB	31	4	615	25		---/300	663
314MB	319	15	1225	34		---/---	AUTO
340MB	340					---/---	
44MB	44	7	733	17		---/300	733
527MB	527					---/---	
540MB	540	7	2466			---/---	

Drive Model	Seek Time	Interface	Encode	Form Factor	cache kb	mtbf	Obsolete? RPM ⇓
94G3201	8	SCSI-2 DIFF		3.5 HH	512k	1000k	5400
94G3203	7.5	SCSI-2 DIFF		3H	512k	1000k	7200
94G3204	8	SCSI-2 DIFF		3.5 HH	512k	1000k	7200
94G3205	8	SCSI-2 DIFF		3.5 HH	512k	1000k	5400
94G3787	8	SCSI-2 FAST		3.5 HH	512k	1000k	5400
94G3794	8	SCSI-2 FAST		3.5 HH	512k	1000k	5400
94G4196	8	IDE AT		3.5 3H	512k	1000k	5400

IBM CORP. (STORAGE SYS DIV)

Drive Model	Seek Time	Interface	Encode	Form Factor	cache kb	mtbf	Obsolete? RPM ⇓
0661-371	12.5	SCSI-2		3.5 HH	64k	300k	Y
0661-371	12	SCSI-2	RLL		64k	30k 4316	Y
0661-437		SCSI		3.5 HH			Y
0661-467	11.5	SCSI-2		3.5 HH	128k	300k	Y
0661-467	11	SCSI-2			128k	30k 4316	Y
0661-467R	11	SCSI-2		3.5 HH	128k	50k 4316	Y
0662-A10	10	IDE AT		3.5 3H	512k	500k 5400	Y
0662-S12	10	SCSI-2 FAST		3.5 3H	512k	800k 5400	Y
0662-S1D	10	SCSI-2FstD		3.5 3H	512k	800k 5400	
0662-SW1	10	SCSI-2 FSTW		3.5 3H	512k	800k 5400	
0662-SWD	10	SCSI-2 FSTW		3.5 3H	512k	800k 5400	
0663-E12	11	SCSI-2 FAST		3.5 HH	256k	50k 4317	
0663-E15	11	SCSI-2 FAST		3.5 HH	256k	50k 4317	
0663-E15R	9	SCSI-2		3.5 FH	256k	75k 4316	
0663-H11	11	SCSI-2	RLL	3.5 HH	256k	400k 4316	
0663-H12	11	SCSI-2	RLL	3.5 HH	256k	400k 4316	
0663-L08	9.8	SCSI-2		3.5 HH		400k	
0663-L11	11	SCSI-2	RLL	3.5 HH	256k	400k 4316	
0663-L12R	11	SCSI-2	RLL	3.5 FH	256k	75k 4316	
0663-W2H	9	SCSI-2 FAST		5.25 FH	256k	300k 4317	
0664-CSH	11	SCSI-2 FAST		5.25 FH		375k 5400	
0664-DSH		SCSI-2 FAST		5.25 FH		375k 5400	
0664-ESH	11	SCSI-2 FAST		5.25 FH		375k 5400	
0664-FSH		SCSI-2 FAST		5.25 FH		375k 5400	
0664-M1H	11	SCSI-2 FAST		3.5 HH	512k	750k 5400	
0664-N1H	11	SCSI-2 FSTW		3.5 HH	512k	750k 5400	
0664-P1S	11	IPI-2				750k 5400	
0665-30	40	ST412/506	MFM	5.25 FH			Y
0665-38	40	ST412/506	MFM	5.25 FH			Y
0665-53	40	ST412/506	MFM	5.25 FH			Y
0667-61	30	ESDI	RLL	5.25 FH			Y
0667-85	30	ESDI		5.25 FH			Y
0669-133		ESDI		5.25 FH			Y
0671-315/S		ESDI		5.25 FH			Y
0671-S11	21.5	SCSI		5.25 FH			Y
0671-S15	21.5	SCSI		5.25 FH			Y
0681-1000	13	SCSI	RLL	5.25 FH		150k	Y
0681-500	13	SCSI	RLL	5.25 FH		150k	Y
115MB	28	ESDI		5.25			Y
120MB	23	ST412/506	MFM	5.25 FH			Y
120MB	23	ST412/506	MFM	5.25 FH			Y
1430	80	ST412/506	MFM	5.25 FH			Y
1431	40	ST412/506	MFM	5.25 FH			Y
1470	40	ST412/506	MFM	5.25 FH			Y
1471	40	ST412/506	MFM	5.25 FH			Y
20MB		ST412/506	MFM	5.25 FH			Y
20MB PS/2	80	ST412/506	MFM	3.5 HH			Y
245MB	15	IDE AT		4H			Y
30MB		ST412/506	MFM	5.25 FH			Y
314MB	23	ESDI		5.25 FH			Y
340MB	14	IDE AT		4H			Y
44MB		ST412/506	MFM	5.25 FH			Y
527MB	9	IDE AT		3.5 3H			Y
540MB	9	SCSI-2		3.5 3H	256k	300k 6300	

Drive Model	Format Size MB	Head	Cyl	Sect/Trac	Translate H/C/S	RWC/WPC	Land Zone
60MB	60	6	762	26		--/--	
70MB	75	7	583	36		--/--	AUTO
DALA 3540	540	2	4892		16/1049/63	--/--	
DALA 3540	528				16/1049/63	--/--	
DALS 3540	541	2				--/--	
DAQA 32160	2160	4	6911			--/--	
DAQA 33240	3240	6	6911			--/--	
DBOA 2360	360	2	3478		16/700/63	--/--	
DBOA 2528	528				16/1024/63	--/--	
DBOA 2540	540	3	3478		16/1050/63	--/--	
DBOA 2720	722	4	3478		16/1400/63	--/--	
DCAA 32880	2880	4	8210			--/--	
DCAA 33610	3610	5	8210			--/--	
DCAA 34330	4330	6	8210			--/--	
DCAS 32160	2160	3	8120			--/--	
DCAS 34330	4330	6	8120			--/--	
DCHC 34550	4550	9				--/--	
DCHC 38700	8700	18				--/--	
DCHC 39100	9100	18				--/--	
DCHS 34550	4550	9				--/--	
DCHS 38700	8700	18				--/--	
DCHS 39100	9100	18				--/--	
DCMS 310800	10800	20				--/--	
DCRA 22160	2160				16/4200/63	--/--	
DDLA 21215	1215	3	5120			--/--	
DDLA 21620	1620	4	5120			--/--	
DESKSTAR 1700AT	1700	2				--/--	
DESKSTAR 540AT	540					--/--	
DESKSTAR XP 1.	1080	2				--/--	
DFHC 31080	1126	4				--/--	
DFHC 32160	2255	8				--/--	
DFHC 32160	2255	8				--/--	
DFHC 34320	4512	16				--/--	
DFHC 34320	4512	16				--/--	
DFHC C4x	4510	16				--/--	
DFHS 31080 S1F	1126	4				--/--	
DFHS 32160	2255	8				--/--	
DFHS 32160 S2D	2255					--/--	
DFHS 32160 S2F	2250					--/--	
DFHS 32160 S2W	2250					--/--	
DFHS 34320	4512	16				--/--	
DFHS 34320 S4D	4512					--/--	
DFHS 34320 S4F	4510					--/--	
DFHS 34320 S4W	4510					--/--	
DFMS 31080	1320	4				--/--	
DFMS 32160	2325	8				--/--	
DFMS 32600	2657	8				--/--	
DFMS 34320	4320	13				--/--	
DFMS 351AV	5106	16				--/--	
DFMS 35250	5318	16				--/--	
DFMS 35250 S5D	5318					--/--	
DFMS 35250 S5F	5318					--/--	
DFMS 35250 S5W	5318					--/--	
DHAA 2270	270	2	2788		16/524/63	--/--	
DHAA 2344	344	3	2788			--/--	
DHAA 2405	405	3	2788		16/785/63	--/--	
DHAA 2540	540	4	2788		16/1047/63	--/--	
DHAS 2270	270	2	2788			--/--	
DHAS 2344	344	3	2788			--/--	
DHAS 2405	405	3	2788			--/--	
DHAS 2540	540	4	2788			--/--	
DHEA 34330	4330	5	8209			--/--	
DHEA 34860	4860	6	8209			--/--	

Drive Model	Seek Time	Interface	Encode	Form Factor	cache kb	mtbf	Obsolete? RPM
60MB	27	ST412/506	MFM	5.25 FH			Y
70MB	30	ESDI		5.25 FH			Y
DALA 3540	12	ATA-2		3.5 3H	128k	350k	4500
DALA 3540	12	ATA-2		3.5 3H	128k	350k	4500
DALS 3540	12	SCSI-2 FAST		3.5 4H	64k	350k	4500
DAQA 32160	9.5	ATA-3		3.5 3H	128k		5400
DAQA 33240	9.5	ATA-3		3.5 3H	128k		5400
DBOA 2360	13	ATA-2		2.5 4H	32k	300k	4000
DBOA 2528	13	ATA-2		2.5 4H	64k	300k	4000
DBOA 2540	13	ATA-2		2.5 4H	32k	300k	4000
DBOA 2720	13	ATA-2		2.5 4H	64k	300k	4000
DCAA 32880	9.5	ATA-3	PRML	3.5 3H	128k	40k	5400
DCAA 33610	9.5	ATA-3	PRML	3.5 3H	128k	40k	5400
DCAA 34330	9.5	ATA-3	PRML	3.5 3H	128k	40k	5400
DCAS 32160	8.5	SCSI-3Ultra	PRML	3.5 3H	512k		5400
DCAS 34330	8.5	SCA-2	PRML	3.5 3H	512k		5400
DCHC 34550	7.5	SSA	PRML	3.5 HH	512k		7200
DCHC 38700	9	SSA		3.5 FH	512k	1000k	7200
DCHC 39100	7.5	SSA		3.5 HH	512k		7200
DCHS 34550	7.5	SCSI-2FstWd	PRML	3.5 3H	512k		7200
DCHS 38700	9	IPI-2		3.5 FH	512k	1000k	7200
DCHS 39100	7.5	SCSI-2Fst20	PRML	3.5 HH	512k		7200
DCMS 310800	9	SCSI-2 FSTW		3.5 FH	512k	1000k	5400
DCRA 22160	12	IDE AT		2.5 4H	96k		4200
DDLA 21215	13	ATA-3	PRML	2.5 4H	128k		4000
DDLA 21620	13	ATA-3	PRML	2.5 4H	128k		4000
DESKSTAR 1700AT	12	ATA-2		3.5 3H	128k	350k	4500
DESKSTAR 540AT	12	ATA-2		3.5 3H	128k	350k	4500
DESKSTAR XP 1.	10.5	ATA-2		3.5 3H	512k	500k	5400
DFHC 31080	9	SSA		3.5 3H	512k	1000k	7200
DFHC 32160	9	SSA		3.5 3H	512k	1000k	7200
DFHC 32160	9	SSA		3.5 3H	512k	1000k	7200
DFHC 34320	9	SSA		3.5 3H	512k	1000k	7200
DFHC 34320	9.5	SSA		3.5 3H	512k	1000k	7200
DFHC C4x	8	SSA		3.5 3H			7200
DFHS 31080 S1F	9	SCSI-2 F/FW		3.5 3H	512k	1000k	7200
DFHS 32160	9	SCSI-2 F/FW		3.5 3H	512k	1000k	7200
DFHS 32160 S2D	7.5	SCSI-2 DIFF		3.5 3H	512k	1000k	7200
DFHS 32160 S2F	7.5	SCSI-2 FAST		3.5 3H	512k	1000k	7200
DFHS 32160 S2W	7.5	SCSI-2 FSTW		3.5 3H	512k	1000k	7200
DFHS 34320	9	SCSI-2 F/FW		3.5 HH	512k	1000k	7200
DFHS 34320 S4D	8	SCSI-2 DIFF		3.5 HH	512k	1000k	7200
DFHS 34320 S4F	8	SCSI-2 FAST		3.5 HH	512k	1000k	7200
DFHS 34320 S4W	8	SCSI-2 FSTW		3.5 HH	512k	1000k	7200
DFMS 31080	7	SCSI-2 FAST		3.5 3H	512k	1000k	5400
DFMS 32160	9	SCSI-2 FAST		3.5 3H	512k	1000k	5400
DFMS 32600	9	SCSI-2 FAST		3.5 3H	512k	1000k	5400
DFMS 34320	9.5	SCSI-2 FAST		3.5 3H	512k	1000k	5400
DFMS 351AV	9.5	SCSI-2 F/FW		3.5 3H	512k	1000k	5400
DFMS 35250	9.5	SCSI-2 FAST		3.5 3H	512k	1000k	5400
DFMS 35250 S5D	8	SCSI-2 DIFF		3.5 3H	512k	1000k	5400
DFMS 35250 S5F	8	SCSI-2 DIFF		3.5 3H	512k	1000k	5400
DFMS 35250 S5W	8	SCSI-2 FSTW		3.5 HH	512k	1000k	5400
DHAA 2270	14	IDE AT		2.5 4H	32k	300k	3800
DHAA 2344	14	IDE AT		2.5 4H	32k	300k	3800 Y
DHAA 2405	14	IDE AT		2.5 4H	32k	300k	3800
DHAA 2540	14	IDE AT		2.5 4H	32k	300k	3800
DHAS 2270	14	SCSI-2 FAST		2.5 4H	32k	300k	3800
DHAS 2344	14	SCSI-2 FAST		2.5 4H	32k	300k	3800 Y
DHAS 2405	14	SCSI-2 FAST		2.5 4H	32k	300k	3800
DHAS 2540	14	SCSI-2 FAST		2.5 4H	32k	300k	3800
DHEA 34330	9.5	ATA-3	PRML	3.5 3H	512k	40k	5400
DHEA 34860	9.5	ATA-3	PRML	3.5 3H	512k	40k	5400

Drive Model	Format Size MB	Head	Cyl	Sect/Trac	Translate H/C/S	RWC/WPC	Land Zone
DHEA 36480	6480	8	8209			---/---	
DHEA 38451	8450	8	9784			---/---	
DLGA 22690	2690	7	5120			---/---	
DLGA 23080	3080	7	5120			---/---	
DMCA 21080	1080	3	4975			---/---	
DMCA 21440	1440	4	4975				
DORS 32160	2160	3				---/---	
DPEA 30540	540				16/1050/63	---/---	
DPEA 30810	812				16/1574/63	---/---	
DPEA 31080	1083				16/2100/63	---/---	
DPES 30540	540	4	4896			---/---	
DPES 30810	810	4	4896			---/---	
DPES 31080	1080	4	4896			---/---	
DPLA 24480	4480	7	6976			---/---	
DPLA 25120	5120	8	6976			---/---	
DPRA 20810	810	16	1572	63		---/---	
DPRA 21215	1215	16	2358	63		---/---	
DPRS 20810	810					---/---	
DPRS 21215	1215	16	2358	63		---/---	
DSAA 3270	270					---/---	
DSAA 3360	364					---/---	
DSAA 3540	548	3	3875			---/---	
DSAA 3720	720	3	3875			---/---	
DSAS 3270	270					---/---	
DSAS 3360	364					---/---	
DSAS 3540	548	4	3875			---/---	
DSAS 3720	720	4	3875			---/---	
DSOA 20540	540				16/1050/63	---/---	
DSOA 20810	810				16/1575/63	---/---	
DSOA 21080	1080				16/2100/63	---/---	
DTCA 23240	3240	5	6976			---/---	
DTCA 24090	4090	6	6976			---/---	
DTNA 21800	1800	5	4928			---/---	
DTNA 22160	2160	6	4928			---/---	
DVAA 2810	810	6	2788		16/1571/63	---/---	
DVAA 2810	810				16/1571/63	---/---	
DVAS 2810	810	6	2788			---/---	
H1172-S2	172	2	2264			---/---	
H2172-A2	172	2	2264			AUTO/AUTO	NA
H2172-S2	172	2	2264			AUTO/AUTO	NA
H2258-A3	258	3	2264			---/---	
H2258-S3	258	3	2264			---/---	
H2344-A4	344	4	2264			---/---	
H2344-S4	344	4	2264			---/---	
H3133-A2	133	2	2420		15/1023/17	---/---	
H3171-A2	171	2	2420		10/984/34	---/---	
H3256-A3	256	3	2420		16/872/36	---/---	
H3342-A4	342	4	2420		16/872/48	---/---	
Ultrastar Ultra 2.16S	2160	3				---/---	
Ultrastar XP 2.25GB	2250	4				---/---	
Ultrastar XP 4.51GB	4510	8				---/---	
WD-12	10	4	306	17		296/296	
WD-2120	126	4	1248	50		---/---	
WD-240	42	2	1120	38		NA/NA	AUTO
WD-240	43	2	1122	38		NA/NA	AUTO
WD-240	42	2	1120	38		---/---	
WD-25	20	8	306	17		296/296	
WD-25A	20					---/---	
WD-25R	20					---/---	
WD-280	85	4	1120	38		---/---	
WD-3158	120	8	920	32		NA/NA	AUTO
WD-3158(PS2/70)	120					---/---	
WD-3160	163	8	1021	39		NA/NA	AUTO

Drive Model	Seek Time	Interface	Encode	Form Factor	cache kb	mtbf	RPM	Obsolete?
DHEA 36480	9.5	ATA-3	PRML	3.5 3H	512k	40k	5400	
DHEA 38451	9.5	ATA-3	PRML	3.5 3H	512k	40k	5400	
DLGA 22690	12	ATA-3	PRML	2.5 4H	128k		4900	
DLGA 23080	12	ATA-3	PRML	2.5 4H	128k		4900	
DMCA 21080	13	ATA-3	PRML	2.5 4H	128k		4000	
DMCA 21440	13	ATA-3	PRML	2.5 4H	128k		4000	
DORS 32160	8.5	SCSI-3Ultra		3.5 3H	512k	800k	5400	
DPEA 30540	10.5	ATA-2		3.5 3H	512k	350k	5400	
DPEA 30810	10.5	IDE AT		3.5 3H	448k	350k	5400	
DPEA 31080	10.5	ATA-2		3.5 3H	448k	350k	5400	
DPES 30540	10.5	SCSI-2 FAST		3.5 3H	512k	1000k	5400	Y
DPES 30810	10.5	SCSI-2 FAST		3.5 3H	512k	1000k	5400	Y
DPES 31080	10.5	SCSI-2 FAST		3.5 3H	512k	1000k	5400	Y
DPLA 24480	12	ATA-3	PRML	2.5 4H	512k		4900	
DPLA 25120	12	ATA-3	PRML	2.5 4H	512k		4900	
DPRA 20810	12	ATA-2		2.5 4H	64k	300k	4900	
DPRA 21215	12	ATA-2		2.5 4H	64k	300k	4900	
DPRS 20810	12	SCSI-2		2.5 4H	64k	300k	4900	
DPRS 21215	12	SCSI-2		2.5 4H	64k	300k	4900	
DSAA 3270	12	IDE AT		3.5 4H	96k	300k	4500	Y
DSAA 3360	12	IDE AT		3.5 3H	96k	300k	4500	Y
DSAA 3540	12	ATA-2		3.5 3H	128k	300k	4500	Y
DSAA 3720	12	ATA-2		3.5 3H	128k	300k	4500	Y
DSAS 3270	12	SCSI-2 FAST		3.5 4H	96k	300k	4500	Y
DSAS 3360	12	SCSI-2 FAST		3.5 3H	96k	300k	4500	Y
DSAS 3540	12	SCSI-2 FAST		3.5 3H	128k	300k	4500	Y
DSAS 3720	12	SCSI-2 FAST		3.5 3H	128k	300k	4500	Y
DSOA 20540	13	IDE AT		2.5 4H	128k		4000	
DSOA 20810	13	IDE AT		2.5 4H	128k		4000	
DSOA 21080	13	IDE AT		2.5 4H	128k		4000	
DTCA 23240	13	ATA-3	PRML	2.5 4H	512k		4000	
DTCA 24090	13	ATA-3	PRML	2.5 4H	512k		4000	
DTNA 21800	13	ATA-3	PRML	2.5 4H	128k		4000	
DTNA 22160	13	ATA-3	PRML	2.5 4H	128k		4000	
DVAA 2810	14	IDE AT		2.5 4H	32k	300k	3800	Y
DVAA 2810	14	IDE AT	1,7 RLL	2.5 4H	32k			3800
DVAS 2810	14	SCSI-2 FAST		2.5 4H	32k	300k	3800	Y
H1172-S2	14	SCSI		2.5 4H	32k	300k	3800	Y
H2172-A2	14	IDE AT		2.5 3H	32k	300k	3800	Y
H2172-S2	14	SCSI-2		2.5 3H	32k	300k	3800	Y
H2258-A3	14	IDE AT		2.5 4H	32k	300k	3800	Y
H2258-S3	14	SCSI		2.5 4H	32k	300k	3800	Y
H2344-A4	14	IDE AT		2.5 4H	32k	300k	3800	Y
H2344-S4	14	SCSI		2.5 4H	32k	300k	3800	Y
H3133-A2	14	IDE AT		3.5 3H	96k	250k	3600	Y
H3171-A2	14	IDE AT		3.5 3H	96k	250k	3600	Y
H3256-A3	14	IDE AT		3.5 3H	96k	250k	3600	Y
H3342-A4	14	IDE AT		3.5 3H	96k	250k	3600	Y
Ultrastar Ultra 2.16S	8.5	Ultra SCSIW		3.5 3H	512k	800k	5400	
Ultrastar XP 2.25GB	7.5	SCSI-2 FAST		3.5 3H	512k	1000k	7200	
Ultrastar XP 4.51GB	8	SCSI-2 FAST		3.5 HH	512k	1000k	7200	
WD-12		ST412/506	MFM	5.25 FH		150k	3600	Y
WD-2120	16	IDE AT	RLL	2.5 4H		150k	3600	Y
WD-240	19	MCA		2.5 4H		150k	3600	Y
WD-240	19	MCA		2.5 4H		150k	3600	Y
WD-240	19	MCA		2.5 4H		150k	3600	Y
WD-25		ST412/506	MFM	5.25 FH		150k	3600	Y
WD-25A		ST412/506	MFM	5.25 FH		150k	3600	Y
WD-25R		ST412/506	MFM	5.25 FH		150k	3600	Y
WD-280	17	MCA		2.5 4H		150k	3600	Y
WD-3158	23	MCA		3.5 FH		45k		Y
WD-3158(PS2/70)		MCA		3.5 HH				Y
WD-3160	16	MCA		3.5 HH		110k		Y

Drive Model	Format Size MB	Head	Cyl	Sect/ Trac	Translate H/C/S	RWC/ WPC	Land Zone
WD-325	21	4	615	17		---/---	
WD-325K	20					---/---	
WD-325N(PS2/50)	21					---/---	
WD-325Q(PS2/30)	21					---/---	
WD-336P(PS2/30E)	31					---/---	
WD-336R(PS2/50Z)	31					---/---	
WD-380	81	4	1021	39		NA/NA	AUTO
WD-380S(PS2/30)	81					---/---	
WD-387(PS2/70)	60	4	928	32		NA/NA	AUTO
WD-387T(PS2/70)	60					---/---	
WD-L320(PS2/30E)	20					---/---	
WD-L330P(PS2/30E)	30					---/---	
WD-L330R(PS2/70)	30					---/---	
WD-L40	41	2	1038	39		NA/NA	AUTO
WD-L40S(PS2/70)	41	2	1038	39		NA/NA	AUTO
WDA-2120R	126	4	1243	50		---/---	
WDA-240	43	2	1122	38		NA/NA	AUTO
WDA-260	63	2	1248	50		---/---	
WDA-280	87	4	1122	38		NA/NA	AUTO
WDA-3160	81	4	1021	39		NA/NA	AUTO
WDA-380	81	4	1021	39		NA/NA	AUTO
WDA-L160	171	4	1923	44	8/966/44	---/---	
WDA-L40	41	2	1040	39		NA/NA	AUTO
WDA-L42	42	2	1067	39		NA/NA	AUTO
WDA-L80	85	2	1923	44		---/---	
WDS-240	43	2	1120	38		NA/NA	AUTO
WDS-260	63	2	1248	50		---/---	
WDS-280	85	4	1120	38		---/---	
WDS-3100	104	2	1990	44		NA/NA	AUTO
WDS-3160	163	8	1021	39		NA/NA	AUTO
WDS-3168	160					---/---	
WDS-3200	209	4	1990	44		---/---	
WDS-380	81	4	1021	39		NA/NA	AUTO
WDS-387	80					---/---	
WDS-L160	171	4	1923	44		---/---	
WDS-L40	41	2	1038	39		NA/NA	AUTO
WDS-L42	42	2	1066	39		NA/NA	AUTO
WDS-L80	85	2	1923	44		---/---	

IMI

Drive Model	Format Size MB	Head	Cyl	Sect/ Trac	Translate H/C/S	RWC/ WPC	Land Zone
5006	5	2	306	17		307/214	
5007	5	2	306	17		---/---	
5012	10	4	306	17		307/214	
5018	15	6	306	17		307/214	
5021H	15			17		---/---	
7720	20			17		---/---	
7740	40			17		---/---	

INTERGRAL PERIPHERALS

Drive Model	Format Size MB	Head	Cyl	Sect/ Trac	Translate H/C/S	RWC/ WPC	Land Zone
105 (VIPER)	105	4				---/---	
170 (VIPER)	171	4				---/---	
1820 (MUSTANG)	21	2	615			NA/NA	AUTO
1842 (STINGRAY)	42	3				NA/NA	AUTO
1862	64	3		V		NA/NA	AUTO
2100	1000	6			16/1900/63	NA/NA	AUTO
260 (VIPER)	262	4				---/---	
340 (VIPER)	341	4				---/---	

JCT (SEE MAXCARD)

Drive Model	Format Size MB	Head	Cyl	Sect/ Trac	Translate H/C/S	RWC/ WPC	Land Zone
100	5			17		---/---	
1000	5			17		---/---	
1005	7			17		---/---	

Drive Model	Seek Time	Interface	Encode	Form Factor	cache kb	mtbf	RPM	Obsolete?
WD-325	88	MCA		3.5 HH				Y
WD-325K		ST412/506	MFM	3.5 HH				Y
WD-325N(PS2/50)		MCA		3.5 HH				Y
WD-325Q(PS2/30)		MCA		3.5 HH				Y
WD-336P(PS2/30E)		MCA		3.5 HH				Y
WD-336R(PS2/50Z)		MCA		3.5 HH				Y
WD-380	16	MCA		3.5 HH		110k		Y
WD-380S(PS2/70)		MCA		3.5 HH				Y
WD-387(PS2/70)	23	MCA		3.5 HH		45k		Y
WD-387T(PS2/70)		MCA		3.5 HH				Y
WD-L320(PS2/30E)		MCA		3.5 HH				Y
WD-L330P(PS2/30E)		MCA		3.5 HH				Y
WD-L330R(PS2/70)		MCA		3.5 HH				Y
WD-L40	17	MCA		3.5 HH		90k		Y
WD-L40S(PS2/70)	17	MCA		3.5 HH		90k		Y
WDA-2120R	16	IDE AT		2.5 HH		25k	3600	Y
WDA-240	19	IDE AT		2.5 4H		150k	3600	Y
WDA-260	16	IDE AT		2.5 4H		150k	3600	Y
WDA-280	17	IDE AT		2.5 4H		150k	3600	Y
WDA-3160	18	IDE AT		3.5 HH		110k		Y
WDA-380	16	IDE AT		3.5 HH		110k		Y
WDA-L160	17	IDE AT		3.5 4H		150k	3600	Y
WDA-L40	17	IDE AT	2,7 RLL	3.5 3H		90k		Y
WDA-L42	17	IDE AT	2,7 RLL	3.5 3H		90k		Y
WDA-L80	16	SCSI-2		3.5 4H		150k	3600	Y
WDS-240	19	SCSI		2.5 4H		150k	3600	Y
WDS-260	16	SCSI-2		2.5 4H		150k	3600	Y
WDS-280	17	SCSI		2.5 4H		150k	3600	Y
WDS-3100	12	SCSI-2		3.5 4H	32k	150k	4320	Y
WDS-3160	16	SCSI-2		3.5 HH		110k		Y
WDS-3168		SCSI		3.5 HH				Y
WDS-3200	12	SCSI-2		3.5 4H	32k	150k	4320	Y
WDS-380	16	SCSI-2		3.5 HH		110k		Y
WDS-387		SCSI		3.5 HH				Y
WDS-L160	16	SCSI-2		3.5 4H		150k	3600	Y
WDS-L40	17	SCSI-2		3.5 FH		90k		Y
WDS-L42	17	SCSI-2		3.5 3H		80k		Y
WDS-L80	16	SCSI-2		3.5 4H		150k	3600	Y

IMI

Drive Model	Seek Time	Interface	Encode	Form Factor	cache kb	mtbf	RPM	Obsolete?
5006	27	ST412/506	MFM					
5007	85	ST412/506	MFM	5.25 FH				
5012	27	ST412/506	MFM					
5018	27	ST412/506	MFM					
5021H	85	ST412/506	MFM	5.25 FH				
7720	85	ST412/506	MFM					
7740	85	ST412/506	MFM					

INTEGRAL PERIPHERALS

Drive Model	Seek Time	Interface	Encode	Form Factor	cache kb	mtbf	RPM	Obsolete?
105 (VIPER)	15	PCMCIA-ATA	1,7 RLL	1.8 IN	32k	250k	4500	
170 (VIPER)	12	PCMCIA-ATA	1,7 RLL	1.8 IN	32k	250k	4500	
1820 (MUSTANG)	18	IDE AT	1,7 RLL	1.8		100k		Y
1842 (STINGRAY)	18	IDE AT	1,7 RLL	1.8		100k		Y
1862	18	IDE AT	1,7 RLL			100k		Y
2100	12	ATA-2	1,7 RLL	2.5 4H	128k	250k	4200	
260 (VIPER)	12	PCMCIA-ATA	1,7 PRML	1.8 IN	32k	250k	4500	
340 (VIPER)	12	PCMCIA-ATA	1,7 PRML	1.8 IN	32k	250k	4500	

JCT (SEE MAXCARD)

Drive Model	Seek Time	Interface	Encode	Form Factor	cache kb	mtbf	RPM	Obsolete?
100	110	ST412/506	MFM	5.25 HH				Y
1000	110	Commodore	MFM	5.25 HH				Y
1005	110	Commodore	MFM	5.25 HH				Y

Drive Model	Format Size MB	Head	Cyl	Sect/Trac	Translate H/C/S	RWC/WPC	Land Zone
1010	14			17		---/---	
105	5	2	306	17		---/---	
110	14			17		---/---	
120	20			17		---/---	

JTS CORPORATION

Drive Model	Format Size MB	Head	Cyl	Sect/Trac	Translate H/C/S	RWC/WPC	Land Zone
C1700-2AF	1700	4	3312			---/---	
C2000-2AF	2000	4	3882			---/---	
C2500-3AF	2500	6	4970			---/---	
C3000-3AF	3000	6	5824			---/---	
Champ Family	1000	4	5050			---/---	
Champ Family	1300	4	5050			---/---	
Champ Family	1700	6	5050			---/---	
Champ Family	2000	6	5050			---/---	
N1080-2AR	1080	4	4032			---/---	
N1440-3AR	1440	6	4032			---/---	
N1620-3AR	1620	6	4032			---/---	
N2160-3AR	2160	6	4435			---/---	

JVC COMPANIES OF AMERICA

Drive Model	Format Size MB	Head	Cyl	Sect/Trac	Translate H/C/S	RWC/WPC	Land Zone
JD-E2042M	42	2	973	43		NA/NA	AUTO
JD-E2085M	85	4	973	43		NA/NA	AUTO
JD-E2825P(A)	21	2	581	36		---/---	AUTO
JD-E2825P(S)	21	2	581	36		---/---	AUTO
JD-E2825P(X)	21	2	581	36		---/---	AUTO
JD-E2850P(A)	42	3	791	35		---/---	AUTO
JD-E2850P(S)	42	3	791	35		---/---	AUTO
JD-E2850P(X)	42	3	791	35		---/---	AUTO
JD-E3824TA	21	2	436	48			AUTO
JD-E3848HA	42	4	436	48			
JD-E3848P(A)	42	2	862	48		---/---	AUTO
JD-E3848P(S)	42	2	862	48		---/---	AUTO
JD-E3848P(X)	42	2	862	48		---/---	AUTO
JD-E3896P(A)	84	4	862	48		---/---	AUTO
JD-E3896P(S)	84	4	862	48		---/---	AUTO
JD-E3896P(X)	84	4	862	48		---/---	AUTO
JD-E3896V(A)	84	4	862	48		NA/NA	AUTO
JD-E3896V(S)	84	4	862	48		NA/NA	AUTO
JD-E3896V(X)	84	4	862	48		NA/NA	AUTO
JD-F2042M	42	2	973	43		NA/NA	AUTO
JD3842HA	21	2	436	48		---/---	
JD3848HA	43	4	436	48		---/---	

KALOK CORPORATION

Drive Model	Format Size MB	Head	Cyl	Sect/Trac	Translate H/C/S	RWC/WPC	Land Zone
KL1000	105	6	978	35		---/---	AUTO
KL3100	105	6	820	48/35	6/979/35	NA/NA	AUTO
KL3120	121	6	820	55/40	6/981/40	NA/NA	AUTO
KL320	21	4	615	17		616/300	
KL330	33	4	615	26		617/617	
KL332	40	4	615			---/---	
KL340	43	4	820	17			
KL341	43	4	676	31			AUTO
KL342	42	4	676	31		---/---	
KL343	43	4	676	31		645/645	AUTO
KL360	66	6	820	26		---/---	
KL381	85	6	820			NA/NA	
KL383	84	6	815	34	6/815/33	NA/NA	AUTO
P3250	251	4	2048	80	16/961/32	NA/NA	AUTO
P3360	362	4	791	56	16/791/56	NA/NA	AUTO
P3540	540	4	1024	63		NA/NA	AUTO
P5-125(A)	125	2	2048			NA/NA	AUTO
P5-125(S)	125	2	2048			NA/NA	AUTO

Drive Model	Seek Time	Interface	Encode	Form Factor	cache kb	mtbf	RPM	Obsolete?
1010	130	Commodore	MFM	5.25 HH				Y
105	110	ST412/506	MFM	5.25 HH				Y
110	130	ST412/506	MFM	5.25 HH				Y
120	100	ST412/506	MFM	5.25 HH				Y

JTS CORPORATION

Drive Model	Seek Time	Interface	Encode	Form Factor	cache kb	mtbf	RPM	Obsolete?
C1700-2AF		EIDE/ATA-3		3.5 3H	256k	500k	5400	
C2000-2AF		EIDE/ATA-3		3.5 3H	256k	500k	5400	
C2500-3AF		EIDE/ATA-3		3.5 3H	256k	500k	5400	
C3000-3AF		EIDE/ATA-3		3.5 3H	256k	500k	5400	
Champ Family		EIDE	1,7 RLL	3.5 4H	128k	500k	4500	
Champ Family		EIDE	1,7 RLL	3.5 4H	128k	500k	4500	
Champ Family		EIDE	1,7 RLL	3.5 4H	128k	500k	4500	
Champ Family		EIDE	1,7 RLL	3.5 4H	128k	500k	4500	
N1080-2AR		EIDE/ATA-3		3.0	128k	500k	4103	
N1440-3AR		EIDE/ATA-3		3.0	128k	500k	4103	
N1620-3AR		EIDE/ATA-3		3.0	128k	500k	4103	
N2160-3AR		EIDE/ATA-3		3.0	128k	500k	4103	

JVC COMPANIES OF AMERICA

Drive Model	Seek Time	Interface	Encode	Form Factor	cache kb	mtbf	RPM	Obsolete?
JD-E2042M	16	IDE AT	1,7 RLL	2.5 4H	32k	130k	3118	Y
JD-E2085M	16	IDE AT	1,7 RLL	2.5 4H	32k	130k	3118	Y
JD-E2825P(A)	25	IDE AT	2,7 RLL	3.5 4H		30k	3109	Y
JD-E2825P(S)	25	SCSI	2,7 RLL	3.5 4H		30k	3109	Y
JD-E2825P(X)	25	IDE XT	2,7 RLL	3.5 4H		30k	3109	Y
JD-E2850P(A)	25	IDE AT	2,7 RLL	3.5 4H	32k	40k	3109	Y
JD-E2850P(S)	25	SCSI	2,7 RLL	3.5 4H	32k	40k	3109	Y
JD-E2850P(X)	25	IDE XT	2,7 RLL	3.5 4H	32k	40k	3109	Y
JD-E3824TA	28		2,7 RLL	3.5 3H		20k		Y
JD-E3848HA	29		2,7 RLL	3.5 3H		20k		Y
JD-E3848P(A)	25	IDE AT	2,7 RLL	3.5 4H		30k	2332	Y
JD-E3848P(S)	25	SCSI	2,7 RLL	3.5 4H		30k	2332	Y
JD-E3848P(X)	25	IDE XT	2,7 RLL	3.5 4H		30k	2332	Y
JD-E3896P(A)	25	IDE AT	2,7 RLL	3.5 4H		30k	3109	Y
JD-E3896P(S)	25	SCSI	2,7 RLL	3.5 4H		30k	3109	Y
JD-E3896P(X)	25	IDE XT	2,7 RLL	3.5 4H		30k	3109	Y
JD-E3896V(A)	25	IDE AT	2,7 RLL	3.5 3H		30k		Y
JD-E3896V(S)	25	SCSI	2,7 RLL	3.5 3H		30k		Y
JD-E3896V(X)	25	IDE XT	2,7 RLL	3.5 3H		30k		Y
JD-F2042M	16	IDE AT	1,7 RLL	2.5 4H	32k	130k	3118	Y
JD3842HA	28		2,7 RLL	3.5 3H		20k		Y
JD3848HA	29		2,7 RLL	3.5 3H		20k		Y

KALOK CORPORATION

Drive Model	Seek Time	Interface	Encode	Form Factor	cache kb	mtbf	RPM	Obsolete?
KL1000	25	IDE AT	2,7 RLL	3.5 HH	32k	50k	3662	Y
KL3100	19	IDE AT	2,7 RLL	3.5 HH		100k	3662	Y
KL3120	19	IDE AT	2,7 RLL	3.5 HH		100k	3663	Y
KL320	40	ST412/506	MFM	3.5 HH		43.5	3600	Y
KL330	40	ST412/506	2,7 RLL	3.5 HH		43.5	3600	Y
KL332	48	MCA	2,7 RLL	3.5 HH				Y
KL340	25	ST412/506	MFM	3.5 HH		50		Y
KL341	33	SCSI	2,7 RLL	3.5 HH	8k	40k	3375	Y
KL342	30	MCA	2,7 RLL	3.5 HH		40k		Y
KL343	28	IDE AT	2,7 RLL	3.5 HH	8k	40k	3375	Y
KL360	25	ST412/506	2,7 RLL	3.5 HH		50k		Y
KL381	25	SCSI	2,7 RLL	3.5 HH		50k		Y
KL383	25	IDE AT	2,7 RLL	3.5 HH		50k		Y
P3250	16.5	IDE AT	1,7 RLL	3.5 4H	128k	250k	3600	Y
P3360	16.5	IDE AT	1,7 RLL	3.5 4H	128k	250k	3600	Y
P3540	11/16.5	IDE AT	1,7 RLL	3.5 4H	128k	250k	4200	Y
P5-125(A)	17	IDE AT	1,7 RLL			100k		Y
P5-125(S)	17	SCSI-2	1,7 RLL			100k		Y

Drive Model	Format Size MB	Head	Cyl	Sect/ Trac	Translate H/C/S	RWC/ WPC	Land Zone
P5-250(A)	251	4	2048			NA/NA	AUTO
P5-250(S)	251	4	2048			NA/NA	AUTO

KYOCERA ELECTRONICS, INC.

KC20A	21	4	615	17		---/---	
KC20B	21	4	615	17		---/---	
KC30A	33	4	615	26		---/---	
KC30B	33	4	615	26		---/---	
KC40GA	40	2	1075	17	4/577	33/---	AUTO
KC80C	87	8	787	28		NA/NA	
KC80GA	78	4	1069	36	8/577/33	NA/NA	AUTO

LANSTOR

LAN-115		15	918	17		---/NONE	1023
LAN-140		8	1024	34		---/NONE	1023
LAN-180		8	1024	26		---/NONE	1023
LAN-64		8	1024	17		---/NONE	1023

LAPINE

LT10	10	2	615	17		616/---	
LT100 (not verified)	10					---/---	
LT20	20	4	615	17		616/---	
LT200	20	4	615	17		615/---	
LT2000	20	4	614	17		615/---	
LT300	32	4	614	17		615/---	
LT3065	10	4	306	17		306/128	
LT3512	10	4	306	17		306/128	
LT3522	10	4	306	17		307/---	
LT3532	32	4	614	26		---/615	
LT3533	20					---/---	
LT4000 (not verified)	40					---/---	
TITAN 20	21	4	615	17		---/---	615
TITAN 30	21	4	615			---/---	
TITAN 40	40					---/---	
TITAN 42	42					---/---	
TITAN 45	45					---/---	

MAXTOR CORPORATION

250837	837	5		66-132		---/---	
250840	840	5		43-67		---/---	
25084A	80	2		43-67	16/569/18	NA/NA	569
251005	1005	6		66-132		---/---	
251010	1010	6		66-132		---/---	
25128A	128	4	1092	NA	14/1024/17	NA/NA	AUTO
251340	1340	8		66-132		---/---	
251350	1350	8		66-132	16/2616/63	---/---	
25252A	252	6			16/569/54	---/---	
25252S	251	6		67		NA/NA	AUTO
2585A	85	4	1092	NA	10/981/17	NA/NA	AUTO
2585S (never made)	85	4	1092	V		NA/NA	AUTO
3053	44	5	1024	17		1024/512	
3085	68	7	1170	17		1170/512	
3130E	112	5	1250	36		1251/512	
3130S	112	5	1255	35		1256/512	
3180E	150	7	1250	36		1251/512	
3180S	153	7	1255	36		1256/512	
3380	338	15	1224	NA		NA/NA	AUTO
7040A	41	2	1155	36	5/981/17	NA/NA	AUTO
7040S	42	2	1155	36		NA/NA	AUTO
7060A	65	2	1498	NA	16/467/17	NA/NA	AUTO
7060S	60	2	1498	42		NA/NA	AUTO

Drive Model	Seek Time	Interface	Encode	Form Factor	cache kb	mtbf	RPM	Obsolete?
P5-250(A)	17	IDE AT	1,7 RLL			100k		Y
P5-250(S)	17	SCSI-2	1,7 RLL			100k		Y

KYOCERA ELECTRONICS, INC.

KC20A	65	ST412/506	MFM	3.5 HH		40k		Y
KC20B	62	ST412/506	MFM	3.5 HH		40k		Y
KC30A	65	ST412/506	2,7 RLL	3.5 HH		40k		Y
KC30B	62	ST412/506	2,7 RLL	3.5 HH		40k		Y
KC40GA	28	IDE AT	2,7 RLL	3.5 HH		40k		Y
KC80C	28	SCSI	2,7 RLL	3.5 HH		28k		Y
KC80GA	23	IDE AT	2,7 RLL	3.5 HH		28k		Y

LANSTOR

LAN-115								
LAN-140								
LAN-180								
LAN-64								

LAPINE

LT10	27	ST412/506	MFM	3.5 HH				
LT100 (not verified)	85			3.5 HH				
LT20		ST412/506	MFM	3.5 HH				
LT200	65	ST412/506	MFM	3.5 HH				
LT2000		ST412/506	MFM	3.5 HH				
LT300		ST412/506	MFM	3.5 HH				
LT3065		ST412/506	2,7 RLL	3.5 HH				
LT3512	65	ST412/506	2,7 RLL	3.5 HH				
LT3522	27	ST412/506	MFM	3.5 HH				
LT3532	65	ST412/506	2,7 RLL	3.5 HH				
LT3533		ST412/506	MFM	3.5 HH				
LT4000 (not verified)	27	SCSI		3.5 HH				
TITAN 20		ST412/506	MFM	3.5 HH				
TITAN 30			RLL?	3.5 HH				
TITAN 40		SCSI		3.5 HH				
TITAN 42		SCSI		3.5 HH				
TITAN 45		SCSI		3.5 HH				

MAXTOR CORPORATION

250837	14	IDE AT	1,7 RLL	2.5 4H	64k	300k	4464	Y
250840	12	IDE AT	1,7 RLL	2.5 4H	128k	350k	4247	Y
25084A	12	IDE AT	1,7 RLL	2.5 4H	128k	350k	4247	Y
251005	14	IDE AT	1,7 RLL	2.5 4H	64k	300k	4464	Y
251010	14	IDE AT	1,7 RLL	2.5 4H	64k	300k	4464	Y
25128A	14	IDE AT	1,7 RLL	2.5 4H		250k	3600	Y
251340	14	IDE AT	1,7 RLL	2.5 4H		250k	3600	Y
251350	13	IDE AT	1,7 RLL	2.5 4H	64k	300k	4464	Y
25252A	12	IDE AT	1,7 RLL	2.5 4H	64k	300k	4464	Y
25252S	12	SCSI	1,7 RLL	2.5 4H	64k	350k	4247	Y
2585A	14	IDE AT	1,7 RLL	2.5 4H	128k	350k	4247	
2585S (never made)	15	SCSI	1,7 RLL	2.5 4H		150k	3600	
3053	25	ST412/506	MFM	5.25 HH		30k	3600	Y
3085	22	ST412/506	MFM	5.25 HH		40k	3600	Y
3130E	17	ESDI	2,7 RLL	5.25 HH		35k	3600	Y
3130S	17	SCSI	2,7 RLL	5.25 HH		35k	3600	Y
3180E	17	ESDI	2,7 RLL	5.25 HH		35k	3600	Y
3180S	17	SCSI	2,7 RLL	5.25 HH		35k	3600	Y
3380	27	SCSI	RLL	5.25 FH		20k	3600	Y
7040A	17	IDE AT	1,7 RLL	3.5 3H	32k	150k	3703	Y
7040S	17	SCSI	1,7 RLL	3.5 3H	32k	150k	3600	Y
7060A	15	IDE AT	1,7 RLL	3.5 3H		150k	3600	Y
7060S	15	SCSI	1,7 RLL	3.5 3H		150k	3600	Y

Drive Model	Format Size MB	Head	Cyl	Sect/Trac	Translate H/C/S	RWC/WPC	Land Zone
7080A	85	4	1166	36	10/981/17	NA/NA	AUTO
7080S	85	4	1166	36		NA/NA	AUTO
71000A	1002	3			16/1946/63	--/--	
71050A	1000	5		77-124	16/2045/63	--/--	
71084A	1084	4	413691-155		16/2105/63	NA/NA	AUTO
71084AP	1084	4	413691-155		16/2105/63	NA/NA	AUTO
7120A	125	4	1498	NA	16/936/17	NA/NA	AUTO
7120S	125	4	1498	42		NA/NA	AUTO
71260A	1200	6		77-124	16/2448/63	--/--	
71260AP	1260	5	413691-155		16/2632/63	NA/NA	AUTO
71260S	1200					--/--	
7131A	125	2	2096		8/1002/32	NA/NA	AUTO
71336A	1336	4	4721		16/2595/63	--/--	
71336AP	1336	4	4721		16/2595/63	--/--	
71350A	1350	4			16/2624/63	--/--	
71350AP	1350	4			16/2624/63	--/--	
7135AV	135	1		72-123	13/966/21	--/--	
71626A	1626	6	413691-155		16/3158/63	NA/NA	AUTO
71626AP	1626	6	413691-155		16/3158/63	NA/NA	AUTO
71670A	1670	5	4721		16/3224/63	--/--	
71670AP	1670	5	4721		16/3224/63	--/--	
71687AP	1687	4			16/3280/63	--/--	
7170A	171	4	1281	48-72	10/984/34	--/--	
7171A	172	4		V	15/866/26	--/--	
72004A	2004	6	4721		16/3893/63	--/--	
72004AP	2004	6	4721		16/3893/63	--/--	
72025AP	2025	6			16/3936/63	--/--	
7213A	213	4	1690	42	16/683/38	NA/NA	AUTO
7213S	213	4	1690	42		NA/NA	AUTO
7245A	234	4		48-72	16/967/31	--/--	
7245S	245	4		48-72		--/--	
72577AP	2577	8			16/4996/63	--/--	
72700AP	2700	8			16/5248/63	--/--	
7270AV	270	2		72-123	11/959/50	--/--	
7273A	273	3		V	16/1012/33	--/--	
7290A	290	4		60-96		NA/NA	AUTO
7290S	290	4				--/--	
7345A	345	4			15/790/57	--/--	
7345S	345	4				--/--	
7405A	4051	4			16/989/50	--/--	
7405AV	405	3		72-123	16/989/50	--/--	
7420AV	420	3		72-123	16/1046/63	--/--	
7425AV	425	2	372176-144		16/1000/52	NA/NA	AUTO
7540AV	540	4		72-123	16/1046/63	--/--	
7541A	541	4	413691-155		16/1052/63	NA/NA	AUTO
7541AP	541	4	413691-155		16/1052/63	NA/NA	AUTO
7546A	547	4		V	16/1024/63	--/--	
7668A	668	2	4721		16/1297/63	--/--	
7668AP	668	2	4721		16/1297/63	--/--	
7850AV	850	4	372176-144		16/1648/63	NA/NA	AUTO
8051A	41	4	745	26	5/981/17	NA/NA	981
8051S	40	4	793	28		NA/NA	AUTO
80875A2	875	2			16/1700/63	--/--	
81080A3	1080	3			16/2100/63	--/--	
81081A2	1081	2			16/2100/63	--/--	
81275A3	1275	3			16/2480/63	--/--	
81280A2	1280	2			16/2481/63	--/--	
81312A3	1312	3			16/2548/63	--/--	
81620A3	1550	3			16/3150/63	--/--	
81630A4	1630	4			16/3168/63	--/--	
81750A2	1750	2			15/3618/63	--/--	
81750A4	1750	4			16/3400/63	--/--	
81750D2	1750	2			15/3618/63	--/--	

Drive Model	Seek Time	Interface	Encode	Form Factor	cache kb	mtbf	RPM	Obsolete?
7080A	17	IDE AT	1,7 RLL	3.5 3H	32k	150k	3703	Y
7080S	17	SCSI	1,7 RLL	3.5 3H	32k	150k	3600	Y
71000A	12	IDE AT	1,7 RLL	3.5 3H		300k		Y
71050A	12	EIDE	1,7 RLL	3.5 3H	256k	300k	4500	Y
71084A	12	IDE AT	1,7 RLL	3.5 3H	64k	300k	4480	Y
71084AP	12	IDE AT	1,7 RLL	3.5 3H	128k	300k	4480	Y
7120A	15	IDE AT	1,7 RLL	3.5 3H	64k	150k	3600	Y
7120S	15	SCSI	1,7 RLL	3.5 3H	64k	150k	3600	Y
71260A	12	EIDE	1,7 RLL	3.5 3H	256k	300k	4500	Y
71260AP	12	IDE AT	1,7 RLL	3.5 3H	128k	300k	4480	Y
71260S	14	ATA-2	1,7 RLL	3.5 3H	256k	300k	4500	Y
7131A	14	IDE AT	1,7 RLL	3.5 3H	64k	300k	3551	Y
71336A		IDE AT	1,7 RLL	3.5 3H	64k	300k	4480	Y
71336AP		IDE AT	1,7 RLL	3.5 3H	128k	300k	4480	Y
71350A		IDE AT	1,7 RLL	3.5 3H	64k	300k	4480	Y
71350AP		IDE AT	1,7 RLL	3.5 3H	128k	300k	4480	Y
7135AV	12	IDE AT	1,7 RLL	3.5 3H	32k	300k	3551	Y
71626A	12	IDE AT	1,7 RLL	3.5 3H	64k	300k	4480	Y
71626AP	12	IDE AT	1,7 RLL	3.5 3H	128k	300k	4480	Y
71670A		IDE AT	1,7 RLL	3.5 3H	64k	300k	4480	Y
71670AP		IDE AT	1,7 RLL	3.5 3H	128k	300k	4480	Y
71687AP		IDE AT	1,7 RLL	3.5 3H	128k	300k	4480	Y
7170A	15	IDE AT	1,7 RLL	3.5 3H	64k	150k	3551	Y
7171A	14	IDE AT	1,7 RLL	3.5 3H	64k	300k	3551	Y
72004A		IDE AT	1,7 RLL	3.5 3H	64k	300k	4480	Y
72004AP		IDE AT	1,7 RLL	3.5 3H	128k	300k	4480	Y
72025AP		IDE AT	1,7 RLL	3.5 3H	128k	300k	4480	Y
7213A	15	IDE AT	1,7 RLL	3.5 3H	64k	150k	3551	Y
7213S	15	SCSI	1,7 RLL	3.5 3H	64k	150k	3551	Y
7245A	15	IDE AT	1,7 RLL	3.5 3H	64k	250k	3551	Y
7245S	15	SCSI	1,7 RLL	3.5 3H	64k	250k	3551	Y
72577AP		IDE AT	1,7 RLL	3.5 3H	128k	300k	4480	Y
72700AP		IDE AT	1,7 RLL	3.5 3H	128k	300k	4480	Y
7270AV	12	IDE AT	1,7 RLL	3.5 3H	32k	300k	3551	Y
7273A	12	IDE AT	1,7 RLL	3.5 3H	256k	300k	4500	Y
7290A	14	IDE AT	1,7 RLL	3.5 3H	64k	300k	3551	Y
7290S	14	SCSI	1,7 RLL	3.5 3H	64k	300k	3551	Y
7345A	14	IDE AT	1,7 RLL	3.5 3H	64k	300k	3551	Y
7345S	14	SCSI	1,7 RLL	3.5 3H	64k	300k	3551	Y
7405A	12	IDE AT	1,7 RLL	3.5 3H	32k	300k	3551	Y
7405AV	12	IDE AT	1,7 RLL	3.5 3H	32k	300k	3551	Y
7420AV	12	IDE AT	1,7 RLL	3.5 3H	32k	300k	3551	Y
7425AV	12	IDE AT	1,7 RLL	3.5 3H	64k	300k	3551	Y
7540AV	12	IDE AT	1,7 RLL	3.5 3H	32k	300k	3551	Y
7541A	12	IDE AT	1,7 RLL	3.5 3H	64k	300k	4480	Y
7541AP	12	IDE AT	1,7 RLL	3.5 3H	128k	300k	4480	Y
7546A	12	IDE AT	1,7 RLL	3.5 3H	256k	300k	4500	Y
7668A		IDE AT	1,7 RLL	3.5 3H	64k	300k	4480	Y
7668AP		IDE AT	1,7 RLL	3.5 3H	128k	300k	4480	Y
7850AV	12	IDE AT	1,7 RLL	3.5 3H	64k	300k	3551	Y
8051A	28	IDE AT	2,7 RLL	3.5 HH	32k	150k	3484	Y
8051S	28	SCSI	2,7 RLL	3.5 HH		30k	3600	Y
80875A2	12	EIDE	1,7 RLL	3.5 3H	128k	400k	4480	
81080A3	12	ATA-3	1,7 RLL	3.5 3H	128k	400k	4480	
81081A2	11	ATA-3	RLL 8,9	3.5 3H	256k	400k	4480	
81275A3	12	IDE AT	1,7 RLL	3.5 3H	128k	400k	4480	
81280A2	10	ATA-3	RLL 8,9	3.5 3H	256k	500k	5400	
81312A3	12	EIDE	1,7 RLL	3.5 3H	128k	400k	4480	
81620A3	11	ATA-3	RLL 8,9	3.5 3H	256k	400k	4480	
81630A4	12	IDE AT	1,7 RLL	3.5 3H	128k	400k	4480	
81750A3	10	ATA-4	RLL 8,9	3.5 3H	256k	500k	5200	
81750A4	12	EIDE	1,7 RLL	3.5 3H	128k	400k	4480	
81750D2	10	ATA-4	RLL 8,9	3.5 3H	256k	500k	5200	

Drive Model	Format Size MB	Head	Cyl	Sect/Trac	Translate H/C/S	RWC/WPC	Land Zone
82100A4	2100	4			16/4092/63	---/---	
82187A5	2187	5			16/4248/63	---/---	
82400A4	2400	4			16/4708/63	---/---	
82559A4	2559	4			16/4960/63	---/---	
82560A3	2560	3			15/5292/63	---/---	
82560A4	2560	4			16/4962/63	---/---	
82560D3	2560	3			15/5292/63	---/---	
82577A6	2577	6			16/5000/63	---/---	
82580A5	2580	5			16/5004/63	---/---	
82625A6	2625	6			16/5100/63	---/---	
83062A7	3062	7			16/5948/63	---/---	
83200A5	3200	5			16/6296/63	---/---	
83200A6	3200	6			15/6296/15	---/---	
83200A8	3200	8			16/6218/63	---/---	
83201A6	3201	6			16/6218/63	---/---	
83202A6	3202	6			16/6296/63	---/---	
83209A5	3209	5			16/6218/63	---/---	
83240A4	3240	4			16/6696/63	---/---	
83240D4	3240	4			15/6696/63	---/---	
83500A4	3500	4			15/7237/63	---/---	
83500A8	3500	8			16/6800/63	---/---	
83500D4	3500	4			15/7237/63	---/---	
83840A6	3840	6			16/7441/63	---/---	
84000A6	4000	6			16/7763/63	---/---	
84004A8	4004	8			16/7758/63	---/---	
84200A8	4200	8			16/8184/63	---/---	
8425S	21	4	612	17		616/128	664
84320A5	4320	5			15/8928/63	---/---	
84320A8	4320	8			16/8400/63	---/---	
84320D5	4320	5			15/8928/63	---/---	
85120A8	5120	8			16/9924/63	---/---	
85121A8	5121	8			15/10585/63	---/---	
85210D6	5210	6			15/10856/63	---/---	
85250A6	5250	6			15/10856/63	---/---	
86480A8	6480	8			15/13392/63	---/---	
86480D8	6480	8			15/13392/63	---/---	
87000A8	7000	8			15/14475/63	---/---	
87000D8	7000	8			15/14475/63	---/---	
9380E	338	15	1224	36		NA/512	AUTO
9380S	336	15	1218	36		NA/512	AUTO
9780E	676	15	1661	53		NA/512	AUTO
9780S	676	15	1661	53		166/512	AUTO
EXT4175	149	7	1224	34		NA/NA	AUTO
EXT4280	234	11	1224	36		NA/NA	AUTO
EXT4380	319	15	1224	34		NA/NA	AUTO
LXT100A	90					---/---	
LXT100S	96	8	733	32		NA/NA	AUTO
LXT200A	191	7	1320	NA	15/816/32	NA/NA	AUTO
LXT200S	207	7	1320	33,53		NA/NA	AUTO
LXT213A	203	7	1320	NA	16/683/38	NA/NA	AUTO
LXT213S	213	7	1320	34-56		NA/NA	AUTO
LXT340A	340	7	1560	47-72	16/654/63	NA/NA	AUTO
LXT340S	340	7	1560	47-72		NA/NA	AUTO
LXT437A (never made)	437	9	1560	V	16/842/63	NA/NA	AUTO
LXT437S (never made)	437	9	1560	V		NA/NA	AUTO
LXT50S	48	4	733	32		NA/NA	AUTO
LXT535A	535	11	1024	63	16/1024/63	NA/NA	AUTO
LXT535S	535	11	1560	47-72		NA/NA	AUTO
MOBILEMAX 105MB	105	4	1254	28-50		---/---	
MOBILEMAX 131MB	131	4	1254	28-50		---/---	
MOBILEMAX 171MB	171	4	1254	28-50		---/---	
MOBILEMAX 262MB	262					---/---	
MX9217SDN	2170	9		100-14		---/---	

Drive Model	Seek Time	Interface	Encode	Form Factor	cache kb	mtbf	RPM	Obsolete?
82100A4	11	ATA-3	RLL 8,9	3.5 3H	256k	400k	4480	
82187A5	12	EIDE	1,7 RLL	3.5 3H	128k	400k	4480	
82400A4	10	ATA-3	RLL 8,9	3.5 3H	256k	500k	5400	
82559A4	10	ATA-3	RLL 8,9	3.5 3H	256k	500k	5400	
82560A3	10	ATA-4	RLL 8,9	3.5 3H	256k	500k	5200	
82560A4	10	ATA-3	RLL 8,9	3.5 3H	256k	500k	5400	
82560D3	10	ATA-4	RLL 8,9	3.5 3H	256k	500k	5200	
82577A6	12	IDE AT	1,7 RLL	3.5 3H	128k	400k	4480	
82580A5	11	ATA-3	RLL 8,9	3.5 3H	128k	400k	4480	
82625A6	12	EIDE	1,7 RLL	3.5 3H	128k	400k	4480	
83062A7	12	EIDE	1,7 RLL	3.5 3H	128k	400k	4480	
83200A5	10	ATA-3	RLL 8,9	3.5 3H	256k	500k	5400	
83200A6	10	ATA-3	RLL 8,9	3.5 3H	256k	500k	5400	
83200A8	12	EIDE	1,7 RLL	3.5 3H	128k	400k	4480	
83201A6	11	ATA-3	RLL 8,9	3.5 3H	256k	500k	5400	
83202A4	10	ATA-3	RLL 8,9	3.5 3H	256k	500k	5400	
83209A5	10	ATA-3	RLL 8,9	3.5 3H	256k	500k	5400	
83240A4	10	ATA-4	RLL 8,9	3.5 3H	256k	500k	5200	
83240D4	10	ATA-4	RLL 8,9	3.5 3H	256k	500k	5200	
83500A4	10	ATA-4	RLL 8,9	3.5 3H	256k	500k	5200	
83500A8	12	EIDE	1,7 RLL	3.5 3H	128k	400k	4480	
83500D4	10	ATA-4	RLL 8,9	3.5 3H	256k	500k	5200	
83840A6	10	ATA-3	RLL 8,9	3.5 3H	256k	500k	5400	
84000A6	10	ATA-3	RLL 8,9	3.5 3H	256k	500k	5400	
84004A8	10	ATA-3	RLL 8,9	3.5 3H	256k	500k	5400	
84200A8	10	ATA-3	RLL 8,9	3.5 3H	256k	500k	5400	
8425S	68	SCSI	MFM	3.5 HH		20k	3600	Y
84320A5	10	ATA-4	RLL 8,9	3.5 3H	256k	500k	5200	
84320A8	11	ATA-4	RLL 8,9	3.5 3H	256k	400k	4480	
84320D5	10	ATA-4	RLL 8,9	3.5 3H	256k	500k	5200	
85120A8	10	ATA-3	RLL 8,9	3.5 3H	256k	500k	5400	
85121A8	10	ATA-3	RLL 8,9	3.5 3H	256k	500k	5400	
85210D6	10	ATA-4	RLL 8,9	3.5 3H	256k	500k	5200	
85250A6	10	ATA-4	RLL 8,9	3.5 3H	256k	500k	5200	
86480A8	10	ATA-4	RLL 8,9	3.5 3H	256k	500k	5200	
86480D8	10	ATA-4	RLL 8,9	3.5 3H	256k	500k	5200	
87000A8	10	ATA-4	RLL 8,9	3.5 3H	256k	500k	5200	
87000D8	10	ATA-4	RLL 8,9	3.5 3H	256k	500k	5200	
9380E	16	ESDI	2,7 RLL	5.25 FH		50k	3600	Y
9380S	16	SCSI	2,7 RLL	5.25 FH		50k	3600	Y
9780E	17	ESDI	1,7 RLL	5.25 FH		50k	3600	Y
9780S	17	SCSI	1,7 RLL	5.25 FH		30k	3600	Y
EXT4175	27	ESDI	RLL	5.25 FH		20k	3600	Y
EXT4280	27	ESDI	RLL	5.25 FH		20k	3600	Y
EXT4380	27	ESDI	RLL	5.25 FH		20k	3600	Y
LXT100A		IDE AT	1,7 RLL	3.5 HH		150k	3600	Y
LXT100S	27	SCSI	2,7 RLL	3.5 HH		150k	3600	Y
LXT200A	15	IDE AT	1,7 RLL	3.5 HH		150k	3600	Y
LXT200S	15	SCSI	1,7 RLL	3.5 HH		150k	3600	Y
LXT213A	15	IDE AT	1,7 RLL	3.5 HH	32k	150k	3600	Y
LXT213S	15	SCSI-2	1,7 RLL	3.5 HH	32k	150k	3600	Y
LXT340A	15	IDE AT	2,7 RLL	3.5 HH	128k	150k	3600	Y
LXT340S	15	SCSI	2,7 RLL	3.5 HH	128k	150k	3600	Y
LXT437A (never made)	12	IDE AT	2,7 RLL	3.5 HH		150k		Y
LXT437S (never made)	13	SCSI	2,7 RLL	3.5 HH		150k		Y
LXT50S	27	SCSI	2,7 RLL	3.5 HH		40k	3600	Y
LXT535A	13	IDE AT	2,7 RLL	3.5 HH	128k	150k	3600	Y
LXT535S	13	SCSI	2,7 RLL	3.5 HH	128k	150k	3600	Y
MOBILEMAX 105MB	19	PCMCIA-ATA	1,7 RLL	1.8 4H	31k	300k	4464	Y
MOBILEMAX 131MB	19	PCMCIA-ATA	1,7 RLL	2.8 4H	31k	300k	4464	Y
MOBILEMAX 171MB	19	PCMCIA-ATA	1,7 RLL	2.8 4H	31k	300k	4464	Y
MOBILEMAX 262MB		PCMCIA-ATA	1,7 RLL	1.8 4H				Y
MX9217SDN	10.5	SE SCSI-2D	1,7 RLL	3.5 3H	512k	800k	5400	Y

Drive Model	Format Size MB	Head	Cyl	Sect/Trac	Translate H/C/S	RWC/WPC	Land Zone
MX9217SDW	2170	9		100-14		---/---	
MX9217SSN	2170	9		100-14		---/---	
MX9217SSW	2170	9		100-14		---/---	
MXT1240S	1240	15	2512	NA		NA/NA	AUTO
MXT540AL	547	7	2466		16/1024/63	NA/NA	AUTO
MXT540SL	547	7	2466	NA		NA/NA	AUTO
P0-12S PANTHER	1045	15	163261-103			NA/NA	AUTO
P1-08E (never made)	696	9	1778	85		NA/NA	AUTO
P1-12E (never made)	1051	15	1778	77		NA/NA	AUTO
P1-13E (never made)	1160	15	1778			NA/NA	AUTO
P1-16E (never made)	1331	19	1778			NA/NA	AUTO
P1-17E (never made)	1470	19	1778	85		NA/NA	AUTO
P1-17S PANTHER	1503	19	177870-101			NA/NA	AUTO
RXT-800HD	786					---/---	
RXT-800HS	786					---/---	
RXT-800S	786					---/---	
XT1050	38	5	902	17		NA/NA	AUTO
XT1065	52	7	918	17		NA/NA	AUTO
XT1085	71	8	1024	17		NA/NA	AUTO
XT1105	84	11	918	17		NA/NA	AUTO
XT1120R	105	8	1024	25		NA/NA	AUTO
XT1140	119	15	918	17		NA/NA	AUTO
XT1240R	196	15	1024	25		NA/NA	AUTO
XT2085	72	7	1224	17		NA/NA	AUTO
XT2140	113	11	1224	17		NA/NA	AUTO
XT2190	159	15	1224	17		NA/NA	AUTO
XT3170	146	9	1224	26		NA/NA	AUTO
XT3280	244	15	1224	26		NA/NA	AUTO
XT3380	319	15	1224	34		NA/NA	AUTO
XT4170E	157	7	1224	35/36	16	NA/NA	AUTO
XT4170S	157	7	1224	35-36		NA/NA	AUTO
XT4175	234	11	1224	34		NA/NA	AUTO
XT4230E	203	9	1224	35/36		NA/NA	AUTO
XT4280SF	338	15	1224	36		NA/NA	AUTO
XT4380E	338	15	1224	36		NA/NA	AUTO
XT4380S	338	15	1224	NA		NA/NA	AUTO
XT81000E	889	15	1632	71		NA/NA	AUTO
XT8380E	361	8	1632	53-54		NA/NA	AUTO
XT8380EH	360	8	1632	54		NA/NA	AUTO
XT8380S	361	8	1632	NA		NA/NA	AUTO
XT8380SH	360	8	1632	NA		NA/NA	AUTO
XT8610E	541	12	1632	53-54		NA/NA	AUTO
XT8702S	616	15	1490	NA		NA/NA	AUTO
XT8760E	676	15	1632	53-54		NA/NA	AUTO
XT8760EH	676	15	1632	54		NA/NA	AUTO
XT8760S	670	15	1632	NA		NA/NA	AUTO
XT8760SH	670	15	1632	NA		NA/NA	AUTO
XT8800E	694	15	1274	54		NA/NA	AUTO

MEGA DRIVE SYSTEMS

Drive Model	Format Size MB	Head	Cyl	Sect/Trac	Translate H/C/S	RWC/WPC	Land Zone
M1-105	105	4	1219			---/---	
M1-120	122	2	1818			---/---	
M1-240	245	4	1818			---/---	
M1-52	52	2	1219			---/---	
MH-1G	1050	13	1974			---/---	
MH-340	338	9	1100			---/---	
MH-425	426	9	1520			---/---	
MH-535	525	9	1476			---/---	
P105	103	6	1019	33		NA/NA	AUTO
P120	120	5	1123			NA/NA	AUTO
P170	168	7	1123			NA/NA	AUTO
P210	210	7	1156			NA/NA	AUTO
P320	320	15	886			NA/NA	AUTO

Drive Model	Seek Time	Interface	Encode	Form Factor	cache kb	mtbf	RPM	Obsolete?
MX9217SDW	10.5	SE SCSI-2DW	1,7 RLL	3.5 3H	512k	800k	5400	Y
MX9217SSN	10.5	SE SCSI-2	1,7 RLL	3.5 3H	512k	800k	5400	Y
MX9217SSW	10.5	SE SCSI-2W	1,7 RLL	3.5 3H	512k	800k	5400	Y
MXT1240S	9	SCSI-2 FAST	1,7 RLL	3.5 HH		300k	6300	
MXT540AL	9	IDE AT	1,7 RLL	3.5 3H		300k	6300	
MXT540SL	9	SCSI-2 FAST	1,7 RLL	3.5 3H		300k	6300	
P0-12S PANTHER	13	SCSI-2	RLL	5.25 FH	256k	150k	3600	Y
P1-08E (never made)	12	ESDI	RLL	5.25 FH		100k	3600	
P1-12E (never made)	13	ESDI	RLL	5.25 FH		100k	3600	
P1-13E (never made)	13	ESDI	RLL	5.25 FH		100k	3600	
P1-16E (never made)	13	ESDI	RLL	5.25 FH		100k	3600	
P1-17E (never made)	13	ESDI	RLL	5.25 FH		100k	3600	
P1-17S PANTHER	13	SCSI-2	RLL	5.25 FH	256k	150k	3600	Y
RXT-800HD		SCSI		5.25 HH				
RXT-800HS		SCSI		5.25 HH				
RXT-800S		SCSI		5.25 HH				
XT1050	30	ST412/506	MFM	5.25 FH		20k	3600	Y
XT1065	30	ST412/506	MFM	5.25 FH		20k	3600	Y
XT1085	28	ST412/506	MFM	5.25 FH		150k	3600	Y
XT1105	27	ST412/506	MFM	5.25 FH		20k	3600	Y
XT1120R	27	ST412/506	2,7 RLL	5.25 FH		150k	3600	Y
XT1140	27	ST412/506	MFM	5.25 FH		20k	3600	Y
XT1240R	27	ST412/506	2,7 RLL	5.25 FH		150k	3600	Y
XT2085	30	ST412/506	MFM	5.25 FH		30k	3600	Y
XT2140	30	ST412/506	MFM	5.25 FH		30k	3600	Y
XT2190	29	ST412/506	MFM	5.25 FH		150k	3600	Y
XT3170	30	SCSI	RLL	3.5 FH		20k	3600	Y
XT3280	30	SCSI	RLL	5.25 FH		20k	3600	Y
XT3380	27	SCSI	RLL	5.25 FH		20k	3600	Y
XT4170E	14	ESDI	1,7 RLL	5.25 FH		150k	3600	Y
XT4170S	14	SCSI	1,7 RLL	5.25 FH		150k	3600	Y
XT4175	27	ESDI	RLL	5.25 FH		20k	3600	Y
XT4230E	16	ESDI	1,7 RLL	5.25 FH		150k	3600	Y
XT4280SF	16	SCSI	1,7 RLL	5.25 FH		150k	3600	Y
XT4380E	16	ESDI	1,7 RLL	5.25 FH		150k	3600	Y
XT4380S	16	SCSI	1,7 RLL	5.25 FH		150k	3600	Y
XT81000E	16	ESDI	1,7 RLL	5.25 FH		150k	3600	
XT8380E	16	ESDI	1,7 RLL	5.25 FH		150k	3600	Y
XT8380EH	13	ESDI	1,7 RLL	5.25 FH		150k	3600	Y
XT8380S	14	SCSI	1,7 RLL	5.25 FH		150k	3600	Y
XT8380SH	14	SCSI	1,7 RLL	5.25 FH		150k	3600	Y
XT8610E	16	ESDI	1,7 RLL	5.25 FH	256k	150k	3600	Y
XT8702S	17	SCSI	1,7 RLL	5.25 FH		150k	3600	Y
XT8760E	16	ESDI	1,7 RLL	5.25 FH		150k	3600	Y
XT8760EH	14	ESDI	1,7 RLL	5.25 FH		150k	3600	Y
XT8760S	16	SCSI	1,7 RLL	5.25 FH		150k	3600	Y
XT8760SH	14	SCSI	1,7 RLL	5.25 FH		150k	3600	Y
XT8800E	14	ESDI	1,7 RLL	5.25 FH	256k	150k	3600	Y

MEGA DRIVE SYSTEMS

Drive Model	Seek Time	Interface	Encode	Form Factor	cache kb	mtbf	RPM	Obsolete?
M1-105	17	SCSI	2,7 RLL	3.5 HH	64k	60k	3662	Y
M1-120	16	SCSI	1,7 RLL	3.5 HH	256k	250k	4306	Y
M1-240	16	SCSI	1,7 RLL	3.5 HH	256k	250k	4306	Y
M1-52	17	SCSI	2,7 RLL	3.5 HH	64k	60k	3662	Y
MH-1G	10	SCSI	1,7 RLL	3.5 HH	256k	300k	5400	
MH-340	13	SCSI	1,7 RLL	3.5 HH	64k	150k	4412	Y
MH-425	14	SCSI	1,7 RLL	3.5 HH	64k	150k	4412	Y
MH-535	14	SCSI	1,7 RLL	3.5 HH	256k	150k	4412	Y
P105	19	SCSI	2,7 RLL	3.5 HH		50k		Y
P120	14	SCSI	1,7 RLL	3.5 HH		50k		Y
P170	14	SCSI	1,7 RLL	3.5 HH		50k		Y
P210	14	SCSI	1,7 RLL	3.5 HH		50k		Y
P320	12.5	SCSI	1,7 RLL	3.5 HH		150k		Y

Drive Model	Format Size MB	Head	Cyl	Sect/ Trac	Translate H/C/S	RWC/ WPC	Land Zone
P42	42	3	834	33		NA/NA	AUTO
P425	426	9	1512			NA/NA	AUTO
P84	84	6	834	33		NA/NA	AUTO

MEMOREX

321	5	2	320	17		321/128	
322	10	4	320	17		321/128	
323	15	6	320	17		321/128	
324	20	8	320	17		321/128	
450	10	2	612	17		321/350	
512	25	3	961	17		321/480	
513	41	5	961	17		321/480	
514	58	7	961	17		961?/480	

MICROPOLIS CORP

1302	20	3	830	17		831/831	AUTO
1303	35	5	830	17		831/831	AUTO
1304	40	6	830	17		831/831	AUTO
1323	35	4	1024	17		1025/1025	AUTO
1323A	44	5	1024	17		1025/1025	AUTO
1324	53	6	1024	17		1025/1025	AUTO
1324A	62	7	1024	17		1025/1025	AUTO
1325	71	8	1024	17		1025/1025	AUTO
1325CT	71		1024	17		1025/1025	AUTO
1333	35	4	1024	17		1025/1025	AUTO
1333A	44	5	1024	17		1025/1025	AUTO
1334	53	6	1024	17		1025/1025	AUTO
1334A	62	7	1024	17		1025/1025	AUTO
1335	71	8	1024	17		1025/1025	AUTO
1352	32	2	1024	36		---/---	
1352A	41	3	1024	36		NA/NA	
1353	75	4	1024	36		NA/NA	AUTO
1353A	94	5	1024	36		NA/NA	AUTO
1354	113	6	1024	36		NA/NA	AUTO
1354A	131	7	1024	36		NA/NA	AUTO
1355	150	8	1024	36		NA/NA	AUTO
1372A	52		1024	36		---/---	
1373	72	4	1024	36		1017/1017	AUTO
1373A	91	5	1024	36		NA/NA	AUTO
1374	109	6	1024	36		1017/1017	AUTO
1374-6	135	6	1245	36		---/---	
1374A	127	7	1024	36		1017/1017	AUTO
1375	145	8	1024	36		1017/1017	AUTO
1516-10S	678	10	1840	72		NA/NA	
1517-13	922	13	1925	72		NA/NA	
1517-14	981	14	1925	71		---/---	
1517-15	1051	15	1925	71		---/---	
1518	1346					---/---	
1518-14	993	14	1925	72		NA/NA	
1518-15	1341	15	2104	83		NA/NA	AUTO
1528	1342	15	2100	84		---/---	
1528-15	1342	15	2100	84		NA/NA	AUTO
1528-15D	1300					---/---	
1538	871	15	1669	68		NA/NA	AUTO
1538-15	910	15	1669	71		NA/NA	AUTO
1548-15	1748	15	2112	V		NA/NA	AUTO
1554-07	157	7	1224	36		NA/NA	AUTO
1555-08	180	8	1224	36		NA/NA	AUTO
1555-09	203	9	1224	36		NA/NA	AUTO
1556-10	225	10	1224	36		NA/NA	AUTO
1556-11	248	11	1224	36		NA/NA	AUTO
1557-12	270	12	1224	36		NA/NA	AUTO

Drive Model	Seek Time	Interface	Encode	Form Factor	cache kb	Obsolete? mtbf	RPM ⇓
P42	19	SCSI	2,7 RLL	3.5 HH		50k	Y
P425	12	SCSI	1,7 RLL	3.5 HH		75k	Y
P84	19	SCSI	2,7 RLL	3.5 HH		50k	Y

MEMOREX

Drive Model	Seek Time	Interface	Encode	Form Factor	cache kb	Obsolete? mtbf	RPM ⇓
321		ST412/506	MFM	5.25 FH			Y
322		ST412/506	MFM	5.25 FH			Y
323		ST412/506	MFM				Y
324		ST412/506	MFM				Y
450		ST412/506	MFM				Y
512		ST412/506	MFM				Y
513		ST412/506	MFM				Y
514		ST412/506	MFM				Y

MICROPOLIS CORP

Drive Model	Seek Time	Interface	Encode	Form Factor	cache kb	Obsolete? mtbf	RPM ⇓
1302	30	ST412/506	MFM	5.25 FH		20k	3600 Y
1303	30	ST412/506	MFM	5.25 FH		20k	3600 Y
1304	30	ST412/506	MFM	5.25 FH		20k	3600 Y
1323	28	SP412/506	MFM	5.25 FH		35k	3600 Y
1323A	28	ST412/506	MFM	5.25 FH		35k	3600 Y
1324	28	ST412/506	MFM	5.25 FH		35k	3600 Y
1324A	28	ST412/506	MFM	5.25 FH		35k	3600 Y
1325	28	ST412/506	MFM	5.25 FH		35k	3600 Y
1325CT	28	ST412/506	MFM	5.25 FH		35k	3600 Y
1333	28	ST412/506	MFM	5.25 FD		25k	3600 Y
1333A	28	ST412/506	MFM	5.25 FH		25k	3600 Y
1334	28	ST412/506	MFM	5.25 FH		25k	3600 Y
1334A	28	ST412/506	MFM	5.25 FH		25k	3600 Y
1335	28	ST412/506	MFM	5.25 FH		25k	3600 Y
1352	23	ESDI	2,7 RLL	5.25 FH			Y
1352A	23	ESDI	2,7 RLL	5.25 FH			Y
1353	23	ESDI	2,7 RLL	5.25 FH		150k	3600 Y
1353A	23	ESDI	2,7 RLL	5.25 FH		150k	3600 Y
1354	23	ESDI	2,7 RLL	5.25 FH		150k	3600 Y
1354A	23	ESDI	2,7 RLL	5.25 FH		150k	3600 Y
1355	23	ESDI	2,7 RLL	5.25 FH		150k	3600 Y
1372A		SCSI	2,7 RLL	5.25 FH			Y
1373	23	SCSI	2,7 RLL	5.25 FH		30k	3600 Y
1373A	23	SCSI	2,7 RLL	5.25 FH		30k	3600 Y
1374	23	SCSI	2,7 RLL	5.25 FH		30k	3600 Y
1374-6	16	SCSI	2,7 RLL	5.25 HH		40k	3600 Y
1374A	23	SCSI	2,7 RLL	5.25 FH		30k	3600 Y
1375	23	SCSI	2,7 RLL	5.25 FH		30k	3600 Y
1516-10S	14	ESDI	2,7 RLL	5.25 FH		150k	Y
1517-13	14	ESDI	2,7 RLL	5.25 FH		150k	Y
1517-14	14	ESDI	2,7 RLL	5.25 FH		150k	Y
1517-15	14	ESDI	2,7 RLL	5.25 FH		150k	Y
1518	14.5	ESDI	1,7 RLL	5.25 FH		150k	Y
1518-14	14	ESDI	2,7 RLL	5.25 FH		150k	Y
1518-15	14	ESDI	2,7 RLL	5.25 FH		150k	3600 Y
1528	14.5	SCSI-2		5.25 FH	256k	150k	3600 Y
1528-15	14	SCSI-2		5.25 FH		150k	3600 Y
1528-15D		SCSI-2 DIFF		5.25 FH			3600 Y
1538		ESDI	1,7 RLL	5.25 FH		150k	3600 Y
1538-15	15	ESDI	2,7 RLL	5.25 FH		150k	3600 Y
1548-15	14	SCSI-2		5.25 FH	256k	150k	3600 Y
1554-07	18	ESDI	2,7 RLL	5.25 FH		150k	3600 Y
1555-08	18	ESDI	2,7 RLL	5.25 FH		150k	3600 Y
1555-09	18	ESDI	2,7 RLL	5.25 FH		150k	3600 Y
1556-10	18	ESDI	2,7 RLL	5.25 FH		150k	3600 Y
1556-11	18	ESDI	2,7 RLL	5.25 FH		150k	3600 Y
1557-12	18	ESDI	2,7 RLL	5.25 FH		150k	3600 Y

Drive Model	Format Size MB	Head	Cyl	Sect/ Trac	Translate H/C/S	RWC/ WPC	Land Zone
1557-13	293	13	1224	36		NA/NA	AUTO
1557-14	315	14	1224	36		1225/1225	
1557-15	338	15	1224	36		1225/1225	
1558	338		1224	36		---/---	
1558-13	293	14	1224	36		NA/NA	AUTO
1558-14	315	14	1224	36		NA/NA	AUTO
1558-15	338	15	1224	36		NA/NA	AUTO
1560-8S	389	8	1224	54		---/---	
1564-07	315	7	1224	54		NA/NA	AUTO
1565-08	360	8	1224	54		NA/NA	AUTO
1565-09	406	9	1224	54		NA/NA	AUTO
1566-10	451	10	1224	54		NA/NA	AUTO
1566-11	496	11	1224	54		NA/NA	AUTO
1567-12	541	12	1632	54		NA/NA	AUTO
1567-13	586	13	1224	54		NA/NA	AUTO
1567-14	631	14	1632	54		---/---	
1568	676		1632	54		---/---	
1568-13	586		1632	54		---/---	
1568-14	631	14	1632	54		NA/NA	AUTO
1568-15	676	15	1632	54		NA/NA	AUTO
1574-07	155	7	1224	36		NA/NA	AUTO
1575-08	177	8	1224	36		NA/NA	AUTO
1575-09	199	9	1224	36		NA/NA	AUTO
1576-10	221	10	1224	36		1224/1224	AUTO
1576-11	243	11	1224	36		1224/1224	AUTO
1577-12	265	12	1224	36		1224/1224	AUTO
1577-13	287	13	1224	36		1224/1224	AUTO
1578	331		1224	36		1224/1224	AUTO
1578-14	310	14	1224	36		1224/1224	AUTO
1578-15	332	15	1224	36		1224/1224	AUTO
1585-8S	344	8	1628	54		---/---	
1586-11	490	11	1628	54		1632/1632	AUTO
1587-12	540	12	1628	54		1632/1632	AUTO
1587-13	579	13	1628	54		1632/1632	AUTO
1587-13	585	13	1628	54		NA/NA	AUTO
1588	668					---/---	
1588-14	624	14	1628	54		1632/1632	AUTO
1588-15	667	15	1632	54		1632/1632	AUTO
1588T-15	676	15	1632	54		NA/NA	AUTO
1596-10S	668	10	1834	72		1835/1835	
1597-13	909	13	1919	72		1835/1835	
1598	1034					---/---	
1598-14	979	14	1919	72		1920/1920	
1598-15	1034	15	1928	71		1920/1920	AUTO
1624	667	7	2089	V		AUTO/AUTO	NA
1624-7	667	7	2112			NA/NA	AUTO
1653-3	92	4	1249	36		NA/NA	AUTO
1653-5	115	5	1249	36		NA/NA	AUTO
1653-6	138	6	1249			---/---	
1654	161		1249	36		---/---	
1654-6	138	6	1249	36		NA/NA	AUTO
1654-7	161	7	1249	36		NA/NA	AUTO
1663-4	197	4	1780	54		NA/NA	AUTO
1663-5	246	5	1780	54		NA/NA	AUTO
1664	345		1780	54		---/---	
1664-6	295	6	1780	54		NA/NA	AUTO
1664-7	344	7	1780	54		NA/NA	AUTO
1670-4	90	4	1245	36		---/---	
1670-5	90		1245	36		---/---	
1670-6	112		1245	36		---/---	
1670-7	135		1245	36		---/---	
1673-4	90	4	1249	36		1250/1250	AUTO
1673-5	112	5	1249	36		1250/1250	AUTO

Drive Model	Seek Time	Interface	Encode	Form Factor	cache kb	mtbf	RPM	Obsolete?
1557-13	18	ESDI	2,7 RLL	5.25 FH		150k	3600	Y
1557-14	18	ESDI	2,7 RLL	5.25 FH		150k	3600	Y
1557-15	18	ESDI	2,7 RLL	5.25 FH		150k	3600	Y
1558	19	ESDI	2,7 RLL	5.25 FH		150k	3600	Y
1558-13	18	ESDI	2,7 RLL	5.25 FH		150k	3600	Y
1558-14	18	ESDI	2,7 RLL	5.25 FH		150k	3600	Y
1558-15	18	ESDI	2,7 RLL	5.25 FH		150k	3600	Y
1560-8S	16	ESDI	2,7 RLL	5.25 FH		150k	3600	Y
1564-07	18	ESDI	2,7 RLL	5.25 FH		150k		Y
1565-08	18	ESDI	2,7 RLL	5.25 FH		150k	3600	Y
1565-09	18	ESDI	2,7 RLL	5.25 FH		150k	3600	Y
1566-10	18	ESDI	2,7 RLL	5.25 FH		150k	3600	Y
1566-11	18	ESDI	2,7 RLL	5.25 FH		150k	3600	Y
1567-12	18	ESDI	2,7 RLL	5.25 FH		150k	3600	Y
1567-13	18	ESDI	2,7 RLL	5.25 FH		150k	3600	Y
1567-14	18	ESDI	2,7 RLL	5.25 FH		150k	3600	Y
1568	16	ESDI	2,7 RLL	5.25 FH		150k	3600	Y
1568-13	16	ESDI	2,7 RLL	5.25 FH		150k	3600	Y
1568-14	16	ESDI	2,7 RLL	5.25 FH		150k	3600	Y
1568-15	16	ESDI	2,7 RLL	5.25 FH		150k	3600	Y
1574-07	16	SCSI	2,7 RLL	5.25 FH		150k	3600	Y
1575-08	16	SCSI	2,7 RLL	5.25 FH		150k	3600	Y
1575-09	16	SCSI	2,7 RLL	5.25 FH		150k	3600	Y
1576-10	16	SCSI	2,7 RLL	5.25 FH		150k	3600	Y
1576-11	16	SCSI	2,7 RLL	5.25 FH		150k	3600	Y
1577-12	16	SCSI	2,7 RLL	5.25 FH		150k	3600	Y
1577-13	16	SCSI	2,7 RLL	5.25 FH		150k	3600	Y
1578	16	SCSI		5.25 FH	64k	150k		Y
1578-14	16	SCSI	2,7 RLL	5.25 FH		150k	3600	Y
1578-15	16	SCSI	2,7 RLL	5.25 FH		150k	3600	Y
1585-8S	16	SCSI	2,7 RLL	5.25 FH		150k		Y
1586-11	16	SCSI	2,7 RLL	5.25 FH		150k		Y
1587-12	16	SCSI	2,7 RLL	5.25 FH		150k		Y
1587-13	16	SCSI	2,7 RLL	5.25 FH		150k		Y
1587-13	16	SCSI	2,7 RLL	5.25 FH		150k		Y
1588	16	SCSI	2,7 RLL	5.25 FH	256k	150k		Y
1588-14	16	SCSI	2,7 RLL	5.25 FH		150k		Y
1588-15	16	SCSI	2,7 RLL	5.25 FH		150k		Y
1588T-15	16	SCSI	2,7 RLL	5.25 FH		150k	3600	Y
1596-10S	14	SCSI	2,7 RLL	5.25 FH		150k		Y
1597-13	14	SCSI	2,7 RLL	5.25 FH		150k		Y
1598	14.5	SCSI-2	2,7 RLL	5.25 FH	256k	150k		Y
1598-14	14	SCSI	2,7 RLL	5.25 FH		150k		Y
1598-15	14	SCSI-2	2,7 RLL	5.25 FH		150k	3600	Y
1624	15	SCSI-2		5.25 FH		150k		Y
1624-7	15	SCSI-2 FAST		5.25 FH		150k	3600	Y
1653-4	16	ESDI	2,7 RLL	5.25 FH		150k	3600	Y
1653-5	16	ESDI	2,7 RLL	5.25 FH		150k	3600	Y
1653-6		ESDI	2,7 RLL	5.25 FH		150k		Y
1654	16	ESDI	2,7 RLL	5.25 FH		150k		Y
1654-6	16	ESDI	2,7 RLL	5.25 FH		150k	3600	Y
1654-7	16	ESDI	2,7 RLL	5.25 FH		150k	3600	Y
1663-4	14	ESDI	2,7 RLL	5.25 FH		150k		Y
1663-5	14	ESDI	2,7 RLL	5.25 FH		150k		Y
1664	15	ESDI	2,7 RLL	5.25 FH		150k		Y
1664-6	14	ESDI	2,7 RLL	5.25 FH		150k		Y
1664-7	14	ESDI	2,7 RLL	5.25 FH		150k	3600	Y
1670-4	16	SCSI		5.25 HH		150k		Y
1670-5		SCSI		5.25 HH		150k		Y
1670-6		SCSI		5.25 HH		150k		Y
1670-7		SCSI		5.25 HH		150k		Y
1673-4	16	SCSI	2,7 RLL	5.25 HH		150k	3600	Y
1673-5	16	SCSI	2,7 RLL	5.25 HH		150k	3600	Y

Drive Model	Format Size MB	Head	Cyl	Sect/ Trac	Translate H/C/S	RWC/ WPC	Land Zone
1674	158		1249	36		---/---	
1674-6	135	6	1249	36		1250/1250	AUTO
1674-7	157	7	1249	36		1250/1250	AUTO
1683-4	193	4	1776	54		1777/1777	AUTO
1683-5	242	5	1776	54		1777/1777	AUTO
1684	340		1776	54		---/---	
1684-6	291	6	1776	54		1777/1777	AUTO
1684-7	339	7	1780	54		1777/1777	AUTO
1743-5	112	5	1140	28		NA/NA	
1744-6	135	6	1140	28		NA/NA	
1744-7	157	7	1140	28		NA/NA	
1745-8	180	8	1140	28		NA/NA	
1745-9	202	9	1140	28		NA/NA	
1773-5	112	5	1140	28		1141/1141	
1774-6	135	6	1140	28		1141/1141	
1774-7	157	7	1140	28		1141/1141	
1775-8	180	8	1140	28		1141/1141	
1775-9	202	9	1140	28		1141/1141	
1908-15	1381	15	2112	V		NA/NA	AUTO
1924-21	2100	21	2267	V		NA/NA	AUTO
1924D	2100		2267	V		---/---	
1926	2158	15		V		NA/NA	AUTO
1926-15	2158	15	2772	V		---/---	
1936	3022	15	2759	V		NA/NA	AUTO
1936-21	3022	21	2772	V		NA/NA	AUTO
1936AV	3022	21	2759	V		NA/NA	AUTO
1936D	3022	21	2759	V		NA/NA	AUTO
1991	9091	27	4446	V		---/---	
1991AV	9090	27	4477	V		---/---	
1991W	9090	27	4477	V		---/---	
1991WAV	9090	27	4477	V		---/---	
2100	512	15	2759	V		NA/NA	AUTO
2105(A)	560	8	1745	V	16/1084/63	NA/NA	AUTO
2105(S)	560	8	1745	V		NA/NA	AUTO
2105-15	560	15	1747	V		NA/NA	AUTO
2105A-15	560	15	1747	V		NA/NA	AUTO
2108(A)	666	10	1745	V		NA/NA	AUTO
2108(S)	666	10	1745	V		NA/NA	AUTO
2112(A)	1050	15	1745	V	16/2034/63	NA/NA	AUTO
2112(D)	1050	15	1744	V		NA/NA	AUTO
2112(S)	1050	15	1745	V		NA/NA	AUTO
2112-15	1050	15	1747	V		NA/NA	AUTO
2112-DW	1050	15	1745	V		NA/NA	AUTO
2112A-15	1050	15	1747	V		NA/NA	AUTO
2121(A)				V		NA/NA	AUTO
2121(S)				V		NA/NA	AUTO
2205	585	5	2360			NA/NA	AUTO
2205A	542	5				NA/NA	AUTO
2207	701	9	2360	V		NA/NA	AUTO
2210	1056	9	2360			NA/NA	AUTO
2210A	976	9	2360			NA/NA	AUTO
2210AV	1056	9	2360			NA/NA	AUTO
2210WD	1056	9	2360	V		---/---	
2217	1765	15	2360	V		NA/NA	AUTO
2217A	1626	15				NA/NA	AUTO
2217AV	1765	15				NA/NA	AUTO
2217WD	1765		2360	V		---/---	
3020	512	21	2759	V		NA/NA	AUTO
3221	2050		3956	V		---/---	
3221AV	2050		3956	V		---/---	
3243	4294	19	4124	V		---/---	
3243AV	4290	19	4081			NA/NA	AUTO
3243S	4294	19	3957	V		---/---	

Drive Model	Seek Time	Interface	Encode	Form Factor	cache kb	mtbf	RPM	Obsolete?
1674	16	SCSI	2,7 RLL	5.25 HH		150k		Y
1674-6	16	SCSI	2,7 RLL	5.25 HH		150k	3600	Y
1674-7	16	SCSI	2,7 RLL	5.25 HH		150k	3600	Y
1683-4	14	SCSI	2,7 RLL	5.25 HH		150k		Y
1683-5	14	SCSI	2,7 RLL	5.25 HH		150k		Y
1684	15	SCSI	2,7 RLL	5.25 HH		150k		Y
1684-6	14	SCSI	2,7 RLL	5.25 HH		150k		Y
1684-7	14	SCSI	2,7 RLL	5.25 HH		150k	3600	Y
1743-5	15	IDE AT	2,7 RLL	3.5 HH				Y
1744-6	15	IDE AT	2,7 RLL	3.5 HH				Y
1744-7	15	IDE AT	2,7 RLL	3.5 HH				Y
1745-8	15	IDE AT	2,7 RLL	3.5 HH				Y
1745-9	15	IDE AT	2,7 RLL	3.5 HH				Y
1773-5	15	SCSI	2,7 RLL	3.5 HH				Y
1774-6	15	SCSI	2,7 RLL	3.5 HH				Y
1774-7	15	SCSI	2,7 RLL	3.5 HH				Y
1775-8	15	SCSI	2,7 RLL	3.5 HH				Y
1775-9	15	SCSI	2,7 RLL	3.5 HH				Y
1908-15	11	SCSI-2 FAST		5.25 FH		150k	5400	Y
1924-21	12	SCSI-2Fast		5.25 FH		250k	5400	Y
1924D	12	SCSI-2Fast		5.25 FH		250k	5400	Y
1926	13	SCSI-2 FAST		5.25 FH	512k	250k	5400	Y
1926-15	13	SCSI-2		5.25 FH		300k		
1936	12	SCSI-2 FAST		5.25 FH	256k	250k	5400	Y
1936-21	11.5	SCSI-2	2,7 RLL	5.25 FH		300k		
1936AV	13	SCSI-2 FAST	MZR	5.25 FH	256k	250k	5400	
1936D	12	SCSI-2 FAST		5.25 FH	256k	250k	5400	Y
1991	12	SCSI-2 Fast		5.25 FH	512k	650k	5400	
1991AV	12	SCSI-2Fast	MZR	5.25 FH	512k	650k	5400	
1991W	12	SCSI-2FstWd	MZR	5.25 FH	512k	650k	5400	
1991WAV	12	SCSI-2FstWd	MZR	5.25 FH	512k	650k	5400	
2100	13	SCSI-2 FAST		5.25 FH	512k	300k	5400	Y
2105(A)	10	IDE AT	RLL	3.5 HH		300k		Y
2105(S)	10	SCSI-2	RLL	3.5 HH		300k		Y
2105-15	10	SCSI-2 FAST		3.5 FH		300k	5400	Y
2105A-15	10	IDE AT		3.5 FH		300k	5400	Y
2108(A)	10	IDE AT	RLL	3.5 HH		300k		Y
2108(S)	10	SCSI-2	RLL	3.5 HH		300k		Y
2112(A)	10	IDE AT	RLL	3.5 FH		300k		Y
2112(D)	10	SCSI-2Diff		3.5 HH		300k		
2112(S)	10	SCSI-2	RLL	5.25 FH		300k		Y
2112-15	10	SCSI-2 FAST	RLL	3.5 FH		300k	5400	Y
2112-DW	10	SCSI-2FstWd	RLL	3.5 FH		300k	5400	Y
2112A-15	10	IDE AT	RLL	3.5 FH		300k	5400	Y
2121(A)	10	IDE AT	RLL	3.5 FH		300k		Y
2121(S)	10	SCSI-2	RLL	5.25 FH		300k		Y
2205	10	SCSI-2 FAST		3.5 FH		300k	5400	Y
2205A	10	IDE AT		3.5 FH		300k	5400	Y
2207	10	SCSI-2 FAST		3.5 FH	512k	300k	5400	Y
2210	10	SCSI-2 FAST		3.5 FH	512k	300k	5400	Y
2210A	10	IDE AT		3.5 FH	512k	300k	5400	Y
2210AV	10	SCSI-2 FAST		3.5 FH	512k	300k	5400	Y
2210WD	10	SCSI-2FstWd		3.5 FH		300k	5400	
2217	10	SCSI-2 FAST		3.5 FH		300k	5400	Y
2217A	10	IDE AT		3.5 FH	512k	300k	5400	Y
2217AV	10	SCSI-2 FAST		3.5 FH	512k	300k	5400	Y
2217WD	10	SCSI-2FstWd		3.5 FH		300k	5400	Y
3020	13	SCSI-2 FAST		5.25 FH	512k	250k	5400	Y
3221	9	SCSI-2Fast		3.5 FH		650k	7200	
3221AV	9	SCSI-2Fast		3.5 FH		650k	7200	
3243	8.5	SCSI-2 Fast		3.5 HH		650k	7200	
3243AV	9	SCSI-2Fast	MZR	3.5 HH	512k	650k	7200	
3243S	9	SSA-SCSI		3.5 HH	512k	650k	7200	

Drive Model	Format Size MB	Head	Cyl	Sect/ Trac	Translate H/C/S	RWC/ WPC	Land Zone
3243W	4294	19	3956	V		---/---	
3243WAV	4294	19	3957	V		NA/NA	AUTO
3243WD	4294	19	3956	V		---/---	
3243WDAV	4294	19	3956	V		---/---	
3387NS	8700		4811	V		---/---	
3387SS	8700		4811	V		---/---	
3387WS	8700		4811	V		---/---	
3391AV	9103		4811	V		---/---	
3391NS	9103		4811	V		---/---	
3391SS	9103		4811	V		---/---	
3391WAV	9103		4811	V		---/---	
3391WD	9103		4811	V		---/---	
3391WS	9103		4811	V		---/---	
3418NS	18250		7308	V		---/---	
3418SS	18250		7308	V		---/---	
3418WS	18250		7308	V		---/---	
3420AV	20270		7308	V		---/---	
3420WAV	20270		7308	V		NA/NA	AUTO
4110	1052	9		V		---/---	
4110A	1052		2415	V		---/---	
4221	200		4150	V	16/1024/63	---/---	
4221AV	2050	9	4050			NA/NA	AUTO
4221W	2050	9	4150	V		NA/NA	AUTO
4221WAV	2050	9	4150	V		NA/NA	AUTO
4221WD	2050	9	4050	V		NA/NA	AUTO
4221WDAV	2050	9	4150	V		---/---	
4341NS	4130		4811	V		---/---	
4341SS	4130		4811	V		---/---	
4341WS	4130		4811	V		---/---	
4345AV	4550		4811	V		---/---	
4345NS	4550		4811	V		---/---	
4345SD	4550		4811	V		---/---	
4345SS	4550		4811	V		---/---	
4345WAV	4550		4811	V		---/---	
4345WD	4550		4811	V		---/---	
4345WS	4550		4811	V		---/---	
4421	2147		4050	V		---/---	
4421AV	2050		4050	V		---/---	
4525A	2500	4	6807		16/4884/63	---/---	
4540A	4000	6	6807		16/7847/63	---/---	
4550A	5000	8	6807		16/9768/63	---/---	
4691AV	9100		7308	V		---/---	
4691NS	9100		7308	V		---/---	
4691SS	9100		7308	V		---/---	
4691WAV	9100		7308	V		---/---	
4691WS	9100		7308	V		---/---	
4721NS	2100		6565	V		---/---	
4743NS	4300		6565	V		---/---	
4743SS	4300		6565	V		---/---	
4743WS	4300		6565	V		---/---	

MICROSCIENCE INTERNATIONAL COR

Drive Model	Format Size MB	Head	Cyl	Sect/ Trac	Translate H/C/S	RWC/ WPC	Land Zone
4050	44	5	1024	17		1025/1025	
4060	67	5	1024	26		---/---	
4070	62	7	1024	17		---/---	
4090	93	7	1024	26		---/---	
5040	45	3	855	35		NA/NA	AUTO
5070	76	5	855	35		NA/NA	AUTO
5070-20	86	5	960	35		NA/NA	AUTO
5100	110	7	855	36		NA/NA	
5100-20	120	7	960	35		NA/NA	AUTO
5160	159	7	1271	35		NA/NA	AUTO

Drive Model	Seek Time	Interface	Encode	Form Factor	cache kb	mtbf	RPM	Obsolete? ⇓
3243W	9	SCSI-2FstWd	MZR	3.5 HH	512k	650k	7200	
3243WAV	9	SCSI-2FstWd	MZR	3.5 HH	512k	650k	7200	
3243WD	9	SCSI-2Diff		3.5 FH	512k	650k	7200	
3243WDAV	9	SCSI-2Diff		3.5 FH	512k	650k	7200	
3387NS	8	Ultra SCSI3		3.5 FH		650k	7200	
3387SS	8	Ultra SCSI3		3.5 FH		650k	7200	
3387WS	8	Ultra SCSI3		3.5 FH		650k	7200	
3391AV	8	Ultra SCSI3		3.5 HH	2mb	650k	7200	
3391NS	8	Ultra SCSI3		3.5 HH		650k	7200	
3391SS	8	SCSI-3Wide		3.5 HH	2mb	650k	7200	
3391WAV	8	SCSI-3Wide		3.5 HH	2mb	650k	7200	
3391WD	8	SCSI-3Wide		3.5 HH		650k	7200	
3391WS	8	Ultra SCSI3		3.5 HH		650k	7200	
3418NS	8	Ultra SCSI3		3.5 3H		1000k	7200	
3418SS	8	SCSI-3Wide		3.5 3H		1000k	7200	
3418WS	8	SCSI-3Wide		3.5 3H		1000k	7200	
3420AV	8	Ultra SCSI3		3.5 3H	2mb	1000k	7200	
3420WAV	8	SCSI-3Wide		3.5 3H	2mb	1000k	7200	
4110	8.5	SCSI-2 FAST		3.5 3H	512k	500k	5400	Y
4110	8.5	SCSI-2Fast		3.5 3H		500k	5400	
4110A	8.5	IDE AT		3.5 3H	512k	500k	5400	Y
4221	9	SCSI-2 FAST		3.5 3H	512k	650k	7200	
4221AV	9	SCSI-2 Fast	MZR	3.5 3H	512k	650k	7200	
4221W	9	SCSI-2FstWd	MZR	3.5 3H	512k	650k	7200	
4221WAV	9	SCSI-2FstWd	MZR	3.5 3H	512k	650k	7200	
4221WD	9	SCSI-2Diff	MZR	3.5 3H	512k	650k	7200	
4221WDAV	9	SCSI-2Diff	MZR	3.5 3H	512k	650k	7200	
4341NS	8	Ultra SCSI3		3.5 3H		650k	7200	
4341SS	8	SCSI-3Wide		3.5 3H		650k	7200	
4341WS	8	SCSI-3Wide		3.5 3H		650k	7200	
4345AV	8	Ultra SCSI3		3.5 3H	2mb	650k	7200	
4345NS	8	Ultra SCSI3		3.5 3H		650k	7200	
4345SD	8	SCSI-3Wide		3.5 3H		650k	7200	
4345SS	8	SCSI-3Wide		3.5 3H		650k	7200	
4345WAV	8	SCSI-3Wide		3.5 3H	2mb	650k	7200	
4345WD	8	SCSI-3Wide		3.5 3H		650k	7200	
4345WS	8	SCSI-3Wide		3.5 3H		650k	7200	
4421	9	SCSI-2Fast		3.5 3H		650k	5400	
4421AV	9	SCSI-2Fast		3.5 3H		650k	5400	
4525A	10.5	EIDE	PRML	3.5 3H		400k	5200	
4540A	10.5	EIDE	PRML	3.5 3H		400k	5200	
4550A	10.5	EIDE	PRML	3.5 3H		400k	5200	
4691AV	7.9	Ultra SCSI3		3.5 3H	2mb	1000k	7200	
4691NS	7.9	Ultra SCSI3		3.5 3H	2mb	1000k	7200	
4691SS	7.9	SCSI-3Wide		3.5 3H	2mb	1000k	7200	
4691WAV	7.9	SCSI-3Wide		3.5 3H	2mb	1000k	7200	
4691WS	7.9	SCSI-3Wide		3.5 3H	2mb	1000k	7200	
4721NS	10	Ultra SCSI3		3.5 3H		400k	5400	
4743NS	10	Ultra SCSI3		3.5 3H		400k	5400	
4743SS	10	SCSI-3Wide		3.5 3H		400k	5400	
4743WS	10	SCSI-3Wide		3.5 3H		400k	5400	

MICROSCIENCE INTERNATIONAL COR

Drive Model	Seek Time	Interface	Encode	Form Factor	cache kb	mtbf	RPM	Obsolete?
4050	18	ST412/506	MFM	3.5 HH		36k		Y
4060	18	ST412/506	2,7 RLL	3.5 HH		36k		Y
4070	18	ST412/506	MFM	3.5 HH		36k		Y
4090	18	ST412/506	2,7 RLL	3.5 HH		36k		Y
5040	18	ESDI	2,7 RLL	3.5 HH		36k		Y
5070	18	ESDI	2,7 RLL	3.5 HH		36k		Y
5070-20	18	ESDI	2,7 RLL	3.5 HH		36k		Y
5100	18	ESDI	2,7 RLL	3.5 HH		36k		Y
5100-20	18	ESDI	2,7 RLL	3.5 HH		36k		Y
5160	18	ESDI	2,7 RLL	3.5 HH		60k		Y

Drive Model	Format Size MB	Head	Cyl	Sect/ Trac	Translate H/C/S	RWC/ WPC	Land Zone
6100	110	7	855	36		NA/NA	AUTO
7040	47	3	855	36		NA/NA	
7070-20	86	5	960	35		NA/960	960
7100	100	7	855	36		NA/NA	
7100-20	120	7	960	35		NA/960	960
7100-21	121	5	1077	44		NA/992	992
7200	200	7	1277	44		---/---	
7400	304	8	1904			NA/NA	AUTO
8040	42	2	1024	40		NA/NA	AUTO
8040MLC 48-000	42	2	1024	40		NA/NA	AUTO
8080	85	2	1768	47		NA/NA	AUTO
8200	152	4	1904			NA/NA	AUTO
FH21200	1062	15	1921	72		NA/NA	AUTO
FH21600	1418	15	2147	86		NA/NA	AUTO
FH2414	366	8	1658	54		NA/NA	AUTO
FH2777	687	15	1658	54		NA/NA	AUTO
FH31200	1062	15	1921	72		NA/NA	AUTO
FH31600	1418	15	2147	86		NA/NA	AUTO
FH3414	366	8	1658	54		NA/NA	AUTO
FH3777	687	15	1658	54		NA/NA	AUTO
HH1050	44	5	1024	17		1025/1025	1023
HH1060	65	5	1024	26		1025/1025	
HH1075	62	7	1024	17		1025/1025	
HH1080	65	5	1024	26		---/---	
HH1090	80	7	1314	17		1315/1315	
HH1095	95	7	1024	26		1025/1025	
HH1120	122	7	1314	26		1315/1315	
HH2012	10	4	306	17		---/---	
HH2120	128	7	1024	35		NA/NA	
HH2160	160	7	1276	35		NA/NA	
HH2160F	160					---/---	
HH312	10	4	306	17		307/307	
HH3120	121	5	1314	36		---/---	
HH3120F	122					---/---	
HH315	10	4	306	17		307/307	
HH3160	170	7	1314	36		---/---	
HH3160F	170					---/---	
HH325	21	4	612	17		613/613	615
HH330	32	4	612	26		613/613	
HH612	10	4	612	17		307/307	
HH625	21	4	612	17		613/613	
HH712	10	2	612	17		613/613	
HH712A	10	2	612	17		---/---	
HH725	21	4	612	17		613/613	615
HH738	32	4	612	26		613/613	
HH825	21	4	615	17		616/616	
HH830	33	4	615	26		616/616	

MINISCRIBE CORPORATION

Drive Model	Format Size MB	Head	Cyl	Sect/ Trac	Translate H/C/S	RWC/ WPC	Land Zone
1006	5	2	306	17		307/128	336
1012	10	4	306	17		307/128	336
2006	5	2	306	17		307/128	336
2012	10	4	306	17		307/128	336
3006	5	2	306	17		307/128	306
3012	10	2	612	19		613/128	656
3053	44	5	1024	17		1024/512	AUTO
3085	68	7	1170	17		1170/512	AUTO
3085E	72	3	1270	36		NA/NA	AUTO
3085S	72	3	1255	125		NA/NA	AUTO
3130E	112	5	1250	36		1251/512	AUTO
3130S	112	5	1255	35		1256/512	AUTO
3180E	150	7	1250	36		1251/512	AUTO
3180S	153	7	1255	36		1256/512	AUTO

Drive Model	Seek Time	Interface	Encode	Form Factor	cache kb	Obsolete? mtbf	RPM ⇓
6100	18	SCSI	2,7 RLL	3.5 HH		36k	Y
7040	18	IDE AT	2,7 RLL	3.5 HH			Y
7070-20	18	IDE AT	2,7 RLL	3.5 HH		36k	Y
7100	18	IDE AT	2,7 RLL	3.5 HH		36k	Y
7100-20	18	IDE AT	2,7 RLL	3.5 HH		60k	3600 Y
7100-21	18	IDE AT	2,7 RLL	3.5 HH		60k	Y
7200	18	IDE AT	2,7 RLL	3.5 HH			Y
7400	15	IDE AT	2,7 RLL	3.5 HH		100k	Y
8040	25	IDE AT	2,7 RLL	3.5 3H		20k	Y
8040MLC 48-000	25	IDE AT	2,7 RLL	3.5 3H		300k	Y
8080	17	IDE AT	2,7 RLL	3.5 3H		100k	Y
8200	16	IDE AT	2,7 RLL	3.5 3H		100k	Y
FH21200	14	ESDI	2,7 RLL	5.25 FH		100k	3600 Y
FH21600	14	ESDI	2,7 RLL	5.25 FH		100k	3600 Y
FH2414	14	ESDI	2,7 RLL	5.25 FH		100k	Y
FH2777	14	ESDI	2,7 RLL	5.25 FH		50k	3600 Y
FH31200	14	SCSI	2,7 RLL	5.25 FH		100k	3600 Y
FH31600	14	SCSI	2,7 RLL	5.25 FH		100k	3600 Y
FH3414	14	SCSI	2,7 RLL	5.25 FH		100k	Y
FH3777	14	SCSI	2,7 RLL	5.25 FH		100k	3600 Y
HH1050	28	ST412/506	MFM	5.25 HH		140k	Y
HH1060	28	ST412/506	2,7 RLL	5.25 HH		140k	Y
HH1075	28	ST412/506	MFM	5.25 HH			Y
HH1080	28	ST412/506	2,7 RLL	5.25 HH		50k	Y
HH1090	28	ST412/506	MFM	5.25 HH		40k	Y
HH1095	28	ST412/506	2,7 RLL	5.25 HH			Y
HH1120	28	ST412/506	2,7 RLL	5.25 HH		40k	Y
HH2012		ST412/506	MFM	5.25 HH			Y
HH2120	28	ESDI (10)	2,7 RLL	5.25 HH		40k	Y
HH2160	28	ESDI (10)	2,7 RLL	5.25 HH		40k	Y
HH2160F		ESDI	2,7 RLL	5.25 HH			Y
HH312	65	ST412/506	MFM	5.25 HH			Y
HH3120	28	SCSI	2,7 RLL	5.25 HH		40k	Y
HH3120F		SCSI	2,7 RLL	5.25 HH			Y
HH315	65	ST412/506	MFM	5.25 HH			Y
HH3160	28	SCSI	2,7 RLL	5.25 HH		40k	Y
HH3160F		SCSI	2,7 RLL	5.25 HH			Y
HH325	80	ST412/506	MFM	5.25 HH			Y
HH330	105	ST412/506	2,7 RLL	5.25 HH			Y
HH612	85	ST412/506	MFM	5.25 HH			Y
HH625	65	ST412/506	MFM	5.25 HH			Y
HH712	105	ST412/506	MFM	5.25 HH			Y
HH712A	75	ST412/506	MFM	5.25 HH			Y
HH725	105	ST412/506	MFM	5.25 HH			Y
HH738	105	ST412/506	2,7 RLL	5.25 HH			Y
HH825	65	ST412/506	MFM	5.25 HH			Y
HH830	65	ST412/506	2,7 RLL	5.25 HH			Y

MINISCRIBE CORPORATION

Drive Model	Seek Time	Interface	Encode	Form Factor	cache kb	Obsolete? mtbf	RPM ⇓
1006	179	ST412/506	MFM	5.25 FH		8k	Y
1012	179	ST412/506	MFM	5.25 FH		8k	Y
2006	93	ST412/506	MFM	5.25 FH		10k	Y
2012	85	ST412/506	MFM	5.25 FH		10k	Y
3006		ST412/506	MFM	5.25 HH			Y
3012	155	ST412/506	MFM	5.25 HH		10k	Y
3053	25	ST412/506	MFM	5.25 HH		30k	3600 Y
3085	22	ST412/506	MFM	5.25 HH		40k	3600 Y
3085E	17	ESDI	2,7 RLL	5.25 HH			Y
3085S	17	SCSI	2,7 RLL	5.25 HH			Y
3130E	17	ESDI	2,7 RLL	5.25 HH		35k	3600 Y
3130S	17	SCSI	2,7 RLL	5.25 HH		35k	3600 Y
3180E	17	ESDI	2,7 RLL	5.25 HH		35k	3600 Y
3180S	17	SCSI	2,7 RLL	5.25 HH		35k	3600 Y

Drive Model	Format Size MB	Head	Cyl	Sect/Trac	Translate H/C/S	RWC/WPC	Land Zone
3180SM	161	7	1250	36		NA/NA	AUTO
3212	10	2	612	17		613/128	656
3212 PLUS	11	2	615	17		613/128	AUTO
3412	10	4	306	17		307/128	336
3425	20	4	615	17		616/128	656
3425 PLUS	20	4	615	17		616/128	656
3425S	21	4	612	17		615/128	656
3438	32	4	615	26		616/128	656
3438 PLUS	32	4	615	26		616/128	656
3650	40	6	809	17		819/128	852
3650F	42	6	809	17		810/128	852
3650R	64	6	809	26		809/128	852
3675	63	6	809	26		810/128	852
4010	8	2	480	17		481/128	520
4020	16	4	480	17		481/128	520
5330	25	6	480	17		481/128	
5338	32	6	612	17		613/306	
5440	32	8	480	17		481/128	
5451	43	8	612	17		613/306	
6032	26	3	1024	17		1024/512	AUTO
6053	44	5	1024	17		1024/512	AUTO
6074	62	7	1024	17		1025/512	
6079	68	5	1024	26		1024/512	AUTO
6085	71	8	1024	17		1024/512	AUTO
6085E	71					---/---	
6128	109	8	1024	26		1024/512	AUTO
6128E	110					---/---	
6170E	130	8	1024	34		NA/NA	AUTO
6212	10	2	612	17		613/128	
7040A	40	2	1159	36	5/981/17	981/512	AUTO
7040S	40	2	1156	36		NA/NA	AUTO
7060A	65	2	1516	42	7/1024/17	NA/NA	AUTO
7060S	65	2	1516	42		NA/NA	AUTO
7080A	81	4	1159	36	10/981/17	981/512	AUTO
7080S	81	4	1156	36		NA/NA	AUTO
7120A	131	2	1516	85	14/1024/17	NA/NA	AUTO
7120S	131	2	1516	85		NA/NA	AUTO
7426	21	4	612	17		613/613	
8048S	40					---/---	
8051A	41	4	745	26	4/745/28	746/128	AUTO
8051S	43	4	745	26		746/128	AUTO
8057A	42					---/---	
80SC-MFM	21	4	615	17		---/---	
80SC-RLL	33	4	615	26		---/---	
8212	10	2	615	17		616/128	664
8225	20	2	771	26		772/128	810
8225A	21	2	747	28	4/615/17	NA/NA	AUTO
8225AT	20	2	747	28		748/128	820
8225S	21	2	804	26		805/128	820
8225XT	20	2	805	26		806/128	820
8412	10	4	306	17		307/128	336
8425	21	4	615	17		616/128	664
8425F	20	4	615	17		616/128	664
8425S	21	4	612	17		616/128	664
8425XT	20	4	615	17		616/128	664
8434F	32	4	615	26		616/128	
8438	31	4	615	26		616/128	664
8438 PLUS	31	4	615	26		615/128	664
8438F	32	4	615	26		616/128	664
8438XT	31	4	615	26		NA/NA	664
8450	39	4	771	26		772/128	810
8450AT	42	4	745	28		746/128	820
8450S	42	4	804	26		805/128	820

Drive Model	Seek Time	Interface	Encode	Form Factor	cache kb	mtbf	RPM	Obsolete?
3180SM	17	SCSI-MAC	RLL	5.25 HH		35k		
3212	85	ST412/506	MFM	5.25 HH		20k	3600	Y
3212 PLUS	53	ST412/506	MFM	5.25 HH		20k	3600	Y
3412	60	ST412/506	MFM	5.25 HH		11k		Y
3425	85	ST412/506	MFM	5.25 HH		20k	3600	Y
3425 PLUS	53	ST412/506	MFM	5.25 HH		20k	3600	Y
3425S	68	SCSI		5.25 HH		20k		
3438	85	ST412/506	2,7 RLL	5.25 HH		20k	3600	Y
3438 PLUS	53	ST412/506	2,7 RLL	5.25 HH		20k	3600	Y
3650	61	ST412/506	MFM	5.25 HH		25k	3600	Y
3650F	46	ST412/506	MFM	5.25 HH		25k	3600	Y
3650R	61	ST412/506	2,7 RLL	5.25 HH		25k	3600	Y
3675	61	ST412/506	2,7 RLL	5.25 HH		25k		Y
4010	133	ST412/506	MFM	5.25 FH		10k		Y
4020	133	ST412/506	MFM	5.25 FH		10k		Y
5330	27	ST412/506	MFM	5.25 FH				Y
5338	27	ST412/506	MFM	5.25 FH				Y
5440	27	ST412/506	MFM	5.25 FH				Y
5451	27	ST412/506	MFM	5.25 FH				Y
6032	28	ST412/506	MFM	5.25 FH		25k	3600	Y
6053	28	ST412/506	MFM	5.25 FH		25k	3600	Y
6074	28	ST412/506	MFM	5.25 FH				Y
6079	28	ST412/506	2,7 RLL	5.25 FH		25k	3600	Y
6085	28	ST412/506	MFM	5.25 FH		25k	3600	Y
6085E		ESDI	MFM	5.25 FH				Y
6128	28	ST412/506	2,7 RLL	5.25 FH		25k	3600	Y
6128E		ESDI	2,7 RLL	5.25 FH				Y
6170E	28	ESDI	RLL	5.25 FH				Y
6212	27	ST412/506	MFM	5.25 FH				Y
7040A	19	IDE AT	1,7 RLL	3.5 3H	32k	40k	3703	Y
7040S	19	SCSI	RLL	3.5 3H		40k		Y
7060A	15	IDE AT	1,7 RLL	3.5 3H		150k		Y
7060S	15	SCSI	1,7 RLL	3.5 3H		150k		Y
7080A	19	IDE AT	1,7 RLL	3.5 3H	32k	40k	3703	Y
7080S	19	SCSI	1,7 RLL	3.5 3H		150k		Y
7120A	15	IDE AT	1,7 RLL	3.5 3H		150k		Y
7120S	15	SCSI	1,7 RLL	3.5 3H		150k		Y
7426	27	ST412/506	MFM	3.5 HH				Y
8048S		SCSI		3.5 HH				
8051A	28	IDE AT	2,7 RLL	3.5 HH	32k	150k	3484	Y
8051S	28	SCSI	2,7 RLL	3.5 HH	32k	150k	3484	Y
8057A		IDE AT		3.5 HH				Y
80SC-MFM	68	ST412/506	MFM	3.5 HH		20k	3600	Y
80SC-RLL	68	ST412/506	2,7 RLL	3.5 HH		20k	3600	Y
8212	68	ST412/506	MFM	3.5 HH		20k	3600	Y
8225	68	ST412/506	2,7 RLL	3.5 HH		30k	3600	Y
8225A		IDE		3.5 HH		30k	3600	Y
8225AT	40	IDE AT	2,7 RLL	3.5 HH		30k	3600	Y
8225S	68	SCSI	2,7 RLL	3.5 HH		30k	3600	Y
8225XT	68	IDE XT	2,7 RLL	3.5 HH		30k	3600	Y
8412	50	ST412/506	MFM	3.5 HH		20k	3600	Y
8425	68	ST506/412	MFM	3.5 HH		20k	3600	Y
8425F	40	ST412/506	MFM	3.5 HH		20k	3600	Y
8425S	68	SCSI	MFM	3.5 HH		20k	3600	Y
8425XT	68	IDE XT	MFM	3.5 HH		20k	3600	Y
8434F	40	ST412/506	RLL	3.5 HH		20k	3600	Y
8438	68	ST412/506	RLL	3.5 HH		20k	3600	Y
8438 PLUS	55	2,7 RLL	2,7 RLL	5.25 HH		20k	3600	Y
8438F	40	ST412/506	2,7 RLL	5.25 HH		20k	3600	Y
8438XT	68	IDE XT	RLL	3.5 HH		20k	3600	Y
8450	45	SCSI	2,7 RLL	3.5 HH		20k	3600	Y
8450AT	40	IDE AT	2,7 RLL	3.5 HH		30k	3600	Y
8450S	45	SCSI	2,7 RLL	3.5 HH		20k	3600	Y

Drive Model	Format Size MB	Head	Cyl	Sect/Trac	Translate H/C/S	RWC/WPC	Land Zone
8450XT	42	4	805	26		806/128	820
9000E	338	15	1224	36		NA/NA	AUTO
9000S	347	15	1220	36		NA/NA	AUTO
9230	203	9	1224	34		0/512	0
9230E	203	9	1224	36		NA/NA	AUTO
9230S	203	9	1224	36		NA/NA	AUTO
9380E	338	15	1224	36		NA/512	AUTO
9380S	336	15	1218	36		NA/512	AUTO
9380SM	319	15	1218			NA/NA	AUTO
9424E	360	8	1661			NA/NA	AUTO
9424S	355	8	1661			NA/NA	AUTO
9780E	676	15	1661	53		NA/512	AUTO
9780S	676	15	1661	53		166/512	AUTO

MITSUBISHI ELECTRONICS

Drive Model	Format Size MB	Head	Cyl	Sect/Trac	Translate H/C/S	RWC/WPC	Land Zone
M2860-1	21			17		---/---	
M2860-2	50			17		---/---	
M2860-3	85			17		---/---	
MR335	69	7	743	26		---/---	
MR521	10	2	612	17		---/---	
MR522	20	4	612	17		---/300	612
MR5310E	65	5	977	26		NA/NA	AUTO
MR533	24	3	971	17		---/NONE	971
MR535	42	5	977	17		300/300	AUTO
MR535-U00	42	5	977	17		300/300	
MR535R	65	5	977	26		NA/NA	AUTO
MR535S	85	5	977	34		NA/NA	AUTO
MR537S	65	5	977	26		NA/NA	AUTO

MITSUMI ELECTRONICS CORP.

Drive Model	Format Size MB	Head	Cyl	Sect/Trac	Translate H/C/S	RWC/WPC	Land Zone
HD2509AA	92	4		52		---/---	
HD2513AA	130	4		52		---/---	

MMI

Drive Model	Format Size MB	Head	Cyl	Sect/Trac	Translate H/C/S	RWC/WPC	Land Zone
M106	5	2	306	17		---/128	
M112	10	4	306	17		---/128	
M125	20	8	306	17		---/128	
M212	10	4	306	17		---/128	
M225	20	8	306	17		---/128	
M306	5	2	306	17		---/128	
M312	10	4	306	17		---/128	
M325	20	8	306	17		---/128	
M350	42	8	612	17		---/288	

NCL AMERICA

SEE BRAND TECHNOLOGIES ---/---

NCR CORP

Drive Model	Format Size MB	Head	Cyl	Sect/Trac	Translate H/C/S	RWC/WPC	Land Zone
6091-5101	323	9				NA/NA	AUTO
6091-5301	675	15				NA/NA	AUTO
H6801-STD1-03-17	53	7	872	17		---/650	
H6801-STD1-07-17	45	3	868	34		NA/NA	AUTO
H6801-STD1-10-17	104	8	776	33		NA/NA	AUTO
H6801-STD1-12-17	42	2	1047	40		NA/NA	AUTO
H6801-STD1-46-46	21	4	615	17		616/128	664
H6801-STD1-47-46	71	8	1024	17		1025/128	AUTO
H6801-STD1-47-46	121	7	969	35		1025/128	AUTO

NEC TECHNOLOGIES INC

Drive Model	Format Size MB	Head	Cyl	Sect/Trac	Translate H/C/S	RWC/WPC	Land Zone
D1711	42	2				---/---	

Drive Model	Seek Time	Interface	Encode	Form Factor	cache kb	mtbf	Obsolete? RPM
8450XT	68	IDE XT	2,7 RLL	3.5 HH		20k	3600 Y
9000E	16	ESDI		5.25 FH		30k	Y
9000S	16	SCSI		5.25 FH		30k	Y
9230	16	ESDI	RLL	5.25 FH			Y
9230E	16	ESDI	RLL	5.25 FH			Y
9230S	16	SCSI	RLL	5.25 FH			Y
9380E	16	ESDI	2,7 RLL	5.25 FH		50k	3600 Y
9380S	16	SCSI	2,7 RLL	5.25 FH		50k	3600 Y
9380SM	16	SCSI-MAC	RLL	5.25 FH		50k	Y
9424E	17	ESDI	2,7 RLL	5.25 FH			Y
9424S	17	SCSI	2,7 RLL	5.25 FH			Y
9780E	17	ESDI	1,7 RLL	5.25 FH		50k	3600 Y
9780S	17	SCSI	1,7 RLL	5.25 FH		30k	3600 Y

MITSUBISHI ELECTRONICS

Drive Model	Seek Time	Interface	Encode	Form Factor	cache kb	mtbf	Obsolete? RPM
M2860-1		ST412/506	MFM				Y
M2860-2		ST412/506	MFM				Y
M2860-3		ST412/506	MFM				Y
MR335	20	ST412/506	MFM	3.5 HH		30k	Y
MR521	85	ST412/506	MFM	5.25 HH			Y
MR522	85	ST412/506	MFM	5.25 HH			Y
MR5310E	28	ESDI	2,7 RLL	5.25 HH		30k	Y
MR533		ST412/506	MFM	5.25 HH			Y
MR535	28	ST412/506	MFM	5.25 HH		30k	3600 Y
MR535-U00	28	ST412/506	MFM	5.25 HH		30k	Y
MR535R	28	ST412/506	2,7 RLL	5.25 HH		30k	3600 Y
MR535S	28	SCSI	2,7 RLL	5.25 HH		30k	Y
MR537S	28	SCSI	2,7 RLL	5.25 HH		30k	Y

MITSUMI ELECTRONICS CORP.

Drive Model	Seek Time	Interface	Encode	Form Factor	cache kb	mtbf	Obsolete? RPM
HD2509AA	16	IDE AT	1,7 RLL	2.5 4H	32k	150k	3600 Y
HD2513AA	16	IDE AT	1,7 RLL	2.5 4H	32k	150k	3600 Y

MMI

Drive Model	Seek Time	Interface	Encode	Form Factor	cache kb	mtbf	Obsolete? RPM
M106	75	ST412/506	MFM	3.5 HH			Y
M112	75	ST412/506	MFM	3.5 HH			Y
M125	75	ST412/506	MFM	3.5 HH			Y
M212	75	ST412/506	MFM	5.25 HH			Y
M225	75	ST412/506	MFM	5.25 HH			Y
M306	75	ST412/506	MFM	5.25 HH			Y
M312	75	ST412/506	MFM	5.25 HH			Y
M325	75	ST412/506	MFM	5.25 HH			Y
M350	75	ST412/506	MFM	5.25 HH			Y

NCL AMERICA

SEE BRAND TECHNOLOGIES

NCR CORP

Drive Model	Seek Time	Interface	Encode	Form Factor	cache kb	mtbf	Obsolete? RPM
6091-5101	27	SCSI	2,7 RLL	5.25			Y
6091-5301	25	SCSI	2,7 RLL	5.25			Y
H6801-STD1-03-17	28	ST412/506	MFM	3.5 HH		20k	Y
H6801-STD1-07-17	18	IDE AT	2,7 RLL	3.5 HH		20k	Y
H6801-STD1-10-17	25	IDE AT	2,7 RLL	3.5 HH		150k	Y
H6801-STD1-12-17	25	IDE AT	2,7 RLL	3.5 3H		150k	Y
H6801-STD1-46-46	28	ST412/506	MFM	3.5 HH		20k	Y
H6801-STD1-47-46	68	ST412/506	MFM	3.5 HH		20k	Y
H6801-STD1-47-46	28	ST412/506	MFM	5.25 HH		40k	Y
H6801-STD1-47-46	16	ESDI (10)	2,7 RLL	5.25 FH		100k	Y

NEC TECHNOLOGIES INC

Drive Model	Seek Time	Interface	Encode	Form Factor	cache kb	mtbf	Obsolete? RPM
D1711	19	IDE/PCMCIA	1,7 RLL	4H	32k	100k	5400 Y

Drive Model	Format Size MB	Head	Cyl	Sect/Trac	Translate H/C/S	RWC/WPC	Land Zone
D1731	85	4				--/--	
D3122	20					--/--	
D3126	21	4	615	17		616/256	
D3126H	21						
D3142	42	8	642	17			
D3146H	40	8	615	17			
D3661	118	7	915	36		NA/NA	AUTO
D3713	345	16	670	63		--/--	
D3717	540	4	2924			--/--	
D3724	426	2			16/827/63	--/--	
D3725-351	730	4	3493		16/1416/63	--/--	
D3725-351	730	4			16/1416/63	--/--	
D3725-540	540	2			16/1416/63	NA/NA	AUTO
D3727	1083	6	3493		16/2100/63	NA/NA	AUTO
D3735	45	2	1084	41	4/542/41	--/--	AUTO
D3741	40					--/--	
D3743	540	2			16/1048/63	--/--	
D3745-301	1080	4			16/2096/63	NA/NA	AUTO
D3745-351	1080	4			16/2096/63	--/--	
D3747	1620	6	3678			--/--	AUTO
D3755	105	4	1250	41	8/625/41	--/--	AUTO
D3756	105					--/--	
D3761	114	7	915	35	7/915/35	--/--	
D3772	330					--/--	
D3781	425	9	1464	63	9/1464/63	--/--	AUTO
D3817	540	4				--/--	
D3825	730	4				--/--	
D3825	1083	6				--/--	
D3827	1083	6				--/--	
D3835	45	2	1084	41		--/--	AUTO
D3841	45	8	440	25		--/--	
D3843	540	2				--/--	
D3845	1080	4				--/--	
D3847	1620	6				--/--	
D3855	105	4	1250	41		--/--	AUTO
D3856	105					--/--	
D3861	114	7	915	35			
D3865	176						
D3872	330					--/--	
D3881	425	9	1464	63			AUTO
D3896	2160	9					
D5114	5	2	306	17		--/--	
D5124	10	4	309	17		310/310	664
D5126	20	4	612	17		613/NONE	664
D5126H	21	4	612	17		613/NONE	664
D5146	40	8	615	17		616/NONE	664
D5146H	42	8	615	17		616/NONE	664
D5244	21					--/--	
D5392	1322	16	615	17		--/--	
D5452	71	10	823	17		--/--	
D5652	143	10	823	34		NA/NA	
D5655	140	7	1224	35		NA/NA	1230
D5662	300	15	1224	35		NA/NA	
D5665	153					--/--	
D5682	664	15	1633	53		NA/NA	AUTO
D5855	153					--/--	
D5862	301	15	1224	53		NA/NA	
D5882	664	15	1633	53		--/--	AUTO
D5892	1404	19	1678	86		--/--	
DSE1700A	1706	4			16/3306/63	--/--	
DSE2010A	2010	4			16/3990/63	--/--	
DSE2100A	2100	5			16/4092/63	--/--	
DSE2550A	2550	6			16/4960/63	--/--	

Drive Model	Seek Time	Interface	Encode	Form Factor	cache kb	mtbf	RPM	Obsolete?
D1731	19	IDE/PCMCIA	1,7 RLL	4H	32k	100k	5400	Y
D3122	85	ST412/506	MFM	3.5 HH				Y
D3126		ST412/506	MFM	3.5 HH				Y
D3126H		ST412/506	MFM	3.5 HH				Y
D3142	28	ST412/506	MFM	3.5 HH		30k		Y
D3146H	35	ST412/506	MFM	3.5 HH				Y
D3661	20	ESDI (10)	2,7 RLL	3.5 HH		30k		Y
D3713	12	IDE			64k			Y
D3717	12	IDE AT	1,7 RLL	3.5 3H	96k	250k	4500	Y
D3724	14	IDE	PRML 8,9	3.5 3H	256k	300k	4090	Y
D3725-351	11	IDE AT	1,7 RLL	3.5 3H	128k	300k	4090	Y
D3725-351	11	IDE AT	1,7 RLL	3.5 3H	128k	300k	4090	Y
D3725-540	11	IDE AT	1,7 RLL	3.5 3H	128k	300k	4090	Y
D3727	11	IDE AT	1,7 RLL	3.5 3H	128k	300k	4090	Y
D3735	25	IDE AT	1,7 RLL	3.5 3H		50k	3456	Y
D3741		IDE AT		3.5 3H				Y
D3743	11	IDE	PRML 8,9	3.5 3H	128k	300k	4500	Y
D3745-301	11	IDE	PRML 8,9	3.5 3H	128k	300k	4500	Y
D3745-351	11	IDE	PRML 8,9	3.5 3H	128k	300k	4500	Y
D3747	11	IDE AT	PRML	3.5 3H	128k	300k	4500	Y
D3755	25	IDE AT	1,7 RLL	3.5 3H		50k	3456	Y
D3756		IDE AT		3.5 3H				Y
D3761	20	IDE AT	2,7 RLL	3.5 3H		30k		Y
D3772		IDE AT		3.5 3H				Y
D3781	15	IDE AT	1,7 RLL	3.5 3H	64k	50k	3600	Y
D3817	12	SCSI-2	1,7 RLL	3.5 3H	64k	250k	4500	Y
D3825	11	SCSI-2	1,7 RLL	3.5 3H	64k	300k	4090	Y
D3825	11	SCSI-2	1,7 RLL	3.5 3H	32k	300k	4090	Y
D3827	11	SCSI-2	1,7 RLL	3.5 3H	64k	300k	4090	Y
D3835	25	SCSI	1,7 RLL	3.5 HH		50k	3456	Y
D3841	28	SCSI	1,7 RLL	3.5 HH		30k		Y
D3843	11	SCSI-2	PRML 8,9	3.5 3H	64k	300k	4500	Y
D3845	11	SCSI-2	PRML	3.5 3H	64k	300k	4500	Y
D3847	11	SCSI-2	PRML8,9	3.5 3H	64k	300k	4500	Y
D3855	25	SCSI	1,7 RLL	3.5 3H		50k	3456	Y
D3856		SCSI		3.5 HH				Y
D3861	20	SCSI	2,7 RLL	3.5 HH		30		Y
D3865		SCSI		3.5 HH				Y
D3872		SCSI-2		3.5 HH				Y
D3881	15	SCSI	1,7 RLL	3.5 HH	64k	50k	3600	Y
D3896	9	SCSI-2	1,7 RLL	3.5 HH	1024k	800k	7200	Y
D5114		ST412/506	MFM	5.25 HH				Y
D5124	80	ST412/506	MFM	5.25 HH				Y
D5126	80	ST412/506	MFM	5.25 HH				Y
D5126H	40	ST412/506	MFM	5.25 HH				Y
D5146	40	ST412/506	MFM	5.25 HH				Y
D5146H	40	ST412/506	MFM	5.25 HH				Y
D5244		ST412/506	MFM	5.25 FH				Y
D5392	14	IPI-2		5.25 FH		100k		Y
D5452		ST412/506	MFM	5.25 FH				Y
D5652	23	ESDI	2,7 RLL	5.25 FH				Y
D5655	18	ESDI	2,7 RLL	5.25 FH		30k		Y
D5662	18	ESDI	2,7 RLL	5.25 FH		30k		Y
D5665		ESDI		5.25 FH				Y
D5682	16	ESDI	RLL 1,7	5.25 FH		50k	3600	Y
D5855		SCSI		5.25 FH				Y
D5862	18	SCSI		5.25 FH		30k		Y
D5882	16	SCSI	1,7 RLL	5.25 FH		50k	3600	Y
D5892	14	SCSI	1,7 RLL	5.25 FH		100k		Y
DSE1700A	11	IDE	PRML 8,9	3.5 3H	128k	300k	5200	Y
DSE2010A	11	IDE	PRML 8,9	3.5 3H	128k	300k	5200	Y
DSE2100A	11	IDE	PRML 8,9	3.5 3H	128k	300k	5200	
DSE2550A	11	IDE	PRML 8,9	3.5 3H	128k	300k	5200	

Drive Model	Format Size MB	Head	Cyl	Sect/ Trac	Translate H/C/S	RWC/ WPC	Land Zone
NEI							
RD3127	10	2	612	17		---/---	
RD3255	20	4	612	17		---/---	
RD4127	10	4	306	17		---/---	
RD4255	20	8	306	17		---/---	
NEWBURY DATA							
NDR1065	55	7	918	17		---/---	
NDR1085	71	8	1024	17		---/NONE	1023
NDR1105	87	11	918	17		---/NONE	1023
NDR1140	120	15	918	17		---/NONE	1023
NDR2085	74	7	1224	17		1224/1224	
NDR2140	117	11	1224	17		1224/1224	
NDR2190	160	15	1224	17		---/NONE	1223
NDR3170S	146	9	1224	26		NA/NA	AUTO
NDR320	21	4	615	17		---/NONE	615
NDR3280S	244	15	1224	26		---/---	
NDR3380S	319	15	1224	34		NA/NA	AUTO
NDR340	42	8	615	17		---/NONE	615
NDR4175	179	7	1224	36		NA/NA	
NDR4380	338	15	1224	36		NA/NA	
NDR4380S	319	15	1224	34		---/---	
PENNY 340	42	8	615	17		615/615	
NPL							
4064	5			17		---/---	
4127	10			17		---/---	
4191S	15			17		---/---	
4255	20			17		---/---	
4362	30			17		---/---	
NP02-13	11	4	320	17		NA/0	320
NP02-26A/26S	22	4	640	17		NA/0	640
NP02-52A	44	8	640	17		NA/640	640
NP03-20	16	6	306	17		NA/0	306
NP04-13T	10	6		17		---/---	
NP04-55	45	7	754	17		NA/0	754
NP04-85	72	11	754	17		NA/0	754
NP05-105	10			17		---/---	
OKIDATA							
OD526	31	4	640	26		651/651	
OD540	51	6	640	26		651/651	
OLIVETTI							
HD662/11	10	2	612	17		---/---	
HD662/12	20	4	612	17		---/---	
XM3220	21	4	612	17		NA/128	656
XM5210	10	2	612	17		---/---	
XM5220/2	20	4	612	17		---/---	
XM5221	21	4	615	17		NA/256	700
XM5340	42	6	820	17		256/256	819
XM5360	42	6	820	17		128/128	819
XM563-12	10					---/---	
OPTIMA TECHNOLOGY CORP							
CONCORDE 1050	990	15				NA/NA	AUTO
CONCORDE 1350	1342					NA/NA	AUTO
CONCORDE 635	640	14				NA/NA	AUTO
CONCORDE 9000	8669					NA/NA	AUTO
CONCORDE 9000W	8669					NA/NA	AUTO

Drive Model	Seek Time	Interface	Encode	Form Factor	cache kb	mtbf	Obsolete? RPM ⇓
NEI							
RD3127		ST412/506	MFM	5.25			
RD3255		ST412/506	MFM	5.25			
RD4127		ST412/506	MFM	5.25			
RD4255		ST412/506	MFM	5.25			
NEWBURY DATA							
NDR1065	25	ST412/506	MFM	5.25 FH			
NDR1085	26	ST412/506	MFM	5.25 FH			
NDR1105	25	ST412/506	MFM	5.25 FH			
NDR1140	25	ST412/506	MFM	5.25 FH			
NDR2085		ST412/506	MFM	5.25 FH			
NDR2140		ST412/506	MFM	5.25 FH			
NDR2190	28	ST412/506	MFM	5.25 FH			
NDR3170S	28	SCSI	2,7 RLL	5.25 FH			
NDR320		SCSI	MFM	5.25 FH			
NDR3280S	28	SCSI	2,7 RLL	5.25 FH			
NDR3380S	28	SCSI	2,7 RLL	5.25 FH		50k	
NDR340	40	ST412/506	MFM	3.5 HH			
NDR4175	28	ESDI	2,7 RLL	5.25 FH			
NDR4380	28	ESDI	2,7 RLL	5.25 FH			
NDR4380S	28	SCSI	RLL	5.25 FH			
PENNY 340		ST412/506	MFM	5.25 HH			
NPL							
4064		ST412/506	MFM	5.25 FH			
4127		ST412/506	MFM	5.25 FH			
4191S		ST412/506	MFM	5.25 FH			
4255		ST412/506	MFM	5.25 FH			
4362		ST412/506	MFM	5.25 FH			
NP02-13	95	ST412/506	MFM	5.25 FH			
NP02-26A/26S	40	ST412/506	MFM	5.25 HH			
NP02-52A	40	ST412/506	MFM	5.25 HH			
NP03-20	85	ST412/506	MFM	3.5 FH			
NP04-13T	85	ST412/506	MFM	5.25 FH			
NP04-55	35	ST412/506	MFM	5.25 FH			
NP04-85	35	ST412/506	MFM	3.5 HH			
NP05-105		ST412/506	MFM	5.25 FH			
OKIDATA							
OD526	85	ST412/506	2,7 RLL	5.25 HH			Y
OD540	85	ST412/506	2,7 RLL	5.25 HH			Y
OLIVETTI							
HD662/11	27	ST412/506	MFM	5.25 HH			Y
HD662/12	27	ST412/506	MFM	5.25 HH			Y
XM3220	85	ST412/506	MFM	3.5 HH			Y
XM5210	65	ST412/506	MFM	5.25 HH			Y
XM5220/2	85	ST412/506	MFM	5.25 HH			Y
XM5221	40	ST412/506	MFM	5.25 HH			Y
XM5340	40	ST412/506	MFM	5.25 HH			Y
XM5360	40	ST412/506	MFM	5.25 HH			Y
XM563-12		ST412/506	MFM	5.25 HH			Y
OPTIMA TECHNOLOGY CORP							
CONCORDE 1050	15	SCSI	2,7 RLL	5.25		150k	
CONCORDE 1350	14	SCSI	2,7 RLL	5.25		150k	Y
CONCORDE 635	16	SCSI	2,7 RLL	5.25		150k	Y
CONCORDE 9000	11	SCSI-2 FAST	2,7 RLL	5.25 FH		500k	5400
CONCORDE 9000W	11	SCSI-2 FSTW	2,7 RLL	5.25 FH		500k	5400

Drive Model	Format Size MB	Head	Cyl	Sect/ Trac	Translate H/C/S	RWC/ WPC	Land Zone
DISKOVERY 1000	1001					NA/NA	AUTO
DISKOVERY 1000	2040					NA/NA	AUTO
DISKOVERY 130	137					NA/NA	AUTO
DISKOVERY 1800DHW	1763					NA/NA	AUTO
DISKOVERY 200	200					NA/NA	AUTO
DISKOVERY 2100W	2040					NA/NA	AUTO
DISKOVERY 325	321					NA/NA	AUTO
DISKOVERY 40	45					NA/NA	AUTO
DISKOVERY 4100	4095					NA/NA	AUTO
DISKOVERY 4100W	4095					NA/NA	AUTO
DISKOVERY 420	416	8				NA/NA	AUTO
DISKOVERY 500	520					NA/NA	AUTO
MINIPAK 100	104	4				NA/NA	AUTO
MINIPAK 1000	1001					NA/NA	AUTO
MINIPAK 200	209	8				NA/NA	AUTO
MINIPAK 2100	2040					NA/NA	AUTO
MINIPAK 2100	2040					NA/NA	AUTO
MINIPAK 300	320					NA/NA	AUTO
MINIPAK 40	45					NA/NA	AUTO
MINIPAK 4100	4095					NA/NA	AUTO
MINIPAK 500	520					NA/NA	AUTO

ORCA TECHNOLOGY CORP

Drive Model	Format Size MB	Head	Cyl	Sect/ Trac	Translate H/C/S	RWC/ WPC	Land Zone
320A	370	9				NA/NA	AUTO
320S	370	9				NA/NA	AUTO
400A	470	9				NA/NA	AUTO
400S	470	9				NA/NA	AUTO
760E	760	15	1564			NA/NA	AUTO
760S	760	15	1564			NA/NA	AUTO

OTARI

Drive Model	Format Size MB	Head	Cyl	Sect/ Trac	Translate H/C/S	RWC/ WPC	Land Zone
SEE DISCTRON						---/---	

PACIFIC MAGTRON

Drive Model	Format Size MB	Head	Cyl	Sect/ Trac	Translate H/C/S	RWC/ WPC	Land Zone
MT3050	50	2	1062	46		---/---	
MT3100	100	4	1062	46		---/---	
MT4115E	115	4	1597			---/---	
MT4115S	115	4	1597			---/---	
MT4140E	140	5	1597			---/---	
MT4140S	140	5	1597			---/---	
MT4170E	170	6	1597			---/---	
MT4170S	170	6	1597			---/---	
MT5760E	676	15	1632	54		NA/NA	AUTO
MT5760S	673	15	1632	54		NA/NA	AUTO
MT6120S	1050	15	1927	71		NA/NA	AUTO

PANASONIC

Drive Model	Format Size MB	Head	Cyl	Sect/ Trac	Translate H/C/S	RWC/ WPC	Land Zone
JU116	20	4	615	17		616/616	
JU128	42	7	733	17		734/734	

PLUS DEVELOPMENT

Drive Model	Format Size MB	Head	Cyl	Sect/ Trac	Translate H/C/S	RWC/ WPC	Land Zone
HARDCARD 20	21	4	615	17		NA/NA	AUTO
HARDCARD 40	42	8	612	17		NA/NA	AUTO
HARDCARD II-40	40	5	925	17		NA/NA	AUTO
HARDCARD II-80	80	10	925	17		NA/NA	AUTO
HARDCARD II-XL105	105	15	806	17		---/---	
HARDCARD II-XL50	52	10	601	17		---/---	
IMPULSE 105AT/LP	105	16	755	17	16/755/17	---/---	AUTO
IMPULSE 105S	105	6	1019			---/---	AUTO
IMPULSE 105S/LP	105	4	1056			---/---	AUTO
IMPULSE 120AT	120	5	1123	42	9/814/32	---/---	AUTO

Drive Model	Seek Time	Interface	Encode	Form Factor	cache kb	mtbf	RPM	Obsolete?
DISKOVERY 1000	9	SCSI-2 FAST	2,7 RLL	3.5 4H		800k	5400	
DISKOVERY 1000	8	SCSI-2 FAST	2,7 RLL	3.5 4H		500k	5400	
DISKOVERY 130	20	SCSI	2,7 RLL	5.25		50k		Y
DISKOVERY 1800DHW	8	SCSI-2 FSTW	2,7 RLL	3.5 HH		500k		
DISKOVERY 200	15	SCSI	2,7 RLL	5.25		150k		
DISKOVERY 2200W	8	SCSI-2 FSTW	2,7 RLL	3.5 4H		500k	7200	
DISKOVERY 325	14	SCSI	2,7 RLL	5.25		150k		Y
DISKOVERY 4	25	SCSI	2,7 RLL	5.25		50k		Y
DISKOVERY 4100	8	SCSI-2 FAST	2,7 RLL	3.5 HH		800k	7200	
DISKOVERY 4100W	8	SCSI-2 FSTW	2,7 RLL	3.5 HH		800k	7200	
DISKOVERY 420	16	SCSI	2,7 RLL	5.25		100k		
DISKOVERY 500	12	SCSI-2 FAST	2,7 RLL	3.5 4H		300k	5411	
MINIPAK 100	25	SCSI	2,7 RLL	3.5 HH		30k		
MINIPAK 1000	9	SCSI	2,7 RLL	3.5 4H		800k	5400	
MINIPAK 200	20	SCSI	2,7 RLL	3.5 HH		40k		
MINIPAK 2100	8	SCSI-2 FAST	2,7 RLL	3.5 4H		500k	7200	
MINIPAK 2100	8	SCSI-2 FSTW	2,7 RLL	3.5 4H		500k	7200	
MINIPAK 300	13	SCSI	2,7 RLL	3.5 HH		150k		Y
MINIPAK 40	25	SCSI	2,7 RLL	3.5 HH		30k		Y
MINIPAK 4100	8	SCSI-2 FAST	2,7 RLL	3.5 HH		800k	7200	
MINIPAK 500	12	SCSI-2 FAST	2,7 RLL	3.5 4H		300k	5411	

ORCA TECHNOLOGY CORP

Drive Model	Seek Time	Interface	Encode	Form Factor	cache kb	mtbf	RPM	Obsolete?
320A	12	IDE AT	2,7 RLL	3.5 HH		100k		
320S	12	SCSI	2,7 RLL	3.5 HH		100k		
400A	12	IDE AT	2,7 RLL	3.5 HH		100k		
400S	12	SCSI	2,7 RLL	3.5 HH		100k		
760E	14	ESDI	2,7 RLL	5.25		50k		
760S	14	SCSI	2,7 RLL	5.25		50k		

OTARI

SEE DISCTRON

PACIFIC MAGTRON

Drive Model	Seek Time	Interface	Encode	Form Factor	cache kb	mtbf	RPM	Obsolete?
MT3050	20	IDE AT	2,7 RLL	5.25 HH		60k		Y
MT3100	20	IDE AT	2,7 RLL	5.25 HH		60k		Y
MT4115E	16	ESDI	2,7 RLL	5.25 HH		100k		Y
MT4115S	16	SCSI	2,7 RLL	5.25 HH		100k		Y
MT4140E	16	ESDI	2,7 RLL	5.25 HH		100k		Y
MT4140S	16	SCSI	2,7 RLL	5.25 HH		100k		Y
MT4170E	16	ESDI	2,7 RLL	5.25 HH		100k		Y
MT4170S	16	SCSI	2,7 RLL	5.25 HH		100k		Y
MT5760E	14	ESDI (15)	1,7 RLL	5.25 FH		150k		Y
MT5760S	14	SCSI	1,7 RLL	5.25 FH		150k		Y
MT6120S	14	SCSI	1,7 RLL	5.25 FH		150k		Y

PANASONIC

Drive Model	Seek Time	Interface	Encode	Form Factor	cache kb	mtbf	RPM	Obsolete?
JU116	85	ST412/506	MFM	3.5 HH		5		Y
JU128	35	ST412/506	MFM	3.5 HH		5		Y

PLUS DEVELOPMENT

Drive Model	Seek Time	Interface	Encode	Form Factor	cache kb	mtbf	RPM	Obsolete?
HARDCARD 20	40	IDE AT	2,7 RLL	3.5 3H		60k		
HARDCARD 40	40	IDE AT	2,7 RLL	3.5 3H		60k		
HARDCARD II-40	25	IDE AT	2,7 RLL	3.5 3H				
HARDCARD II-80	25	IDE AT	2,7 RLL	3.5 3H				
HARDCARD II-XL105	17	IDE AT	2,7 RLL	CARD 3H				
HARDCARD II-XL50	17	IDE AT	2,7 RLL	CARD 3H				
IMPULSE 105AT/LP	17	IDE AT	2,7 RLL	3.5 3H		60k		Y
IMPULSE 105S	19	SCSI-2	2,7 RLL	3.5 HH		50k		Y
IMPULSE 105S/LP	17	SCSI-2	2,7 RLL	3.5 3H		60k		Y
IMPULSE 120AT	15	IDE AT	1,7 RLL	3.5 HH		50k	3605	Y

Drive Model	Format Size MB	Head	Cyl	Sect/ Trac	Translate H/C/S	RWC/ WPC	Land Zone
IMPULSE 120S	120	5	1123	42		---/---	AUTO
IMPULSE 170AT	169	7	1123	42	10/966/34	---/---	AUTO
IMPULSE 170S	169	7	1123	42		---/---	AUTO
IMPULSE 210AT	174	7	1156	42	13/873/36	---/---	AUTO
IMPULSE 210S	174	7	1156	42		---/---	AUTO
IMPULSE 330AT	331					---/---	AUTO
IMPULSE 330S	331					---/---	AUTO
IMPULSE 40AT	41	5	965	17	5/968/17	NA/NA	AUTO
IMPULSE 40S	42	3	834			---/---	AUTO
IMPULSE 425AT	425					---/---	AUTO
IMPULSE 425S	425					---/---	AUTO
IMPULSE 52AT/LP	52	8	751	17	8/751/17	---/---	AUTO
IMPULSE 52S/LP	52	2				---/---	AUTO
IMPULSE 80AT	83	10	965	17	6/611/17	NA/NA	AUTO
IMPULSE 80AT/LP	85	16	616	17	6/611/17	---/---	AUTO
IMPULSE 80S	84	6	918			---/---	AUTO
IMPULSE 80S/LP	85	4				---/---	AUTO

PRAIRIETEK CORP

Drive Model	Format Size MB	Head	Cyl	Sect/ Trac	Translate H/C/S	RWC/ WPC	Land Zone
PRAIRIE 120	21	2	615	34		---/---	
PRAIRIE 140	42	4	615	34		NA/NA	AUTO
PRAIRIE 220A	20	4	612	16		---/---	
PRAIRIE 220S	20	4	612	16		---/---	
PRAIRIE 240	42	4	615	34		---/---	
PRAIRIE 242A	42	4	615	34		NA/NA	AUTO
PRAIRIE 242S	42	4	615	34		NA/NA	AUTO
PRAIRIE 282A	82	4		34		NA/NA	AUTO
PRAIRIE 282S	82	4		34		NA/NA	AUTO

PRIAM CORPORATION

Drive Model	Format Size MB	Head	Cyl	Sect/ Trac	Translate H/C/S	RWC/ WPC	Land Zone
160A	62					---/---	
185A	73					---/---	
330	338					---/---	
3504	32	4	820	26		---/---	
502	46	7	755	17		756/756	
504	46	7	755	17		756/756	
514	117	11	1224	17		---/---	
519	160	15	1224	17		1225/1225	
519	244	11	1224	26		---/---	
617	153	7	1225			NA/NA	
628	241	11	1225			NA/NA	
638	329	15	1225			NA/NA	
717	153	7	1225			1226/1226	
728	241	11	1225			1226/1226	
738	329	15	1225			1226/1226	
ID/ED040	42	5	987	17		---/---	
ID/ED045	50	5	1166	17		---/---	
ID/ED060	62	7	1018	17		---/---	
ID/ED062	71	7	1166	17		---/---	
ID/ED075	74	5	1166	17		---/---	
ID/ED100	122	7	1314	26		---/---	
ID/ED1000	1046	15	1919	71		---/---	AUTO
ID/ED120	121	7	1024	33		NA/NA	AUTO
ID/ED130	159	15	1224	17		---/---	
ID/ED150	160	7	1276	35		NA/NA	AUTO
ID/ED160	158	7	1225	36		NA/NA	AUTO
ID/ED230	235	15	1224	25		---/---	
ID/ED240	243	15	1220	26		---/---	
ID/ED250	248	11	1225	36		NA/NA	AUTO
ID/ED660	675	15	1628	54		---/---	AUTO
ID100	103	7	1166	25		---/---	
ID1000	1034	15	1919	71		NA/NA	AUTO

Drive Model	Seek Time	Interface	Encode	Form Factor	cache kb	mtbf	RPM	Obsolete?
IMPULSE 120S	15	SCSI-2	1,7 RLL	3.5 HH		50k	3605	Y
IMPULSE 170AT	15	IDE AT	1,7 RLL	3.5 HH		50k	3605	Y
IMPULSE 170S	15	SCSI-2	1,7 RLL	3.5 HH		50k	3605	Y
IMPULSE 210AT	15	IDE AT	1,7 RLL	3.5 HH		50k	3605	Y
IMPULSE 210S	15	SCSI-2	1,7 RLL	3.5 HH		50k	3605	Y
IMPULSE 330AT	14	IDE AT	1,7 RLL	3.5 HH		75k		Y
IMPULSE 330S	14	SCSI-2	1,7 RLL	3.5 HH		75k		Y
IMPULSE 40AT	19	IDE AT	2,7 RLL	3.5 HH		50k	3660	Y
IMPULSE 40S	19	SCSI-2	2,7 RLL	3.5 HH		50k	3660	Y
IMPULSE 425AT	14	IDE AT	1,7 RLL	3.5 HH		75k		Y
IMPULSE 425S	14	SCSI-2	1,7 RLL	3.5 HH		75k		Y
IMPULSE 52AT/LP	17	IDE AT	2,7 RLL	3.5 3H		60k		Y
IMPULSE 52S/LP	17	SCSI-2	2,7 RLL	3.5 3H		60k		Y
IMPULSE 80AT	19	IDE AT	2,7 RLL	3.5 HH		50k	3660	Y
IMPULSE 80AT/LP	17	IDE AT	2,7 RLL	3.5 3H		50k	3660	Y
IMPULSE 80S	19	SCSI-2	2,7 RLL	3.5 HH		50k	3660	Y
IMPULSE 80S/LP	17	SCSI-2	2,7 RLL	3.5 3H		60k		Y

PRAIRIETEK CORP

Drive Model	Seek Time	Interface	Encode	Form Factor	cache kb	mtbf	RPM	Obsolete?
PRAIRIE 120	23	IDE AT	2,7 RLL	2.5 4H		20k		
PRAIRIE 140	23	IDE AT	2,7 RLL	2.5 4H		20k		
PRAIRIE 220A	28	IDE AT	2,7 RLL	2.5 3H		20k		
PRAIRIE 220S	28	SCSI	2,7 RLL	2.5 3H		20k		
PRAIRIE 240	28	IDE AT	2,7 RLL	2.5 3H		20k		
PRAIRIE 242A	23	IDE XT-AT	2,7 RLL			20k		
PRAIRIE 242S	23	SCSI	2,7 RLL			20k		
PRAIRIE 282A	28	IDE AT	2,7 RLL			20k		
PRAIRIE 282S	23	SCSI	2,7 RLL			20k		

PRIAM CORPORATION

Drive Model	Seek Time	Interface	Encode	Form Factor	cache kb	mtbf	RPM	Obsolete?
160A		ST412/506	MFM	5.25 FH				Y
185A		ST412/506	MFM	5.25 FH				Y
330		ST412/506	MFM	5.25 FH				Y
3504	27	ST412/506	2,7 RLL	3.5 HH				Y
502	22	ST412/506	MFM	5.25 FH				Y
504	22	ST412/506	MFM	5.25 FH				Y
514	22	ST412/506	MFM	5.25 FH				Y
519	22	ST412/506	MFM	5.25 FH		40k		Y
519	22	ST412/506	2,7 RLL	5.25 FH		40		Y
617	20	ESDI	2,7 RLL	5.25 FH		40k		Y
628	20	ESDI	2,7 RLL	5.25 FH		40k		Y
638	20	ESDI	2,7 RLL	5.25 FH		40k		Y
717	20	SCSI	2,7 RLL	5.25 FH		40k		Y
728	20	SCSI	2,7 RLL	5.25 FH		40k		Y
738	20	SCSI	2,7 RLL	5.25 FH		40k		Y
ID/ED040	23	ST412/506	MFM	5.25 FH		40k		Y
ID/ED045	23	ST412/506	MFM	5.25 FH		40k		Y
ID/ED060	30	ST412/506	MFM	5.25 FH		40k		Y
ID/ED062	23	ST412/506	MFM	5.25 FH		40k		Y
ID/ED075	23	ST412/506		5.25 FH		40k		Y
ID/ED100	15	ST412/506	2,7 RLL	5.25 HH		40k		Y
ID/ED1000	14	SCSI		5.25 FH		150k		Y
ID/ED120	28	ESDI	2,7 RLL	5.25 FH				Y
ID/ED130	13	ST412/506	MFM	5.25 HH		40k		Y
ID/ED150	28	ESDI	2,7 RLL	5.25 FH				Y
ID/ED160	18	ESDI	2,7 RLL	5.25 FH				Y
ID/ED230	11	ST412/506		5.25 FH		40k		Y
ID/ED240	28	ST412/506	2,7 RLL	5.25 FH				Y
ID/ED250	18	ESDI		5.25 FH				Y
ID/ED660	16	SCSI		5.25 FH		150k		Y
ID100	15	ST412/506	2,7 RLL	5.25 FH		40k		Y
ID1000	14	ESDI		5.25 FH		150k		Y

Drive Model	Format Size MB	Head	Cyl	Sect/ Trac	Translate H/C/S	RWC/ WPC	Land Zone
ID120	119	7	1024	33		NA/NA	
ID130	132	15	1224	17		---/---	
ID150	158	7	1276	35		NA/NA	
ID160	158	7	1218	36		---/---	AUTO
ID160H	156	7	1225	36		NA/NA	AUTO
ID20	25	3	987	17		---/---	
ID230	233	15	1224	25		---/---	
ID250	246	11	1225	36		NA/NA	
ID330	339	15	1218	36		---/---	
ID330D	337	15	1225	36		NA/NA	
ID330E	337	15	1218	36		---/---	
ID330E-PS/2	330	15	1195	36		---/---	
ID330S	338	15	1225	36		NA/NA	AUTO
ID340H	340	7	1218	36		---/---	AUTO
ID40	42	5	987	17		---/---	
ID40AT	40	5	1018	17		---/---	
ID45	44	5	1018	17		---/---	
ID45H	44	5	1024	17		---/---	
ID60	59	7	1018	17		---/---	
ID60AT	59	7	1018	17		---/---	
ID62	62	7	1166	17		---/---	
ID660	660	15	1632	54		NA/NA	AUTO
ID75	73	5	1166	25		---/---	
V130	39	3	987	26		988/988	987
V150	42	5	987	17		988/988	987
V160	50	5	1166	17		1167/1167	
V170	60	7	987	17		988/988	987
V170R	91	7	987	26		988/988	987
V185	72	7	1166	17		1167/1167	1165
V519	159	15	1224	17		---/NONE	1223

PROCOM TECHNOLOGY

Drive Model	Format Size MB	Head	Cyl	Sect/ Trac	Translate H/C/S	RWC/ WPC	Land Zone
ATOM-AT1300	1350					---/---	
ATOM-AT1302	1350					---/---	
ATOM-AT2001	2160					---/---	
ATOM-AT3000	3050					---/---	
ATOM-AT340	340					NA/NA	AUTO
ATOM-AT500	528					---/---	
ATOM-AT800	811					---/---	
BRAVOPAQ120	124	14	1024	17		---/---	AUTO
BRAVOPAQ40	42	5	977	17		---/---	AUTO
HIPER 145	150	8	1024	36		---/---	
HIPER 155	160	9	966	36		---/---	
HIPER 20	21	4	615	17		---/---	
HIPER 30	33	4	615	26		---/---	
HIPER 330	337	15	1224	36		---/---	
HIPER 380	388	16	755	63		---/---	
HIPER 48	48	6	615	26		---/---	
HIPER/II 155	157	64	150	32		---/---	
HIPER/II 380	383	64	365	32		---/---	
HIPER/II 65	65	9	925	17		---/---	
MD100	104	64	102	32		---/---	
MD1003 (external)	1080	4	4826	116		---/---	
MD20	21	64	21	32		---/---	
MD200	209	32	200	32		---/---	
MD2003 (external)	2160	5	2149	148		---/---	
MD2103 (external)	2147	11	371	186-125			
MD2103W (external)	2100						
MD30	30	64	30	32		---/---	
MD320	337	64	317	32		---/---	
MD420	433	64	415	32		---/---	
MD4303 (external)	4350						
MD4303W (external)	4294						

Drive Model	Seek Time	Interface	Encode	Form Factor	cache kb	mtbf	RPM	Obsolete?
ID120	28	ESDI	2,7 RLL	5.25 FH				Y
ID130	13	ST412/506	MFM	5.25 FH				Y
ID150	28	ESDI	2,7 RLL	5.25 FH		40k		Y
ID160	28	ESDI		5.25 FH		150k		Y
ID160H	28	ESDI	2,7 RLL	5.25 FH		150k		Y
ID20	23	ST412/506	MFM	5.25 FH		40k		Y
ID230	11	ST412/506	2,7 RLL	5.25 FH		40k		Y
ID250	18	ESDI	2,7 RLL	5.25 FH				Y
ID330	18	SCSI	2,7 RLL	5.25 FH				Y
ID330D	18	ESDI	2,7 RLL	5.25 FH				Y
ID330E	18	ESDI	2,7 RLL	5.25 FH				Y
ID330E-PS/2	18	PS/2	2,7 RLL	5.25 FH				Y
ID330S	18	SCSI	2,7 RLL	5.25 FH				Y
ID340H	14	ESDI	2,7 RLL	5.25 FH		150k		Y
ID40	23	ST412/506	MFM	5.25 FH		40k		Y
ID40AT	23	ST412/506	MFM	5.25 FH		150k		Y
ID45	23	ST412/506	MFM	5.25 FH		150k		Y
ID45H	25	ST412/506	MFM	5.25 HH		40k		Y
ID60	30	ST412/506	MFM	5.25 FH		40k		Y
ID60AT	23	ST412/506	MFM	5.25 FH		150k		Y
ID62	23	ST412/506	MFM	5.25 FH		40k		Y
ID660	16	ESDI	2,7 RLL	5.25 FH		150k		Y
ID75	23	ST412/506	2,7 RLL	5.25 FH		40k		Y
V130		ST412/506	2,7 RLL	5.25 FH				Y
V150		ST412/506	MFM	5.25 FH				Y
V160		ST412/506	MFM	5.25 FH				Y
V170	28	ST412/506	MFM	5.25 FH				Y
V170R	28	ST412/506	MFM	5.25 FH				Y
V185	28	ST412/506	MFM	5.25 FH				Y
V519	20		MFM	5.25 FH				Y

PROCOM TECHNOLOGY

Drive Model	Seek Time	Interface	Encode	Form Factor	cache kb	mtbf	RPM	Obsolete?
ATOM-AT1300	13	ATA-2		2.5 4H	128k	300k	4200	
ATOM-AT1302	13	ATA-2		2.5 4H	128k	300k	4200	
ATOM-AT2001	13	ATA-2		2.5 4H	128k	300k	4200	
ATOM-AT3000	13	ATA-2		2.5 4H	128k	300k	4852	
ATOM-AT340	16	IDE		2.5 4H	120k	300k		
ATOM-AT500	13	IDE		2.5 4H	128k	300k		
ATOM-AT800	13	IDE		2.5 4H	128k	300k		
BRAVOPAQ120	19	IDE AT	RLL	3.5 HH		150k		Y
BRAVOPAQ40	25	IDE AT	RLL	3.5 HH		150k		Y
HIPER 145	23	ESDI		5.25 FH		30		Y
HIPER 155	16.5	SCSI	RLL	5.25 FH		150k		Y
HIPER 20	40	ST412/506	MFM			100k		Y
HIPER 30	28	ST412/506	RLL			150k		Y
HIPER 330	18	ESDI		5.25 FH		30k		Y
HIPER 380	16	SCSI		5.25 FH		100k		Y
HIPER 48	28	ST412/506	RLL			150k		Y
HIPER/II 155	16.5	SCSI	RLL	5.25 FH		100k		Y
HIPER/II 380	16	ESDI	RLL	5.25 FH		100k		Y
HIPER/II 65	28	ST412/506	MFM	5.25 FH		40k		Y
MD100	18	SCSI	RLL			70k		Y
MD1003 (external)	12.5	SCSI-2 FAST		3.5	128k	300k	5376	
MD20	28	SCSI	RLL			150k		Y
MD200	18	SCSI	RLL			70k		Y
MD2003 (external)	8.5	SCSI-2 FAST		3.5	448k	800k	5400	
MD2103 (external)	9	SCSI-2 FAST		3.5	512k	800k	7200	
MD2103W (external)	8	SCSI-2 FSTW		3.5			7200	
MD30	28	SCSI	RLL			150k		Y
MD320	12	SCSI	RLL			100k		Y
MD420	16	SCSI	RLL			100k		Y
MD4303 (external)	8	SCSI-2 FAST		3.5 HH	512k	1000k	7200	
MD4303W (external)	8	SCSI-2 FSTW		3.5	1024k	800k	7200	

Drive Model	Format Size MB	Head	Cyl	Sect/ Trac	Translate H/C/S	RWC/ WPC	Land Zone
MD45	45	64	45	32		---/---	
MD544 (external)	541	2	4901	108		---/---	
MD80	83	64	80	32		---/---	
MD9103	9100					---/---	
MD9103W	9100					---/---	
MTD1000	1037	64	989	32		---/---	
MTD320-10	337	64	317	32		---/---	
MTD585	601	64	573	32		---/---	
MTD650	676	64	650	32		---/---	
MTD9000 (external)	9090					---/---	
PAT100	110	14	535	29		---/---	AUTO
PAT40	42	4	805	26		---/---	AUTO
PH.D20	21	4	615	17		---/---	
PH.D2520	21	4	615	17		---/---	
PH.D2545	45	7	733	17		---/---	
PH.D30	33	4	615	26		---/---	
PH.D30-CE	33	4	615	17		---/---	
PH.D3020	21	4	615	17		---/---	
PH.D45	45	7	773	17		---/---	
PH.D48	49	6	615	26		---/---	
PH.D5045	45	7	773	17		---/---	
PIRA 100	101	8	776	33		---/---	
PIRA 120	124	14	1024	17		---/---	AUTO
PIRA 200	210	12	954	36		---/---	AUTO
PIRA 40	42	5	977	17		---/---	AUTO
PIRA 50-120	210	14	1024	36		---/---	AUTO
PIRA 50-200	210	12	954	36		---/---	AUTO
PIRA 50-270	270					---/---	
PIRA 50-340	340					---/---	
PIRA 50-420	420					---/---	
PIRA 55-120	130					---/---	
PIRA 55-200	212					---/---	
PIRA 55-270	270					---/---	
PIRA 55-340	340					---/---	
PIRA 55-420	420					---/---	
PIRA 55-500	510					---/---	
PR-IDE1000	1080					---/---	
PR-IDE1200	1200					---/---	
PR-IDE1600	1629					---/---	
PR-IDE2000	2113					---/---	
PR-IDE210	210					---/---	
PR-IDE270	270					---/---	
PR-IDE340	340					---/---	
PR-IDE420	420					---/---	
PR-IDE500	510					---/---	
PR-IDE800	800					---/---	
PROPAQ/N100	101	8	776	33		---/---	AUTO
PROPAQ/N120-19	124	14	1024	17		---/---	AUTO
PROPAQ/N185-15	189	12	1023	33		---/---	AUTO
PROPAQ/N40	40	4	805	26		---/---	AUTO
PROPAQ/N40N	40	6	560	26		---/---	AUTO
PROPAQ/S100	101	8	776	33		---/---	AUTO
PROPAQ/S120-19	124	14	1024	17		---/---	AUTO
PROPAQ/S185-15	189	12	1023	33		---/---	AUTO
PROPAQ/S40	40	4	805	26		---/---	AUTO
PROPAQ/S40N	40	6	560	26		---/---	AUTO
PROPAQ100	101	8	776	33		---/---	AUTO
PROPAQ120-19	124	14	1024	17		---/---	AUTO
PROPAQ185-15	189	12	1023	33		---/---	AUTO
PROPAQ185-15	189	5				NA/NA	AUTO
PROPAQ40	40	4	805	26		---/---	AUTO
PROPAQ40N	40	6	560	26		---/---	AUTO
SI100	104	64	102	32		---/---	

Drive Model	Seek Time	Interface	Encode	Form Factor	cache kb	mtbf	RPM	Obsolete?
MD45	28	SCSI	RLL			150k		Y
MD544 (external)	12	SCSI-2 FAST		3.5	64k	300k	5400	
MD80	24	SCSI	RLL			150k		Y
MD9103	9	Ultra SCSI			2024k	1000k	7200	
MD9103W	9	WIDE SCSI			2024k	1000k	7200	
MTD1000	15	SCSI	RLL ZBR			100k		Y
MTD320-10	10.7	SCSI	RLL ZBR			100k		Y
MTD585	16.5	SCSI	RLL ZBR			100k		Y
MTD650	15.5	SCSI	RLL ZBR			100k		Y
MTD9000 (external)	11	SCSI-2 FAST			1024k	500k		
PAT100	15	IDE AT	RLL	3.5 HH		150		Y
PAT40	25	IDE AT	RLL	5.25 HH		150k		Y
PH.D20	40	ST412/506	MFM	3.5 HH		150		Y
PH.D2520	40	ST412/506	MFM	3.5 HH		30k		Y
PH.D2545	25	ST412/506	MFM	3.5 HH		30k		Y
PH.D30	28	ST412/506	RLL	3.5 HH		150		Y
PH.D30-CE	28	ST412/506	RLL	3.5 HH		150		Y
PH.D3020	40	ST412/506	MFM	3.5 HH		30k		Y
PH.D45	25	ST412/506	RLL	3.5 HH		150		Y
PH.D48	28	ST412/506	MFM	3.5 HH		150		Y
PH.D5045	25	ST412/506	MFM	3.5 HH		150		Y
PIRA 100	25	IDE AT		3.5 HH		150k		Y
PIRA 120	18	IDE AT	RLL	3.5 HH		20k		Y
PIRA 200	15	IDE AT	RLL	3.5 HH		150		Y
PIRA 40	28	IDE AT	RLL	3.5 HH		150k		Y
PIRA 50-120	19	IDE AT	RLL	3.5 HH		150k		Y
PIRA 50-200	15	IDE AT	RLL	3.5 HH		150k		Y
PIRA 50-270	14	IDE AT	RLL	3.5 HH		150k		Y
PIRA 50-340	15	IDE AT	RLL	3.5 HH		150k		
PIRA 50-420	14	IDE AT	RLL	3.5 HH		150k		
PIRA 55-120	16	IDE	2,7 RLL		32k	150k	3211	Y
PIRA 55-200	15	IDE	1,7 RLL		64k	150k	3551	Y
PIRA 55-270	14	IDE				150k		
PIRA 55-340	15	IDE				150k		
PIRA 55-420	14	IDE				150k		
PIRA 55-500	12	IDE	2,7 RLL		256k	150k	4500	
PR-IDE1000	14	ATA-2		3H	128k	350k	3800	
PR-IDE1200	10	IDE		3H				
PR-IDE1600	12	ATA-2			128k	300k	4480	
PR-IDE2000	10.5	ATA-2			256k	500k	5400	
PR-IDE210	14	IDE		3H				Y
PR-IDE270	14	IDE		3H				Y
PR-IDE340	12	IDE		3H				
PR-IDE420	14	IDE		3H				
PR-IDE500	12	IDE		3H				
PR-IDE800	12	IDE		3H				
PROPAQ/N100	25	IDE AT	RLL	3.5 HH		100k		Y
PROPAQ/N120-19	19	IDE AT	RLL	3.5 HH		150k		Y
PROPAQ/N185-15	15	IDE AT	RLL	3.5 HH		150k		Y
PROPAQ/N40	25	IDE AT	RLL	3.5 HH		100k		Y
PROPAQ/N40N	25	IDE AT	RLL	3.5 HH		150k		Y
PROPAQ/S100	25	IDE AT	RLL	3.5 HH		20k		Y
PROPAQ/S120-19	19	IDE AT	RLL	3.5 HH		150k		Y
PROPAQ/S185-15	15	IDE AT	RLL	3.5 HH		150k		Y
PROPAQ/S40	25	IDE AT	RLL	3.5 HH		100k		Y
PROPAQ/S40N	25	IDE AT	RLL	3.5 HH		150k		Y
PROPAQ100	25	IDE AT	RLL	3.5 HH		150k		Y
PROPAQ120-19	19	IDE AT	RLL	3.5 HH		150k		Y
PROPAQ185-15	15	IDE AT	RLL	3.5 HH		150k		Y
PROPAQ185-15		IDE AT	RLL	3.5 HH		70k		Y
PROPAQ40	25	IDE AT	RLL	3.5 HH		100k		Y
PROPAQ40N	25	IDE AT	RLL	3.5 HH		150k		Y
SI100	18	SCSI	RLL			70k		Y

Drive Model	Format Size MB	Head	Cyl	Sect/Trac	Translate H/C/S	RWC/WPC	Land Zone
SI1000	1037	64		32		---/---	
SI1000/S5	1037	8				NA/NA	AUTO
SI1003	1080	4	4826	116		---/---	
SI1003/C	1080	4	4826	116		---/---	
SI200	209	64	200	32		---/---	
SI200/PS3	209	4				NA/NA	AUTO
SI2003	2160	5	2149	148		---/---	
SI2003/C	2160	5	2149	148		---/---	
SI2103	2147	11	371186-125			---/---	
SI2103/C	2147	11	371186-125			---/---	
SI2103W/C	2100						
SI320-10	337	64	317	32		---/---	
SI320H	331	64	339	32		---/---	
SI420H	435	64	415	32		---/---	
SI4303	4350	10	5288	165		---/---	
SI4303/C	4350	10	5288	165		---/---	
SI4303W/C	4300						
SI45	48	64	45	32		---/---	
SI544	541	2	4901	108		---/---	
SI544/C	544	2	4901	108		---/---	
SI585	601	64	415	32		---/---	
SI585/PS5	601	8				NA/NA	AUTO
SI585/S5	601	8				NA/NA	AUTO
SI650	662	64	632	32		---/---	
SI80	83	64	80	32		---/---	
SI9000/S5	9090						
SI9103	9100	20	5273153-23			---/---	
SI9103W	9100	20	5273153-23			---/---	
SI9103W/C	9100	20	5273153-23			---/---	

PTI (PERIPHERAL TECHNOLOGY)

Drive Model	Format Size MB	Head	Cyl	Sect/Trac	Translate H/C/S	RWC/WPC	Land Zone
PL100 TURBO	105	4				NA/NA	AUTO
PL200 TURBO	210	7				NA/NA	AUTO
PL32 TURBO	320	14				NA/NA	AUTO
PT225	21	4	615	17		---/---	
PT234	28	4	820	17		---/---	
PT238A	32	4	615	26		NA/NA	
PT238R	32	4	615	26		---/---	
PT238S	32	4	615	26		---/---	
PT251A	51	4	820	26		---/---	
PT251R	44	4	820	26		---/---	
PT251S	44	4	820	26		---/---	
PT338	32	6	615	17		---/---	
PT351	42	6	820	17		---/---	
PT357A	49	6	615	26		---/---	
PT357R	49	6	615	26		---/---	
PT357S	49	6	615	26		---/---	
PT376A	65	6	820	26		NA/NA	
PT376R	65	6	820	26		---/---	
PT376S	65	6	820	26		---/---	
PT4102A	87	8	820	26		---/---	
PT4102R	87	8	820	26		---/---	
PT4102S	87	8	820	26		---/---	
PT468	57	8	820	17		---/---	

QUANTUM CORPORATION

Drive Model	Format Size MB	Head	Cyl	Sect/Trac	Translate H/C/S	RWC/WPC	Land Zone
ATLAS II 2.2S	2275	5		V		---/---	
ATLAS II 4.5S	4550	10		V		---/---	
ATLAS II 9.1S	9100	20		V		---/---	
ATLAS III 18.2S 1-98	18200	20				---/---	
ATLAS III 18.2S 1-98	18200	20				---/---	
ATLAS III 18.2S 1-98	18200	20				---/---	

Drive Model	Seek Time	Interface	Encode	Form Factor	cache kb	mtbf	RPM	Obsolete?
SI1000	15	SCSI	RLL	5.25 FH		100k		
SI1000/S5	15	SCSI		5.25		40k		
SI1003	12	SCSI-2 FAST		3.5 3H	128k	300k	5376	
SI1003/C	12	SCSI-2 FAST		3.5 3H	128k	300k	5376	
SI200	18	SCSI	RLL			70k		Y
SI200/PS3	18	SCSI	2,7 RLL	3.5 HH		70k		Y
SI2003	8.5	SCSI-2 FAST		3.5 3H		800k	5400	
SI2003/C	8.5	SCSI-2 FAST		3.5 3H		800k	5400	
SI2103	9	SCSI-2 FAST		3.5 3H	512k	800k	7200	
SI2103/C	9	SCSI-2 FAST		3.5 3H	512k	800k	7200	
SI2103W/C	8	SCSI-2 FSTW		3.5 3H			7200	
SI320-10	10.7	SCSI	RLL	5.25 FH		100k		Y
SI320H	14	SCSI	RLL	5.25 FH		100k		Y
SI420H	16	SCSI	RLL	5.25 FH		100k		Y
SI4303	8	SCSI-2 FAST		3.5 HH	512k	1000k	7200	
SI4303/C	8	Ultra SCSI			512k	1000k	7200	
SI4303W/C	8	SCSI-2 FSTW		3.5 HH	1024k	800k	7200	
SI45	28	SCSI	RLL			150k		Y
SI544	12	SCSI-2 FAST		3.5 3H	64k	300k	5400	
SI544/C	12	SCSI-2 FAST		3.5 3H	64k	300k	5400	
SI585	16.5	SCSI	RLL	5.25 FH		100k		
SI585/PS5	17	SCSI		5.25		100k		
SI585/S5	17	SCSI		5.25		100k		
SI650	15.5	SCSI	RLL	5.25 FH		100k		
SI80	24	SCSI	RLL			150k		Y
SI9000/S5	11	SCSI-2 FAST		5.25 FH	024k	500k		
SI9103	9	Ultra SCSI			2024k	1000k	7200	
SI9103W	9	SCSI WIDE			2024k	1000k	7200	
SI9103W/C	9	WIDE SCSI			2024k	1000k	7200	

PTI (PERIPHERAL TECHNOLOGY)

Drive Model	Seek Time	Interface	Encode	Form Factor	cache kb	mtbf	RPM	Obsolete?
PL100 TURBO	19	SCSI	2,7 RLL	3.5 HH		60k		
PL200 TURBO	19	SCSI	2,7 RLL	3.5 HH		50k		
PL32 TURBO	12	SCSI	2,7 RLL	3.5 HH		100k		
PT225	35	ST412/506	MFM	3.5 HH				
PT234	35	ST412/506	MFM	3.5 HH				
PT238A	35	IDE AT	2,7 RLL	3.5 HH				
PT238R	35	ST412/506	2,7 RLL	3.5 HH				
PT238S	35	SCSI	2,7 RLL	3.5 HH				
PT251A	35	IDE AT	2,7 RLL	3.5 HH		25k		
PT251R	35	ST412/506	2,7 RLL	3.5 HH		25		
PT251S	35	SCSI	2,7 RLL	3.5 HH		25k		
PT338	35	ST412/506	MFM	3.5 HH		25k		
PT351	35	ST412/506	MFM	3.5 HH		25k		
PT357A	35	IDE AT	2,7 RLL	3.5 HH		25k		
PT357R	35	ST412/506	2,7 RLL	3.5 HH				
PT357S	35	SCSI	2,7 RLL	3.5 HH		25k		
PT376A	35	IDE AT	2,7 RLL	3.5 HH		25k		
PT376R	35	ST412/506	2,7 RLL	3.5 HH		25k		
PT376S	35	SCSI	2,7 RLL	3.5 HH		25k		
PT4102A	35	IDE AT	2,7 RLL	3.5 HH		25k		
PT4102R	35	ST412/506	2,7 RLL	3.5 HH		25k		
PT4102S	35	SCSI		3.5 HH		25k		
PT468	35	ST412/506	MFM	3.5 HH		25k		

QUANTUM CORPORATION

Drive Model	Seek Time	Interface	Encode	Form Factor	cache kb	mtbf	RPM	Obsolete?
ATLAS II 2.2S	8	SCSI-3	1,7 RLL	3.5 3H	512k	1000k	7200	
ATLAS II 4.5S	8	SCSI-3	1,7 RLL	3.5 3H	512k	1000k	7200	
ATLAS II 9.1S	8	SCSI-3	1,7 RLL	3.5 HH	1024k	1000k	7200	
ATLAS III 18.2S 1-98	7.5	ULTRA2LVD	PRML	16,173.5 HH	024k		7200	
ATLAS III 18.2S 1-98	7.5	FC	PRML	16,173.5 HH	024k		7200	
ATLAS III 18.2S 1-98	7.5	UL SE SCSI3	PRML	16,173.5 HH	024k		7200	

Drive Model	Format Size MB	Head	Cyl	Sect/ Trac	Translate H/C/S	RWC/ WPC	Land Zone
ATLAS III 4.5S 1-98	4550	5				---/---	
ATLAS III 4.5S 1-98	4550	5				---/---	
ATLAS III 4.5S 1-98	4550	5				---/---	
ATLAS III 9.1S 1-98	9100	10				---/---	
ATLAS III 9.1S 1-98	9100	10				---/---	
ATLAS III 9.1S 1-98	9100	10				---/---	
ATLAS XP31070S	1075	5		80-134			
ATLAS XP32150S	2150	10		80-134			
ATLAS XP34300S	4350	20		80-134			
BIGFOOT 1275	1275	2		144-23	16/2492/63		
BIGFOOT 2.1	2110	4		149-27			
BIGFOOT 2550	2550	4		144-23	16/4994/63		
BIGFOOT CY 2.1	2111	2			16/4092/63		
BIGFOOT CY 4.3	4335	4			15/8960/63		
BIGFOOT CY 6.4	6510	6			15/13456/63		
CAPELLA VP31110S	1108	4		97-149		---/---	
CAPELLA VP32210S	2216	8		97-149		---/---	
DAYTONA 127AT	127	2		54-92	9/677/41	NA/NA	AUTO
DAYTONA 127S	127	2		54-92		NA/NA	AUTO
DAYTONA 170AT	256	3		54-92	10/538/62	NA/NA	AUTO
DAYTONA 170S	170	3		54-92		NA/NA	AUTO
DAYTONA 256AT	256	4		54-92	11/723/63	NA/NA	AUTO
DAYTONA 256S	256	4		54-92		NA/NA	AUTO
DAYTONA 341AT	341	6		54-92	15/1011/44	NA/NA	AUTO
DAYTONA 341S	341	6		54-92		NA/NA	AUTO
DAYTONA 514AT	514	8		54-92	16/996/63	NA/NA	AUTO
DAYTONA 514S	514	8		54-92		NA/NA	AUTO
DSP3053LS	535	4		59-119		---/---	
DSP3107LS	1070	8		59-119		---/---	
DSP3133LS	1337	10		59-119		---/---	
DSP3210S	2148	16		59-119		---/---	
ELS127AT	127	3	1536	V	16/919/17	NA/NA	AUTO
ELS127S	127	3	1536	V		NA/NA	AUTO
ELS170AT	170	4	1536	V	15/1011/22	NA/NA	AUTO
ELS170S	170	4	1536	V		NA/NA	AUTO
ELS42AT	42	1	1536	V	5/968/17	NA/NA	AUTO
ELS42S	42	1	1536	V		NA/NA	AUTO
ELS85AT	85	2	1536	V	10/977/17	NA/NA	AUTO
ELS85S	85	2	1536	V		NA/NA	AUTO
EMPIRE 1080S	1080	8		72-137			
EMPIRE 1400S	1400	8		72-137			
EMPIRE 2100S	2100	12		72-137			
EMPIRE 540S	540	4				NA/NA	AUTO
EMPIRE II VP32181S	2180	5				---/---	
EMPIRE II VP34360S	4360	10				---/---	
EMPIRE II VP39100S	9100	20		311586-126		---/---	
EUROPA 1080AT	1080	4		66-110	15/2362/60	---/---	
EUROPA 540AT	540	4		66-110	15/1179/60	---/---	
EUROPA 810AT	810	6		66-110	15/1771/63	---/---	
FIREBALL 1080AT	1089	4		88-177	16/2112/63	---/---	
FIREBALL 1080S	1093	4		88-177		---/---	
FIREBALL 1280AT	1280	4		95-177	16/2484/63	---/---	
FIREBALL 1280S	1280	4		95-177		---/---	
FIREBALL 540AT	544	2		88-177	16/1056/63	---/---	
FIREBALL 540S	545	2		88-177		---/---	
FIREBALL 640AT	640	2		95-177	16/1244/63	---/---	
FIREBALL 640S	640	2		95-177		---/---	
FIREBALL SE2.1AT1-98	2111	2			16/4092/63	---/---	
FIREBALL SE2.1S1-98	2111	2				---/---	
FIREBALL SE3.2AT1-98	3228	3			16/6256/63	---/---	
FIREBALL SE3.2S1-98	3228	3				---/---	
FIREBALL SE4.3AT1-98	4310	4			9/14848/63	---/---	
FIREBALL SE4.3S1-98	4310	4				---/---	

Drive Model	Seek Time	Interface	Encode	Form Factor	cache kb	mtbf	Obsolete? RPM
ATLAS III 4.5S 1-98	7.5	UL SE SCSI3	PRML16,173.5	3H	1024k		7200
ATLAS III 4.5S 1-98	7.5	FC	PRML16,173.5	3H	1024k		7200
ATLAS III 4.5S 1-98	7.5	Ultra 2 LVD	PRML16,173.5	3H	1024k		7200
ATLAS III 9.1S 1-98	7.5	FC	PRML16,173.5	3H	1024k		7200
ATLAS III 9.1S 1-98	7.5	UL SE SCSI3	PRML16,173.5	3H	1024k		7200
ATLAS III 9.1S 1-98	7.5	Ultra 2 LVD	PRML16,173.5	3H	1024k		7200
ATLAS XP31070S	8	SCSI-2 FAST	1,7 RLL	3.5 3H	1024k		7200
ATLAS XP32150S	8	SCSI-2 FAST	1,7 RLL	3.5 3H	1024k	800k	7200
ATLAS XP34300S	8	SCSI-2 FAST	1,7 RLL	3.5 HH	1024k	800k	7200
BIGFOOT 1275	15.5	ATA-2 Fast	PRML16,175.25	4H	128k	300k	3600
BIGFOOT 2.1	15.5	ATA-2 Fast	PRML16,175.25	4H	128k	300k	3600
BIGFOOT 2550	15.5	ATA-2 Fast	PRML16,175.25	4H	128k	300k	3600
BIGFOOT CY 2.1		ATA-2 Fast		5.25 4H	128k	300k	3600
BIGFOOT CY 4.3		ATA-2 Fast		5.25 3H	128k	300k	3600
BIGFOOT CY 6.4		ATA-2 Fast		5.25 3H	128k	300k	3600
CAPELLA VP31110S	9	SCSI-2 FAST	1,7 RLL	3.5 3H	1024k	800k	5400
CAPELLA VP32210S	9	SCSI-2 FAST	1,7 RLL	3.5 3H	1024k	800k	5400
DAYTONA 127AT	17	IDE AT	1,7 RLL	2.5 4H	96k	350k	4500 Y
DAYTONA 127S	17	SCSI-2	1,7 RLL	2.5 4H	96k	350k	4500 Y
DAYTONA 170AT	17	IDE AT	1,7 RLL	2.5 4H	96k	350k	4500 Y
DAYTONA 170S	17	SCSI-2	1,7 RLL	2.5 4H	96k	350k	4500 Y
DAYTONA 256AT	17	IDE AT	1,7 RLL	2.5 4H	96k	350k	4500
DAYTONA 256S	17	SCSI-2	1,7 RLL	2.5 4H	96k	350k	4500
DAYTONA 341AT	17	IDE AT	1,7 RLL	2.5 4H	96k	350k	4500
DAYTONA 341S	17	SCSI-2	1,7 RLL	2.5 4H	96k	350k	4500
DAYTONA 514AT	17	IDE AT	1,7 RLL	2.5 4H	96k	350k	4500
DAYTONA 514S	17	SCSI-2	1,7 RLL	2.5 4H	96k	350k	4500
DSP3053LS	9.5	SCSI-2 FAST	1,7 RLL	3.5 3H	512k	500k	5400 Y
DSP3107LS	9.5	SCSI-2 FAST	1,7 RLL	3.5 3H	512k	500k	5400 Y
DSP3133LS	9.5	SCSI-2 FAST	1,7 RLL	3.5 3H	512k	500k	5400 Y
DSP3210S	9.5	SCSI-2 FAST	1,7 RLL	3.5 HH	512k	500k	5400 Y
ELS127AT	17	IDE AT	1,7 RLL	3.5 3H	32k	250k	3663 Y
ELS127S	17	SCSI	1,7 RLL	3.5 3H	32k	250k	3663 Y
ELS170AT	17	IDE AT	1,7 RLL	3.5 3H	32k	250k	3663 Y
ELS170S	17	SCSI	1,7 RLL	3.5 3H	32k	250k	3663 Y
ELS42AT	19	IDE AT	2,7 RLL	3.5 3H		250k	Y
ELS42S	19	SCSI	2,7 RLL	3.5 3H		250k	Y
ELS85AT	17	IDE XT	2,7 RLL	3.5 3H		250k	Y
ELS85S	17	SCSI	2,7 RLL	3.5 3H		250k	Y
EMPIRE 1080S	9.5	SCSI-3		3.5 3H	512k	500k	5400 Y
EMPIRE 1400S	11	SCSI-3 FAST	PRML0,4,43.5	3H	512k	500k	5400
EMPIRE 2100S	11	SCSI-3 FAST	PRML0,4,43.5	HH	512k	500k	5400
EMPIRE 540S	9.5	SCSI-3		3.5 3H	512k	500k	5400 Y
EMPIRE II VP32181S	9	SCSI-3	PRML	3.5 3H	512k	1000k	4800
EMPIRE II VP34360S	9	SCSI-3	PRML	3.5 3H	512k	1000k	4800
EMPIRE II VP39100S	9	SCSI-3	PRML	3.5 HH	512k	1000k	4800
EUROPA 1080S	14	ATA-2 FAST	PRML	2.5 4H	128k	350k	3800
EUROPA 540AT	14	ATA-2 FAST	PRML	2.5 4H	128k	350k	3800
EUROPA 810AT	14	ATA-2 FAST	PRML	2.5 4H	128k	350k	3800
FIREBALL 1080AT	12	ATA-2 Fast	PRML16,173.5	3H	128k	500k	5400
FIREBALL 1080S	12	SCSI-3	PRML	3.5 3H	128k	500k	5400
FIREBALL 1280AT	12	ATA-2 Fast	PRML16,173.5	3H	128k	400k	5400
FIREBALL 1280S	12	SCSI-3	PRML16,173.5	3H	128k	400k	5400
FIREBALL 540AT	12	ATA-2	PRML	3.5 3H	128k	500k	5400
FIREBALL 540S	12	SCSI-3	PRML	3.5 3H	128k	500k	5400
FIREBALL 640AT	12	ATA-2 Fast	PRML16,173.5	3H	128k		5400
FIREBALL 640S	12	SCSI-3	PRML16,173.5	3H	128k		5400
FIREBALL SE2.1AT1-98	9.5	ULTRA ATA		3.5 3H	128k		5400
FIREBALL SE2.1S1-98	9.5	Ultra SCSI3		3.5 3H	128k		5400
FIREBALL SE3.2AT1-98	9.5	ULTRA ATA		3.5 3H	128k		5400
FIREBALL SE3.2S1-98	9.5	Ultra SCSI3		3.5 3H	128k		5400
FIREBALL SE4.3AT1-98	9.5	ULTRA ATA		3.5 3H	128k		5400
FIREBALL SE4.3S1-98	9.5	ULTRA SCSI3		3.5 3H	128k		5400

Drive Model	Format Size MB	Head	Cyl	Sect/Trac	Translate H/C/S	RWC/WPC	Land Zone
FIREBALL SE6.4AT1-98	6448	6			15/13328/63	---/---	
FIREBALL SE6.4S1-98	6448	6				---/---	
FIREBALL SE8.4AT1-98	8455	8			16/16383/63	---/---	
FIREBALL SE8.4S1-98	8455	8				---/---	
FIREBALL ST 1.6	1614	2			16/3128/63	---/---	
FIREBALL ST 2.1	2111	3				---/---	
FIREBALL ST 3.2AT	3228	4			16/6256/63	---/---	
FIREBALL ST 3.2S	3228	4				---/---	
FIREBALL ST 4.3AT	4310	6			9/14848/63	---/---	
FIREBALL ST 4.3S	4310	6				---/---	
FIREBALL ST 6.4AT	6448	8			15/13328/63	---/---	
FIREBALL ST 6.4S	6448	8				---/---	
FIREBALL TM 1.0	1089	2	104-23	16/2112/63		---/---	
FIREBALL TM 1.2AT	1281	2	104-23	16/2484/63		---/---	
FIREBALL TM 1.2S	1281	2	104-23			---/---	
FIREBALL TM 2.1AT	2111	4	104-23	16/4092/63		---/---	
FIREBALL TM 2.1S	2111	4	104-23			---/---	
FIREBALL TM 2.5AT	2564	4	104-23	16/4969/63		---/---	
FIREBALL TM 3.2AT	3216	5	104-23	16/6232/63		---/---	
FIREBALL TM 3.2S	3216	5	104-23			---/---	
FIREBALL TM 3.8AT	3860	6	104-23	16/7480/63		---/---	
GODRIVE 120AT	127	4	1097	V	13/731/26	NA/NA	AUTO
GODRIVE 120S	127	4	1097	V		NA/NA	AUTO
GODRIVE 40AT	43	2	957		6/820/17	---/---	AUTO
GODRIVE 40S	43	2	957			NA/NA	AUTO
GODRIVE 60AT	63	2	1097	V	9/526/26	NA/NA	AUTO
GODRIVE 60S	63	2				NA/NA	AUTO
GODRIVE 80AT	84	2		NA	10/991/17	NA/NA	AUTO
GODRIVE 80S	84	2				NA/NA	AUTO
GODRIVE GLS127AT	127	3			9/677/41	NA/NA	AUTO
GODRIVE GLS127S	127	3				NA/NA	AUTO
GODRIVE GLS170AT	170	4			10/538/62	NA/NA	AUTO
GODRIVE GLS170S	170	4				NA/NA	AUTO
GODRIVE GLS256AT	256	6			11/723/63	NA/NA	AUTO
GODRIVE GLS256S	256	6				NA/NA	AUTO
GODRIVE GLS85AT	85	2			10/722/23	NA/NA	AUTO
GODRIVE GLS85S	85	2				NA/NA	AUTO
GODRIVE GRS160AT	169	4			10/966/34	NA/NA	AUTO
GODRIVE GRS160S	169	4				NA/NA	AUTO
GODRIVE GRS80AT	84	2	45-73		5/966/34	NA/NA	AUTO
GODRIVE GRS80S	84	2				NA/NA	AUTO
GrandPrix XP32151S	2150	10	118			---/---	
GrandPrix XP34301S	4300	20	118			---/---	
HARDCARD EZ 42	42	5	977	17		NA/NA	AUTO
Lightning 365AT	366	2	61-128	12/976/61		NA/NA	AUTO
Lightning 365S	365	2	64-128			NA/NA	AUTO
Lightning 540AT	541	4	61-128	16/1120/59		NA/NA	AUTO
Lightning 540S	541	3	64-128			NA/NA	AUTO
Lightning 730AT	731	4	61-128	16/1416/63		NA/NA	AUTO
Lightning 730S	732	4	54-128			NA/NA	AUTO
MAVERICK 270AT	271	2	58-118	14/944/40		NA/NA	AUTO
MAVERICK 270S	271	2	58-118			NA/NA	AUTO
MAVERICK 540AT	541	4	58-118	16/1049/63		NA/NA	AUTO
MAVERICK 540S	542	4	58-118			NA/NA	AUTO
PIONEER SG 1.0	1082	2		16/2097/63		---/---	
PIONEER SG 2.1	2111	4		16/4092/63		---/---	
PRODRIVE 100E	103					NA/NA	
PRODRIVE 1050AT	1050	12	2442	NA		NA/NA	AUTO
PRODRIVE 105AT	104	10	1219	17	16/755/17	NA/NA	AUTO
PRODRIVE 105S	105	6	1019			---/---	AUTO
PRODRIVE 120AT	120	5	1123		9/814/32	NA/NA	AUTO
PRODRIVE 120S	120	5	1123			---/---	AUTO
PRODRIVE 1225AT	1225	14	2444	NA		NA/NA	AUTO

Drive Model	Seek Time	Interface	Encode	Form Factor	cache kb	mtbf	RPM	Obsolete?
FIREBALL SE6.4AT1-98	9.5	ULTRA ATA		3.5 3H	128k		5400	
FIREBALL SE6.4S1-98	9.5	ULTRA SCSI3		3.5 3H	128k		5400	
FIREBALL SE8.4AT1-98	9.5	ULTRA ATA		3.5 3H	128k		5400	
FIREBALL SE8.4S1-98	9.5	ULTRA SCSI3		3.5 3H	128k		5400	
FIREBALL ST 1.6		ULTRA ATA		3.5 3H	128k	400k	5400	
FIREBALL ST 2.1		ULTRA SCSI3		3.5 3H	128k	400k	5400	
FIREBALL ST 3.2AT		ULTRA ATA		3.5 3H	128k	400k	5400	
FIREBALL ST 3.2S		ULTRA SCSI3		3.5 3H	128k	400k	5400	
FIREBALL ST 4.3AT		ULTRA ATA		3.5 3H	128k	400k	5400	
FIREBALL ST 4.3S		ULTRA SCSI3		3.5 3H	128k	400k	5400	
FIREBALL ST 6.4AT		ULTRA ATA		3.5 3H	128k	400k	5400	
FIREBALL ST 6.4S		ULTRA SCSI3		3.5 3H	128k	400k	5400	
FIREBALL TM 1.0	12	ATA-2 Fast	PRML16,17	3.5 3H	128k	400k	4500	
FIREBALL TM 1.2AT	12	ATA-2 Fast	PRML16,17	3.5 3H	128k	400k	4500	
FIREBALL TM 1.2S	12	ULTRA SCSI3	PRML16,17	3.5 3H	128k	400k	4500	
FIREBALL TM 2.1AT	10.5	ULTRA ATA	PRML16,17	3.5 3H	128k	400k	4500	
FIREBALL TM 2.1S	10.5	ULTRA SCSI3	PRML16,17	3.5 3H	128k	400k	4500	
FIREBALL TM 2.5AT	10.5	ULTRA ATA	PRML16,17	3.5 3H	128k	400k	4500	
FIREBALL TM 3.2AT	10.5	ULTRA ATA	PRML16,17	3.5 3H	128k	400k	4500	
FIREBALL TM 3.2S	10.5	ULTRA SCSI3	PRML16,17	3.5 3H	128k	400k	4500	
FIREBALL TM 3.8AT	10.5	ULTRA ATA	PRML16,17	3.5 3H	128k	400k	4500	
GODRIVE 120AT	17	IDE AT	1,7 RLL	2.5 3H	32k	150k		Y
GODRIVE 120S	17	SCSI	1,7 RLL	2.5 3H	32k	150k		Y
GODRIVE 40AT	19	IDE AT	1,7 RLL	2.5 4H	32k	80k		Y
GODRIVE 40S	19	SCSI	1,7 RLL	2.5 4H	32k	80k		Y
GODRIVE 60AT	17	IDE AT	1,7 RLL	2.5 3H		150k		Y
GODRIVE 60S	17	SCSI	1,7 RLL	2.5 3H		150k		Y
GODRIVE 80AT	17	IDE AT	1,7 RLL	2.5 4H		80k		Y
GODRIVE 80S	19	SCSI	1,7 RLL	2.5 4H		80k		Y
GODRIVE GLS127AT	17	IDE AT		2.5	128k	350k		Y
GODRIVE GLS127S	17	SCSI-2		2.5	128k	350k		Y
GODRIVE GLS170AT	17	IDE AT		2.5	128k	350k		Y
GODRIVE GLS170S	17	SCSI-2		2.5	128k	350k		Y
GODRIVE GLS256AT	17	IDE AT		2.5	128k	350k		Y
GODRIVE GLS256S	17	SCSI-2		2.5	128k	350k		Y
GODRIVE GLS85AT	17	IDE AT		2.5	128k	350k		Y
GODRIVE GLS85S	17	SCSI-2		2.5	128k	350k		Y
GODRIVE GRS160AT	17	IDE AT		2.5	32k	150k		Y
GODRIVE GRS160S	17	SCSI		2.5	32k	150k		Y
GODRIVE GRS80AT	17	IDE AT	1,7 RLL	2.5 4H	32k	150k	3600	Y
GODRIVE GRS80S	17	SCSI		2.5	32k	150k		Y
GrandPrix XP32151S	10	SCSI-3	PRML0,4,5	3.5 HH	512k	800k	7200	
GrandPrix XP34301S	10	SCSI-3	PRML0,4,5	3.5 HH	512k	800k	7200	
HARDCARD EZ 42		IDE AT		3.5				
Lightning 365AT	11	IDE AT	1,7 RLL	3.5 3H	128k	300k	4500	
Lightning 365S	11	SCSI-2	1,7 RLL	3.5 3H	128k	300k	4500	
Lightning 540AT	11.5	IDE AT	1,7 RLL	3.5 3H	128k	300k	4500	
Lightning 540S	11.5	SCSI-2	1,7 RLL	3.5 3H	128k	300k	4500	
Lightning 730AT	11.5	IDE AT	1,7 RLL	3.5 3H	128k	300k	4500	
Lightning 730S	11.5	SCSI-2	1,7 RLL	3.5 3H	128k	300k	4500	
MAVERICK 270AT	14	IDE AT	1,7 RLL	3.5 3H	128k	300k	3600	
MAVERICK 270S	14	SCSI-2	1,7 RLL	3.5 3H	128k	300k	3600	
MAVERICK 540AT	14	IDE AT	1,7 RLL	3.5 3H	128k	300k	3600	
MAVERICK 540S	14	SCSI-2	1,7 RLL	3.5 3H	128k	300k	3600	
PIONEER SG 1.0	12	ATA-2 Fast		3.5 3H	64k	300k	4500	
PIONEER SG 2.1	12	ATA-2 Fast		3.5 3H	64k	300k	4500	
PRODRIVE 100E	19	ESDI	2,7 RLL	3.5 HH				Y
PRODRIVE 1050S	10	SCSI		3.5 HH	512k	350k	4500	Y
PRODRIVE 105AT	17	IDE AT	2,7 RLL	3.5 HH		60k		Y
PRODRIVE 105S	19	SCSI	2,7 RLL	3.5 HH	64k	50k		Y
PRODRIVE 120AT	15	IDE AT	1,7 RLL	3.5 HH	64k	500k	3605	Y
PRODRIVE 120S	15	SCSI	1,7 RLL	3.5 HH	64k	50k		Y
PRODRIVE 1225S	10	SCSI		3.5 HH	512k	350k	4500	Y

Drive Model	Format Size MB	Head	Cyl	Sect/Trac	Translate H/C/S	RWC/WPC	Land Zone
PRODRIVE 145E	145					NA/NA	
PRODRIVE 160AT	168	4	839			NA/NA	AUTO
PRODRIVE 160S	168	4	839			NA/NA	AUTO
PRODRIVE 170AT	168	7	1123		10/968/34	---/---	AUTO
PRODRIVE 170S	168	7	1123			---/---	AUTO
PRODRIVE 1800S	1800	14				NA/NA	
PRODRIVE 210AT	209	7	1156		13/873/36	NA/NA	AUTO
PRODRIVE 210S	210	7	1156			---/---	AUTO
PRODRIVE 330AT	331	7	1156			---/---	AUTO
PRODRIVE 330S	331	7	1156			---/---	AUTO
PRODRIVE 40AT	42	3	834		5/965/17	NA/NA	AUTO
PRODRIVE 40S	42	3	834			---/---	AUTO
PRODRIVE 425AT	426	9	1520	V	16/1021/51	NA/NA	AUTO
PRODRIVE 425S	426	9				---/---	AUTO
PRODRIVE 525S	525	6	2446	NA		NA/NA	
PRODRIVE 700S	700	8	2443	NA		NA/NA	
PRODRIVE 80AT	84	6	834	35	10/965/17	NA/NA	AUTO
PRODRIVE 80S	84	6	834	35		---/---	AUTO
PRODRIVE LPS105AT	105	4	1219		16/755/17	NA/NA	AUTO
PRODRIVE LPS105S	105	4	1219			---/---	AUTO
PRODRIVE LPS120AT	122	2			5/901/53	NA/NA	AUTO
PRODRIVE LPS120S	122	2	1818			---/---	AUTO
PRODRIVE LPS127AT	128	2		65-91	16/919/17	NA/NA	AUTO
PRODRIVE LPS127S	127	2				---/---	AUTO
PRODRIVE LPS170AT	171	2		52-91	15/1011/22	NA/NA	AUTO
PRODRIVE LPS170S	170	2				NA/NA	AUTO
PRODRIVE LPS210AT	211	2		55-104	15/723/38	NA/NA	AUTO
PRODRIVE LPS240AT	245	4			13/723/51	NA/NA	AUTO
PRODRIVE LPS240S	245	4	1818	V	13/723/51	NA/NA	AUTO
PRODRIVE LPS270AT	270	2		V	14/944/40	NA/NA	AUTO
PRODRIVE LPS270S	270	2				NA/NA	AUTO
PRODRIVE LPS340AT	342	4			15/1011/44	NA/NA	AUTO
PRODRIVE LPS340S	342	4				NA/NA	AUTO
PRODRIVE LPS420AT	420	4		55-104	16/1010/51	NA/NA	AUTO
PRODRIVE LPS525AT	525	6			16/1017/63	NA/NA	AUTO
PRODRIVE LPS525S	525	6				NA/NA	AUTO
PRODRIVE LPS52AT	52	2	1219		8/751/17	NA/NA	AUTO
PRODRIVE LPS52S	52	2	1219			---/---	AUTO
PRODRIVE LPS540AT	541	4		V	16/1120/59	NA/NA	AUTO
PRODRIVE LPS540S	541	4				---/---	AUTO
PRODRIVE LPS80AT	85				16/616/17	NA/NA	AUTO
PRODRIVE LPS80S	86	4				NA/NA	AUTO
SATURN VP31080S	1080	5				---/---	
SATURN VP32170S	2170	10				---/---	
SIROCCO 1700AT	1700	4		90-180	16/3309/63	NA/NA	AUTO
SIROCCO 1700S	1700	4		90-180		NA/NA	AUTO
SIROCCO 2550AT	2550	6		90-180	16/4969/63	NA/NA	AUTO
SIROCCO 2550S	2550	6		90-180		NA/NA	AUTO
TRAILBLAZER 420AT	422	2		76-141	16/1010/51	---/---	
TRAILBLAZER 420S	425	2		76-141		---/---	
TRAILBLAZER 635AT	636	3		76-141	16/1234/63	---/---	
TRAILBLAZER 635S	636	3		76-141		---/---	
TRAILBLAZER 850AT	850	4		76-141	16/1647/63	---/---	
TRAILBLAZER 850S	852	4		76-141		---/---	
VIKING 2.1S	2180	4				---/---	
VIKING 4.3S	4360	8				---/---	
VIKING II 4.5 1-98	4550	5				---/---	
VIKING II 4.5 1-98	4550	5				---/---	
VIKING II 9.1 1-98	9100	10				---/---	
VIKING II 9.1 1-98	9100	10				---/---	

RICOH

RH5130		10	2	612	17	613/400	

Drive Model	Seek Time	Interface	Encode	Form Factor	cache kb	mtbf	RPM	Obsolete?
PRODRIVE 145E	19	ESDI		3.5 HH				Y
PRODRIVE 160AT	19	IDE AT	1,7 RLL	3.5 4H		80k		Y
PRODRIVE 160S	19	SCSI	1,7 RLL	3.5 4H		80k		Y
PRODRIVE 170AT	15	IDE AT	1,7 RLL	3.5 HH	56k	50k	3605	Y
PRODRIVE 170S	15	SCSI	1,7 RLL	3.5 HH	64k	50k		Y
PRODRIVE 1800S	10	SCSI		3.5 HH	512k	350k	4500	Y
PRODRIVE 210AT	15	IDE AT	1,7 RLL	3.5 HH	56k	50k	3605	Y
PRODRIVE 210S	15	SCSI	1,7 RLL	3.5 HH	64k	50k	3606	Y
PRODRIVE 330AT	14	IDE AT	1,7 RLL	3.5 HH	64k	150k	3606	Y
PRODRIVE 330S	14	SCSI	1,7 RLL	3.5 HH	64k	150k		Y
PRODRIVE 40AT	19	IDE AT	2,7 RLL	3.5 HH		50k		Y
PRODRIVE 40S	19	SCSI	2,7 RLL	3.5 HH		50k		Y
PRODRIVE 425AT	14	IDE AT	1,7 RLL	3.5 HH	56k	150k	3606	Y
PRODRIVE 425S	14	SCSI	1,7 RLL	3.5 HH	64k	150k	3606	Y
PRODRIVE 525S		SCSI		3.5 HH				Y
PRODRIVE 700S	10	SCSI		3.5 HH	512k	350k	4500	Y
PRODRIVE 80AT	19	IDE AT	2,7 RLL	3.5 HH		50k		Y
PRODRIVE 80S	19	SCSI	2,7 RLL	3.5 HH		50k		Y
PRODRIVE LPS105AT	17	IDE AT	2,7 RLL	3.5 3H	64k	60k		Y
PRODRIVE LPS105S	17	SCSI	2,7 RLL	3.5 3H	64k	60k		Y
PRODRIVE LPS120AT	16	IDE AT	1,7 RLL	3.5 3H	256k	250k		Y
PRODRIVE LPS120S	16	SCSI	1,7 RLL	3.5 3H	256k	250k	4306	Y
PRODRIVE LPS127AT	14	IDE AT	1,7 RLL	3.5 3H	128k	300k	3600	Y
PRODRIVE LPS127S	14	SCSI-2	1,7 RLL	3.5 3H	128k	300k	3600	Y
PRODRIVE LPS170AT	14	IDE AT	1,7 RLL	3.5 3H	128k	300k	3600	Y
PRODRIVE LPS170S	14	SCSI-2	1,7 RLL	3.5 3H	128k	300k	3600	Y
PRODRIVE LPS210AT	15	IDE AT	1,7 RLL	3.5 3H	256k	250k	4306	Y
PRODRIVE LPS240AT	16	IDE AT	1,7 RLL	3.5 3H	256k	250k	4306	Y
PRODRIVE LPS240S	17	SCSI	1,7 RLL	3.5 3H	128k	300k	3600	Y
PRODRIVE LPS270AT	14	IDE AT	1,7 RLL	3.5 3H	256k	250k	4306	Y
PRODRIVE LPS270S	12	SCSI-2	1,7 RLL	3.5 3H	128k	300k	3600	Y
PRODRIVE LPS340AT	12	IDE AT		3.5 3H	128k	300k	4500	Y
PRODRIVE LPS340S	12	SCSI-2		3.5 3H	128k	300k	4500	Y
PRODRIVE LPS420AT	13	IDE AT	1,7 RLL	3.5 3H	128k	300k	3600	Y
PRODRIVE LPS525AT	10	IDE AT		3.5 3H	512k	350k	4500	Y
PRODRIVE LPS525S	10	SCSI		3.5 3H	512k	350k	4500	Y
PRODRIVE LPS52AT	17	IDE AT	2,7 RLL	3.5 3H	64k	60k		Y
PRODRIVE LPS52S	17	SCSI	2,7 RLL	3.5 3H	64k	60k		Y
PRODRIVE LPS540AT	14	IDE AT	1,7 RLL	3.5 3H	128k	300k	3600	Y
PRODRIVE LPS540S	12	SCSI-2	1,7 RLL	3.5 3H	128k	300k	4500	Y
PRODRIVE LPS80AT		SCSI		3.5 3H				Y
PRODRIVE LPS80S	19	SCSI	2,7 RLL	3.5 3H		60k		Y
SATURN VP31080S	8.5	SCSI-2	1,7 RLL	3.5 3H	512k		5400	
SATURN VP32170S	8.5	SCSI-3Fast	1,7 RLL	3.5 3H	512k		5400	
SIROCCO 1700AT	11	ATA-2	PRML16,17	3.5 3H	128k	400k	4500	
SIROCCO 1700S	11	ATA-2	PRML16,17	3.5 3H	128k	400k	4500	
SIROCCO 2550AT	11	ATA-2	PRML16,17	3.5 3H	128k		4500	
SIROCCO 2550S	11	SCSI-3	PRML16,17	3.5 3H	128k		4500	
TRAILBLAZER 420AT	14	ATA-2 FAST	1,7 RLL	3.5 3H	128k	300k	4500	
TRAILBLAZER 420S	14	SCSI-2 FAST	1,7 RLL	3.5 3H	128k	300k	4500	
TRAILBLAZER 635AT	14	ATA-2 Fast	1,7 RLL	3.5 3H	128k	300k	4500	
TRAILBLAZER 635S	14	SCSI-3	1,7 RLL	3.5 3H	128k	300k	4500	
TRAILBLAZER 850AT	14	ATA-2 Fast	1,7 RLL	3.5 3H	128k	300k	4500	
TRAILBLAZER 850S	14	SCSI-2 FAST	1,7 RLL	3.5 3H	128k	300k	4500	
VIKING 2.1S	8.5	Ultra SCSI3		3.5 3H	512k	800k	7200	
VIKING 4.3S	8.5	Ultra SCSI3		3.5 3H	512k	800k	7200	
VIKING II 4.5 1-98	8	ULTRA LVD	PRML16,17	3.5 3H	512k		7200	
VIKING II 4.5 1-98	8	UL SE SCSI3	PRML16,17	3.5 3H	512k		7200	
VIKING II 9.1 1-98	8	UL SE SCSI3	PRML16,17	3.5 3H	512k		7200	
VIKING II 9.1 1-98	8	ULTRA LVD	PRML16,17	3.5 3H	512k		7200	

RICOH

Drive Model	Seek Time	Interface	Encode	Form Factor	cache kb	mtbf	RPM	Obsolete?
RH5130	85	ST412/506	MFM					Y

Hard Drives   391

Drive Model	Format Size MB	Head	Cyl	Sect/Trac	Translate H/C/S	RWC/WPC	Land Zone
RH5260	10	2	615	17		---/---	
RH5261	10	2	612	17		---/---	
RH5500	100	2	1285	76		NA/NA	AUTO
RS9150AR	100	2	1285	76		NA/NA	AUTO

RMS

RMS503	2.5	2	153	17		77/77	
RMS506	5	4	153	17		77/77	
RMS509	8	6	153	17		77/77	
RMS512	10	8	153	17		77/77	

RODIME SYSTEMS, INC

COBRA 1000E (Mac)	1000					---/---	AUTO
COBRA 110AT	110	4				---/---	AUTO
COBRA 210AT	210	5				---/---	AUTO
COBRA 330E (Mac)	330					---/---	AUTO
COBRA 40AT	40	2	1170	36	4/585/36	---/---	AUTO
COBRA 650E (Mac)	650					---/---	AUTO
COBRA 80AT	80	4	1159	36	8/579/36	---/---	AUTO
RO101	6	2	192	17		96/192	
RO102	12	4	192	17		96/192	
RO103	18	6	192	17		96/192	
RO104	24	8	192	17		---/132	
RO200	11	4	320	17		132/300	
RO201	5	2	321	17		132/300	
RO201E	11	2	640	17		264/300	
RO202	10	4	321	17		132/300	
RO202E	21	4	640	17		264/300	640
RO203	15	6	321	17		132/300	321
RO203E	32	6	640	17		264/300	640
RO204	21	8	320	17		132/300	321
RO204E	43	8	640	17		264/300	640
RO251	5	2	306	17		307/307	
RO252	11	4	306	17		64/128	
RO3045	37	5	872	17		873/---	
RO3051	44					---/---	
RO3055	45	6	872	17		873/---	
RO3055A	49					---/---	
RO3055T	45	3	1053	26		NA/NA	AUTO
RO3057S	45	5	680			---/---	
RO3058A	45	3	868	17	3/868/34	---/---	
RO3058T	45	3	868	17		---/---	
RO3059A	46	2	1216	17		---/---	
RO3059T	46	2	1216	34		---/---	
RO3060R	50	2	1216	17		---/---	
RO3065	53	7	872	17		---/650	
RO3070S	71					---/---	
RO3075R	59	6	750			---/650	
RO3085A	78					---/---	
RO3085R	69	7	750			---/650	
RO3085S	69	7	750			---/650	
RO3085T	80					---/---	
RO3088A	75	5	868	34	5/868/34	---/---	
RO3088T	75	5	868	34		---/---	
RO3089A	70	3	1216	34		---/---	
RO3089T	70	3	1216	34		---/---	
RO3090T	75	5	1053	28		NA/NA	AUTO
RO3095A	80	3	1216	34	5/923/34	---/---	
RO3099A	80	4	1030		15/614/17	NA/NA	AUTO
RO3099AP	80	4	1030		15/614/17	NA/NA	AUTO
RO3128A	105	7	868	34		---/---	
RO3128T	105	7	868	17		---/---	

Drive Model	Seek Time	Interface	Encode	Form Factor	cache kb	mtbf	RPM	Obsolete?
RH5260	85	ST412/506	MFM					Y
RH5261	85	SCSI	MFM					Y
RH5500	25	SCSI	2,7 RLL	5.25 HH		20k		Y
RS9150AR	25	SCSI	2,7 RLL	5.25 HH		20k		Y

RMS

Drive Model	Seek Time	Interface	Encode	Form Factor	cache kb	mtbf	RPM	Obsolete?
RMS503		ST412/506	MFM	5.25				Y
RMS506		ST412/506	MFM	5.25				Y
RMS509		ST412/506	MFM	5.25 FH				Y
RMS512		ST412/506	MFM	5.25				Y

RODIME SYSTEMS, INC

Drive Model	Seek Time	Interface	Encode	Form Factor	cache kb	mtbf	RPM	Obsolete?
COBRA 1000E (Mac)	15	SCSI			45k	100k	3600	Y
COBRA 110AT	19	IDE AT	2,7 RLL	3.5 HH		40k		Y
COBRA 210AT		IDE AT	2,7 RLL	3.5 HH		40k		Y
COBRA 330E (Mac)	14.5	SCSI			45k	50k	3600	Y
COBRA 40AT	19	IDE AT	2,7 RLL	3.5 HH		40k		Y
COBRA 650E (Mac)	16.5	SCSI			45k	50k	3600	Y
COBRA 80AT	20	IDE AT	2,7 RLL	3.5 HH		40k		Y
RO101		ST412/506	MFM	5.25 FH				Y
RO102		ST412/506	MFM	5.25 FH				Y
RO103	55	ST412/506	MFM	5.25 FH				Y
RO104		ST412/506	MFM	5.25 FH				Y
RO200		ST412/506	MFM	5.25 FH				Y
RO201	85	ST412/506	MFM	5.25 FH				Y
RO201E	55	ST412/506	MFM	5.25 HH				Y
RO202	85	ST412/506	MFM	5.25 HH				Y
RO202E	55	ST412/506	MFM	5.25 HH				Y
RO203	85	ST412/506	MFM	5.25 HH				Y
RO203E	55	ST412/506	MFM	5.25 HH				Y
RO204	85	ST412/506	MFM	5.25 HH				Y
RO204E	55	ST412/506	MFM	5.25 HH				Y
RO251	85	ST412/506	MFM	5.25 HH				Y
RO252	85	ST412/506	MFM	5.25 HH				Y
RO3045	28	ST412/506	MFM	3.5 HH				Y
RO3051		SCSI	2,7 RLL	3.5 HH				Y
RO3055	28	ST412/506	MFM	3.5 HH				Y
RO3055A		IDE AT	2,7 RLL	3.5 HH				Y
RO3055T		SCSI	RLL	3.5 HH				Y
RO3057S	28	SCSI	2,7 RLL	3.5 HH				Y
RO3058A	18	IDE AT	2,7 RLL	3.5 HH		20k		Y
RO3058T	18	SCSI	2,7 RLL	3.5 HH		20k		Y
RO3059A	18	IDE AT	2,7 RLL	3.5 HH		20k		Y
RO3059T	18	SCSI	2,7 RLL	3.5 HH		20k		Y
RO3060R	28	ST412/506	2,7 RLL	3.5 HH		20k		Y
RO3065	28	ST412/506	MFM	3.5 HH		20k		Y
RO3070S	28	SCSI	2,7 RLL	3.5 HH				Y
RO3075R	28	ST412/506	2,7 RLL	3.5 HH		20k		Y
RO3085A		IDE AT	2,7 RLL	3.5 HH				Y
RO3085R	28	ST412/506	2,7 RLL	3.5 HH		20k		Y
RO3085S	28	SCSI	2,7 RLL	3.5 HH				Y
RO3085T		SCSI	2,7 RLL	3.5 HH				Y
RO3088A	18	IDE AT	2,7 RLL	3.5 HH		20k		Y
RO3088T	18	SCSI	2,7 RLL	3.5 HH		20k		Y
RO3089A	18	IDE AT	2,7 RLL	3.5 HH		20k		Y
RO3089T	18	SCSI	2,7 RLL	3.5 HH		20k		Y
RO3090T		SCSI	2,7 RLL	3.5 HH				Y
RO3095A	18	IDE AT	2,7 RLL	3.5 HH		20k		Y
RO3099A	19	IDE AT	2,7 RLL	3.5 HH				Y
RO3099AP	19	IDE AT	2,7 RLL	3.5 HH				Y
RO3128A	18	IDE AT	2,7 RLL	3.5 HH		20k		Y
RO3128T	18	SCSI	2,7 RLL	3.5 HH		20k		Y

Drive Model	Format Size MB	Head	Cyl	Sect/Trac	Translate H/C/S	RWC/WPC	Land Zone
RO3129A	105	5	1090			--/--	
RO3129T	105	5	1090	17		--/--	
RO3130A	109					--/--	
RO3130S	105	7	1047	30		--/--	
RO3130T	105	7	1053	28		NA/NA	AUTO
RO3135A	112	7	923	34	7/923/34	--/--	
RO3139A	112	5	1168	17	15/861/17	--/--	
RO3139AP	112	5	1168		15/861/17	NA/NA	AUTO
RO3139S	112	5	1148			NA/NA	AUTO
RO3139TP	112	5	1148			NA/NA	AUTO
RO3258TS	210					--/--	
RO3259A	210				15/976/28		
RO3259AP	212	9	1235		15/990/28	NA/NA	AUTO
RO3259T	210					--/--	
RO3259TP	210	9	1148	V		NA/NA	AUTO
RO3259TS	210	9	1216			NA/NA	AUTO
RO351	5	2	306	17		307/307	
RO352	11	4	306	17		64/128	
RO365	21	4	612	17		613/613	
RO5040S	38	3		17		--/--	
RO5060ST	60						
RO5065	63	5		17		--/--	
RO5070	63						
RO5075E	65	3	1224	35		NA/NA	AUTO
RO5075S	76					--/--	
RO5078S	62	3	1224	33		NA/NA	AUTO
RO5090	89	7	1224	17		--/--	
RO5095R	81	5	1219	26		NA/NA	AUTO
RO5125-1F2	106	5	1224	34		--/--	
RO5125E	106	5	1224	34		NA/NA	AUTO
RO5125S	106	5	1219	34		NA/NA	AUTO
RO5128S	103	5	1224	33		NA/NA	AUTO
RO5130R	114	7	1224	26		--/--	
RO5178S	144	7	1219			--/--	
RO5180-1F2	148	7	1219	34		NA/NA	AUTO
RO5180E	149	7	1224	34		--/--	
RO5180S	144	7	1219	34		NA/NA	AUTO
RO652	20	4	306	33		--/--	
RO652A	20					--/--	
RO652B	20	4	306	33		--/--	
RO752	20	4	306	33		NA/NA	AUTO
RO752A	25					--/--	

SAMSUNG

Drive Model	Format Size MB	Head	Cyl	Sect/Trac	Translate H/C/S	RWC/WPC	Land Zone
ACB20811A (Rel. 10-96)	810					--/--	
ACE21021A (Rel. 10-96)	1020					--/--	
PLS30854A	850	4	386872-132		16/1647/63	--/--	
PLS30854S	850	4	3868	VAR		--/--	
PLS31084A	1080	5	384072-144		16/2093/63	--/--	
PLS31084S	1080	5	384072-144		16/2093/63	--/--	
PLS31274A	1273	5	384472-132			--/--	
PLS31274S	1273	5	384472-132			--/--	
SHD2040N	44	4	820	26		--/544	819
SHD2041	47	4	820	28		NA/NA	AUTO
SHD30280A	280					NA/NA	AUTO
SHD30420A	421	3	276872-120			--/--	
SHD30560A	561	4	276872-120		16/1086/70	--/--	
SHD3061A	60	2	1478	40	7/993/17	NA/NA	AUTO
SHD3062A	121	4	1479	40	15/927/17	NA/NA	AUTO
SHD3101B	105	4	1282	40		NA/NA	AUTO
SHD3121A	125	2	1956	79		--/--	
SHD3122A	251	4	1956	79		--/--	
SHD3171A	178	2				--/--	

Drive Model	Seek Time	Interface	Encode	Form Factor	cache kb	mtbf	RPM	Obsolete?
RO3129A	18	IDE AT	2,7 RLL	3.5 HH		20k		Y
RO3129T	18	SCSI	2,7 RLL	3.5 HH		20k		Y
RO3130A		IDE AT	2,7 RLL	3.5 HH				Y
RO3130S	22	SCSI	2,7 RLL	5.25 HH		20k		Y
RO3130T	22	SCSI	2,7 RLL	5.25 HH		20k		Y
RO3135A	19	IDE AT	2,7 RLL	3.5 HH		20k		Y
RO3139A	18	IDE AT	2,7 RLL	3.5 HH		20k		Y
RO3139AP	18	IDE AT	2,7 RLL	3.5 HH		20k		Y
RO3139S	18	SCSI	2,7 RLL	3.5 HH				Y
RO3139TP		SCSI	RLL ZBR	3.5 HH				Y
RO3258TS		SCSI		3.5 HH				Y
RO3259A	18	IDE AT	2,7 RLL	3.5 HH				Y
RO3259AP		IDE AT		3.5 HH				Y
RO3259T	18	SCSI	2,7 RLL	3.5 HH				Y
RO3259TP		SCSI	2,7 RLL	3.5 HH				Y
RO3259TS	18	SCSI	2,7 RLL	3.5 HH				Y
RO351	85	ST412/506	MFM	3.5 HH				Y
RO352	85	ST412/506	MFM	3.5 HH				Y
RO365		ST412/506	MFM	3.5 HH				Y
RO5040S	28	SCSI	MFM	5.25 HH				Y
RO5060ST		SCSI		5.25 HH				Y
RO5065	28	ST412/506	MFM	5.25 HH				Y
RO5070		ST412/506	MFM	5.25 HH				Y
RO5075E	28	ESDI		5.25 HH				Y
RO5075S	28	SCSI		5.25 HH				Y
RO5078S		SCSI		5.25 HH				Y
RO5090	28	ST412/506	MFM	5.25 HH				Y
RO5095R		ST412/506	2,7 RLL	5.25 HH				Y
RO5125-1F2	18	SCSI	2,7 RLL	5.25 HH		20k		Y
RO5125E	18	ESDI	2,7 RLL	5.25 HH		25k		Y
RO5125S	28	SCSI	2,7 RLL	5.25 HH		20k		Y
RO5128S		SCSI		5.25 HH				Y
RO5130R	28	ST412/506	2,7 RLL	5.25 FH		20k		Y
RO5178S	19	SCSI	2,7 RLL	5.25 HH				Y
RO5180-1F2	19	SCSI	2,7 RLL	5.25 HH		20k		Y
RO5180E	18	ESDI	2,7 RLL	5.25 HH		25k		Y
RO5180S	28	SCSI	2,7 RLL	5.25 HH				Y
RO652	85	SCSI	2,7 RLL	3.5 HH				Y
RO652A	85	SCSI		3.5 HH				Y
RO652B	85	SCSI	2,7 RLL	3.5 HH				Y
RO752	85	SCSI		3.5 HH				Y
RO752A	85	SCSI		5.25 HH				Y

SAMSUNG

Drive Model	Seek Time	Interface	Encode	Form Factor	cache kb	mtbf	RPM	Obsolete?
ACB20811A (Rel. 10-96)	12	ATA-2 Fast		2.5				
ACE21021A (Rel. 10-96)	12	ATA-2 Fast		2.5				
PLS30854A	11	EIDE	1,7 RLL	3.5 3H	256k	300k	4500	
PLS30854S	11	SCSI-2Fast	1,7 RLL	3.5 3H	256k	300k	4500	
PLS31084A	11	ATA-2	1,7 RLL	3.5 3H	256k	300k	4500	
PLS31084S	11	SCSI-2	1,7 RLL	3.5 3H	256k	300k	4500	
PLS31274A	11	ATA-2	1,7 RLL	3.5 3H	256k	300k	4500	
PLS31274S	11	SCSI-2	1,7 RLL	3.5 3H	256k	300k	4500	
SHD2040N	39	ST412/506	2,7 RLL	3.5 HH		30k	3568	Y
SHD2041	29	IDE AT	2,7 RLL	3.5 HH		30k	3525	Y
SHD30280A	12	ATA		3.5 HH	64k			Y
SHD30420A	12	IDE AT	1,7 RLL	3.5 3H	128k	250k	3600	
SHD30560A	12	IDE AT	1,7 RLL	3.5 3H	128k	250k	3600	
SHD3061A	16	IDE AT	1,7 RLL	3.5 3H		200k		
SHD3062A	16	IDE AT	1,7 RLL	3.5 3H		200k		
SHD3101B	19	IDE AT	1,7 RLL	3.5 3H	32k	40k	3600	Y
SHD3121A	16	IDE AT	1,7 RLL	3.5 3H	64k	250k	3600	Y
SHD3122A	16	IDE AT	1,7 RLL	3.5 3H	64k	250k	3600	Y
SHD3171A	13	IDE AT	1,7 RLL	3.5 3H	64k	250k	3600	Y

Drive Model	Format Size MB	Head	Cyl	Sect/Trac	Translate H/C/S	RWC/WPC	Land Zone
SHD3172A	356	4	2223	96		---/---	
SHD3202	212	7	1376	43		NA/NA	AUTO
SHD3210S	212	7	1376	43		NA/NA	AUTO
SHD3211A	213	2	2570	55-95		---/---	
SHD3212A	426					NA/NA	AUTO
SHD3272A	545	4				---/---	
SHD3272S	545	4				---/---	
STG31271A	1280	4			16/2483/63	---/---	
STG31601A	1610				16/3104/63	---/---	
TBR31080A	1080				16/2092/63	---/---	
TBR31081A	1080	4	4308			---/---	
VG33402A	3400	4				---/---	
VG34202A	4250	5				---/---	
VG35102A	5100	6				---/---	
WN310820A	1080	2	6022			---/---	
WN312016A	1207	5	5389			---/---	
WN312021A	1207	2	6077			---/---	
WN31273A	1270	2	6333			---/---	
WN316025A	1620	3	5891			---/---	
WN32101S	2160	6				---/---	
WN321620A	2160	4	6022			---/---	
WN32162U	2160	4	5909			---/---	
WN32543A	2540	4	6331			---/---	
WN33203A	3175	5	6331			---/---	
WN34003A	4000	6				---/---	
WN34003U	4000	6				---/---	
WNR31601A	1610	4	5589			---/---	
WNR32100A	2104	6				---/---	
WNR32101A	2060	5	5589			---/---	
WNR32501A	2415	6				---/---	

SEAGATE TECHNOLOGIES

Drive Model	Format Size MB	Head	Cyl	Sect/Trac	Translate H/C/S	RWC/WPC	Land Zone
ELITE12G	1050	17				---/---	AUTO
SABRE1123	964	19				---/---	AUTO
SABRE1150	990	19				---/---	AUTO
SABRE1230	1050	15	1635			---/---	AUTO
SABRE2270	1948	15				---/---	AUTO
SABRE2500	2145	19				---/---	AUTO
SABRE368	368	10	1635			---/---	AUTO
SABRE500	500	10	1217			---/---	AUTO
SABRE736	741	15	1217			---/---	AUTO
SABRE850	851	15	1635			---/---	AUTO
ST1057A	53	3	1024	17	6/1024/17	NA/NA	AUTO
ST1057N	49	3	1024	34		---/---	AUTO
ST1090A	79	5	1072	29	16/335/29	NA/NA	AUTO
ST1090N	79	5	1068	29		NA/NA	AUTO
ST1096N	84	7	906	26		NA/NA	AUTO
ST1100	83	9	1072	17		1073/1073	AUTO
ST1102A	89	5	1024	17	10/1024/17	NA/NA	AUTO
ST1102N	84	5	945	34		---/---	AUTO
ST1106R	91	7	977	26		NA/NA	AUTO
ST1111A	98	5	1072	36	10/536/36	NA/NA	AUTO
ST1111E	98	5	1072	36		NA/NA	AUTO
ST1111N	98	5	1068	36		NA/NA	AUTO
ST11200N	1054	15	1872	73		---/---	AUTO
ST11200ND	1050	15	1877			---/---	AUTO
ST11201N (never made)	1054	15	1872	73		---/---	AUTO
ST11201ND	1050	15	1877			---/---	AUTO
ST1126A	111	7	1072	29	16/469/29	NA/NA	AUTO
ST1126N	107	7	1068	29		NA/NA	AUTO
ST1133A	117	5	1272	36	10/636/36	NA/NA	AUTO
ST1133NS	113	5	1268	36		NA/NA	AUTO
ST1144A	131	7	1024	32	15/1001/17	NA/NA	AUTO

Drive Model	Seek Time	Interface	Encode	Form Factor	cache kb	mtbf	RPM	Obsolete?
SHD3172A	13	IDE AT	1,7 RLL	3.5 3H	64k	250k	3600	Y
SHD3202	16	SCSI	1,7 RLL	3.5 HH		50k		Y
SHD3210S	16	SCSI	1,7 RLL	3.5 HH		50k		Y
SHD3211A	13	IDE AT	1,7 RLL	3.5 3H	64k	250k	3600	
SHD3212A	13	ATA		3.5 HH	128k			
SHD3272A	12	IDE AT	1,7 RLL		256k			
SHD3272S	12	SCSI-2 FAST	1,7 RLL		256k		4510	Y
STG31271A	12	ATA-2 Fast					4510	Y
STG31601A	12	ATA-2 Fast		3.5 3H	128k	300k	4500	
TBR31080A	9	ATA-2 Fast		3.5	128k		4500	
TBR31081A	9	ATA-2 Fast		3.5	256k		5400	
VG33402A	11						5400	
VG34202A	11				128k	500k	5400	
VG35102A	11				128k	500k	5400	
WN310820A		ATA-2 Fast	RLL 8,9	3.5 3H	128k	500k	4500	
WN312016A	11	ATA-2 Fast	RLL 8,9	3.5 3H	128k	500k	4500	
WN312021A	10	ATA-2 Fast	RLL 8,9	3.5 3H	128k	500k	4500	
WN31273A	11	ATA-2 Fast	RLL 8,9	3.5 3H	128k	500k	4500	
WN316025A	10	ATA-2 Fast	RLL 8,9	3.5 3H	128k	500k	4500	
WN32101S	11	SCSI-2Fast		3.5 3H	128k	500k	5400	
WN321620A		ATA-2 Fast	RLL 8,9	3.5 3H	128k	500k	5400	
WN32162U	9.5		RLL 8,9	3.5 3H	512k	500k	5400	
WN32543A	10	ATA-2 Fast	RLL 8,9	3.5 3H	128k	500k	5400	
WN33203A	10	ATA-2 Fast	RLL 8,9	3.5 3H	128k	500k	5400	
WN34003A	10	ATA-2 Fast	RLL 8,9	3.5 3H	128k	500k	5400	
WN34003U	10	Ultra SCSI	RLL 8,9	3.5 3H	128k	500k	5400	
WNR31601A	11	ATA-2 Fast	RLL 8,9	3.5 3H	128k	500k	5400	
WNR32100A	11			3.5 3H	128k	500k	5400	
WNR32101A	11	ATA-2 Fast	RLL 8,9	3.5 3H	128k	500k	5400	
WNR32501A	11	ATA-2 Fast	PRML	3.5 3H	128k	500k	5400	

SEAGATE TECHNOLOGIES

Drive Model	Seek Time	Interface	Encode	Form Factor	cache kb	mtbf	RPM	Obsolete?
ELITE12G	12	SMD	RLL	5.25 FH		100k		Y
SABRE1123	15	SMD	RLL	8.0 FH		100k		Y
SABRE1150	15	IPI-2	RLL	8.0 FH		100k		Y
SABRE1230	15	SMD/SCSI	RLL	8.0 FH		100k		Y
SABRE2270	12	SMD	RLL	8.0 FH		100k		Y
SABRE2500	12	SMD/SCSI	RLL	8.0 FH		100k		Y
SABRE368	182	SMD/SCSI	RLL	8.0 FH		100k		Y
SABRE500	18	SMD/SCSI	RLL	8.0 FH		100k		Y
SABRE736	15	SMD/SCSI	RLL	8.0 FH		50k		Y
SABRE850	15	SMD/SCSI	RLL	8.0 FH		50k		Y
ST1057A	19	IDE AT	RLL ZBR	3.5 HH	8/32k	50k	3528	Y
ST1057N	19	SCSI-2	2,7 RLL	3.5 HH	8/32k	50k	3528	Y
ST1090A	15	IDE AT	2,7 RLL	3.5 HH		70k	3600	Y
ST1090N	15	SCSI	2,7 RLL	3.5 HH		70k	3600	Y
ST1096N	20	SCSI	2,7 RLL	3.5 HH	8k	150k	3600	Y
ST1100	15	ST412/506	MFM	3.5 HH		150k	3600	Y
ST1102A	19	IDE AT	RLL ZBR	3.5 HH	8k	150k	3528	Y
ST1102N	19	SCSI-2	RLL ZBR	3.5 HH	8/32k	50k	3528	Y
ST1106R	24	ST412/506	RLL	3.5 HH		50k	3600	Y
ST1111A	15	IDE AT	2,7 RLL	3.5 HH		70k	3600	Y
ST1111E	15	ESDI (10)	2,7 RLL	3.5 HH		150k	3600	Y
ST1111N	15	SCSI	2,7 RLL	3.5 HH		70k	3600	Y
ST11200N	11	SCSI-2 FAST	RLL ZBR	3.5 HH	256k	200k	5411	Y
ST11200ND	12	SCSI-2 FAST	1,7 RLL	3.5 HH	256k	200k	5400	Y
ST11201N (never made)	10	SCSI-2 FSTW	ZBR,1,7RLL	3.5 HH	256k	200k	5411	
ST11201ND	12	SCSI-2 FSTW	1,7 RLL	3.5 HH	256k	200k	5400	
ST1126A	15	IDE AT	2,7 RLL	3.5 HH	32k	150k	3600	Y
ST1126N	15	SCSI	RLL	3.5 HH	32k	150k	3600	Y
ST1133A	15	IDE AT	2,7 RLL	3.5 HH	64k	150k	3600	Y
ST1133NS	15	SCSI	RLL	3.5 HH	64k	150k	3600	Y
ST1144A	19	IDE AT	RLL ZBR	3.5 HH	32k	70k	3528	Y

Drive Model	Format Size MB	Head	Cyl	Sect/Trac	Translate H/C/S	RWC/WPC	Land Zone
ST1144N	126	7		32		---/---	AUTO
ST1150R	128	9		26		NA/300	AUTO
ST1156A	138	7	1072	36	14/536/36	NA/NA	AUTO
ST1156E	138	7	1072	36		NA/NA	AUTO
ST1156N	138	7	1068	36		---/---	AUTO
ST1156NS	138	7	1068	36		NA/NA	AUTO
ST1162A	143	9	1072	29	16/603/29	NA/NA	AUTO
ST1162N	138	9	1068	29		NA/NA	AUTO
ST11700N	1430	13	2626			---/---	
ST11700ND	1430	13	2626			---/---	
ST11701N	1430	13	2626			---/---	
ST11701ND	1430	13	2626			---/---	
ST11750N	1437		2756			---/---	
ST11750ND	1437		2756			---/---	
ST11751N	1437		2756			---/---	
ST11751ND	1437		2756			---/---	
ST1186A	164	7	1272	36	12/742/36	NA/NA	AUTO
ST1186NS	159	7	1268	36		NA/NA	AUTO
ST11900N	1700	15	2621	83		NA/NA	AUTO
ST11900NC	1700	15	2621	83		NA/NA	AUTO
ST11900ND	1700	15	2621	83		NA/NA	AUTO
ST11900W	1700	15	2621	83		NA/NA	AUTO
ST11900WC	1700	15	2621	83		NA/NA	AUTO
ST11900WD	1700	15	2621	83		NA/NA	AUTO
ST11950N	1690	15	2706	81		NA/NA	AUTO
ST11950ND	1690					NA/NA	AUTO
ST11950W	1690	15	2706	81		NA/NA	AUTO
ST11950WD	1690					NA/NA	AUTO
ST1201A	177	9	1072	36	9/804/48	NA/NA	AUTO
ST1201E	177	9	1072	36		NA/NA	AUTO
ST1201N	172	9	1068	36		---/---	AUTO
ST1201NS	177	9	1068	36		NA/NA	AUTO
ST1239NS	211	9	1272	36	14/817/36	NA/NA	AUTO
ST1239NS	204	9	1268	36		NA/NA	AUTO
ST124	21	4	615	17		616/616	670
ST12400N	2148	19	2621	83		NA/NA	AUTO
ST12400NC	2148	19	2621	83		NA/NA	AUTO
ST12400ND	2100	19	2626			---/---	
ST12400WD	2148	19	2621	83		NA/NA	AUTO
ST12400W	2148	19	2621	84		NA/NA	AUTO
ST12400WC	2148	19	2621	84		NA/NA	AUTO
ST12400WD	2148	19	2621	84		NA/NA	AUTO
ST12401N	2100	19	2626			NA/NA	AUTO
ST12401ND	2100	19	2626			---/---	
ST12450W	1849	18	2710	149		NA/NA	AUTO
ST12450WD	1781					NA/NA	AUTO
ST125-0	21	4	615	17		NA/NA	AUTO
ST125-1	21	4	615	17		NA/NA	AUTO
ST12550N	2139	19	2707	81		NA/NA	AUTO
ST12550ND	2139		2756			NA/NA	AUTO
ST12550W	2139	19	2707	81		NA/NA	AUTO
ST12550WD	2139					NA/NA	AUTO
ST12551N	2100		2756			---/---	
ST12551ND	2100		2756			---/---	
ST125A-0	21	4	404	26	4/615/17	NA/NA	AUTO
ST125A-1	21	4	404	26	4/615/17	NA/NA	AUTO
ST125N-0	21	4	407	26		NONE/NA	NA
ST125N-1	21	4	407	26		NA/NA	AUTO
ST125R	21.5	4	404	26		---/---	AUTO
ST1274A	230	4	407	26	4/407/26		
ST137R	33	4	615	26		---/---	AUTO
ST138-0	32	6	615	17		NA/NA	AUTO
ST138-1	32	6	615	17		NA/NA	AUTO

Drive Model	Seek Time	Interface	Encode	Form Factor	cache kb	mtbf	RPM	Obsolete?
ST1144N	19	SCSI-2	RLL ZBR	3.5 HH	8/32k	50k	3528	Y
ST1150A	15	ST412/506	RLL	3.5 HH		150k	3600	Y
ST1156A	15	IDE AT	2,7 RLL	3.5 HH		70k	3600	Y
ST1156E	15	ESDI	RLL	3.5 HH		70k	3600	Y
ST1156N	15	SCSI	RLL	3.5 HH		70k	3600	Y
ST1156NS	15	SCSI	RLL	3.5 HH		70k	3600	Y
ST1162A	15	IDE AT	2,7 RLL	3.5 HH	32k	150k	3600	Y
ST1162N	15	SCSI	2,7 RLL	3.5 HH	64k	70k	3600	Y
ST11700N	9	SCSI-2 FAST	1,7 RLL	3.5 HH	256k	500k	5400	Y
ST11700ND	10	SCSI-2 FSTW	1,7 RLL	3.5 HH	256k	500k	5400	Y
ST11701N	9	SCSI-2 FAST	1,7 RLL	3.5 HH	256k	500k	5400	Y
ST11701ND	10	SCSI-2 FSTW	1,7 RLL	3.5 HH	256k	500k	5400	Y
ST11750N	8	SCSI-2 FAST	1,7 RLL	3.5 HH	1024k	500k	7200	Y
ST11750ND	9	SCSI-2 FAST	1,7 RLL	3.5 HH	1024k	500k	7200	Y
ST11751N	8	SCSI-2 FAST	1,7 RLL	3.5 HH	1024k	500k	7200	Y
ST11751ND	9	SCSI-2 FAST	1,7 RLL	3.5 HH	1024k	500k	7200	Y
ST1186A	15	IDE AT	2,7 RLL	3.5 HH		150k	3600	Y
ST1186NS	15	SCSI	2,7 RLL	3.5 HH	64k	150k	3600	Y
ST11900N	10	SCSI	1,7 RLL	3.5 HH		500k	5411	Y
ST11900ND	10	SCSI-2 FAST	1,7 RLL	3.5 HH		500k	5411	Y
ST11900W	10	SCSI-2 FSTW	RLL ZBR	3.5 HH		500k	5411	Y
ST11900WC	10	SCSI-2 FSTW	RLL ZBR	3.5 HH		500k	5411	Y
ST11900WD	10	SCSI-2 FSTW	RLL ZBR	3.5 HH		500k	5411	Y
ST11950N	9	SCSI-2	RLL ZBR	3.5 HH	1024k	500k	7200	Y
ST11950ND	9	SCSI-2 FAST		3.5 HH	1024k	500k	7200	Y
ST11950W	9	SCSI-2 FSTW	RLL ZBR	3.5 HH	1024k	500k	7200	Y
ST11950WD	9	SCSI-2 FSTW		3.5 HH	1024k	500k	7200	Y
ST1201A	15	IDE AT	2,7 RLL	3.5 HH	32k	150k	3600	Y
ST1201E	15	ESDI (10)	2,7 RLL	3.5 HH		150k	3600	Y
ST1201N	15	SCSI	2,7 RLL	3.5 HH	64k	150k	3600	Y
ST1201NS	15	SCSI-2	2,7 RLL	3.5 HH		70k		Y
ST1239A	15	IDE AT	2,7 RLL	3.5 HH	32k	150k	3600	Y
ST1239NS	15	SCSI-2	2,7 RLL	3.5 HH	64k	150k	3600	Y
ST124	40	ST412/506	MFM	3.5 HH		150k	3600	Y
ST12400N	9	SCSI-2 FAST	RLL ZBR	3.5 HH	256k	500k	5411	Y
ST12400NC	9	SCSI-2 FAST	RLL ZBR	3.5 HH	256k	500k	5411	Y
ST12400ND	10	SCSI-2 FAST	1,7 RLL	3.5 HH	256k	500k	5400	Y
ST12400W	9	SCSI-2 FSTW	RLL ZBR	3.5 HH	256k	500k	5411	Y
ST12400WC	10.5	SCSI-2 FSTW	RLL ZBR	3.5 HH	256k	500k	5411	Y
ST12400WD	10.5	SCSI-2 FSTW	RLL ZBR	3.5 HH	256k	500k	5411	Y
ST12401N	9	SCSI-2 FAST	RLL ZBR	3.5 HH	256k	500k	5411	Y
ST12401ND	10	SCSI-2 FSTW	1,7 RLL	3.5 HH	256k	500k	5400	Y
ST12450W	9	SCSI-2 FSTW	1,7RLL,ZBR	3.5 HH	1024k	500k	7200	Y
ST12450WD	9	SCSI-2 FSTW		3.5 HH	1024	500k	7200	Y
ST125-0	40	ST412/506	MFM	3.5 HH		150k	3600	Y
ST125-1	28	ST412/506	MFM	3.5 HH		150k	3600	Y
ST12550N	8	SCSI-2 FAST	1,7 RLL	3.5 HH	1024k	500k	7200	Y
ST12550ND	9	SCSI-2 FAST	1,7 RLL	3.5 HH	1024k	500k	7200	Y
ST12550W	9	SCSI-2 FSTW	1,7RLL,ZBR	3.5 HH	1024k	500k	7200	Y
ST12550WD	9	SCSI-2 FSTW		3.5 HH	1024k	500k	7200	Y
ST12551N	8	SCSI-2 FAST	1,7 RLL	3.5 HH	1024k	500k	7200	Y
ST12551ND	9	SCSI-2 FAST	1,7 RLL	3.5 HH	1024k	500k	7200	Y
ST125A-0	40	IDE AT	RLL	3.5 HH	2k	150k	3600	Y
ST125A-1	28	IDE AT	RLL	3.5 HH	2k	150k	3600	Y
ST125N-0	40	SCSI	RLL	3.5 HH	2k	150k	3600	Y
ST125N-1	28	SCSI	RLL	3.5 HH	2k	150k	3600	Y
ST125R		ST412/506	2,7 RLL	3.5 HH		150k		
ST1274A	18	IDE AT	2,7 RLL	3.5 HH		70k		Y
ST137R	40	ST412/506	2,7 RLL	3.5 HH		70k		Y
ST138-0	40	ST412/506	MFM	3.5 HH	2k	150k	3600	Y
ST138-1	28	ST412/506	MFM	3.5 HH	2k	70k	3600	Y

Drive Model	Format Size MB	Head	Cyl	Sect/Trac	Translate H/C/S	RWC/WPC	Land Zone
ST138A-0	32	4	604	26	6/615/17	NA/NA	AUTO
ST138A-1	32	4	604	26	6/615/17	NA/NA	AUTO
ST138N-0	32	4	615	26		NA/NA	AUTO
ST138N-1	32	4	615	26		NA/NA	AUTO
ST138R-0	32	4	615	26		NA/NA	AUTO
ST138R-1	32	4	615	26		NA/NA	AUTO
ST1400A	331	7	1475	NA	12/1018/53	NA/NA	AUTO
ST1400N	331	7	1476	62		NA/NA	AUTO
ST1401A	340	9	1132		15/726/61	NA/NA	AUTO
ST1401N	338	9	1100	66		NA/NA	AUTO
ST14207N Cayman	4294	20	4016	104		NA/NA	AUTO
ST14207W Cayman	4294	20	4016	104		NA/NA	AUTO
ST1480A	426	9	1474	NA	15/895/62	NA/NA	AUTO
ST1480N	426	9	1476	62		NA/NA	AUTO
ST1480NV	426	9	1478	V		NA/NA	AUTO
ST1481N	426	9	1476	62		NA/NA	AUTO
ST151	42	5	977	17		NA/NA	AUTO
ST15150DC	4294	21	3711			NA/NA	AUTO
ST15150FC	4294	21	3711			NA/NA	AUTO
ST15150N	4294	21	3711	81		NA/NA	AUTO
ST15150ND	4294	21	3711			NA/NA	AUTO
ST15150W	4294	21	3711			NA/NA	AUTO
ST15150WC	4294	21	3711			NA/NA	AUTO
ST15150WD	4294	21	3711			NA/NA	AUTO
ST15230DC	4294	19	3892			NA/NA	AUTO
ST15230N	4294	19	3892			NA/NA	AUTO
ST15230ND	4294	19	3892			NA/NA	AUTO
ST15230W	4294	19	3892			NA/NA	AUTO
ST15230WC	4294	19	3892			NA/NA	AUTO
ST15230WD	4294	19	3892			NA/NA	AUTO
ST157A-0	45	6	560	26	7/733/17	NA/NA	AUTO
ST157A-1	45	6	560	26	7/733/17	NA/NA	AUTO
ST157N-0	49	6	615	26		NA/NA	AUTO
ST157N-1	49	6	615	26		NA/NA	AUTO
ST157R-0	49	6	615	26		NA/NA	AUTO
ST157R-1	49	6	615	26		NA/NA	AUTO
ST1581N	525	9	1476	77		NA/NA	AUTO
ST177N	60	5	921	26		NA/NA	AUTO
ST1830N	702	13	1325			--/--	AUTO
ST18771DC	8700	20	5333			NA/NA	AUTO
ST18771FC	8700	20	5333			NA/NA	AUTO
ST18771N	8700	20	5333			NA/NA	AUTO
ST18771ND	8700	20	5333			NA/NA	AUTO
ST18771W	8700	20	5333			NA/NA	AUTO
ST18771WC	8700	20	5333			NA/NA	AUTO
ST18771WD	8700	20	5333			NA/NA	AUTO
ST19101DC	9100	16	6526			--/--	
ST19101FC	9100	16	6526			--/--	
ST19101N	9100	16	6526			--/--	
ST19101W	9100	16	6526			--/--	
ST19101WC	9100	16	6526			--/--	
ST19101WD	9100	16	6526			--/--	
ST19171DC	9100	20	5274			--/--	
ST19171FC	9100	20	5274			--/--	
ST19171N	9100	20	5274			--/--	
ST19171W	9100	20	5274			--/--	
ST19171WC	9100	20	5274			--/--	
ST19171WD	9100	20	5274			--/--	
ST1950N	803	13	1575			--/--	AUTO
ST1980N	860	13	1730	74		NA/NA	AUTO
ST1980NC	860	13	1730			NA/NA	AUTO
ST1980ND	860	13	1730			--/--	AUTO
ST206	5	2	306	17		307/128	

Drive Model	Seek Time	Interface	Encode	Form Factor	cache kb	mtbf	RPM	Obsolete? ⇓
ST138A-0	40	IDE AT	2,7 RLL	3.5 HH	2k	150k	3600	Y
ST138A-1	28	IDE AT	2,7 RLL	3.5 HH	2k	150k	3600	Y
ST138N-0	40	SCSI	2,7 RLL	3.5 HH	2k	150k	3600	Y
ST138N-1	28	SCSI	2,7 RLL	3.5 HH	2k	150k	3600	Y
ST138R-0	40	ST412/506	2,7 RLL	3.5 HH	2k	150k	3600	Y
ST138R-1	28	ST412/506	2,7 RLL	3.5 HH	2k	150k	3600	Y
ST1400A	14	IDE AT	1,7 RLL	3.5 HH	64k	150k	4412	Y
ST1400N	14	SCSI-2	1,7RLL,ZBR	3.5 HH	64k	150k	4412	Y
ST1401A	12	IDE AT	1,7 RLL	3.5 HH	64k	150k	4412	Y
ST1401N	12	SCSI-2	1,7RLL,ZBR	3.5 HH	64k	150k	4412	Y
ST14207N Cayman	9	SCSI-2Fast	1,7 RLL	3.5 HH	512k	1000k	7200	
ST14207W Cayman	9	SCSI-2FstWd	1,7 RLL	3.5 HH	512k	1000k	7200	
ST1480A	14	IDE AT	ZBR	3.5 HH	64k	150k	4412	Y
ST1480N	14	SCSI-2	ZBR	3.5 HH	64k	150k	4412	Y
ST1480NV	14	SCSI-2	1,7 RLL	3.5 HH	64k	150k	4412	Y
ST1481N	14	SCSI-2 FAST	ZBR, 1,7 RLL	3.5 HH	64k	150k	4412	Y
ST151	24	ST412/506	MFM	3.5 HH		150k	3600	Y
ST15150DC	9	SCSI-2 DIFF	1,7 RLL	3.5 HH	1024k	800k	7200	
ST15150FC	9	FC	1,7 RLL	3.5 HH	1024k	800k	7200	
ST15150N	9	SCSI-2 FAST	1,7 RLL	3.5 HH	1024k	800k	7200	
ST15150ND	9	SCSI-2 DIFF	1,7 RLL	3.5 HH	1024k	800k	7200	
ST15150W	9	SCSI-2 FSTW	1,7 RLL	3.5 HH	1024k	800k	7200	
ST15150WC	9	SCSI-2 FSTW	1,7 RLL	3.5 HH	1024k	800k	7200	
ST15150WD	9	SCSI-2 FSTW	1,7 RLL	3.5 HH	1024k	800k	7200	
ST15230DC	10	SCSI-2 FSTW	ZBR, 1,7 RLL	3.5 HH	512k	800k	5411	
ST15230N	9	SCSI-2 FAST	1,7 RLL	3.5 HH	512k	800k	5411	
ST15230ND	9	SCSI-2 FAST	1,7 RLL	3.5 HH	512k	800k	5411	
ST15230W	10	SCSI-2 FSTW	ZBR, 1,7 RLL	3.5 HH	512k	800k	5411	
ST15230WC	10	SCSI-2 FSTW	ZBR, 1,7 RLL	3.5 HH	512k	800k	5411	
ST15230WD	10	SCSI-2 FSTW	ZBR, 1,7 RLL	3.5 HH	512k	800k	5411	
ST157A-0	40	IDE AT	2,7 RLL	3.5 HH	2k	150k	3600	Y
ST157A-1	28	IDE AT	2,7 RLL	3.5 HH	2k	150k	3600	Y
ST157N-0	40	SCSI	2,7 RLL	3.5 HH	2k	150k	3600	Y
ST157N-1	28	SCSI	2,7 RLL	3.5 HH	2k	150k	3600	Y
ST157R-0	40	ST412/506	2,7 RLL	3.5 HH	2k	150k	3600	Y
ST157R-1	28	ST412/506	2,7 RLL	3.5 HH	2k	150k	3600	Y
ST1581N	14	SCSI-2 FAST	RLL ZBR	3.5 HH	64k	150k	4412	Y
ST177N	24	SCSI	ZBR,1,7RLL	3.5 HH	8k	150k	3600	Y
ST1830N		SCSI-2 FAST	ZBR,1,7RLL	3.5 HH	256k	200k	4535	Y
ST18771DC	9	ULTRA SCSI	PRML0,6,6	3.5 HH	512k	1000k	7200	
ST18771FC	9	FC	PRML0,6,6	3.5 HH	512k	1000k	7200	
ST18771N	9	ULTRA SCSI	PRML0,6,6	3.5 HH	512k	1000k	7200	
ST18771ND	9	ULTRA SCSI	PRML0,6,6	3.5 HH	512k	1000k	7200	
ST18771W	9	ULTRA SCSI	PRML0,6,6	3.5 HH	512k	1000k	7200	
ST18771WC	9	ULTRA SCSI	PRML0,6,6	3.5 HH	512k	1000k	7200	
ST18771WD	9	ULTRA SCSI	PRML0,6,6	3.5 HH	512k	1000k	7200	
ST19101DC	8	ULTRA SCSI	PRML0,4,4	3.5 HH	512k	1000k	1003	
ST19101FC	8	FC	PRML0,4,4	3.5 HH	1024k	1000k	1003	
ST19101N	8	Ultra SCSI	PRML0,4,4	3.5 HH	512k	1000k	1003	
ST19101W	8	Ultra SCSI	PRML0,4,4	3.5 HH	512k	1000k	1003	
ST19101WC	8	Ultra SCSI	PRML0,4,4	3.5 HH	512k	1000k	1003	
ST19101WD	8	Ultra SCSI	PRML0,4,4	3.5 HH	512k	1000k	1003	
ST19171DC	9	FC-AL	PRML0,4,4	3.5 HH	512k	1000k	7200	
ST19171FC	9	FC-AL	PRML0,4,4	3.5 HH	512k	1000k	7200	
ST19171N	9	Ultra SCSI	PRML0,4,4	3.5 HH	512k	1000k	7200	
ST19171W	9	FC-AL	PRML0,4,4	3.5 HH	512k	1000k	7200	
ST19171WC	9	FC-AL	PRML0,4,4	3.5 HH	512k	1000k	7200	
ST19171WD	9	FC-AL	PRML0,4,4	3.5 HH	512k	1000k	7200	
ST1950N		SCSI-2 FAST	ZBR	3.5 HH	256k	200k	4535	Y
ST1980N	10	SCSI-2 FAST	ZBR,1,7RLL	3.5 HH	256k	200k	5411	Y
ST1980NC	11	SCSI-2 FAST		3.5 HH	256k	200k	5400	Y
ST1980ND	11	SCSI-2 FAST	1,7 RLL	3.5 HH	256k	200k	5400	Y
ST206		ST412/506	MFM	5.25 FH				Y

Drive Model	Format Size MB	Head	Cyl	Sect/Trac	Translate H/C/S	RWC/WPC	Land Zone
ST2106E	89	5	1024	34		NA/NA	AUTO
ST2106N	91	5	1022	36		NA/NA	AUTO
ST2106NM	94	5	1022	35		NA/NA	AUTO
ST212	10	4	306	17		307/128	319
ST2125N	107	3	1544	45		NA/NA	AUTO
ST2125NM	107	3	1544	45		NA/NA	AUTO
ST2125NV	107	3	1544	45		NA/NA	AUTO
ST213	10	2	615	17		616/300	670
ST2182E	160	4	1453	54		NA/NA	AUTO
ST2209N	179	5	1544	45		NA/NA	AUTO
ST224N	21	2				---/---	
ST225	21	4	615	17		NONE/300-614	670
ST225N	21	4	615	17		NA/NA	670
ST225R	21	2	667	31		NA/NA	670
ST2274A	241	5	1747	54	16/536/55	NA/NA	AUTO
ST2383A	338	7	1747	54	16/737/56	NA/NA	AUTO
ST2383E	338	7	1747	54		NA/NA	AUTO
ST2383N	332	7	1261	74		NA/NA	AUTO
ST2383ND	332	7	1261	NA		NA/NA	AUTO
ST2383NM	332	7	1261	NA		NA/NA	AUTO
ST238R	32	4	615	26		NA/NA	670
ST2502N	435	7	1755	NA		NA/NA	AUTO
ST2502ND	435	7	1765	NA		NA/NA	AUTO
ST2502NM	435	7	1765	NA		NA/NA	AUTO
ST2502NV	435	7	1765	NA		NA/NA	AUTO
ST250N	42	4	667			NA/NA	AUTO
ST250R	42	4	667	31		NA/NA	AUTO
ST251-0	42	6	820	17		NA/NA	AUTO
ST251-1	42	6	820	17		NA/NA	AUTO
ST251N-0	43	4	820	26		NA/NA	AUTO
ST251N-1	43	4	820	26		NA/NA	AUTO
ST251R	43	4	820	26		NA/NA	AUTO
ST252	42	6	820	17		NA/NA	AUTO
ST253	43	5	989	17		NA/128	AUTO
ST274A	65	5	948	26	8/940/17	NA/NA	AUTO
ST277N-0	65	6	628	34		NA/NA	AUTO
ST277N-1	65	6	628	34		NA/NA	AUTO
ST277R-0	65	6	820	26		NA/NA	AUTO
ST277R-1	65	6	820	26		NA/NA	AUTO
ST278R	65	6	820	26		NA/NA	AUTO
ST279R	65	5	989	26		NA/128	AUTO
ST280A	71	4	1032	26	10/516/27	NA/NA	AUTO
ST296N	85	6	820	34		NA/NA	AUTO
ST3025A	21	1	615	17	2/808/26	NA/NA	AUTO
ST3025N	21	1	1616	26		NA/NA	AUTO
ST3051A	43	6	820	17	6/820/17	NA/NA	AUTO
ST3057A	53	*	1024	17		NA/NA	AUTO
ST3057N	49	3	940	34		NA/NA	AUTO
ST3096A	90	10	1024	17	8/836/26	NA/NA	AUTO
ST3096N	84	3	1024	35		NA/NA	AUTO
ST31051N	1060	4	4176			NA/NA	AUTO
ST31051W	1060	4	4176			NA/NA	AUTO
ST31051WC	1060	4	4176			NA/NA	AUTO
ST31055N	1060	4	4176			---/---	
ST31055W	1060	4	4176			---/---	
ST31055WC	1060	4	4176			---/---	
ST31081A	1081	4	3924		16/2097/63	NA/NA	AUTO
ST31082A	1082				4/2097/63	---/---	
ST31200N	1052	9	2700	84		NA/NA	AUTO
ST31200NC	1052					NA/NA	AUTO
ST31200ND	1052	9	2626			NA/NA	AUTO
ST31200W	1052	9	2700	84		NA/NA	AUTO
ST31200WC	1052	9	2700	84		NA/NA	AUTO

Drive Model	Seek Time	Interface	Encode	Form Factor	cache kb	Obsolete? mtbf	RPM
ST2106E	18	ESDI (10)	2,7 RLL	5.25 HH		100k	3600 Y
ST2106N	18	SCSI	2,7 RLL	5.25 HH	32k	100k	3600 Y
ST2106NM	18	SCSI	2,7 RLL	5.25 HH	32k	100k	3600 Y
ST212	65	MFM	MFM	5.25 FH		11k	3600 Y
ST2125N	18	SCSI	ZBR,2,7RLL	5.25 HH	32k	100k	3600 Y
ST2125NM	18	SCSI	ZBR,2,7RLL	5.25 HH	32k	100k	3600 Y
ST2125NV	18	SCSI	ZBR,2,7RLL	5.25 HH	32k	100k	3600 Y
ST213	65	ST412/506	MFM	5.25 FH		20k	3600 Y
ST2182E	16	ESDI (15)	2,7 RLL	5.25 HH		100k	3600 Y
ST2209N	18	SCSI	ZBR,2,7RLL	5.25 HH	32k	100k	3600 Y
ST224N	70	SCSI	2,7 RLL	5.25 HH		100k	
ST225	65	ST412/506	MFM	5.25 HH		100k	3600 Y
ST225N	65	SCSI	2,7 RLL	5.25 HH		100k	3600 Y
ST225R	70	ST412/506	2,7 RLL	5.25 HH		100k	3000 Y
ST2274A	16	IDE AT	2,7 RLL	5.25 HH	32k	100k	3600 Y
ST2383A	16	IDE AT	2,7 RLL	5.25 HH	32k	100k	3600 Y
ST2383E	16	ESDI	2,7 RLL	5.25 HH		100k	3600 Y
ST2383N	14	SCSI	ZBR,2,7RLL	5.25 HH	64k	100k	3600 Y
ST2383ND	14	SCSI	RLL ZBR	5.25 HH	64k	100k	3600 Y
ST2383NM	14	SCSI	RLL ZBR	5.25 HH	64k	100k	3600 Y
ST238R	65	ST412/506	RLL	5.25 HH		100k	3600 Y
ST2502N	16	SCSI	ZBR,2,7RLL	5.25 HH	64k	100k	3600 Y
ST2502ND	16	SCSI	RLL ZBR	5.25 HH	64k	100k	Y
ST2502NM	16	SCSI	RLL ZBR	5.25 HH	64k	100k	Y
ST2502NV	16	SCSI	RLL ZBR	5.25 HH	64k	100k	Y
ST250N	70	SCSI	2,7 RLL	5.25 HH		100k	Y
ST250R	70	ST412/506	2,7 RLL	5.25 HH		100k	3600 Y
ST251-0	40	ST412/506	MFM	5.25 HH		100k	3600 Y
ST251-1	28	ST412/506	MFM	5.25 HH		70k	3600 Y
ST251N-0	40	SCSI	RLL	5.25 HH		70k	3600 Y
ST251N-1	28	SCSI	RLL	5.25 HH		70k	3600 Y
ST251R	40	ST412/506	2,7 RLL	5.25 HH		100k	Y
ST252	40	ST412/506	MFM	5.25 HH		100k	3600 Y
ST253	28	ST412/506	MFM	5.25 HH		40k	3600 Y
ST274A	29	IDE AT	RLL	5.25 HH		40k	3600 Y
ST277N-0	40	SCSI	RLL	5.25 HH	2k	70k	3600 Y
ST277N-1	28	SCSI	RLL	5.25 HH	2k	70k	3600 Y
ST277R-0	40	ST412/506	2,7 RLL	5.25 HH		70k	3600 Y
ST277R-1	28	ST412/506	2,7 RLL	5.25 HH		70k	3600 Y
ST278R	40	ST412/506	2,7 RLL	5.25 HH		100k	3600 Y
ST279R	28	ST412/506	RLL	5.25 HH		40k	3600 Y
ST280A	29	IDE AT	RLL	5.25 HH		40k	3600 Y
ST296N	28	SCSI	2,7 RLL	5.25 HH	8k	70k	3600 Y
ST3025A	19	IDE AT	2,7 RLL	3.5 3H	8/32k	50k	3600 Y
ST3025N	19	SCSI-2	2,7 RLL	3.5 3H	8/32k	50k	3600 Y
ST3051A	16	IDE AT	2,7 RLL	3.5 3H	32k	150k	3211 Y
ST3057A	19	IDE AT	2,7 RLL	3.5 3H	8/32k	50k	3600 Y
ST3057N	19	SCSI-2	2,7 RLL	3.5 3H	8/32k	50k	3600 Y
ST3096A	14	IDE AT	2,7 RLL	3.5 3H	32k	150k	3211 Y
ST3096N	20	SCSI-2	2,7 RLL	3.5 3H	8/32k	50k	3528 Y
ST31051N	10.5	SCSI-3Fast	RLL 0,4,4	3.5 3H	256k	800k	5411 Y
ST31051W	10.5	SCSI-3Fast	RLL 0,4,4	3.5 3H	512k	800k	5411 Y
ST31051WC	10.5	SCSI-3Fast	RLL 0,4,4	3.5 3H	512k	800k	5411 Y
ST31055N	9	Ultra SCSI	RLL 0,4,4	3.5 3H	256k	800k	5411 Y
ST31055W	9	Ultra SCSI	RLL 0,4,4	3.5 3H	512k	800k	5411 Y
ST31055WC	9	Ultra SCSI	RLL 0,4,4	3.5 3H	512k	800k	5411 Y
ST31081A	14	ATA	1,7 RLL	3.5 3H	64k	300k	3600 Y
ST31082A	12.5	ATA-3	1,7 RLL	3.5 3H	64k	300k	4500 Y
ST31200N	10	SCSI-2 FAST	ZBR,1,7RLL	3.5 3H	256k	500k	5411 Y
ST31200NC	10.5	SCSI-2 FAST		3.5 3H	256k	500k	5400 Y
ST31200ND	10	SCSI-2 FAST	1,7 RLL	3.5 3H	256k	500k	5400 Y
ST31200W	10.5	SCSI-2 FSTW	ZBR,1,7RLL	3.5 3H	256k	500k	5411 Y
ST31200WC	10.5	SCSI-2 FSTW	1,7 RLL	3.5 3H	256k	500k	5411 Y

Drive Model	Format Size MB	Head	Cyl	Sect/Trac	Translate H/C/S	RWC/WPC	Land Zone
ST31200WD	1052	9	2700	84		NA/NA	AUTO
ST3120A	107	12	1024	NA	12/1024/17	NA/NA	AUTO
ST31220A	1083	6	3876		16/2099/63	NA/NA	AUTO
ST31230DC	1050	5	3892			NA/NA	AUTO
ST31230N	1050	5	3892			NA/NA	AUTO
ST31230NC	1050	5	3898			NA/NA	AUTO
ST31230ND	1050	5	3892			NA/NA	AUTO
ST31230W	1050	5	3892			NA/NA	AUTO
ST31230WC	1050	5	3898			NA/NA	AUTO
ST31230WD	1050	5	3898			NA/NA	AUTO
ST31231N	1060	5	3992			NA/NA	AUTO
ST3123A	106	2			12/1024/17	NA/NA	AUTO
ST31250N	1021	5	3711	107		NA/NA	AUTO
ST31250ND	1021	5	3711			NA/NA	AUTO
ST31250W	1021	5	3711			NA/NA	AUTO
ST31250WC	1021	5	3711			NA/NA	AUTO
ST31250WD	1021	5	3711			NA/NA	AUTO
ST31270A	1283	6	3876		16/2485/63	NA/NA	AUTO
ST31275A	1275	6	3640		16/2477/63	NA/NA	AUTO
ST31276A	1281	4	4893		16/2482/63	NA/NA	AUTO
ST3144A	130	15	1001	17	15/1001/17	NA/NA	AUTO
ST3145A	130	2				NA/NA	AUTO
ST31621A	1621	6	3924		16/3146/63	NA/NA	AUTO
ST31640A	1625		4834		16/3150/63	NA/NA	AUTO
ST31720A	1700	2			16/3306/63	—/—	AUTO
ST31930N	1700	7	3898			NA/NA	AUTO
ST31930ND	1700	7	3898			NA/NA	AUTO
ST3195A	170	4			10/981/34	NA/NA	AUTO
ST32132A	2113	6			6/4095/63	—/—	AUTO
ST32140A	2113	8	4834		16/4200/63	NA/NA	AUTO
ST32151N	2148	8	4176			NA/NA	AUTO
ST32151W	2148	8	4176			NA/NA	AUTO
ST32151WC	2148	8	4176			NA/NA	AUTO
ST32155N	2148	8	4176			—/—	AUTO
ST32155W	2148	8	4176			—/—	AUTO
ST32155WC	2148	8	4176			—/—	AUTO
ST32171DC	2150	6	5178			NA/NA	AUTO
ST32171FC	2150	6	5178			NA/NA	AUTO
ST32171N	2150	6	5178			NA/NA	AUTO
ST32171ND	2150	6	5178			NA/NA	AUTO
ST32171W	2150	6	5178			NA/NA	AUTO
ST32171WC	2150	6	5178			NA/NA	AUTO
ST32171WD	2150	6	5178			NA/NA	AUTO
ST32271DC	2260	6	5178			—/—	AUTO
ST32271N	2260	6	5178			—/—	AUTO
ST32271W	2260	6	5178			—/—	AUTO
ST32271WC	2260	6	5178			—/—	AUTO
ST32271WD	2260	6	5178			—/—	AUTO
ST32272DC	2260	4	6311			—/—	AUTO
ST32272N	2260	4	6311			—/—	AUTO
ST32272W	2260	4	6311			—/—	AUTO
ST32272WC	2260	4	6311			—/—	AUTO
ST32272WD	2260	4	6311			—/—	AUTO
ST3240A	211	2				NA/NA	AUTO
ST32430DC	2147	9	3892			NA/NA	AUTO
ST32430N	2147	9	3892			NA/NA	AUTO
ST32430NC	2147	9	3898			NA/NA	AUTO
ST32430ND	2147	9	3898			NA/NA	AUTO
ST32430W	2147	9	3892			NA/NA	AUTO
ST32430WC	2147	9	3892			NA/NA	AUTO
ST32430WD	2147	9	3892			NA/NA	AUTO
ST3243A	214	4	1024	34	12/1024/34	NA/NA	AUTO
ST3250A	213	2			12/1024/34	NA/NA	AUTO

Drive Model	Seek Time	Interface	Encode	Form Factor	cache kb	mtbf	RPM	Obsolete?
ST31200WD	10.5	SCSI-2 FSTW	ZBR,1,7RLL	3.5 3H	256k	500k	5411	Y
ST3120A	15	IDE AT	RLL ZBR	3.5 3H	32k	150k	3211	Y
ST31220A	12	ATA-2 FAST	1,7 RLL	3.5 3H	256k	300k	4500	
ST31230DC	10.5	SCSI-2 DIFF	1,7 RLL	3.5 3H	512k	800k	5411	
ST31230N	10.5	SCSI-2 FAST	1,7 RLL	3.5 3H	512k	800k	5411	
ST31230NC	10.5	SCSI-2 FAST	ZBR,1,7RLL	3.5 3H		800k	5411	Y
ST31230ND	10.5	SCSI-2 DIFF	1,7 RLL	3.5 3H	512k	800k	5411	
ST31230W	10.5	SCSI-2 FSTW	1,7 RLL	3.5 3H	512k	800k	5411	
ST31230WC	10.5	SCSI-2 FSTW	1,7 RLL	3.5 3H	512k	800k	5411	
ST31230WD	10.5	SCSI-2 DIFF	1,7 RLL	3.5 3H	512k	800k	5411	
ST31231N	10	SCSI-2-Fast	RLL ZBR	3.5 3H	256k	800k	5411	
ST3123A	16	IDE AT	ZBR,1,7RLL	3.5 3H	32k	250k	3811	Y
ST31250A	9	SCSI-2 FAST	1,7 RLL	3.5 3H	512k	800k	7200	
ST31250ND	9	SCSI-2 DIFF	1,7 RLL	3.5 3H	512k	800k	7200	
ST31250W	9	SCSI-2 FSTW	1,7 RLL	3.5 3H	512k	800k	7200	
ST31250WC	9	SCSI-2 DIFF	1,7 RLL	3.5 3H	512k	800k	7200	
ST31250WD	9	SCSI-2 DIFF	1,7 RLL	3.5 3H	512k	800k	7200	
ST31270A	12	ATA	RLL ZBR	3.5 3H	256k	300k	4500	
ST31275A	14	ATA	RLL ZBR	3.5 3H	64k	300k	3600	
ST31276A	12	ATA	RLL ZBR	3.5 3H	64k	300k	4500	
ST31344A	16	IDE AT	2,7 RLL	3.5 3H	32k	150k	3211	Y
ST3145A	16	IDE AT	1,7 RLL	3.5 3H		250k	3811	Y
ST31621A	14	ATA	RLL ZBR	3.5 3H	64k	300k	3600	
ST31640A	10	ATA-2 FAST	1,7 RLL	3.5 3H	256k	300k	5400	
ST31720A	12	ATA-2 FAST	1,7 RLL	3.5 3H	128k	300k	4500	
ST31930N	10.5	SCSI-2 FAST	ZBR,1,7RLL	3.5 3H		800k	5411	Y
ST31930ND	10.5	SCSI-2 FAST	ZBR,1,7RLL	3.5 3H		800k	5411	Y
ST3195A	16	IDE AT	ZBR,1,7RLL	3.5 3H	64k	250k	3811	Y
ST32132A	12.5	ATA-3	PRML	6,12,8	3.5 3H	128k	300k	4500
ST32140A	10	ATA-2 FAST	1,7 RLL	3.5 3H	128k	500k	5400	
ST32151N	10.5	SCSI-3Fast	RLL 0,4,4	3.5 3H	256k	800k	5411	
ST32151W	10.5	SCSI-3Fast	RLL 0,4,4	3.5 3H	512k	800k	5411	
ST32151WC	10.5	SCSI-3Fast	RLL 0,4,4	3.5 3H	512k	800k	5411	
ST32155N	9	Ultra SCSI	RLL 0,4,4	3.5 3H	256k	800k	5411	
ST32155W	9	Ultra SCSI	RLL 0,4,4	3.5 3H	512k	800k	5411	
ST32155WC	9	Ultra SCSI	RLL 0,4,4	3.5 3H	512k	800k	5411	
ST32171DC	9	ULTRA SCSI	PRML	3.5 3H	512k	1000k	7200	
ST32171FC	9	FC-AL	PRML	3.5 3H	512k	1000k	7200	
ST32171N	9	ULTRA SCSI	PRML	3.5 3H	512k	1000k	7200	
ST32171ND	9	ULTRA SCSI	PRML	3.5 3H	512k	1000k	7200	
ST32171W	9	ULTRA SCSI	PRML	3.5 3H	512k	1000k	7200	
ST32171WC	9	ULTRA SCSI	PRML	3.5 3H	512k	1000k	7200	
ST32171WD	9	ULTRA SCSI	PRML	3.5 3H	512k	1000k	7200	
ST32271DC	9	Ultra SCSI	PRML	3.5 3H	512k	1000k	7200	
ST32271N	9	Ultra SCSI	PRML	3.5 3H	512k	1000k	7200	
ST32271W	9	Ultra SCSI	PRML	3.5 3H	512k	1000k	7200	
ST32271WC	9	Ultra SCSI	PRML	3.5 3H	512k	1000k	7200	
ST32271WD	9	Ultra SCSI	PRML	3.5 3H	512k	1000k	7200	
ST32272DC	9	Ultra SCSI	PRML	3.5 3H	512k	1000k	7200	
ST32272N	9	Ultra SCSI	PRML	3.5 3H	512k	1000k	7200	
ST32272W	9	Ultra SCSI	PRML	3.5 3H	512k	1000k	7200	
ST32272WC	9	Ultra SCSI	PRML	3.5 3H	512k	1000k	7200	
ST32272WD	9	Ultra SCSI	PRML	3.5 3H	512k	1000k	7200	
ST3240A	8	IDE AT	RLL ZBR	3.5 3H	120k	300k	3811	Y
ST32430DC	10.5	SCSI-2 FAST	1,7 RLL	3.5 3H	512k	800k	5411	
ST32430N	10.5	SCSI-2 FAST	1,7 RLL	3.5 3H	512k	800k	5411	
ST32430NC	10.5	SCSI-2 FAST	ZBR,1,7RLL	3.5 3H		800k	5411	Y
ST32430ND	10.5	SCSI-2 DIFF	1,7 RLL	3.5 3H	512k	800k	5411	
ST32430W	10.5	SCSI-2 FSTW	1,7 RLL	3.5 3H	512k	800k	5411	
ST32430WC	10.5	SCSI-2 FSTW	1,7 RLL	3.5 3H	512k	800k	5411	
ST32430WD	10.5	SCSI-2 DIFF	1,7 RLL	3.5 3H	512k	800k	5411	
ST3243A	16	IDE AT	ZBR,1,7RLL	3.5 3H	32k	250k	3811	Y
ST3250A	15	IDE AT	ZBR,1,7RLL	3.5 3H	120k	300k	3811	Y

Drive Model	Format Size MB	Head	Cyl	Sect/ Trac	Translate H/C/S	RWC/ WPC	Land Zone
ST32530A	2558	6			16/4958/63	NA/NA	AUTO
ST32531N	2557	6			6/4956/63	---/---	
ST32550DC	2147	11	3711	V		NA/NA	AUTO
ST32550N	2147	11	3711	V		NA/NA	AUTO
ST32550ND	2147	11	3711	V		NA/NA	AUTO
ST32550W	2147	11	3510	108		NA/NA	AUTO
ST32550W	2147	11	3711	V		NA/NA	AUTO
ST32550WC	2147	11	3711	V		NA/NA	AUTO
ST32550WD	2147	11	3711	V		NA/NA	AUTO
ST325A,X	21	2	615	17	4/615/17	NA/NA	AUTO
ST325N	21	2	654	32		NA/NA	AUTO
ST325X	21	2	615	17		NA/NA	
ST3271A	265	2	2805		10/977/53	NA/NA	AUTO
ST3283A	245				14/978/35	NA/NA	AUTO
ST3283N	248	5	1691	57		NA/NA	AUTO
ST3285N	248	5	1691			NA/NA	AUTO
ST3290A	260				15/1001/34	NA/NA	AUTO
ST3291A	272	4			14/761/50	NA/NA	AUTO
ST3295A	273	2			14/761/50	NA/NA	AUTO
ST33240A	3227	8			8/6253/63	---/---	
ST3385A	340	5	767	62	14/767/62	NA/NA	AUTO
ST3390A	341				14/768/62	NA/NA	AUTO
ST3390N	344	3	2676	83		NA/NA	AUTO
ST3391A	341	4			14/768/62	NA/NA	AUTO
ST34217N	4294	10	6028			---/---	
ST34217W	4294	10	6028			---/---	
ST34217WC	4294	10	6028			---/---	
ST34217WD	4294	10	6028			---/---	
ST34340A	4303	8			8/8894/63	---/---	
ST34371DC	4350	10	5288			NA/NA	AUTO
ST34371FC	4350	10	5288			NA/NA	AUTO
ST34371N	4350	10	5288			NA/NA	AUTO
ST34371ND	4350	10	5288			NA/NA	AUTO
ST34371W	4350	10	5288			NA/NA	AUTO
ST34371WC	4350	10	5288			NA/NA	AUTO
ST34371WD	4350	10	5288			NA/NA	AUTO
ST34501DC	4550	8	6526			---/---	
ST34501FC	4550	8	6526			---/---	
ST34501N	4550	8	6526			---/---	
ST34501W	4550	8	6526			---/---	
ST34501WC	4550	8	6526			---/---	
ST34501WD	4550	8	6526			---/---	
ST34572DC	4550	8	6311			---/---	
ST34572N	4550	8	6311			---/---	
ST34572W	4550	8	6311			---/---	
ST34572WC	4550	8	6311			---/---	
ST34572WD	4550	8	6311			---/---	
ST3491A	428	4			15/899/62	NA/NA	AUTO
ST3500A	426	7	1547		15/895/62	NA/NA	AUTO
ST3500N	426	7	1547	V		NA/NA	AUTO
ST351A,X	43	2	820	17	6/820/17	NA/NA	AUTO
ST352A,X	42	2		17	5/980/17	NA/NA	AUTO
ST3550A	452	5	1018	62	14/1018/62	NA/NA	AUTO
ST3550N	456	5	2126	83		NA/NA	AUTO
ST3600A	528	7	1872		16/1024/63	NA/NA	AUTO
ST3600N	525	7	1872	79		NA/NA	AUTO
ST3600ND	525	7	1872			NA/NA	AUTO
ST3610N	535	7	1872	79		NA/NA	AUTO
ST3610NC	535					NA/NA	AUTO
ST3610ND	535	7	1872			NA/NA	AUTO
ST3620N	545	5	2700	78		NA/NA	AUTO
ST3620NC	545	5	2700	78		NA/NA	AUTO
ST3620ND	545	5	2700	78		NA/NA	AUTO

Drive Model	Seek Time	Interface	Encode	Form Factor	cache kb	Obsolete? mtbf	RPM
ST32530A	10.5	ATA-3	ZBR PRML	3.5 3H	128k	500k	5376
ST32531A	12	ATA-3	1,7 RLL	3.5 3H	128k	300k	5400
ST32550DC	8	SCSI-2 DIFF	1,7 RLL	3.5 3H	512k	800k	7200
ST32550N	8	SCSI-2 FAST	1,7 RLL	3.5 3H	512k	800k	7200
ST32550ND	8	SCSI-2 DIFF	1,7 RLL	3.5 3H	512k	800k	7200
ST32550W	8	SCSI-2 FSTW	RLL ZBR	3.5 3H	512k	800k 7200	Y
ST32550W	8	SCSI-2 FSTW	1,7 RLL	3.5 3H	512k	800k	7200
ST32550WC	8	SCSI-2 FSTW	1,7 RLL	3.5 3H	512k	800k	7200
ST32550WD	8	SCSI-2 DIFF	1,7 RLL	3.5 3H	512k	800k	7200
ST325A,X	28	IDE AT	ZBR,2,7RLL	3.5 HH/b	32k	150k 3048	Y
ST325N	28	SCSI	2,7 RLL	3.5 HH	2k/8k	50k 3600	Y
ST325X	45	IDE XT	RLL	3.5 HH	8/32k	150k 3600	Y
ST3271A	10.5	ATA	RLL ZBR	3.5 3H	256k	300k	4500
ST3283A	12	IDE AT	RLL ZBR	3.5 3H	128k	200k 4500	Y
ST3283N	12	SCSI-2 FAST	RLL ZBR	3.5 3H	128k	250k 4500	Y
ST3285N	12	SCSI-2 FAST	ZBR,1,7RLL	3.5 3H	128k	250k 4500	Y
ST3290A	16	IDE AT	1,7 RLL	3.5 3H		250k	3811
ST3291A	13	IDE AT	ZBR,1,7RLL	3.5 3H	120k	300k 3811	Y
ST3295A	14	IDE AT	1,7 RLL	3.5 3H	120k	300k	3811
ST33240A	12	ATA-3	1,7 RLL	3.5 3H	128k	300k	4500
ST3385A	12	IDE AT	ZBR,1,7RLL	3.5 3H	256k	250k 4500	Y
ST3390A	12	IDE AT	1,7 RLL	3.5 3H		250k	4500
ST3390N	12	SCSI-2 FAST	ZBR,1,7RLL	3.5 3H	256k	250k 4500	Y
ST3391A	14	IDE AT	1,7 RLL	3.5 3H		300k 3811	Y
ST34217N	9	Ultra SCSI	8,9RLL	3.5 3H	512k	1000k	7200
ST34217W	9	Ultra SCSI	8,9RLL	3.5 3H	512k	1000k	7200
ST34217WC	9	Ultra SCSI	8,9RLL	3.5 3H	512k	1000k	7200
ST34217WD	9	Ultra SCSI	8,9RLL	3.5 3H	512k	1000k	7200
ST34340A	12	ATA-3	1,7 RLL	3.5 3H	128k	300k	4500
ST34371DC	9	ULTRA SCSI	RLL 0,4,4	3.5 3H	512k	1000k	7200
ST34371FC	9	FC-AL	RLL 0,4,4	3.5 3H	512k	1000k	7200
ST34371N	9	ULTRA SCSI	RLL 0,4,4	3.5 3H	512k	1000k	7200
ST34371W	9	ULTRA SCSI	RLL 0,4,4	3.5 3H	512k	1000k	7200
ST34371WC	9	ULTRA SCSI	RLL 0,4,4	3.5 3H	512k	1000k	7200
ST34371WD	9	ULTRA SCSI	RLL 0,4,4	3.5 3H	512k	1000k	7200
ST34501DC	7.5	Ultra SCSI	PRML0,4,43.5 3H		1024k	1000k	1003
ST34501FC	7.5	FC	PRML	3.5 3H	512k	1000k	1003
ST34501N	7.5	Ultra SCSI	PRML0,4,43.5 3H		512k	1000k	1003
ST34501W	7.5	Ultra SCSI	PRML0,4,43.5 3H		512k	1000k	1003
ST34501WC	7.5	Ultra SCSI	PRML0,4,43.5 3H		512k	1000k	1003
ST34501WD	7.5	Ultra SCSI	PRML0,4,43.5 3H		512k	1000k	1003
ST34572DC	9	Ultra SCSI	PRML	3.5 3H	512k	1000k	7200
ST34572N	9	Ultra SCSI	PRML	3.5 3H	512k	1000k	7200
ST34572W	9	Ultra SCSI	PRML	3.5 3H	512k	1000k	7200
ST34572WC	9	Ultra SCSI	PRML	3.5 3H	512k	1000k	7200
ST34572WD	9	Ultra SCSI	PRML	3.5 3H	512k	1000k	7200
ST3491A	14	ATA FAST	ZBR,1,7RLL	3.5 3H	120k	300k 3811	Y
ST3500A	10	AT BUS	RLL ZBR	3.5 3H	256k	200k 4535	Y
ST3500N	11	SCSI-2 FAST	ZBR,1,7RLL	3.5 3H	240k	200k 4535	Y
ST351A,X	28	IDE AT	2,7 RLL	3.5 3H	32k	150k 3048	Y
ST352A,X	28	AT/XT	ZBR,2,7RLL	3.5 3H		150k 3048	Y
ST3550A	12	IDE AT	ZBR,1,7RLL	3.5 3H	256k	250k 4500	Y
ST3550N	12	SCSI-2 FAST	ZBR,1,7RLL	3.5 3H	256k	250k 4500	Y
ST3600A	11	IDE AT	1,7 RLL	3.5 3H	256k	200k 4535	Y
ST3600ND	12	SCSI-2 FAST	1,7 RLL	3.5 3H	256k	200k 5400	Y
ST3610N	12	SCSI-2 FAST	ZBR,1,7RLL	3.5 3H	256k	200k 5400	Y
ST3610NC	12	SCSI-2 FAST		3.5 3H	256k	200k 5400	Y
ST3610ND	12	SCSI-2 FAST	1,7 RLL	3.5 3H	256k	200k 5400	Y
ST3620N	10.5	SCSI-2 FAST	ZBR,1,7RLL	3.5 3H	256k	500k 5411	Y
ST3620NC	10.5	SCSI-2 FAST	ZBR,1,7RLL	3.5 3H	256k	500k 5411	Y
ST3620ND	10.5	SCSI-2 FAST	ZBR,1,7RLL	3.5 3H	256k	500k 5411	Y

Drive Model	Format Size MB	Head	Cyl	Sect/Trac	Translate H/C/S	RWC/WPC	Land Zone
ST3620W	546	5	2700	78		NA/NA	AUTO
ST3636A	640	2	4893		16/1241/63	NA/NA	AUTO
ST3655A	528	5			16/1024/63	NA/NA	AUTO
ST3655N	545	5	2393	89		NA/NA	AUTO
ST3660A	545				16/1057/63	NA/NA	AUTO
ST3780A	722	4	3876		16/1399/63	NA/NA	AUTO
ST3852A	850	1			16/1653/63	---/---	
ST4026	20	4	615	17		NA/NA	AUTO
ST4038	31	5	733	17		NA/300	AUTO
ST4038N	30	5	733			NA/NA	977
ST4051	40	5	977	17		NA/NA	AUTO
ST4053	44	5	1024	17		NA/NA	AUTO
ST406	5	2	306	17		NA/128	319
ST4077N	67	5	1024	26		1025/1025	
ST4077R	65	5	1024	26		1025/1025	
ST4085	71	8	1024	17		NA/NA	AUTO
ST4086	72	8	925	17		NA/NA	AUTO
ST4096	80	9	1024	17		NA/NA	AUTO
ST4096N	83	4				---/---	AUTO
ST4097	80	9	1024	17		NA/NA	AUTO
ST410800N	9090	27	4925	133		NA/NA	AUTO
ST410800ND	9090	27	4925	133		NA/NA	AUTO
ST410800W	9090	27	4925	133		NA/NA	AUTO
ST410800WD	9090	27	4925	133		NA/NA	AUTO
ST41097J	1097	17	2101			NA/NA	AUTO
ST412	10	4	306	17		307/128	319
ST41200N	1037	15	1931	71		NA/NA	AUTO
ST41200ND	1037	15	1931	NA		NA/NA	AUTO
ST41200NM	1037	15	1931	NA		NA/NA	AUTO
ST41200NV	1037	15	1931	NA		NA/NA	AUTO
ST41201J	1200U	17	2101			NA/NA	AUTO
ST41201K	1200U	17	2101	NA		NA/128	AUTO
ST4135R	115	9	960	26		NA/NA	AUTO
ST4144N	122	9	1024	26		NA/NA	1023
ST4144R	122	9	1024	26		NA/NA	AUTO
ST41520N	1370	17	2101	NA		NA/NA	AUTO
ST41520ND	1370	17	2101	NA		NA/NA	AUTO
ST41600N	1370	17	2101	NA		NA/NA	AUTO
ST41600ND	1370	17	2101	NA		NA/NA	AUTO
ST41601N	1370	17	2101	V		NA/NA	AUTO
ST41601ND	1370	17	2101	V		NA/NA	AUTO
ST41650N	1415	15	2107	87		NA/NA	AUTO
ST41650ND	1415	15	2107	NA		NA/NA	AUTO
ST41651N	1415	15	2107	87		NA/NA	AUTO
ST41651ND	1415	15	2107	NA		NA/NA	AUTO
ST41800K	1986U	18	2627	NA		NA/NA	AUTO
ST4182E	151	9	969	34		NA/NA	AUTO
ST4182N	155	9	967	36		NA/NA	AUTO
ST4182NM	155	9	967	36		NA/NA	AUTO
ST419	15	6	306	32		307/128	319
ST4192E	169	8	1147	36		NA/NA	AUTO
ST4192N	168	8	1147	36		1148/1148	
ST42000N,ND	1792	16	2627	83		NA/NA	AUTO
ST42100N	1900	15	2573	96		NA/NA	AUTO
ST423451N	23.2	28	6876	237		---/---	
ST423451W	23.2	28	6876	237		---/---	
ST423451WD	23.2	28	6876	237		NA/NA	AUTO
ST42400N,ND	2129	19	2627	83		307/128	AUTO
ST425	20	8	306	17		NA/NA	AUTO
ST43200K	3386U	20	2738			NA/NA	AUTO
ST43200N	3338			NA		NA/NA	AUTO
ST43400N	2912	21	2738	99		NA/NA	AUTO
ST43400ND	2912	21	2738	99		NA/NA	AUTO

Drive Model	Seek Time	Interface	Encode	Form Factor	cache kb	mtbf	RPM	Obsolete?
ST3620W	10	SCSI-2 FSTW	RLL ZBR	3.5 3H	256k	500k	5411	Y
ST3636A	12.5	ATA	RLL ZBR	3.5 3H	64k	300k	4500	Y
ST3655A	12	IDE AT	1,7 RLL	3.5 3H	256k	250k	4500	Y
ST3655N	12	SCSI-2 FAST	ZBR,1,7RLL	3.5 3H		250k	4500	Y
ST3660A	14	ATA FAST	1,7 RLL	3.5 3H	120k	300k	3811	
ST3780A	14	IDE AT	RLL ZBR	3.5 3H	256k	300k	4500	Y
ST3852A	12	ATA-2	1,7 RLL	3.5 3H	128k	500k	4500	Y
ST4026	40	ST412/506	MFM	5.25 FH		15k	3600	Y
ST4038	40	ST412/506	MFM	5.25 FH		25k	3600	Y
ST4038N		SCSI		5.25 FH				Y
ST4051	40	ST412/506	MFM	5.25 FH		15k	3600	Y
ST4053	28	ST412/506	MFM	5.25 FH		40k	3600	Y
ST406	85	ST412/506	MFM	5.25 FH		11k	3600	Y
ST4077N	28	SCSI	2,7 RLL	5.25 FH				Y
ST4077R	28	ST412/506	2,7 RLL	5.25 FH				Y
ST4085	28	ST412/506	MFM	5.25 FH		40k	3600	Y
ST4086	28	ST412/506	MFM	5.25 FH		40k	3600	Y
ST4096	28	ST412/506	MFM	5.25 FH		40k	3600	Y
ST4096N	17	SCSI		5.25 FH				Y
ST4097	28	ST412/506	MFM	5.25 FH		40k	3600	Y
ST410800N	12	SCSI-2 FAST	1,7 RLL	5.25 FH	1024k	500k	5400	Y
ST410800ND	12	SCSI-2 FAST	1,7 RLL	5.25 FH	1024k	500k	5400	Y
ST410800W	12	SCSI-2 FSTW	1,7 RLL	5.25 FH	1024k	500k	5400	Y
ST410800WD	12	SCSI-2 FSTW	1,7 RLL	5.25 FH	1024k	500k	5400	Y
ST411097J	11	SMD-O/E	2,7 RLL	5.25 FH		150k	5400	Y
ST412	85	ST412/506	MFM	5.25 FH		110k		
ST41200N	15	SCSI-2	1,7RLL,ZBR	5.25 FH	256k	150k	3600	Y
ST41200ND	15	SCSI-2	RLL ZBR	5.25 FH	256k	150k		Y
ST41200NM	15	SCSI-2	RLL ZBR	5.25 FH	256k	150k		Y
ST41200NV	15	SCSI-2	RLL ZBR	5.25 FH	256k	150k		Y
ST41201J	11	SMD-O/E	2,7 RLL	5.25 FH		150k	5400	Y
ST41201K	11	IPI-2	2,7 RLL	5.25 FH		150k	5400	Y
ST4135R	28	ST412/506	RLL	5.25 FH		40k	3600	Y
ST4144N	28	SCSI	2,7 RLL	5.25 FH				Y
ST4144R	28	ST412/506	2,7 RLL	5.25 FH		40k	3600	Y
ST41520N	11	SCSI-2	ZBR,2,7RLL	5.25 FH	48k	150k	5400	Y
ST41520ND	11	SCSI-2	ZBR	5.25 FH	48k	150k	5400	Y
ST41600N	11	SCSI-2	ZBR,2,7RLL	5.25 FH	48k	150k	5400	Y
ST41600ND	11	SCSI-2	ZBR	5.25 FH	48k	150k	5400	Y
ST41601N	11	SCSI-2 FAST	ZBR,2,7RLL	5.25 FH	256k	150k	5400	Y
ST41601ND	11	SCSI-2 FAST	2,7 RLL	5.25 FH	256k	150k	5400	Y
ST41650N	15	SCSI-2	ZBR,1,7RLL	5.25 FH	256k	150k	3600	Y
ST41650ND	15	SCSI-2 DIFF	RLL ZBR	5.25 FH	256k	150k		Y
ST41651N	15	SCSI-2	ZBR,1,7RLL	5.25 FH	256k	150k	3600	Y
ST41651ND	15	SCSI-2 DIFF	1,7 RLL	5.25 FH	256k	150k		Y
ST41800K	11	IPI-2	2,7 RLL	5.25 FH		150k	5400	Y
ST4182E	16	ESDI	RLL	5.25 FH		100k	3600	Y
ST4182N	16	SCSI	2,7 RLL	5.25 FH		100k	3600	Y
ST4182NM	16	SCSI	2,7 RLL	5.25 FH	32k	100k	3600	Y
ST419	85	ST412/506	MFM	5.25 FH		11k		Y
ST4192E	17	ESDI	2,7 RLL	5.25 FH		20k		Y
ST4192N	17	SCSI	2,7 RLL	5.25 FH		20k		Y
ST42000N,ND	11	SCSI-2 FAST	ZBR,2,7RLL	5.25 FH		150k	5400	Y
ST42100N	13	SCSI-2 FSTW	ZBR,1,7RLL	5.25 FH	256k	150k	3600	Y
ST423451N	13	Ultra SCSI	PRML0,4,45,25	5.25 FH	2048k	500k	5400	
ST423451W	13	Ultra SCSI	PRML0,4,45,25	5.25 FH	2048k	500k	5400	
ST423451WD	13	Ultra SCSI	PRML0,4,45,25	5.25 FH	2048k	500k	5400	
ST42400N,ND	11	SCSI-2 FAST	ZBR,2,7RL	5.25 FH	512k	150k	5400	Y
ST425		ST412/506	MFM	5.25 FH				
ST43200K	11	IPI-2	1,7 RLL	5.25 FH	512k	200k	5400	Y
ST43200K	11	IPI-2	RLL ZBR	5.25 FH		300k		
ST43400N	11	SCSI-2 FAST	1,7 RLL	5.25 FH	512k	200k	5400	Y
ST43400ND	11	SCSI-2 FAST	1,7 RLL	5.25 FH	512k	200k	5400	Y

Drive Model	Format Size MB	Head	Cyl	Sect/ Trac	Translate H/C/S	RWC/ WPC	Land Zone
ST43401N	2912	21	2738			NA/NA	AUTO
ST43401ND	2912	21	2738			NA/NA	AUTO
ST43402N	2912	21	2738	99		NA/NA	AUTO
ST43402ND	2912	21	2738	99		NA/NA	AUTO
ST4350N	300	9	1412	46		NA/NA	AUTO
ST4350NM	307	9	1412	NA		NA/NA	AUTO
ST4376N	330	9	1549	45		NA/NA	AUTO
ST4376NM	330	9	1549	NA		NA/NA	AUTO
ST4376NV	330	9	1549	NA		NA/NA	AUTO
ST4383E	319	13	1412	34		NA/NA	AUTO
ST4384E	319	15	1224	34		NA/NA	AUTO
ST4385N	330	15	791	55		NA/NA	AUTO
ST4385NM	330	15	791	NA		NA/NA	AUTO
ST4385NV	330	15	791	NA		NA/NA	AUTO
ST4442E	368	15	1412	34		NA/NA	AUTO
ST4702E	601	15	1546	50		NA/NA	AUTO
ST4702NM	601	15	1546	NA		NA/NA	AUTO
ST4766E	664	15	1632	53		NA/NA	AUTO
ST4766N	676	15	1632	54		NA/NA	AUTO
ST4766NM	663		1632	54		NA/NA	AUTO
ST4766NV	663		1632	54		NA/NA	AUTO
ST4767E	676	15	1399	63		NA/NA	AUTO
ST4767N	665	15	1356	64		NA/NA	AUTO
ST4767ND	665	15	1356	64		NA/NA	AUTO
ST4767NM	665	15	1356	64		NA/NA	AUTO
ST4767NV	665	15	1356	64		NA/NA	AUTO
ST4769E	631	15	1552	53		NA/NA	AUTO
ST506	5	4	153	17		128/128	157
ST51080A	1080	4	4771		16/2114/63	NA/NA	AUTO
ST51080N	1000					---/---	
ST51270A	1282	4	5414		16/2485/63	NA/NA	AUTO
ST52160A	2113	4			16/4095/63	---/---	
ST52520A	2560	4			16/4970/63	---/---	
ST5540A	541	2	4834		16/1050/63	NA/NA	AUTO
ST5660A	545	4	3420		16/1057/63	NA/NA	AUTO
ST5660N	545	4	3420	77		NA/NA	AUTO
ST5850A	855	4	4085		16/1656/63	NA/NA	AUTO
ST6165J	165	10	823			---/---	
ST6315J	315	19	823			---/---	
ST6344J	344	24	711			---/---	AUTO
ST6515J	516	24	711			---/---	AUTO
ST6515K	516u	24	711			---/---	
ST6516J	516	24	711			---/---	
ST683J	83	5	823			NA/NA	AUTO
ST7050P	42	2				---/---	
ST706	5	2	306	17		307/128	AUTO
ST81123J	1123U	15	1635			---/---	AUTO
ST81154K	1154U	14	1635			---/---	
ST81236J	1236	15	1635			---/---	AUTO
ST81236K	1236	15	1635			---/---	
ST81236N	1056	15	1635	NA		NA/NA	AUTO
ST82030J	2030U	19	2120			---/---	
ST82030K	2030U	19	2120			---/---	AUTO
ST82038J	2038U	19	2611			---/---	
ST82105K	2105U	16	2611			---/---	AUTO
ST82272J	2272U	19	2611			---/---	
ST82368J	2368U	18	2611			---/---	
ST82500J	2500	19	2611			---/---	AUTO
ST82500K	2500 (U)	19	2611			---/---	
ST82500N	2140	19	2611	NA		NA/NA	AUTO
ST83050K	3050U	18	2655	NA		NA/NA	AUTO
ST83050N	3050U	18	2655	NA		NA/NA	AUTO
ST83073J	3073u	19	2655			NA/NA	

Drive Model	Seek Time	Interface	Encode	Form Factor	cache kb	mtbf	RPM	Obsolete?
ST43401N	11	SCSI-2 FSTW	1,7 RLL	5.25 FH	512k	200k	5400	Y
ST43401ND	11	SCSI-2 FSTW	1,7 RLL	5.25 FH	512k	200k	5400	Y
ST43402N	11	SCSI-2 2POR	ZBR,1,7RLL	5.25 FH	2048k	200k	5400	Y
ST43402ND	11	SCSI-2 2POR	ZBR,1,7RLL	5.25 RH	894k	200k	5400	Y
ST4350N	16	SCSI				100k		Y
ST4350NM	16	SCSI	RLL ZBR	5.25 FH	32k	100k	3600	Y
ST4376N	17	SCSI	ZBR,2,7RLL	5.25 FH	32k	100k	3600	Y
ST4376NM	17	SCSI	ZBR,2,7RLL	5.25 FH	32k	100k		Y
ST4376NV	17	SCSI	RLL ZBR	5.25 FH	32k	100k		Y
ST4383E	18	ESDI	2,7 RLL	5.25 FH		100k	3600	Y
ST4384E	14	ESDI	2,7 RLL	5.25 FH		100k	3600	Y
ST4385N	10	SCSI	ZBR,2,7RLL	5.25 FH	32k	100k	3600	Y
ST4385NM	10	SCSI	RLL ZBR	5.25 FH	32k	100k		Y
ST4385NV	10	SCSI	RLL ZBR	5.25 FH	32k	100k		Y
ST4442E	16	ESDI	RLL	5.25 FH		100k	3600	Y
ST4702N	16	SCSI	ZBR,2,7RLL	5.25 FH	32k	100k	3600	Y
ST4702NM	16	SCSI	RLL ZBR	5.25 FH	32k	100k		Y
ST4766E	16	ESDI (15)	RLL	5.25 FH		150k	3600	Y
ST4766N	15	SCSI	RLL	5.25 FH	32k	150k	3600	Y
ST4766NM	15	SCSI	2,7 RLL	5.25 FH	32k	150k		Y
ST4766NV	15	SCSI	2,7 RLL	5.25 FH	32k	150k		Y
ST4767E	11	ESDI (24)	1,7 RLL	5.25 FH		150k	4800	Y
ST4767N	11	SCSI-2	ZBR,1,7RLL	5.25 FH	256k	150k	4800	Y
ST4767ND	11	SCSI-2	RLL ZBR	5.25 FH	256k	150k	4800	Y
ST4767NM	11	SCSI-2	RLL ZBR	5.25 FH	256k	150k	4800	Y
ST4767NV	11	SCSI-2	RLL ZBR	5.25 FH	256k	150k	4800	Y
ST4769E	14	ESDI	1,7 RLL	5.25 FH		150k	4800	Y
ST506	85	ST412/506	MFM	3.5 4H		11k		Y
ST51080A	10	ATA-2 FAST	1,7 RLL	3.5 4H	256	300k	5400	Y
ST51080N		SCSI		2.5 4H				Y
ST51270A	10.5	ATA	RLL ZBR	3.5 4H	128k	300k	5376	Y
ST52160A	11	ATA-2 Fast	PRML	3.5 3H	128k	300k	5400	Y
ST52520A	11	ATA-2 Fast	PRML	3.5 4H	128k	500k	5400	Y
ST5540A	10.5	ATA	RLL ZBR	3.5 4H	128k	300k	5376	Y
ST5660A	12	IDE AT	1,7 RLL	3.5 4H		300k	4500	Y
ST5660N	12	SCSI-2 FAST	ZBR,1,7RLL	3.5 4H	256k	300k	4500	Y
ST5850A	11	ATA-2 FAST	1,7 RLL	3.5 4H		300k	5400	Y
ST6165J	30	SMD	2,7 RLL	8		10k	3600	Y
ST6315J	20	SMD-E	MFM	9		30k	3600	Y
ST6344J	18	SMD-O/E	MFM	9		30k	3600	Y
ST6515J	18	SMD	2,7 RLL	9		30k	3600	Y
ST6515K	18	IPI-2	2,7 RLL	9		30k	3600	Y
ST6516J	18	SMD-E	2,7 RLL	9		30k	3600	Y
ST683J	30	SMD	2,7 RLL	8		8k	3600	Y
ST7050P	18	PCMCIA/ATA	1,7 RLL	1.8 4H	32k	150k	3545	Y
ST706		ST412/506	MFM	5.25 FH			706	
ST81123J	15	SMD-E	2,7 RLL	8		150k	3600	Y
ST81154K	15	IPI-2	2,7 RLL	8		150k	3600	Y
ST81236J	15	SMD-E	2,7 RLL	8		150k	3600	Y
ST81236K	15	IPI-2	2,7 RLL	8		150k	3600	Y
ST81236N	15	SCSI	2,7 RLL	8		150k	3600	Y
ST82030J	11	SMD-O/E	2,7 RLL	8		150k	3600	Y
ST82030K	11	IPI-2	2,7 RLL	8		150k	3600	Y
ST82038J	12	SMD-E	2,7 RLL	8		150k	3600	Y
ST82105K	12	IPI-2	2,7 RLL	8		80k	3600	Y
ST82272J	12	SMD-E	2,7 RLL	8		150k		Y
ST82368K	12	IPI-2	2,7 RLL	8		80k	3600	Y
ST82500J	12	SMD-E	2,7 RLL	8		150k	3600	Y
ST82500K	12	IPI-2	2,7 RLL	8		150k	3600	Y
ST82500N	12	SCSI	2,7 RLL	8		150k	3600	Y
ST83050K	12	IPI-2	1,7 RLL	8		150k	4365	Y
ST83050N	12	IPI-2	1,7 RLL	8		150k	4365	Y
ST83073J	12	SMD-O/E	1,7 RLL	8 FH		150k	4235	Y

Drive Model	Format Size MB	Head	Cyl	Sect/Trac	Translate H/C/S	RWC/WPC	Land Zone
ST83220K	3220U	19	2655	NA		NA/NA	AUTO
ST8368J	368U	10	1217			---/---	
ST8368N	316	10	1217	NA		---/---	AUTO
ST8500J	500U	10	1217			---/---	
ST8500N	427	10	1217	NA		NA/NA	AUTO
ST8741J	741U	15	1635			---/---	
ST8741N	637	15	1635	NA		---/---	AUTO
ST8851J	851	15	1381			---/---	
ST8851K	851	15	1381			---/---	
ST8851N	727	15	1381			NA/NA	AUTO
ST8885N	727			NA		NA/NA	AUTO
ST9025A	21	4	1024		4/615/17	NA/NA	AUTO
ST9051A	43	4	654	32	6/820/17	NA/NA	AUTO
ST9052A	42	16	1024	63	5/980/17	---/---	
ST9077A	64	4	802	39	11/669/17	NA/NA	
ST9080A	64	2		38	4/823/38	NA/NA	
ST9096A	85	4		34	10/980/17	NA/NA	
ST9100A	85					NA/NA	
ST9100AG	85	2		63	14/748/16	NA/NA	AUTO
ST91350AG	1350				16/2616/63	---/---	
ST9140AG	127	4			15/980/17	NA/NA	
ST9144A	128	6			15/980/17	NA/NA	
ST9145A	128	4	1463		15/980/17	NA/NA	AUTO
ST9145AG	127	4	1463		15/980/17	NA/NA	
ST9150AG	131	2			13/419/47	NA/NA	
ST91685AG	1680				8/3256/63	---/---	
ST9190AG	171	4			16/873/24	NA/NA	
ST92255AG	2250				10/4360/63	---/---	
ST9235AG	209	6	985	32	13/985/32	NA/NA	
ST9235N	209	13	985	NA		NA/NA	AUTO
ST9240AG	210	4			8/988/52	NA/NA	AUTO
ST9295AG	261	16	1024	63		---/---	
ST9295N (never made)	250 NA		NA	NA		NA/NA	AUTO
ST9300AG	262	4			15/569/60	NA/NA	AUTO
ST9385AG	341	6			16/934/51	NA/NA	AUTO
ST9420AG	420				16/988/32	---/---	
ST9550AG	455	6			16/942/59	NA/NA	AUTO
ST9655AG	524	6			14/1016/63	NA/NA	AUTO
ST9816AG	810				16/1571/63	NA/NA	AUTO
ST9840AG	840	4			16/1628/63	NA/NA	AUTO

SEQUEL, INC

Drive Model	Format Size MB	Head	Cyl	Sect/Trac	Translate H/C/S	RWC/WPC	Land Zone
5300	3000	21		V		---/---	
5350	3572	25		V		---/---	
5400	4000	26		V		---/---	
EXT4175	149	7	1224	34		NA/NA	AUTO
EXT4280	234	11	1224	36		NA/NA	AUTO
EXT4380	319	15	1224	34		NA/NA	AUTO
XT1050	38	5	902	17		NA/NA	AUTO
XT1065	52	7	918	17		NA/NA	AUTO
XT1085	71	8	1024	17		NA/NA	AUTO
XT1105	84	11	918	17		NA/NA	AUTO
XT1120R	105	8	1024	25		NA/NA	AUTO
XT1140	119	15	918	17		NA/NA	AUTO
XT1240R	196	15	1024	25		NA/NA	AUTO
XT2085	72	7	1224	17		NA/NA	AUTO
XT2140	113	11	1224	17		NA/NA	AUTO
XT2190	159	15	1224	17		NA/NA	AUTO
XT3170	146	9	1224	26		---/---	
XT3280	244	15	1224	26		---/---	
XT3380	319	15	1224	34		---/---	
XT4170E	157	7	1224	35/36	16	NA/NA	AUTO
XT4170S	157	7	1224	35-36		NA/NA	AUTO

Drive Model	Seek Time	Interface	Encode	Form Factor	cache kb	mtbf	RPM	Obsolete?
ST83220K	12	IPI-2	1,7 RLL	8		150k	4365	Y
ST8368J	18	SMD-E	2,7 RLL	8 FH		35k	3600	Y
ST8368N	18	SCSI	2,7 RLL	8		30k	3600	Y
ST8500J	18	SMD-E	2,7 RLL	8		30k	3600	Y
ST8500N	18	SCSI	2,7 RLL	8		30k	3600	Y
ST8741J	15	SMD-E	2,7 RLL	8		50k	3600	Y
ST8741N	15	SCSI	2,7 RLL	8		50k	3600	Y
ST8851J	15	SMD-E	2,7 RLL	8		100k	3600	Y
ST8851K	15	IPI-2	2,7 RLL	8		100k	3600	Y
ST8851N	12	SCSI	2,7 RLL	8		100k	3600	Y
ST8885N	15	SCSI	2,7 RLL	8		150k		Y
ST9025A		IDE AT	2,7 RLL	2.5 4H		150k	3631	Y
ST9051A		IDE AT	2,7 RLL	2.5 4H		150k	3631	Y
ST9052A	16	IDE AT	2,7 RLL	2.5 4H	32k	150k	3450	Y
ST9077A	19	IDE AT	2,7 RLL	2.5 4H	32k	150k	3546	Y
ST9080A	16	IDE AT	ZBR,2,7RLL	2.5 4H	32k	150k	3449	Y
ST9096A	16	IDE AT	ZBR	2.5 4H	64k	150k	3450	Y
ST9100A	16	IDE AT		2.5 4H	120k	300k		Y
ST9100AG	16	IDE AT	ZBR,1,7RLL	2.5 4H	120k	300k	3545	Y
ST91350AG	12	ATA-2 Fast	RLL ZBR	2.5 4H	103k	300k	4508	Y
ST9140AG	16	IDE AT	ZBR,1,7RLL	2.5 4H	64k	300k	3545	Y
ST9144A	16	IDE AT	ZBR,2,7RLL	2.5 4H	64k	150k	3450	Y
ST9145A	16	AT BUS	RLL ZBR	2.5 4H		150k	3449	Y
ST9145AG	16	IDE AT	ZBR,1,7RLL	2.5 4H	32k	150k	3449	Y
ST9150AG	16	IDE AT	ZBR,1,7RLL	2.5 4H	120k	300k	3980	Y
ST91685AG	12	ATA-2 Fast	RLL ZBR	2.5 4H	103k	300k	4508	Y
ST9190AG	16	IDE AT	ZBR,1,7RLL	2.5 4H	120k	300k	3545	Y
ST92255AG	12	ATA-2 Fast		2.5 4H	103k	300k	4508	Y
ST9235AG	16	IDE AT	RLL ZBR	2.5 4H	64k	150k	3449	Y
ST9235N	16	SCSI	ZBR,2,7RLL	2.5 4H	64k	150k	3449	Y
ST9240AG	16	ATA FAST	ZBR,1,7RLL	2.5 4H	120k	300k	3980	Y
ST9295AG	16	IDE AT	2,7 RLL	2.5 4H	120k	300k	3450	Y
ST9295N (never made)	16	SCSI	2,7 RLL	2.5 4H	64k	150k	3450	Y
ST9300AG	16	ATA FAST	ZBR,1,7RLL	2.5 4H	120k	300k	3980	Y
ST9385AG	16	ATA FAST	ZBR,1,7RLL	2.5 4H	120k	300k	3980	Y
ST9420AG	16	ATA-2 FAST		2.5 4H	120k	300k	4500	Y
ST9550AG	16	IDE AT	ZBR,1,7RLL	2.5 4H	120k	300k	3980	Y
ST9655AG	16	ATA FAST	ZBR,1,7RLL	2.5 4H	120k	300k	3980	Y
ST9816AG	16	ATA-2 FAST		2.5 4H	120k	300k	4500	Y
ST9840AG	14	ATA	PRML8,9	3.5 4H	107k	300k	4500	Y

SEQUEL, INC

5300	12	SCSI-2 FSTW	1,7 RLL	5.25 FH	512	300k	5400	Y
5350	12	SCSI-2 FSTW	1,7 RLL	5.25 FH	512k	300k	5400	Y
5400	12	SCSI-2 FSTW	1,7 RLL	5.25 FH	1024k	300k	5400	Y
EXT4175	27	ESDI	RLL	5.25 FH		20k	3600	Y
EXT4280	27	ESDI	RLL	5.25 FH		20k	3600	Y
EXT4380	27	ESDI	RLL	5.25 FH		20k	3600	Y
XT1050	30	ST412/506	MFM	5.25 FH		20k	3600	Y
XT1065	30	ST412/506	MFM	5.25 FH		20k	3600	Y
XT1085	28	ST412/506	MFM	5.25 FH		150k	3600	
XT1105	27	ST412/506	MFM	5.25 FH		20k	3600	Y
XT1120R	27	ST412/506	2,7 RLL	5.25 FH		150k	3600	
XT1140	27	ST412/506	MFM	5.25 FH		150k	3600	
XT1240R	27	ST412/506	2,7 RLL	5.25 FH		150k	3600	
XT2085	30	ST412/506	MFM	5.25 FH		30k	3600	Y
XT2140	30	ST412/506	MFM	5.25 FH		30k	3600	Y
XT2190	29	ST412/506	MFM	5.25 FH		150k	3600	
XT3170	30	SCSI	RLL	5.25 FH		20k	3600	
XT3280	30	SCSI		5.25 FH		20k	3600	
XT3380	27	SCSI		5.25 FH		20k	3600	
XT4170E	14	ESDI	1,7 RLL	5.25 FH		150k	3600	
XT4170S	14	SCSI	1,7 RLL	5.25 FH		150k	3600	

Drive Model	Format Size MB	Head	Cyl	Sect/ Trac	Translate H/C/S	RWC/ WPC	Land Zone
XT4380E	338	15	1224	36		NA/NA	AUTO
XT4380S	338	15	1224	36		NA/NA	AUTO
XT8380E	361	8	1632	53-54		NA/NA	AUTO
XT8380S	361	8	1632	54		NA/NA	AUTO
XT8760E	676	15	1632	53-54		NA/NA	AUTO
XT8760EH	676	15	1632	54		NA/NA	AUTO
XT8760S	670	15	1632	NA		NA/NA	AUTO
XT8760SH	670	15	1632	NA		NA/NA	AUTO
XT8800E	694	15	1274	54		NA/NA	AUTO

SHUGART

Drive Model	Format Size MB	Head	Cyl	Sect/ Trac	Translate H/C/S	RWC/ WPC	Land Zone
1002	5			17		---/---	
1004	10			17		---/---	
1006	30					---/---	
4004	14			17		---/---	
4008	29			17		---/---	
4100	56			17		---/---	
604	5	4	160	17		128/128	AUTO
606	7	6	160	17		128/128	AUTO
612	10	4	306	17		307/128	AUTO
706	6	2	320	17		321/128	AUTO
712	10	4	320	17		321/128	AUTO
725	20					---/---	

SIEMENS

Drive Model	Format Size MB	Head	Cyl	Sect/ Trac	Translate H/C/S	RWC/ WPC	Land Zone
1200	174	8	1216	35		NA/NA	AUTO
1300	261	12	1216	35		NA/NA	AUTO
2200	174	8	1216			NA/NA	AUTO
2300	261	12	1216	35		NA/NA	AUTO
4410	322	11	1100	52		NA/NA	AUTO
4420	334	11	1100	54		NA/NA	AUTO
5710	655	15				NA/NA	AUTO
5720	655	15				NA/NA	AUTO
5810	777	16				NA/NA	AUTO
5820	777	16				NA/NA	AUTO
6200	1200					NA/NA	AUTO
7520	655	15				NA/NA	AUTO

SONY

Drive Model	Format Size MB	Head	Cyl	Sect/ Trac	Translate H/C/S	RWC/ WPC	Land Zone
2020A	20					---/---	
2040A	40					---/---	
3080L	80					---/---	

STORAGE DIMENSIONS

Drive Model	Format Size MB	Head	Cyl	Sect/ Trac	Translate H/C/S	RWC/ WPC	Land Zone
AT100	109	8	1024	26		---/NONE	1023
AT1000S	1000	15				NA/NA	AUTO
AT100S	105	3				NA/NA	AUTO
AT120	119	15	918	17		NA/NA	AUTO
AT133	133	15	1024	17		---/NONE	1023
AT140	142	8	1024	34		---/NONE	1023
AT155E	158	9	1224	36		---/---	
AT155S	156	9	1224	36		---/---	
AT160	160	15	1224	17		---/NONE	1023
AT200	204	15	1024	26		---/NONE	1023
AT200S	204	7				---/---	
AT320S	320	15	1224	36		---/---	
AT335E	338	15	1224	36		---/---	
AT40	44	5	1024	17		---/NONE	1023
AT650E	651	15	1632	54		---/---	
AT650S	651	15	1632	54		---/---	
AT70	70			17		---/---	

Drive Model	Seek Time	Interface	Encode	Form Factor	cache kb	mtbf	RPM	Obsolete?
XT4380E	16	ESDI	1,7 RLL	5.25 FH		150k	3600	
XT4380S	16	SCSI	1,7 RLL	5.25 FH		150k	3600	
XT8380E	16	ESDI	1,7 RLL	5.25 FH		150k	3600	
XT8380S	14	SCSI	1,7 RLL	5.25 FH		150k	3600	
XT8760E	16	ESDI	1,7 RLL	5.25 FH		150k	3600	
XT8760EH	14	ESDI	1,7 RLL	5.25 FH		150k	3600	
XT8760S	16	SCSI	1,7 RLL	5.25 FH		150k	3600	
XT8760SH	14	SCSI	1,7 RLL	5.25 FH 256k		150k	3600	
XT8800E	14	ESDI	1,7 RLL	5.25 FH		150k	3600	

SHUGART

Drive Model	Seek Time	Interface	Encode	Form Factor	cache kb	mtbf	RPM	Obsolete?
1002		ST412/506	MFM	8.0 FH				Y
1004		ST412/506	MFM	8.0 FH				Y
1006		ST412/506	MFM	8.0				Y
4004		ST412/506	MFM					Y
4008		ST412/506	MFM	14.0				Y
4100		ST412/506	MFM					Y
604	27	ST412/506	MFM	5.25 FH				Y
606	27	ST412/506	MFM	5.25 FH				Y
612	27	ST412/506	MFM	5.25 FH				Y
706	27	ST412/506	MFM	5.25 FH				Y
712	27	ST412/506	MFM	5.25 FH				Y
725		ST412/506	MFM	5.25 HH				Y

SIEMENS

Drive Model	Seek Time	Interface	Encode	Form Factor	cache kb	mtbf	RPM	Obsolete?
1200	25	ESDI	2,7 RLL	5.25 FH				Y
1300	25	ESDI	2,7 RLL	5.25 FH				Y
2200	25	ESDI	2,7 RLL	5.25 FH				Y
2300	25	ESDI	2,7 RLL	5.25 FH				Y
4410	18	ESDI	2,7 RLL	5.25 FH		30k		Y
4420	16	SCSI	2,7 RLL	5.25 FH		40k		Y
5710	16	SCSI	2,7 RLL	5.25 FH				Y
5720	14	SCSI	2,7 RLL	5.25 FH				Y
5810	18	ESDI	2,7 RLL	5.25 FH				Y
5820	14	SCSI	2,7 RLL	5.25 FH				Y
6200	14	SCSI	2,7 RLL	5.25 FH				Y
7520	16	SCSI	2,7 RLL	5.25 FH				Y

SONY

Drive Model	Seek Time	Interface	Encode	Form Factor	cache kb	mtbf	RPM	Obsolete?
2020A		SCSI		3.5 HH				
2040A		SCSI		3.5 HH				
3080L		SCSI		3.5 3H				

STORAGE DIMENSIONS

Drive Model	Seek Time	Interface	Encode	Form Factor	cache kb	mtbf	RPM	Obsolete?
AT100		ST412/506	2,7 RLL					Y
AT1000S		SCSI				100k		Y
AT100S	19	SCSI	2,7 RLL	3.5 HH		150k		Y
AT120	26	ST412/506	MFM	5.25 FH		40k		Y
AT133		ST412/506	MFM					Y
AT140								Y
AT155E	14	ESDI	2,7 RLL	5.25 FH		40k		Y
AT155S	17	SCSI	2,7 RLL	5.25 FH		40k		Y
AT160	28	ST412/506	MFM	5.25 FH		40k		Y
AT200		ST412/506	2,7 RLL	3.5 HH				Y
AT200S	16	SCSI	2,7 RLL	3.5 HH		150k		Y
AT320S	17	SCSI	2,7 RLL	5.25 FH		40k		Y
AT335E	16	ESDI	2,7 RLL	5.25 FH		40k		Y
AT40		ST412/506	MFM					Y
AT650E	16	ESDI	2,7 RLL	5.25 FH		40k		Y
AT650S	16	SCSI	2,7 RLL	5.25 FH		40k		Y
AT70	27	ST412/506	MFM	5.25 FH		40k		Y

Drive Model	Format Size MB	Head	Cyl	Sect/ Trac	Translate H/C/S	RWC/ WPC	Land Zone
CDASM-1051F	1000					---/---	
CDASM-2105F	2100					---/---	
CDASM-4005F	4300					---/---	
DMH-A02W	2100					---/---	
DMH-A04W	4300					---/---	
DMH-B02W	2100					---/---	
DMH-B04W	4300					---/---	
DMH-B09W	9100					---/---	
LAN1050F	1050					---/---	
LAN2101F	2101					---/---	
LAN2105F	2105					---/---	
LAN4005	4300					---/---	
LAN9000F	9000					---/---	
MAC-195	195	7				NA/NA	AUTO
PS155E	156	9	1224	36		---/---	
PS155S	156	9	1224	36		---/---	
PS320S	320	15	1224	36		---/---	
PS335E	338	15	1224	36		---/---	
PS650S	651	15	1632	16		---/---	
XT100	109	8	1024	26		---/NONE	1023
XT120	119	15	918	17		---/NONE	
XT200	204	15	1024	26		---/NONE	1023
XT40	44	5	1024	17		---/NONE	1023
XT70	71	8	1024	17		---/NONE	1023

SYQUEST TECHNOLOGY

Drive Model	Format Size MB	Head	Cyl	Sect/ Trac	Translate H/C/S	RWC/ WPC	Land Zone
EZ135 (removable)	135					---/---	
EZ135 (removable)	135					---/---	
EZ230 (removable)	230					---/---	
EZ230 (removable)	230					---/---	
SQ105 (removable)	105					---/---	
SQ200	200					---/---	
SQ225F	20			17		---/---	
SQ270 (removable)	270					---/---	
SQ306F	5			17		---/---	
SQ306R	5	2	306	17		---/---	
SQ306RD	5	2	306	17		307/307	
SQ3105 (removable)	105	2			16/420/32	---/---	
SQ312	10	2	615	17		---/---	
SQ312RD	10	2	615	17		616/616	
SQ319	10	2	612	17		---/---	
SQ325	21	4	612	17		612/612	
SQ325F	20	4	615	17		616/616	
SQ3270 (removable)	256	2			16/1024/32	---/---	
SQ338F	30	6	615	17		616/616	
SQ340AF	38	6	640	17		616/616	
SQ5110C (removable)	89					---/---	
SQ5200C (removable)	200					---/---	
SQ555 (removable)	44					---/---	
SQ88	88					---/---	
SYJET 1.3 (removeable)	1300					---/---	
SYJET 1.5 (removeable)	1500					---/---	
SYJET 1.5 (removeable)	1500					---/---	
SYJET 650 (removeable)	650					---/---	

TANDON COMPUTER CORPORATION

Drive Model	Format Size MB	Head	Cyl	Sect/ Trac	Translate H/C/S	RWC/ WPC	Land Zone
TM2085	74	9	1004	17		1005/1005	
TM2128	115	9	1004	26		1005/1005	
TM2170	154	9	1344	26		1345/1345	
TM244	41	4	782	26		783/783	
TM246	62	6	782	26		783/783	
TM251	5	2	306	17		---/---	

Drive Model	Seek Time	Interface	Encode	Form Factor	cache kb	mtbf	RPM	Obsolete?
CDASM-1051F	9.5	SCSI-2 FAST		3.5		800k	5400	
CDASM-2105F	8.5	SCSI-2 FAST		3.5		800k	7200	
CDASM-4005F	8.5	SCSI-2 FAST		3.5		800k	7200	
DMH-A02W	9.5	SCSI-2 FAST		3.5		800k	5400	
DMH-A04W	9.5	SCSI-2 FAST		3.5		800k	5400	
DMH-B02W	8.5	SCSI-2 FSTW		3.5		800k	7200	
DMH-B04W	8.5	SCSI-2 FSTW		3.5		800k	7200	
DMH-B09W	9	SCSI-2FstWd		3.5		1000k	7200	
LAN1050F	9.5	SCSI-2 FAST		3.5		500k	5400	
LAN2101F	9	SCSI-2 FAST		3.5		500k	5400	
LAN2105F	8.5	SCSI-2 FAST		3.5		500k	7200	
LAN4005	8.5	SCSI-2 FAST		3.5		800k	7200	
LAN9000F	11.5	SCSI-2 FAST		5.25 FH		500k	5400	
MAC-195	15	SCSI	2,7 RLL	3.5 HH		150k		Y
PS155E	14	ESDI	2,7 RLL	5.25 FH		70k		Y
PS155S	14	SCSI	2,7 RLL	5.25 FH		70k		Y
PS335S	16	SCSI	2,7 RLL	5.25 FH		150k		Y
PS335E	15	ESDI	2,7 RLL	5.25 FH		70k		Y
PS650S	15	SCSI	2,7 RLL	5.25 FH		100k		Y
XT100		ST412/506	2,7 RLL					Y
XT120		ST412/506						Y
XT200		ST412/506	2,7 RLL					Y
XT40		ST412/506	MFM					Y
XT70		ST412/506	MFM					Y

SYQUEST TECHNOLOGY

Drive Model	Seek Time	Interface	Encode	Form Factor	cache kb	mtbf	RPM	Obsolete?
EZ135 (removable)	13	SCSI-2	1,7 RLL	3.5 3H	64k	200k	3600	
EZ135 (removable)	13	ATA-2	1,7 RLL	3.5 3H	64k	200k	3600	
EZ230 (removable)	13.5	SCSI		3.5 3H		200k		
EZ230 (removable)	13.5	EIDE		3.5 3H		200k		
SQ200	18			5.25 HH	64k	200k		
SQ105 (removable)	14.5	IDE AT		3.5 3H	64k	100k	3600	
SQ225F	99		MFM	5.25 HH				Y
SQ270 (removable)	13.5	IDE AT		3.5 3H	128k	100k	3600	
SQ306F	99	ST412/506	MFM	5.25 HH				Y
SQ306R	99	ST412/506	MFM	5.25 HH				Y
SQ306RD	99	ST412/506	MFM	5.25 HH				Y
SQ3105 (removable)	14.5	ATA-2	1,7 RLL	3.5 3H	64k	100k	3600	
SQ312	80	ST412/506	MFM	5.25 HH				Y
SQ312RD	80	ST412/506	MFM	5.25 HH				Y
SQ319	80	ST412/506	RLL	5.25 HH				Y
SQ325	80	ST412/506	MFM	5.25 HH				Y
SQ325F	80	ST412/506	MFM	5.25 HH				Y
SQ3270 (removable)	13.5	ATA-2	1,7 RLL	3.5 3H	128k	100k	3600	
SQ338F	80	ST412/506	MFM	5.25 HH				Y
SQ340AF	80	ST412/506	MFM	5.25 HH				Y
SQ5110C (removable)	20	SCSI-2		5.25 HH	64k	100k	3220	
SQ5200C (removable)	18	SCSI-2		5.25 HH	64k	100k	3220	
SQ555 (removable)	20	SCSI-2		5.25 HH	64k	100k	3220	
SQ88	20			5.25 HH	32k	100k		
SYJET 1.3 (removable)		SCSI		3.5 HH	256k	250k	5400	
SYJET 1.5 (removeable)	12	SCSI-2		3.5 HH	512k	250k		
SYJET 1.5 (removeable)		EIDE		3.5 HH	512k	250k		
SYJET 650 (removeable)		SCSI		3.5 HH	256k	250k	5400	

TANDON COMPUTER CORPORATION

Drive Model	Seek Time	Interface	Encode	Form Factor	cache kb	mtbf	RPM	Obsolete?
TM2085	25	SCSI	MFM	5.25 FH				Y
TM2128	25	SCSI	2,7 RLL	5.25 FH				Y
TM2170	25	SCSI	2,7 RLL	5.25 FH				Y
TM244	37	ST412/506	2,7 RLL	3.5 HH				Y
TM246	37	ST412/506	2,7 RLL	3.5 HH				Y
TM251		ST412/506	MFM	5.25				Y

Drive Model	Format Size MB	Head	Cyl	Sect/Trac	Translate H/C/S	RWC/WPC	Land Zone
TM252	10	4	306	17		307/307	
TM261	10	2	615	17		616/616	
TM262	21	4	615	17		616/616	AUTO
TM262R	20	2	782	26		783/783	
TM264	41	4	782	26		783/783	
TM3085	71	8	1024	17		1024/1024	
TM3085R	105	8	1024	26		1024/1024	
TM344	41	4	782	26		783/783	
TM346	62	6	782	26		783/783	
TM361	10	2	615	17		616/616	
TM362	20	4	615	17		616/616	615
TM362R	20	2	782	26		783/783	
TM364	41	4	782	26		783/783	
TM501	5	2	306	17		128/153	
TM502	10	4	306	17		128/153	
TM503	15	6	306	17		128/153	
TM601	3					---/---	
TM602S	5	4	153	17		128/128	
TM602SE	12		153	17		---/---	
TM603S	10	6	153	17		128/128	
TM603SE	12	6	230	17		128/128	
TM702	20	4	615	26		616/616	AUTO
TM702AT	21	4	615	17		616/616	615
TM703	30	5	733	17		734/734	695
TM703AT	31	5	733	17		733/733	733
TM703C	25	17	733				
TM705	41	5	962	17		---/NONE	962
TM755	42	5	981	17		982/982	981

TANDY CORP

25-1045	28					---/---	AUTO
25-1046	43	4	782	27		NA/NA	AUTO
25-4130	100	4	1219			NA/NA	AUTO

TEAC AMERICA, INC.

Drive Model	Format Size MB	Head	Cyl	Sect/Trac	Translate H/C/S	RWC/WPC	Land Zone
SD150	10	4	306	17		---/---	
SD240	43	2	1000	42		NA/NA	AUTO
SD260	63	2	1226	50		NA/NA	AUTO
SD3105A	105	4	1282	40	8/641/40	NA/NA	AUTO
SD3105S	105	4	1282	40		NA/NA	AUTO
SD3210A	215	4	1695	62	8/847/62	NA/NA	AUTO
SD3210S	215	4	1695	62		NA/NA	AUTO
SD3240	245	4	1930		8/965/62	---/---	
SD3250N (removable)	252					NA/NA	AUTO
SD3360N (removable)	363					NA/NA	AUTO
SD340A	43	2	1050	40	4/525/40	NA/NA	AUTO
SD340HA	43	2	1050	40		NA/NA	AUTO
SD340HS	43	2	1050	40		---/---	AUTO
SD340S	43	2	1050	40		NA/NA	AUTO
SD3540N (removable)	540					---/---	AUTO
SD380	86	4	1025	40	8/965/62	NA/300	1025
SD380HA	86	4	1050	40		NA/NA	AUTO
SD380HS	86	4	1050	40		---/---	AUTO
SD380S	86	4	1050	40		---/---	AUTO
SD510	10	4	306	17		128/128	
SD520	20	4	615	17		128/128	
SD540	40	8	615	17		---/---	

TEXAS INSTRUMENTS

525-122	20					---/---	
DB260	212	8				NA/NA	AUTO
DB380	333	15				64/64	

Drive Model	Seek Time	Interface	Encode	Form Factor	cache kb	Obsolete? mtbf	RPM ⇓
TM252	85	ST412/506	MFM	5.25 HH			Y
TM261		ST412/506	MFM	5.25			Y
TM262	65	ST412/506	MFM	3.5 HH			Y
TM262R	85	ST412/506	2,7 RLL	3.5 HH			Y
TM264	85	ST412/506	2,7 RLL	3.5 HH			Y
TM3085	35	ST412/506	MFM	5.25			Y
TM3085R	35	ST412/506	2,7 RLL	5.25			Y
TM344	35	ST412/506	2,7 RLL	3.5 HH			Y
TM346	35	ST412/506	2,7 RLL	3.5 HH			Y
TM361	27	ST412/506	MFM	5.25			Y
TM362	85	ST412/506	MFM	5.25			Y
TM362R	85	ST412/506	2,7 RLL	3.5 HH			Y
TM364	85	ST412/506	2,7 RLL	3.5 HH			Y
TM501	85	ST412/506	MFM	5.25 FH			Y
TM502	85	ST412/506	MFM	5.25 FH			Y
TM503	85	ST412/506	MFM	5.25 FH			Y
TM601		ST412/506	MFM	5.25 FH			Y
TM602S	85	ST412/506	MFM	5.25 FH			Y
TM602SE		ST412/506	MFM	5.25 FH			Y
TM603S		ST412/506	MFM	5.25 FH			Y
TM603SE		ST412/506	MFM	5.25 FH			Y
TM702	27	ST412/506	MFM	5.25 FH			Y
TM702AT	27	ST412/506	MFM	5.25 FH			Y
TM703	40	ST412/506	MFM	5.25 FH			Y
TM703AT	40	ST412/506	MFM	5.25 FH			Y
TM703C		ST412/506	MFM	5.25 FH			Y
TM705		ST412/506	MFM	5.25 FH			Y
TM755	27	ST412/506	MFM	5.25 FH			Y

TANDY CORP

Drive Model	Seek Time	Interface	Encode	Form Factor	cache kb	Obsolete? mtbf	RPM ⇓
25-1045	28	IDE XT		3.5 HH			Y
25-1046	28	IDE XT	2,7 RLL	3.5 HH		40k	Y
25-4130	17	IDE XT	2,7 RLL	3.5 HH			Y

TEAC AMERICA, INC.

Drive Model	Seek Time	Interface	Encode	Form Factor	cache kb	Obsolete? mtbf	RPM ⇓
SD150		ST412/506	MFM	5.25			Y
SD240	19	IDE AT	1,7 RLL	2.5	32k	100k	3600 Y
SD260	19	IDE AT	1,7 RLL	2.5	32k	100k	3600 Y
SD3105A	19	IDE AT	2,7 RLL	3.5 3H	64k	30k	3600 Y
SD3105S	19	SCSI	2,7 RLL	3.5 3H	64k	30k	3600 Y
SD3210A	17	IDE AT	1,7 RLL	3.5 3H	65k	100k	3600 Y
SD3210S	17	SCSI	1,7 RLL	3.5 3H	63k	100k	3600 Y
SD3240	17	IDE AT	1,7 RLL	3.5 3H	64k	100k	3600 Y
SD3250N (removable)	17	IDE		5.25 HH		250k	3600
SD3360N (removable)	17	IDE		5.25 HH		250k	3600
SD340A	23	IDE AT	2,7 RLL	3.5 3H	64k	30k	2358 Y
SD340HA	19	IDE AT	2,7 RLL	3.5 3H		30k	2358 Y
SD340HS	19	SCSI	2,7 RLL	3.5 3H		30k	2358 Y
SD340S	23	SCSI	2,7 RLL	3.5 3H	28k	30k	2358 Y
SD3540N (removable)	11	IDE		5.25 HH		250k	4201
SD380	22	IDE AT	2,7 RLL	3.5 3H		30k	2358 Y
SD380HA	19	IDE AT	2,7 RLL	3.5 3H		30k	2358 Y
SD380HS	19	SCSI	2,7 RLL	3.5 3H		30k	2358 Y
SD380S	22	SCSI	2,7 RLL	3.5 3H		30k	2358 Y
SD510	27	ST412/506	MFM	5.25 FH			Y
SD520	27	ST412/506	MFM	5.25 FH			Y
SD540	40			5.25 HH		20k	3600 Y

TEXAS INSTRUMENTS

Drive Model	Seek Time	Interface	Encode	Form Factor	cache kb	Obsolete? mtbf	RPM ⇓
525-122		ST412/506	MFM	5.25 FH			Y
DB260	16	SCSI		3.5 HH			Y
DB380	16	SCSI	MFM	5.25 FH			Y

Drive Model	Format Size MB	Head	Cyl	Sect/Trac	Translate H/C/S	RWC/WPC	Land Zone
TI5	5	4	153	17		64/64	

TOSHIBA AMERICA, INC.

Drive Model	Format Size MB	Head	Cyl	Sect/Trac	Translate H/C/S	RWC/WPC	Land Zone
HDD2616	2160					---/---	
HDD2712	1350					---/---	
MK1002MAV	1602500/3					---/---	
MK1034FC	107	4	1345		8/664/39	---/---	
MK1122FC	43	2	977		5/988/17	---/---	
MK130	53	7	733			---/---	
MK1301MAV	1350					---/---	
MK132FA	18					---/---	
MK133FA	30					---/---	
MK134FA	44	7	733	17		---/---	
MK134FA(R)	65	7	733	26		---/---	
MK1401MAV	1440					---/---	
MK1422FCV	86	2	988		10/988/17	---/---	
MK1522FCV	126	2	812		8/812/38	NA/NA	AUTO
MK153FA	74	5	830	35		NA/NA	
MK153FA-I	74	5	830	35		NA/NA	AUTO
MK153FB	76	5	830	35		---/---	
MK154FA	104	7	830	35		NA/NA	
MK154FA-I	104	7	830	35		NA/NA	AUTO
MK154FB	106	7	830	35		---/---	
MK156FA	148	10	830	35		NA/NA	
MK156FB	152	10	830	35		---/---	
MK158FA	173u	10	830			---/---	
MK1624FCV	213	4			16/684/38	NA/NA	AUTO
MK1722FCV	131	2			8/842/38	---/---	
MK1724FCV	262	4	841		16/842/38	NA/NA	AUTO
MK1824FBV	352	4	2050			---/---	
MK1824FCV	353	4		63	16/682/63	NA/NA	AUTO
MK182FB	83	5	823			---/---	
MK184FB	116	7	823			---/---	
MK186FB	166	10	823			---/---	
MK1924FBV	543	4	2920			---/---	
MK1924FCV	543	4			16/1053/63	NA/NA	AUTO
MK1926FBV	815	6	2920			---/---	
MK1926FCV	815	6			16/1579/63	NA/NA	AUTO
MK2024FC	86	4	977	43	10/988/17	NA/NA	AUTO
MK2101MAN	2160				16/4200/63	---/---	
MK2103MAV	2160				16/4200/63	---/---	
MK2124FC	130	4	934	55	16/934/17	NA/NA	AUTO
MK2224FB	213	4	1560	83		NA/NA	AUTO
MK2224FC	213	4	684		16/684/38	NA/NA	AUTO
MK2326FB	340	6	1830	74		NA/NA	AUTO
MK2326FC	340	6			14/969/49	NA/NA	AUTO
MK2326FCH	340					---/---	
MK232FB	45	3	845	35		---/---	AUTO
MK232FBS	45	3	845	35		NA/NA	
MK232FC	45	3	845	35		NA/NA	
MK233FB	75	5	845	35		---/---	AUTO
MK234FB	106	7	845	35		---/---	AUTO
MK234FBS	106	7	845	35		---/---	
MK234FC	106	7	845	35	7/845/35	---/---	
MK234FCH	106	7	845	35	7/845/35	---/---	AUTO
MK2428FB	524	8	1920	83		NA/NA	AUTO
MK2428FC	524	8		63	16/1016/63	NA/NA	AUTO
MK250FA	382	10	1224	35		NA/NA	
MK250FB	382	10	1224	35		NA/NA	
MK2526FC	528	6		63	16/1023/63	NA/NA	AUTO
MK2528FC	704	8			16/1365/63	NA/NA	AUTO
MK253FA	162					---/---	
MK253FB	158					---/---	

Drive Model	Seek Time	Interface	Encode	Form Factor	cache kb	mtbf	RPM	Obsolete?
TI5	27	ST412/506	MFM	5.25 FH				Y

TOSHIBA AMERICA, INC.

Drive Model	Seek Time	Interface	Encode	Form Factor	cache kb	mtbf	RPM	Obsolete?
HDD2616	13	ATA-2		2.5 4H	128k		300k	
HDD2712	13	ATA-2		2.5 4H	128k			
MK1002MAV	13	ATA-2		2.5 4H	128k		4200	
MK1034FC	16	IDE AT	2,7 RLL	3.5 3H	64k	40k	3414	
MK1122FC	23	IDE AT	2,7 RLL	3.5 HH	32k	40k	3600	Y
MK130	25	ST412/506	MFM	3.5 HH		30k		Y
MK1301MAV	13	ATA-2 Fast	PRML	2.5 4H	128k	300k	4200	
MK132FA		ST412/506	MFM	3.5 HH		300k	4200	
MK133FA		ST412/506	MFM	3.5 HH				Y
MK134FA	25	ST412/506	MFM	3.5 HH		30k	3600	Y
MK134FA(R)	23	ST412/506	2,7 RLL	3.5 HH				Y
MK1401MAV	13	ATA-2		2.5 4H	128k		4200	
MK1422FCV	15	IDE AT		2.5 4H	128k	150k	3600	Y
MK1522FCV	15	IDE AT		2.5 4H	128k	150k	3600	Y
MK153FA	23	ESDI		5.25 FH		30k		Y
MK153FA-I	23	ESDI	2,7 RLL	5.25 FH		30k		Y
MK153FB	23	ESDI	2,7 RLL	5.25 FH	32k	30k	3600	Y
MK154FA	23	SCSI	2,7 RLL	5.25 FH		30k	3600	Y
MK154FA-I	23	ESDI	2,7 RLL	5.25 FH		30k		Y
MK154FB	23	SCSI	2,7 RLL	5.25 FH	32k	30k	3600	Y
MK156FA	23	ESDI	2,7 RLL	5.25 FH		30k		Y
MK156FB	23	SCSI	2,7 RLL	5.25 FH	32k	30k	3600	Y
MK158FA	23	ESDI	2,7 RLL	5.25 FH		30k	3600	Y
MK1624FCV	13	IDE AT		2.5 4H	128k	150k	4000	Y
MK1722FCV	13	IDE AT		2.5 4H	128k		4000	Y
MK1724FCV	12	IDE AT		2.5 4H	128k	150k	4000	
MK1824FBV	13	SCSI-2	1,7 RLL	2.5 4H	128k	300k	4200	
MK1824FCV	13	ATA-2		2.5 4H	128k	300k	4200	
MK182FB	18	SMD/CMD	2,7 RLL	8.00 FH		20k	3600	
MK184FB	18	SMD/CMD	2,7 RLL	8.00 FH		20k	3600	
MK186FB	18	SMD/CMD	2,7 RLL	8.00 FH		20k	3600	
MK1924FBV	13	SCSI-2	8,9RLL	2.5 4H	128k		4200	
MK1924FCV	13	ATA-2		2.5 4H	128k	300k	4200	
MK1926FBV	13	SCSI-2	8,9RLL	2.5 4H	128k		4200	
MK1926FCV	13	ATA-2		2.5 4H	128k	300k	4200	
MK2024FC	19	IDE AT	2,7 RLL	2.5 4H	32k	80k	3600	Y
MK2101MAN	13	ATA-2	PRML	2.5 4H	128k	300k	4200	
MK2103MAV	13	ATA-3		2.5 4H	128k	300k	4200	
MK2124FC	17	IDE AT	2,7 RLL	2.5 4H	32k	150k	3600	Y
MK2224FC	12	SCSI-2 FAST		2.5 4H	128k	150k	4000	Y
MK2224FC	12	IDE AT		2.5 4H	128k	150k	4000	Y
MK2326FB	12	SCSI-2 FAST		2.5 4H	128k	150k	4200	
MK2326FC	12	IDE AT		2.5 4H	128k	150k	4200	
MK2326FCH		IDE AT		2.5 4H	128k	150k	4200	
MK232FB	25	SCSI		3.5 HH		30k	3600	Y
MK232FBS	19	SCSI		3.5 HH		30k		Y
MK232FC	25	IDE AT	2,7 RLL	3.5 HH		30k		Y
MK233FB	25	SCSI	2,7 RLL	3.5 HH		30	3600	Y
MK234FB	25	SCSI	2,7 RLL	3.5 HH		30k	3600	Y
MK234FBS	19	SCSI	2,7 RLL	3.5 HH		30k		Y
MK234FC	25	IDE AT	2,7 RLL	3.5 HH		30k	3600	Y
MK234FCH	25	IDE AT	2,7 RLL	3.5 HH		30k		Y
MK2428FB	12	SCSI-2 FAST		2.5 4H	512k	150k	4000	
MK2428FC	12	IDE AT		2.5 4H	512k	150k	4000	
MK250FA	18	ESDI	2,7 RLL	5.25 FH		30k		
MK250FB	18	SCSI	2,7 RLL	5.25 FH		30k		
MK2526FC	13	IDE AT		2.5 4H	128k		4200	
MK2528FC	13	IDE AT		2.5 4H	128k		4200	
MK253FA		ESDI		5.25 FH				Y
MK253FB		SCSI		5.25 FH				Y

Drive Model	Format Size MB	Head	Cyl	Sect/ Trac	Translate H/C/S	RWC/ WPC	Land Zone
MK254FA	227					---/---	
MK254FB	221					---/---	
MK256FA	325					---/---	
MK256FB	316					---/---	
MK256FB	315					---/---	
MK2616	2160	10				---/---	
MK2628FC	811	8			16/1571/63	NA/NA	AUTO
MK2712	1350					---/---	
MK2720FC	1350	10			16/2633/63	NA/NA	AUTO
MK2728FC	1080	8			16/1579/63	---/---	
MK286FC	374	11	823			---/---	
MK288FC	510	15	823			---/---	
MK3003MAN	3008				16/6409/63	---/---	
MK3303	3300					---/---	
MK355FA	405	9	1661	53		---/---	
MK355FB	405	9	1661	53		---/---	
MK356FA	495					---/---	
MK358FA	675	15	1661	53		---/---	
MK358FB	675	15	1661	53		---/---	
MK388FA	720	15	1162			NA/NA	AUTO
MK438FB	900	11	1980			NA/NA	AUTO
MK537FB	1064	13	1980	NA		NA/NA	AUTO
MK538FB	1230	15	1980	NA		---/512	830
MK53FA	36	5	830	17		830/512	830
MK53FA(M)	36	5	830	26		831/831	
MK53FA(R)	43	5	830	17		830/512	
MK53FB	36	5	830	17		830/512	
MK53FB(M)	36	5	830	26		831/831	
MK53FB(R)	64	5	830	17		830/512	
MK53FB-I	36	5	830	17		831/512	830
MK54FA(M)	60	7	830	26		831/831	
MK54FA(R)	90	7	830	17		830/512	
MK54FB(M)	60	7	830	26		831/831	
MK54FB(R)	90	7	830	17		830/512	830
MK54FB-I	50	7	830			NA/NA	
MK556FA	152	10	830	17		831/831	
MK56FA(M)	86	10	830	26		---/512	830
MK56FA(R)	129	10	830	17		830/512	
MK56FB(M)	86	10	830	26		831/831	
MK56FB(R)	129	10	830	17		830/512	830
MK56FB-I	72	10	830	17		---/---	
MK72PC	72	10	830	26		---/---	
MK72PCR	109	10	830	17		830/512	830
MKM0351E	36	5	830	17		830/512	830
MKM0351J	36	5	830	17		---/512	830
MKM0352E	50	7	830	17		---/512	830
MKM0352J	50	7	830	17		830/512	830
MKM0353E	72	10	830	17		830/512	830
MKM0353J	72	10	830	35		NA/NA	AUTO
MKM0363A	74	5	830	35		NA/NA	AUTO
MKM0363J	74	5	830	35		NA/NA	AUTO
MKM0364A	104	7	830	35		NA/NA	AUTO
MKM0364J	104	7	830	17		830/512	
MKM0381E	36	5	830	17		830/512	830
MKM0381J	36	5	830	17		---/512	830
MKM0382E	50	7	830	17		---/512	830
MKM0382J	50	7	830	17		830/512	830
MKM0383E	72	10	830	17		830/512	830
MKM0383J	72	10	830	17		830/512	830

TULIN

Drive Model	Format Size MB	Head	Cyl	Sect/ Trac	Translate H/C/S	RWC/ WPC	Land Zone
TL213	10	2	640	17		656/656	640
TL226	22	4	640	17		656/656	656

Drive Model	Seek Time	Interface	Encode	Form Factor	cache kb	mtbf	RPM	Obsolete?
MK254FA		ESDI		5.25 FH				Y
MK254FB		SCSI		5.25 FH				Y
MK256FA		ESDI		5.25 FH				
MK256FB		SCSI		5.25 FH				
MK256FB		SCSI		5.25 FH				
MK2616	13	ATA-2		2.5 4H	128k		4200	
MK2628FC	13	ATA-2		2.5 4H	128k	300k	4200	
MK2712	13	ATA-2		2.5 4H	128k		4200	
MK2720FC	13	ATA-2		2.5 4H	128k	300k	4200	
MK2728FC	13	ATA-2		2.5 4H	128k	300k	4200	
MK286FC	18	HSMD	2,7 RLL	8.00 FH		35k	3600	
MK288FC	18	HSMD	2,7 RLL	8.00 FH		35k	3600	
MK3003MAN	13	ATA-2		2.5 4H	128k		4852	
MK3303	13	ATA-3		2.5 4H		300k	4852	
MK355FA	16	ESDI	1,7 RLL	5.25 FH	64k	30k	3600	
MK355FB	16	SCSI	2,7 RLL	5.25 FH	64k	30k	3600	
MK356FA		SCSI	RLL	5.25 FH				
MK358FA	16	ESDI	1,7 RLL	5.25 FH	64k	30k	3600	
MK358FB	16	SCSI-2	2,7 RLL	5.25 FH	64k	30k		
MK388FA	18	HSMD	2,7 RLL	8.00 FH		35k	3600	
MK438FB	12	SCSI-2	1,7 RLL	3.5 HH	512k	200		
MK537FB	12	SCSI-2	1,7 RLL	3.5 HH	512k	200k		
MK538FB	12	SCSI-2	1,7 RLL	3.5 HH	512k	200k		
MK53FA	30	ST412/506	MFM	5.25 FH		20k		Y
MK53FA(M)	25	ST412/506	MFM	5.25 FH		20k		Y
MK53FA(R)	30	ST412/506	2,7 RLL	5.25 FH		20k		Y
MK53FB	25	ST412/506	MFM	5.25 FH		20k		Y
MK53FB(M)	25	ST412/506	MFM	5.25 FH		20k		Y
MK53FB(R)	30	ST412/506	2,7 RLL	5.25 FH		20k		Y
MK53FB-I		ST412/506	MFM	5.25 FH		20k		Y
MK54FA	30	ST412/506	MFM	5.25 FH		20k		Y
MK54FA(M)	25	ST412/506	MFM	5.25 FH		20k		Y
MK54FA(R)	30	ST412/506	2,7 RLL	5.25 FH		20k		Y
MK54FB(M)	25	ST412/506	MFM	5.25 FH		20k		Y
MK54FB(R)	25	ST412/506	2,7 RLL	5.25 FH		20k		Y
MK54FB-I	25	ST412/506	MFM	5.25 FH		20k		Y
MK556FA	23	ESDI		5.25 FH		30k		Y
MK56FA(M)	30	ST412/506	MFM	5.25 FH		20k		Y
MK56FA(R)	30	ST412/506	2,7 RLL	5.25 FH		20k		Y
MK56FB(M)	25	ST412/506	MFM	5.25 FH		20k		Y
MK56FB(R)	25	ST412/506	2,7 RLL	5.25 FH		20k		Y
MK56FB-I	25	ST412/506	MFM	5.25 FH		20k		Y
MK72PC	25	ST412/506	MFM	3.5 HH				Y
MK72PCR	25	ST412/506	2,7 RLL	3.5 HH				Y
MKM0351E	25	ST412/506	MFM	5.25 FH		20k		Y
MKM0351J	25	ST412/506	MFM	5.25 FH		20k		Y
MKM0352E	30	ST412/506	MFM	5.25 FH		20k		Y
MKM0352J	30	ST412/506	MFM	5.25 FH		20k		Y
MKM0353E	25	ST412/506	MFM	5.25 FH		20k		Y
MKM0353J	25	ST412/506	MFM	5.25 FH		20k		Y
MKM0363A	23	ESDI	2,7 RLL	5.25 FH		30k		Y
MKM0363J	23	SCSI	2,7 RLL	5.25 FH		30k		Y
MKM0364A	23	ESDI	2,7 RLL	5.25 FH		30k		Y
MKM0364J	23	ESDI	2,7 RLL	5.25 FH		30k		Y
MKM0381E	25	ST412/506	MFM	5.25 FH		20k		Y
MKM0381J	25	ST412/506	MFM	5.25 FH		20k		Y
MKM0382E	30	ST412/506	MFM	5.25 FH		20k		Y
MKM0382J	30	ST412/506	MFM	5.25 FH		20k		Y
MKM0383E	25	ST412/506	MFM	5.25 FH		20k		Y
MKM0383J	25	ST412/506	MFM	5.25 FH		20k		Y

TULIN

Drive Model	Seek Time	Interface	Encode	Form Factor	cache kb	mtbf	RPM	Obsolete?
TL213	27	ST412/506	MFM	5.25 HH				Y
TL226	85	ST412/506	MFM	5.25 HH				Y

Drive Model	Format Size MB	Head	Cyl	Sect/ Trac	Translate H/C/S	RWC/ WPC	Land Zone
TL238	22	4	640	17		---/NONE	640
TL240	33	6	640	17		656/656	656
TL258	32	6	640	17		---/NONE	640
TL326	22	4	640	17		641/641	640
TL340	33	6	640	17		641/641	640

VERTEX (SEE PRIAM)

| | | | | | | ---/--- | |

WESTERN DIGITAL

Drive Model	Format Size MB	Head	Cyl	Sect/ Trac	Translate H/C/S	RWC/ WPC	Land Zone
PhD1000	1083					---/---	
PhD1400	1400					---/---	
PhD2100	2168					---/---	
PIRANHA 105A	1104	4				NA/NA	AUTO
PIRANHA 105S	1104	4				NA/NA	AUTO
PIRANHA 210A	210					---/---	
PIRANHA 210S	210					---/---	
WD140	40					---/---	
WD2120	125					---/---	
WD262	20	4	615	17		616/616	616
WD280	80					---/---	
WD344R	40	4	782	26		783/783	783
WD362	20	4	615	17		616/616	616
WD382R	20	2	782	26		783/783	782
WD383R	30	4	615	26		616/616	616
WD384R	40	4	782	26		783/783	783
WD544R	40	4	782	26		783/783	783
WD562-5	21	4	615	17		---/---	
WD582R	20	2	782	26		783/783	783
WD583R	30	4	615	26		616/616	616
WD584R	40	4	782	26		783/783	783
WD93018-A	21					---/---	
WD93020-XE1	20	4	615	17		NA/NA	616
WD93023-A	21					---/---	
WD93024-A	21	2	782	27	4/615/17	NA/NA	783
WD93024-X	21	2	782	27		NA/NA	783
WD93028-A	21	2	782	27		NA/NA	783
WD93028-AD	21	2	782	27	4/615/17	NA/NA	783
WD93028-X	21	2	782	27		NA/NA	783
WD93034-X	32	3	782	27		NA/NA	783
WD93038-X	32	3	782	27		NA/NA	783
WD93044-A	43	4	782	27	5/977/17	NA/NA	783
WD93044-X	43	4	782	27		NA/NA	862
WD93048-A	40	4	782	27		NA/NA	783
WD93048-AD	43	4	782	27		NA/NA	783
WD93048-X	43	4	782	27		NA/NA	783
WD95024-A	21	2	782	27	4/615/17	NA/NA	783
WD95024-X	21	2	782	27		783/783	783
WD95028-A	20	2	782	27		NA/NA	783
WD95028-AD	21	2	782	27		783/783	783
WD95028-X	20	2	782	27		NA/NA	783
WD95034-X	32	3	782	27		783/783	783
WD95038-X	30	3	782	27		NA/NA	783
WD95044-A	43	4	782	27	4/782/27	783/783	783
WD95044-X	43	4	782	27	4/782/27	783/783	783
WD95048-A	40	4	782	27	4/782/27	NA/NA	783
WD95048-AD	43	4	782	27	4/782/27	NA/NA	783
WD95048-X	40	4	782	27	4/782/27	NA/NA	783
WDAB130 (Tidbit)	31	5	733	17	4/916/17	734/734	AUTO
WDAB140	42	2	1390		5/980/17	---/---	
WDAB260 (Tidbit)	62	4	1020	17		NA/NA	AUTO
WDAC11000	1056	16	2046	63		---/---	

Drive Model	Seek Time	Interface	Encode	Form Factor	cache kb	mtbf	RPM	Obsolete?
TL238		ST412/506	MFM	5.25 HH				Y
TL240	85	ST412/506	MFM	5.25 HH				Y
TL258		ST412/506	MFM	5.25 HH				Y
TL326	40	ST412/506	MFM	5.25 HH				Y
TL340	40	ST412/506	MFM	5.25 HH				Y

VERTEX (SEE PRIAM)

WESTERN DIGITAL

Drive Model	Seek Time	Interface	Encode	Form Factor	cache kb	mtbf	RPM	Obsolete?
PhD1000	14	PCMIDE		3.0 4H	128k	300k	4536	
PhD1400	14	PCMIDE		3.0 4H	256k	350k	4000	
PhD2100	14	PCMIDE		3.0 4H	256k	350k	4000	
PIRANHA 105A	15	IDE AT	2,7 RLL	3.5 HH		50k		Y
PIRANHA 105S	15	SCSI	2,7 RLL	3.5 HH		50k		Y
PIRANHA 210A		IDE AT		3.5 HH				Y
PIRANHA 210S		SCSI		3.5 HH				Y
WD140		IDE AT		3.5 3H				Y
WD2120		IDE AT		3.5 3H				Y
WD260		IDE AT		3.5 3H				Y
WD262	80	ST412/506	MFM	3.5 HH				Y
WD344R	40	ST412/506	2,7 RLL	3.5 HH				Y
WD362	80	ST412/506	MFM	3.5 HH				Y
WD382R	85	ST412/506	2,7 RLL	3.5 HH				Y
WD383R	85	ST412/506	2,7 RLL	3.5 HH				Y
WD384R	85	ST412/506	2,7 RLL	3.5 HH				Y
WD544R	40	ST412/506	2,7 RLL	3.5 HH				Y
WD562-5	80	ST412/506	MFM	3.5 HH		40k		Y
WD582R	85	ST412/506	2,7 RLL	3.5 HH				Y
WD583R	85	ST412/506	2,7 RLL	3.5 HH				Y
WD584R	85	ST412/506	2,7 RLL	3.5 HH				Y
WD93018-A		IDE AT		3.5 HH				Y
WD93020-XE1	85	IDE XT	2,7 RLL	3.5 HH				Y
WD93023-A		IDE AT		3.5 HH				Y
WD93024-A	28	IDE AT	2,7 RLL	3.5 HH		40k		Y
WD93024-X	39	IDE XT	2,7 RLL	3.5 HH	1k	50k		Y
WD93028-A	70	IDE XT	2,7 RLL	3.5 HH		40k		Y
WD93028-AD	69	IDE AT	2,7 RLL	3.5 HH		40k		Y
WD93028-X	70	IDE XT	2,7 RLL	3.5 HH		40k		Y
WD93034-X	39	IDE XT	2,7 RLL	3.5 HH	1k	50k		Y
WD93038-X	70	IDE XT	2,7 RLL	3.5 HH		40k		Y
WD93044-X	28	IDE XT	2,7 RLL	3.5 HH	640k	40k		Y
WD93044-X	39	IDE XT	2,7 RLL	3.5 HH	1k	50k		Y
WD93048-X	69	IDE XT	2,7 RLL	3.5 HH		40k		Y
WD93048-AD	69	IDE AT	2,7 RLL	3.5 HH		40k		Y
WD93048-X	70	IDE XT	2,7 RLL	3.5 HH		40k		Y
WD95024-A	28	IDE AT	2,7 RLL	5.25 HH		40k		Y
WD95024-X	39	IDE XT	2,7 RLL	3.5 HH	1k	50k		Y
WD95028-X	70	IDE XT	2,7 RLL	5.25 HH		40k		Y
WD95028-AD	69	IDE AT	2,7 RLL	5.25 HH		40k		Y
WD95028-X	70	IDE XT	2,7 RLL	5.25 HH		40k		Y
WD95034-X	39	IDE XT	2,7 RLL	3.5 HH	1k	50k		Y
WD95038-X	70	IDE XT	2,7 RLL	5.25 HH		40k		Y
WD95044-A	28	IDE XT	2,7 RLL	5.25 HH		40k		Y
WD95044-X	39	IDE XT	2,7 RLL	3.5 HH	1k	50k		Y
WD95048-A	70	IDE XT	2,7 RLL	5.25 HH		40k		Y
WD95048-AD	69	IDE AT	2,7 RLL	5.25 HH		40k		Y
WD95048-X	70	IDE XT	2,7 RLL	5.25 HH		40k		Y
WDAB130 (Tidbit)	19	IDE AT-XT	2,7 RLL	2.50 4H	32k			Y
WDAB140	16	IDE	2,7 RLL	2.5 4H				
WDAB260 (Tidbit)	19	IDE XT-AT	2,7 RLL	2.5 4H		50k		Y
WDAC11000								

Drive Model	Format Size MB	Head	Cyl	Sect/ Trac	Translate H/C/S	RWC/ WPC	Land Zone
WDAC11200	1282				16/2484/63	---/---	
WDAC1170 (Caviar)	170	2	2233	56-96	6/1010/55	NA/NA	AUTO
WDAC1210 (Caviar)	212	2	2720	55-99	12/989/35	NA/NA	AUTO
WDAC1270 (Caviar)	270	2			12/917/48	NA/NA	AUTO
WDAC1365 (Caviar)	364	2			16/708/63	---/---	
WDAC140 (Caviar)	42	2	1082	39	5/980/17	NA/NA	AUTO
WDAC1425 (Caviar)	427	2			16/827/63	---/---	
WDAC160 (Caviar)	62	7	1024	17	7/1024/171	023/1023	
WDAC21000 (Caviar)	1083	4			16/2100/63	---/---	
WDAC2120 (Caviar)	125	8	872	35	8/872/35	872/872	AUTO
WDAC21200 (Caviar)	1282	4			16/2484/63	---/---	
WDAC21600 (Caviar)	1625	4			16/3148/63	NA/NA	AUTO
WDAC2170 (Caviar)	171	4	1584	48-56	6/1010/55	NA/NA	AUTO
WDAC21700	1707	16	3308	63		---/---	
WDAC2200 (Caviar)	213	4	1971	48-56	12/989/35	NA/NA	AUTO
WDAC22000	2000				16/3876/63	---/---	
WDAC22100	2112				16/4092/63	---/---	
WDAC2250 (Caviar)	256	3	2233	56-96	9/1010/55	NA/NA	AUTO
WDAC22500	2559				16/4960/63	---/---	
WDAC2340 (Caviar)	341	4	2233	56-96	12/1010/55	NA/NA	AUTO
WDAC2420 (Caviar)	425	4	2720	55-99	15/989/56	NA/NA	AUTO
WDAC2540 (Caviar)	540	3			16/1048/63	NA/NA	AUTO
WDAC2635 (Caviar)	640	3			16/1240/63	---/---	
WDAC2700 (Caviar)	730	4			16/1416/63	---/---	
WDAC280 (Caviar)	85	10	980	17	10/980/17	NA/NA	981
WDAC2850 (Caviar)	854	4			16/1654/63	---/---	
WDAC31000 (Caviar)	1084	6			16/2100/63	---/---	
WDAC31200 (Caviar)	1282	6			16/2484/63	---/---	
WDAC31600 (Caviar)	1625	6			16/3148/63	---/---	
WDAC3210 (Caviar)	1250					---/---	
WDAC32100 (Caviar)	2112	5			16/4092/63	NA/NA	AUTO
WDAC32500 (Caviar)	2560	6			16/4960/63	NA/NA	AUTO
WDAC33100 (Caviar)	3166					---/---	
WDAC34000	4001				16/7752/63	---/---	
WDAC34300	4304				15/8896/63	---/---	
WDAC35100	15/15108723					---/---	
WDAC36400	6449				15/13328/63	---/---	
WDAH260 (Tidbit)	62	4	1024	17	7/1024/17	NA/NA	AUTO
WDAH280	86	4	1390	V	10/980/17	NA/NA	AUTO
WDAL1100	100					---/---	
WDAL2120	120	15	1001	17	8/872/35	NA/NA	AUTO
WDAL2170	170					---/---	
WDAL2200	200					---/---	
WDAL2540	541	4			16/1048/63	---/---	
WDAP2120 (Piranha)	125	8	872	35		NA/NA	AUTO
WDAP4200 (Pirahna)	212	8	1280	41	12/987/35	NA/NA	AUTO
WDCU140	42	2	1050	30-35	5/980/17	NA/NA	AUTO
WDE2170-0003	2170					---/---	
WDE2170-0007	2170					---/---	
WDE2170-0008	2170					---/---	
WDE2170-0023	2170					---/---	
WDE4360-0003	4360					---/---	
WDE4360-0007	4360					---/---	
WDE4360-0008	4360					---/---	
WDE4360-0023	4360					---/---	
WDMI130-44 (44 PIN)	31	2	920	33		NA/NA	AUTO
WDMI130-72 (72 PIN)	30	2	928	32		NA/NA	AUTO
WDMI4120-72 (72 PIN)	125	8	925	33		NA/NA	AUTO
WDSC8320 (Condor)	320	14	949	48		NA/NA	AUTO
WDSC8400 (Condor)	400	15	1199	48		NA/NA	AUTO
WDSP2100 (Piranha)	104	4	1265	41		NA/NA	AUTO
WDSP4200 (Piranha)	209	8	1265	41		NA/NA	AUTO
WDTM262R (Tandon)	20	2	782	26		783/783	784

Drive Model	Seek Time	Interface	Encode	Form Factor	cache kb	mtbf	RPM	Obsolete?
WDAC11200	11	EIDE		3.5 3H	256k	350k	5200	
WDAC1170 (Caviar)	13	IDE AT		3.5 3H	32k	250k	3322	Y
WDAC1210 (Caviar)	13	IDE AT	1,7 RLL	3.5 3H	64k	250k	3314	Y
WDAC1270 (Caviar)	11	IDE AT	1,7 RLL	3.5 3H	64k	250k	4500	Y
WDAC1365 (Caviar)	10	IDE AT		3.5 3H	64k	300k	4500	Y
WDAC140 (Caviar)	18	IDE AT	2,7 RLL	3.5 3H	32k	50k		Y
WDAC1425 (Caviar)	10	IDE AT		3.5 3H	64k	300k	4500	Y
WDAC160 (Caviar)	17	IDE AT	2,7 RLL	3.5 3H			3605	Y
WDAC21000 (Caviar)		EIDE		3.5 3H	128k	300k	5200	
WDAC2120 (Caviar)	15	IDE AT	2,7 RLL	3.5 3H	32k	100k	3600	Y
WDAC21200 (Caviar)		EIDE		3.5 3H	128k	300k	5200	
WDAC21600 (Caviar)	12	EIDE		3.5 3H	128k	300k	5200	
WDAC2170 (Caviar)	14	IDE AT	2,7 RLL	3.5 3H	64k	100k	3652	Y
WDAC21700								
WDAC2200 (Caviar)	14	IDE AT	2,7 RLL	3.5 3H	64k	100k	3652	Y
WDAC22100	12	EIDE		3H	128k		5200	
WDAC22250 (Caviar)	11	EIDE		3.5 3H	256k	250k	3322	
WDAC22500 (Caviar)	11	EIDE		3.5 3H	256k	350k	5200	
WDAC2340 (Caviar)	13	IDE AT	1,7 RLL	3.5 3H	64k	250k	3322	
WDAC2420 (Caviar)	13	IDE AT	1,7 RLL	3.5 3H	128k	250k	3314	
WDAC2540 (Caviar)	11	IDE AT		3.5 3H	64k	300k	4500	
WDAC2635 (Caviar)	10	IDE AT		3.5 3H	64k	300k	4500	
WDAC2700 (Caviar)	10	IDE AT		3.5 3H	64k	300k	4500	
WDAC280 (Caviar)	17	IDE AT	2,7 RLL	3.5 3H	32k	100k	3595	Y
WDAC2850 (Caviar)	10	IDE AT		3.5 3H	64k	300k	4500	
WDAC31000 (Caviar)	10	EIDE		3.5 3H	128k	250k	4500	
WDAC31200 (Caviar)	10	IDE AT		3.5 3H	64k	250k	4500	
WDAC31600 (Caviar)		EIDE		3.5 3H	128k	300k	5200	
WDAC3210 (Caviar)	13	IDE		3H	128k		4500	
WDAC32100 (Caviar)		EIDE		3.5 3H	128k	300k	5200	
WDAC32500 (Caviar)		EIDE		3.5 3H	128k	300k	5200	
WDAC33100 (Caviar)		EIDE		3.5 3H	128k	300k	5200	
WDAC34000	11.5	EIDE		3H	128k	350k	5200	
WDAC34300	11	EIDE		3.5 3H	256k	350k	5400	
WDAC35100	11	EIDE		3.5 3H	256k	350k	5400	
WDAC36400	9.5	EIDE		3.5 3H	256k	350k	5400	
WDAH260 (Tidbit)	19	IDE XT-AT	2,7 RLL	2.5 4H		50k	3383	Y
WDAH280	19	IDE XT-AT	2,7 RLL	2.5 4H		50k		Y
WDAL1100	17	IDE AT		2.5 4H		100k		Y
WDAL2120		IDE AT	2,7 RLL	2.5 3H	32k	100k		
WDAL2170	16	IDE AT		2.5 4H	32k	100k		
WDAL2200	14	IDE AT		2.5 4H	32k	100k		
WDAL2540	9.5	EIDE		2.5 4H	128k	300k	4500	
WDAP2120 (Piranha)	13	IDE AT	2,7 RLL	3.5 HH	64k	100k	3605	Y
WDAP4200 (Pirahna)	14	IDE AT	2,7 RLL	3.5 HH	64k	50k		Y
WDCU140	19	PCMCIA-ATA		1.8 4H	32k	255k	4503	Y
WDE2170-0003	8	Ultra Fast	PRML	3.5	512k	1000k	7200	
WDE2170-0007	8	Ultra FastW	PRML	3.5	512k	1000k	7200	
WDE2170-0008	8	SCA-2	PRML	3.5	512k	1000k	7200	
WDE2170-0023	8	Ultra FstDf	PRML	3.5	512k	1000k	7200	
WDE4360-0003	8	Ultra Fast	PRML	3.5	512k	1000k	7200	
WDE4360-0007	8	Ultra FastW	PRML	3.5	512k	1000k	7200	
WDE4360-0008	8	SCA-2	PRML	3.5	512k	1000k	7200	
WDE4360-0023	8	Ultra FstDf	PRML	3.5	512k	1000k	7200	
WDMI130-44 (44 PIN)	19	MCA	RLL	3.5 3H		45k		Y
WDMI130-72 (72 PIN)	19	MCA	RLL	3.5 3H		45k		Y
WDMI4120-72 (72 PIN)	23	MCA	2,7 RLL	3.5 3H		45k		Y
WDSC8320 (Condor)	14	SCSI-2	1,7 RLL	3.5 HH	64k	150k	4316	Y
WDSC8400 (Condor)	16	SCSI-2	1,7 RLL	3.5 HH	128k	150k	4316	Y
WDSP2100 (Piranha)	14	SCSI-2	2,7 RLL	3.5 HH	64k	50k		Y
WDSP4200 (Piranha)	14	SCSI-2	2,7 RLL	3.5 HH	64k	50k		Y
WDTM262R (Tandon)	85	ST412/506	2,7 RLL	3.5 HH				Y

Drive Model	Format Size MB	Head	Cyl	Sect/ Trac	Translate H/C/S	RWC/ WPC	Land Zone
WDTM364 (Tandon)	41	4	782	26		783/783	784

XEBEC

Drive Model	Format Size MB	Head	Cyl	Sect/ Trac	Translate H/C/S	RWC/ WPC	Land Zone
OWL I	25	4				---/---	
OWL II	38	4				---/---	
OWL III	52	4				---/---	
XE3100	105	6	979	35		---/---	

Y-E DATA AMERICA, INC

Drive Model	Format Size MB	Head	Cyl	Sect/ Trac	Translate H/C/S	RWC/ WPC	Land Zone
YD3042	43	4	788	28		789/789	AUTO
YD3081B	45	2	1057	42		NA/NA	AUTO
YD3082	87	8	788	28		789/789	AUTO
YD3082B	90	4	1057	42		NA/NA	AUTO
YD3083B	136	6	1057	42		NA/NA	AUTO
YD3084B	181	8	1057	42		NA/NA	AUTO
YD3161B	45	2	1057	42		NA/NA	AUTO
YD3162B	90	4	1057	42		NA/NA	AUTO
YD3181B	45	2	1057	42		NA/NA	AUTO
YD3182B	90	4	1057	42		NA/NA	AUTO
YD3530	32	5	731	17		732/732	AUTO
YD3540	42	7	733	32		732/732	AUTO
YD3541	45	8	731	15		732/732	AUTO

ZENTEC

Drive Model	Format Size MB	Head	Cyl	Sect/ Trac	Translate H/C/S	RWC/ WPC	Land Zone
DRACO	518	6	2142	V		---/---	
ZH3100(A)	86					NA/NA	AUTO
ZH3100(S)	86					NA/NA	AUTO
ZH3140(A)	121					NA/NA	AUTO
ZH3140(S)	121					NA/NA	AUTO
ZM3180	170					---/---	
ZM3272	260	4	2076	55		---/---	
ZM3360	340					---/---	
ZM3540	518					---/---	
ZQ2140	126	4	1410	44		---/---	

Drive Model	Seek Time	Interface	Encode	Form Factor	cache kb	mtbf	RPM	Obsolete?
WDTM364 (Tandon)	85	ST412/506	2,7 RLL	3.5 HH				Y

XEBEC

Drive Model	Seek Time	Interface	Encode	Form Factor	cache kb	mtbf	RPM	Obsolete?
OWL I	55	SCSI	MFM	5.25 HH				Y
OWL II	40	SCSI	MFM	5.25 HH				Y
OWL III	38	SCSI	MFM	5.25 HH				Y
XE3100		IDE AT						Y

Y-E DATA AMERICA, INC

Drive Model	Seek Time	Interface	Encode	Form Factor	cache kb	mtbf	RPM	Obsolete?
YD3042	28	SCSI	2,7 RLL	3.5 HH		40k		
YD3081B	28	SCSI	2,7 RLL	3.5 HH		30k		Y
YD3082	28	SCSI	2,7 RLL	3.5 HH		40k		Y
YD3082B	28	SCSI	2,7 RLL	3.5 HH		30k		Y
YD3083B	28	SCSI	2,7 RLL	3.5 HH		30k		Y
YD3084B	28	SCSI	2,7 RLL	3.5 HH		30k		Y
YD3161B	19	IDE AT	2,7 RLL	3.5 3H		40k		Y
YD3162B	19	IDE AT	2,7 RLL	3.5 3H		40k		Y
YD3181B	19	SCSI	2,7 RLL	3.5 3H		40k		Y
YD3182B	19	SCSI	2,7 RLL	3.5 3H		40k		Y
YD3530	26	ST412/506	MFM	3.5 HH				Y
YD3540	29	ST412/506	MFM	3.5 HH		20k	3600	Y
YD3541	29	SCSI	2,7 RLL	3.5 HH		20k	3600	Y

ZENTEC

Drive Model	Seek Time	Interface	Encode	Form Factor	cache kb	mtbf	RPM	Obsolete?
DRACO	12	SCSI-2 FAST	1,7 RLL	3.5 3H	512k	150k	4200	
ZH3100(A)	20	IDE AT		3.5 HH		50k		
ZH3100(S)	20	SCSI		3.5 HH		50k		
ZH3140(A)	20	IDE AT		3.5 HH		50k		
ZH3140(S)	20	SCSI		3.5 HH		50k		
ZM3180	12	IDE AT		3.5 3H		150k		
ZM3272	13	IDE AT	1,7 RLL	3.5 3H	64k	150k	3600	
ZM3360	12	IDE AT		3.5 3H		150k		
ZM3540	12	IDE AT		3.5 3H		150k		
ZQ2140	18	IDE AT	1,7 RLL	2.5 4H	32k	150k	3600	

Hard Drive Source Notes

Information contained in the hard drive chapter was derived from numerous sources, including the manufacturers of the drives. When compiling tables this large, the chance for typing and resource error is great. The authors and publisher would greatly appreciate being notified of any inaccurate or missing information. Some of the older drives (especially those from companies who have gone out of business) are very difficult to obtain accurate and verifiable specifications for. If you have access to old specification sheets, etc please send us a copy so that we may add the information to future editions.

The following are important resources:

ONTRACK Computer Systems Disk Manager Series
Eden Prairie, Minnesota, 1985 to 1990
The Hard Disk Technical Guide by Douglas T. Anderson
PCS Publications, Clearwater, FL, 1990, 1991
The Micro House Encyclopedia of Hard Drives edited
by Douglas T. Anderson, Boulder, CO, 1990 to 1995
Numerous public domain and BBS hard drive listings.
SpeedStor Hard Disk Preparation/Diagnostics
Storage Dimensions, 1985, 1988
Numerous manufacturer specification sheets
Reseller's Resource - Hard Drives, Volume 2, No 1
Technology Publishing, Inc, Livonia, MI   January 1990
Buyer's Guide-Hard Drives 40MB to 400MB
Computer Shopper, March 1990
THEREF by F. Robert Falbo, Rome, New York, 1991
Western Digital BBS Listing, 6-6-91

Chapter 8

Floppy Drive Specifications

Many thanks to Bottom Line Industries, 9556 Cozycroft Ave, Chatsworth, California, 91311, (818) 700-1922, (800) 344-6044 for providing Sequoia with additional floppy drive information included in this chapter. If you need to have a floppy or hard drive rebuilt or would like to purchase a rebuilt floppy or hard drive, Bottom Line Industries is an excellent source!

Floppy Drive Manufacturers

The following table is a general summary of companies that have manufactured and/or are still manufacturing floppy drives. If you have information concerning the status of any of these companies, such as "XYZ Company went bankrupt in August, 1990" or "XYZ Company was bought by Q Company", please let us know so we can keep this section current. If a phone number is listed in the Status column, the company is in business.

Manufacturer	Status
Alps	800-449-2577
Aurora Tech	697-290-4800
Bachelor	Unknown
BASF	800-343-4600
Burroughs	Unknown
Calcomp	800-225-2667
Canon	800-423-2366
C.D.C	Unknown
Century Data	919-821-5696; Not a manufacturer
Chinon	310-533-0274
Citizen	310-453-0614
Disc Tec	407-671-5500
Epson	310-787-6300
Fuji	510-438-9700; Do not manufacture floppy or hard drives anymore.
Fujitsu	408-432-6333; Made in Japan
Hewlett Packard	800-752-0900
Hi-Tech (China)	886-2-773-3555
Hitachi	800-448-2244
IBM	914-765-1900
Iomega	801-778-1000
JVC	714-816-6500 Never manufactured floppy drives
MFE	210-997-9663
MPI	Unknown
Maple Tech	Unknown
Memorex	804-342-9620
Micropolis	800-847-8153; No longer manufactures floppy drives

Manufacturer	Status
Mitac	Unknown
Mitsubishi	408-730-5900 Corporate
Mitsumi	972-550-7300
NEC	508-264-8000
Newtronic	Unknown
Okidata	609-235-2600
Olivetti	Out of Business
Pacific Rim	510-782-1013
Panasonic	800-854-4536
Persci	Unknown
Pertec	Unknown
Phillips	719-593-7900
Qume	Unknown
Remex	Unknown
Samsung	800-726-7864
Sanyo (Japan)	81-64-432-949
Seiko	800-888-0817; Never manufactured floppy drives
Shugart	Unknown
Siemans	Out of Business
Sony	800-222-7669; Do not manufacture floppy drives?
Tandon	Filed Chapter 11 bankruptcy 9-95
Teac Corp.	213-726-0303
Tec	Unknown
Tecmate	Unknown
Texas Peripherals	Unknown
Toshiba	714-457-0777
Victor	800-628-2420
Weltec	302-737-1260
World Storage	Unknown
Y-E Data	708-855-0890

GENERAL FLOPPY DRIVE SPECS

Formatted Capacity	Sides	Tracks	Sectors	ID Byte	Media Type*	Media Agent
5-1/4 inch diameter						
160 kb**	1	40	8	FE	SSDD	Ferrite
180 kb**	1	40	9	FC	SSDD	Ferrite
320 kb**	2	40	8	FF	DSDD	Ferrite
360 kb	2	40	9	FD	DSDD	Ferrite
1.2 Mb	2	80			DSQD	Ferrite
1.2 Mb	2	80	15	F9	DSHD	Cobalt
3-1/2 inch diameter						
720 kb	2	80	9	F9	DSDD	Cobalt
1.44 Mb	2	80	18	F0	DSHD	Cobalt
2.8 Mb	2	80	36	F0	DSEHD	Barium

* SS = Single Sided, DS=Double Sided
  DD = Double Density
  HD = High Density
  QD = Quad Density (now obsolete)
  EHD or ED = Extra High Density

** Obsolete drives

Maximum Entries in the Root Directory:
  5-1/4 DD and 3.5 DD = 112 Entries
  5-1/4 HD and 3.5 HD = 224 Entries
  3.5 EHD = 240 Entries

All floppy drives currently produced rotate at 300 RPM, except for the 1.2Mb, 5-1/4 HD drives, which rotate at 360 RPM.

All floppy drives are formatted at 512 Bytes Per Sector.

Floppy disks have 2 FATs, 12 Bit Type

Sequoia needs your help! If you have specifications on new or obsolete floppy drives, please send them to us for future editions of PCRef

FLOPPY DRIVE SPECS BY MODEL

Manufacturer	Model Number	Width (Inch)	Height (Inch)	Format Capacity	Media Density
Alps	413(PS2)	3.50	Half	720kb	DSHD
	713(PS2)	3.50	Half	1.44Mb	DSHD
	723	3.50	1/3	1.44Mb	DSHD
	723(PS2)	3.50	Half	1.44Mb	DSHD
	2124	5.25	Half	180kb	SSDD
	2124A	5.25	Full	360kb	DSDD
	2624-BKI	5.25	Half	360kb	DSDD
	DF328N	3.50	1/4	2.88Mb	DSHD
	DFC 222 B02A,01A	5.25	Half	360kb	DSDD
	DFC 222A05A	5.25	Half	360kb	DSDD
	DFC 642 B01B	5.25	Half	1.2Mb	DSDD
Aurora Tech	FD350(SCSI)	3.50	Half		
	FD525(SCSI)	5.25	Half		
Bachelor	FD-104	5.25	Half	360kb	DSDD
BASF	6106	5.25	Full	180kb	SSDD
	6128	5.25	Half	360kb	DSDD
	6138	5.25	Half	720kb	DSDD
Burroughs	B9489-1	8.00	Full	1.6Mb	DSDD
Calcomp	142	8.00	Full	800kb	SSDD
	143	8.00	Full	1.6Mb	DSDD
Canon	221	5.25	Half	720kb	DSDD
	530	5.25	Half	720kb	DSDD
	531	5.25	Half	360kb	DSDD
	3361	3.50	1/4	1.44Mb	DSHD
	5201	5.25	Half	360kb	DSDD
	5501	5.25	1/3	1.2Mb	DSHD
	5511	5.25/3.5	Half	1.2/1.44Mb	DUAL
C.D.C.	9404	8.00	Full	800kb	SSDD
	9406-3	8.00	Full	800kb	SSDD
	9406-4	8.00	Full	1.6Mb	DSDD
	9408	5.25	Full	180kb	SSDD
	9409	5.25	Full	360kb	DSDD
	9409T	5.25	Full	720kb	DSQD
	9428	5.25	Half	360kb	DSDD
	9428-01	5.25	Half	180kb	SSDD
	9428-02	5.25	Half	360kb	DSDD
	9429	5.25	Half	720kb	DSQD
	9429-01	5.25	Half	360kb	SSQD
	BR8B1A	5.25	Full	360kb	DSDD
Century Data	140	8.00	Full	800kb	SSDD
Chinon	506-L	5.25	Half	1.2Mb	DSDD
	C354	3.50	Half	720kb	DSDD
	FX354	3.50	1.0"	720kb	DSDD
	FZ357	3.50	1.0"	1.4Mb	DSHD
	C359	3.50	Half	1.4Mb	DSHD
	F,FZ,C502	5.25	Half	360kb	DSDD
	C506	5.25	Half	1.2Mb	DSHD
Citizen	OSDA-01D	3.50	1/3	720kb	DSQD
	OSDA-14A	3.50	1/3	1.44Mb	DSHD

FLOPPY DRIVE SPECS BY MODEL

Manufacturer	Model Number	Width (Inch)	Height (Inch)	Format Capacity	Media Density
	OSDA-39D	3.50	1/3	1.44Mb	DSDD
	OSDA-51B	3.50	1/3	1.44Mb	DSHD
	OSDA-52B	3.50	1/3	1.44Mb	DSHD
	OSDA-53B	3.50	1/3	1.44Mb	DSHD
	OSDA-77D	3.50	1/3	720kb	DSQD
	OSDA-81F	3.50	Half	1.44Mb	DSHD
	OSDA-90E-U	3.50	1/3	720kb	DSQD
	OPDB-22A-U	3.50	Half	720kb	DSQD
	OSDD-05B	3.50	1/3	720kb	DSQD
	OSDD-57	3.50	1/3	720kb	DSQD
	OSDD-57B	3.50	1/3	720kb	DSQD
	U1DA-14A	3.50	1/4	1.44Mb	DSHD
	V1DA-10A	3.50	1/4	1.44Mb	DSHD
	V1DA-27A	3.50	1/4	1.44Mb	DSHD
	V1DA-31B	3.50	1/4	1.44Mb	DSHD
	V9DA-55A	3.50	1/4	1.44Mb	DSHD
	V9DA-55B	3.50	1/4	1.44Mb	DSHD
	V9DA-71B	3.50	1/4	1.44Mb	DSHD
Digital	PBXRX-AA	3.50	1.0"	1.44Mb	DSHD
	PBXRX-AB	3.50	1.0"	1.44Mb	DSHD
Epson	170-SMD	3.50	Half	400kb	SSDD
	180	3.50	Half	720kb	DSDD
	200P-053	3.50	Half	720kb	DSDD
	200P-055	3.50	Half	720kb	DSDD
	200P-073	3.50	Half	720kb	DSDD
	280	3.50	Half	720kb	DSDD
	300	3.50	1/3	1.44Mb	DSHD
	340	3.50	1/3	1.44Mb	DSHD
	400 W/FRAME	3.50	1/3	1.44Mb	DSHD
	400P-4	3.50	1/3	1.44Mb	DSHD
	500	5.25	Half	360kb	DSDD
	521	5.25	Half	360kb	DSDD
	521L	5.25	Half	360kb	DSDD
	621L	5.25	Half	360kb	DSDD
	700/800	5.25/3.5		1.2/1.44Mb	DUAL
	1000	3.50	1/3	1.44Mb	DSHD
	1000P	3.50	1/4	1.44Mb	DSHD
	DYO-211	3.50	Half	1.44Mb	DSHD
	DYO-212	3.50	Half	1.44Mb	DSHD
	SD-321	5.25	1/3	360kb	DSDD
	SD-520	5.25	Half	360kb	DSDD
	SD-521	5.25	Half	360kb	DSDD
	SD-581	5.25	Half		
	SD-621L	5.25	Half	328kb	DSDD
	SD-680L	5.25	Half	1.02Mb	DSHD
	SMD-1040	3.50	0.7"	1.44Mb	DSHD
	SMD-1060	3.50	0.7"	2.8Mb	DSEHD
	SMD-1340	3.50	1.0"	1.44Mb	DSHD
	SMD-340	3.50	1.0"	1.47Mb	DSHD
	SMD-349	3.50	Half	1.4Mb	DSHD
	SMD-380	3.50	1.0"	656kb	DSDD
	SMD-389	3.50	Half	720kb	DSDD
	SMD-400P-4	3.50	1/3	1.44Mb	DSHD

FLOPPY DRIVE SPECS BY MODEL

Manufacturer	Model Number	Width (Inch)	Height (Inch)	Format Capacity	Media Density
Fuji/Toshiba....	FDD4206AOK	3.50	Half	720kb	DSDD
	FDD421GOK	3.50	1.0"	720kb	DSDD
	FDD5452BOK	5.25	Half	360kb	DSDD
	FDD6471LOK	5.25	Half	360kb	DSDD
Fujitsu	2551 A08	5.25	Half	360kb	DSDD
	2552K	5.25	Half	720kb	DSQD
	2553A,K	5.25	Half	1.2Mb	DSHD
	2553 K03B	5.25	Half	1.2Mb	DSQD
	2554	5.25	Half	720kb	DSQD
	M2537K	3.50	1/3	1.44Mb	DSHD
	N02B-0112-B001	3.50	Half	720kb	DSDD
	N02B-0112-B201	3.50	Half	720kb	DSDD
Hewlett Packard					
	J455-3	5.25	Half	360kb	DSDD
	J475-1	5.25	Half	1.2Mb	DSQD
Hi-Tech..........	548-25	5.25	Half	180kb	SSDD
	548-50	5.25	Half	360kb	DSDD
	548-A	5.25	Half	360kb	DSDD
	596-10	5.25	Full	720kb	DSQD
Hitachi	HFD 305S	5.25	Half	360kb	SSDD
	FD532EIU	5.25	Half	2.4Mb	DSHD
	FDD412A	5.25	Half	1.2Mb	DSDD
IBM	0384-002	5.25	Full	360kb	DSDD
JVC.................	MDP-100	5.25	Half	720kb	DSQD
MFE................	M700	8.00	Full	1.6Mb	DSDD
	M750	8.00	Full	1.6Mb	DSDD
MPI	501	5.25	Half	180kb	SSDD
	502B	5.25	Half	360kb	DSDD
	51M	5.25	Full	180kb	SSDD
	52M	5.25	Full	360kb	DSDD
	52S	5.25	Full	360kb	DSDD
	91M	5.25	Full	360kb	SSQD
	92M-002	5.25	Full	720kb	DSQD
	B101M-S	5.25	Full	180kb	SSQD
	B102M-S	5.25	Full	360kb	DSQD
	B51S	5.25	Full	180kb	SSDD
	B52S	5.25	Full	360kb	DSDD
	B91S	5.25	Full	360kb	SSQD
	B92M	5.25	Full	720kb	DSQD
	B92S	5.25	Full	720kb	DSQD
Maple Tech	MT-502	5.25	Half	360kb	DSQD
Matsushita ...	EME-263TL	3.50	1/4	1.44Mb	DSHD
	EME-278T	3.50	1/4	1.44Mb	DSHD
	EME-278TA	3.50	1/4	1.44Mb	DSHD
Memorex	651	8.00	Full	1.2Mb	DSDD
Micropolis	1006-4N	5.25	Full	720kb	DSQD
	1015-2	5.25	Full	360kb	SSQD
	1015-4	5.25	Full	720kb	DSQD

FLOPPY DRIVE SPECS BY MODEL

Manufacturer	Model Number	Width (Inch)	Height (Inch)	Format Capacity	Media Density
Micropolis (cont.)	1015-6	5.25	Full	720kb	DSQD
	1016-2	5.25	Full	360kb	DSDD
	1115-4	5.25	Full	720kb	DSQD
	1115-5	5.25	Full	360kb	SSDD
	1115-6	5.25	Full	720kb	DSQD
	1117-6	5.25	Full	720kb	DSQD
Mitac	MC-490	5.25	Half	360kb	DSDD
Mitsubishi	2894	8.00	Full	1.6Mb	DSDD
	2894-63	8.00	Full	1.6Mb	DSDD
	2896	8.00	Half	1.6Mb	DSDD
	2896-63	8.00	Half	1.6Mb	DSDD
	353AF	3.50	Half	720kb	DSDD
	353B-12	3.50	Half	720kb	DSDD
	353B-82	3.50	1/3	720kb	DSDD
	353B,C	3.50	Half	720kb	DSDD
	353C	3.50	1/3	720kb	DSDD
	353-12	3.50	1/3	720kb	DSDD
	355A,B,C	3.50	1.0"	1.4Mb	DSHD
	355B-52	3.50	Half	1.44Mb	DSHD
	355B-82UF	3.50	Half	1.44Mb	DSHD
	355BA-82UF/W51/4	3.50	Half	1.44Mb	DSHD
	355BA-88UF/W51/4	3.50	Half	1.44Mb	DSHD
	355B-88UF	3.50	Half	1.44Mb	DSHD
	355C-12	3.50	1/3	1.44Mb	DSHD
	355C-215	3.50	1/3	1.44Mb	DSHD
	355C-222	3.50	1/3	1.44Mb	DSHD
	355C-258MC	3.50	1/3	1.44Mb	DSHD
	355C-352	3.50	1/3	1.44Mb	DSHD
	355C-37/W51/4	3.50	1/3	1.44Mb	DSHD
	355C-526	3.50	1/3	1.44Mb	DSHD
	355C-58UF	3.50	1/3	1.44Mb	DSHD
	355C599MA(PS2)	3.50	Half	1.4Mb	DSHD
	355C599MB(PS2)	3.50	Half	1.4Mb	DSHD
	355C599MR4(PS2)	3.50	Half	1.4Mb	DSHD
	355C599MQ4(PS2)	3.50	Half	1.4Mb	DSHD
	355C599MQ41(PS2)	3.50	Half	1.4Mb	DSHD
	355C-82UF/W51/4	3.50	Half	1.44Mb	DSHD
	355C-88UF/W51/4	3.50	Half	1.44Mb	DSHD
	355F258	3.50	1/3	1.4Mb	DSHD
	355F3250UG	3.50	Full	1.44Mb	DSHD
	355F3252UG	3.50	Full	1.44Mb	DSHD
	355F3258UG	3.50	Full	1.44Mb	DSHD
	355H-120MG	3.50	Half	1.44Mb	DSHD
	355H-212MG	3.50	Half	1.44Mb	DSHD
	355H-218MG	3.50	Half	1.44Mb	DSHD
	355H-240MG	3.50	Half	1.44Mb	DSHD
	355H-242MG	3.50	Half	1.44Mb	DSHD
	355H-248MG	3.50	Half	1.44Mb	DSHD
	355W99M1(PS2)	3.50	Half	1.4Mb	DSHD
	355W99M2(PS2)	3.50	Half	1.4Mb	DSHD
	355W99M3(PS2)	3.50	Half	1.4Mb	DSHD
	355W99WI(PS2)	3.50	Half	1.4Mb	DSHD
	356F-250UG	3.50	Full	2.8MB	DSHD

FLOPPY DRIVE SPECS BY MODEL

Manufacturer	Model Number	Width (Inch)	Height (Inch)	Format Capacity	Media Density
Mitshbishi (cont.)	356F-252UG	3.50	Full	2.8MB	DSHD
	356F-258UG	3.50	Full	2.8MB	DSHD
	4851	5.25	Half	360kb	DSDD
	4852	5.25	Full	720kb	DSQD
	4853	5.25	Half	720kb	DSQD
	4854	5.25	Half	1.2Mb	DSQD
	501A	5.25	Half	360kb	DSDD
	501B	5.25	Half	360kb	DSDD
	501C	5.25	Half	360kb	DSDD
	503	5.25	Half	720kb	DSQD
	504A	5.25	Half	1.2Mb	DSHD
	504B	5.25	Half	1.2Mb	DSQD
	504C	5.25	Half	1.2Mb	DSQD
	504S	5.25	Half	1.2Mb	DSHD
	LS-120	3.50	Full	1.44Mb	DSHD
Mitsumi		3.50		720kb	DSDD
		3.50		1.44Mb	DSHD
	D353F2	3.50	Half	1.44Mb	DSHD
	D353F2E	3.50	Half	1.44Mb	DSHD
	D353G	3.50	Half	1.44Mb	DSHD
	D353T5	3.50	Full	1.44Mb	DSHD
	D359C	3.50	1/4	1.44Mb	DSHD
	D359F2	3.50	Half	1.44Mb	DSHD
	D359F2E	3.50	Half	1.44Mb	DSHD
	D359G	3.50	Half	1.44Mb	DSHD
	D359T2	3.50	1/3	1.44Mb	DSHD
	D359T3	3.50	1/3	1.44Mb	DSHD
	D359T5	3.50	1/3	1.44Mb	DSHD
	D359T7	3.50	Full	1.44Mb	DSHD
	D503	5.25	Half	360kb	DSDD
	D509V	5.25	Half	1.2Mb	DSQD
	D509V5	5.25	Full	1.2Mb	DSQD
	DP119F2	3.50	Full	1.44Mb	DSHD
MPI	51-S	5.25	Full	180kb	SSDD
	52-S	5.25	Full	360kb	DSDD
NEC	1035	3.50	Half	720kb	DSDD
	1036A	3.50	1/3	720kb	DSDD
	1037A	3.50	1/3	720kb	DSDD
	1053	5.25	Half	360kb	DSDD
	1055	5.25	Half	720kb	DSQD
	1137H	3/50	1/3	1.44Mb	DSHD
	1155C	5.25	Half	1.2Mb	DSQD
	1157C	5.25	Half	1.2Mb	DSQD
	1158C	5.25	1/3	1.2Mb	DSHD
	1165A	8.00	Half	1.6Mb	DSDD
	1165FQ	8.00	Half	1.6Mb	DSDD
	5138A	3.50	1/3	1.44Mb	DSHD
	FD1035	3.50	Half	720kb	DSDD
	FD1138H	3.50	.75"	1.44Mb	DSHD
	FD1139H	3.50	0.6"	1.44Mb	DSHD
	FD1148H	3.50	0.78"	1.44Mb	DSHD
	FD1155C	5.25	1.6"	1.2Mb	DSQD
	FD1157C	5.25	1.6"	1.2Mb	DSQD

FLOPPY DRIVE SPECS BY MODEL

Manufacturer	Model Number	Width (Inch)	Height (Inch)	Format Capacity	Media Density
NEC (cont.)	FD1158C	5.25	1.6"	1.2Mb	DSQD
	FD1165F	8.00	Half	1.6Mb	DSDD
	FD1165H	8.00	Half	1.6Mb	DSDD
	FD1165S	8.00	Half	1.6Mb	DSDD
	FD1177C	5.25	1.6"	1.2Mb	DSHD
	FD1231H	3.50	1.0"	1.44Mb	DSHD
	FD1238H	3.50	0.5"	1.44Mb	DSHD
	FD1335H	3.50	1.0"	1.44Mb	DSHD
	FD5839H	5.25/3.5	1.63"	1.2/1.44Mb	DUAL
Newtronic	D357	3.50	1/3	720kb	DSDD
Okidata	3305	5.25	Half	360kb	DSDD
	3305BU	5.25	1/3	360kb	DSDD
	3305U	5.25	Half	360kb	DSDD
	3315B	5.25	Half	360kb	DSDD
Olivetti	4311	5.25	Half	360kb	DSDD
	4311-3	5.25	Half	360kb	DSDD
Pacific Rim	U1.2	5.25	Half	1.2Mb	DSHD
	U1.44	3.50		1.44Mb	DSHD
	U4	3.50	1.0"	2.88Mb	DSEHD
	U720	3.50		720kb	DSDD
	U360	5.25	Half	360kb	DSDD
Panasonic	253	3.50	1/3	720kb	DSDD
	257	3.50	1/3	1.44Mb	DSHD
	257 W/FRAME	3.50	1/3	1.44Mb	DSHD
	455	5.25	Half	360kb	DSDD
	465	5.25	Half	720kb	DSQD
	475	5.25	Half	1.2Mb	DSQD
	551	5.25	Half	360kb	DSDD
	595	5.25	Half	1.2Mb	DSQD
Persci	277(6N)	8.00	Full	1.2Mb	SSDD
	299	8.00	Full	2.0Mb	DSDD
Pertec	FD200	5.25	Full	180kb	SSDD
	FD250	5.25	Full	360kb	DSDD
	FD400	8.00	Full	800Kb	SSDD
	FD410	8.00	Full	800kb	SSDD
	FD500	8.00	Full	800kb	SSDD
	FD510	8.00	Full	800kb	DSDD
	FD511	8.00	Full	800kb	SSDD
	FD514-U2	8.00	Full	800kb	SSDD
	FD650	8.00	Full	1.6Mb	DSDD
Phillips	3121		Half	360kb	SSDD
	3132	5.25	Half	360kb	DSDD
	3133	5.25	Half	720kb	DSDD
	3134	5.25	Half	1.0Mb	DSDD
Qume	142	5.25	Half	360kb	DSDD
	242	8.00	Half	1.6Mb	DSDD
	542	5.25	Full	360kb	DSDD
	841	8.00	Full	800kb	DSDD
	842	8.00	Full	1.6Mb	DSDD
	DT/5	5.25	Full	360kb	DSDD

FLOPPY DRIVE SPECS BY MODEL

Manufacturer	Model Number	Width (Inch)	Height (Inch)	Format Capacity	Media Density
Qume (cont.)	DT/8	8.00	Full	1.6Mb	DSDD
Remex	RFD 2000	8.00	Full	800kb	SSDD
	RFD 4000	8.00	Full	1.6Mb	DSDD
	RFD 480	5.25	Half	360kb	DSDD
Richoh	5100	5.25	Half	720kb	DSQD
	RF8160	8.00	Half	1.6Mb	DSDD
Samsung	SFD500K	5.25	Half	360kb	DSDD
	SFD-560DT	5.25	Half	1.2Mb	DSHD
	SFD-321DT	3.50	Half	1.44Mb	DSHD
Sanyo	500C	5.25	Half	360kb	DSDD
	FDA5200	5.25	Half	360kb	DSDD
Seiko	8640	5.25	Full	640kb	DSDD
Shugart	SA200	5.25	Half	180kb	SSDD
	SA210	5.25	Half	360kb	DSDD
	SA215	5.25	Half	180kb	DSDD
	SA300	3.50	Half	360kb	SSDD
	SA390	5.25	Full	180kb	SSDD
	SA400	5.25	Full	180kb	SSDD
	SA400L	5.25	Full	180kb	SSDD
	SA410	5.25	Full	360kb	SSQD
	SA450	5.25	Full	360kb	DSDD
	SA455	5.25	Half	360kb	DSDD
	SA460	5.25	Full	720kb	DSQD
	SA465	5.25	Half	720kb	DSQD
	SA475	5.25	Half	1.2Mb	DSQD
	SA551	5.25	Half	360kb	DSDD
	SA561	5.25	Half	720kb	DSQD
	SA800-1	8.00	Full	800kb	SSDD
	SA800-1R	8.00	Full	800kb	SSDD
	SA800-2	8.00	Full	800k	SSDD
	SA800-2R	8.00	Full	800kb	SSDD
	SA800-4	8.00	Full	800kb	SSDD
	SA801	8.00	Full	800kb	SSDD
	SA801-R	8.00	Full	800kb	SSDD
	SA810	8.00	Half	800kb	SSDD
	SA850	8.00	Full	1.6Mb	DSDD
	SA850R	8.00	Full	1.6Mb	DSDD
	SA851	8.00	Full	1.6Mb	DSDD
	SA851R	8.00	Full	1.6Mb	DSDD
	SA860	8.00	Half	1.6Mb	DSDD
	SA860-1	8.00	Half	1.6Mb	DSDD
	SA900-1	8.00	Full	800kb	SSDD
	SA901	8.00	Full	800kb	SSSD
Siemans	FDD100-5	5.25	Full	180kb	SSDD
	FDD100-8	8.00	Full	800kb	SSDD
	FDD220-8	8.00	Full	800kb	SSDD
	FDD121-5	5.25	Full	360kb	SSDD
	FDD196-5	5.25	Full	360kb	SSDD
	FDD221-5	5.25	Full	360kb	DSDD

FLOPPY DRIVE SPECS BY MODEL

Manufacturer	Model Number	Width (Inch)	Height (Inch)	Format Capacity	Media Density
Sony	120-04	3.50	1/3	1.44Mb	DSHD
	17W	3.50	1/3	1.44Mb	DSHD
	17W-5PF	3.50	1/3	1.44Mb	DSHD
	17W-10/W51/4	3.50	1/3	1.44Mb	DSHD
	17W-34/W51/4	3.50	1/3	1.44Mb	DSHD
	17W-42/W51/4	3.50	1/3	1.44Mb	DSHD
	17W-55	3.50	Half	1.44Mb	DSHD
	17W-90	3.50	1/3	1.44Mb	DSHD
	17W-WFP	3.50	1/3	1.44Mb	DSHD
	40W-00(PS2)	3.50	1/3	2.8Mb	DSHD
	40W-9E	3.50	1/3	2.8Mb	DSHD
	40W-15	3.50	Half	2.8Mb	DSHD
	40W-KO	3.50	Half	2.8Mb	DSHD
	420-6	3.50	1/3	1.44Mb	DSHD
	53	3.50	1/3	1.44Mb	DSHD
	53W	3.50	1/3	720kb	DSQD
	63W	3.50	1/3	720kb	DSQD
	73W	3.50	3/4	1.44Mb	DSHD
	73W-34D/W51/4	3.50	3/4	1.44Mb	DSHD
	77W(PS2)	3.50	1/3	1.44Mb	DSHD
	MFD51W	3.50	1/3	800kb	DSQD
Tandon	TM100-1A	5.25	Full	180kb	SSDD
	TM100-2A	5.25	Full	360kb	DSDD
	TM100-3	5.25	Full	360kb	SSQD
	TM100-3M	5.25	Full	360kb	DSDD
	TM100-4	5.25	Full	720kb	DSQD
	TM100-4A	5.25	Full	720kb	DSQD
	TM101-2	5.25	Full	360kb	DSDD
	TM101-3	5.25	Full	360kb	SSQD
	TM101-4	5.25	Full	720kb	DSQD
	TM50-1	5.25	Half	180kb	SSDD
	TM50-2	5.25	Half	360kb	DSDD
	TM55-1	5.25	Half	180kb	SSDD
	TM55-2	5.25	Half	360kb	DSDD
	TM55-4	5.25	Half	720kb	DSQD
	TM65-1L	5.25	Half	180kb	SSDD
	TM65-2L	5.25	Half	360kb	DSDD
	TM65-4	5.25	Half	720kb	DSQD
	TM65-8	5.25	Half	1.2Mb	SSQD
	TM75-2	5.25	Half	360kb	DSDD
	TM75-8	5.25	Half	1.2Mb	DSQD
	TM848-1	8.00	Half	800kb	SSDD
	TM848-1E	8.00	Half	800kb	SSDD
	TM848-2	8.00	Half	1.6Mb	DSDD
	TM848-2E	8.00	Half	1.6Mb	DSDD
	TM965-2	5.25	Full	360kb	DSDD
Teac	35F	3.50	Half	720kb	DSDD
	35FN	3.50	Half	720kb	DSDD
	35HFN	3.50	1/3	1.44Mb	DSHD
	50A	5.25	Full	180kb	SSDD
	53B	5.25	Half	360kb	DSDD
	54B	5.25	Half	360kb	DSDD
	55A	5.25	Half	180kb	SSDD

FLOPPY DRIVE SPECS BY MODEL

Manufacturer	Model Number	Width (Inch)	Height (Inch)	Format Capacity	Media Density
Teac (cont.)	55B	5.25	Half	360kb	DSDD
	55BR	5.25	Half	360kb	DSDD
	55BV	5.25	Half	360kb	DSDD
	55E	5.25	Half	360kb	DSDD
	55FR	5.25	Half	720kb	DSQD
	55FV	5.25	Half	720kb	DSQD
	55G	5.25	Half	1.2Mb	DSQD
	55GFR	5.25	Half	1.2Mb	DSQD
	55GR	5.25	Half	1.2Mb	DSHD
	55GS (SCSI)	5.25	Half	1.2Mb	DSHD
	55GV	5.25	Half	1.2Mb	DSQD
	55GVF	5.25	Half	1.2Mb	DSQD
	135FN	3.50	1/3	720kb	DSDD
	135HF	3.50	1/3	1.44Mb	DSHD
	135HFN	3.50	1/3	720kb	DSDD
	235F	3.50	1/3	720kb	DSDD
	235GF	3.50	1.0"	1.6Mb	DSDD
	235HF	3.50	1/3	1.44Mb	DSHD
	235HG	3.50	1/3	1.44Mb	DSHD
	235HS (SCSI)	3.50	1.0"	1.44Mb	DSHD
	235J	3.50	1.0"	2.88Mb	DSEHD
	235JS (SCSI)	3.50	1.0"	2.88Mb	DSEHD
	335F	3.50	0.75"	720kb	DSDD
	335HF	3.50	0.75"	1.4Mb	DSHD
	335HS (SCSI)	3.50	0.75"	1.4Mb	DSHD
	335J	3.50	0.75"	2.88Mb	DSEHD
	335JS (SCSI)	3.50	0.75"	2.88Mb	DSEHD
	505	5.25/3.5	Half	1.2/1.44Mb	DSHD
	05HF-030	3.50	1/3	1.44Mb	DSHD
Tec	FB501	5.25	Half	180kb	SSDD
	FB503	5.25	Half	360kb	DSDD
	FB504	5.25	Half	720kb	DSQD
Tecmate	1103	5.25	Half	3.3Mb	DSDD
Texas Peripherals					
	10-5355-001	5.25	Full	180kb	SSDD
Toshiba	0202A	5.25	Full	720kb	DSQD
	0242A	5.25	Half	360kb	DSDD
	0401GR	5.25	Half	360kb	DSDD
	0801GR	5.25	Half	1.2Mb	DSHD
	0802GR	5.25	Half	1.2Mb	DSHD
	352TH	3.50	1/3	720kb	DSQD
	3527H	3.50	1/3	720kb	DSDD
	3527TH	3.50	1/3	720kb	DSQD
	3561	3.50	1/3	1.44Mb	DSHD
	3564	3.50	1/3	1.44Mb	DSHD
	3567	3.50	1/3	1.44Mb	DSHD
	4210	3.50	1/3	720kb	DSDD
	4202-AOK	3.50	1/3	720kb	DSDD
	4207-AOK	3.50	1.0"	720kb	DSQD
	4207-AOK	3.50	1/3	720kb	DSDD
	4261	3.50	1/3	720kb	DSDD
	4449-AOZ(PS2)	3.50	Half	720kb	DSQD

FLOPPY DRIVE SPECS BY MODEL

Manufacturer	Model Number	Width (Inch)	Height (Inch)	Format Capacity	Media Density
Toshiba (cont.)	5401	5.25	Half	360kb	DSDD
	5406	5.25	Half	360kb	DSDD
	5426	5.25	Half	360kb	DSDD
	5451	5.25	Half	360kb	DSDD
	5454	5.25	Half	360kb	DSDD
	5471	5.25	Half	360kb	DSDD
	5472	5.25	Half	360kb	DSDD
	5474	5.25	Half	360kb	DSDD
	5629	5.25	Half	720kb	DSQD
	5861	5.25	Half	1.2Mb	DSHD
	5862	5.25	Half	1.2Mb	DSHD
	5863	5.25	Half	1.2Mb	DSHD
	5881	5.25	Half	1.2Mb	DSHD
	5882	5.25	Half	1.2Mb	DSQD
	6371	5.25	Half	360kb	DSDD
	6374	5.25	Half	360kb	DSDD
	6471	5.25	Half	360kb	DSDD
	6474-T2P	5.25	Half	360kb	DSDD
	6782	5.25	Half	1.2Mb	DSHD
	6784	5.25	Half	1.2Mb	DSHD
	6881	5.25	Half	1.2Mb	DSHD
	6882	5.25	Half	1.2Mb	DSHD
	6890	5.25	Half	1.2Mb	DSHD
	M48D-12	5.25	Half	360kb	DSDD
	ND-04	5.25	Half	360kb	DSDD
	ND-08	5.25	Half	1.2Mb	DSHD
	ND-352T,S	3.50	1.0"	720kb	DSDD
	ND-354A	3.50	1.0"	720kb	DSDD
	ND-356	3.50	1/3	1.44Mb	DSHD
	ND-3565-A	3.50	1/3	1.44Mb	DSHD
	ND-3571	3.50	1.0"	2.88Mb	DSEHD
	PD-211	3.50	1.0"	2.88Mb	DSEHD
Victor	TM100-3	5.25	Full	360kb	SSQD
	TM100-4	5.25	Full	720kb	DSQD
Weltec	M16-A22	5.25	Half	1.0Mb	DSDD
	M16-P12	5.25	Half	720kb	DSDD
	M-16-R12	5.25	Half	1.0Mb	DSDD
	M16-R12/910	5.25	Half	720kb	DSDD
	M48D-1	5.25	Half	360kb	DSDD
	M48D-14	5.25	Half	360kb	DSDD
	N96-12	5.25	Half	720kb	DSDD
World Storage	FD100-5	5.25	Full	180kb	SSDD
	FD100-8	8.00	Full	800kb	SSDD
	FD200-5	5.25	Full	360kb	DSDD
	FD200-8	8.00	Full	1.6Mb	DSDD
YE-Data	YD180	8.00	Half	1.6Mb	DSDD
	YD280	5.25	Full	720kb	DSQD
	YD380	5.25	Half	1.2Mb	DSHD
	YD380B	5.25	Half	1.2Mb	DSHD
	YD380C	5.25	Half	1.2Mb	DSHD
	YD580	5.25	Half	360kb	DSDD
	YD580B	5.25	Half	360kb	DSDD
	YD701	3.50	1/3	1.44Mb	DSHD
	YD701(PS2)	3.50	1/3	1.44Mb	DSHD

Chapter 9

PC Phone Book

The following information has been included in this phone book:

    Company Name:State .... Main Phone
    Toll Free Phone .... Fax Line .... Tech Support

We ran out of space in the phone book this year so we had to eliminate the Fax on Demand and BBS phone numbers. If you need additional info on companies, Sequoia now publishes a shirt pocket reference book titled *Pocket PC DIRectory* which contains complete company address, and additional phone numbers such as BBS, Fax on Demand, and Toll Free/900 Tech support numbers. Internet, Web, Compuserve, AOL and Microsoft Network addresses are also included!! See also the Hard Drive and Floppy Drive manufacturers directories on pages 294 and 432 for additional information.

1776 Inc:CA .... **Main: (310) 215-1776**
  Fax:(310) 216-1107   Tech:(310) 215-1776
1st Class Software:ON .... **Main: (905) 302-9988**
  Fax:(905) 608-2422
1st Tech Corp:TX .... **Main: (512) 258-3570**
  TFree:(800) 533-1744   Fax:(512) 258-3689 Tech:(512) 258-3570
20/20 Software:OR .... **Main: (503) 520-0504**
  TFree:(800) 735-2020   Fax:(503) 520-9118 Tech:(503) 520-0504
3Com Corp:CA .... **Main: (408) 764-5000**
  TFree:(800) 876-3266   Fax:(408) 764-5001 Tech:(800) 876-3266
3D Visions (see Visual Numerics):
3Dlabs Inc:CA .... **Main: (408) 436-3455**
  Fax:(408) 436-3458
3DTV Corp:OR .... **Main: (541) 988-9634**
  Fax:(541) 988-9627
3G Graphics:WA .... **Main: (206) 774-3518**
  TFree:(800) 456-0234   Fax:(206) 771-8975 Tech:(206) 774-3518
3M Data Storage Products Div:MN .... **Main: (612) 736-1866**
  TFree:(800) 328-6276   Fax:(800) 437-6264 Tech:(800) 328-9438
3PM Inc:IA .... **Main: (319) 393-7932**
  Fax:(319) 393-8549
4Q Technologies:CA .... **Main: (818) 333-6688**
  Fax:(818) 333-6637
7 Sigma:MN .... **Main: (612) 721-4280**
  Fax:(612) 722-0493

7th Level Inc:TX .... **Main: (972) 498-8100**
  Fax:(972) 437-2717   Tech:(972) 498-8060

A & G Graphics Interface Inc:MA .... **Main: (617) 492-0120**
  Fax:(617) 492-2133

A.R.S.:VA .... **Main: (804) 974-1726**
  TFree:(800) 443-5894 Fax:(804) 973-2004

A4 Technology Inc:CA .... **Main: (909) 468-0071**
  Fax:(909) 468-2231   Tech:(909) 468-0071

Abaco Software Inc:NH .... **Main: (603) 883-1818**
  Fax:(603) 883-2019   Tech:(603) 883-1818

Abacus Accounting Systems Inc: .... **Main: (403) 488-8100**
  TFree:(800) 992-0616 Fax:(403) 488-8150 Tech:(403) 488-8100
  Canada:(800) 665-6657

Abacus Concepts Inc:CA .... **Main: (510) 540-1949**
  TFree:(800) 666-7828 Fax:(510) 540-0260 Tech:(510) 540-1949

Abacus Software Inc:MI .... **Main: (616) 698-0330**
  TFree:(800) 451-4319 Fax:(616) 689-0325 Tech:(616) 698-0330

Abaton (see Everex Systems):

Abbeon Cal:CA .... **Main: (805) 966-0810**
  TFree:(800) 922-0977 Fax:(805) 966-7659

Ability Systems Corp:PA .... **Main: (215) 657-4338**
  Fax:(215) 657-7815

Able Soft (Out of Business):

Abra Cadabra Software:FL .... **Main: (813) 579-1111**
  TFree:(800) 424-9392 Fax:(813) 578-2178 Tech:(813) 579-1111

Absoft Corp:MI .... **Main: (248) 853-0050**
  Fax:(248) 853-0108   Tech:(248) 853-0095

Absolute Battery Co:NJ .... **Main: (908) 534-1560**
  TFree:(800) 829-8296 Fax:(908) 534-1792 Tech:(908) 534-1560

Abstract Technologies Inc:TX .... **Main: (512) 441-4040**
  Fax:(512) 416-0310

Abudoe Software Inc (NWNexus):

ACC dotCom:MD .... **Main: (800) 242-0739**
  TFree:(800) 242-0739 Fax:(410) 635-9801 Tech:(888) 444-7854
  Tech Fax:(301) 831-8289

Accent Software International Ltd:CA .... **Main: (714) 223-0620**
  TFree:(800) 535-5216 Fax:(800) 535-5257 Tech:(800) 535-5216

Access Micro Products (All Amer Semi):CA Main: (408) 441-1300
  TFree:(800) 639-4366 Fax:(408) 437-4355 Tech:(800) 639-4366

Access Software:UT .... **Main: (801) 359-2900**
  TFree:(800) 800-4880 Fax:(801) 596-9128 Tech:(800) 793-0324

AccessData Corp:UT .... **Main: (801) 224-6970**
  TFree:(800) 489-5199 Fax:(801) 224-6009 Tech:(800) 489-5199

Accolade Inc:CA .... **Main: (408) 985-1700**
  TFree:(800) 245-7744 Fax:(408) 246-0231 Tech:(408) 296-8400

Accton Technology Corp:CA .... **Main: (408) 452-8900**
  TFree:(800) 926-9288 Fax:(408) 452-8988 Tech:(800) 926-9288

Acculogic Inc (ACC Technology Group):CA Main: (619) 530-8170
  Fax:(619) 586-1540

Accurate Research Inc:CA .... **Main: (408) 523-4788**
  TFree:(800) 799-8802 Fax:(408) 523-4789 Tech:(408) 523-4788

Accurite Technologies Inc:CA .... **Main: (510) 668-4900**
  Fax:(510) 668-4905

Accutek Inc:AL .... Main: **(205) 931-8000**
Fax:(205) 931-8251

Acecad Inc:CA .... Main: **(408) 655-1900**
TFree:(800) 676-4223 Fax:(408) 655-1919 Tech:(408) 655-9911

Acer America Corp:CA .... Main: **(408) 432-6200**
TFree:(800) 733-2237 Fax:(408) 922-2933 Tech:(800) 445-6495
Extra Support:(900) 555-2237

Acer Sertek Inc:CA .... Main: **(408) 733-3174**
Fax:(408) 733-2569   Tech:(408) 733-3174

Aces Research Inc:CA .... Main: **(510) 683-8855**
Fax:(510) 683-8875   Tech:(510) 661-2093

Aci Us Inc:CA .... Main: **(408) 252-4444**
TFree:(800) 881-3466 Fax:(408) 252-4829

ACL Staticide:IL .... Main: **(847) 981-9212**
TFree:(800) 782-8420 Fax:(847) 981-9278 Tech:(847) 981-9212

Acme Electric Corp:NY .... Main: **(716) 968-2400**
TFree:(800) 325-5848 Fax:(716) 968-3948

Acorn Computers:WA .... Main: **(206) 443-8004**
Fax:(206) 443-5838

ACT Networks Inc:CA .... Main: **(805) 388-2474**
TFree:(800) 367-2281 Fax:(805) 388-3504
Customer Service Fax:(805) 389-3180

Action Image Systems Technology Inc:NJ...Main: **(908) 232-2166**
Fax:(908) 232-1621   Tech:(908) 232-2166

Action Technologies Inc:CA .... Main: **(510) 521-6190**
TFree:(800) 967-5356 Fax:(510) 769-0596

Active Voice Corp:WA .... Main: **(206) 441-4700**
Fax:(206) 441-4784

Activision:CA .... Main: **(310) 473-9200**
TFree:(800) 477-3650 Fax:(310) 479-7355 Tech:(310) 479-5644

Actix Systems Inc:CA .... Main: **(408) 986-1625**
TFree:(800) 927-5557 Fax:(408) 986-1646 Tech:(408) 986-1625

Adaptec Inc:CA .... Main: **(408) 945-8600**
TFree:(800) 959-7274 Fax:(408) 262-2533 Tech:(408) 934-7274
Tech Fax:(408) 957-6776

Adaptiv Software Corp:CA .... Main: **(714) 789-7300**
TFree:(800) 598-1222 Fax:(714) 789-7320 Tech:(714) 789-7311

Adaptive Solutions Inc:OR .... Main: **(503) 690-1236**
TFree:(800) 482-6277 Fax:(503) 690-1249

Adax Inc:CA .... Main: **(510) 548-7047**
Fax:(510) 548-5526

ADC Fibermux corp (See ADC Kentrox):

ADC Kentrox:OR .... Main: **(503) 643-1681**
TFree:(800) 733-5511 Fax:(503) 641-3341 Tech:(800) 733-5511

Addison-Wesley Publishing Co:CA .... Main: **(617) 944-3700**
TFree:(800) 447-2226 Fax:(617) 944-9338

Adept Computer Solutions Inc:CA .... Main: **(619) 597-1776**
TFree:(800) 578-6277 Fax:(619) 597-1774

ADI Systems Inc:CA .... Main: **(408) 944-0100**
TFree:(800) 228-0530 Fax:(408) 944-0300 Tech:(408) 944-0100

Adobe Systems Inc (Mac):CA .... Main: **(408) 536-6000**
TFree:(800) 833-6687 Fax:(408) 537-6000
Main reception number Seattle:(206) 622-5500

Adobe Systems Inc (PC):CA .... Main: (408) 536-6000
 TFree:(800) 447-3577 Fax:(408) 537-6000
 Main receptionnumber Seattle:(206) 622-5500
Adtran:AL .... Main: (205) 971-8000
 TFree:(800) 827-0807 Fax:(205) 971-7941 Tech:(205) 971-8716
 tech support:(800) 726-8663
Advanced Digital Information (ADIC):WA ...... Main: (206) 881-8004
 TFree:(800) 336-1233 Fax:(206) 881-2296 Tech:(206) 883-4357
Advanced Digital Systems:CA .... Main: (562) 926-1928
 TFree:(800) 888-5244 Fax:(562) 926-0518 Tech:(562) 926-4338
Advanced Graphics Software Inc:CA .... Main: (760) 931-1919
 TFree:(800) 795-4754 Fax:(760) 931-9313
Advanced Gravis Computer Tech Ltd:BC .... Main: (604) 431-5020
 TFree:(800) 663-8558 Fax:(604) 431-5155 Tech:(604) 431-1807
 Tech Fax:(604) 451-9358
Advanced Logic Research (ALR Inc):CA Main: (714) 581-6770
 TFree:(800) 444-4257 Fax:(714) 581-9240 Tech:(800) 257-1230
 Tech Fax:(714) 458-0532
Advanced Matrix Technology Inc:CA .... Main: (805) 388-5799
 TFree:(800) 637-7878 Fax:(805) 494-3087 Tech:(805) 388-5799
Advanced Media:CA .... Main: (714) 957-1616
 TFree:(800) 292-4264 Fax:(714) 957-5977 Tech:(714) 957-1616
Advanced Media:NY .... Main: (516) 244-1616
 Fax:(516) 244-1415
Advanced Micro Devices:CA .... Main: (408) 732-2400
 TFree:(800) 538-8450 Fax:(800) 222-9323 Tech:(800) 222-9323
 windows tech support:(408) 749-3060
Advanced Network Solutions:WA .... Main: (425) 644-6082
 TFree:(800) 837-4180 Fax:(206) 222-7622
Advanced RISC Machines Inc:CA .... Main: (408) 399-5199
 Fax:(408) 399-8854
Advanced Software (see Prairie Group):
Advanced Storage Concepts Inc:TX .... Main: (409) 744-2129
 Fax:(409) 744-2181
AdvanSys Inc:CA .... Main: (408) 383-9400
 TFree:(800) 525-7443 Fax:(408) 383-9612 Tech:(800) 525-7440
 Tech Support:(408) 467-2930
Advantage Memory:CA .... Main: (714) 453-8111
 TFree:(800) 245-5299 Fax:(714) 453-8158 Tech:(800) 245-5299
 Tech Fax:(714) 453-1357
Advisor Publications Inc:CA .... Main: (619) 278-5600
 TFree:(800) 336-6060 Fax:(619) 278-0300
AEC Management (see AEC Software):
AEC Software:VA .... Main: (703) 450-1980
 TFree:(800) 346-9413 Fax:(703) 450-9786 Tech:(703) 450-2318
Aeronics Inc:TX .... Main: (512) 258-2303
 Fax:(512) 258-4392   Tech:(512) 258-2303
AG Group, The:CA .... Main: (510) 937-7900
 TFree:(800) 466-2447 Fax:(510) 937-2479 Tech:(800) 446-2447
AgData:CA .... Main: (916) 846-6203
 TFree:(800) 382-4328
Agfa Compugraphics (Bayer Corp):NJ .... Main: (201) 440-2500
 TFree:(800) 424-8973 Fax:(201) 440-5733 Tech:(800) 879-2432

Agile Networks Inc:MA .... Main: **(508) 287-9000**
TFree:(800) 286-9526   Fax:(508) 287-9050

Ahead Systems Inc:CA .... Main: **(510) 623-0900**
Fax:(510) 623-0960

Ahern Communications Corp:MA .... Main: **(617) 471-1100**
TFree:(800) 451-5067   Fax:(617) 328-9070

Aim Tech:NH .... Main: **(603) 883-0220**
TFree:(800) 289-2884   Fax:(603) 883-5582   Tech:(800) 801-2884

Aladdin Software Security Inc:NY .... Main: **(212) 564-5678**
TFree:(800) 223-4277   Fax:(212) 564-3377

Aladdin Systems Inc:CA .... Main: **(408) 761-6200**
Fax:(408) 761-6206   Tech:(408) 761-6200

Alberta Printed Circuits LTD:AL .... Main: **(403) 250-3406**

Aldus Corp (see Adobe Systems Inc):

Alexander LAN Inc:NH .... Main: **(603) 880-8800**
Fax:(603) 880-8881

Algorithm Inc:GA .... Main: **(770) 232-4949**
Fax:(770) 232-4951

Alias Research (see Wavefront):

Alki Software Corp:WA .... Main: **(206) 286-2600**
TFree:(800) 669-9673   Fax:(206) 286-2785   Tech:(206) 286-2780

All Components Inc:TX .... Main: **(972) 233-0203**
TFree:(800) 779-0234   Fax:(972) 851-1998   Tech:(972) 233-0203

Allaire Corp:MA .... Main: **(617) 761-2000**
TFree:(888) 939-2545   Fax:(617) 761-2001   Tech:(617) 761-2100
Sales:(617) 761-2100

Allegiant:CA .... Main: **(619) 587-0500**
TFree:(800) 255-8258   Fax:(619) 587-1314   Tech:(619) 587-0500

Allegro New Media (Software Publishing):

Allegro Systems Ltd:AZ .... Main: **(520) 795-6000**
Fax:(520) 795-0158

Alliance Research/ORA Elect/Dataspec:CA .Main: **(818) 772-2700**
TFree:(800) 877-7448   Fax:(818) 718-8626   Tech:(818) 772-2700
Other Fax:(818) 718-8667

Alliant Tech Systems Inc:MD .... Main: **(410) 266-1700**
Fax:(410) 224-0887

Allied Telesyn International (ATI):CA ...... Main: **(408) 730-0950**
TFree:(800) 424-4284   Fax:(408) 736-0100   Tech:(800) 424-4284

AllMicro (Fore Front Direct):FL .... Main: **(813) 539-7283**
TFree:(800) 653-4933   Fax:(813) 531-0200   Tech:(813) 539-7283

Allsop Computer Accessories:WA .... Main: **(360) 734-9090**
TFree:(800) 426-4303   Fax:(360) 734-9858   Tech:(360) 734-9090

Alltech Electronics:CA .... Main: **(714) 543-5011**
Fax:(714) 543-0553

Almo Corp:PA .... Main: **(215) 698-4000**
TFree:(800) 878-5758   Fax:(215) 698-4080   Tech:(800) 878-5758

Almo Distributing (see Almo Corp):

ALOS Micrographics Corporation:NY .... Main: **(914) 457-4400**
TFree:(800) 431-7105   Fax:(914) 457-9083   Tech:(914) 457-4400

Alpha Software Corp:MA .... Main: **(617) 229-2924**
TFree:(800) 451-1018   Fax:(617) 272-4876   Tech:(800) 225-3766
Tech Fax:(617) 272-8222

AlphaBlox Corp:CA .... Main: **(415) 526-1700**
  Fax:(415) 526-1701

Alpharel Inc:CA .... Main: **(619) 625-3000**
  TFree:(800) 992-6784   Fax:(619) 546-7671 Tech:(800) 633-6784

Alps Electric USA:CA .... Main: **(408) 432-6000**
  TFree:(800) 825-2577   Fax:(408) 432-6035 Tech:(800) 449-2577
  Customer Service:(800) 825-2577

ALR Inc (Advanced Logic Research):CA ...... Main: **(800) 444-4257**
  TFree:(800) 444-4257   Fax:(714) 581-9240 Tech:(800) 257-1230
  Tech Fax:(714) 458-0532

Alsoft:TX .... Main: **(281) 353-4090**
  TFree:(800) 257-6381   Fax:(281) 353-9868 Tech:(281) 353-1510

Alta Technology Corp:UT .... Main: **(801) 562-1010**
  Fax:(801) 254-2020

Altec Lansing Consumer Prod:PA .... Main: **(717) 296-4434**
  TFree:(800) 258-3288   Fax:(717) 296-1222 Tech:(800) 258-3288

Altex Electronics Corp:TX .... Main: **(512) 814-8882**
  TFree:(800) 531-5369   Fax:(512) 814-8812

Altex Electronics-Austin:TX .... Main: **(512) 832-9131**
  TFree:(800) 531-5369   Fax:(512) 832-9213

Altex Electronics-Dallas:TX .... Main: **(972) 386-8882**
  TFree:(800) 531-5369   Fax:(972) 386-9182

Altex Electronics-Mail Ord:TX .... Main: **(210) 637-3200**
  TFree:(800) 531-5369   Fax:(210) 637-3264

Altex Electronics-San Antonio:TX .... Main: **(210) 828-0503**
  TFree:(800) 531-5369   Fax:(210) 340-2409

Altsys (see Macromedia):

Alysis:CA .... Main: **(415) 566-2263**
  TFree:(800) 825-9747   Fax:(415) 928-2896 Tech:(800) 825-9747

Amber Wave Systems (see U.S. Robotics):

Amcom Corp:NV .... Main: **(702) 261-9992**
  TFree:(800) 807-1117   Fax:(702) 261-9230 Tech:(702) 261-9992

Amdahl Corp:CA .... Main: **(408) 746-6000**
  TFree:(800) 538-8460   Fax:(408) 773-0833

Amdek Corp (WYSE Technology):CA .... Main: **(408) 473-1200**
  TFree:(800) 438-9973   Fax:(408) 922-5729 Tech:(800) 800-9973

America Online:VA .... Main: **(703) 448-8700**
  TFree:(800) 827-6364   Fax:(703) 883-1509 Tech:(800) 827-3338

American Bible Society:NY .... Main: **(212) 408-1200**
  TFree:(800) 322-4253   Fax:(212) 408-1512 Tech:(212) 408-1200

American Business Info (CDROM Div):NE ... Main: **(402) 596-7575**
  Fax:(402) 331-6184

American Business System:MA .... Main: **(508) 250-9600**
  TFree:(800) 356-4034   Fax:(508) 250-8027 Tech:(508) 250-9600

American Covers:UT .... Main: **(801) 553-0600**
  TFree:(800) 228-8987   Fax:(801) 553-1212 Tech:(800) 228-8987

American Cybernetics:AZ .... Main: **(602) 968-1945**
  TFree:(800) 899-0100   Fax:(602) 966-1654 Tech:(602) 968-1945

American Ink Jet Corp:MA .... Main: **(508) 670-9200**
  TFree:(800) 332-6538   Fax:(508) 670-5637 Tech:(508) 670-9200

American Laser Games:NM .... Main: **(505) 880-1718**
  TFree:(800) 880-1718   Fax:(505) 880-1557 Tech:(505) 880-1718

American Megatrends Inc:GA .... Main: (770) 246-8600
TFree:(800) 828-9264 Fax:(770) 246-8791 Tech:(770) 246-8645
American MPC Research:CA .... Main: (562) 801-0108
Fax:(562) 801-0138   Tech:(562) 801-0108
American Ntl Standards Institute:NY .... Main: (212) 642-4900
Fax:(212) 398-0023
American On-Line (See Ventana):NC .... Main: (919) 544-9404
TFree:(800) 332-7450 Fax:(919) 544-9472
American Power Conversion Corp:RI .... Main: (401) 789-5735
TFree:(800) 541-8896 Fax:(401) 789-3710 Tech:(800) 800-4272
American Small Bus Computer (ViaGrafix):
AmeriQuest Technologies:FL .... Main: (305) 967-2397
TFree:(800) 255-4489 Fax:(305) 967-1143
Amicus Networks Inc:TX .... Main: (512) 418-8828
Fax:(512) 418-8829
AMP Inc:PA .... Main: (717) 986-7777
TFree:(800) 522-6752 Fax:(717) 986-7575 Tech:(800) 526-0721
2nd Fax on Demand line:(717) 986-3500
Ampex Corp:CA .... Main: (415) 367-2011
TFree:(800) 752-7590 Tech:(719) 570-3714
AMS Tech:CA .... Main: (818) 814-8851
TFree:(800) 980-8889 Fax:(818) 814-0782 Tech:(800) 886-3536
Amtex Software Corp:ON .... Main: (613) 967-7900
TFree:(800) 810-7345 Fax:(613) 967-7902 Tech:(613) 967-7900
ANA Tech:CO .... Main: (303) 973-6722
Fax:(303) 973-7092
Analog Devices Inc:MA .... Main: (617) 329-4700
TFree:(800) 262-5643 Fax:(617) 461-3091 Tech:(800) 426-2564
Anawave Software Inc:CA .... Main: (714) 250-7262
TFree:(800) 711-6030 Fax:(714) 250-7265 Tech:(714) 250-7263
Ancom Inc:CA .... Main: (714) 692-8899
Fax:(714) 692-0956   Tech:(714) 692-8899
Andataco On-The-Net:CA .... Main: (619) 453-9191
TFree:(800) 334-9191 Fax:(619) 453-9294 Tech:(619) 453-9809
Anderson Investor's Software Inc:MO ...... Main: (314) 918-0990
TFree:(800) 286-4106 Fax:(314) 918-0980
Andromeda Research:OH .... Main: (513) 831-9708
Fax:(513) 831-7562
Andyne Computing Ltd:ON .... Main: (613) 548-4355
Fax:(613) 548-7801
ANGOSS Software International:ON .... Main: (416) 593-1122
Fax:(416) 593-5077   Tech:(416) 593-1122
AniCom (Animated Communications):NC .... Main: (919) 967-2890
TFree:(800) 949-4559 Fax:(919) 933-9503
Annabooks:CA .... Main: (619) 674-6155
TFree:(800) 462-1042 Fax:(619) 673-1432
Ansoft Corp:PA .... Main: (412) 261-3200
Fax:(412) 471-9427   Tech:(800) 323-9504
Antec Inc:CA .... Main: (510) 770-1200
TFree:(888) 542-6832 Fax:(510) 770-1288 Tech:(800) 222-6832
Anthem Technology Systems:CA .... Main: (408) 453-1200
TFree:(800) 359-3580 Fax:(408) 441-4504

Anvil Cases:CA .... Main: **(818) 968-4100**
 TFree:(800) 359-2684   Fax:(818) 968-1703

Aonix:CA .... Main: **(415) 543-0900**
 TFree:(800) 972-6649   Fax:(415) 543-0145

Apertus Technologies Inc:MN .... Main: **(612) 828-0300**
 TFree:(800) 328-3998   Fax:(612) 828-0773

Apex Data Inc:CA .... Main: **(510) 623-1231**
 TFree:(800) 841-2739   Fax:(510) 249-1600   Tech:(510) 249-1605
 Tech Fax:(510) 249-1604

APEX Software Corp:PA .... Main: **(412) 681-4343**
 TFree:(800) 858-2739   Fax:(412) 681-4384   Tech:(412) 681-4738

Apogee Software Inc:CA .... Main: **(408) 369-9001**
 TFree:(800) 854-6705   Fax:(408) 369-9018

Apple Computer Inc:CA .... Main: **(408) 996-1010**
 TFree:(800) 776-2333   Fax:(408) 974-9976   Tech:(800) 919-2775

Applications Techniques Inc:MA .... Main: **(508) 433-5201**
 TFree:(800) 433-5201   Fax:(508) 433-8466   Tech:(508) 433-8464

Applied Computer Systems:CA .... Main: **(408) 739-8676**
 TFree:(888) 422-0867   Fax:(408) 739-7169

Applied Microsystems Corp:WA .... Main: **(425) 882-2000**
 TFree:(800) 426-3925   Fax:(206) 883-3049   Tech:(800) 275-4262

Applied Optical Media:PA .... Main: **(610) 429-3701**
 TFree:(800) 321-7259   Fax:(610) 429-3810   Tech:(800) 321-7259

Applix Inc:MA .... Main: **(508) 870-0300**
 TFree:(800) 827-7549   Fax:(508) 366-2278   Tech:(800) 827-7549

Approach Software (see Lotus Develop):

APS Technologies:MO .... Main: **(800) 235-8935**
 TFree:(800) 235-8935   Tech:(816) 483-6200

Apsylog Inc:CA .... Main: **(510) 275-0200**
 TFree:(800) 277-9564   Fax:(510) 275-0225   Tech:(510) 275-0200

AR Industries (Road Warrior Intl):CA ...... Main: **(714) 418-1400**
 TFree:(800) 274-4277   Fax:(714) 839-6282   Tech:(800) 274-4277

Arabesque Software (see NetManage):

Arcada Software (Seagate Software):FL ... Main: **(407) 333-7500**
 TFree:(800) 327-2232   Fax:(407) 333-7730   Tech:(800) 468-2587

Archetype Interactive:CA .... Main: **(510) 849-4045**
 Fax:(510) 849-4046   Tech:(510) 849-4045

Archive Software (see Seagate):

Arco Computer Products Inc:FL .... Main: **(954) 925-2688**
 TFree:(800) 458-1666   Fax:(954) 925-2889   Tech:(954) 925-2688

Areal Technology Inc (Out Of Business):

Ares Software:CA .... Main: **(415) 578-9090**
 TFree:(800) 783-2737   Fax:(415) 378-8999   Tech:(415) 578-9090

Argent Software:CA .... Main: **(408) 996-0938**
 Fax:(408) 343-1191

Arista Enterprises:NY .... Main: **(516) 435-0200**
 TFree:(800) 274-7824   Fax:(516) 435-4545   Tech:(800) 274-7824

Aristo Computers Inc:OR .... Main: **(503) 626-6333**
 TFree:(800) 327-4786   Fax:(503) 626-6492

Aristosoft Inc (Software Made Simple):CA
 TFree:(800) 338-2629   Fax:(510) 328-1117

Arnet Corp (See Digi International):

Arrow Electronics Inc:NY .... **Main: (516) 391-1300**
TFree:(800) 932-7769   Fax:(516) 391-1640

Arrowfield International Inc:CA .... **Main: (714) 669-0101**
TFree:(800) 227-9628   Fax:(714) 669-0526

Ars Nova Software:WA .... **Main: (425) 889-0927**
TFree:(800) 445-4866   Fax:(425) 889-8699   Tech:(425) 889-0927

Artecon Inc:CA .... **Main: (760) 931-5500**
TFree:(800) 833-2783   Fax:(760) 931-5527   Tech:(760) 931-5500

Articulate Systems:MA .... **Main: (617) 935-5656**
TFree:(800) 443-7077   Fax:(617) 935-0490   Tech:(617) 935-2220

Artisoft:AZ .... **Main: (520) 670-7100**
TFree:(800) 846-9726   Fax:(520) 670-7101   Tech:(520) 670-4287

Artisoft Inc:AZ .... **Main: (520) 670-7100**
TFree:(800) 846-9726   Fax:(520) 670-7101   Tech:(520) 670-7101

Artist Graphics Inc:MN .... **Main: (612) 631-7800**
TFree:(800) 627-8478   Fax:(612) 631-7802   Tech:(612) 631-7888

Asante Technologies:CA .... **Main: (408) 435-8388**
TFree:(800) 662-9686   Fax:(408) 432-7511   Tech:(800) 622-7464

Ascend Communications:CA .... **Main: (510) 769-6001**
TFree:(800) 621-9578   Fax:(510) 814-2300   Tech:(800) 272-3634

ASCII Group Inc, The:MD .... **Main: (301) 718-2600**
Fax:(301) 718-0435

ASD Software Inc:CA .... **Main: (909) 624-2594**
Fax:(909) 624-9574   Tech:(909) 624-2594

Ashlar Inc:CA .... **Main: (408) 746-1800**
TFree:(800) 877-2745   Fax:(408) 487-9815   Tech:(800) 877-2745

Ashton-Tate (see Borland):

ASIC Northwest Inc:OR .... **Main: (541) 923-3755**
Fax:(541) 923-8752

AskSam Systems:FL .... **Main: (904) 584-6590**
TFree:(800) 800-1997   Fax:(904) 584-7481   Tech:(904) 584-6590
Another BBS:(904) 584-8287

Aspect Software Engineering (see Microsoft):

Association for Computing Machinery:NY **Main: (212) 626-0500**
TFree:(800) 342-6626   Fax:(212) 944-1318

AST Research:CA .... **Main: (714) 727-4141**
TFree:(800) 876-4278   Fax:(714) 727-9355   Tech:(800) 727-1278

Astec Standard Power:CA .... **Main: (760) 757-1880**
Fax:(760) 930-4700   Tech:(760) 757-1880

Astound Inc:CA .... **Main: (415) 845-6200**
TFree:(800) 982-9888   Fax:(415) 845-6201   Tech:(905) 602-5292
Mac tech support:(905) 602-0395

Astrobyte:CO .... **Main: (303) 861-4861**
Fax:(303) 861-4876

Asus Computer International:CA .... **Main: (408) 474-0567**
Fax:(408) 474-0568

Asymetrix Corp:WA .... **Main: (425) 462-0501**
TFree:(800) 448-6523   Fax:(206) 455-3071   Tech:(206) 637-1600

AT&T Global Info. Solutions (NCR):OH ...... **Main: (800) 746-4722**
TFree:(800) 746-4722   Tech:(800) 831-4314

AT&T National Parts Sales Center:CO ...... **Main: (800) 222-7278**
TFree:(800) 222-7278   Fax:(800) 527-4360   Tech:(800) 628-2888

Atcom/Info:CA .... Main: (619) 699-4000
  TFree:(888) 552-8266 Fax:(619) 699-4040
ATI Technologies Inc:ON .... Main: (905) 882-2600
  Fax:(905) 882-2620   Tech:(905) 882-2626
ATS Inc:TX .... Main: (214) 265-8787
  Fax:(214) 265-1019
Attachmate Corp:WA .... Main: (425) 644-4010
  TFree:(800) 426-6283 Fax:(425) 649-6461 Tech:(800) 388-3270
Attain (Out of Business):
Attar Software:MA .... Main: (508) 456-3946
  TFree:(800) 456-3966 Fax:(508) 456-8383
AudioNet:TX .... Main: (214) 748-6660
  Fax:(214) 748-6657
Aura Memories:CA .... Main: (408) 252-2872
  Fax:(408) 252-2876
Auspex:CA .... Main: (408) 986-2000
  TFree:(800) 735-3177 Fax:(408) 986-2020 Tech:(408) 986-2000
Autodesk:CA .... Main: (415) 507-5000
  TFree:(800) 964-6432 Fax:(415) 507-5100 Tech:(206) 487-2934
Automap (see Microsoft):
AVA Instrumentation Inc:CA .... Main: (408) 336-2281
  Fax:(408) 461-1883
Avalan Technology Inc:MA .... Main: (508) 429-6482
  Fax:(508) 429-3179
Avalon Hill Game (Monarch Avalon):MD ...... Main: (410) 254-9200
  TFree:(800) 999-3222 Fax:(410) 254-0991 Tech:(410) 426-9600
Avantos Performance Systems:CA .... Main: (510) 654-4600
  TFree:(800) 282-6867 Fax:(510) 654-5199 Tech:(510) 654-4727
Avatar/DCA (see Attachmate):
Avax International:ON .... Main: (519) 833-2900
  Fax:(519) 833-7469
Avery Dennison International:TX .... Main: (214) 283-9176
  TFree:(800) 252-8379 Tech:(214) 888-2699
Avery Label:CA .... Main: (818) 969-3311
  TFree:(800) 252-8379 Fax:(818) 969-5262 Tech:(972) 389-3699
Avnet Inc:NY .... Main: (516) 466-7000
  Fax:(516) 466-1203
Award Software International Inc:CA .... Main: (650) 237-6800
  Fax:(650) 968-0274 Tech:(650) 968-4433
Axis Communications Inc:MA .... Main: (617) 938-1188
  TFree:(800) 444-2947 Fax:(617) 938-6161
  Tech Fax:(617) 938-0774
Az-Tech Software:MO .... Main: (816) 776-2700
  TFree:(800) 227-0644 Fax:(816) 776-8398 Tech:(816) 776-2700
Azerty Inc:NY .... Main: (716) 662-0200
  TFree:(800) 888-8080 Fax:(716) 662-7616 Tech:(716) 662-7616
Azure Technologies Inc (GN Nettest):MA ..... Main: (800) 233-3800
  TFree:(800) 233-3800 Fax:(508) 435-0448
B & L Associates Inc:MA .... Main: (617) 444-1404
  Fax:(617) 444-5805
Baker & Taylor Entertainment:IL .... Main: (847) 965-8060
  Fax:(847) 470-7860 Tech:(847) 965-8060

Balboa Software:ON .... **Main: (800) 763-8542**
TFree:(800) 763-8542 Fax:(416) 730-9715 Tech:(416) 730-8980
Baler Software Corp (see Tech Tools):
Balt Inc:TX .... **Main: (817) 697-4953**
TFree:(800) 749-2258 Fax:(800) 529-7577 Tech:(817) 697-4953
Fax:(800) 697-6258
Banana Programming:MT .... **Main: (406) 543-1928**
Fax:(406) 549-3522
Banner Blue Software (see Broderbund):
Banyan Systems Inc:MA .... **Main: (508) 898-1000**
TFree:(800) 222-6926 Fax:(508) 898-1755 Tech:(508) 898-1000
Barbey Electronics:PA .... **Main: (610) 376-7451**
Fax:(610) 372-8622 Tech:(610) 376-7451
BASF Magnetics Corp:MA .... **Main: (617) 271-4000**
TFree:(800) 343-4600 Fax:(617) 275-9602 Tech:(800) 225-3326
Basic Needs:CA .... **Main: (760) 738-7020**
TFree:(800) 633-3703 Fax:(760) 738-0515 Tech:(800) 633-3703
Bate Tech Software Inc (Ixchange Inc):CO ... **Main: (303) 763-8333**
TFree:(800) 743-6238 Fax:(303) 763-2783
Battery Express:WV .... **Main: (800) 666-2296**
TFree:(800) 666-2296 Fax:(304) 428-2297 Tech:(304) 428-2296
Battery Technology Inc (BTI):CA ...... **Main: (213) 728-7874**
TFree:(800) 982-8284 Fax:(213) 728-7996 Tech:(800) 982-8284
Bay Networks Inc:CA .... **Main: (408) 988-2400**
TFree:(800) 822-9638 Fax:(408) 988-5525 Tech:(800) 252-6926
Public Relations:(408) 764-7548
Bayer Corp. (AGFA Division):NJ .... **Main: (201) 440-2500**
TFree:(800) 424-8973 Fax:(201) 440-5733 Tech:(800) 879-2432
BayWare Inc (Transparent Language):
BBN Inc:MA .... **Main: (617) 873-2000**
TFree:(800) 472-4565 Fax:(617) 873-5011
BCAM Int Inc (HumanCAD Systems Inc):ON **Main: (905) 761-7681**
TFree:(800) 248-3746 Fax:(905) 761-7682 Tech:(516) 752-3507
BE Inc:CA .... **Main: (415) 462-4100**
Fax:(415) 462-4129
Beckman Industrial (see Wavetek):
Belden Wire And Cable:IN .... **Main: (765) 983-5200**
TFree:(800) 235-3361 Fax:(765) 983-5737 Tech:(765) 983-5200
Belkin Components:CA .... **Main: (310) 898-1100**
TFree:(800) 223-5546 Fax:(310) 898-1111 Tech:(800) 223-5546
Belmont Distributing (see Almo Corp):
Benefit Software Inc:CA .... **Main: (805) 568-0240**
TFree:(800) 533-1388 Fax:(805) 568-0239
Bentley Systems Inc:PA .... **Main: (610) 458-5000**
TFree:(800) 236-8539 Fax:(610) 458-1060
Berkeley Software Design Inc:CO ..... **Main: (719) 593-9445**
TFree:(800) 800-4273 Fax:(719) 598-4238 Tech:(800) 487-2738
toll free order:(800) 776-2734
Berkeley Systems Inc:CA .... **Main: (510) 540-5535**
TFree:(800) 757-7707 Fax:(510) 849-9426 Tech:(510) 549-2300
Berkshire Products:GA .... **Main: (770) 271-0088**
Fax:(770) 932-0082

Best Data Products Inc:CA .... Main: **(818) 773-9600**
  Fax:(818) 773-9619   Tech:(818) 773-9600

Best Power:WI .... Main: **(608) 565-7200**
  TFree:(800) 356-5794   Fax:(608) 565-2221 Tech:(800) 356-5737

Best Programs Inc:VA .... Main: **(703) 709-5200**
  TFree:(800) 368-2405   Fax:(703) 318-0499 Tech:(800) 331-8514

BestWare Inc:NJ .... Main: **(201) 586-2200**
  TFree:(800) 322-6962   Fax:(201) 586-8885 Tech:(800) 322-6962
  Marketing Fax on Demand:(201) 586-2200

Bethesda Softworks:MD .... Main: **(301) 926-8300**
  TFree:(800) 677-0700   Fax:(301) 926-8010 Tech:(301) 963-2002

Beverly Hills Software:CA .... Main: **(310) 358-8311**
  Fax:(310) 358-0326

Bible Research Systems:TX .... Main: **(512) 251-7541**
  TFree:(800) 423-1228   Fax:(512) 251-4401 Tech:(512) 251-7541

Biblesoft:WA .... Main: **(206) 824-8360**
  TFree:(800) 877-0778   Fax:(206) 824-1828 Tech:(206) 870-1463

Bindview:TX .... Main: **(800) 749-8439**
  TFree:(800) 749-8439   Fax:(713) 881-9200

BitShop:MD .... Main: **(301) 345-6789**
  Fax:(301) 345-6745

Bitstream Inc:MA .... Main: **(617) 497-6222**
  TFree:(800) 522-3668   Fax:(617) 868-0784 Tech:(617) 497-7514
  Tech support Fax:(617) 354-7954

Biz Base Inc (see Santa Fe Software):

Black Belt Systems:MT .... Main: **(406) 228-8945**
  Fax:(406) 228-8943   Tech:(406) 228-8944

Black Box Corp:PA .... Main: **(412) 746-5500**
  Fax:(412) 746-0746   Tech:(412) 746-5565

Black Ice Software Inc:NH .... Main: **(603) 673-1019**
  Fax:(603) 672-4112   Tech:(603) 673-1019

Blackstar Publishing Company:NY .... Main: **(212) 679-3288**
  Fax:(212) 889-2052

Blastronix:CA .... Main: **(209) 795-0738**
  Fax:(209) 795-0646

Blue Ribbon Sound Works, The:GA .... Main: **(404) 315-0212**
  TFree:(800) 226-0212   Fax:(404) 315-0213 Tech:(404) 315-0212

Blue Willow Inc:CO .... Main: **(303) 932-1600**
  TFree:(800) 932-1600   Fax:(303) 932-1800

BlueSky Software:CA .... Main: **(619) 459-6365**
  TFree:(800) 793-0364   Fax:(619) 459-6366 Tech:(619) 551-5680

Bluestone:NJ .... Main: **(609) 727-4600**
  Fax:(609) 727-5077   Tech:(609) 778-7900

BMDP Statistical Software Inc (SEE SPSS):

Boardwatch Magazine:CO .... Main: **(303) 973-6038**
  TFree:(800) 933-6038   Fax:(303) 973-3731
  Subscriptions:(800) 973-6038

Boca Research:FL .... Main: **(561) 997-6227**
  Fax:(561) 995-9456   Tech:(561) 241-8084

Boffin Limited:MN .... Main: **(612) 894-0595**
  TFree:(800) 248-5328   Fax:(612) 894-6175

BookMaker Corp:CA .... Main: **(415) 354-8160**
  TFree:(800) 766-8531   Fax:(415) 856-4734 Tech:(415) 354-8166

Borland International:CA .... Main: (408) 431-1000
... C++ DOS (900 Advisor) .... Main: (900) 555-1004
... C++ DOS (Credit Card Advisor) .... Main: (800) 368-3366
... C++ Installation .... Main: (408) 461-9133
... C++ OS/2 (900 Advisor) .... Main: (900) 555-1005
... C++ OS/2 (Credit Card Advisor) .... Main: (800) 437-8884
... C++ WIN (900 Advisor) .... Main: (900) 555-1002
... C++ WIN (Credit Card Advisor) .... Main: (800) 782-5558
... Customer Service .... Main: (510) 354-3828
    Fax:(408) 431-4122
    credit card orders:(800) 932-9994
... D-Base DOS (Credit Card Advisor) .... Main: (800) 368-9222
... D-Base DOS Installation .... Main: (408) 431-9060
... D-Base for DOS (900 Advisor) .... Main: (900) 555-1003
... D-Base WIN (900 Advisor) .... Main: (900) 555-1009
... D-Base WIN (Credit Card Advisor) .... Main: (800) 285-1118
... D-Base WIN Installation .... Main: (408) 461-9110
... Database Engine Installation .... Main: (408) 461-9123
... Database Engine Support .... Main: (800) 839-9777
... Delphi (900 Advisor) .... Main: (900) 555-1015
... Delphi (Credit Card Advisor) .... Main: (800) 330-3372
... Delphi Installation .... Main: (408) 461-9195
... Local Interbase Server (900 Advisor) .... Main: (900) 555-1013
... Local Interbase Server Installation .... Main: (408) 461-9189
... Local Interbase Server(Credit Card) .... Main: (800) 819-8881
... Paradox DOS (900 Advisor) .... Main: (900) 555-1000
... Paradox DOS (Credit Card Advisor) .... Main: (800) 468-9990
... Paradox DOS Installation .... Main: (408) 461-9155
... Paradox WIN (900 Advisor) .... Main: (900) 555-1006
... Paradox WIN (Credit Card Advisor) .... Main: (800) 452-1333
... Paradox WIN Installation .... Main: (408) 461-9166
... Pascal (900 Advisor) .... Main: (900) 555-1007
... Pascal (Credit Card Advisor) .... Main: (800) 344-2266
... Pascal Installation .... Main: (408) 461-9177
... ReportSmith (900 Advisor) .... Main: (900) 555-1011
... ReportSmith (Credit Card Advisor) .... Main: (800) 673-2288
... ReportSmith Installation .... Main: (408) 461-9150
Boston Computer Exchange:MA .... Main: (617) 542-4414
    TFree:(800) 262-6399 Fax:(617) 542-8849 Tech:(617) 542-4414
Bottom Line Industries Inc:CA .... Main: (818) 700-1922
    TFree:(800) 344-6044 Fax:(818) 700-4549 Tech:(818) 700-1922
Bourbaki Inc:ID .... Main: (208) 342-5849
    TFree:(800) 289-1347 Fax:(208) 342-5823 Tech:(208) 342-5849
Box Hill Systems Corp:NY .... Main: (212) 989-4455
    TFree:(800) 727-3863 Fax:(212) 989-6817
Boxer Software:AZ .... Main: (602) 485-1635
    TFree:(800) 982-6937 Fax:(602) 485-1636
BradyGames (MacMillian Publishing):IN ...... Main: (317) 581-3500
    TFree:(800) 545-5914 Fax:(317) 581-4596 Tech:(317) 581-3500
Brain-Storm Technologies Inc:CA .... Main: (818) 760-7974
    TFree:(800) 829-7974 Tech:(818) 760-7974
Breakthrough Technologies Inc:AZ .... Main: (602) 258-2715
    TFree:(800) 323-1809 Fax:(602) 258-2805

Brightwork Developement (see MacAvee):
Brilliance Labs Inc:FL .... Main: (407) 306-9554
BroadVision:CA .... Main: (415) 943-3600
   TFree:(888) 825-5121 Fax:(415) 943-3699
Broderbund Software Inc:CA .... Main: (415) 382-4400
   TFree:(800) 521-6263 Fax:(415) 382-4419 Tech:(415) 382-4700
Brother International:NJ .... Main: (908) 356-8880
   TFree:(800) 284-4357 Fax:(800) 947-1445 Tech:(901) 373-6256
... Dealer parts .... Main: (901) 373-6371
... Fax Service .... Main: (800) 284-4329
... Printer service .... Main: (800) 276-7746
   Fax:(714) 859-2272
... Word Processor Service .... Main: (901) 373-6256
   Fax:(901) 373-6213
BTG Inc:VA .... Main: (703) 383-8000
   TFree:(800) 899-6200 Fax:(703) 383-8999 Tech:(800) 899-6200
Buerg Software And Computers:CA .... Main: (707) 769-5477
   TFree:(800) 442-8374 Fax:(707) 769-5479
Buffalo Creek Software:IA .... Main: (515) 225-9552
Buffalo Inc:OR .... Main: (503) 585-3414
   TFree:(800) 345-2356 Fax:(503) 585-4505 Tech:(503) 585-4174
Bulldog Computer Products:IL .... Main: (800) 438-6039
Bureau of Electronic Publishing (see Thynx):
Burr-Brown Corp:AZ .... Main: (520) 746-1111
   TFree:(800) 227-3947 Fax:(520) 746-7401 Tech:(800) 548-6132
Business Resource Software Inc:TX .... Main: (512) 251-7541
   TFree:(800) 423-1228 Fax:(512) 251-4401 Tech:(512) 251-7541
BusLogic Inc (SEE Mylex Corp):
Button Ware Inc (see Outlook Software):
BYTE Magazine:NH .... Main: (603) 924-9281
   Fax:(603) 924-2683
C H Products:CA .... Main: (760) 598-2518
   TFree:(800) 624-5804 Fax:(760) 598-2524 Tech:(760) 598-7833
C-Star Technology:MN .... Main: (612) 943-1565
   Fax:(612) 943-0291
Cable Connection:CA .... Main: (408) 395-6700
   Fax:(408) 354-3980
Cables To Go (CTG):OH .... Main: (513) 275-0886
   TFree:(800) 826-7904 Fax:(800) 331-2841 Tech:(513) 275-0886
   sales:(800) 506-9606
Cabletron Systems Inc:NH .... Main: (603) 332-9400
   Fax:(603) 337-2211 Tech:(603) 332-9400
Cactus Development Company:TX .... Main: (512) 453-2244
   TFree:(800) 336-9444 Fax:(512) 453-3757 Tech:(512) 453-2244
Cadix International Inc:GA .... Main: (770) 804-9951
   TFree:(800) 876-4605 Fax:(770) 804-9949 Tech:(770) 804-9951
CADRE Technologies (Cayenne Software):
Caere Corp:CA .... Main: (408) 395-7000
   TFree:(800) 535-7226 Fax:(408) 354-2743 Tech:(408) 395-8319
   Another BBS:(408) 773-9068
Cake Walk Music Software:MA .... Main: (617) 926-2480
   TFree:(888) 225-3925 Fax:(617) 924-6657 Tech:(617) 924-6275

Cal-Abco:CA .... Main: **(818) 704-9100**
  TFree:(800) 669-2226   Fax:(818) 704-7733 Tech:(800) 473-8325

CalComp Inc:CA .... Main: **(714) 821-2000**
  TFree:(800) 225-2667   Fax:(714) 821-2832 Tech:(800) 225-2667

Calculus Inc:CA .... Main: **(415) 854-3130**
  Fax:(415) 854-1248

Caldera Inc:UT .... Main: **(801) 377-7687**
  TFree:(800) 850-7779   Fax:(801) 377-8752 Tech:(801) 377-7687

Calera Recognition Systems (see Caere):

Caligari Corporation:CA .... Main: **(415) 390-9600**
  TFree:(800) 351-7620   Fax:(415) 390-9755 Tech:(415) 390-9600

Caliper Corp:MA .... Main: **(617) 527-4700**
  Fax:(617) 527-5113   Tech:(617) 527-4700

Cambrix Publishing:CA .... Main: **(818) 992-8484**
  TFree:(800) 992-8781   Fax:(818) 992-8781 Tech:(818) 992-8484

Camelot Corporation:TX .... Main: **(972) 733-3005**
  TFree:(800) 528-7822   Fax:(972) 733-0574 Tech:(972) 733-3005

Camintonn/Z-Ram:CA .... Main: **(714) 454-1500**
  TFree:(800) 368-4726   Fax:(714) 830-4726 Tech:(714) 454-1500

Campbell Services Inc:MI .... Main: **(248) 559-5955**
  TFree:(800) 559-5955   Fax:(248) 559-1034 Tech:(900) 454-8324

Canon Business Machines Inc:CA .... Main: **(714) 556-4700**

Canon Computer Systems Inc:CA .... Main: **(714) 438-3000**
  TFree:(800) 423-2366   Fax:(714) 438-3099 Tech:(800) 423-2366

Canon Financial Services Inc:NJ .... Main: **(609) 387-8555**
  TFree:(800) 220-0200

Canon Information Systems Inc:CA .... Main: **(714) 438-7100**

Canon Research Center America Inc:CA ..... Main: **(415) 354-1200**

Canon Software America Inc:NY .... Main: **(516) 228-7070**

Canon Trading USA Inc:CA .... Main: **(714) 753-4170**

Canon USA Inc:NY .... Main: **(516) 488-6700**
  Fax:(516) 354-5805   Tech:(800) 423-2366

... Broadcast Equipment Division .... Main: **(201) 816-2900**

... Custom Integrated Technology Inc .... Main: **(757) 881-6300**
  Fax:(757) 881-6400

... Industrial Resource Technologies Inc ..... Main: **(804) 695-7000**
  Fax:(804) 695-7099

... MCS Business Solutions Inc .... Main: **(212) 850-1000**

Canon USA Inc (E):NJ .... Main: **(908) 521-7000**
  TFree:(800) 221-3333   Tech:(908) 521-7000

Canon USA Inc (E):VA .... Main: **(703) 807-3400**
  Tech:(703) 807-3400

Canon USA Inc (Hawaii):HI .... Main: **(808) 522-5930**
  Tech:(808) 522-5930

Canon USA Inc (MW):IL .... Main: **(630) 250-6200**
  Fax:(630) 250-1572   Tech:(630) 250-6200

Canon USA Inc (S):GA .... Main: **(770) 849-7700**
  Tech:(770) 849-7700

Canon USA Inc (SW):TX .... Main: **(214) 830-9600**
  Tech:(214) 830-9600

Canon USA Inc (W):CA .... Main: **(714) 753-4000**
  Tech:(714) 753-4000

Canon USA Inc (W):CA .... Main: (408) 982-5200
Tech:(408) 982-5200
... **Affiliated Business Solutions Inc** .... Main: (609) 387-8700
... **Ambassador Business Solutions Inc** .... Main: (847) 706-3400
... **Astro Business Solutions Inc** .... Main: (310) 217-3000
... **C S Polymer Inc** .... Main: (804) 249-5500
... **South Tech Inc** .... Main: (804) 443-8000
Canon Virginia Inc:VA .... Main: (804) 881-6000
TFree:(800) 423-2366   Tech:(804) 881-6000
Canyon Software:CA .... Main: (415) 453-9779
TFree:(800) 280-3691   Fax:(415) 453-6195   Tech:(415) 453-9779
CAP Automation:TX .... Main: (817) 560-7007
TFree:(800) 826-5009   Fax:(817) 560-8249   Tech:(817) 560-7007
Capital Computing Services:NC .... Main: (919) 828-7770
Fax:(919) 833-8975
Capsoft Development Corporation:UT .... Main: (801) 354-8000
TFree:(800) 500-3627   Fax:(801) 354-8099   Tech:(801) 354-8080
Capstone (Intracorp Entertainment):FL .... Main: (305) 373-7700
Fax:(305) 577-6173   Tech:(305) 373-3770
Caravelle Networks Corp:ON .... Main: (613) 225-1172
TFree:(800) 363-5292   Fax:(613) 225-4777   Tech:(613) 225-1172
Cardiff Software Inc:CA .... Main: (760) 752-5200
TFree:(800) 659-8755   Fax:(760) 752-5222   Tech:(760) 931-4565
Cardinal Technologies Inc:GA .... Main: (770) 840-2157
Fax:(770) 729-6513
Carina Software:CA .... Main: (510) 355-1266
TFree:(800) 493-8555   Fax:(510) 355-1268   Tech:(510) 355-1266
Cartesia Software:NJ .... Main: (609) 397-1611
TFree:(800) 334-4291   Fax:(609) 397-5724
Casady & Greene Inc:CA .... Main: (408) 484-9228
TFree:(800) 359-4920   Fax:(408) 484-9218   Tech:(408) 484-9228
Cascade:MA .... Main: (508) 692-2600
Fax:(508) 692-9214
Casio Inc:NJ .... Main: (201) 442-5707
TFree:(800) 634-1895   Fax:(201) 361-3819   Tech:(800) 962-2746
Castelle:CA .... Main: (408) 496-0474
TFree:(800) 289-7555   Fax:(408) 492-1964   Tech:(408) 496-0474
Cayenne Software Inc:MA .... Main: (617) 273-9003
TFree:(800) 528-2388   Fax:(617) 229-9904   Tech:(800) 356-2224
Cayman Systems:MA .... Main: (617) 279-1101
TFree:(800) 473-4776   Fax:(617) 438-4680   Tech:(617) 279-1101
Tech support Fax:(617) 438-5560
CCOM Information Systems:NJ .... Main: (732) 603-7750
Fax:(732) 603-7751
CD Concepts Inc:IN .... Main: (317) 651-9848
Fax:(317) 651-1223   Tech:(317) 651-9848
CD Technologies:CA .... Main: (408) 752-8500
Fax:(408) 752-8501   Tech:(408) 752-8499
CD World Publishing Plus:AZ .... Main: (602) 839-3031
TFree:(800) 839-1140   Fax:(602) 839-2872   Tech:(602) 839-2847
CD-ROM Direct:MA .... Main: (617) 332-2445
TFree:(800) 332-2404   Fax:(617) 332-1783

CD-Rom Strategies Inc (DV Studio Inc):CA ..Main: **(714) 453-1702**
TFree:(800) 454-1702   Fax:(714) 453-1311   Tech:(714) 453-1702

CDB Systems Inc:CO ....Main: **(303) 444-7071**
Fax:(303) 444-0035   Tech:(303) 444-7071

CE Software:IA ....Main: **(515) 221-1801**
TFree:(800) 523-7638   Fax:(515) 221-1806   Tech:(515) 221-1803
Another BBS:(515) 221-2167

Cedar Software:VT ....Main: **(802) 888-5275**
Fax:(802) 888-3009

Centerline:MA ....Main: **(617) 498-3000**
TFree:(800) 669-2687   Fax:(617) 868-6655

Centigram Communications Corp:CA ....Main: **(408) 944-0250**
Fax:(408) 428-3732

Central Data Corp:IL ....Main: **(217) 359-8010**
TFree:(800) 482-0315   Fax:(217) 359-6904

Central Point Software (see Symantec):

Centron Software Inc:NC ....Main: **(910) 215-5708**
TFree:(800) 848-2424   Fax:(910) 692-2173   Tech:(910) 215-5708

Centura Software Corp:CA ....Main: **(650) 596-3400**
TFree:(800) 444-8782

Centura Software Corp:CA ....Main: **(415) 321-9500**
TFree:(800) 444-8782   Fax:(415) 321-5471

Century Microelectronics Inc:CA ....Main: **(408) 748-7788**
Fax:(408) 748-8686

Century Software Inc:UT ....Main: **(801) 268-3088**
TFree:(800) 877-3088   Fax:(801) 268-2772   Tech:(800) 877-3088

Certus (see Symantec):

CH Products:CA ....Main: **(760) 598-2518**
TFree:(800) 624-5804   Fax:(760) 598-2524   Tech:(760) 598-7833

Chaco Communications Inc:CA ....Main: **(408) 996-1115**
Fax:(408) 865-0571

Chain Store Guide Info Services (CSGIS):FL:Main: **(813) 664-6800**
TFree:(800) 778-9794   Fax:(813) 664-6882

Champion Business Systems Inc:CO ....Main: **(303) 792-3606**
TFree:(800) 243-2626   Fax:(303) 792-0255

Changeling Inc:TX ....Main: **(512) 419-7085**
TFree:(800) 769-2768   Fax:(512) 419-7288   Tech:(512) 419-7085

Chaplet Systems USA Inc:CA ....Main: **(408) 732-7950**
Fax:(408) 732-6050

Chase Advanced Technologies:CT ....Main: **(203) 526-2400**
TFree:(800) 511-3477   Fax:(203) 526-2410   Tech:(203) 526-2400

Chatsworth Products Inc:CA ....Main: **(818) 735-6111**
Fax:(818) 735-6199

CheckFree:OH ....Main: **(614) 825-3000**
TFree:(800) 882-5280   Tech:(614) 825-3000

CheckMark Software:CO ....Main: **(970) 225-0522**
TFree:(800) 444-9922   Fax:(970) 225-0611   Tech:(970) 225-0387

Chemtronics Inc:GA ....Main: **(770) 424-4888**
TFree:(800) 645-5244   Fax:(770) 424-4267   Tech:(800) 424-9300

Cherry Electrical Products:IL ....Main: **(847) 662-9200**
Fax:(708) 360-3566

Cheyenne Software Inc:NY ....Main: **(516) 465-5000**
TFree:(800) 243-9462   Fax:(516) 484-2489   Tech:(800) 243-9832

Chicago Case Co:IL .... Main: **(312) 927-1600**
TFree:(800) 927-2602   Fax:(312) 927-2820   Tech:(312) 927-1600

Chicago-Soft Ltd:NH .... Main: **(603) 643-4002**
Fax:(603) 643-4571

Chinon America (Electronic Imaging):NJ ..... Main: **(908) 654-0404**
TFree:(800) 932-0374   Fax:(908) 654-6656

Chinon America (Info Equipment Div):CA .... Main: **(310) 533-0274**
TFree:(800) 441-0222   Fax:(310) 533-1727   Tech:(800) 441-0222

Chipcom Corp (see 3Com Corp):

Chips And Technologies Inc:CA .... Main: **(408) 434-0600**
TFree:(800) 944-6284   Fax:(408) 894-2082

ChipSoft Inc (see Intuit):

Chorus Systems:CA .... Main: **(408) 879-4100**
TFree:(800) 972-4678   Fax:(408) 879-4102

Chuck Atkinson Programs (CAP):TX .... Main: **(817) 560-7007**
TFree:(800) 826-5009   Fax:(817) 560-8249   Tech:(817) 829-4005

Cipher Data Products (see Overland Data):

Ciprico Inc:MN .... Main: **(612) 551-4035**
TFree:(800) 727-4669   Fax:(612) 551-4002   Tech:(612) 551-4131

Cirque Corp:UT .... Main: **(801) 467-1100**
TFree:(800) 454-3375   Fax:(801) 467-0208   Tech:(801) 467-1100

Cirrus Logic Inc:CA .... Main: **(510) 623-8300**
Fax:(510) 252-6020   Tech:(510) 623-8300

Cisco Systems:CA .... Main: **(408) 526-4000**
TFree:(800) 553-6387   Fax:(408) 526-4100   Tech:(800) 553-2447

Citizen America Corp:CA .... Main: **(310) 453-0614**
TFree:(800) 556-1234   Fax:(310) 315-1881   Tech:(310) 453-0614

Citizen CBM America Corp:CA .... Main: **(310) 781-1460**
TFree:(800) 218-9045   Fax:(310) 781-9152   Tech:(800) 843-8270

Citrix Systems Inc:FL .... Main: **(954) 267-2256**
TFree:(800) 437-7503   Fax:(954) 267-9319   Tech:(800) 424-8749

CLARiiON:MA .... Main: **(800) 672-7729**
TFree:(800) 672-7729   Fax:(508) 480-7950   Tech:(800) 344-1314

Clarion Software (see Top Speed Corp):

Claris Corp:CA .... Main: **(408) 987-7000**
TFree:(800) 325-2747   Fax:(408) 987-7447   Tech:(408) 727-9004
Mac tech support:(408) 727-9054

Clarity Software:CA .... Main: **(415) 691-0320**
TFree:(800) 235-6736   Fax:(415) 964-4383

Clark Development Company:UT .... Main: **(801) 261-1686**
Fax:(801) 261-8987   Tech:(801) 261-1686

Clary Corp:CA .... Main: **(818) 359-4486**
TFree:(800) 442-5279   Fax:(818) 305-0254   Tech:(800) 551-6111

Classic IPO Partners:CA .... Main: **(818) 564-8106**
TFree:(800) 370-2746   Fax:(818) 564-8554   Tech:(818) 564-8106

Classic Software Inc:OH .... Main: **(513) 232-6764**
TFree:(800) 677-2952   Fax:(513) 232-9844   Tech:(513) 232-6764

CLEAR Software Inc:MA .... Main: **(617) 965-6755**
TFree:(800) 338-1759   Fax:(617) 965-5310   Tech:(617) 965-5019

Cleo Communications (Interface Systems):

Clickable Software (See Virtual Publisher):

Client/Server Connection:NY .... Main: **(914) 921-0800**
Fax:(914) 921-3276

Clipper Products:OH .... Main: **(513) 528-7011**
TFree:(800) 829-0824   Fax:(513) 528-7676

CMD Technology Inc:CA .... Main: **(714) 454-0800**
TFree:(800) 426-3832   Fax:(714) 455-1656   Tech:(714) 454-0800
Tech Fax:(714) 454-8314

CMH Software:MT .... Main: **(406) 293-3616**
TFree:(800) 680-7638   Fax:(406) 293-5075

CMS Enhancements:CA .... Main: **(714) 424-5520**
TFree:(800) 327-5773   Fax:(714) 435-9504

CMS Enhancements (Ameriquest Tech.):

CNet Technology Inc:CA .... Main: **(408) 934-0800**
TFree:(800) 486-2638   Fax:(408) 934-0900   Tech:(408) 954-8800

Coconut Computing (ITU Engineering):

Codenoll Technology Corp:NY .... Main: **(914) 965-6300**
TFree:(800) 553-7978   Fax:(914) 965-9811   Tech:(914) 965-6300

Cogent Data Tech Inc (Adaptec):WA .... Main: **(206) 603-0333**
TFree:(800) 426-4368   Fax:(206) 603-9223

CogniTech Corp:GA .... Main: **(770) 518-4577**
TFree:(800) 947-5075   Fax:(770) 518-4588   Tech:(770) 518-3285

Cognitronix:CA .... Main: **(619) 549-8955**
TFree:(800) 217-0932   Fax:(619) 549-8327   Tech:(619) 549-8955

Cognos Corporation:MA .... Main: **(617) 229-6600**
TFree:(800) 426-4667   Fax:(617) 229-9844

Coleman Research Corp:FL .... Main: **(407) 244-3700**

Collabra Software Inc:CA .... Main: **(415) 254-1900**
TFree:(800) 639-0939   Fax:(415) 528-4124   Tech:(800) 639-0939

Colorado Memory Systems (HP):CO .... Main: **(970) 669-8000**
Fax:(970) 667-0997   Tech:(970) 635-1501

ColorAge Inc:MA .... Main: **(508) 667-8585**
TFree:(800) 437-3336   Fax:(508) 667-8821   Tech:(508) 663-8213

Columbia Data Products Inc:FL .... Main: **(407) 869-6700**
TFree:(800) 613-6288   Fax:(407) 862-4725   Tech:(407) 869-6700

Columbia Power & Data (see Computer Sys&Edu):

Com-Kyle Inc:CA .... Main: **(408) 734-9660**
TFree:(800) 722-1123   Fax:(408) 744-1650

Comark Inc:IL .... Main: **(630) 924-6700**
TFree:(800) 888-5390   Fax:(708) 351-7204   Tech:(800) 955-1488

Comfy:CA .... Main: **(408) 865-1777**
TFree:(800) 992-6639   Fax:(408) 865-1877   Tech:(617) 746-2929

Command Communications Inc:CO .... Main: **(303) 751-7000**
TFree:(800) 288-6794   Fax:(303) 752-1903   Tech:(800) 288-6794

Command Software Systems Inc:FL .... Main: **(561) 575-3200**
TFree:(800) 423-9147   Fax:(561) 575-3026   Tech:(561) 575-3200

Common Ground Software:CA .... Main: **(415) 917-2360**
TFree:(800) 598-3821   Fax:(415) 917-2369   Tech:(800) 598-3821

CommTouch Software Inc:CA .... Main: **(408) 245-8682**
Fax:(408) 245-3466

Compaq Computer Corp:TX .... Main: **(281) 370-0670**
TFree:(800) 888-5858   Fax:(281) 514-1740   Tech:(800) 652-6672

```
... Customer Service ..................................... Main: (800) 345-1518
... Enduser Techsupport.............................. Main: (800) 652-6672
... Servers Techsupport............................... Main: (800) 386-2172
Compatible Systems Corp:CO ..................... Main: (303) 444-9532
   TFree:(800) 356-0283   Fax:(303) 444-9595 Tech:(800) 356-0283
Compex Inc:CA ............................................ Main: (714) 630-7302
   TFree:(800) 279-8891   Fax:(714) 630-6521 Tech:(714) 630-5451
Compex Technology Inc (see Kenpax):
Compix Media Inc:CA ................................... Main: (213) 487-8222
   Fax:(213) 487-9251   Tech:(213) 487-3215
Complete PC, The (see Boca Research):
Compsee Inc:NC ........................................... Main: (407) 724-4321
   TFree:(800) 628-3888   Fax:(407) 723-2895 Tech:(407) 724-4321
Compton's NewMedia:CA ............................ Main: (800) 862-2206
   Fax:(716) 871-7591   Tech:(800) 893-5458
Compu-Teach:WA .......................................... Main: (206) 885-0517
   TFree:(800) 448-3224   Fax:(206) 883-9169 Tech:(206) 867-0767
CompuCover Inc:FL ...................................... Main: (904) 862-4448
   TFree:(800) 874-6391   Fax:(904) 863-2200
CompuLink Management Center Inc:CA ...... Main: (310) 212-5465
   Fax:(310) 212-5064   Tech:(310) 212-5465
   Another BBS:(310) 212-5045
CompuMart (James Publishing):TX ............. Main: (512) 992-6400
   TFree:(800) 864-1155   Fax:(512) 888-6073
CompUSA Inc:TX .......................................... Main: (214) 982-4000
   TFree:(800) 266-7872   Tech:(800) 266-7872
   Alaska toll free:(800) 998-9967
CompuServe Inc:OH ..................................... Main: (614) 457-8600
   TFree:(800) 848-8990   Tech:(800) 944-9871
   MAC support:(800) 998-9622
Computational Mechanics Inc:TX ............... Main: (512) 467-0618
   Fax:(512) 467-1382
Computer Associates Inc:NY ...................... Main: (516) 342-5224
   TFree:(800) 773-5445   Fax:(516) 342-5125 Tech:(516) 342-5466
Computer Associates International Inc . Main: (516) 342-5224
   TFree:(800) 637-5858   Fax:(516) 342-5329 Tech:(516) 342-4100
Computer Discount Warehouse (CDW):IL .. Main: (847) 465-6000
   TFree:(800) 840-4239   Fax:(847) 465-7700 Tech:(800) 383-4239
Computer Friends Inc:OR ............................ Main: (503) 626-2291
   TFree:(800) 547-3303   Fax:(503) 643-5379
Computer Hotline Magazine:TX .................. Main: (972) 233-5131
   TFree:(800) 866-3241
Computer Industry Almanac:NV .................. Main: (702) 749-5053
   TFree:(800) 377-6810   Fax:(702) 749-5864 Tech:(702) 749-5053
Computer Intelligence InfoCorp:CA ............ Main: (619) 450-1667
   Fax:(619) 452-7491
Computer Knacks Inc:NJ .............................. Main: (908) 530-0262
   TFree:(800) 551-1433   Fax:(908) 741-0972 Tech:(908) 530-0262
Computer Library (Information Access):NY . Main: (212) 503-4400
   Fax:(212) 503-4414   Tech:(212) 503-4444
Computer Parts Outlet Inc:FL ..................... Main: (561) 265-1206
   TFree:(800) 475-1655   Fax:(561) 265-1209 Tech:(561) 265-1655
```

Computer Parts Unlimited:CA .... Main: (805) 532-2500
 TFree:(800) 644-4494   Fax:(805) 532-2599

Computer Peripherals Inc:CA .... Main: (714) 454-2441
 TFree:(800) 854-7600   Fax:(714) 454-8527   Tech:(714) 454-2441

Computer Products Plus (see AR Industry):

Computer Reseller News Magazine:NY .... Main: (516) 733-6700
 TFree:(800) 521-3463   Fax:(516) 733-8636

Computer Retail Week Magazine (CMP):NY .Main: (516) 733-6700
 TFree:(800) 842-0780   Fax:(516) 733-8636

Computer Shopper Magazine:NY .... Main: (212) 503-3800
 TFree:(800) 274-6384

Computer Support Corp:TX .... Main: (972) 661-8960
 Fax:(972) 661-5429   Tech:(972) 661-8960

Computer Systems And Education:WA .... Main: (360) 693-6165
 Fax:(360) 693-6109   Tech:(800) 791-1181

Computer Teaching Corp:IL .... Main: (217) 352-6363
 Fax:(217) 352-3104

Computer Technology Review:CA .... Main: (213) 208-1335
 Fax:(310) 208-1054

Computer Tyme Software Lab:MO .... Main:(417) 866-1222
 TFree:(800) 548-5353   Fax:(417) 866-1665

ComputerPREP Inc:AZ .... Main: (602) 275-7700
 TFree:(800) 228-1027   Fax:(602) 275-1603

ComputerTrend Systems(Premio Com):CA .Main: (818) 333-5121
 TFree:(800) 677-6477   Fax:(818) 369-6803
 Tech Fax:(818) 330-9749

Computone Corp:GA .... Main: (770) 475-2725
 TFree:(800) 241-3946   Fax:(770) 664-1510   Tech:(770) 475-2725
 another BBS:(770) 664-1210

Computron Software Inc:NJ .... Main: (201) 935-3400
 TFree:(800) 828-7660   Fax:(201) 935-7678

Compuware Corp:MI .... Main: (248) 737-7300
 Fax:(248) 737-7119

Comtech Publishing:NV .... Main: (702) 825-9000
 TFree:(800) 456-7005   Fax:(702) 825-1818   Tech:(702) 825-9000

Comtech Research:OH .... Main: (419) 278-6790
 Fax:(419) 278-7744

Comtrol Corp:MN .... Main: (612) 631-7654
 TFree:(800) 926-6876   Fax:(612) 631-8117   Tech:(800) 926-6876

Concentric Data:MA .... Main: (508) 366-1122
 TFree:(800) 325-9035   Fax:(508) 366-2954   Tech:(800) 325-9035
 support contract:(800) 487-8622

Concept Software:OH .... Main: (216) 943-4341
 Fax:(216) 943-4346

Concord Communications:MA .... Main: (508) 460-4646
 TFree:(800) 851-8725   Fax:(508) 481-9772

Connectix Corp:CA .... Main: (415) 571-5100
 TFree:(800) 950-5880   Fax:(415) 571-0850   Tech:(800) 839-3627
 Tech Fax:(415) 571-5195

ConnectSoft Inc:WA .... Main: (206) 827-6467
 TFree:(800) 234-9497   Fax:(206) 822-9095   Tech:(800) 234-9497

Conner Peripherals Inc (see Seagate):

Conner Tape Products:CA .... **Main: (714) 641-1230**
  Fax:(714) 966-5534   Tech:(800) 426-6637

Contact East:MA .... **Main: (508) 682-2000**
  TFree:(888) 925-2960 Fax:(800) 225-5317

Contact Software International Inc:TX .... **Main: (214) 418-1866**
  Tech:(214) 484-4349

Contango Inc (Creative Insights):CA .... **Main: (415) 548-0283**
  Fax:(415) 548-9512   Tech:(415) 548-0283

Contour Design Inc:NH .... **Main: (603) 893-4556**
  TFree:(800) 462-6678 Fax:(603) 893-4558 Tech:(603) 893-4556

Control Data Systems (CDC):MN .... **Main: (612) 415-2999**
  TFree:(888) 742-5864 Fax:(612) 415-3000 Tech:(800) 257-6736

Copia International Ltd:IL .... **Main: (630) 682-8898**
  TFree:(800) 689-8898 Fax:(630) 665-9841 Tech:(630) 682-8898

Core International:FL .... **Main: (561) 997-6055**
  Fax:(561) 997-6202   Tech:(561) 997-6033
  Core Engineering:(561) 998-3800

Corel Corporation:ON .... **Main: (613) 728-3733**
  TFree:(800) 772-6735 Fax:(613) 761-9176 Tech:(613) 728-7070
  Fax:(613) 761-1295

... CorelVENTURA 7.0
  Tech:(613) 728-6398
  extended support:(800) 792-6735

... Artshow (all versions)
  Tech:(613) 728-6173

... CD Office Companion
  Tech:(613) 728-6173

... CD+ for A&M CD's
  Tech:(613) 728-6514

... Corel CADD 3D
  Tech:(613) 728-6418
  :(800) 291-4434

... Corel CD Home
  Tech:(613) 728-1010

... Corel Click & Create
  extended support:(800) 754-8209

... Corel Family Tree Suite
  Tech:(613) 728-6891

... Corel GALLERY
  Tech:(613) 728-6173

... Corel GALLERY 2
  Tech:(613) 728-6173

... Corel Graphics Pack
  Tech:(613) 728-6891
  extended support:(800) 205-4295

... Corel Learning Series
  Tech:(613) 728-6548

... Corel MEGA GALLERY
  Tech:(613) 728-6173

... Corel Office Professional Suite (Win 3.1)..Main: (801) 765-4043
... Corel Office Professional Suite 7 ....Main: (801) 765-4045
... **Corel PHOTO-PAINT 5.0+**
  Tech:(613) 728-6398
   extended support:(800) 792-6735
... **Corel PHOTO-PAINT 6.0**
  Tech:(613) 728-6398
   extended support:(800) 792-6735
... **Corel PHOTO-PAINT 7.0+**
  Tech:(613) 728-6398
   extended support:(800) 792-6735
... **Corel Print House (all versions)**
  Tech:(613) 728-6891
... **Corel SCSI**
  Tech:(613) 728-1010
... **Corel VisualCADD**
  Tech:(613) 728-6418
   extended support:(800) 291-4434
... **Corel WEB.DATA**
  Tech:(613) 728-6625
   extended support:(800) 856-5650
... **Corel WEB.DESIGNER**
  Tech:(613) 728-6625
   extended support:(800) 856-5650
... **Corel WEB.GALLERY**
  Tech:(613) 728-6173
... **Corel WEB.GRAPHICS Suite**
  Tech:(613) 728-6625
   extended support:(800) 856-5650
... **Corel WebMaster Suite**
  Tech:(613) 728-6625
   extended support:(800) 856-5650
... Corel Word Perfect 7 Suite ....Main: (801) 765-4044
  TFree:(800) 757-2133
  Fee support:(900) 555-2123
... Corel Word Perfect 8 Suite ....Main: (801) 765-4080
... Corel WordPerfect Suite (Win 3.1) ....Main: (801) 765-4041
  TFree:(800) 310-2122
  Fee support:(900) 555-2120
... **Corel WP BBS**
  how to use BBS:(801) 765-4033
... **Corel XARA**
  Tech:(613) 728-6891
   extended support:(800) 992-6735
... **CorelDRAW 2.5 for OS/2**
  Tech:(613) 728-6641
   extended support:(800) 582-6735
... **CorelDRAW 3.0**
  Tech:(613) 728-6641
   extended support:(800) 582-6735
... **CorelDRAW 4.0**
  Tech:(613) 728-6641
   extended support:(800) 582-6735

... CorelDRAW 5.0
  Tech:(613) 728-6641
  extended support:(800) 818-1848

... CorelDRAW 6.0
  Tech:(613) 728-7070
  extended support:(800) 205-4295

... CorelDRAW 7.0
  Tech:(613) 728-7070
  extended support:(800) 205-4295

... CorelDRAW for MAC
  Tech:(613) 728-4201
  extended support:(800) 205-4295

... CorelDRAW for UNIX .... Main: (801) 765-4019

... CorelFLOW 2.0
  Tech:(613) 728-6173
  extended support:(800) 856-5650

... CorelFLOW 3.0
  Tech:(613) 728-6173
  extended support:(800) 856-5650

... CorelVENTURA 5.0
  Tech:(613) 728-6398
  extended support:(800) 792-6735

... DOS/WIN version 6.x (Priority Service)
  TFree:(800) 861-2160
  (900) 555-4010:(800) 861-2310

... DOS/WIN version 7 & higher(Priority Service)
  TFree:(800) 861-2160
  (900) 555-2123:(800) 757-2133

... Envoy/Quickfinder 7 .... Main: (801) 765-4058
... InfoCentral (Win 3.1) .... Main: (801) 765-4012
... Intellitag/SGML (Win 3.1) .... Main: (801) 765-4013
... IVAN .... Main: (801) 765-4038
... Language Modules (DOS) .... Main: (801) 765-4013
... MAC & DOS/WIN ver 5.x & lower(Priority Serv)
  TFree:(800) 861-2160
  (900) 555-2233:(800) 861-2410

... Make-It-Perfect .... Main: (801) 765-4030
... Novell GroupWise Support .... Main: (801) 431-3400
  TFree:(800) 861-2140
... Paradox 7 (Connectivity/Database Dsgn) . Main: (888) 761-6909
... Paradox 7 (DOS (CC#)) .... Main: (800) 468-9990
... Paradox 7 (DOS Contract) .... Main: (800) 529-1999
... Paradox 7 (Up & running pre-sales) ... Main: (801) 765-4062
... Paradox 7 (Windows (CC#)) .... Main: (800) 452-1333
... Paradox 7 (Windows Contract) .... Main: (800) 553-5512
... PerfectWorks Support (Arkose) .... Main: (801) 228-9936
... Presentations 2.1 (DOS) .... Main: (801) 765-4031
... Presentations 3.0 (Win 3.1) .... Main: (801) 765-4016
... Presentations 7 .... Main: (801) 765-4057
... Product Orders .... Main: (800) 772-6735
... Professional Photos
  Tech:(613) 728-6173
... Quattro Pro 5.6 (DOS) .... Main: (801) 765-4017
  TFree:(800) 862-8222

```
        Fee support:(900) 555-1001
... Quattro Pro 6.0 (Win 3.1) .....................Main: (801) 765-4029
    TFree:(800) 862-8222
    Fee support:(900) 555-1008
... Quattro Pro 7 .........................................Main: (801) 765-4056
... Service Sales .........................................Main: (800) 861-2160
... SGML 7 ..................................................Main: (801) 765-4059
    TFree:(800) 861-2025
    Fee support:(900) 555-5040
... UNIX (Priority Service) ..........................Main: (801) 765-4019
... WordPerfect 3.51 and higher (MAC) .......Main: (801) 765-4020
... WordPerfect 5.1 and higher (UNIX) .........Main: (801) 765-4019
... WordPerfect 5.1+ (DOS) ........................Main: (801) 765-4022
... WordPerfect 6.1 (DOS) ...........................Main: (801) 765-4024
... WordPerfect 6.1 (Win 3.1) ......................Main: (801) 765-4027
... WordPerfect 6.2 (DOS) ...........................Main: (801) 765-4024
... WordPerfect 7 ........................................Main: (801) 765-4055
... WordPerfect French Canadian Support ....Main: (613) 728-9035
... WordPerfect Spanish Support .................Main: (801) 765-4034
Cornerstone Imaging:CA ............................Main: (408) 435-8900
    TFree:(800) 562-2552   Fax:(408) 435-8998  Tech:(800) 562-2552
Cornerstone Training:NJ ............................Main: (908) 251-6300
CoStar:CT ..................................................Main: (203) 661-9700
    TFree:(800) 426-7827   Fax:(203) 661-1540  Tech:(203) 661-9700
    Tech Fax:(203) 661-6534
Cougar Mountain Software Inc:ID ...............Main: (208) 375-4455
    TFree:(800) 388-3038   Fax:(208) 375-4455  Tech:(800) 727-0656
Covey Leadership Center (Franklin Covey):
Cox Recorders/Energy Reserve Inc:NC ......Main: (704) 825-8146
    Fax:(704) 825-4498
    Sales:(909) 946-4441
Cray Research Inc:MN ................................Main: (612) 683-3800
    Fax:(612) 683-3599
Creative Assistance Software:NC ...............Main: (704) 544-0001
    Fax:(704) 544-8031    Tech:(704) 544-0001
Creative Labs Inc:CA .................................Main: (408) 428-6600
    TFree:(800) 998-1000  Fax:(408) 428-6611  Tech:(405) 742-6622
    Tech Fax:(405) 742-6633
Creative Multimedia Corp:OR .....................Main: (503) 241-4351
    Fax:(503) 241-4370     Tech:(503) 241-1530
Crescent Software:MA ................................Main: (617) 280-3000
    TFree:(800) 352-2742  Fax:(617) 280-4025  Tech:(617) 280-3000
... CD+ for Sony CD's
    Tech:(613) 761-9330
Crosstalk Communication(Attachmate):GA .Main: (770) 442-4000
    TFree:(800) 426-6283  Fax:(770) 944-2435  Tech:(206) 957-7764
Crosswise Corp:CA ....................................Main: (408) 459-9060
    TFree:(800) 747-9060  Fax:(408) 426-3859  Tech:(800) 747-9060
Crystal Services (see Seagate):BC .............Main: (604) 681-3435
    TFree:(800) 877-2340  Fax:(604) 681-2934  Tech:(604) 669-8379
CS Electronics:CA .....................................Main: (714) 475-9100
    Fax:(714) 475-9119
```

CTX International Inc:CA .... **Main: (818) 839-0500**
TFree:(800) 888-2012   Fax:(818) 810-6703   Tech:(800) 282-2205

Cubix Corp:NV .... **Main: (702) 888-1000**
TFree:(800) 829-0550   Fax:(702) 888-1001

Curtis Manufacturing Co (Rolodex):NJ   Main: (800) 727-7656
TFree:(800) 955-5544   Fax:(201) 348-0239   Tech:(800) 955-5544

Cway Software:PA .... **Main: (215) 368-9494**
Fax:(215) 368-7233   Tech:(215) 368-9494

CyberMedia Inc:CA .... **Main: (310) 581-4700**
TFree:(800) 721-7824   Fax:(310) 581-4720   Tech:(310) 581-4710
Tech Fax:(310) 581-4737

Cybex Corp:AL .... **Main: (205) 430-4000**
TFree:(800) 793-3758   Fax:(205) 430-4030

CyLink Corp:CA .... **Main: (408) 735-5800**
Fax:(408) 735-6643   Tech:(800) 545-6608

Cyma Systems Inc:AZ .... **Main: (602) 303-2962**
TFree:(800) 292-2962   Fax:(602) 303-2969

Cypress Research:CA .... **Main: (408) 486-7900**
Fax:(408) 486-7952   Tech:(408) 486-0444

Cypress Semiconductor Corp:CA .... **Main: (408) 943-2600**
Fax:(408) 943-2843   Tech:(800) 858-1810

Cyrix Corp:TX .... **Main: (972) 968-8388**
TFree:(800) 462-9749   Fax:(972) 699-9857   Tech:(972) 462-9749

D-Link Systems Inc:CA .... **Main: (714) 455-1688**
TFree:(800) 326-1688   Fax:(714) 455-1261   Tech:(714) 598-8150

DacEasy Inc:TX .... **Main: (972) 248-0305**
TFree:(800) 322-3279   Fax:(972) 713-6331   Tech:(972) 248-0205

Dalco Electronics:OH .... **Main: (513) 743-8042**
TFree:(800) 445-5342   Fax:(513) 743-9251   Tech:(800) 543-2526

Dallas Semiconductor:TX .... **Main: (972) 788-2197**
Fax:(972) 980-4290   Tech:(972) 371-4167

Damark International Inc:MN .... **Main: (800) 729-9000**
TFree:(800) 729-9000   Tech:(800) 729-9000

Danpex Corp:CA .... **Main: (408) 437-7557**
TFree:(800) 452-1551   Fax:(408) 434-1699   Tech:(408) 434-1688

Dantz Development Corp:CA .... **Main: (510) 253-3000**
TFree:(800) 225-4880   Fax:(510) 253-9099   Tech:(510) 253-3050

Dariana Software (see E-Ware):

Data Access Corp:FL .... **Main: (305) 238-0012**
TFree:(800) 451-3539   Fax:(305) 238-0017   Tech:(305) 238-0012

Data Assist Inc:OH .... **Main: (614) 888-8088**
TFree:(800) 326-8088   Fax:(614) 888-8072   Tech:(800) 326-8088

Data Code Inc:FL .... **Main: (407) 351-3441**
TFree:(800) 762-1480   Fax:(407) 351-5019

Data Conversion Laboratory:NY .... **Main: (718) 357-8700**
Fax:(718) 357-8776

Data Depot Inc:CA
TFree:(800) 432-8233

Data Fellows:CA .... **Main: (408) 938-6700**
Fax:(408) 938-6701   Tech:(408) 244-9090

Data General Corp:MA .... **Main: (508) 898-5000**
TFree:(800) 328-2436   Fax:(508) 366-1319   Tech:(800) 344-3577

Data I/O Corp:WA .... Main: **(206) 881-6444**
TFree:(800) 426-1045   Fax:(425) 882-1043   Tech:(800) 247-5700

Data Pro Accounting Software:FL .... Main: **(813) 885-9459**
TFree:(800) 836-6377   Fax:(813) 882-8143   Tech:(813) 888-5847

Data Race:TX .... Main: **(210) 263-2000**
TFree:(800) 329-7223   Fax:(210) 263-2075   Tech:(210) 263-2010

Data Storage Marketing:CO .... Main: **(303) 442-4747**
TFree:(800) 543-6090   Fax:(303) 442-7985   Tech:(800) 543-6098

Data Storage Marketing:TX .... Main: **(214) 407-0222**
TFree:(800) 654-6311   Fax:(214) 407-9732

Data Technology Corp (DTC):CA .... Main: **(408) 942-4000**
Fax:(408) 942-4027   Tech:(408) 262-7700

Data Views Corp:MA .... Main: **(413) 586-4144**
Fax:(413) 586-3805

Data Watch:MA .... Main: **(508) 988-9700**
TFree:(800) 988-4739   Fax:(508) 988-2040   Tech:(508) 988-9700
Tech Fax:(508) 988-0697

Database America:NJ .... Main: **(201) 476-2000**
TFree:(888) 362-2533   Fax:(201) 476-2419   Tech:(201) 476-2000

DataCal Corp:AZ .... Main: **(602) 813-3100**
TFree:(800) 223-0123   Fax:(602) 545-8090   Tech:(602) 545-8089

DataEase International:CT .... Main: **(203) 374-8000**
TFree:(800) 243-5123   Fax:(203) 365-2397   Tech:(203) 374-2825

Dataproducts Corporation:CA .... Main: **(805) 578-4000**
TFree:(800) 887-8848   Fax:(805) 578-4001   Tech:(805) 578-4455

DataQuest Interactive:CA .... Main: **(408) 468-8000**
TFree:(800) 419-3282   Fax:(408) 954-1780   Tech:(408) 748-1111

Datashield Unison (Tripp Lite Worldwide):IL Main: **(312) 755-5400**
Fax:(312) 644-6505   Tech:(312) 755-5401

DataSoft:AZ .... Main: **(602) 930-5380**
TFree:(800) 824-2371   Fax:(602) 930-5241   Tech:(602) 930-5380

Datasouth Computer Corp:NC .... Main: **(704) 523-8500**
TFree:(800) 476-2120   Fax:(704) 523-9298   Tech:(800) 476-2450

DataSpec (see Alliance Research):

Datastor:CA .... Main: **(714) 833-8000**
TFree:(800) 777-6621   Fax:(714) 833-9600

Datastorm Technologies(Quarterdeck):MO Main: **(573) 443-3282**
TFree:(800) 354-3222   Fax:(800) 354-3329   Tech:(573) 875-0530

DataViz Inc:CT .... Main: **(203) 268-0030**
TFree:(800) 733-0030   Fax:(203) 268-4345   Tech:(203) 268-0030

Dataware Technologies Inc:MA .... Main: **(617) 621-0820**
Fax:(617) 494-0740

Datum Inc:CA .... Main: **(714) 380-8880**
Fax:(714) 380-8555

Dauphin Technology Inc:IL .... Main: **(847) 358-4406**
Fax:(847) 358-4407

David Systems Inc (see 3Com Corp):

Davidson & Associates (CUC Intl):CA..Main: **(310) 793-0600**
TFree:(800) 545-7677   Fax:(310) 793-0601   Tech:(800) 556-6141

Day Runner:CA .... Main: **(714) 680-3500**
TFree:(800) 232-9786   Fax:(714) 441-4848

Dayna Communications:UT................ Main: **(801) 269-7200**
TFree:(800) 531-0600   Fax:(801) 269-7363   Tech:(801) 569-7200

DayStar Digital Inc:GA .... Main: **(770) 967-2077**
  TFree:(800) 962-2077   Fax:(770) 967-3018   Tech:(770) 967-2077
Db-Tech Inc:NJ .... Main: **(732) 329-9000**
  TFree:(800) 234-4500   Fax:(732) 329-0066
DCA/IRMA (see Attachmate):
DDC Publishing:NY .... Main: **(212) 986-7300**
  TFree:(800) 528-3897   Fax:(212) 689-6851   Tech:(800) 955-5284
Deadly Games:NY .... Main: **(516) 537-6060**
  Fax:(516) 537-3299   Tech:(516) 537-6060
DEC PC Support BBS: .... Main: **(508) 496-8800**
  TFree:(800) 987-9995   Fax:(415) 528-4321
Decisive Technology Corp:CA .... Main: **(415) 528-4300**
Deep River Publishing Inc:ME .... Main: **(207) 871-1684**
  TFree:(800) 643-5630   Fax:(207) 871-1683   Tech:(207) 871-1684
Dell Computer Corp:TX .... Main: **(512) 338-4400**
  TFree:(800) 289-3355   Fax:(800) 727-8320   Tech:(800) 624-9896
DeLorme Mapping:ME .... Main: **(207) 846-7000**
  TFree:(800) 452-5931   Fax:(800) 575-2244   Tech:(207) 846-8900
  Tech Suppport Fax:(207) 846-7050
Delphi (News Corp/MCI Online Ventures):
Delrina Software (See Symantec):ON .... Main: **(416) 441-3676**
  TFree:(800) 268-6082   Fax:(416) 441-0333   Tech:(800) 268-6082
Delta Software Systems Inc:TN .... Main: **(901) 758-0123**
  Fax:(901) 758-0211
DeltaPoint:CA .... Main: **(408) 648-4000**
  TFree:(800) 446-6825   Fax:(408) 648-4020   Tech:(408) 375-4700
  Tech Support Fax:(408) 648-4048
Deltec:CA .... Main: **(619) 291-4211**
  TFree:(800) 854-2658   Fax:(619) 296-8039   Tech:(800) 848-4734
Deneba Software:FL .... Main: **(305) 596-5644**
  TFree:(800) 733-6322   Fax:(305) 273-9069   Tech:(305) 596-5644
Derby And Associates:CO .... Main: **(303) 979-6054**
  Fax:(303) 972-8043
DeScribe Inc (Out of Business):
DesignCAD:OK .... Main: **(918) 825-7555**
  TFree:(800) 233-3223   Fax:(918) 825-6359   Tech:(918) 825-4844
Develcon Electronics Ltd: .... Main: **(306) 933-3300**
  TFree:(800) 667-9333   Fax:(306) 931-1370
DFI USA:CA .... Main: **(916) 568-1234**
  Fax:(916) 568-1233   Tech:(916) 568-1234
Dia-Nielsen:NJ .... Main: **(609) 829-9441**
  TFree:(800) 893-6361   Fax:(609) 829-8814   Tech:(609) 829-9381
Diagnostic Technologies Inc:ON .... Main: **(905) 542-8674**
  Fax:(905) 542-8458   Tech:(905) 347-0486
DiagSoft Inc:FL .... Main: **(813) 207-7000**
  TFree:(800) 342-4763   Fax:(813) 207-7001
Dialogic Corp:NJ .... Main: **(201) 993-3000**
  TFree:(800) 755-4444   Fax:(201) 993-3093
Dialogic GammaLink:NJ .... Main: **(973) 993-3000**
  TFree:(800) 329-4727   Fax:(973) 993-3093   Tech:(408) 745-2250

Diamond Computer (Diamond Multimedia):
Diamond Entertainment Corp:NJ.................Main: (908) 431-0700
Diamond Flower Electric Inst (see DFI USA):
Diamond Multimedia Systems:CA.................Main: (408) 325-7000
TFree:(800) 468-5846 Fax:(408) 325-7070 Tech:(408) 325-7100
Digi International:TN.................Main: (615) 834-8000
Fax:(615) 834-5399 Tech:(800) 366-8844
Digi International:MN.................Main: (612) 912-3444
TFree:(800) 344-4273 Fax:(612) 912-4952
Tech Fax:(612) 912-4958
Digi-Data Corp:MD.................Main: (301) 498-0200
Fax:(301) 498-0771 Tech:(301) 498-0200
Digi-Key Corporation:MN.................Main: (218) 681-6674
TFree:(800) 344-4539 Fax:(218) 681-3380
Digiboard Inc (see Digi International):
Digicom Systems Inc:CA.................Main: (408) 262-1277
TFree:(800) 833-8900 Fax:(408) 262-1390 Tech:(408) 934-1601
Digimarc Corp:OR.................Main: (503) 223-0118
TFree:(800) 344-4627 Fax:(503) 223-6015 Tech:(503) 626-8811
Digit Head Inc:VA.................Main: (703) 524-0101
Fax:(703) 524-0102 Tech:(703) 524-0101
Digital Dynamics:CA.................Main: (408) 438-4444
Fax:(408) 438-6825 Tech:(408) 438-4444
Digital Equipment Corp:MA.................Main: (800) 354-9000
TFree:(800) 332-4636
Digital Equipment Corp:MA.................Main: (508) 841-3111
TFree:(800) 354-9000 Fax:(508) 841-6100
Digital Equipment Corp:NH.................Main: (603) 884-5111
TFree:(800) 354-9000
... Computer Systems Division.................Main: (800) 354-9000
TFree:(800) 332-7378 Tech:(800) 722-9332
... Digital Components and Peripherals.................Main: (800) 777-4343
... Digital Learning Center.................Main: (800) 332-5656
Fax:(603) 884-6655
... Digital Semiconductor.................Main: (508) 568-6872
... Digital Storage Information.................Main: (800) 786-7967
... Internet Business Group.................Main: (800) 344-4825
... Mobile Software Business.................Main: (508) 486-2111
Digital Impact:OK.................Main: (918) 742-2022
TFree:(800) 775-4232 Fax:(918) 742-8176 Tech:(918) 742-2022
Digital Vision:MA.................Main: (617) 329-5400
TFree:(800) 346-0090 Fax:(617) 329-6286 Tech:(617) 329-5400
Dimension X Inc (see Microsoft):
Disc Distributing Corp:CA.................Main: (310) 787-6800
TFree:(800) 688-4545 Fax:(310) 787-6810
Discis Knowledge Research:ON.................Main: (416) 250-6537
Fax:(416) 250-6540 Tech:(416) 250-6537
Disctec:FL.................Main: (407) 671-5500
Fax:(407) 671-6606
Disney Interactive:CA.................Main: (818) 543-4300
Fax:(818) 846-0454 Tech:(800) 228-0988

Distinct Corp:CA .... Main: (408) 366-8933
  Fax:(408) 366-0153   Tech:(408) 342-3216
  Tech Fax:(408) 342-3216

Distributed Processing Tech:FL .... Main: (407) 830-5522
  TFree:(800) 322-4378 Fax:(407) 260-5366 Tech:(407) 830-5522

Diversified Technology:MS .... Main: (601) 856-4121
  TFree:(800) 443-2667 Fax:(601) 856-2888

DMA (see Symantec):

DocuMagix Inc:CA .... Main: (408) 434-1138
  TFree:(800) 362-8624 Fax:(408) 434-0915 Tech:(408) 434-1001

Dorak International Corp:CA .... Main: (818) 288-9171
  Fax:(818) 288-6205   Tech:(818) 288-9171

Dr. Dobb's Journal (Miller Freeman):CA ... Main: (650) 358-9500
  TFree:(800) 444-4881 Fax:(650) 358-9749

Dr. Solomon's Software:MA .... Main: (617) 273-7400
  TFree:(888) 377-6566 Fax:(617) 273-7474 Tech:(617) 273-7400

Dr. T's Music Software:MA .... Main: (617) 272-9000
  Fax:(617) 272-9097   Tech:(770) 428-0008

Dragon Systems Inc:MA .... Main: (617) 965-5200
  TFree:(800) 825-5897 Fax:(617) 527-0372 Tech:(617) 965-7670

Dream Theater:CA .... Main: (818) 773-4979
  Fax:(818) 773-8314   Tech:(818) 773-4979

Dresselhaus Computer Products:CA .... Main: (909) 937-1137
  TFree:(800) 368-7737 Fax:(909) 937-1150 Tech:(909) 937-1137

DS Design:NC .... Main: (919) 319-1770
  TFree:(800) 745-4037 Fax:(919) 460-5983

DSP Group Inc:CA .... Main: (408) 986-4300
  Fax:(408) 986-4323

DSP Solutions Inc:CA .... Main: (650) 919-4000
  Fax:(650) 919-4040 Tech:(650) 919-4100

DTK Computer Inc:CA .... Main: (626) 810-0098
  TFree:(800) 289-2385 Fax:(626) 810-0090 Tech:(626) 810-0098

Dukane Corporation:IL .... Main: (630) 584-2300
  Fax:(630) 584-5156

Durand Communications Inc:CA .... Main: (805) 961-8700
  Fax:(805) 961-8701

Dynacomp Inc:NY .... Main: (716) 346-9788

Dynalink Technologies:QC .... Main: (514) 489-3007
  Fax:(514) 486-2901   Tech:(514) 489-3007

Dynatech Computer Power (S.L. Waiber):

Dynatran:OR .... Main: (503) 646-9045
  TFree:(800) 423-7650 Fax:(503) 641-4697 Tech:(503) 646-9045

E-mu Systems Inc:CA .... Main: (408) 438-1921
  Fax:(408) 439-8612   Tech:(408) 438-1921

E-Tech Research Inc:CA .... Main: (510) 438-6700
  TFree:(888) 609-8885 Fax:(408) 438-6701 Tech:(888) 413-7433

E-Ware Systems Inc:NY .... Main: (212) 581-5858

Eagle Data Protection Inc:UT .... Main: (801) 363-7300
  TFree:(800) 909-3141 Fax:(801) 538-0200 Tech:(801) 363-7300

Eagle Point Software Corp:IA .... Main: (319) 556-8392

Eagle Technology:WI .... Main: (414) 241-3845
  TFree:(800) 388-3268 Fax:(414) 241-5248 Tech:(414) 241-3845

Eastman Kodak Co:NY .... Main: **(716) 724-9977**
  TFree:(800) 242-2424 Fax:(716) 724-3282 Tech:(800) 235-6325
  Help Line:(716) 781-5224
Easy Software Products:MD .... Main: **(301) 373-9603**
  Fax:(301) 373-9604
EBM Corporation:MI .... Main: **(517) 426-6327**
  TFree:(800) 815-5719 Fax:(517) 426-7354
Eccentric Software:WA .... Main: **(206) 628-2687**
  TFree:(800) 436-6758 Fax:(206) 628-2681 Tech:(206) 628-2687
Echo Speech Corporation:CA .... Main: **(805) 684-4593**
  Tech:(805) 684-4593
Eclipse Tech Inc:CA .... Main: **(408) 523-5700**
Edmark Corp:WA .... Main: **(206) 556-8400**
  TFree:(800) 691-2986 Fax:(206) 556-8430 Tech:(206) 556-8480
  Customer service:(206) 556-8484
EDS Internet New Media: .... Main: **(972) 604-7445**
  TFree:(800) 890-1841
EDS Unigraphics:MO .... Main: **(314) 344-5900**
  Fax:(314) 344-4180
EDUCORP Multimedia:CA .... Main: **(619) 536-9999**
  TFree:(800) 843-9497 Fax:(619) 536-2345 Tech:(619) 693-4030
Efficient Field Service:MA .... Main: **(508) 251-7800**
  TFree:(800) 257-4745 Fax:(508) 251-4882
EFI Electronics Corp:UT .... Main: **(801) 977-9009**
  TFree:(800) 877-1174 Fax:(801) 977-0200 Tech:(800) 877-1174
Egghead Software:WA .... Main: **(425) 391-0800**
  TFree:(800) 344-4323 Fax:(425) 391-0880
Eicon Technology Corp:TX .... Main: **(972) 490-3270**
  TFree:(800) 342-6660 Fax:(972) 239-8069
Eigentech Inc:NJ .... Main: **(609) 985-9185**
  TFree:(800) 676-8689 Fax:(609) 985-9185
Elan Computer Group:CA .... Main: **(415) 964-2200**
  TFree:(800) 536-3526 Fax:(415) 964-8588
Elan Software Corp (Goldmine Softwr):CA .. Main: **(310) 454-6800**
  TFree:(800) 654-3526 Fax:(310) 454-4848 Tech:(310) 459-1222
  Tech Fax:(310) 459-8222
Electronic Arts:CA .... Main: **(415) 571-7171**
  Fax:(415) 571-7995 Tech:(415) 572-2787
Electronic City:CA .... Main: **(818) 842-5275**
  Fax:(818) 842-0419
Electronic Data Systems Corp (EDS):TX ...... Main: **(972) 605-6000**
  TFree:(800) 566-9337 Fax:(972) 604-3562 Tech:(972) 605-6000
Electronic Energy Control Inc:OH .... Main: **(800) 842-7714**
  TFree:(800) 842-7714 Fax:(614) 464-9656 Tech:(614) 464-4470
Electronic Multimedia Enterprises:CT .... Main: **(203) 406-4040**
  TFree:(800) 548-7322 Fax:(203) 406-4043 Tech:(800) 548-7322
Electronic Press Services:MA .... Main: **(617) 225-9023**
  TFree:(800) 680-6856 Fax:(617) 225-7983 Tech:(800) 680-6856
Electronics Of Salina:KS .... Main: **(913) 827-7377**
  TFree:(800) 874-8204 Fax:(913) 827-7611
Electronix Corp:OH .... Main: **(937) 878-9878**
  Fax:(937) 878-1972

Elgin Interactive Software:IL .... Main: (847) 697-9654
    Fax:(847) 697-9689
Elite Products:MD .... Main: (800) 576-2349
    TFree:(800) 576-2349   Fax:(410) 987-3258
Elitegroup Computer System (ECS):CA .... Main: (510) 226-7333
    Fax:(415) 226-7350   Tech:(510) 226-7333
Elo TouchSystems Inc:CA .... Main: (510) 651-2340
    TFree:(800) 356-8682   Fax:(510) 651-3511   Tech:(615) 220-4299
Emblem Corp:FL .... Main: (305) 541-4331
    TFree:(800) 323-8324   Fax:(305) 541-0074   Tech:(305) 541-4331
Emerald Systems (NCE Storage Solutions):
EMPaC International Corp:CA .... Main: (510) 683-8800
    Fax:(510) 683-8662   Tech:(510) 226-4754
    Tech Support:(510) 683-8762
Empress Software Inc:MD .... Main: (301) 220-1919
    Fax:(301) 220-1997
Emulex:CA .... Main: (714) 662-5600
    TFree:(800) 854-7112   Fax:(714) 241-0792   Tech:(714) 513-8270
Enable Software Inc:NY .... Main: (518) 877-8600
    TFree:(800) 888-0684   Fax:(518) 877-3337   Tech:(518) 877-8236
Encore Computer Corp:FL .... Main: (954) 587-2900
    TFree:(800) 933-6267   Fax:(954) 797-5793
    :(800) 933-6267
Endl Publications:CA .... Main: (408) 867-6642
    Fax:(408) 867-2115
Enhance Memory Products Inc:CA .... Main: (818) 343-3066
    TFree:(800) 343-0100   Fax:(818) 343-1436   Tech:(818) 343-3066
ENSONIQ Corp:PA .... Main: (610) 647-3930
    TFree:(800) 553-5151   Fax:(610) 647-8908
Envirogen International:CA .... Main: (714) 574-1440
    TFree:(800) 228-8839   Fax:(714) 574-1432   Tech:(714) 574-1440
Environmental Systems Research Inst:CA ..Main: (909) 793-2853
    TFree:(800) 447-9778   Fax:(909) 793-5953   Tech:(909) 792-0960
EO (see AT&T):
Epilogue Technology Corp:CA .... Main: (408) 542-1500
    Fax:(408) 542-1961   Tech:(617) 245-0804
    Tech Fax:(617) 245-8122
Epson America Inc:CA .... Main: (310) 782-0770
    TFree:(800) 289-3776   Fax:(310) 782-5220   Tech:(800) 922-8911
Equilibrium Inc:CA .... Main: (415) 332-4343
    Fax:(415) 332-4433   Tech:(415) 332-4343
Equinox Systems Inc:FL .... Main: (305) 746-9000
    TFree:(800) 275-3500   Fax:(305) 746-9101   Tech:(800) 275-3500
Ergo Computing Inc:MA .... Main: (508) 535-7510
    Fax:(508) 535-7512   Tech:(800) 633-1922
ESoft Product Support:CO .... Main: (303) 699-6565
    Fax:(303) 699-6872   Tech:(303) 699-1300
EST (Engineering Service Technology):NH .Main: (603) 673-9907
    Fax:(603) 673-9913
Europa Software:OR .... Main: (503) 417-2900
    Fax:(503) 227-7344
Evans & Sutherland:UT .... Main: (801) 588-1000
    Fax:(801) 588-4500

Everex Systems:CA .... Main: **(510) 498-1111**
  TFree:(800) 383-7391 Fax:(510) 683-2186 Tech:(510) 498-4411
  Tech Support:(800) 262-3312

Evolution Computing:AZ .... Main: **(602) 967-8633**
  TFree:(800) 874-4028 Fax:(602) 968-4325 Tech:(800) 874-4028

Ex Machina Inc (Air Media):NY .... Main: **(212) 842-0000**
  TFree:(800) 238-4738 Fax:(212) 545-7992 Tech:(212) 843-0000

Exabyte Corp:CO .... Main: **(303) 417-7792**
  TFree:(800) 445-7736 Fax:(303) 417-7160 Tech:(800) 445-7736

Excalibur Communications Inc:OK .... Main: **(918) 488-9801**
  TFree:(800) 392-2522 Fax:(918) 491-0033 Tech:(918) 488-9801

Excite Inc:CA .... Main: **(415) 568-6000**
  Fax:(415) 568-6030 Tech:(415) 943-1200

Expert Software:FL .... Main: **(305) 567-9990**
  TFree:(800) 759-2562 Fax:(305) 443-0786 Tech:(305) 567-9990

ExperVision Inc:CA .... Main: **(510) 623-7071**
  TFree:(800) 732-3897 Fax:(510) 623-9290 Tech:(800) 732-3897

Exponent Corp:NJ .... Main: **(973) 808-9424**
  TFree:(800) 772-7077 Fax:(973) 808-9419

Express Systems Inc (See WRQ):WA ..... Main: **(206) 728-8300**
  TFree:(800) 321-4606 Fax:(206) 728-8301 Tech:(800) 321-4606

Extended Systems Inc:ID .... Main: **(208) 322-7800**
  TFree:(800) 235-7576 Fax:(406) 587-9170 Tech:(800) 235-7576

EZI America Corp:CA .... Main: **(805) 987-5885**
  Fax:(805) 987-7677

Fairhaven Software:MA .... Main: **(508) 994-6400**
  TFree:(800) 582-4747 Fax:(508) 994-6465 Tech:(508) 994-6464

Fantazia Concepts Inc:OH .... Main: **(216) 951-5666**
  Fax:(216) 951-9241 Tech:(216) 951-0877

Farallon Computing:CA .... Main: **(510) 814-5100**
  TFree:(800) 344-7489 Fax:(510) 814-5023 Tech:(510) 814-5000

Fargo Electronics Inc:MN .... Main: **(612) 941-9470**
  TFree:(800) 327-4622 Fax:(612) 941-7836 Tech:(612) 941-0050
  Tech Support:(612) 941-1852

FastComm Communications Corp:VA ...... Main: **(703) 318-7750**
  TFree:(800) 521-2496 Fax:(703) 787-4625

Faulkner Information Services:NJ .... Main: **(609) 662-2070**
  TFree:(800) 843-0460 Fax:(609) 662-3380

FaxBack Inc:OR .... Main: **(503) 645-1114**
  TFree:(800) 329-2225 Fax:(503) 690-6399 Tech:(503) 614-5360

Fedco Electronics Inc (Energy+):WI ...... Main: **(414) 922-6490**
  TFree:(800) 542-9761 Fax:(414) 922-6750 Tech:(800) 542-9761

FedWorld Info Net:VA .... Main: **(703) 487-4650**

Fessenden Technologies:MO .... Main: **(417) 485-2501**
  TFree:(800) 606-5542 Fax:(417) 485-3133

FGS (see Symantec):

Fibermux (see ADC Kentrox):

Ficus Systems:MA .... Main: **(617) 938-7055**
  TFree:(800) 342-8799 Fax:(617) 938-7054 Tech:(617) 938-7055

Fidelity International Technologies:NJ ... Main: **(908) 417-2230**
  Fax:(908) 417-5994 Tech:(908) 417-2230

Fifth Generation Sys (see Symantec):

Filenet Corp:CA .... Main: **(714) 966-3400**
TFree:(800) 345-3638

Financial Navigator Int'l:CA .... Main: **(415) 962-0300**
TFree:(800) 468-3636   Fax:(415) 962-0730   Tech:(415) 962-8510

Firefox Inc (FTP Software Inc):CA .... Main: **(408) 321-8344**
TFree:(800) 230-6090   Fax:(408) 467-1105   Tech:(206) 827-9066

First Floor Inc:CA .... Main: **(650) 968-1101**
TFree:(800) 639-6387   Fax:(650) 968-1193   Tech:(650) 968-1101

First Things First:OR .... Main: **(503) 246-6200**
Fax:(503) 452-1198   Tech:(503) 246-6200

Fitnesoft Inc:UT .... Main: **(801) 221-7777**
TFree:(800) 607-7637   Fax:(801) 221-7707   Tech:(801) 221-7708

Flagship Systems Inc:TX .... Main: **(972) 458-8828**
Fax:(972) 458-8728

Flambeaux Software Inc:CA .... Main: **(818) 500-0044**
TFree:(800) 833-7355   Fax:(818) 957-0194   Tech:(818) 957-0097

Fluke Corporation:WA .... Main: **(206) 347-6100**
TFree:(800) 443-5853   Fax:(206) 356-5116   Tech:(800) 443-5853

Focus Enhancements:MA .... Main: **(508) 371-2000**
TFree:(800) 538-8865   Fax:(617) 938-7741   Tech:(508) 371-8500
Customer Service:(800) 538-8862

Foley Hi-Tech Systems:CA .... Main: **(510) 597-1621**
Fax:(510) 595-0862   Tech:(510) 597-1621

Folio Corp:UT .... Main: **(801) 229-6700**
TFree:(800) 543-6546   Fax:(801) 229-6787   Tech:(801) 229-6650

Fore Systems Inc:PA .... Main: **(412) 742-4444**
TFree:(888) 404-0444   Fax:(412) 635-3625   Tech:(412) 772-6600

Forefront:TX .... Main: **(713) 961-1101**
TFree:(800) 475-5831   Fax:(713) 961-1149

Foresight Resources Corp (Softdesk):

FormGen Inc:AZ .... Main: **(602) 443-4109**
Fax:(602) 951-6810   Tech:(602) 443-4109

Forte Inc:CA .... Main: **(760) 431-6400**
Fax:(760) 431-6465

Fractal Design Corp:CA .... Main: **(408) 430-4000**
TFree:(800) 846-0111   Fax:(408) 438-9673   Tech:(408) 430-4200
Tech Fax:(408) 438-9672

Frame Technology (see Adobe Systems):

Franklin Covey:UT .... Main: **(801) 975-1776**
TFree:(800) 654-1776   Fax:(800) 446-1492   Tech:(800) 975-9999

Frederick Engineering:MD .... Main: **(410) 290-9000**
TFree:(888) 866-9008   Fax:(410) 381-7180   Tech:(410) 290-9000

FreeSoft Co:PA .... Main: **(412) 846-2700**
Fax:(412) 847-4436   Tech:(412) 846-2700

Fry's Electronics:CA .... Main: **(415) 496-6000**

Frye Computer (see Seagate EMS):

FTP Software Inc:MA .... Main: **(508) 685-4000**
TFree:(800) 382-4387   Fax:(508) 794-4488   Tech:(508) 685-3600

Fujitsu America Inc:CA .... Main: **(408) 432-1300**
Fax:(408) 432-1318

Fujitsu Computer Products of America:CA .. Main: **(408) 432-6333**
TFree:(800) 626-4686   Fax:(408) 894-1709   Tech:(800) 826-4686

24hr automated support #:(408) 894-3950

Fujitsu Personal Systems Inc:CA .... Main: (408) 982-9500
TFree:(800) 831-3183 Fax:(408) 496-0609 Tech:(408) 982-9500

Fullmark International:CA .... Main: (310) 539-1880
TFree:(800) 233-3855 Fax:(800) 233-3855 Tech:(800) 233-3855

Funk Software Inc:MA .... Main: (617) 497-6339
TFree:(800) 828-4146 Fax:(617) 547-1031 Tech:(617) 497-6339

Future Domain Corp:CA .... Main: (714) 253-0400
Fax:(714) 253-0913   Tech:(714) 253-0440

Future Thinking:MN .... Main: (612) 332-9262
Fax:(612) 332-9200   Tech:(612) 332-9262

FutureSoft Engineering Inc:TX .... Main: (281) 496-9400
TFree:(800) 989-8908 Fax:(281) 496-1090 Tech:(281) 588-6868
another BBS:(281) 588-6805

FutureTense Inc:MA .... Main: (508) 263-5480
Fax:(508) 263-1769

Futurus Corp (Novell):

FWB Software LLC:CA .... Main: (415) 482-4800
Fax:(415) 482-4858

G.V.C.:ON .... Main: (905) 738-9300
TFree:(888) 482-8324 Fax:(905) 738-5563 Tech:(905) 738-5736

Galacticomm Inc:FL .... Main: (954) 583-5990
TFree:(800) 328-1128 Fax:(954) 583-7846 Tech:(954) 321-2404

Gametek:CA .... Main: (415) 289-0220
Tech:(910) 222-5190

Gamma Productions Inc:CA .... Main: (619) 794-6399
TFree:(800) 974-2662 Fax:(619) 794-7294

Gammalink (Dialogic Sunnyvale):CA .... Main: (408) 744-1400
TFree:(800) 329-4720 Fax:(408) 744-1900

Gap Development:CA .... Main: (714) 496-3774
Fax:(714) 496-3774   Tech:(714) 496-3774
Another BBS:(714) 493-9851

Gates Arrow:CA .... Main: (510) 489-5371
TFree:(800) 332-2222 Fax:(510) 489-9393 Tech:(800) 332-2315
Customer service:(800) 332-2299

Gateway 2000 Inc:SD .... Main: (605) 232-2000
TFree:(800) 846-2000 Fax:(605) 232-2023 Tech:(800) 846-2301
Another Fax on Demand:(605) 232-2561

Gateway BBS:SD .... Main: (605) 632-2000
TFree:(800) 846-2000 Fax:(605) 232-2023 Tech:(800) 846-2301
Fax Back:(800) 846-4526

Gateway Electronics:MO .... Main: (314) 427-6116
TFree:(800) 669-5810 Fax:(314) 427-3147 Tech:(800) 669-5810

Gateway Electronics:CO .... Main: (303) 458-5444
TFree:(800) 669-5810 Fax:(303) 458-6988 Tech:(800) 669-5810

Gateway Electronics:CA .... Main: (619) 279-6802
TFree:(800) 669-5810 Fax:(619) 279-7294 Tech:(800) 669-5810

Gazelle Systems (see GTM Software):

GBC Technologies:NJ .... Main: (609) 767-2500
TFree:(800) 229-6581 Fax:(609) 753-1123

GCC Technologies:MA .... Main: (617) 275-5800
TFree:(800) 422-7777 Fax:(617) 275-1115 Tech:(617) 276-8620

GDT Softworks:BC .... Main: **(604) 473-3600**
   TFree:(800) 663-6222 Fax:(604) 473-3699 Tech:(604) 473-3678
   Tech Fax:(604) 473-3636
General Computer Engineering:CA .... Main: **(714) 999-2894**
   Fax:(714) 999-2793
General DataComm Inc:CT .... Main: **(203) 574-1118**
   Fax:(203) 758-8507
General Magic Inc:CA .... Main: **(408) 774-4000**
   Fax:(408) 774-4010
General Signal Networks (Telenex):NJ .... Main: **(609) 234-7900**
   TFree:(800) 222-0187 Fax:(609) 778-8700
General Software:WA .... Main: **(425) 454-5755**
   TFree:(800) 850-5755 Fax:(425) 454-5744
Generic Software (see AutoDesk):
Genicom:VA .... Main: **(703) 802-9200**
   TFree:(800) 436-4266 Fax:(703) 802-9039 Tech:(703) 802-9200
Genoa Systems Corp:CA .... Main: **(408) 362-2900**
   Fax:(408) 362-2998 Tech:(408) 362-2990
Genovation:CA .... Main: **(714) 833-3355**
   TFree:(800) 822-4333 Fax:(714) 833-0322
Geographic Data Technologies Inc:NH .... Main: **(603) 643-2815**
   TFree:(800) 331-7881 Fax:(603) 643-6808
GeoWorks:CA .... Main: **(510) 814-1660**
   TFree:(800) 224-2411 Fax:(510) 814-4250 Tech:(510) 814-5745
Gibson Research:CA .... Main: **(714) 348-7100**
   TFree:(800) 736-0637 Fax:(714) 348-7110 Tech:(714) 362-8900
Giga-Byte Technology Co Ltd:CA .... Main: **(818) 854-9339**
   Fax:(818) 854-9339   Tech:(818) 854-9334
GigaTrend:CA .... Main: **(760) 931-9122**
   TFree:(800) 743-4442 Fax:(760) 929-0846 Tech:(760) 931-9122
Gilmore Systems:CA .... Main: **(805) 379-3210**
   Fax:(805) 379-1341   Tech:(805) 379-3210
Global Computer Supply:CA .... Main: **(800) 845-6225**
   TFree:(800) 845-6225 Fax:(310) 637-6191
Global Engineering Documents:CO .... Main: **(303) 792-2181**
   TFree:(800) 854-7179 Fax:(303) 397-2740
Global Village Communications:CA .... Main: **(408) 523-1000**
   TFree:(800) 736-4821 Fax:(408) 523-2407 Tech:(408) 523-1050
   Another Fax on Demand:(800) 890-4562
Globalink Inc:VA .... Main: **(703) 273-5600**
   TFree:(800) 255-5660 Fax:(703) 273-3866 Tech:(703) 904-2734
Globe Manufacturing Inc:NJ .... Main: **(908) 232-7300**
   TFree:(800) 227-3258 Fax:(908) 232-4729 Tech:(800) 227-3258
Globelle Corporation:MN .... Main: **(612) 947-1000**
   TFree:(800) 745-7000 Fax:(612) 996-5566
Go Ahead Software Inc:WA .... Main: **(425) 882-1900**
   Fax:(425) 882-1117
Gold Disk Inc (see Astound Inc):
Gold Standard Multimedia Inc:FL .... Main: **(813) 287-1775**
   TFree:(800) 375-0943 Fax:(813) 287-1810 Tech:(813) 287-1775
Golden Bow Systems:CA .... Main: **(619) 298-9349**
   TFree:(800) 284-3269 Fax:(619) 298-9950 Tech:(800) 284-3269

Golden Coast Information Systems:CA .... Main: (619) 268-8447
  Fax:(619) 278-0948
Golden Ribbon:CO.. Main: (303) 443-6966
  Fax:(303) 443-1660
Golden Software:CO... Main: (303) 279-1021
  TFree:(800) 972-1021   Fax:(303) 729-0909   Tech:(303) 279-1021
GoldStar USA Inc (LGEAI):AL .... Main: (201) 816-2000
  Tech:(800) 777-1192
Good Software (see Outlook Software):
GRACE Electronic Materials:MA..................... Main: (617) 861-6600
  TFree:(800) 832-4929   Fax:(617) 933-4318   Tech:(800) 832-4929
Gradient Technologies Inc:MA........................ Main: (508) 624-9600
  TFree:(800) 525-4343   Fax:(508) 229-0338
Grand Junction Network (Cisco Systems):
Granite Communications Inc:NH .... Main: (603) 881-8666
  Fax:(603) 881-4042
Graphic Utilities Inc:CA .... Main: (408) 577-0334
  TFree:(800) 400-5253   Fax:(408) 577-0348   Tech:(800) 669-4723
  Tech Support:(207) 473-7587
Graphix Zone:CA .... Main: (714) 833-3838
  TFree:(800) 828-3838   Fax:(714) 833-3990   Tech:(812) 829-1007
GraphOn Corp:CA.. Main: (408) 370-4080
  Fax:(408) 370-5047
GraphPad Software:CA...................................... Main: (619) 457-3909
  TFree:(800) 388-4723   Fax:(619) 457-8141
Graphsoft Inc:MD.. Main: (410) 290-5114
  Fax:(410) 290-8050   Tech:(410) 290-5114
Gravis:BC.. Main: (604) 431-5020
  Fax:(604) 431-5155   Tech:(604) 431-1807
  Tech Fax:(604) 451-9358
Graymark:CA .... Main: (800) 854-7393
Great Falls Computer (see Microtec):
Great Plains Software:ND .... Main: (701) 281-0555
  TFree:(800) 456-0025   Fax:(701) 281-3328   Tech:(800) 456-0025
Great Wave Software:CA................................... Main: (408) 438-1990
  TFree:(800) 423-1144   Fax:(408) 438-7171   Tech:(800) 423-1144
Greenview Data:MI .... Main: (313) 996-1300
  TFree:(800) 458-3348   Fax:(313) 996-1308   Tech:(313) 996-1300
Grolier Interactive Inc:CT .... Main: (203) 797-3703
  TFree:(800) 621-1115   Fax:(203) 797-3130   Tech:(203) 796-2536
  Tech Fax:(203) 797-3835
Group 1 Software:MD.. Main: (301) 731-2300
  TFree:(800) 368-5806   Fax:(301) 731-0360   Tech:(301) 731-2300
  PC support:(800) 578-8324
Gruber Industries:AZ .... Main: (602) 863-2655
  TFree:(800) 658-5883   Fax:(602) 257-4313   Tech:(800) 581-1697
Gryphon Software Corp:CA.............................. Main: (619) 536-8815
  TFree:(800) 795-0981   Fax:(619) 536-8932   Tech:(619) 536-8815
GSI Inc:CA .... Main: (714) 261-7949
  TFree:(800) 486-7800   Fax:(714) 757-1778   Tech:(714) 261-9744
GT Interactive Software Corp:NY.................... Main: (212) 726-6500
  TFree:(800) 621-4847   Fax:(212) 679-6858

GTCO Corp (Graphic Technology):MD .... Main: **(410) 381-6688**
Fax:(410) 290-9065

GTEK Inc:MS .... Main: **(800) 282-4835**
TFree:(800) 282-4835   Fax:(601) 467-0935   Tech:(601) 467-8048

GTM Software:UT .... Main: **(801) 235-7000**
TFree:(800) 786-3278   Fax:(801) 235-7099   Tech:(801) 235-7000

Gupta Corp (see Centura Software Corp):

GVC Technologies Inc (see MaxTech GVC):

GW Instruments Inc:MA .... Main: **(617) 625-4096**
Fax:(617) 625-1322

HAHT Software Inc:NC .... Main: **(919) 786-5100**
TFree:(888) 438-4248   Fax:(919) 786-5250

Hal Computer Systems (Fujitsu):CA .... Main: **(408) 379-7000**
TFree:(800) 425-0329   Fax:(408) 341-5401   Tech:(800) 425-9111

Harbinger Corp:GA .... Main: **(404) 467-3000**
Fax:(404) 841-4399   Tech:(404) 841-4334

Harbor Electronics:CA .... Main: **(408) 988-6544**
Fax:(408) 988-2948

Hard Drive Associates Inc:OR .... Main: **(503) 233-2821**
Fax:(503) 233-2911

Harlequin Incorporated:MA .... Main: **(617) 374-2400**
Fax:(617) 252-6505

Harris Computer Systems (Concurrent):FL . Main: **(954) 974-1700**
TFree:(800) 666-4544   Fax:(954) 977-5580
Customer Service:(800) 245-6453

Hauppauge Computer Works Inc:NY .... Main: **(516) 434-1600**
TFree:(800) 443-6284   Fax:(516) 434-3198   Tech:(516) 434-3197

HavenTree Software Ltd:ON .... Main: **(613) 544-6035**
TFree:(800) 267-0668   Fax:(613) 544-9632   Tech:(613) 544-6035

Hayes Microcomputer Products Inc:GA ...... Main: **(770) 840-9200**
TFree:(800) 377-4377   Fax:(770) 441-1213   Tech:(770) 441-1617
Tech Support Fax:(770) 449-0087

HDC Computer (see WRQ):

HDS Network Systems:PA .... Main: **(610) 277-8300**
TFree:(800) 437-1551   Fax:(610) 275-5739

Heathkit Educational Systems:MI .... Main: **(616) 925-6000**
TFree:(800) 253-0570   Fax:(616) 925-2898   Tech:(616) 925-6000

Helix Software Company Inc:NY .... Main: **(718) 392-3100**
TFree:(800) 451-0551   Fax:(718) 392-4212   Tech:(718) 392-3735

Helpful Programs Inc (HPI):AL .... Main: **(205) 880-8782**
TFree:(800) 448-4154   Fax:(205) 880-8705   Tech:(205) 880-8702

Hercules Computer Technology Inc:CA ...... Main: **(510) 623-6030**
TFree:(800) 323-0601   Fax:(510) 623-1112   Tech:(510) 623-6050
Tech Support Fax:(510) 623-4215

Hermann Marketing:MO .... Main: **(800) 523-9009**
TFree:(800) 854-1199   Fax:(314) 432-1818

Herne Data Systems Ltd:ON .... Main: **(519) 366-2732**
Fax:(519) 366-2732

Heurikon Corp:WI .... Main: **(608) 831-5500**
TFree:(800) 356-9602   Fax:(608) 831-4249

Hewlett-Packard:CA .... Main: **(301) 670-4300**
TFree:(800) 752-0900   Tech:(208) 323-2551

```
... Disk Memory Division ............................................. Main: (208) 396-6000
   Fax:(208) 333-3182          Tech:(208) 323-2551
... Fax Information - Canada ..................................... Main: (208) 344-4809
... Information Storage Group ................................ Main: (970) 679-6000
... Mass Storage Division ....................................... Main: (970) 635-1000
   TFree:(800) 231-9300        Tech:(970) 635-1000
... Peripheral Group ............................................. Main: (408) 447-6440
... Personal Computer Products ........................... Main: (800) 752-0900
... Personal Information Products Group ........ Main: (800) 762-0900
   TFree:(800) 762-0900
... RISC Systems ................................................... Main: (800) 752-0900
... Windows Client ............................................... Main: (800) 752-0900
Hi-Image:CA ............................................................ Main: (415) 358-8500
   TFree:(800) 345-3540       Fax:(415) 345-9535
Hilbert Computing:KS ............................................ Main: (913) 780-5051
   Fax:(913) 829-2450          Tech:(913) 780-5051
Hilgraeve Inc:MI ..................................................... Main: (313) 243-0576
   TFree:(800) 826-2760       Fax:(313) 243-0645    Tech:(313) 243-0576
Hitachi America:NY ................................................ Main: (914) 332-5800
   TFree:(800) 323-9712       Fax:(914) 332-5555    Tech:(800) 448-2244
Hitachi America:CA ................................................ Main: (510) 661-0777
   Fax:(510) 661-6300
Hitachi America (Computer Division):CA ..... Main: (415) 589-8300
   TFree:(800) 448-2244       Fax:(415) 583-4207
Hitachi Home Electronics America:CA .... Main: (714) 517-6000
   TFree:(800) 369-0422       Fax:(714) 517-6003    Tech:(800) 241-6558
HockWare Inc:NC .................................................. Main: (919) 380-0616
   Fax:(919) 380-0757          Tech:(919) 380-0616
Hollywood Interactive Digital Entertain:CA .. Main: (818) 897-2020
   TFree:(800) 423-7779       Fax:(818) 897-1878    Tech:(818) 897-2020
Home Office Computing:DC .................................. Main: (202) 663-8452
Hopkins Tech:MN .................................................. Main: (612) 931-9376
   TFree:(800) 397-9211       Fax:(612) 931-9377    Tech:(800) 397-9211
Horizons Technology Inc:CA ............................... Main: (619) 292-8331
   TFree:(800) 828-3808       Fax:(619) 292-9439    Tech:(619) 292-8320
   Another Fax:(619) 292-7321
Hot Wire Data Security Inc:PA ........................... Main: (610) 435-7700
   TFree:(888) 468-9473       Fax:(610) 435-6449
Houston Instrument (see Summagraphics):
Howard W. Sams (Bell Atlantic):IN ............... Main: (317) 298-5400
   TFree:(800) 428-7267       Fax:(317) 298-5604
Howling Dog Systems Inc:ON ............................ Main: (613) 376-3868
   TFree:(800) 267-4695       Fax:(613) 376-3584    Tech:(613) 599-7927
HPS Simulation:CA ............................................... Main: (408) 554-8381
   Fax:(408) 241-6886          Tech:(408) 554-8381
HSC Software (see MetaTools Inc):
Hughes Network Systems:MD ........................... Main: (301) 428-5500
   Fax:(301) 428-1868          Tech:(301) 428-5500
Hummingbird Communications Ltd:ON .......... Main: (416) 496-2200
   Fax:(416) 496-2207          Tech:(416) 496-2200
HyperGlot Software:TN ........................................ Main: (615) 558-8270
   TFree:(800) 726-5087       Fax:(615) 588-6569    Tech:(800) 726-5087
```

Hyperion Software:CT .... Main: (203) 703-3000	
Fax:(203) 329-4541	Tech:(203) 703-3000
Hyundai Electronics America:CA .... Main: (408) 232-8000	
Fax:(408) 232-8121	
Ibex Technologies Inc:CA .... Main: (916) 939-8888	
TFree:(800) 975-4239 Fax:(916) 939-8899 Tech:(916) 939-8888	
Fax Back:(916) 939-8875	
IBM Corporation:TX .... Main: (800) 426-3333	
IBM Corporation:NY .... Main: (914) 288-3000	
IBM Corporation:GA .... Main: (404) 238-7000	
... 3151 ASCII Terminal Hotline .... Main: (800) 426-3151	
... ACIS Ordering Information .... Main: (800) 222-7257	
... AIX Systems Support Center .... Main: (800) 547-1283	
... Ambra Technical Support .... Main: (800) 363-0066	
... Ambra Telemarketing/Order (Canada) ...... Main: (800) 252-6272	
... Anti-Virus Services .... Main: (800) 742-2493	
... Anti-Virus Services (Canada) .... Main: (416) 946-3786	
... ARTIC Technical Support .... Main: (800) 241-1620	
... Asia Pacific South Developer Asst .... Main: (612) 354-7684	
... Authorized Dealer Locator .... Main: (800) 447-4700	
... Automated Fax System .... Main: (800) 426-3395	
... Boca Raton Tech Serv Sftwr Sys Test .... Main: (800) 426-2622	
... Bulletin Board System .... Main: (919) 517-0001	
... CAD Assistance .... Main: (303) 924-7262	
... Canada BBS .... Main: (905) 316-4244	
... Catalog Solutions Center .... Main: (800) 426-2255	
... Continuous Speech Series (ICSS) Ord .... Main: (800) 426-2255	
... Continuous Speech Series Mbr CAN .... Main: (800) 561-5293	
... Continuous Speech Series Mbr Info .... Main: (800) 627-8363	
... Continuous Speech Series Tech Supt .... Main: (800) 553-1623	
... Credit Card Support Center .... Main: (800) 345-9186	
... Credit Corporation .... Main: (203) 973-5100	
... Cross System Product Ordering, Pre .... Main: (800) 426-2279	
... Customer Education Schedules .... Main: (800) 426-8322	
... Customer Relations Department .... Main: (201) 930-3443	
... Customer Support Center .... Main: (800) 967-7882	
... Customized Operational Services .... Main: (800) 999-0052	
... DB2/2 Developer Asst Prgm Info/Reg .... Main: (404) 627-8363	
... DB2/2 Technical Conference Enroll .... Main: (800) 955-1238	
... Dealer Support .... Main: (800) 426-7763	
... Desktop Software Support Hotline .... Main: (800) 336-5430	
... Developer Assistance Program Info .... Main: (800) 285-2936	
... Developer Connection for OS/2 .... Main: (800) 633-8266	
... Direct (Supplies, Orders, Price Info) .... Main: (800) 426-2468	
... Direct Response Marketing PCs, S/W .... Main: (800) 426-2968	
... Direct Response Marketing-Education .... Main: (800) 426-4190	
... DisplayWrite End-User Support .... Main: (800) 336-5430	
... Drake Training and Technologies .... Main: (800) 959-3926	
... Easy Options Technical Support .... Main: (800) 933-7573	
... EduQuest Software Ordering .... Main: (800) 426-3327	
TFree:(800) 426-3327 Tech:(800) 426-6378	
... Employee Sales Department .... Main: (800) 426-3675	
... End User Support .... Main: (800) 772-2227	
... End User Support–Fee Help Desk .... Main: (800) 937-3737	

... OS/2 Support BBS (Toronto, Canada)...... Main:	(416) 492-1823
... OS/2 Support BBS (Toronto/Markham)....... Main:	(416) 946-4255
... OS/2 Support BBS (Vancouver, Can.) .... Main:	(604) 664-6466
... OS/2 Support Center .... Main:	(800) 992-4777
... Part Number ID and Lookup .... Main:	(303) 924-4015
... PartnerLink (CSS/RICS) Dealer Supt ...... Main:	(800) 426-3325
... Parts Order Center .... Main:	(800) 388-7080
... PC Company Bulletin Board System........ Main:	(919) 517-0001
... PC Company Product Info Faxback .... Main:	(800) 426-4329
... PC Company Tech Support Faxback .... Main:	(800) 426-3395
... PC Direct Sales and Information............. Main:	(800) 426-2968
... PC Factory Outlet.................................. Main:	(800) 426-7015
... PC Help Center .... Main:	(800) 772-2227
... PCC Education Registration.................... Main:	(800) 937-3737
... PenAssist Developer's Program............... Main:	(404) 238-2200
... Personal Dictation Series(IPDS) Order .... Main:	(800) 426-2255
... Personal Software Solutions Ctr.............. Main:	(800) 992-4777
... Personal Systems Card Repair Service .... Main:	(800) 759-6995
... Personal Systems Direct Sales(PCs) .... Main:	(800) 426-2969
... Personal Systems HelpCenter .... Main:	(800) 772-2227
TFree:(800) 772-2227 Fax:(800) 426-3395	
... Personal Systems Tech Presentations ..... Main:	(800) 547-1283
... Platinum Accounting Software Support ... Main:	(800) 333-5242
... Platinum OEM Add-on Database Prod ... Main:	(800) 999-1809
... Porting/Technical Consulting Workshp ... Main:	(800) 678-3187
... PowerPC Sales..................................... Main:	(800) 472-7693
... Prospective Industry Remarketer Info ..... Main:	(800) 426-8277
... Prospective Reseller Information .... Main:	(800) 426-3333
... PS/1 Bulletin Board System .... Main:	(404) 835-8230
... PS/1 Dealer Locator .... Main:	(800) 426-3377
... PS/1 Help Line .... Main:	(800) 765-4747
... PS/2 Lease from IBM Credit Corp .... Main:	(800) 237-4824
... PS/2 Loan For Learning Program .... Main:	(800) 634-9308
... PS/2 Trade-in Program .... Main:	(800) 331-0589
... PSP Developer Support Marketing Cntr ... Main:	(407) 982-6408
TFree:(800) 285-2936	
... PSP Product Information & Sales (US) ..... Main:	(800) 342-6672
... PSP Support Center .... Main:	(800) 992-4777
... PSP Technical Interchange Registraion ... Main:	(800) 872-7109
... Publications ordering............................. Main:	(800) 879-2755
... RISC System/6000............................... Main:	(800) 426-7378
... Software & Publications Order (Dealer) ... Main:	(800) 327-5711
... Software Defect Support (Dealer/Tech) ... Main:	(800) 237-5511
... Software Installer 1.2 for OS/2 Info........ Main:	(800) 426-2279
... Software Manufacturing & Delivery Ctr... Main:	(800) 879-2755
... Software Manufacturing Company .... Main:	(800) 926-0364
... Software Store..................................... Main:	(800) 342-6672
... Software Support Line .... Main:	(800) 237-5511
... Solution Validation Lab .... Main:	(800) 742-2493
... Special Needs Info and Referral Center ... Main:	(800) 426-4832
... Speech Recognition Education .... Main:	(800) 426-8322
... Speech Recognition Information .... Main:	(800) 825-5263
... Speech Server Series (ISSS) Ordering ..... Main:	(800) 426-2255
... Storage Systems Division...................... Main:	(507) 286-4200
Fax:(507) 253-4111 Tech:(507) 253-4110	

... Supplies Technical Hotline	Main: (800) 426-1484
... Surplus PC Reseller Program Info	Main: (716) 987-2318
... Systems Storage Division (Ad/Star)	Main: (408) 284-6039
... SystemXtra for Personal Systems	Main: (800) 547-1283
... Tax Deferred Savings Plan (TDSP)	Main: (800) 726-1000
... Technical Books Hotline	Main: (800) 426-7282
... Technical Coordinator Program	Main: (800) 547-1283
... Technical Solutions Magazine Circul.	Main: (800) 551-5832
... Think Magazine Circulation Dept	Main: (914) 288-5800
... ThinkPad Helpdesk for NBA Coaches	Main: (800) 622-8465
... Triumph! Workstation Mgr Service	Main: (972) 644-1344
... Video Display Terminal Project Off	Main: (919) 766-3488
... VoiceType Inquires (Dragon Systems)	Main: (800) 825-5897
... VoiceType Ordering	Main: (800) 426-2968
... VoiceType Tech Support, End Users	Main: (800) 241-1620
... Warranty Claims Ctr (Dealers only)	Main: (800) 759-7483
IBM Desktop Software:CT	Main: (800) 426-7699
IBM Desktop Software (Talklink Info):	Main: (800) 547-1283
IBM North America:NY	Main: (520) 574-4600
TFree:(800) 426-3333	
IBM PC Company:NC	Main: (800) 772-2227
TFree:(800) 772-2227 Tech:(800) 426-7378	
IBM Personal Sys Card Rpr:TX	Main: (512) 823-9561
TFree:(800) 759-6995 Fax:(512) 823-5872	
IBM Personal Sys Tech Sol Mag:	
... Subscriptions	Main: (800) 678-8014
TFree:(800) 678-8014 Fax:(214) 518-2507	
IBM Technical Directory:WI	Main: (414) 633-8108
IC Systems (IC Verify):CA	Main: (510) 553-7500
TFree:(800) 900-6133 Tech:(800) 811-1371	
IC Verify Inc (See IC Systems):CA	Main: (510) 553-7500
Fax:(510) 553-7553	
ICA (International Communications):TX	Main: (972) 620-7020
TFree:(800) 422-4636 Fax:(972) 488-9985	
Iceberg Software LLC:VA	Main: (703) 435-3427
Fax:(703) 435-9049	
$2.00 per minute:(900) 288-2345	
Iconovex Corp:MN	Main: (612) 896-5100
TFree:(800) 943-0292 Fax:(612) 896-5101 Tech:(612) 896-5100	
IDG Books Worldwide Inc:CA	Main: (416) 293-8464
TFree:(800) 762-2974 Fax:(416) 655-3299 Tech:(416) 655-3000	
Canada Toll Free:(800) 667-1115	
IEEE Computer Society:CA	Main: (714) 821-8380
TFree:(800) 272-6657 Fax:(714) 821-4010	
Illinois Lock Co (Eastern Comp):IL	Main: (847) 537-1800
TFree:(800) 733-3907 Fax:(847) 537-1881 Tech:(800) 733-3907	
Illustra Information Technologies:CA	Main: (510) 652-8000
Fax:(510) 869-6388 Tech:(510) 652-8000	
Image Club Graphics Inc:AB	Main: (800) 387-9193
TFree:(800) 387-9193 Fax:(403) 261-7013 Tech:(403) 262-8008	
Image Control Corp:ON	Main: (416) 694-7509
Fax:(416) 694-7929 Tech:(416) 694-7747	
Image Smith:CA	Main: (408) 460-9155
TFree:(800) 876-6679 Fax:(408) 460-9154 Tech:(408) 457-0854	

Image-In (see Hi Image):

Imageline Inc:VA .... **Main: (804) 644-0766**
Fax:(804) 644-0769   Tech:(804) 644-0766

Imagine Publishing Inc:CA .... **Main: (415) 468-4684**
Fax:(415) 468-4686   Tech:(415) 468-4684

IMAJA:CA .... **Main: (510) 526-4621**
Fax:(510) 559-9571

IMC Networks Corp:CA .... **Main: (714) 724-1070**
TFree:(800) 624-1070   Fax:(714) 724-1020 Tech:(800) 624-1070

Impediment Inc:MA .... **Main: (617) 834-3800**
Fax:(617) 834-3666

IMSI Software:CA .... **Main: (415) 257-3000**
TFree:(800) 833-8082 Fax:(415) 257-3565 Tech:(415) 257-3000

IMT Systems Inc:TX .... **Main: (713) 937-2115**
Fax:(713) 937-2125

In Focus Systems Inc:OR .... **Main: (503) 685-8888**
TFree:(800) 294-6400 Fax:(503) 685-8887 Tech:(800) 294-6400

InContext Systems Inc:ON .... **Main: (905) 819-1173**
TFree:(888) 819-2500 Fax:(905) 819-9245 Tech:(905) 819-1173

Indiana Cash Drawer Co:IN .... **Main: (317) 398-6643**
TFree:(800) 227-4379 Fax:(317) 392-0958 Tech:(800) 227-4832
Tech Fax:(317) 392-6726

Individual Software Inc:CA .... **Main: (510) 734-6767**
TFree:(800) 822-3522 Fax:(510) 734-8337 Tech:(800) 331-3313

Infinite Technologies:MD .... **Main: (410) 363-1097**
TFree:(800) 678-1097 Fax:(410) 363-0846 Tech:(410) 363-1097

InfiniText Software:CA .... **Main: (714) 651-0640**
Fax:(714) 651-0640

Info Access Inc:WA .... **Main: (425) 201-1915**
TFree:(800) 344-9737 Fax:(425) 201-1922

InfoGold American Multisystems:CA .... **Main: (408) 945-2296**
TFree:(800) 888-6615 Fax:(408) 945-2299

InfoMagic Inc:AZ .... **Main: (520) 526-9565**
TFree:(800) 800-6613 Fax:(520) 526-9573

Infonet Communications Inc:CA .... **Main: (209) 446-2360**
TFree:(800) 470-1555 Fax:(209) 438-8064 Tech:(209) 446-2360

Inforite Corp (see PennWare):

Information Builders Inc:NY .... **Main: (212) 736-4433**
TFree:(800) 969-4636 Fax:(212) 967-6406
Customer Support:(800) 736-6130

Information Cybernetics Inc:MA .... **Main: (617) 354-8585**
TFree:(888) 354-8585 Fax:(617) 354-8899

Informative Graphics Corp:AZ .... **Main: (602) 971-6300**
Fax:(602) 971-1714   Tech:(602) 971-6061

Informix Software Inc:CA .... **Main: (415) 926-6300**
TFree:(800) 331-1763

Inforonics Inc:MA .... **Main: (508) 486-8976**
Fax:(508) 486-0027

InfoVision Technologies Inc:MA .... **Main: (508) 366-3660**
Fax:(508) 366-2544

Infoworld:CA .... **Main: (650) 572-7341**
TFree:(800) 227-8365 Fax:(650) 312-0580

Ingram Book:TN .... Main: **(800) 937-8000**

Ingram Micro:CA .... Main: **(714) 566-1000**
TFree:(800) 274-4800 Fax:(714) 566-7720 Tech:(800) 234-9220
Orders:(800) 456-8000

Inline Inc:CA .... Main: **(714) 921-4100**
TFree:(800) 882-7117 Fax:(714) 921-4160 Tech:(800) 882-7117

Inline Software:MA .... Main: **(617) 938-8088**
Fax:(617) 938-7741 Tech:(617) 935-1515

Inmagic Inc:MA .... Main: **(617) 938-4442**
Fax:(617) 938-6393 Tech:(617) 938-4442

Inmark Development (see Rogue Wave Software):

Innovative Data Design (IDD):CA .... Main: **(510) 680-6818**
Fax:(510) 680-1165 Tech:(510) 680-6818

Innovative Electronics Corp:CO .... Main: **(303) 288-5000**
TFree:(800) 765-4432 Fax:(303) 288-5099

Innovative Quality Software:NV .... Main: **(702) 435-9077**
TFree:(800) 844-1554 Fax:(702) 435-9106 Tech:(702) 435-9077

Inset Systems Inc (see Quarterdeck Office):

Insight Development Corp:CA .... Main: **(510) 244-2000**
TFree:(800) 825-4115 Fax:(510) 244-2020 Tech:(510) 244-2000

Insight Software Solutions:UT .... Main: **(801) 295-1890**
Fax:(801) 299-1781

Insignia Solutions:CA .... Main: **(408) 327-6000**
TFree:(800) 848-7677 Fax:(408) 327-6105 Tech:(408) 327-6000

INSO Corporation:IL .... Main: **(312) 329-0700**
TFree:(800) 333-1395 Fax:(312) 670-0820 Tech:(312) 527-4357

Int'l Electronic Research (IERC):CA .... Main: **(818) 842-7277**
Fax:(818) 848-8872

Integral Peripherals Inc:CO .... Main: **(303) 449-8009**
TFree:(800) 333-8009 Fax:(303) 449-8089 Tech:(303) 449-8009

Integrated Data Systems Inc:GA .... Main: **(912) 236-4374**
Fax:(912) 236-6792 Tech:(912) 236-4374

Integrated Electronics Corp:CO .... Main: **(303) 292-5537**
Fax:(303) 292-0114

Integrated Information Tech (See 8X8):CA ... Main: **(408) 727-1885**
TFree:(888) 843-9898 Fax:(408) 980-0432 Tech:(408) 727-1676

Integrated Systems Inc:CA .... Main: **(408) 542-1500**
TFree:(800) 543-7767 Fax:(408) 542-1950 Tech:(800) 458-7767

Intel Application Support BBS: .... Main: **(916) 356-3600**

Intel Corp:CA .... Main: **(408) 765-8080**
TFree:(800) 238-0486 Fax:(408) 765-9904 Tech:(800) 321-4044

Intel PC Enhancement Division:OR .... Main: **(503) 696-8080**
TFree:(800) 538-3373 Fax:(503) 228-9707 Tech:(503) 264-7000

Intelitool Inc:IL .... Main: **(630) 406-1041**
TFree:(800) 227-3805 Fax:(630) 406-1079

Intellicom Inc:CA .... Main: **(818) 407-3900**
TFree:(800) 992-2882 Fax:(818) 882-2404 Tech:(818) 407-3900

IntelliMedia Corp:MI .... Main: **(616) 925-3675**
TFree:(800) 706-0077 Fax:(616) 925-3668 Tech:(800) 706-0077

InterCon Systems (See Ascend):VA .... Main: **(816) 463-1412**
Tech:(800) 272-3634
tech support:(816) 463-2021

Interface Group, The:MA .... Main: (617) 449-6600
  Fax:(617) 449-2674
Interface Systems:MI .... Main: (313) 769-5900
  TFree:(800) 544-4072   Fax:(313) 769-1047   Tech:(800) 544-4072
Intergraph Corp:AL .... Main: (205) 730-5441
  TFree:(800) 345-4856   Fax:(205) 730-9441   Tech:(800) 633-7248
  Hardware Products:(800) 763-0242
Interleaf Inc:MA .... Main: (617) 290-0710
  TFree:(800) 955-5323   Fax:(617) 290-4943   Tech:(800) 688-5151
International Jensen (see Specialty Auto):
International Transware:CA .... Main: (650) 903-2300
  TFree:(800) 999-6387   Fax:(650) 903-9544   Tech:(650) 903-2300
Internex Information Services:CA .... Main: (408) 327-2355
  Fax:(408) 496-5485   Tech:(408) 327-2200
  Sales:(408) 327-2388
Interphase Corp:TX .... Main: (214) 654-5000
  TFree:(800) 327-8638   Fax:(214) 654-5500
  Customer Service:(214) 654-5555
Interplay Productions:CA .... Main: (714) 553-6655
  TFree:(800) 468-7529   Fax:(714) 252-2820   Tech:(714) 553-6678
Interse Corp (Microsoft):CA .... Main: (408) 732-0932
  Fax:(408) 732-7038   Tech:(800) 936-3400
Intersolv:MD .... Main: (301) 838-5000
  TFree:(800) 547-4000   Fax:(919) 461-4526   Tech:(800) 876-3101
Intex Solutions:MA .... Main: (617) 449-6222
  Fax:(617) 444-2318   Tech:(617) 449-6222
IntraServer Technology Inc:MA .... Main: (508) 429-0425
  Fax:(508) 429-0430
Intuit Inc:CA .... Main: (415) 322-0573
  TFree:(800) 446-8848   Fax:(415) 852-9911   Tech:(415) 322-0573
Invisible Software Inc:CA .... Main: (415) 570-5967
  TFree:(800) 982-2962   Fax:(407) 260-1841   Tech:(407) 260-5007
IOMEGA Corp:UT .... Main: (801) 778-1000
  TFree:(800) 697-8833   Fax:(801) 778-3460   Tech:(800) 456-5522
IPC Peripherals:CA .... Main: (510) 354-0800
  Fax:(510) 354-0808   Tech:(510) 354-0800
Ipsilon:CA .... Main: (415) 846-4600
  TFree:(888) 477-4566   Fax:(415) 855-1414   Tech:(415) 846-4600
IQ Software:GA .... Main: (770) 446-8880
  TFree:(800) 458-0386   Fax:(770) 448-4088
IQ Technologies Inc (Smart Cable):WA .... Main: (253) 474-9967
  TFree:(800) 752-6526   Fax:(253) 474-9940   Tech:(206) 823-2273
Irwin Magnetic Systems (see Conner):
ISDN*tek:CA .... Main: (415) 712-3000
  Fax:(415) 712-3003
Island Software:CA .... Main: (415) 372-1966
  TFree:(800) 255-4499   Fax:(415) 884-4500   Tech:(415) 884-4400
Isys/Odyssey Development Inc:CO .... Main: (303) 689-9998
  Fax:(303) 689-9997
IT Designs USA Inc:CA .... Main: (408) 342-0435
  TFree:(800) 437-7339   Fax:(408) 342-0435
ITAC Systems Inc:TX .... Main: (972) 494-3073
  TFree:(800) 533-4822   Fax:(972) 494-4159

ITT Pomona Electronics:CA .... Main: **(909) 469-2900**
Fax:(909) 629-3317

ITU Engineering:CA .... Main: **(619) 456-2002**
Fax:(619) 456-1905   Tech:(619) 456-2002

IVI Publishing:MN .... Main: **(612) 996-6000**
TFree:(800) 952-4773   Fax:(612) 996-6001

J-Mark Computer Corp:CA .... Main: **(818) 856-5800**
Fax:(818) 960-5937   Tech:(818) 856-5800

J. D. Edwards:CO .... Main: **(303) 488-4000**
TFree:(800) 727-5333   Fax:(303) 488-4141 Tech:(800) 289-2999

J. River Inc:MN .... Main: **(612) 339-2521**
Fax:(612) 339-4445

Jade Computer:CA .... Main: **(310) 370-7474**
TFree:(800) 421-1550   Fax:(310) 370-1328 Tech:(800) 421-5500

Jameco Electronics:CA .... Main: **(415) 592-8097**
TFree:(800) 831-4242   Fax:(415) 592-2503 Tech:(415) 592-8097
Toll Free Fax:(800) 237-6948

JASC Inc:MN .... Main: **(612) 930-9171**
TFree:(800) 622-2793   Fax:(612) 930-9172 Tech:(612) 930-9171

Jasmine Multimedia Publishing:CA .... Main: **(818) 780-3344**
TFree:(800) 798-7535   Fax:(818) 780-8705 Tech:(818) 780-3344

Jazz Multimedia Inc:CA .... Main: **(408) 727-8900**
Fax:(408) 727-9092   Tech:(408) 727-8900

JC Systems Inc:DE .... Main: **(302) 764-7455**

JDR Microdevices:CA .... Main: **(408) 494-1400**
TFree:(800) 538-5000   Fax:(800) 538-5005 Tech:(800) 538-5002
Fax:(408) 494-1420

Jensen Tools Inc:AZ .... Main: **(602) 968-6241**
TFree:(800) 426-1194   Fax:(602) 438-1690 Tech:(602) 968-6241

JETFAX Inc:CA .... Main: **(650) 324-0600**
TFree:(800) 753-8329   Fax:(650) 326-6003 Tech:(650) 324-0600

JetForm Corp:ON .... Main: **(613) 230-3676**
TFree:(800) 224-4104   Fax:(613) 751-4804 Tech:(613) 230-4700

JIAN:CA .... Main: **(415) 254-5600**
TFree:(800) 346-5426   Fax:(415) 254-5640 Tech:(415) 254-5600

JL Chatcom Inc:CA .... Main: **(818) 709-1778**
TFree:(800) 456-1333   Fax:(818) 882-9134

JL Cooper Electronics:CA .... Main: **(310) 322-9990**
Fax:(310) 335-0110   Tech:(310) 322-9990

Johnson-Grace Co (See America Online):

Joseph Electronics:IL .... Main: **(847) 297-4200**
Fax:(847) 297-6923

Jostens Home Learning:CA .... Main: **(619) 587-0087**
TFree:(800) 548-8372   Fax:(619) 587-1629 Tech:(800) 548-8372

Jovian Logic Corp:CA .... Main: **(510) 651-4823**
Fax:(510) 651-1343   Tech:(510) 651-4823

JTS Corporation:CA .... Main: **(888) 587-0945**
Fax:(408) 468-1619   Tech:(888) 587-0945

Just Logic Technologies Inc:QC .... Main: **(514) 943-3749**
TFree:(800) 267-6887   Fax:(514) 642-6480

JVC (Victor Company Of Japan Ltd):CA ...... Main: **(714) 261-1292**
Fax:(714) 261-9690   Tech:(714) 816-6500

Kaetron Software:TX .... Main: **(281) 298-1500**
TFree:(800) 938-8900   Fax:(281) 298-2520   Tech:(281) 298-1547

Kalok Corp (see JTS):

Kalpana (see Cisco Systems):

Kasco Technologies Inc:NY .... Main: **(212) 725-0220**
Fax:(212) 725-8062   Tech:(212) 725-0220

Katz and Associates:NJ .... Main: **(908) 464-7048**
TFree:(800) 348-3774   Fax:(908) 464-4636

KDS (Korea Data Systems):CA .... Main: **(714) 379-5599**
Fax:(714) 379-5591   Tech:(714) 379-5599

Kennsco Inc:MN .... Main: **(612) 559-5100**
Fax:(612) 559-5548

Kenpax:CA .... Main: **(818) 855-7988**
Fax:(818) 855-7980

Kensington Microware:CA .... Main: **(650) 572-2700**
TFree:(800) 535-4242   Fax:(650) 572-9675   Tech:(800) 535-4242

Kent Marsh Ltd (Citadel Computer Syst):TX Main: **(713) 522-5625**
TFree:(800) 962-0701   Fax:(713) 522-8965   Tech:(800) 325-3587

Kerr Publications:MT .... Main: **(406) 356-2126**

Key Tronic Corp:WA .... Main: **(509) 928-8000**
TFree:(800) 262-6006   Fax:(509) 927-5248   Tech:(800) 262-6006
Tech Support Fax:(509) 927-5252

Keyfile Corp:NH .... Main: **(603) 883-3800**
TFree:(800) 453-9345   Fax:(603) 889-9259
International Phone:(603) 598-8284

Kidasa Software Inc:TX .... Main: **(512) 328-0168**
TFree:(800) 765-0167   Fax:(512) 328-0247   Tech:(800) 765-0167

KidSoft L.L.C.:CA .... Main: **(408) 255-3434**
TFree:(800) 354-6150   Fax:(408) 342-3500   Tech:(408) 255-1328

Kinetix:CA .... Main: **(415) 547-2000**

Kingston Technology Corp:CA .... Main: **(714) 437-3334**
TFree:(800) 337-8410   Fax:(714) 438-1820   Tech:(800) 435-0640
Tech Support Fax:(714) 437-3310

KL Group:ON .... Main: **(416) 594-1026**
TFree:(800) 663-4723   Fax:(416) 594-1919

Knowledge Adventure:CA .... Main: **(818) 246-4400**
TFree:(800) 542-4240   Fax:(818) 246-8412   Tech:(818) 246-4811
Tech Fax:(818) 246-5604

Knowledge Based Systems Inc:TX .... Main: **(409) 260-5274**
TFree:(800) 808-5274   Fax:(409) 260-1965

Knowledge Garden Inc:FL .... Main: **(561) 615-8209**
Fax:(561) 615-8461   Tech:(561) 615-8209

Knowledge Media Inc:CA .... Main: **(916) 872-7487**
TFree:(800) 782-3766   Fax:(916) 872-3826   Tech:(916) 872-7487

Knowledge Quest:CA .... Main: **(714) 376-8150**
Tech:(714) 376-8150

KnowledgePoint Software:CA .... Main: **(707) 762-0333**
TFree:(800) 727-1133   Fax:(707) 762-0802   Tech:(707) 762-0333

Kodak (see Eastman Kodak Co):

Konami Of America Inc:IL .... Main: **(847) 215-5100**

Korenthal Associates Inc:NY .... Main: **(212) 242-1790**
TFree:(800) 527-7647   Fax:(212) 242-2599   Tech:(212) 242-1790

KorTeam International Inc:CA .... Main: **(408) 733-7888**
  TFree:(800) 763-1688   Fax:(408) 733-9888   Tech:(408) 523-4757

Koss Corp:WI .... Main: **(414) 964-5000**
  TFree:(800) 872-5677   Fax:(414) 964-8615   Tech:(800) 558-8305

Kyocera Electronics Inc:NJ .... Main: **(908) 560-3400**
  TFree:(800) 459-6329   Fax:(908) 560-8380   Tech:(908) 560-3400

LA Computer:CA .... Main: **(310) 533-7177**
  Fax:(310) 533-6955

LAB Tech:MA .... Main: **(508) 657-5400**
  TFree:(800) 879-5228   Fax:(508) 658-9972   Tech:(800) 879-5228
  Toll Free Fax:(800) 899-1609

Labtec Enterprises Inc:WA .... Main: **(360) 896-2000**
  Fax:(360) 896-2020

LaCie Limited:OR .... Main: **(503) 844-4500**
  TFree:(800) 999-1179   Fax:(503) 844-4501

LAN Source Technologies Inc: .... Main: **(416) 535-3555**
  TFree:(800) 677-2727   Fax:(416) 535-6225   Tech:(416) 535-2668

LAN Times:CA .... Main: **(415) 513-6800**
  Fax:(415) 513-6985

LAN Times Testing Center:UT .... Main: **(801) 342-6800**
  Fax:(801) 342-6837

LANart Corp:MA .... Main: **(617) 444-1994**
  TFree:(800) 292-1994   Fax:(617) 444-3692   Tech:(800) 292-1994

Landmark Research (see Quarterdeck Select):

LANshark Systems Inc:OH .... Main: **(614) 751-1111**
  Fax:(614) 751-1112   Tech:(614) 751-1111

Lantec:UT .... Main: **(801) 375-7050**
  Fax:(801) 375-7043   Tech:(800) 352-6832

Lantronix:CA .... Main: **(714) 453-3990**
  TFree:(800) 422-7055   Fax:(714) 453-3995   Tech:(800) 422-7044
  International tech support:(714) 453-7198

Lapis Technologies (Focus Enhancements):

Laser Age (Cartridges USA):CA
  TFree:(888) 866-3787   Fax:(714) 994-8030

Laser Magnetic Storage Intl(see Phillips Mag:

Laser Master Technologies:MN .... Main: **(612) 944-9330**
  TFree:(800) 477-7714   Fax:(619) 943-3695   Tech:(800) 925-0563

Laser Printers Accessories (see PCPI):

LaserGo Inc:CA .... Main: **(619) 578-3100**
  Fax:(619) 578-4502   Tech:(619) 578-3100

LaserMaster Corp (Mac):MN .... Main: **(612) 944-9330**
  TFree:(800) 477-7714   Fax:(612) 944-0522   Tech:(800) 925-0563

LaserMaster Corp (PC):MN .... Main: **(612) 944-9330**
  TFree:(800) 477-7714   Fax:(612) 944-0522   Tech:(800) 925-0563

LaserSoft Inc:MN .... Main: **(612) 944-8161**
  Fax:(612) 944-8648   Tech:(612) 944-7699

LaserTools Corp:CA .... Main: **(510) 420-8777**
  Fax:(510) 420-1150   Tech:(510) 420-1319

Lasonic Electronics Corp:CA .... Main: **(818) 281-3957**
  Fax:(818) 576-7314   Tech:(818) 281-3957

Lattice Incorporated:IL .... Main: **(630) 769-4060**
  TFree:(800) 444-4309   Fax:(630) 769-4083   Tech:(630) 769-4060

Lazer Impact:TX .... Main: **(512) 832-9151**
TFree:(800) 777-4323   Fax:(512) 832-9321   Tech:(512) 966-3621

Lead Technologies Inc:NC .... Main: **(704) 332-5532**
TFree:(800) 637-4699   Fax:(704) 372-8116   Tech:(704) 372-9681
Tech Fax:(704) 332-5868

Leader Technologies:CA .... Main: **(714) 757-1700**
TFree:(800) 922-1787   Fax:(714) 822-1241   Tech:(505) 822-0700

Learned-Mahn Inc:ID .... Main: **(208) 336-2281**
TFree:(800) 727-5009   Fax:(208) 343-2105   Tech:(208) 342-0979
Health Info:(800) 727-5008

Learning Company, The:TN .... Main: **(423) 670-2020**
TFree:(800) 852-2255   Fax:(423) 670-2021   Tech:(423) 670-2020

LearnIT Corp:FL .... Main: **(352) 375-6655**
TFree:(888) 532-7648   Fax:(352) 376-0022   Tech:(352) 375-6655
Fax:(800) 594-8436

LearnKey Inc:UT .... Main: **(801) 674-9733**
TFree:(800) 865-0165   Fax:(801) 674-9734   Tech:(520) 717-1733

Legato Systems:CA .... Main: **(415) 812-6000**
Fax:(415) 812-6032   Tech:(415) 812-6100

Legi-tech:CA .... Main: **(916) 447-1886**
Fax:(916) 447-1109   Tech:(916) 447-1887

Lenel Systems International Inc:NY .... Main: **(716) 248-9720**
TFree:(800) 225-3635   Fax:(716) 248-9185   Tech:(716) 248-9720

Leverage Technologists Inc:MD .... Main: **(301) 309-8783**

Lexmark International Inc:KY .... Main: **(606) 232-2000**
TFree:(800) 539-6275   Fax:(606) 232-5179   Tech:(800) 453-9872
Another Fax on Demand:(606) 232-2380

... Customer Support .... Main: **(800) 258-8575**

... Hardware Service Support .... Main: **(800) 426-7378**

... Printer Technical Support .... Main: **(606) 232-3000**
TFree:(800) 253-9778

LG Electronics USA Inc:NJ .... Main: **(201) 816-2000**
TFree:(800) 243-0000   Fax:(201) 816-0636

Liant Software Corp:MA .... Main: **(508) 872-8700**
Fax:(508) 626-2221

Liant Software Corp (Product Div):TX .... Main: **(512) 719-7060**
TFree:(800) 349-9222   Fax:(512) 345-8010

Liant Software Corp (R.M. Division):TX ...... Main: **(512) 343-1010**
TFree:(800) 349-9222   Fax:(512) 343-9487   Tech:(512) 343-1010

Liant Software Corp (Software Serv):TX ...... Main: **(512) 371-7028**
Fax:(512) 371-7609

Libra Corp:UT .... Main: **(801) 943-2084**
TFree:(800) 453-3827

Lifeboat Assoc (Programmers Paradise):NJ Main: **(908) 389-8950**
TFree:(800) 445-7899   Fax:(908) 389-9227   Tech:(908) 389-0037

Lifestyle Software Group:FL .... Main: **(904) 794-7070**
TFree:(800) 289-1157   Fax:(904) 825-0223   Tech:(904) 794-7955

Light Source Computer Images Inc:CA .... Main: **(415) 446-4200**
TFree:(800) 231-7226   Fax:(415) 492-8011   Tech:(415) 499-9390
sales:(800) 994-2650

Lighten Inc:CA .... Main: **(510) 528-4376**
TFree:(800) 398-4545   Fax:(510) 528-0246   Tech:(510) 528-4376

Lilly Software Associates Inc:NH .... Main: **(603) 926-9696**
Fax:(603) 926-9698
Lind Electronic Design:MN .... Main: **(612) 927-6303**
TFree:(800) 659-5956 Fax:(612) 927-7444 Tech:(800) 659-5956
Link Instruments Inc:NJ .... Main: **(973) 808-8990**
Fax:(973) 808-8786
Link Technologies (see Wyse Technology):
Linksys Group Inc:CA .... Main: **(714) 261-1288**
TFree:(800) 546-5797 Fax:(714) 261-8868 Tech:(714) 261-1288
Liuski International Inc:GA .... Main: **(404) 447-9454**
TFree:(800) 454-8754 Fax:(404) 368-8095 Tech:(800) 347-5454
Locus Computing Corp:IL .... Main: **(630) 620-5000**
TFree:(800) 442-6861 Fax:(630) 691-0718 Tech:(310) 337-5995
Logical Connection Inc (see Buffalo Inc):
Logicode Technology Inc:CA .... Main: **(805) 388-9000**
TFree:(800) 735-6442 Fax:(805) 383-2508 Tech:(805) 388-9000
Tech Support Fax:(805) 383-2509
Logitech Inc:CA .... Main: **(510) 795-8500**
TFree:(800) 231-7717 Fax:(510) 792-8901 Tech:(510) 795-8500
Lotus:MA .... Main: **(617) 577-8500**
TFree:(800) 343-5414 Fax:(617) 693-4551 Tech:(508) 988-2500
... Academic .... Main: **(800) 343-5414**
Tech:(800) 343-5414
... Business Sales and Service .... Main: **(800) 343-5414**
Tech:(800) 343-5414
... CC:Mail .... Main: **(415) 961-8800**
TFree:(800) 448-2500 Tech:(800) 448-2500
... Notes Support .... Main: **(800) 828-7086**
TFree:(800) 828-7086 Tech:(508) 988-2750
... Passport .... Main: **(800) 266-8720**
Tech:(800) 266-8720
... Word Processing .... Main: **(770) 391-0011**
TFree:(800) 343-5414 Fax:(770) 698-7659 Tech:(508) 988-2500
LSI Logic Corp:CA .... Main: **(408) 433-8000**
TFree:(800) 433-8778 Fax:(408) 433-8989
LucasArts Entertainment:CA .... Main: **(800) 985-8227**
TFree:(800) 985-8227 Fax:(818) 587-6629 Tech:(415) 507-4545
Tech Fax:(415) 507-0300
Lucid Corp:TX .... Main: **(972) 644-0198**
Fax:(972) 480-9610   Tech:(972) 644-0198
Order Fax:(972) 480-9610
Lynx Real-Time Systems Inc:CA .... Main: **(408) 879-3900**
TFree:(800) 255-5969 Fax:(408) 879-3920
Lytec Systems Inc:UT .... Main: **(801) 562-0111**
TFree:(800) 735-1991 Fax:(801) 562-0256 Tech:(801) 562-0111
M-USA Business Systems:TX .... Main: **(972) 386-6100**
TFree:(800) 280-6872 Fax:(972) 404-1957 Tech:(972) 407-9059
MA Laboratories Inc:CA .... Main: **(408) 954-9388**
Fax:(408) 954-0944
Mackie Designs Inc:WA .... Main: **(206) 487-4333**
TFree:(800) 258-6883 Fax:(206) 487-4337
MacMillan Computer Publishing:IN .... Main: **(317) 228-4366**
TFree:(800) 716-0044 Fax:(800) 882-8583 Tech:(800) 545-5914

Customer Service:(800) 858-7674

Macmillan New Media (see Elect Press):

Macromedia:TX .... Main: **(214) 680-2060**
Tech:(214) 680-2093

Macromedia Inc:CA .... Main: **(415) 252-2000**
TFree:(800) 888-9335   Fax:(415) 626-0554   Tech:(415) 252-9080

Madge Networks:CA .... Main: **(408) 955-0700**
TFree:(800) 876-2343   Fax:(408) 955-0970   Tech:(800) 876-2343

MaeDae Enterprises:CO .... Main: **(719) 683-3860**
TFree:(888) 683-3860   Fax:(719) 683-5199

MAG InnoVision Inc:CA .... Main: **(714) 751-2008**
TFree:(800) 827-3998   Fax:(714) 751-5522   Tech:(714) 751-2008

Magee Enterprises Inc:GA .... Main: **(770) 446-6611**
TFree:(800) 662-4330   Fax:(770) 368-0719   Tech:(770) 662-5387

Magic Solutions Inc:NJ .... Main: **(201) 587-1515**
TFree:(800) 966-9695   Fax:(201) 587-8005   Tech:(800) 966-9695

Magna:CA .... Main: **(408) 879-7900**
TFree:(800) 806-2462   Fax:(408) 879-7979   Tech:(408) 879-7911

Magnavox (Phillips Consumer Elec):TN .... Main: **(423) 521-4316**
Tech:(800) 531-0039

Magnetic Music:CA .... Main: **(408) 684-2654**
Fax:(408) 662-3134

Magus Software Inc:CA .... Main: **(415) 940-1109**
Fax:(415) 940-1238   Tech:(415) 940-1109

Mailer's Software:CA .... Main: **(714) 492-7000**
TFree:(800) 800-6245   Fax:(714) 492-7086   Tech:(714) 492-7000

Mainstay:CA .... Main: **(805) 484-9400**
TFree:(800) 484-9817   Fax:(805) 484-9428   Tech:(805) 484-9400

Maintenance Troubleshooting:DE .... Main: **(302) 738-0532**
Fax:(302) 738-3028

Mannesmann Tally:WA .... Main: **(206) 251-5500**
TFree:(800) 843-1347   Fax:(206) 251-5520   Tech:(206) 251-5532

Mansfield Software Group Inc:CT .... Main: **(860) 429-8402**
Fax:(860) 487-1185   Tech:(860) 429-8402

ManTech Systems/InSync:VA .... Main: **(703) 218-6000**
Tech:(703) 218-6000

Manugistics Inc:MD .... Main: **(301) 984-5000**
TFree:(800) 592-0050   Fax:(301) 984-5370   Tech:(301) 984-5489

MapInfo:NY .... Main: **(518) 285-6000**
TFree:(800) 327-8627   Fax:(518) 285-6060   Tech:(518) 285-7283

MapLinx Corp:TX .... Main: **(972) 231-1400**
TFree:(800) 352-3414   Fax:(972) 248-2690   Tech:(972) 231-1400

Mark IV Industries Inc:NY .... Main: **(716) 689-4972**
Fax:(716) 689-1529   Tech:(716) 689-4972

Mark Of The Unicorn Inc:MA .... Main: **(617) 576-2760**
Fax:(617) 576-3609   Tech:(617) 576-3066
Tech Support Fax:(617) 354-3068

MarketArts (Window on Wallstreet):TX .... Main: **(972) 235-9594**
TFree:(800) 998-8439   Fax:(972) 783-6798   Tech:(972) 783-6793

MarketForce:TX .... Main: **(817) 277-3000**
TFree:(800) 766-7355   Fax:(817) 274-6700   Tech:(817) 277-3000

Marlin P. Jones & Assoc Inc:FL .... Main: **(561) 848-8236**
TFree:(800) 652-6733   Fax:(561) 844-8764   Tech:(561) 848-8236

Marshall Industries:CA .... Main: (818) 307-6000
TFree:(800) 877-9839   Fax:(818) 307-6187   Tech:(818) 307-6033

Masque Publishing:CO .... Main: (303) 290-9853
TFree:(800) 765-4223   Fax:(303) 290-6303   Tech:(303) 290-9853

Mass Micro Systems Mega Tape:
... A Division of Restore Technology .... Main: (408) 946-9207
TFree:(800) 950-9025   Fax:(408) 946-4746

Masterclips Graphics (see IMSI Software):

MasterSoft Inc (see Adobe Systems):

MathSoft Inc:MA .... Main: (617) 577-1017
TFree:(800) 628-4223   Fax:(617) 577-8829   Tech:(970) 339-7119

MathSoft Inc (see Adobe):

MathWorks Inc, The:MA .... Main: (508) 647-7000
Fax:(508) 647-7001   Tech:(508) 647-7000

Matrox Graphics Inc (MGA):QC .... Main: (514) 969-6320
TFree:(800) 361-1408   Fax:(514) 969-6363   Tech:(514) 685-0270

Maxell Corp Of America:NJ .... Main: (201) 794-5900
TFree:(800) 533-2836   Fax:(201) 796-8790   Tech:(201) 795-5900
tech support:(800) 377-5887

Maxi Switch Inc:AZ .... Main: (520) 294-5450
Fax:(520) 294-6890   Tech:(520) 746-9378

Maximized Software:CA .... Main: (714) 428-0999
TFree:(800) 629-7638   Fax:(714) 428-0998

Maximum Strategy Inc:CA .... Main: (408) 383-1600
TFree:(800) 352-1000   Fax:(408) 383-1616

Maxis Software:CA .... Main: (510) 933-5630
TFree:(800) 336-2947   Fax:(510) 927-3736   Tech:(510) 927-3905

Maxoptix Corp:CA .... Main: (510) 353-9700
TFree:(800) 848-3092   Fax:(510) 353-1845   Tech:(800) 848-3092

MaxTech Corporation:CA .... Main: (562) 921-1698
TFree:(800) 936-7629   Fax:(562) 802-9605   Tech:(562) 921-4438

MaxTech GVC:NJ .... Main: (201) 586-3008
TFree:(800) 289-4821   Fax:(201) 586-3308   Tech:(201) 586-8686
Tech Support Fax:(201) 586-2264

Maxtor Corp:CO .... Main: (303) 678-2012
TFree:(800) 262-9867   Fax:(303) 678-2146   Tech:(800) 262-9867

Maxtor Corp:CA .... Main: (408) 432-1700
TFree:(800) 262-9867   Fax:(408) 922-2085   Tech:(800) 262-9867
Tech Fax:(408) 922-2050

Maxus Group:OH .... Main: (216) 292-3434
Fax:(216) 292-6084

Maynard Electronic (see Seagate):

McAfee Associates Inc:CA .... Main: (408) 988-3832
TFree:(888) 847-8766   Fax:(408) 970-9727   Tech:(408) 988-3832

McAfee East:NJ .... Main: (908) 530-0440
TFree:(800) 552-9876   Fax:(908) 530-0622   Tech:(908) 530-9650

McGraw-Hill Inc (Direct Marketing):OH .... Main: (800) 262-4729
TFree:(800) 262-4729   Fax:(614) 759-3641

MCM Electronics:OH .... Main: (937) 434-0031
TFree:(800) 543-4330   Fax:(937) 434-6959   Tech:(800) 824-8324

MCS Products Inc:TX .... Main: (972) 659-1514
Fax:(972) 659-1624

MECA Software LLC:CT .... **Main: (203) 268-2797**
　TFree:(800) 288-6322　Tech:(888) 808-6322
MECC (Minnesota Educational Compt):MN.. Main: (612) 569-1500
　TFree:(800) 685-6322　Fax:(612) 569-1551
Media Vision Inc (Silicon Valley Tech.):
　Fax:(408) 934-8459　Tech:(408) 934-0880
MediaForm Inc:PA .... **Main: (610) 458-9200**
　TFree:(800) 220-1215　Fax:(610) 458-9554　Tech:(610) 458-9200
Mediamagic (see IPC Technology):
Meditools Inc:CA .... **Main: (805) 566-6200**
　TFree:(800) 472-9025　Fax:(805) 566-6385　Tech:(805) 566-6239
　Catalog:(800) 472-9022
Mega Drive Systems:CA .... **Main: (818) 700-7600**
　TFree:(800) 322-4744　Fax:(818) 700-7611　Tech:(818) 700-7676
Megahertz Corp:UT .... **Main: (801) 320-7000**
　TFree:(800) 527-8677　Fax:(801) 320-6010　Tech:(801) 320-7777
Megalmage Inc:CA .... **Main: (714) 522-8500**
　TFree:(800) 250-1876　Fax:(714) 522-2890　Tech:(800) 555-4736
Megamedia Corp:CA .... **Main: (510) 623-1100**
　TFree:(800) 634-2633　Fax:(510) 440-9924
Megatech Software:CA .... **Main: (310) 320-8287**
　TFree:(800) 258-6342　Fax:(310) 320-8286　Tech:(310) 320-8287
Memorex Telex Corp:TX .... **Main: (972) 444-3500**
　TFree:(800) 944-4455　Fax:(972) 444-3501
Mentat Inc:CA .... **Main: (310) 208-2650**
　Fax:(310) 208-3724
Mentor Electronics Inc:OH .... **Main: (216) 951-1884**
　Fax:(216) 951-0107　Tech:(216) 951-1884
Mercury Interactive Corp:CA .... **Main: (408) 523-9900**
　TFree:(800) 837-8911　Fax:(408) 523-9911
Mergent Intl (Utimaco Safeware):CT .... **Main: (860) 688-4454**
　TFree:(800) 688-1199　Fax:(860) 688-4496　Tech:(800) 688-3227
Meridian Data Inc:CA .... **Main: (408) 438-3100**
　TFree:(800) 342-1129　Fax:(408) 438-6816　Tech:(800) 755-8324
　Tech Fax:(408) 438-8001
Meridian Software Inc:NC .... **Main: (919) 518-1070**
　Fax:(919) 518-1170
Merisel:CA .... **Main: (310) 615-3080**
　TFree:(800) 637-4735　Tech:(800) 832-4003
Merit Studios Inc:TX .... **Main: (214) 385-2353**
　Fax:(214) 385-8205　Tech:(214) 385-2957
Meritec:OH .... **Main: (440) 354-3148**
　TFree:(888) 637-4832　Fax:(440) 354-0509
Merritt Computer Products Inc:TX ...... **Main: (214) 339-0753**
　TFree:(800) 530-1693　Fax:(214) 339-1313　Tech:(214) 339-0753
Metacard Corp:CO .... **Main: (303) 447-3936**
　Fax:(303) 499-9855
MetaTools Inc:CA .... **Main: (805) 566-6200**
　Fax:(805) 566-6385　Tech:(805) 566-6200
Methode Electronics Inc:IL .... **Main: (708) 867-9600**
　TFree:(800) 323-6858　Fax:(708) 867-9130　Tech:(708) 867-9600
Metrics Technology Inc:NM .... **Main: (505) 761-9630**
　TFree:(800) 398-1490　Fax:(505) 761-9641

Metro Software Inc:AZ..**Main: (520) 292-0313**
Fax:(520) 292-1563

Metz Software Inc:WA..**Main: (425) 641-4525**
TFree:(800) 447-1712 Fax:(425) 644-6026 Tech:(425) 641-4525

Micah Development Corp:MA......................................**Main: (617) 641-1500**
TFree:(800) 653-1783 Fax:(617) 641-1973 Tech:(617) 641-2017

Micro 2000 Inc:CA..**Main: (818) 547-0125**
TFree:(800) 864-8008 Fax:(818) 547-0397 Tech:(800) 511-3032

Micro Accessories Inc:CA..**Main: (510) 226-6310**
TFree:(800) 777-6687 Fax:(510) 226-6316 Tech:(510) 226-6310

Micro Computer Cable Company:MI ....**Main: (313) 946-9700**
Fax:(313) 946-9645 Tech:(801) 796-8700

Micro Design International Inc:FL..........**Main: (407) 677-8333**
TFree:(800) 920-8205 Fax:(407) 677-8365
Tech Fax:(407) 677-0221

Micro Firmware Inc:OK..**Main: (405) 321-8333**
TFree:(800) 767-5465 Fax:(405) 573-5535 Tech:(405) 321-8333

Micro Focus:CA..**Main: (415) 856-4161**
Fax:(415) 856-6134 Tech:(610) 263-3550
Tech Fax:(610) 263-3555

Micro House International Inc:CO..............**Main: (303) 443-3388**
TFree:(800) 926-8299 Fax:(303) 443-3323 Tech:(303) 443-3389

Micro Solutions:IL..**Main: (815) 756-3411**
TFree:(800) 890-7227 Fax:(815) 756-2928 Tech:(815) 754-4500
Tech Support Fax:(815) 756-4986

Micro Sports Inc:TN..**Main: (615) 877-6310**
TFree:(800) 937-7737 Tech:(706) 673-4715

Micro Star:CA..**Main: (760) 931-4949**
TFree:(800) 444-1343 Fax:(760) 931-4950 Tech:(760) 931-4955
Tech Support Fax:(760) 931-4944

MicroBiz Corp:NJ..**Main: (201) 512-0900**
TFree:(800) 637-8268 Fax:(201) 512-1919 Tech:(201) 512-0900
Tech Support Fax:(201) 512-5919

Microchip Technology Inc:AZ......................**Main: (602) 786-7200**

Microcom Inc:MA..**Main: (617) 551-1000**
TFree:(800) 822-8224 Fax:(617) 551-1006 Tech:(617) 551-1414

MicroData Corp:FL..**Main: (813) 573-5900**
TFree:(800) 539-0123 Fax:(813) 572-5085 Tech:(408) 261-7090

Microdyne Corp:FL..**Main: (352) 687-4633**
TFree:(800) 255-3967 Fax:(352) 687-3392 Tech:(800) 255-3967

Microdyne Corp (Corporate Hq):VA ....**Main: (703) 329-3700**
TFree:(800) 255-3967 Fax:(703) 329-3716 Tech:(800) 255-3967

Micrografx Inc:TX..**Main: (972) 234-1769**
TFree:(800) 671-0144 Fax:(972) 234-2410 Tech:(972) 234-2694
Tech Support Fax:(972) 644-3688

MicroHelp Inc:GA..**Main: (770) 516-0899**
Fax:(770) 516-1099

Microid Research Inc:MA..**Main: (508) 686-6468**
Fax:(508) 683-1630 Tech:(617) 985-6432

Microleague Interactive Sftr(Out of Bus):

MicroLogic Software Inc:CA......................................**Main: (510) 652-5464**
TFree:(800) 888-9078 Fax:(510) 652-7079 Tech:(510) 652-5464

Microlytics & Selectronics:NY .... Main: (716) 248-9150
  Fax:(716) 248-3868   Tech:(716) 248-9150
Micromedia:CA .... Main: (415) 252-2000
  Tech:(415) 252-2000
MicroMedium Inc:NC .... Main: (919) 558-9225
  TFree:(800) 561-2098   Fax:(919) 303-6011
Micron Technology Inc:ID .... Main: (208) 368-4400
  TFree:(800) 964-2766   Fax:(208) 368-4431   Tech:(888) 349-6972
MicroNet Technology Inc:CA .... Main: (714) 453-6100
  TFree:(800) 800-3475   Fax:(714) 453-6101   Tech:(714) 453-6060
Micronetics Design Corp:MD .... Main: (301) 258-2605
  TFree:(800) 433-7581   Fax:(301) 840-8943
Micronics Computers Inc:CA .... Main: (510) 651-2300
  TFree:(800) 577-0977   Fax:(510) 651-6982   Tech:(510) 661-3000
  Customer Service Fax:(510) 651-6692
Microplex Systems Ltd:BC .... Main: (604) 444-4232
  TFree:(800) 665-7798   Fax:(604) 444-4239
Micropolis Corp:CA .... Main: (818) 709-3325
  TFree:(800) 395-3748   Fax:(818) 701-2809   Tech:(818) 709-3325
  Tech Support Fax:(818) 709-3408
MicroProcessors Unlimited:OK .... Main: (918) 267-4961
  Fax:(918) 267-9879   Tech:(918) 267-4961
Microprose Software:CA .... Main: (510) 522-1164
  Fax:(510) 522-9357
MicroRidge Systems Inc:OR .... Main: (541) 593-1656
  Fax:(541) 593-5652   Tech:(541) 689-3265
Microrim Inc:WA .... Main: (425) 649-9500
  TFree:(800) 628-6990   Fax:(425) 649-2785   Tech:(425) 649-9551
  Customer Service:(800) 248-2001
Microsoft Corporation:WA .... Main: (425) 882-8080
  TFree:(800) 426-9400   Fax:(206) 936-7329   Tech:(800) 322-1233
... Access .... Main: (425) 635-7050
  Canada:(905) 568-2294
... Authorized Support Centers .... Main: (800) 936-3500
... Authorized Training Center Referral .... Main: (800) 636-7544
  Canada:(800) 563-9048
... Automap .... Main: (425) 635-7146
  Canada:(905) 568-3503
... Basic PDS .... Main: (425) 635-7053
... Bob .... Main: (425) 635-7044
  Canada:(905) 568-3503
... Bulletin Board System .... Main: (206) 936-6735
... C/C++ .... Main: (425) 635-7007
... Canadian Support .... Main: (905) 568-3503
... CD-ROM Installation .... Main: (206) 635-7033
... Certified Professionals .... Main: (800) 636-7544
  Canada:(905) 712-0333
... Consulting Line .... Main: (800) 936-5200
... Consulting Services .... Main: (800) 426-9400
  Canada:(905) 712-0333
... Delta .... Main: (425) 635-7019
... Developer Network .... Main: (800) 759-5474
  Canada:(800) 759-5474

```
... Download Service-USA .......................... Main: (206) 936-6735
... Excel for the Macintosh ...................... Main: (425) 635-7080
    Canada:(905) 568-2294
... Excel for Windows and OS/2 ................ Main: (425) 635-7070
    Canada:(905) 568-2294
... Excel SDK ............................................ Main: (425) 635-7048
... Fast Tips, Advanced Syst. (NT, MS Mail) .. Main: (800) 936-4400
    Canada:(800) 936-4400
... Fast Tips, Desktop Applications ............ Main: (800) 936-4100
    Canada:(800) 936-4100
... Fast Tips, Development Tools ................ Main: (800) 936-4300
    Canada:(800) 936-4300
... Fast Tips, Home Products ...................... Main: (800) 936-4100
    Canada:(800) 936-4100
... Fast Tips, Personal Op Systems ............ Main: (800) 936-4200
... FORTRAN ............................................. Main: (425) 635-7015
... Forum on CompuServe .......................... Main: (800) 848-8199
... Fox prods, MS-DOS, Windows & UNIX ... Main: (425) 635-7191
... Fox products, Macintosh ........................ Main: (425) 635-7192
... Front Page .......................................... Main: (425) 635-7088
    Canada:(905) 568-3503
... FTP Site - http://ftp.microsoft.com
... Hardware-Mouse, BallPoint, etc. ............ Main: (425) 635-7040
... Internet Explorer .................................. Main: (425) 635-7123
    Canada:(905) 568-2294
... Macro Assembler (MASM) ...................... Main: (425) 646-5109
... Magic School Bus and Kids Products ...... Main: (425) 635-7140
    Canada:(905) 568-3503
... Microsoft Press .................................... Main: (800) 677-7377
... Microsoft Wish Line ............................. Main: (425) 936-9474
... Money ................................................. Main: (425) 635-7131
    Canada:(905) 568-3503
... MS Plus ............................................... Main: (425) 635-7122
... MS-DOS 6.0/MS-DOS 6.2 Upgrades ......... Main: (425) 646-5104
... MSDL (Supported Products) .................. Main: (425) 936-6735
    Canada:(905) 507-3022
... Multimedia Products ............................. Main: (425) 635-7172
    Canada:(905) 568-3503
... Office - Switcher Line ............................ Main: (425) 635-7041
    Canada:(905) 568-2294
... Office for the Macintosh ........................ Main: (425) 635-7055
    Canada:(905) 568-2294
... Office for Windows ............................... Main: (425) 635-7056
    Canada:(905) 568-2294
... Outlook ............................................... Main: (425) 635-7031
    Canada:(905) 568-3503
... PowerPoint ........................................... Main: (425) 635-7145
    Canada:(905) 568-3503
```

... Premier Support/Sales & Info	Main: (800) 936-3500
... Priority Comprehensive	
... Priority Comprehensive-CC	Main: (800) 936-5900
... Priority Desktop App-CC (Canada)	Main: (800) 668-7975
... Priority Desktop Applications	Main: (900) 555-2000
... Priority Desktop Applications-CC	Main: (800) 936-5700
... Priority Develop. w/Desktop-CC	Main: (800) 936-5800
... Priority Development w/Desktop	Main: (900) 555-2300
... Priority Home Products	Main: (900) 555-2400
... Priority Home Products-CC	Main: (800) 936-5600
Canada credit card:(800) 668-7975	
... Priority Personal Op Sys-CC	Main: (800) 936-5700
... Priority Personal Operating Sys	Main: (900) 555-2000
... Profiler	Main: (425) 635-7015
... Profit	Main: (800) 723-3333
... Project	Main: (425) 635-7155
Canada:(905) 568-3503	
... Publisher	Main: (425) 635-7140
Canada:(905) 568-3503	
... QuickBasic	Main: (425) 646-5101
... QuickC	Main: (425) 635-7010
... Scenes and Games	Main: (425) 637-9308
Canada:(905) 568-3503	
... Schedule	Main: (425) 635-7049
Canada:(905) 568-2294	
... Solution Provider Line	Main: (800) 765-7768
... Solution Provider Sales & Info	Main: (800) 765-7768
Canada:(800) 563-9048	
... Source Safe	Main: (425) 635-7014
... Support Consulting Line	Main: (800) 936-1565
... Support Network Sales & Info	Main: (800) 936-3500
... TechNet	Main: (800) 344-2121
Canada:(800) 344-2121	
... Test for Windows	Main: (425) 635-7052
... Toronto, Canada BBS	Main: (905) 507-3022
... TT/TDD (Text Telephone)	Main: (425) 635-4948
Canada:(905) 568-9641	
... Video for Windows	Main: (425) 635-7172
Canada:(905) 568-4494	
... Visual Basic	Main: (425) 646-5105
... Visual Basic Professional Toolkit	Main: (425) 646-5105
... Visual C/C++	Main: (425) 635-7007
... Visual InterDev	Main: (425) 635-7016
... Visual J++	Main: (425) 635-7011
... Windows 95	Main: (425) 635-7000
... Windows Developer Stds Support	Main: (206) 635-3329
... Windows Entertainment Products	Main: (425) 637-9308
Canada:(905) 568-3503	
... Windows NT(Installation Support)	Main: (206) 635-7018
... Windows/Windows for Workgroups	Main: (425) 637-7098
... Word for MS-DOS	Main: (425) 635-7210
Canada:(905) 568-2294	

... Word for the Macintosh.............................Main: (425) 635-7200
  Canada:(905) 568-2294
... Word for Windows.....................................Main: (425) 462-9673
  Canada:(905) 568-2294
... Works for MS-DOS...................................Main: (425) 635-7150
  Canada:(905) 568-3503
... Works for the Macintosh.........................Main: (425) 635-7160
  Canada:(905) 568-3503
... Works for Windows..................................Main: (425) 635-7130
  Canada:(905) 568-3503
... World Wide Web - http://www.microsoft.com
Microspeed Inc:CA......................................Main: (510) 259-1270
  TFree:(800) 232-7888 Fax:(510) 259-1291 Tech:(800) 232-7888
Microspot:CA...Main: (408) 253-2000
  TFree:(800) 622-7568 Fax:(408) 253-2055 Tech:(408) 257-4000
Microstar Laboratories Inc:WA ....Main: (425) 453-2345
  Fax:(425) 453-3199
Microstar Software Ltd:ON..........................Main: (613) 596-2233
  TFree:(800) 267-9975 Fax:(613) 596-5934
MicroSupply (Corporate):WA......................Main: (206) 885-5420
  Fax:(206) 885-9181 Tech:(206) 885-5420
MicroSupply: AZ:AZ.....................................Main: (602) 829-1258
  Fax:(602) 829-1966 Tech:(602) 829-1258
MicroSupply: CO:CO....................................Main: (303) 792-5474
  Fax:(303) 792-5667 Tech:(303) 792-5474
MicroSupply: NV:NV......................................Main: (702) 739-3393
  Fax:(702) 798-9897 Tech:(702) 739-3393
MicroSupply: OH:OH.....................................Main: (216) 498-9916
  Fax:(216) 498-9948 Tech:(216) 498-9916
MicroSupply: OR:OR.....................................Main: (503) 627-0359
  Fax:(503) 627-0360 Tech:(503) 627-0359
MicroSupply: UT:UT......................................Main: (801) 972-3680
  Fax:(801) 972-3808 Tech:(801) 972-3680
MicroSupply: WA:WA....................................Main: (206) 922-1127
  Fax:(206) 922-1224 Tech:(206) 922-1127
MicroSystems Development Tech:CA...........Main: (408) 296-4000
  Fax:(408) 296-5877 Tech:(408) 296-4000
Microsystems Software:MA.........................Main: (508) 416-1000
  TFree:(800) 828-2608 Fax:(508) 626-8515 Tech:(508) 879-9000
MicroTac Software (see Globalink Inc):
Microtec:CA..Main: (408) 487-7000
  TFree:(800) 950-5554 Fax:(408) 487-7001
Microtech Corp:VA.......................................Main: (540) 937-3298
  TFree:(800) 223-3693 Fax:(540) 937-3299
Microtech International:CT..........................Main: (203) 468-6223
  TFree:(800) 220-9489 Fax:(203) 469-3926 Tech:(800) 666-9689
Microtek Lab:CA...Main: (310) 297-5000
  TFree:(800) 654-4160 Fax:(310) 297-5050 Tech:(310) 297-5100
Microtest Inc:AZ..Main: (602) 952-6400
  TFree:(800) 526-9675 Fax:(602) 952-6401 Tech:(800) 638-3497
  Tech Fax:(800) 419-8991
MicroTouch Systems Inc:MA.......................Main: (508) 659-9000
  TFree:(800) 642-7686 Fax:(508) 659-9100 Tech:(508) 659-9200

Microware Education Ctrs (IT Bridge):CA .... Main: (408) 567-9700
TFree:(800) 444-7300 Fax:(408) 567-9797

MicroWay Inc:MA .... Main: (508) 746-7341
Fax:(508) 746-4678 Tech:(508) 746-7341

Midak:AZ .... Main: (602) 266-9029
TFree:(800) 264-9029 Fax:(602) 266-6252

MIDI Solutions Inc:BC .... Main: (604) 794-3013
TFree:(800) 561-6434 Fax:(604) 794-3396 Tech:(604) 794-3013

Midisoft Corporation:WA .... Main: (425) 391-3610
TFree:(800) 776-6434 Fax:(425) 391-3422 Tech:(425) 391-3495
Tech Support Fax:(425) 313-3491

Milan Technology (Digi Lan Connect):CA ... Main: (408) 744-2770
TFree:(800) 466-4526 Fax:(408) 744-2793 Tech:(408) 744-2751
Tech Support Fax:(408) 744-2771

Miles Tek:TX .... Main: (817) 455-7444
TFree:(800) 524-7444 Fax:(940) 484-9402

Miller Freeman Inc:CA .... Main: (415) 905-2200
TFree:(800) 227-4675 Fax:(415) 905-2232 Tech:(415) 905-2200

Mindscape:CA .... Main: (415) 897-9900
TFree:(800) 234-3088 Fax:(415) 897-8286 Tech:(415) 898-5157
Tech Support Fax:(415) 897-5186

Ministor Peripherals (Out of Business):

Miramar Systems:CA .... Main: (805) 966-2432
TFree:(800) 862-2526 Fax:(805) 965-1824 Tech:(805) 965-5161

Misco Power Up:NJ .... Main: (908) 264-8200
TFree:(800) 876-4726 Fax:(908) 264-5955 Tech:(800) 876-4726

Mitsubishi Electronics Am(Display Prod:CA Main: (714) 220-2500
TFree:(800) 344-6352 Fax:(714) 229-3854 Tech:(800) 344-6352

Mitsumi Electronics Corp:NY .... Main: (516) 752-7730
TFree:(800) 648-7864 Fax:(516) 752-7490 Tech:(415) 691-4465

Mitsumi Electronics Corp:TX .... Main: (972) 550-7300
Fax:(972) 550-7424 Tech:(415) 691-4465

MKS (Mortice Kern Systems):ON .... Main: (519) 884-2251
TFree:(800) 265-2797 Fax:(519) 884-8861 Tech:(519) 884-2270

MMB Development Corporation:CA .... Main: (310) 318-1322
TFree:(800) 832-6022 Fax:(310) 318-2162

MMF Industries:IL .... Main: (847) 537-7890
TFree:(800) 323-8181 Fax:(847) 537-1120 Tech:(800) 323-8181

Mobius Computer Corp:CA .... Main: (510) 556-1500
TFree:(800) 662-4871 Fax:(510) 556-1550

Monotype Typography Inc:IL .... Main: (847) 718-0400
TFree:(800) 803-6964 Fax:(847) 718-0500 Tech:(800) 666-6897

Monster Cable:CA .... Main: (415) 871-6000
Fax:(415) 871-0641 Tech:(415) 871-6000

Moon Valley Software:CA .... Main: (805) 781-3890
TFree:(800) 473-5509 Fax:(805) 781-3898 Tech:(800) 473-5509

Most Significant Bits Inc:OH .... Main: (216) 934-1385
TFree:(800) 755-4619 Fax:(216) 934-1386 Tech:(216) 934-1397

Motion Works Inc:BC .... Main: (604) 685-9975
Fax:(604) 685-6105

Motorola Inc:IL .... Main: (708) 576-5000
Fax:(708) 576-7653 Tech:(800) 311-6456

Motorola Inc:TX .... Main: **(512) 891-2000**
  Fax:(512) 891-2652
Motorola ISG:AL .... Main: **(205) 430-8000**
  TFree:(800) 221-4380 Fax:(203) 430-8973 Tech:(205) 726-0798
Motorola ISG:MA .... Main: **(508) 261-4307**
  TFree:(800) 544-0062 Fax:(508) 339-1105 Tech:(508) 261-0366
MountainGate:NV .... Main: **(702) 851-9393**
  TFree:(800) 556-0222 Fax:(702) 851-5533 Tech:(800) 447-8302
  Tech Support Fax:(800) 447-8303
Mouse Systems Corp:CA .... Main: **(510) 656-1117**
  TFree:(800) 886-6423 Fax:(510) 770-1924 Tech:(510) 656-1117
Mouser Electronics:TX .... Main: **(817) 483-4422**
  TFree:(800) 346-6873 Fax:(817) 483-0931
MPI Media Group:IL .... Main: **(708) 460-0555**
  TFree:(800) 777-2223 Fax:(708) 460-0175 Tech:(708) 460-0555
Mueller Technical Research:IL .... Main: **(708) 726-0709**
  Fax:(708) 726-0710
Multi-Ad Services:IL .... Main: **(309) 692-1530**
  TFree:(800) 447-1950 Fax:(309) 692-6566 Tech:(515) 288-2628
Multi-Net Communications:OR .... Main: **(503) 883-8099**
  TFree:(800) 235-7789 Fax:(503) 883-7879
Multi-Tech Systems Inc:MN .... Main: **(612) 785-3500**
  TFree:(800) 328-9717 Fax:(612) 785-9874 Tech:(800) 972-2439
Multicom Publishing:WA .... Main: **(206) 622-5530**
  TFree:(800) 850-7272 Fax:(206) 622-4380 Tech:(800) 850-7272
Multimedia Integrated:CA .... Main: **(415) 872-7100**
  Fax:(415) 872-7133   Tech:(415) 872-7120
Multimedia Learning Inc:TX .... Main: **(972) 869-8282**
  TFree:(800) 870-6608 Fax:(972) 869-8280 Tech:(972) 869-8282
Music Quest Inc:TX .... Main: **(214) 881-7408**
  TFree:(800) 876-1376 Fax:(972) 422-7094 Tech:(214) 881-7408
Musicator:CA .... Main: **(916) 759-9424**
  TFree:(800) 551-4050 Fax:(916) 759-8852 Tech:(916) 756-9807
Musicware Inc:WA .... Main: **(206) 881-9797**
  TFree:(800) 997-4266 Fax:(206) 881-9664 Tech:(206) 881-1419
Musitek:CA .... Main: **(805) 646-8051**
  TFree:(800) 676-8055 Fax:(805) 646-8051 Tech:(805) 646-5841
Mustang Software Inc:CA .... Main: **(805) 873-2500**
  TFree:(800) 999-9619 Fax:(805) 873-2599 Tech:(805) 873-2550
Mustek Inc:CA .... Main: **(714) 250-8855**
  TFree:(800) 468-7835 Fax:(714) 250-3372 Tech:(714) 247-1300
Mutoh America:AZ .... Main: **(602) 276-5533**
  TFree:(800) 445-8782 Fax:(602) 276-7823 Tech:(800) 445-8782
  Tech Fax:(602) 276-9007
Mylex Corp:CA .... Main: **(510) 796-6100**
  TFree:(800) 776-9539 Fax:(510) 745-7654 Tech:(510) 796-6100
Mylex Corp:CA .... Main: **(510) 608-2400**
  Fax:(510) 745-7715
Nanao USA Corp (EIZO Nanao Tech):CA ...... Main: **(310) 325-5202**
  TFree:(800) 800-5202 Fax:(310) 530-1679 Tech:(310) 325-5202
Narrative Communications:MA .... Main: **(617) 290-5300**
  TFree:(800) 978-8670 Fax:(617) 290-5312

National Assoc Of Service Managers:CA ..... Main: (619) 562-7004
  TFree:(888) 562-7004   Fax:(619) 562-7153
National Computer Dist (see AmeriQuest):
National Computer Systems Inc:MN .... Main: (612) 829-3000
  TFree:(800) 431-1421
National Semiconductor:CA .... Main: (408) 721-5000
  TFree:(800) 272-9959   Fax:(408) 721-7662   Tech:(800) 231-6072
National Technical Info Service:VA .... Main: (703) 487-4600
  Fax:(703) 321-8547
Natural Intelligence Inc:MA .... Main: (617) 876-4876
  TFree:(800) 999-4649   Fax:(617) 492-7425   Tech:(617) 876-7680
NavPress Software:TX .... Main: (512) 835-6900
  Fax:(512) 834-1888
NCE Storage Systems (NCE Computer):CA. Main: (619) 452-7974
  TFree:(800) 446-6456   Fax:(619) 452-3271   Tech:(619) 658-9720
  Sales Fax:(619) 658-9736
NCR Microelectronics (see Symbios Logic):
NDC Communications Inc:CA .... Main: (408) 730-0888
  TFree:(800) 632-1118   Fax:(408) 730-0889   Tech:(408) 428-9108
Neamco:MA .... Main: (617) 269-7600
  TFree:(800) 937-1300   Fax:(617) 268-0473   Tech:(617) 269-7600
NEBS Software (One-Write Plus):NH .... Main: (603) 880-5100
  TFree:(800) 225-9550   Fax:(603) 880-5102   Tech:(603) 880-5100
NEC Technologies Inc:MA .... Main: (630) 775-7900
  TFree:(800) 632-4636   Fax:(800) 366-0476   Tech:(800) 388-8888
  CDROM Main Line:(415) 528-6000
net.Genesis Corp:MA .... Main: (617) 577-9800
  Fax:(617) 577-9850
Net2Net Corp:MA .... Main: (508) 568-0600
  TFree:(888) 638-2638   Fax:(508) 568-8858
NetCarta Corporation:CA .... Main: (408) 461-8920
  Fax:(408) 461-8939   Tech:(408) 461-8920
Netcom Online Communications Serv:CA ... Main: (408) 881-5000
  TFree:(800) 638-2661   Fax:(408) 325-6479   Tech:(408) 881-1810
NetManage Inc:CA .... Main: (408) 973-7171
  TFree:(800) 457-4243   Fax:(408) 257-6405   Tech:(408) 973-8181
Netrix:VA .... Main: (703) 742-6000
  Fax:(703) 742-4049   Tech:(800) 776-1477
  Tech Fax:(703) 793-1002
Netscape Communications Corp:CA .... Main: (415) 254-1900
  Fax:(415) 528-4124
Network 1 Software & Technology Inc:NY ... Main: (212) 293-3068
  TFree:(800) 638-9751   Fax:(212) 293-3090
Network Appliance (NetApp):CA .... Main: (408) 367-3000
  Tech:(888) 463-8277
Network Computing Devices:CA .... Main: (415) 694-0650
  TFree:(800) 800-9599   Fax:(415) 961-7711   Tech:(415) 691-7445
Network General Corp:CA .... Main: (415) 473-2000
  TFree:(800) 764-3337
Network Peripherals:CA .... Main: (408) 321-7300
  TFree:(800) 674-8855   Fax:(408) 321-9218   Tech:(408) 321-9218
Networth Inc (Netelligent):TX .... Main: (214) 929-1700
  TFree:(800) 544-5255   Fax:(214) 929-1720   Tech:(214) 929-6984

New Horizons Computer Learning Ctr:CA....Main: (714) 556-1220
 TFree:(800) 811-2530 Fax:(714) 438-9499
New Media Corp:CA ....Main: (714) 453-0100
 TFree:(800) 227-3748 Fax:(714) 453-0114 Tech:(888) 545-2195
 Tech Support Fax:(714) 453-0614
New Vision Technology Inc:ON ....Main: (613) 727-8184
 Fax:(613) 727-8190 Fax:(613) 727-0884
New World Computing Inc (3DO):CA ....Main: (415) 261-3000
 TFree:(800) 336-3506 Fax:(415) 261-3419 Tech:(415) 261-3454
New-Ware:CA ....Main: (619) 455-6225
Newbridge Networks Corp:VA ....Main: (703) 834-3600
 Fax:(703) 471-7080
Newer Technology Inc:KS ....Main: (316) 943-0222
 TFree:(800) 678-3726 Fax:(316) 943-0555
NewGen Systems Corp:CA......................Main: (714) 641-8099
 TFree:(800) 756-0556 Fax:(714) 641-2800 Tech:(714) 436-5150
Newport Systems (see Cisco Systems):
News Corp/MCI Online (Delphi Internet):MA Main: (617) 441-4801
 TFree:(800) 695-4005 Fax:(617) 441-4902 Tech:(617) 441-4801
NexGen Inc (AMD):CA ....Main: (408) 435-0202
 TFree:(800) 222-9323 Fax:(408) 435-0262 Tech:(408) 749-3060
NHC Communications:QC ....Main: (514) 735-2741
 TFree:(800) 361-1965 Fax:(514) 735-8057 Tech:(800) 361-1965
Nimax Inc:CA......................................Main: (619) 452-2220
 TFree:(800) 876-4629 Fax:(619) 452-6669 Tech:(619) 452-2220
 Tech Fax:(619) 452-6341
Nirvana Systems Inc:TX ....Main: (512) 345-2545
 TFree:(800) 880-0338 Fax:(512) 345-4225 Tech:(512) 345-2592
Nisus Software Inc:CA ....Main: (619) 481-1477
 TFree:(800) 922-2993 Fax:(619) 481-6154 Tech:(619) 481-1477
Nolo Press:CA ....Main: (510) 704-2248
 TFree:(800) 728-3555 Fax:(800) 645-0895 Tech:(510) 549-4660
Nombas Inc:MA ....Main: (617) 391-6595
 Fax:(617) 391-3842
NORTEL:TX ....Main: (214) 684-1000
 TFree:(800) 667-8437 Fax:(214) 684-3866
North Edge Software (see Timeslips Corp):
Northgate Computer Systems:MN ....Main: (612) 947-4600
 TFree:(800) 548-1993 Fax:(612) 947-4608 Tech:(800) 446-5037
Norton-Lambert Corp:CA.......................Main: (805) 964-6767
 Fax:(805) 683-5679 Tech:(805) 964-6767
 Tech Support Fax:(805) 683-4652
NovaStor Corporation:CA......................Main: (805) 579-6700
 Fax:(805) 579-6710 Tech:(805) 579-6700
NovaWeb Technologies Inc:CA ....Main: (510) 249-9500
 TFree:(888) 722-6932 Fax:(510) 249-9380
Novell Corporation:UT ....Main: (800) 526-7937
 TFree:(800) 526-7937 Tech:(800) 638-9273
Novell Corporation:UT ....Main: (801) 429-7000
 TFree:(800) 453-1267 Tech:(800) 638-9273
 ... Applications...................................Main: (800) 228-9907
 ... Borland Office ....Main: (900) 555-5020
 TFree:(800) 861-2725

```
... Quattro Pro (WIN)...........................................Main: (801) 765-4029
    TFree:(800) 862-8222
    Fee support:(900) 555-1008
... Sales, CAN/French Speaking ........................Main: (800) 321-2318
... Sales, Certification ......................................Main: (800) 233-3382
... Sales, Customer Registration......................Main: (801) 222-4500
... Sales, Direct Sales .....................................Main: (801) 226-6800
    TFree:(800) 321-4566
... Sales, Easy Move/Special Lic .....................Main: (800) 526-5040
... Sales, Educational Institutions ..................Main: (800) 321-3220
... Sales, Hearing Impaired (TDD) ...................Main: (801) 228-9906
    TFree:(800) 321-3256
... Sales, International ......................................Main: (801) 229-1667
... Sales, Mini-Main Info/Orders .....................Main: (801) 228-9911
    TFree:(800) 321-3280
... Sales, Orders Resolution ............................Main: (800) 321-2319
... Sales, Software Subscription ......................Main: (800) 282-2892
... Sales, Workgroups/Office ...........................Main: (800) 861-2507
... Shell 4.0..................................................... Main: (801) 228-9937
... Shell 4.0 Macros ........................................Main: (801) 228-9928
... Soft Shoppe ................................................Main: (800) 526-6215
... SoftSolutions ..............................................Main: (800) 861-2146
... Spanish .......................................................Main: (800) 321-8492
... Word Perfect ...............................................See Corel Corporation
Now Software:OR............................................Main: (503) 274-2800
    TFree:(800) 237-2078   Fax:(503) 274-0670  Tech:(503) 274-2815
NuIQ Software Inc:NY.....................................Main: (914) 833-3479
    TFree:(800) 844-6526   Fax:(914) 833-3623  Tech:(914) 833-3479
NuKote International Inc:TX ............................Main: (214) 250-2785
    TFree:(800) 448-1422   Fax:(615) 794-4424  Tech:(800) 251-3365
Number Nine Computer Corp:MA.....................Main: (617) 674-0009
    TFree:(800) 438-6463   Fax:(617) 674-2919  Tech:(617) 674-8595
    Tech Support Fax:(617) 273-0899
Numera Software Corp:WA..............................Main: (206) 622-2233
    TFree:(800) 956-2233   Fax:(206) 622-5382  Tech:(206) 292-8324
NVIDIA Corp:CA..............................................Main: (408) 617-4000
    Fax:(408) 617-4100      Tech:(408) 617-4000
O'Reilly and Associates Inc:CA .....................Main: (707) 829-0515
    TFree:(800) 998-9938   Fax:(707) 829-0104
    toll free:(800) 889-8969
O.R. Technologies, Inc.:CA.............................Main: (408) 866-3000
    Fax:(408) 866-3008
Oak Technology:CA .........................................Main: (408) 737-0888
    Fax:(408) 737-3838
Oberon Software:MA .......................................Main: (617) 494-0990
    TFree:(800) 654-1215   Fax:(617) 494-0414  Tech:(800) 654-1364
Object Design Inc:MA .....................................Main: (617) 674-5000
    TFree:(800) 962-9620   Fax:(617) 674-5010  Tech:(617) 674-5040
Ocean Information Systems Inc:CA ................Main: (818) 339-8888
    TFree:(800) 325-2496   Fax:(818) 859-7668
Ocean Isle Soft (see Stac Electronics):
OCLI (Optical Coating Laboratory):CA..........Main: (707) 545-6440
    TFree:(800) 545-6254   Fax:(707) 525-7410  Tech:(800) 545-6254
```

Octel Communications Inc:CA .... Main: **(408) 321-2000**
  Fax:(408) 324-2702
Odyssey Computing Inc:CA .... Main: **(619) 675-3660**
  TFree:(800) 965-7224   Fax:(619) 675-1130
Oki Semiconductor:CA .... Main: **(408) 720-1900**
  TFree:(800) 832-6654   Fax:(408) 720-1918   Tech:(800) 832-6654
Oki Telecom:GA .... Main: **(770) 995-9800**
  TFree:(800) 554-3112   Fax:(770) 822-2681
Okidata (Division of Oki America Inc):NJ ..... Main: **(609) 235-2600**
  TFree:(800) 654-3282   Fax:(609) 778-4184   Tech:(800) 634-0089
Okna Corp:NJ .... Main: **(201) 909-8600**
  TFree:(800) 438-6562   Fax:(201) 909-0688   Tech:(201) 909-8600
Olicom USA:TX .... Main: **(972) 423-7560**
  TFree:(800) 265-4266   Fax:(972) 423-7261   Tech:(800) 654-2661
Olivr Corp:MA .... Main: **(617) 861-6111**
  Fax:(617) 863-6155
Omni Data Systems:MO .... Main: **(314) 230-3200**
  TFree:(800) 766-2449
Omni Development Inc:WA .... Main: **(206) 523-4152**
  TFree:(800) 315-6664   Fax:(206) 523-5896
Omnicomp Graphics Corp:TX .... Main: **(713) 464-2990**
  Fax:(713) 827-7540
OmniData International Inc:UT .... Main: **(801) 753-7760**
  Fax:(801) 753-6756
Omniprint Inc:NJ .... Main: **(201) 857-0901**
  TFree:(800) 469-2205   Fax:(201) 857-0607
Omnitech Gencorp:FL .... Main: **(305) 599-9898**
  TFree:(800) 222-9618   Fax:(305) 594-2997
Omnitrend:CT .... Main: **(860) 673-8910**
  Fax:(860) 673-3023   Tech:(860) 673-8910
Omron Advanced Systems Inc:CA .... Main: **(408) 727-6644**
  TFree:(800) 362-4411   Fax:(408) 727-5540   Tech:(408) 727-1444
On Technology Corp:MA .... Main: **(617) 374-1400**
  TFree:(800) 767-6683   Fax:(617) 374-1433   Tech:(800) 767-6683
Ontrack Computer Systems:MN .... Main: **(612) 937-5161**
  TFree:(800) 872-2599   Fax:(612) 937-5815   Tech:(612) 937-2121
OnTrack Media Corp:CA .... Main: **(415) 331-1692**
  TFree:(800) 505-5627   Fax:(415) 331-1695   Tech:(415) 331-1692
OnWord Press:NM .... Main: **(505) 474-5120**
  TFree:(888) 763-8786   Fax:(505) 474-5020
Opcode Systems:CA .... Main: **(415) 856-3333**
  Fax:(415) 856-3332   Tech:(415) 812-3205
  Mac support:(415) 856-3331
Open Doors Software:MN .... Main: **(800) 923-8463**
  TFree:(800) 923-8463
Open Environment:MA .... Main: **(617) 562-0900**
Open Systems Inc:MN .... Main: **(612) 829-0011**
  TFree:(800) 328-2276   Fax:(612) 829-1493   Tech:(800) 582-5000
  Tech Fax:(612) 829-1454
OPTi Inc:CA .... Main: **(408) 486-8000**
  Fax:(408) 486-8001
Optibase Inc:CA .... Main: **(408) 557-9670**
  TFree:(800) 451-5101   Fax:(408) 244-0545

Optical Data Systems Inc:TX .... **Main: (972) 234-6400**
  Fax:(972) 234-1467
Optima Technology Corp:CA .... **Main: (714) 476-0515**
  TFree:(800) 411-4237 Fax:(714) 476-0613
ORA Electronics (see Alliance Research):
Oracle Corp:CA.. **Main: (415) 506-7000**
  TFree:(800) 542-1170 Fax:(415) 506-7200 Tech:(415) 506-1500
Orange Cherry/New Media Schoolhouse:NY **Main: (914) 764-4387**
  TFree:(800) 672-6002 Fax:(914) 764-0104 Tech:(914) 764-4104
  orders:(888) 843-6674
Orange Micro Inc:CA .... **Main: (714) 779-2772**
  Fax:(714) 779-9332   Tech:(518) 283-8860
  Sales Fax:(714) 779-9332
Orchid Technology:CA................................ **Main: (510) 661-3000**
  TFree:(800) 577-0977 Fax:(510) 651-6982 Tech:(510) 661-3000
  Tech Support Fax:(510) 651-6982
Origin Systems Inc:TX.............................. **Main: (512) 434-4263**
  TFree:(800) 245-4525 Fax:(512) 794-8959 Tech:(512) 434-4357
  Tech Fax:(512) 795-8014
Osborne/McGraw Hill:CA .... **Main: (510) 549-6600**
  TFree:(800) 227-0900 Fax:(510) 549-6603
OSC (see Micromedia):
Osicom Tech. (Digital Products):MA .... **Main: (781) 647-1234**
  TFree:(800) 243-2333 Fax:(781) 647-4474 Tech:(781) 647-1234
OTC (See Output Tech Corp):
Outlook Software:TX .... **Main: (214) 774-0708**
  TFree:(800) 925-5700 Fax:(214) 774-0689
Output Tech Corp (OTC):WA...................... **Main: (509) 536-0468**
  TFree:(800) 468-8788 Fax:(509) 533-1290 Tech:(509) 536-0468
  Tech Support Fax:(509) 533-1295
Overland Data Inc:CA .... **Main: (619) 571-5555**
  TFree:(800) 729-8725 Fax:(619) 571-0982 Tech:(619) 571-5555
P.A.C.E.:UT .... **Main: (801) 753-1067**
  TFree:(800) 359-6670
P.N.Y. Electronics Inc:NJ .... **Main: (201) 438-6300**
  TFree:(800) 234-4597 Fax:(201) 560-5590 Tech:(201) 438-6300
Pacific Data Products:CA .... **Main: (619) 552-0880**
  TFree:(800) 737-7105 Fax:(619) 552-0889 Tech:(619) 587-4690
Pacific HiTech:UT .... **Main: (801) 261-1024**
  TFree:(800) 765-8369 Fax:(801) 261-0310 Tech:(801) 261-1024
Pacific Magtron Inc:CA .... **Main: (408) 956-8888**
  Fax:(408) 956-8488   Tech:(408) 956-8888
Pacific Micro Data Inc:CA .... **Main: (714) 955-9090**
  TFree:(800) 933-7575 Fax:(714) 955-9490 Tech:(714) 955-9090
Pacific Microelectronics (Net USA Soft.):CA **Main: (415) 948-6200**
  TFree:(800) 628-3475 Fax:(415) 948-6296 Tech:(415) 948-6200
Packard Bell:CA .... **Main: (818) 865-1555**
  TFree:(800) 733-4411 Fax:(801) 579-0093 Tech:(800) 733-4433
Palindrome Corp (Seagate Software):IL...... **Main: (630) 505-3300**
  TFree:(800) 327-2232 Fax:(630) 505-7917 Tech:(800) 288-4912
  Tech Support Fax:(407) 333-7750
... Sales, Marketing, and Tech Support .... **Main: (508) 275-6128**
  TFree:(800) 788-9994 Fax:(508) 275-6200 Tech:(508) 970-0440

Panacea (Spacetec):
Panamax:CA .... **Main: (415) 499-3900**
    TFree:(800) 472-5555   Fax:(415) 472-5540   Tech:(800) 472-5555
Panasonic Comm & Systems (Corp Hq):NJ . Main: (201) 348-7000
    TFree:(800) 233-8182   Tech:(800) 222-0584
Panasonic Office Automation:CA .... **Main: (714) 373-7412**
    TFree:(800) 726-2797   Tech:(800) 726-2797
    Sales:(800) 662-3537
... CD Rom/Opticals/Monitors/Scanners .... **Main: (800) 726-2797**
... Laptop Computer Information .... **Main: (800) 527-8675**
... Manuals and Repair Parts .... **Main: (800) 833-9626**
... Printer Products .... **Main: (800) 222-0584**
.. Window Drivers .... **Main: (800) 993-2333**
Pantheon:WA .... **Main: (206) 628-3411**
    TFree:(800) 668-1647   Fax:(206) 628-3412
PaperClip Software Inc:NJ .... **Main: (201) 487-3503**
    Fax:(201) 487-0613   Tech:(201) 487-3503
Paperless Corp:TX .... **Main: (972) 235-4008**
    TFree:(800) 658-6486   Fax:(972) 680-2566
Paracel Online Systems Inc:TX .... **Main: (818) 666-6688**
    TFree:(888) 727-2235   Fax:(818) 666-6677   Tech:(816) 666-6688
ParaCom Corp:MA .... **Main: (617) 935-6614**
    Fax:(617) 938-1760
Paradigm Software Development Inc:WA ..... **Main: (206) 728-2281**
    TFree:(800) 967-5947   Fax:(206) 728-8401   Tech:(206) 728-4508
Paradise (see Western Digital Corp):
Paragraph International:CA .... **Main: (408) 364-7700**
Parallax Inc:CA .... **Main: (916) 624-8333**
    TFree:(888) 512-1024   Fax:(916) 624-8003   Tech:(916) 624-8333
Parana Supplies Corp:CA .... **Main: (310) 793-1325**
    TFree:(800) 472-7262   Fax:(310) 793-1343   Tech:(800) 472-7262
Parc Place Digitalk:CA .... **Main: (408) 481-9090**
    TFree:(800) 759-7272   Fax:(408) 481-9095   Tech:(800) 253-3415
    Tech Fax:(408) 773-7474
Parsons Technology:IA .... **Main: (319) 395-9626**
    TFree:(800) 779-6000   Fax:(319) 395-0102   Tech:(319) 395-7314
Parts Now Inc:WI .... **Main: (608) 276-8688**
    TFree:(800) 886-6688   Fax:(608) 276-9593   Tech:(608) 276-9415
Passport Designs Inc:CA .... **Main: (415) 349-6224**
    TFree:(800) 443-3210   Fax:(415) 349-8008   Tech:(415) 349-8090
Patton & Patton Software Corp:CA .... **Main: (408) 778-6557**
    TFree:(800) 525-0082   Fax:(408) 778-9972   Tech:(408) 778-6557
Paul Mace Software Inc:OR .... **Main: (503) 488-2322**
    TFree:(800) 944-0191   Fax:(503) 488-1549   Tech:(503) 488-0224
PC & MAC Connection:NH .... **Main: (603) 446-7721**
    TFree:(800) 800-5555   Fax:(603) 446-7791
PC Checks & Supplies Inc:AL .... **Main: (205) 969-0024**
    TFree:(800) 322-5317   Fax:(800) 322-5318
PC DOCS:MA .... **Main: (617) 273-3800**
    TFree:(800) 933-3627   Fax:(904) 656-5559   Tech:(850) 942-5000
PC Dynamics Inc:CA .... **Main: (818) 889-1741**
    TFree:(800) 888-1741   Fax:(818) 889-1014   Tech:(818) 889-1742

PC Guardian:CA .... Main: **(415) 459-0190**
TFree:(800) 288-8126 Fax:(415) 459-1162 Tech:(415) 459-0190
PC Magazine (Ziff-Davis):NY .... Main: **(212) 503-5255**
Fax:(212) 503-5799
PC Power & Cooling Inc:CA .... Main: **(760) 931-5700**
TFree:(800) 722-6555 Fax:(760) 931-6988
PC Repair Corporation:PA .... Main: **(717) 232-7272**
TFree:(800) 727-3724
PC Service Source:TX .... Main: **(972) 406-8583**
TFree:(800) 727-2787 Fax:(972) 406-9081
PC Today (Peed Corp):NE .... Main: **(402) 479-2141**
TFree:(800) 544-1426 Fax:(402) 458-4569
PC-Kwik Corp (MDI Web): .... Main: **(407) 677-8333**
TFree:(800) 920-8205 Fax:(407) 677-0221
PC-Sig/Spectra Pub (see CD World):
PC411 Inc:CA .... Main: **(310) 645-1114**
TFree:(800) 243-8411 Fax:(310) 645-1112 Tech:(310) 645-1114
PCMCIA:CA .... Main: **(408) 433-2273**
Fax:(408) 433-9558
PCPI:CA .... Main: **(619) 485-8411**
Fax:(619) 487-5809   Tech:(619) 485-8411
Peachtree Software:GA .... Main: **(770) 724-4000**
TFree:(800) 247-3224 Fax:(770) 564-8888 Tech:(770) 492-6311
DOS support:(770) 492-6312
Pegasus:CA .... Main: **(510) 938-5340**
Fax:(510) 938-5341   Tech:(510) 938-5340
Pelikan Inc (see NuKote International):
Pen Magic Software (see Pivotal Graphics):
Penril Datability Networks (Access Beyond) Main: **(301) 921-8600**
TFree:(800) 456-7844 Fax:(301) 921-8376 Tech:(800) 456-7844
Tech Support Fax:(301) 840-1528
Pentax Technologies Corp:CO .... Main: **(303) 460-1600**
TFree:(800) 543-6144 Fax:(303) 460-1628 Tech:(303) 460-1820
PeopleSoft:CA .... Main: **(510) 225-3000**
TFree:(888) 773-8277 Fax:(510) 225-3100
Perceptive Solutions Inc:TX .... Main: **(214) 954-1774**
TFree:(800) 486-3278 Fax:(214) 953-1774 Tech:(214) 954-1774
PerfectData Corp:CA .... Main: **(805) 581-4000**
TFree:(800) 973-7332 Fax:(805) 522-5788
Persoft Inc:WI .... Main: **(608) 273-6000**
TFree:(888) 657-3776 Fax:(608) 273-8227 Tech:(608) 273-6090
Persona Technologies (Monster Cable):
Personal Training Systems:CA .... Main: **(415) 614-5950**
TFree:(800) 832-2499 Fax:(415) 463-2522 Tech:(800) 832-2499
Personics Corp (Data Watch Corp):MA .... Main: **(508) 988-9700**
TFree:(800) 445-3311 Fax:(508) 988-2040 Tech:(508) 658-0040
Phase3 Software Inc:CA .... Main: **(805) 644-7185**
TFree:(800) 851-5650 Fax:(805) 644-4572 Tech:(805) 644-0870
PHD - Professional Help Desk:CT .... Main: **(203) 356-7700**
TFree:(800) 474-3725 Fax:(203) 356-7900 Tech:(203) 356-7700
Philips Consumer Electronics:TN .... Main: **(423) 521-4316**
TFree:(800) 531-0039 Fax:(615) 521-4586 Tech:(615) 475-8869

Phillips Laser Magnetic Storage:CO .... Main: **(719) 593-7900**
Tech:(719) 593-4393

Phoenix Technologies:MA .... Main: **(617) 551-4000**
TFree:(800) 677-7300 Fax:(617) 551-3750 Tech:(617) 551-4000

Phoenix Technologies:CA .... Main: **(408) 570-1000**
TFree:(800) 677-7305 Fax:(408) 570-1001 Tech:(312) 541-0262

PhotoDisc Inc:WA .... Main: **(206) 441-9355**
TFree:(800) 528-3472 Fax:(206) 441-9379 Tech:(206) 441-9355

Physician Micro Systems Inc:WA .... Main: **(206) 441-8490**
Fax:(206) 441-8915

Piiceon:CA .... Main: **(408) 432-8030**
TFree:(800) 366-2983 Fax:(408) 943-1309 Tech:(800) 366-2983

Pinnacle Data Systems Inc:OH .... Main: **(614) 487-1150**
TFree:(800) 882-8282 Fax:(614) 487-8568

Pinnacle Micro Inc:CA .... Main: **(714) 789-3000**
TFree:(800) 553-7070 Fax:(714) 789-3150 Tech:(714) 789-3200

Pinnacle Publishing:GA .... Main: **(770) 565-1763**
TFree:(800) 788-1900 Fax:(770) 565-8232 Tech:(206) 251-3513

Pinnacle Software:PQ .... Main: **(514) 345-9578**
Fax:(514) 733-8644 Tech:(514) 345-9578

Pinpoint Publishing:CA .... Main: **(707) 523-0400**
TFree:(800) 788-5236 Fax:(707) 523-0469

Pioneer New Media Technologies:CA .... Main: **(310) 952-2111**
TFree:(800) 444-6784 Fax:(310) 952-2990 Tech:(800) 872-4159

Pivotal Graphics Inc:CA .... Main: **(408) 954-2700**
Fax:(408) 954-0118 Tech:(408) 954-2700

Pivotal Software:BC .... Main: **(604) 988-9982**
TFree:(888) 275-7486 Fax:(604) 988-0035 Tech:(604) 988-9982

Pixar Interactive:CA .... Main: **(510) 236-4000**
TFree:(800) 888-9856 Fax:(510) 236-0388 Tech:(800) 937-3179

PKware Inc:WI .... Main: **(414) 354-8699**
Fax:(414) 354-8559 Tech:(414) 354-8699

PlainTree Systems:MA .... Main: **(617) 965-5811**
TFree:(800) 370-2724 Fax:(617) 965-2466 Tech:(800) 831-1095
Tech Support Fax:(613) 831-6120

Platinum Software Corp:CA .... Main: **(714) 453-4000**
TFree:(800) 999-1809 Fax:(714) 453-4091

Platinum Technology Inc:VA .... Main: **(630) 620-5000**
TFree:(800) 890-7528 Fax:(630) 691-0718 Tech:(800) 890-7528
Tech Support Fax:(708) 691-0708

Play Inc:CA .... Main: **(916) 851-0800**
TFree:(800) 306-7529 Fax:(916) 851-0801 Tech:(916) 851-0900
Tech Fax:(916) 853-9831

Plextor:CA .... Main: **(408) 980-1838**
TFree:(800) 886-3935 Fax:(408) 986-1010 Tech:(800) 886-3935
another BBS:(408) 986-1474

Plus Development Corp (see Quantum Corp):

PNY Electronics:NJ .... Main: **(201) 438-6300**
TFree:(800) 234-4597 Fax:(201) 560-5590 Tech:(201) 438-6300
Tech support:(800) 234-4597

Polaris Software:CA .... Main: **(760) 735-2300**
TFree:(800) 338-5943 Fax:(760) 738-0113 Tech:(760) 735-2300

Polaroid Corporation:MA .... Main: (617) 386-2000
TFree:(800) 343-5000   Fax:(617) 386-3263   Tech:(800) 432-5355
Polygon Inc:MO .... Main: (314) 432-4142
Fax:(314) 997-9696   Tech:(314) 432-4142
Port Inc:CT .... Main: (203) 852-1102
TFree:(800) 242-3133   Fax:(203) 866-0221   Tech:(800) 350-7678
Portable Graphics Inc:TX .... Main: (512) 719-8000
TFree:(800) 574-7333   Fax:(512) 832-0752   Tech:(800) 574-7333
Tech Support Fax:(801) 588-4540
Portrait Display Labs:CA .... Main: (510) 227-2700
POSitive Software Co:WA .... Main: (509) 735-9194
TFree:(800) 735-6860   Fax:(509) 735-6299   Tech:(509) 735-9194
Power BBS Computing:NY .... Main: (516) 938-0506
Fax:(516) 681-3226   Tech:(516) 822-7396
Power Computing Corp:TX .... Main: (512) 246-7807
TFree:(800) 671-6227   Fax:(512) 388-6798   Tech:(800) 708-6227
Powercom America Inc:CA .... Main: (714) 632-8889
TFree:(800) 666-8931   Fax:(714) 632-8868
Powercore Inc (see CE Software):
PowerProduction Software:CA .... Main: (408) 358-2358
Fax:(408) 358-1186
PowerQuest Corp:UT .... Main: (801) 437-8900
TFree:(800) 379-2566   Fax:(801) 226-8941   Tech:(801) 226-6834
Powersoft Corp:MA .... Main: (508) 287-1500
TFree:(800) 395-3525   Fax:(508) 287-1600   Tech:(508) 287-1500
Practical Peripherals:GA .... Main: (770) 441-0896
TFree:(800) 934-2937   Fax:(770) 734-4615   Tech:(770) 840-9966
Tech Fax:(770) 734-4601
Prairie Group:IA .... Main: (515) 225-3720
TFree:(800) 346-5392   Fax:(515) 225-2422   Tech:(515) 225-4122
Orders only:(800) 346-5392
Precision Digital Images Corp:WA .... Main: (425) 882-0218
TFree:(800) 678-6505   Fax:(206) 867-9177
Premenos Corp:CA .... Main: (510) 602-2000
TFree:(800) 426-3836   Fax:(510) 688-2895   Tech:(800) 578-4334
Prentice Hall Inc (Simon & Schuster):NJ ...... Main: (201) 767-5937
TFree:(800) 947-7700
Prescience (Waterloo Maple Software):
Priam Systems (see AST Research):
Primavera Systems, Inc:PA .... Main: (610) 667-8600
TFree:(800) 423-0245   Fax:(610) 667-7894   Tech:(610) 668-3030
Princeton Graphic Systems:CA .... Main: (714) 751-8405
Printronix, Inc:CA .... Main: (714) 863-1900
Fax:(714) 660-8682   Tech:(714) 863-1900
Pro CD Inc (Acxiom Corp):MA .... Main: (508) 750-0055
Fax:(508) 750-0070   Tech:(508) 777-7766
Pro-C Limited:OT .... Main: (519) 742-9521
Fax:(519) 742-1099   Tech:(519) 725-5143
Process Software Corp:MA .... Main: (508) 879-6994
TFree:(800) 722-7770   Fax:(508) 879-0042   Tech:(508) 879-6994
Processor Magazine (Peed Corp):NE .... Main: (402) 479-2141
TFree:(800) 247-4880   Fax:(402) 479-2120   Tech:(800) 247-4880

Procom Technology:CA .... Main: (714) 852-1000
  TFree:(800) 800-8600 Fax:(714) 852-1221 Tech:(800) 800-8600
  Tech Support Fax:(714) 261-6452
PRODIGY Service Information: .... Main: (800) 776-0845
Prodigy Services Company:NY .... Main: (914) 448-8000
  TFree:(800) 776-3449 Fax:(914) 448-8083 Tech:(800) 284-5933
Programmer's Paradise Inc:NJ .... Main: (908) 389-8950
  TFree:(800) 445-7899 Fax:(908) 389-9227 Tech:(908) 389-8950
Programmer's Super Shop:MA .... Main: (617) 740-2510
  TFree:(800) 421-8006 Fax:(617) 740-2728
Programmers Warehouse (see Breakthrough):
Progress Software Corp:MA .... Main: (617) 280-4000
  TFree:(800) 477-6473 Fax:(617) 280-4895
Progressive Networks Inc:WA .... Main: (206) 674-2700
  Fax:(206) 674-2699 Tech:(206) 674-2650
Prometheus Products:OR
  TFree:(800) 477-3473 Fax:(503) 684-2464 Tech:(503) 968-9246
Promise Technology Inc:CA .... Main: (408) 452-0948
  TFree:(800) 888-0245 Fax:(408) 452-1534 Tech:(408) 452-1180
Prostar Interactive MediaWorks:BC .... Main: (604) 273-4099
  TFree:(800) 432-2949 Fax:(604) 273-4046 Tech:(604) 273-4099
Proteon Inc (Open Route Networks Inc):MA Main: (508) 898-2800
  TFree:(800) 545-7464 Fax:(508) 366-9146 Tech:(508) 898-3100
Proteq Technologies Pte Ltd:MO .... Main: (314) 434-0588
  TFree:(800) 426-0522 Fax:(314) 434-1993 Tech:(800) 426-0522
Provantage Corp:OH .... Main: (330) 494-8715
  TFree:(800) 336-1166 Fax:(330) 494-5260 Tech:(330) 494-8715
ProVUE Development:CA .... Main: (714) 841-7779
  TFree:(800) 966-7878 Fax:(714) 841-1479 Tech:(714) 841-8779
Proxim Inc:CA .... Main: (415) 960-1630
  TFree:(800) 229-1630 Fax:(415) 960-1984 Tech:(415) 526-3640
  Tech Fax:(415) 960-1106
Proxima Corp:CA .... Main: (619) 457-5500
  TFree:(800) 447-7692 Fax:(619) 457-9647 Tech:(800) 447-7692
PSI Integration (see Supra Corp):
Psion Inc:MA .... Main: (508) 371-0310
  TFree:(800) 997-7466 Fax:(508) 371-9611
Psygnosis Ltd (see Sony Interactive):
Public Software Library:TX .... Main: (713) 524-6394
  TFree:(800) 242-4775 Fax:(713) 524-6398
PureData (Wild Card Technologies):ON .... Main: (905) 731-6444
  TFree:(800) 661-8210 Fax:(905) 731-7017 Tech:(800) 396-7877
QLogic:CA .... Main: (800) 662-4471
  TFree:(800) 662-4471 Fax:(714) 668-5090 Tech:(800) 737-6524
QMS Inc:AL .... Main: (334) 633-4300
  TFree:(800) 523-2696 Tech:(334) 633-4500
QNX Software Systems Ltd:ON .... Main: (613) 591-0931
  TFree:(800) 676-0566 Fax:(613) 591-3579
Quadralay Corp:TX .... Main: (512) 719-3399
  Fax:(512) 719-3606
Quadtel Corp (see Phoenix Technologies):
Qualcomm Inc:CA .... Main: (619) 587-1121
  Fax:(619) 658-2100

Qualitas:MD .... **Main: (301) 589-8872**
TFree:(800) 733-1377 Fax:(301) 718-6061 Tech:(301) 907-7400

Qualix Group Inc:CA .... **Main: (650) 572-0200**
TFree:(800) 253-4559 Fax:(650) 572-1300

Qualtec Data Products Inc:CA .... **Main: (510) 490-8911**
TFree:(800) 628-4413 Fax:(510) 490-8471 Tech:(800) 628-4413

Quantum Corp:CA .... **Main: (408) 894-4000**
TFree:(800) 624-5545 Fax:(408) 894-3282 Tech:(800) 826-8022

Quark Inc:CO .... **Main: (303) 894-8888**
TFree:(800) 676-4575 Fax:(303) 894-3399 Tech:(303) 894-8899
Tech Fax:(303) 894-3398

Quarter-Inch Cartridge Dr Stds:CA .... **Main: (805) 963-3853**
Fax:(805) 962-1541

Quarterdeck Office Systems:CA .... **Main: (310) 309-3700**
TFree:(800) 225-8148 Fax:(813) 523-2331 Tech:(310) 309-4250
Tech Support Fax:(310) 314-3217

Quarterdeck Select:FL .... **Main: (813) 523-9700**
TFree:(800) 683-6696 Fax:(813) 532-4222 Tech:(800) 683-0854

Que Corp:IN .... **Main: (317) 581-3500**
TFree:(800) 428-5331 Fax:(800) 448-3804 Tech:(317) 581-3833
Customer Service:(800) 858-7674

Quercus Systems:CA .... **Main: (408) 372-7399**
TFree:(800) 440-5944 Fax:(408) 372-5776 Tech:(408) 867-7399

Qume:CA .... **Main: (408) 473-1500**
TFree:(800) 457-4447 Fax:(408) 473-1510

Qume Corp (see Data Technology):

Quyen Systems Inc:MD .... **Main: (301) 258-5087**
TFree:(800) 827-1856 Fax:(301) 258-5088 Tech:(301) 258-5087

Rabbit Software (see Tangram):

Racal-Datacom Inc:FL .... **Main: (954) 846-1601**
TFree:(800) 722-2555 Fax:(954) 846-4942 Tech:(954) 846-6080

RAD:NJ .... **Main: (201) 529-1100**
Fax:(201) 529-5777

Radio Shack:TX .... **Main: (817) 390-3200**
TFree:(800) 843-7422 Fax:(817) 390-3240 Tech:(800) 843-7422

Radius Inc:CA .... **Main: (408) 541-6100**
TFree:(800) 227-2795 Fax:(408) 541-6150 Tech:(408) 541-5700
Automated Tech support:(800) 332-9225

RAG Electronics Inc:CA .... **Main: (805) 498-9933**
TFree:(800) 950-3457 Fax:(805) 498-3733
Marketing:(805) 375-7320

Rail Systems Center:PA .... **Main: (412) 751-8470**
Fax:(412) 754-0176

Raima Corp:WA .... **Main: (206) 515-9477**
TFree:(800) 327-2462 Fax:(206) 748-3200 Tech:(206) 557-5333

Rainbow Technology:CA .... **Main: (510) 252-0708**
Fax:(510) 252-0716 Tech:(510) 252-0708

Rancho Technology, Inc.:CA .... **Main: (909) 987-3966**
Fax:(909) 989-2365

Raosoft Inc (Northwest Nexus):WA .... **Main: (206) 525-4025**
Fax:(206) 525-4947 Tech:(206) 525-4025

Raster OPS (see True Vision Raster OPS):

Ray Dream (Fractal Design):CA .... Main: (415) 960-0765
   TFree:(800) 846-0111   Fax:(415) 960-1198   Tech:(415) 960-0767

Rayovac Corp:WI .... Main: (608) 275-4694
   TFree:(800) 237-7000   Fax:(608) 275-4577

Reach Software:CA .... Main: (408) 733-8685
   TFree:(800) 624-5356   Fax:(408) 733-9265

ReadMe.DOC:PA .... Main: (717) 264-0843
   TFree:(800) 678-1473   Fax:(717) 264-8614

Ready-To-Run Software Inc:MA .... Main: (508) 692-9922
   TFree:(800) 743-1723   Fax:(508) 692-9990

Real Time Integration Inc:WA .... Main: (425) 462-5817
   TFree:(888) 675-1122   Fax:(888) 670-1122

Reality Online Inc:PA .... Main: (610) 277-7600
   TFree:(800) 346-2024   Fax:(610) 278-6115   Tech:(800) 777-7424

Reality Tech (see Reality Online Inc):

RealWorld Corp:NH .... Main: (603) 641-0200
   TFree:(800) 678-6336   Fax:(603) 641-0230   Tech:(603) 288-3433

Red Wing Business Systems Inc:MN .... Main: (612) 388-1106
   TFree:(800) 732-9464   Fax:(612) 388-7950

Relay Technology Inc:VA .... Main: (703) 506-0500
   TFree:(800) 795-8674   Fax:(703) 506-0510   Tech:(703) 902-8700

Relialogic Corp:CA .... Main: (510) 770-3990
   TFree:(800) 998-3966   Fax:(510) 770-3994   Tech:(510) 770-3990

Remco Software Inc:ND .... Main: (701) 225-8336

Remote Control Intl (see Telemagic):

Reply Corp (See Radius Inc):

Research Information Systems:CA .... Main: (760) 438-5526
   TFree:(800) 722-1227   Fax:(760) 438-5573

Reseller Management:MA .... Main: (617) 558-4723
   Fax:(617) 558-4757

ResNova Software Inc:CA .... Main: (714) 379-9000
   Fax:(714) 379-9014   Tech:(714) 379-9018

Responsive Software:CA .... Main: (415) 945-3876
   TFree:(800) 669-4611   Fax:(510) 644-1013

Retix:CA .... Main: (310) 828-3400
   Fax:(310) 828-2255   Tech:(800) 255-2333

Revelation Technologies Inc:MA .... Main: (617) 577-0300
   TFree:(800) 262-4747   Fax:(617) 494-0008   Tech:(800) 262-4747

Rexon Data Storage (Tecmar Technologies):

RGB Spectrum:CA .... Main: (510) 814-7000
   Fax:(510) 814-7026

Rhode Island Soft Systems Inc:RI .... Main: (401) 767-3106
   TFree:(800) 959-7477   Fax:(401) 767-3108   Tech:(401) 767-3106

Ricoh Corp (Scanners):CA .... Main: (714) 259-1310
   TFree:(800) 955-3453   Fax:(714) 556-3505   Tech:(210) 520-0951

Ricoh Corp-Peripherals Products:CA .... Main: (800) 955-3453
   TFree:(800) 955-3453   Fax:(408) 432-9266   Tech:(800) 955-3453

Rinda Technologies Inc:IL .... Main: (312) 736-6633
   Fax:(312) 736-2950

Ring King Visibles Inc:IA .... Main: (319) 263-8144
   TFree:(800) 272-2366   Fax:(800) 272-2382   Tech:(800) 553-9647

RKS Software Inc:VA.....................................Main: (703) 534-1726
Fax:(703) 534-4358

RNS Inc:CA...Main: (805) 968-4262
TFree:(800) 262-8023   Fax:(805) 968-6478

Road Scholar Software:TX..........................Main: (714) 266-7623
TFree:(800) 243-7623   Fax:(713) 266-4525   Tech:(713) 266-7623

Rocket Science Games Inc:CA...................Main: (415) 442-5000
TFree:(800) 987-6253   Fax:(415) 442-5001   Tech:(916) 939-1008
Tech Support Fax:(415) 442-5002

Rogue Wave Software:CA.............................Main: (415) 691-9000
TFree:(888) 442-9641   Fax:(415) 691-9099

Roland Corp US:CA......................................Main: (213) 685-5141
Fax:(213) 722-0911

Roland DG America (Plotters):CA..............Main: (714) 727-2100
TFree:(800) 542-2307   Fax:(714) 727-2112   Tech:(800) 542-2307

Ross Systems:GA...Main: (770) 351-9600
Fax:(770) 351-0036

Ross Technology Inc:TX..............................Main: (512) 349-3108
TFree:(800) 767-7937   Fax:(512) 349-3101   Tech:(512) 436-2061

RSA Data Security (Security Dynamics):CA. Main: (415) 595-8782
Fax:(415) 595-1873

RTZ Software:CA ....Main: (408) 252-2946
Fax:(408) 257-5274

Rupp Technology Corporation:AZ ....Main: (602) 941-4789
TFree:(800) 844-7775   Fax:(602) 941-5505   Tech:(602) 941-5602

Rybs Electronics:CO....................................Main: (303) 444-6073
Fax:(303) 449-9259   Tech:(303) 444-7927

S3 Incorporated:CA.....................................Main: (408) 980-5400
Fax:(408) 980-5444

Saber Software (see McAfee):

SAI Inc (Microleague Multimedia):PA...........Main: (717) 872-6567
TFree:(800) 545-9009   Fax:(717) 871-1959   Tech:(717) 872-2442

Sampo Corp Of America:GA........................Main: (770) 449-6220
Fax:(770) 447-1109   Tech:(770) 449-6220

Sams Publishing:IN ....Main: (317) 581-3500
TFree:(800) 545-5914   Fax:(317) 581-4669   Tech:(800) 545-5914

Samsung America Inc:CA............................Main: (562) 802-2211
TFree:(800) 229-2239   Fax:(562) 802-3011

Samsung Electronics America (Info Sys):NJ Main: (201) 229-7000
TFree:(800) 726-7864   Fax:(201) 229-7030   Tech:(201) 229-4000

SanDisk Corp:CA...Main: (408) 542-0500
Fax:(408) 542-0503   Tech:(408) 562-3400

Santa Cruz Operations:CA..........................Main: (408) 425-7222
TFree:(800) 726-8649   Fax:(408) 458-4227   Tech:(800) 347-4381

Santa Fe Software (ACE Contact Mgr):CA...Main: (619) 673-5313
TFree:(800) 833-5822   Fax:(619) 673-7399   Tech:(619) 673-5313

SAP America Inc:PA.....................................Main: (610) 725-4500
Fax:(610) 725-4555

Saros Corp (FileNet Enterprise Doc Man).....Main: (206) 646-1066
TFree:(800) 345-3638   Fax:(425) 462-0879   Tech:(206) 450-1500

SAS Institute Inc:NC....................................Main: (919) 677-8000
Fax:(919) 677-8123

Savin Corp:CT .... Main: **(203) 967-5000**
Fax:(203) 967-5014   Tech:(203) 967-5460
Sayett Technology Inc:NY .... Main: **(716) 264-1290**
TFree:(800) 678-7469   Fax:(716) 624-6080   Tech:(800) 836-7730
SBT Accounting Systems:CA .... Main: **(415) 444-9900**
TFree:(800) 944-1000   Fax:(415) 444-9901   Tech:(415) 444-9700
Scala Inc:VA .... Main: **(703) 713-0900**
Fax:(703) 713-1960   Tech:(703) 713-6900
SCi:CA .... Main: **(310) 577-1518**
SciTech Software Inc:CA .... Main: **(916) 894-8400**
Fax:(916) 894-9069
Scitor Corp:CA .... Main: **(415) 462-4200**
Fax:(415) 462-4201   Tech:(415) 462-4200
SCO (See Santa Cruz Operations):
Scopus Technology Inc:CA .... Main: **(510) 597-5800**
Fax:(510) 597-8600
Seagate Enterprise Mgmt Software:MA .... Main: **(407) 531-7500**
TFree:(800) 327-2232   Fax:(407) 333-7767   Tech:(617) 451-5400
Seagate Technologies:CA .... Main: **(408) 438-8111**
TFree:(800) 468-3472   Fax:(408) 456-4496   Tech:(408) 438-8222
Tech Fax:(408) 944-9120
Sealevel Systems:SC .... Main: **(864) 843-4343**
Fax:(864) 843-3067   Tech:(864) 843-4343
Searchlight Software:OH .... Main: **(216) 631-9290**
TFree:(800) 988-5483   Fax:(216) 631-9289   Tech:(800) 988-9290
Seattle Lab:WA .... Main: **(425) 402-6003**
Fax:(425) 828-9011   Tech:(425) 481-7619
Seiko Instruments USA:CA .... Main: **(408) 922-5806**
TFree:(800) 553-5312   Fax:(408) 922-5840   Tech:(800) 553-5312
Tech Support Fax:(408) 922-5867
SemWare Corp:GA .... Main: **(770) 641-9002**
TFree:(800) 467-3692   Fax:(770) 640-6213   Tech:(770) 641-9002
Sequel Inc:CA .... Main: **(408) 987-1000**
Fax:(800) 848-5837   Tech:(408) 987-1417
Sequent Computer Systems Inc:OR .... Main: **(503) 626-5700**
TFree:(800) 257-9044
Product or literature info:(800) 257-9044
Sequoia Publishing Inc:CO .... Main: **(303) 972-4167**
TFree:(800) 873-7126   Fax:(303) 972-0158   Tech:(303) 972-4167
Server Technology:CA .... Main: **(408) 745-0300**
TFree:(800) 835-1515   Fax:(408) 745-0392   Tech:(800) 835-1515
Service 2000 (see Kennsco Inc):
Service News Magazine:ME .... Main: **(207) 856-0600**
Fax:(207) 846-0657
SES (Scientific & Engin Software):TX .... Main: **(512) 328-5544**
TFree:(800) 759-6333   Fax:(512) 327-6646   Tech:(512) 328-3377
Set Enterprises Inc:AZ .... Main: **(602) 837-3628**
TFree:(800) 351-7765   Fax:(602) 837-5644   Tech:(602) 837-3628
SGS-Thomson Microelectronics:AZ .... Main: **(602) 485-6201**
Fax:(602) 485-6330
Shaffstall Corp:IN .... Main: **(317) 842-2077**
TFree:(800) 248-3475   Fax:(317) 842-8294   Tech:(317) 842-2077

Shapeware (Out of Business):

Sharp Electronics Corp:NJ .... Main: **(201) 529-8200**
TFree:(800) 237-4277 Fax:(201) 529-8425 Tech:(800) 237-4277

Sherwood Terminals:CA .... Main: **(510) 623-8900**
TFree:(800) 777-8755 Fax:(510) 623-8945 Tech:(800) 777-8755

Shiva Corporation:MA .... Main: **(617) 270-8300**
TFree:(800) 458-3550 Fax:(617) 270-8599 Tech:(617) 270-8400

ShowCase Corporation:MN .... Main: **(507) 288-5922**
TFree:(800) 829-3555 Fax:(507) 287-2803 Tech:(507) 288-5922

Shugart Corporation:CA
Fax:(714) 367-8843   Tech:(714) 770-1100

Sierra On-Line (CUC International Inc):WA ..Main: **(425) 649-9800**
TFree:(800) 757-7707 Fax:(425) 644-7697 Tech:(425) 746-5771
Tech Fax:(402) 393-3224

Sigma Data:NH .... Main: **(603) 526-6909**
TFree:(800) 446-4525 Fax:(603) 526-6915

Sigma Designs Inc:CA .... Main: **(510) 770-0100**
TFree:(800) 845-8086 Fax:(510) 770-2640 Tech:(970) 339-7120

Silicon Graphics Inc:CA .... Main: **(415) 933-3900**
TFree:(800) 800-7441 Fax:(415) 960-0197 Tech:(800) 800-4744

Simon & Schuster Software:NY .... Main: **(212) 698-7000**
TFree:(800) 223-2348 Tech:(317) 581-3833
Order Line:(800) 428-5331

Sir-Tech Software Inc:NY .... Main: **(315) 393-6451**
TFree:(800) 447-1230 Fax:(315) 393-1525 Tech:(315) 393-6644

Sirius Publishing:AZ .... Main: **(602) 951-3288**
TFree:(800) 247-0307 Fax:(602) 951-3884 Tech:(602) 951-8405

Skill Dynamics (Canada) (IBM Teach): .... Main: **(800) 661-2131**

Skill Dynamics (IBM Teach): .... Main: **(800) 426-8322**

SkiSoft:MA .... Main: **(617) 863-1876**
Fax:(617) 861-0086

SL Waber Inc:NJ .... Main: **(609) 866-8888**
TFree:(800) 634-1485 Fax:(609) 866-1945 Tech:(800) 257-8384

Smartronics Inc:NH .... Main: **(603) 437-1975**
Fax:(603) 434-5470

SMC (Standard Microsystems Corp):NY ...... Main: **(516) 435-6000**
TFree:(800) 762-4968 Fax:(516) 273-1803 Tech:(516) 435-6250

Smith Micro Software Inc:CA .... Main: **(714) 362-5800**
Fax:(714) 362-2300

SMS Technology (Televido Multimedia):CA .Main: **(408) 954-8333**
TFree:(800) 345-6050 Fax:(408) 954-0622

Snow Software:FL .... Main: **(813) 784-8899**
Fax:(813) 786-5904

Socket Communications:CA .... Main: **(510) 744-2700**
TFree:(800) 552-3300 Fax:(510) 744-2727 Tech:(510) 744-2720

SoftArc Inc:ON .... Main: **(905) 415-7000**
TFree:(800) 763-8272 Fax:(905) 415-7151 Tech:(905) 415-7000

Softbank Comdex Inc:MA .... Main: **(617) 433-1755**
Fax:(617) 444-4806

Softbite International:IL .... Main: **(630) 833-0006**
Fax:(630) 833-0584   Tech:(800) 336-6060

SoftBooks Inc:CA .... Main: **(714) 225-1463**
TFree:(800) 992-6464 Tech:(714) 586-1039

SoftCad USA:CA .... Main: **(510) 376-0117**
TFree:(800) 763-8223   Fax:(510) 376-0118   Tech:(800) 763-8223

SoftCraft Inc:WI .... Main: **(608) 257-3300**
TFree:(800) 351-0500   Fax:(608) 257-6733   Tech:(608) 257-3300

Softdesk Retail Products:MO .... Main: **(816) 891-1040**
TFree:(800) 231-8574   Fax:(816) 891-8018   Tech:(816) 891-8418

SoftKey International (Learning Co):MA .... Main: **(617) 494-1200**
TFree:(800) 227-5609   Fax:(617) 494-5898   Tech:(423) 670-2020

Softklone:FL .... Main: **(904) 878-8564**
TFree:(800) 634-8670   Fax:(904) 877-9763   Tech:(904) 878-8564

SofTouch Systems Inc:OK .... Main: **(405) 947-8080**
TFree:(800) 944-3036   Fax:(405) 947-8169   Tech:(800) 944-3028

SoftQuad Inc: .... Main: **(416) 544-9000**
TFree:(800) 387-2777   Fax:(416) 544-0300   Tech:(416) 544-8879

Softronics Inc:CO .... Main: **(719) 593-9540**
TFree:(800) 225-8590   Fax:(719) 548-1878   Tech:(719) 593-9550

SoftTalk Inc (Callware Technologies):UT ..... Main: **(801) 984-1100**
TFree:(800) 888-4226   Fax:(801) 984-1120

Software Business Technologies (SBT):

Software Directions Inc:CA .... Main: **(408) 763-0606**
Fax:(408) 763-1608

Software Marketing (see Softkey Intl):

Software Publishers Assoc:DC .... Main: **(202) 452-1600**
TFree:(800) 388-7478   Fax:(202) 223-8756

Software Publishing Corp:CA .... Main: **(408) 537-3000**
TFree:(800) 336-8360   Fax:(408) 537-3500   Tech:(408) 988-6005

Software Support Inc:FL .... Main: **(800) 873-4357**
TFree:(800) 756-4463   Fax:(407) 333-9080   Tech:(800) 873-4357

Software Toolworks (Mindscape):

Software Ventures:CA .... Main: **(510) 644-9277**
TFree:(800) 336-6477   Fax:(510) 848-0885   Tech:(510) 644-1325

Sola Electric:IL .... Main: **(708) 439-2800**
TFree:(800) 289-7652   Fax:(708) 439-1160   Tech:(800) 289-7652

Solectek Accessories:CA .... Main: **(619) 450-1220**
TFree:(800) 437-1518   Fax:(619) 457-2681   Tech:(800) 437-1518

Solidex (Unitech Industries):AZ .... Main: **(602) 991-7626**
TFree:(800) 328-6483   Fax:(602) 991-8860   Tech:(800) 722-1888

Solomon Software:OH .... Main: **(419) 424-1422**
TFree:(800) 476-5666   Fax:(419) 422-2044   Tech:(419) 424-0422

Solsource Computers:CA .... Main: **(760) 929-7800**
TFree:(800) 858-4405   Fax:(760) 929-7810

Sonera Technologies:NJ .... Main: **(908) 747-6886**
TFree:(800) 932-6323   Fax:(908) 747-4523   Tech:(908) 747-6886

Sonic:PA .... Main: **(610) 437-1000**
TFree:(800) 899-2595   Fax:(610) 437-4568   Tech:(610) 437-1000

Sonic Foundry:WI .... Main: **(608) 256-3133**
TFree:(800) 577-6642   Fax:(608) 256-7300   Tech:(608) 256-3133

Sonic Systems:CA .... Main: **(408) 736-1900**
TFree:(888) 222-6563   Fax:(408) 736-7228   Tech:(408) 736-1900

Sony Corp Of America:NJ .... Main: **(201) 930-1000**
TFree:(800) 222-7669   Tech:(201) 930-7669

Sony Electronics:CA .... Main: **(714) 489-3556**
TFree:(800) 352-7669   Tech:(800) 326-9551

... CD-Rom Discman Support .... Main: (800) 766-9236
... Computer Peripheral - TechFax (Canada) Main: (800) 961-7669
... Computer Peripheral - TechFax (USA) ...... Main: (800) 883-7669
... Magic Link Personal Comm Supt............. Main: (800) 326-9551
... Media Support .... Main: (800) 766-9328
... Monitors .... Main: (800) 222-7669
    TFree:(800) 222-7669   Fax:(941) 731-4370   Tech:(800) 222-7669
    Another Fax on Demand:(800) 282-2848
... PlayStation Support .... Main: (800) 345-7669
... Service Centers .... Main: (800) 282-2848
... Service Parts - Monitors .... Main: (800) 488-7669
... Service Parts - Storage Devices.............. Main: (408) 922-0699
Sony Interactive Studios:CA .... Main: (415) 655-8000
    Fax:(415) 655-8001   Tech:(415) 655-5683
Sophisticated Circuits:WA .... Main: (425) 485-7979
    TFree:(800) 827-4669   Fax:(425) 485-7172   Tech:(425) 485-7979
Sound Source Unlimited:CA .... Main: (818) 878-0505
    TFree:(800) 877-4778   Fax:(818) 878-0007
SourceMate Information Systems Inc:CA..... Main: (414) 381-1011
    TFree:(800) 877-8896   Fax:(415) 381-6902   Tech:(414) 381-1793
Spalding Software:GA .... Main: (770) 449-0594
    Fax:(770) 449-0052   Tech:(770) 449-0594
SPARC International Inc:CA .... Main: (408) 748-9111
    Fax:(408) 748-9777
Specialix:CA .... Main: (408) 378-7919
    TFree:(800) 423-5364   Fax:(408) 378-0786   Tech:(800) 423-5364
Specialized Products Co:TX .... Main: (214) 550-1923
    TFree:(800) 866-5353   Fax:(214) 550-1386   Tech:(800) 527-5018
Spectragraphics:CA .... Main: (619) 450-0611
    TFree:(800) 821-4822   Fax:(619) 450-0218   Tech:(900) 934-3200
    order:(619) 450-3213
Spectrum HoloByte Inc:CA.......................... Main: (510) 522-1164
    Fax:(510) 522-9357   Tech:(510) 522-1164
    Game Hint:(900) 773-4468
Spectrum Multimedia:WI .... Main: (608) 274-2778
    Fax:(608) 274-2791   Tech:(608) 274-2778
Spider Island Software:CA.......................... Main: (714) 453-8095
    Fax:(714) 453-8044   Tech:(714) 453-8095
Spinnaker Software (see Softkey):
Sprague Magnetics:CA .... Main: (818) 364-1800
    TFree:(800) 553-8712   Fax:(818) 364-1810   Tech:(800) 553-8712
Spry Inc:WA .... Main: (425) 957-8000
    TFree:(800) 957-8956   Fax:(425) 957-6000
    MAC Support:(425) 957-8998
SPSS:IL .... Main: (312) 329-2400
    TFree:(800) 521-1337   Fax:(312) 329-3668   Tech:(800) 543-2185
Spyglass:IL .... Main: (630) 505-1010
    TFree:(888) 677-9452   Fax:(630) 505-4944
SRW Computer Components:CA .... Main: (714) 963-5500
    TFree:(800) 547-7766   Fax:(714) 259-8037   Tech:(800) 547-7766
Stac Electronics (Mac):CA .... Main: (619) 794-4300
    TFree:(800) 305-7822   Fax:(619) 794-3717   Tech:(619) 794-3700

Stallion Technologies Inc:CA .... **Main: (408) 477-0440**
TFree:(800) 347-7979 Fax:(408) 477-0444 Tech:(800) 729-2342

Stampede Technologies Inc:OH .... **Main: (937) 291-5035**
TFree:(800) 763-3423 Fax:(937) 291-5040

Standard Microsystems Corp (see SMC):

Star Media Systems Corp (DPS Software):IL Main: (708) 305-4843
TFree:(800) 775-3314 Fax:(708) 355-4843 Tech:(708) 305-4843

Star Micronics America:NJ .... **Main: (732) 572-4512**
Fax:(732) 572-5095 Tech:(732) 572-9512

Starfish Software:CA .... **Main: (408) 461-5800**
TFree:(888) 782-7347 Fax:(408) 461-5900 Tech:(970) 522-4610
Questions about an order:(800) 765-7839

Starquest Connectivity Software:CA .... **Main: (510) 704-2000**
TFree:(800) 763-0050 Fax:(510) 704-2001 Tech:(510) 704-2570

State Of The Art:CA .... **Main: (916) 791-7730**
TFree:(800) 447-5700 Fax:(916) 791-5525 Tech:(800) 447-5700

STB Systems Inc:TX .... **Main: (972) 234-8750**
TFree:(800) 234-4334 Fax:(972) 234-1306 Tech:(972) 669-0989
Tech Support Fax:(972) 669-1326

Steinberg/Jones:CA .... **Main: (818) 993-4091**
Fax:(818) 701-7452 Tech:(818) 993-4161

STF Technologies Inc:MO .... **Main: (816) 463-7972**
TFree:(800) 771-6202 Fax:(816) 463-7958 Tech:(816) 463-2021

Storage Dimensions:CA .... **Main: (408) 954-0710**
TFree:(800) 765-7895 Fax:(408) 944-1200 Tech:(408) 894-1325

Storage Technology Corporation:CO .... **Main: (303) 673-5151**
TFree:(800) 786-7835 Fax:(303) 673-7577

Storm Technology:CA .... **Main: (650) 691-6600**
TFree:(800) 275-5734 Fax:(650) 691-9825 Tech:(650) 969-9555

Strata Distributing Inc:CA .... **Main: (510) 656-9848**
Fax:(510) 656-9891 Tech:(510) 656-9848

Strata Inc:UT .... **Main: (801) 628-5218**
TFree:(800) 678-7282 Fax:(801) 628-9756 Tech:(801) 628-9751
Tech Fax:(801) 652-5408

Strategic Mapping (see Software Support):

Strategic Networks Consulting Inc:MA .... **Main: (617) 912-8300**
TFree:(800) 999-7621 Fax:(617) 871-5339

Strategic Simulations Inc:CA .... **Main: (408) 737-6800**
TFree:(800) 601-7529 Fax:(408) 737-6814 Tech:(408) 737-6850

Strategic Studies Group:FL .... **Main: (904) 469-8880**
Fax:(904) 469-8885 Tech:(904) 469-8880

Street Electronics (see Echo Speech Corp):

Streetwise Software:CA .... **Main: (310) 829-7827**
TFree:(800) 743-6765 Fax:(310) 828-8258 Tech:(310) 998-3361

Structured Software (Facet Corp):TX .... **Main: (972) 985-9901**
TFree:(800) 235-9901 Fax:(972) 612-2035
Fax:(800) 982-9901

Structured Software Services Group:TX .... **Main: (972) 960-7555**
TFree:(800) 767-6547 Fax:(972) 991-3244

SubLOGIC:IL .... **Main: (217) 359-8482**
Fax:(217) 352-1472 Tech:(800) 637-4983

Summagraphics Corp (Cal Comp):CA .... **Main: (714) 821-2000**
TFree:(800) 451-7568 Fax:(714) 821-2832 Tech:(800) 444-3425

Sun Microsystems Computer Co:CA .... Main: **(415) 960-1300**
  TFree:(800) 821-4643 Fax:(650) 968-9506 Tech:(800) 872-4786
  PR Fax:(415) 786-8416
SunSoft (see Sun Microsystems Computer):
Superbase Inc:NY .... Main: **(516) 244-1500**
  TFree:(800) 315-7944 Fax:(516) 244-0250 Tech:(800) 315-7940
Supermac Technology (see Radius):
Supra Corp:OR .... Main: **(541) 967-2400**
  TFree:(800) 468-5846 Fax:(541) 967-2401 Tech:(541) 967-2400
  Reseller support:(541) 967-2495
... A Division of Diamond Multimedia Corp.. Main: **(360) 604-1400**
  TFree:(800) 727-8772 Fax:(360) 604-1401 Tech:(800) 727-8772
  Tech Support Fax:(541) 967-2401
... Amiga and other systems .... Main: **(541) 967-2493**
... Dealer .... Main: **(541) 967-2495**
... faxcilitate .... Main: **(541) 967-2492**
... International.. Main: **(360) 604-1400**
... MAC .... Main: **(541) 967-2492**
... PC.. Main: **(541) 967-2490**
Surflogic LLC:CA .... Main: **(415) 731-2732**
  Fax:(415) 731-0584
SusTeen Inc:CA .... Main: **(310) 787-1589**
  Fax:(310) 787-1590 Tech:(310) 787-1589
Swan Technologies Corp:MA......................... Main: **(800) 533-1131**
  TFree:(800) 446-2499 Fax:(508) 480-0156 Tech:(800) 468-7926
  Sales Fax:(814) 237-4450
Swfte International (Expert Software):
Sybase Inc:CA .... Main: **(510) 922-3555**
  TFree:(800) 879-2273 Fax:(510) 658-9441 Tech:(800) 879-2273
Sybex Inc:CA.. Main: **(510) 523-8233**
  TFree:(800) 227-2346 Fax:(510) 523-6840 Tech:(800) 227-2346
  Order Fax:(510) 523-2373
Symantec Corp:CA... Main: **(408) 253-9600**
  TFree:(800) 441-7234 Fax:(408) 253-3968 Tech:(900) 555-7700
  Customer Service:(800) 685-2349
... ACT! for Windows and MAC .... Main: **(408) 253-9600**
  TFree:(800) 441-7234 Tech:(541) 465-8645
  Tech support per incident fee:(800) 927-3989
... Enterprise Developer .... Main: **(408) 253-9600**
  TFree:(800) 441-7234 Tech:(541) 465-7860
  Tech support:(800) 927-6036
... Norton Admstr-Ntwrks,Dsklck,& NAV ...... Main: **(310) 453-4600**
  TFree:(800) 441-7234 Fax:(310) 453-0636 Tech:(541) 465-8484
  Tech support:(800) 927-4017
... Norton AntiVirus & SAM .... Main: **(310) 453-4600**
  TFree:(800) 441-7234 Fax:(310) 453-0636 Tech:(541) 465-8420
  Tech support per incident fee:(800) 927-3991
... Norton Desktop .... Main: **(310) 453-4600**
  TFree:(800) 441-7234 Fax:(310) 453-0636 Tech:(541) 465-8420
  Tech support per incident fee:(800) 927-3991
... Norton PC Anywhere................................... Main: **(310) 453-4600**
  TFree:(800) 441-7234 Fax:(310) 453-0636 Tech:(541) 465-8430
  Tech support per incident fee:(800) 927-4012

... Norton Utilities & DiskDoubler .... Main: **(310) 453-4600**
  TFree:(800) 441-7234 Fax:(310) 453-0636 Tech:(541) 465-8420
  Tech support per incident fee:(800) 927-3991

... Symantec C++ .... Main: **(408) 253-9600**
  TFree:(800) 441-7234 Fax:(541) 465-8470
  Tech support per incident fee:(800) 927-4014

... Customer Operations .... Main: **(541) 345-3322**
  TFree:(800) 441-7234 Fax:(541) 334-7473 Tech:(541) 465-8430
  Toll Free Fax on Demand:(800) 554-4403

Symbios Logic:CO .... Main: **(719) 596-5795**
  TFree:(800) 856-3093 Fax:(719) 536-3301 Tech:(800) 334-5454

Symbol Technologies:NY .... Main: **(516) 738-2400**
  TFree:(800) 722-6234 Fax:(516) 738-2831

Synchronics:TN .... Main: **(901) 761-1166**
  TFree:(800) 852-5852 Fax:(901) 683-8303 Tech:(800) 852-8755

Synergy Interactive Corp:CA .... Main: **(415) 437-2000**
  TFree:(800) 734-9466 Fax:(415) 431-3684 Tech:(800) 734-9466

Synergy Software:PA .... Main: **(610) 779-0522**
  TFree:(800) 876-8376 Fax:(610) 370-0548 Tech:(610) 779-0522

Synergy Solutions (see Artisoft):

Synex:NY .... Main: **(718) 499-6293**
  TFree:(800) 447-9639 Fax:(718) 768-3997 Tech:(718) 369-2944

SynOptics Commun (see Bay Network):

SyQuest Technology:CA .... Main: **(510) 226-4000**
  TFree:(800) 245-2278 Fax:(510) 226-4100 Tech:(800) 249-2440

SysKonnect:CA .... Main: **(408) 437-3857**
  TFree:(800) 752-3334 Fax:(408) 437-3866 Tech:(408) 437-3857

Systems Compatibility (see Inso):

Systems Plus Inc:CA .... Main: **(415) 969-7047**
  TFree:(800) 222-7701 Fax:(415) 969-8936 Tech:(415) 969-7066

SystemSoft Corp:MA .... Main: **(508) 651-0088**
  TFree:(800) 449-7973 Fax:(508) 651-8188 Tech:(508) 651-0088

Sytron Corp (see Arcada):

T/Maker Company:CA .... Main: **(415) 962-0195**
  TFree:(800) 986-2537 Fax:(415) 962-0201 Tech:(415) 962-0195

Tab Books/McGraw-Hill:PA .... Main: **(717) 794-2191**
  TFree:(800) 233-1128 Fax:(717) 794-2103

Tadiran:NY .... Main: **(516) 621-4980**
  TFree:(800) 537-1368 Fax:(516) 621-4517

Tadpole Technology Inc:TX .... Main: **(512) 219-2200**
  TFree:(800) 232-6656 Fax:(512) 219-2222 Tech:(800) 232-1881
  Sales:(800) 232-6656

Tallgrass Technologies (see Exabyte):

Talyon Software Corp:TX .... Main: **(713) 984-7626**
  Fax:(713) 984-7576

Tandem Computers Inc.:CA .... Main: **(408) 285-6000**
  TFree:(800) 482-6336 Tech:(800) 255-5010

Tandon (TSL Holdings Inc):CA .... Main: **(805) 582-6119**

Tandy Corp (see Radio Shack):

Tangent Computers Inc:CA .... Main: **(800) 342-9388**
  TFree:(888) 826-4368 Fax:(415) 342-9380 Tech:(800) 399-8324

Tangram:NC .... Main: **(919) 462-9096**
  TFree:(800) 482-6472 Fax:(919) 851-6004 Tech:(800) 722-2482

Tech Support Fax:(919) 851-6247

Targus:CA .... Main: **(714) 523-5429**
Fax:(714) 523-0153   Tech:(714) 523-5429

Tatung Company Of America:CA .... Main: **(310) 637-2105**
TFree:(800) 827-2850   Fax:(310) 637-8484   Tech:(800) 827-2850

Taylored Graphics:MI .... Main: **(313) 295-3302**
TFree:(800) 346-3629   Fax:(313) 295-3308

TDA/IPC:WA .... Main: **(425) 402-7000**
TFree:(800) 624-2101   Fax:(425) 402-1900   Tech:(425) 402-7000

TDA/WINK Data Products (see TDA/IPC):

TDK Electronics Corp:NY .... Main: **(516) 625-0100**
TFree:(800) 835-8273   Fax:(516) 625-0651   Tech:(800) 835-8273

TEAC America Inc:CA .... Main: **(213) 726-0303**
Fax:(213) 727-7656   Tech:(213) 726-4860

Tech Data Corp:FL .... Main: **(813) 539-7429**
TFree:(800) 237-8931   Fax:(813) 538-7816   Tech:(800) 553-7976

Tech Smith Corp:MI .... Main: **(517) 333-2100**
Fax:(517) 333-1888

Tech Tools:NH .... Main: **(603) 888-8400**
TFree:(800) 501-2677   Fax:(603) 888-8413   Tech:(603) 888-6721
Tech Fax:(603) 429-3833

Techmar Technologies Inc:CO .... Main: **(303) 682-3700**
TFree:(800) 422-2587   Fax:(303) 776-7706

Techni-Tool Inc:PA .... Main: **(610) 941-2400**
Fax:(610) 828-5623   Tech:(610) 941-2400

Technical Communications Corp:CO .... Main: **(303) 693-2408**

Technology Concepts (see Prometheus):

Technology Group Inc, The:MD .... Main: **(410) 576-2040**
Fax:(410) 576-1968   Tech:(410) 576-2040

Technology Works:TX .... Main: **(512) 794-8533**
TFree:(800) 814-3306   Fax:(512) 794-8520   Tech:(800) 688-7466

Tecmar (see Rexon Data Storage):

Tecmar Technologies:CO .... Main: **(303) 682-3700**
TFree:(800) 422-2587   Fax:(303) 776-7706

Tecra Tool:CO .... Main: **(303) 338-9224**
TFree:(800) 284-0808   Fax:(303) 338-9289   Tech:(800) 284-0808

Teknosys Inc (Total Recall):CO .... Main: **(719) 380-1616**
TFree:(800) 743-0566   Fax:(719) 380-7022   Tech:(719) 380-1616

Tekram Technology:TX .... Main: **(512) 833-6550**
TFree:(800) 556-6218   Fax:(512) 833-7276   Tech:(512) 833-8158

TekSoft Inc:AZ .... Main: **(602) 942-4982**
Fax:(602) 866-9016   Tech:(602) 942-4982

Tektronix:OR .... Main: **(503) 682-7737**
TFree:(800) 835-9433   Fax:(503) 682-2980   Tech:(800) 547-8949

Teldar Corp:AZ .... Main: **(602) 814-8400**

Telebit Corp:MA .... Main: **(508) 441-2181**
TFree:(800) 835-3248   Fax:(508) 441-9060   Tech:(800) 835-3248

Telemagic:CA .... Main: **(760) 431-4000**
Fax:(760) 438-7318   Tech:(760) 929-0193

Televideo Multimedia:CA .... Main: **(408) 954-8333**
TFree:(800) 345-6050   Fax:(408) 954-0931   Tech:(800) 345-6050

Teltone Corp:WA .... Main: **(206) 487-1515**
TFree:(800) 426-3926   Fax:(206) 487-2288

Template Graphics Software:CA .... Main: (619) 457-5359
   Fax:(619) 452-2547

Teradyne:MA .... Main: (617) 482-2700
   Fax:(617) 422-2910

Texas Instruments Inc:TX.................................. Main: (214) 995-6611
   TFree:(800) 848-3927   Fax:(800) 443-2984   Tech:(800) 848-3927

Texas Memory Systems Inc:TX........................... Main: (713) 266-3200
   Fax:(713) 266-0332

Texas Microsystems:TX...................................... Main: (713) 541-8200
   TFree:(800) 627-8700   Fax:(713) 541-8226

The Coriolis Group Inc:AZ.................................. Main: (602) 483-0192
   TFree:(800) 410-0192   Fax:(602) 483-0193

The Inference Corp:CA.. Main: (415) 893-7200
   TFree:(800) 332-9923   Fax:(415) 899-9080

The Other 90% Technologies Inc:CA .... Main: (415) 460-9710
   Fax:(415) 460-1919   Tech:(415) 460-9710

Thermalloy Inc:TX.. Main: (972) 243-4321
   Fax:(972) 241-4656   Fax:(972) 243-4321

Thomas Computer Corporation:FL .... Main: (407) 855-2020
   TFree:(800) 621-3906   Fax:(407) 851-9700

Thomas-Conrad Corp (see Compaq Computer Gp):

Three-Sixty Intracorp:TX .... Main: (409) 776-0876
   TFree:(800) 468-7226   Fax:(409) 774-0960   Tech:(409) 776-2187

Thrust Master Inc:OR .... Main: (503) 615-3200
   Fax:(503) 615-3300

Thynx:NJ... Main: (609) 514-1600
   Fax:(609) 514-1818   Tech:(609) 514-1600

Tiara Computer Sys (see Internex Info Serv):

TigerSoftware:FL .... Main: (305) 229-1119
   TFree:(800) 879-1597   Fax:(305) 228-3400

Timberline Software:OR .... Main: (503) 626-6775
   Fax:(503) 641-7498

Time Motion Tools:CA... Main: (619) 679-0303
   TFree:(800) 779-8170   Fax:(619) 679-8171   Tech:(619) 679-0303

Timeslips Corp:TX... Main: (972) 248-9232
   TFree:(800) 285-0999   Fax:(972) 248-9245   Tech:(508) 768-7490
   Tech Fax:(508) 768-7532

Tivoli Systems:TX .... Main: (512) 794-9070
   Fax:(512) 794-0623   Tech:(512) 794-9070

TMS Sequoia:OK.. Main: (405) 377-0880
   TFree:(800) 944-7654   Fax:(405) 372-9288
   Tech Fax:(405) 377-0450

Tool Kit Specialists (see Com-Kyle):

Top Speed Corp:FL .... Main: (954) 785-4555
   TFree:(800) 354-5444   Fax:(954) 946-1650   Tech:(954) 785-4556

Toray Industries:CA .... Main: (415) 341-7152
   TFree:(800) 867-9273   Fax:(415) 341-0845   Tech:(415) 341-7152

Toshiba Amer Consumer Products:IL .... Main: (201) 628-8000
   TFree:(800) 253-5429   Fax:(201) 628-1875   Tech:(201) 628-8000

Toshiba Amer Information Systems:CA .... Main: (714) 583-3000
   TFree:(800) 457-7777   Fax:(800) 950-4373   Tech:(714) 455-0407

Toshiba America:NY .... Main: (212) 596-0600
   Fax:(212) 593-3875

Toshiba America:
... CD Rom Support .... Main: (312) 380-4047
... Disk Products Division .... Main: (714) 457-0777
   Tech:(714) 455-0407
... Disk Products Repair Center .... Main: (408) 428-6435
... Laptop Support .... Main: (800) 999-4273
... PC Support .... Main: (800) 999-4273
... Printer Support .... Main: (800) 468-6744
... Warranty
   TFree:(800) 999-4273
Tosoh USA Inc:CA .... Main: (415) 286-2385
   TFree:(800) 238-6764 Fax:(415) 286-2392 Tech:(415) 286-2385
Total Computer Supplies:MI .... Main: (810) 673-5000
Total Management Inc:IN .... Main: (812) 476-5049
   TFree:(800) 553-5783 Fax:(812) 476-5145 Tech:(800) 553-5783
Totally Hip Software Inc:BC .... Main: (604) 685-6525
   Fax:(604) 685-4057   Tech:(604) 685-0984
TouchStone Software Corp:CA .... Main: (714) 969-7746
   TFree:(800) 531-0450 Fax:(714) 969-4444 Tech:(714) 374-2801
Trade'Ex Electronic Commerce System:FL..Main: (813) 222-2050
   Fax:(813) 222-5658
Transcend Information Inc:CA .... Main: (714) 921-2000
   TFree:(800) 886-5590 Fax:(714) 921-2111 Tech:(714) 921-2000
Transparent Language Inc:NH .... Main: (603) 465-2230
   Fax:(603) 465-2779
Trantor Systems Ltd (see Adaptec):
Traquair Data Systems Inc:NY .... Main: (607) 266-6000
   Fax:(607) 266-8221
Traveling Software:WA .... Main: (425) 483-8088
   TFree:(800) 343-8080 Fax:(425) 485-6786 Tech:(425) 487-8803
Trend Micro Devices Inc:CA .... Main: (408) 257-1500
   TFree:(800) 586-7803 Fax:(408) 257-2003 Tech:(310) 936-1188
Tri-Mark Engineering:TN .... Main: (615) 966-3667
   Fax:(615) 675-3458   Tech:(615) 966-3667
Tri-Star Computer:AZ .... Main: (602) 731-4926
   TFree:(800) 844-2993 Fax:(602) 731-4979 Tech:(602) 731-4926
Tribe Computer Works (Zoom Telephon) ..... Main: (617) 423-1072
   TFree:(800) 778-7423 Tech:(617) 753-0700
Trident Microsystems Inc:CA .... Main: (415) 691-9211
   Fax:(415) 691-9260   Tech:(415) 934-2123
TriniTech Inc:FL .... Main: (813) 442-8882
   TFree:(800) 909-3424 Fax:(813) 581-4411 Tech:(813) 442-8882
Trio Information Systems:NC .... Main: (919) 846-4990
   Fax:(919) 846-4997   Tech:(919) 846-4985
Tripp Lite/Datashield:IL .... Main: (312) 755-5400
   Fax:(312) 644-6505   Tech:(312) 755-5401
   Order desk:(312) 755-5408
Trius Inc:MA .... Main: (508) 794-9377
   TFree:(800) 468-7487 Fax:(508) 688-6312 Tech:(508) 794-0140
Truevision:CA .... Main: (317) 841-0332
   TFree:(800) 522-8783 Fax:(317) 576-7770 Tech:(800) 522-8783

Tseng Laboratories Inc:PA .... Main: **(215) 968-0502**
Fax:(215) 860-7713   Tech:(215) 968-0502
TSSI/Rexon Service:CA .... Main: **(805) 778-1773**
TFree:(800) 286-0651   Fax:(805) 373-3000   Tech:(800) 992-9916
Tucker Electronics:TX .... Main: **(214) 348-8800**
TFree:(800) 527-4642   Fax:(214) 348-0367
Tulin Technology:MA .... Main: **(508) 283-2100**
Fax:(508) 281-3125
Turbopower Software Company:CO .... Main: **(719) 260-9136**
TFree:(800) 333-4160   Fax:(719) 260-7151   Tech:(719) 260-6641
Turtle Beach Systems:NY .... Main: **(810)**
TFree:(800) 233-9377   Fax:(914) 966-1102   Tech:(914) 966-2150
Tut Systems (Tutankhamon Elec):CA .... Main: **(510) 682-6510**
TFree:(800) 998-4888   Fax:(510) 682-4125   Tech:(800) 998-4888
Twelve Tone Systems (Cake Walk Music):
Twilight Technologies:MI .... Main: **(810) 695-8933**
Fax:(810) 695-8706
TwinBridge Software Corp:CA .... Main: **(213) 263-3926**
TFree:(800) 894-6114   Fax:(213) 263-8126   Tech:(213) 263-5931
Twinhead Corp:CA .... Main: **(510) 492-0828**
TFree:(800) 995-8946   Fax:(510) 492-0832   Tech:(510) 492-0828
Tyan Computer Corp:CA .... Main: **(408) 956-8000**
Fax:(408) 956-8044   Tech:(408) 935-7884
Typhoon Software:CA .... Main: **(805) 966-7633**
TFree:(800) 499-0888   Fax:(805) 962-6811   Tech:(805) 966-7633
U.S. Robotics Inc:IL .... Main: **(847) 982-5010**
TFree:(800) 550-7800   Fax:(847) 982-0823   Tech:(800) 982-5151
UB Networks Inc:CA .... Main: **(408) 496-0111**
Ulead Systems Inc:CA .... Main: **(310) 523-9393**
TFree:(800) 858-5323   Fax:(310) 523-9399   Tech:(310) 523-9391
Ultra-X Inc:CA .... Main: **(408) 261-7090**
TFree:(800) 722-3789   Fax:(408) 261-7077   Tech:(408) 261-7090
UltraCoach:CA .... Main: **(909) 625-0463**
TFree:(800) 400-1390   Fax:(909) 625-4504   Tech:(909) 398-1870
UMAX Technologies Inc:CA .... Main: **(510) 651-4000**
TFree:(800) 562-0311   Fax:(510) 651-2610   Tech:(510) 651-8883
Underware:MA .... Main: **(617) 267-9743**
TFree:(800) 343-7308   Fax:(617) 424-1839
Unicorn Multimedia:NV .... Main: **(702) 597-0818**
Fax:(702) 597-0008
Unimark Inc:KS .... Main: **(913) 649-2424**
TFree:(800) 255-6356   Fax:(913) 649-5795
Unison Software Inc:CA .... Main: **(408) 988-2800**
TFree:(800) 298-4149   Fax:(408) 988-2236   Tech:(408) 988-2800
Unisys Corp:NY .... Main: **(716) 924-0480**
TFree:(800) 448-1424   Fax:(716) 742-6671   Tech:(800) 328-0440
Univel (see Novell):
Universal Software:CA .... Main: **(310) 866-1274**
University Research & Development:PA ...... Main: **(412) 363-0990**
TFree:(800) 338-0517

Unixware (see Novell):
USA Flex (see Comark Inc):
V Communications Inc:CA..**Main: (408) 965-4000**
TFree:(800) 648-8266   Fax:(408) 965-4014   Tech:(408) 965-4018
V-One Corp:MD...**Main: (301) 515-5200**
Fax:(301) 515-5280
ValueStor Inc:CA..**Main: (408) 437-2300**
TFree:(800) 873-8258   Fax:(408) 437-9333   Tech:(408) 437-2310
ValueWare Software:TN...**Main: (423) 675-7958**
TFree:(800) 441-7604   Fax:(423) 675-0657
Varta Batteries:NY..**Main: (914) 592-2500**
TFree:(800) 468-2782   Fax:(914) 592-2667
Vartech Inc (Out of Business):
VDONet Corp:CA..**Main: (415) 846-7700**
Fax:(415) 846-7900
Velocity Inc:CA..**Main: (415) 274-8840**
TFree:(800) 856-2489   Fax:(415) 776-8099   Tech:(415) 274-8840
Velocity Inc:CA..**Main: (415) 776-8000**
TFree:(800) 856-2489   Fax:(415) 776-8099   Tech:(415) 776-8000
Ven-Tel Inc:CA...**Main: (408) 436-7400**
TFree:(800) 538-5121   Fax:(408) 436-7451   Tech:(800) 538-5121
Ventana Communications Group:NC............**Main: (919) 544-9404**
TFree:(800) 332-7450   Fax:(919) 544-9472   Tech:(919) 544-9404
Ventura Software (see Corel):
VenturCom Inc:MA..**Main: (617) 661-1230**
TFree:(800) 334-8649   Fax:(617) 577-1607
Verbatim Corp:CA...**Main: (408) 773-3807**
TFree:(800) 538-8589   Fax:(746) 746-3877   Tech:(800) 538-8589
Verbatim Corp:NC...**Main: (704) 547-6500**
TFree:(888) 837-2284   Fax:(704) 547-6565
Verbex Voice Systems Inc:NJ.....................................**Main: (908) 225-5225**
TFree:(888) 483-7239   Fax:(908) 225-7764   Tech:(888) 483-7239
VeriFone:CA...**Main: (415) 591-5504**
TFree:(800) 654-1674   Fax:(415) 598-5504
VeriSign Inc:CA...**Main: (415) 961-7500**
Fax:(415) 961-7300   Tech:(415) 429-3400
Verity Inc:CA...**Main: (408) 541-1500**
Fax:(408) 541-1600   Tech:(408) 542-2222
Tech Fax:(408) 542-2031
Vermont Microsystems:VT..**Main: (802) 655-2860**
TFree:(800) 354-0055   Fax:(802) 655-9058   Tech:(800) 354-0055
Versant Object Technology:CA.....................................**Main: (510) 789-1500**
TFree:(800) 837-7268   Fax:(510) 789-1515
Vertex Industries:NJ..**Main: (201) 503-1919**
Fax:(201) 472-0814   Tech:(201) 777-3500
Vertisoft Systems:SC..**Main: (803) 295-5875**
TFree:(800) 466-5875   Fax:(800) 466-4719   Tech:(803) 269-9969
Vertisoft Systems (Corporate):CA.............................**Main: (415) 956-5999**
Fax:(415) 956-5355
Viacom New Media C/O Star Pak:CO...........................**Main: (303) 339-7114**
TFree:(800) 469-2539   Fax:(303) 339-7022   Tech:(303) 339-7114
ViaGrafix Corp:OK...**Main: (918) 825-7555**
TFree:(800) 233-3223   Fax:(918) 825-6359   Tech:(918) 825-4844

Victory Enterprises Tech:TX .... Main: **(512) 450-0801**
TFree:(800) 727-3475 Fax:(512) 450-0869

Video Electronic Standards Assn:CA .... Main: **(408) 435-0333**
Fax:(408) 435-8225

Videodiscovery Inc:WA .... Main: **(206) 285-5400**
TFree:(800) 548-3472 Fax:(206) 285-9245 Tech:(800) 548-3472

VideoLogic Inc:CA .... Main: **(415) 875-0606**
TFree:(800) 578-5644 Fax:(415) 875-4167

Viewpoint DataLabs:UT .... Main: **(801) 229-3000**
TFree:(800) 328-2738 Fax:(801) 229-3300 Tech:(801) 229-3000
Tech Fax:(801) 229-3384

ViewSonic Corp:CA .... Main: **(909) 869-7976**
TFree:(800) 888-8583 Fax:(909) 869-7958 Tech:(909) 468-5800

Vireo Software Inc:MA .... Main: **(508) 264-9200**
Fax:(508) 264-9205

Virgil Corp:CA .... Main: **(415) 433-9025**
TFree:(800) 662-8256 Fax:(415) 433-8411 Tech:(415) 433-9025

Virgin Interactive Entertainment:CA .... Main: **(714) 833-1999**
Fax:(714) 833-8717 Tech:(714) 833-1999

Virtual Comtech International Inc:MI .... Main: **(616) 399-8934**
Fax:(616) 399-8934 Tech:(616) 399-8934
another BBS:(616) 399-8791

Virtual I/O:WA .... Main: **(206) 382-7410**
TFree:(800) 646-3759 Fax:(206) 382-8810 Tech:(206) 382-4558

Virtual Publisher: .... Main: **(702) 833-0622**
Fax:(702) 833-0677

Virtual Reality Laboratories:CA .... Main: **(805) 545-8515**
TFree:(800) 829-8754 Fax:(805) 781-2259 Tech:(805) 545-8515

Virtual Technologies (Virtual Comtech):

Virtual Vegas:CA .... Main: **(310) 581-3636**
TFree:(800) 958-3427 Fax:(310) 581-3645 Tech:(310) 581-3649

Virtus Corp:NC .... Main: **(919) 467-9700**
TFree:(800) 847-8871 Fax:(919) 460-4530 Tech:(919) 467-9700

Visio Corp:WA .... Main: **(206) 521-4500**
TFree:(800) 248-4746 Fax:(206) 521-4501 Tech:(541) 882-8687
Tech Fax:(541) 882-8446

Vision Imaging (see Advanced Media):

Vision Research Inc:NJ .... Main: **(201) 696-4500**
TFree:(800) 737-6588 Fax:(201) 696-0560

Visionary Software (see First Things First):

Visioneer Communications:CA .... Main: **(510) 608-0300**
TFree:(800) 787-7007 Fax:(415) 493-0399 Tech:(541) 884-5548
Tech Fax:(716) 871-2138

Visiware:NY .... Main: **(212) 737-6967**
Fax:(212) 794-5038 Fax:(212) 737-6967

Visual Business Systems:MA .... Main: **(508) 263-9900**
Fax:(508) 263-9957

Visual Numerics:TX .... Main: **(713) 784-3131**
TFree:(800) 222-4675 Fax:(713) 781-9260

Viziflex Seels:NJ .... Main: **(201) 487-8080**
TFree:(800) 307-3357 Fax:(201) 487-6637

VMark Software Inc:MA .... Main: **(508) 366-3888**
TFree:(800) 486-9636 Fax:(508) 366-3669 Tech:(800) 729-3553

VocalTec Inc:NJ .... Main: (201) 768-9400
  Fax:(201) 768-8893   Tech:(201) 768-9400

Voxware Inc:NJ .... Main: (609) 514-4100
  Fax:(609) 514-4101

Voyager Company, The:NY .... Main: (212) 431-5199
  TFree:(800) 446-2001 Fax:(212) 431-5799 Tech:(212) 219-2522

Voyetra Technologies:NY .... Main: (914) 966-0600
  TFree:(800) 233-9377 Fax:(914) 966-1102 Tech:(914) 966-0600

VST Power Systems:MA .... Main: (508) 287-4600
  Fax:(508) 287-4068   Tech:(508) 287-4600

Wacom Technology Corp:WA .... Main: (360) 750-8882
  TFree:(800) 922-9348 Fax:(360) 750-8924 Tech:(360) 750-8882

Waite Group Press:CA .... Main: (415) 924-2575
  TFree:(800) 368-9369 Fax:(415) 924-2576 Tech:(317) 581-3833

Walker Richer & Quinn Inc:WA .... Main: (206) 217-7500
  TFree:(800) 872-2829 Fax:(206) 217-0293 Tech:(206) 217-7000

Wall Data Inc:WA .... Main: (415) 812-1600
  TFree:(800) 915-9255 Fax:(415) 856-9265 Tech:(800) 915-9255

Walnut Creek CDROM:CA .... Main: (510) 674-0783
  TFree:(800) 786-9907 Fax:(510) 674-0821 Tech:(510) 603-1234

Wang Laboratories Inc:MA .... Main: (508) 967-5000
  TFree:(800) 225-0654 Fax:(508) 967-0829 Tech:(800) 247-9264

Wangtek/WangDAT (see Tecmar Tech):

Warever Corp:UT .... Main: (801) 572-2555
  TFree:(800) 766-7229 Fax:(801) 572-2444 Tech:(801) 572-8923

Washburn & Co:NY .... Main: (716) 385-5200
  TFree:(800) 836-8026 Fax:(716) 381-7549 Tech:(800) 836-8026

Watergate Software Inc:CA .... Main: (510) 596-1770
  Fax:(510) 596-2092   Tech:(510) 704-0160

Waterloo Maple Software:ON .... Main: (519) 747-2373
  TFree:(800) 267-6583 Fax:(519) 747-5284 Tech:(800) 267-6583

Watermark Business Unit:MA .... Main: (617) 229-2600
  Fax:(617) 229-2989   Tech:(714) 850-7680

Wavefront:ON .... Main: (416) 362-9181
  Fax:(416) 362-1276   Tech:(800) 465-0868

Wavefront Communications:MN .... Main: (612) 638-9594
  Fax:(612) 603-0269

Wavetek Corp:CA .... Main: (619) 279-2200
  TFree:(800) 854-2708 Fax:(619) 627-0130 Tech:(619) 279-2200

Wayzata Technology Inc (Out of Business):

WebManage Technologies Inc:NH .... Main: (603) 594-9226
  Fax:(603) 594-9227

WebMaster Inc:CA .... Main: (408) 345-1800
  Fax:(408) 247-9372

WeiSheng Enterprise Co (Compucase):CA .. Main: (310) 464-2646
  Fax:(310) 464-2648

Weitek Corp:CA .... Main: (408) 526-0300
  TFree:(800) 880-2885 Fax:(408) 577-1066 Tech:(408) 522-7600

Westbrook Technologies Inc:CT .... Main: (203) 483-6666
  Fax:(203) 483-3350   Tech:(203) 483-6666

Westech Corp:NJ .... Main: **(201) 729-6584**
TFree:(800) 829-4767   Fax:(201) 729-0431   Tech:(800) 745-4378

Western Digital Corp:CA .... Main: **(714) 932-5000**
TFree:(800) 832-4778   Fax:(714) 932-6294   Tech:(800) 832-4778

Western Micro Technology Inc:CA .... Main: **(408) 379-0177**
TFree:(800) 338-1600   Fax:(408) 341-4762

Western Scientific Inc:CA .... Main: **(619) 565-6699**
TFree:(800) 443-6699   Fax:(619) 565-6938

Western Telematic Inc:CA .... Main: **(714) 586-9950**
TFree:(800) 854-7226   Fax:(714) 583-9514   Tech:(800) 854-7226

Westwood Studios (see Virgin Interactive):

White Pine Software Inc:NH .... Main: **(603) 886-9050**
TFree:(800) 241-7463   Fax:(603) 886-9051

Whittaker Xyplex:MA .... Main: **(508) 952-4700**
TFree:(800) 338-5316   Fax:(508) 952-4702   Tech:(800) 435-7997

Wholesale Computer Exchange:CT .... Main: **(203) 459-8222**
Fax:(203) 459-8022

WildCard Technologies Inc:ON .... Main: **(905) 731-6444**
Fax:(905) 731-7017

Willies Computer Software:TX .... Main: **(281) 360-4232**
TFree:(800) 966-4832   Fax:(281) 360-3231   Tech:(281) 360-3187

Willow Peripherals (Pulse Systems):NY ...... Main: **(516) 329-4222**
TFree:(800) 444-1585   Fax:(718) 402-9603   Tech:(800) 933-6003

Windata:MA .... Main: **(508) 952-0170**
TFree:(800) 553-8008   Fax:(508) 952-0168   Tech:(508) 952-0170

Windows User Magazine:NY .... Main: **(212) 302-2626**

Windsoft International Inc:FL .... Main: **(407) 240-2300**
TFree:(800) 542-4455   Fax:(407) 240-2323   Tech:(407) 240-3350

Windsor Technologies Inc:CA .... Main: **(415) 456-2200**
Fax:(415) 456-2244   Tech:(415) 456-2200

Wingra Technologies Inc:WI .... Main: **(608) 238-4454**
TFree:(800) 544-5465   Fax:(608) 238-8986   Tech:(608) 238-4454

WinSoft Corp:CA .... Main: **(714) 833-8838**
TFree:(800) 494-6763   Fax:(714) 833-8862   Tech:(714) 833-8838

WinWay Corp:CA .... Main: **(916) 965-7878**
TFree:(800) 494-6929   Fax:(916) 965-7879   Tech:(916) 965-7878

Wired Magazine:CA .... Main: **(415) 276-5000**
TFree:(800) 769-4733   Fax:(415) 276-5100

Wiz Technology Inc:CA .... Main: **(714) 443-3000**
Fax:(714) 443-2333   Tech:(714) 443-2374

Wizardware Multimedia Ltd:PA .... Main: **(610) 866-9613**
TFree:(800) 548-7969   Fax:(610) 691-8258   Tech:(900) 225-5570

Wizardworks Group Inc:MN .... Main: **(612) 559-5301**
TFree:(800) 229-2714   Fax:(612) 577-0631   Tech:(612) 559-5301

Wollongong (Attachmate):WA .... Main: **(425) 644-4010**
TFree:(800) 426-6283   Fax:(512) 480-8429   Tech:(425) 957-4607

Wonderware Corp:CA .... Main: **(714) 727-3200**
Fax:(714) 727-3270   Tech:(714) 727-3299

WordPerfect Corporation (Corel):

WordStar International (see Softkey):

Wordstar USA (see Softkey Intl):

Working Software Inc:CA .... Main: **(408) 423-5696**
TFree:(800) 229-9675   Fax:(408) 423-5699

World Software Corp:NJ .... Main: (201) 444-3228
  TFree:(800) 962-6360 Fax:(201) 444-9065 Tech:(201) 444-3290
Worldcomm Systems Inc (Globecomm Sys) Main: (516) 231-9800
  Fax:(516) 231-1557
Worthington Data Solutions:CA .... Main: (408) 458-9938
  TFree:(800) 345-4220 Fax:(408) 458-9964
Wrox Press:IL .... Main: (312) 397-1900
  TFree:(800) 814-4527 Fax:(312) 397-8990
WRQ:WA .... Main: (206) 217-7500
  TFree:(800) 872-2829 Fax:(206) 217-0293 Tech:(206) 217-7515
Wyse Technology:CA .... Main: (408) 473-1200
  TFree:(800) 438-9973 Fax:(408) 473-2401 Tech:(888) 997-3435
X-10 (USA) Inc:NJ .... Main: (201) 784-9700
  TFree:(800) 411-2888 Fax:(201) 784-9464 Tech:(201) 784-1936
X3 Secretarist (see ICA):
XBR Communication:PQ .... Main: (514) 735-9040
  Fax:(514) 735-4969
XcelleNet Inc:GA .... Main: (770) 804-8100
  Fax:(770) 804-8102
Xconsortium (The Open Group):MA .... Main: (617) 621-8700
  Fax:(617) 621-0631
Xebec (Out of Business):
XenoSoft (Cisin, Fred):CA .... Main: (510) 644-9366
Xerox Corp:NY .... Main: (800) 821-2797
Xerox Corporation:NY .... Main: (716) 423-5090
  Tech:(800) 822-2979
Xerox Imaging Systems (Xerox DDS):MA ..... Main: (508) 977-2000
  TFree:(800) 248-6550 Tech:(800) 248-6550
Xerox/X-Soft:CA .... Main: (415) 424-0111
  TFree:(800) 334-6200 Fax:(415) 813-7181
Xinet Inc:CA .... Main: (510) 845-0555
  Fax:(510) 644-2680
Xing Technology Corp:CA .... Main: (805) 783-0400
  TFree:(800) 298-6448 Fax:(805) 783-4930
Xircom Inc:CA .... Main: (805) 376-9300
  TFree:(800) 438-4526 Fax:(805) 376-9311 Tech:(805) 376-9200
  Support Fax:(805) 376-9100
Xtend Micro Products:CA .... Main: (714) 699-1400
  TFree:(800) 232-9836 Fax:(714) 699-1434
XTree Company (see Symantec Corp):
Xylogics Inc (see Bay Networks):
Yamaha Corporation Of America:CA .... Main: (714) 522-9011
  TFree:(800) 823-6414 Fax:(714) 527-5782 Tech:(714) 522-9000
Yamaha Systems Technology Inc:CA .... Main: (408) 467-2300
  TFree:(800) 543-7457 Fax:(408) 437-8791
YBM Magnex Inc:PA .... Main: (215) 956-9300
  TFree:(800) 692-5296 Fax:(215) 579-3444 Tech:(215) 579-0400
Young Chang America:CA .... Main: (562) 926-3200
  Fax:(310) 404-0748
Young Minds Inc:CA .... Main: (909) 335-1350
  TFree:(800) 964-4964 Fax:(909) 798-0488
Z-Code Software (NetMet Manage):CA .... Main: (415) 898-8649
  Fax:(415) 898-8299

Z-Ram (see Camintonn Z-Ram):
Zebra Technologies:IL .... Main: **(847) 634-6700**
  TFree:(800) 423-0422 Fax:(847) 913-8766 Tech:(847) 634-6700
Zedcor:AZ .... Main: **(520) 881-8101**
  TFree:(800) 482-4567 Fax:(520) 881-1841 Tech:(520) 881-2310
Zenith Data Systems Crp (Packard Bell):VA Main: **(703) 713-3023**
  TFree:(800) 654-1394 Fax:(703) 713-3001 Tech:(800) 227-3360
Zenographics Inc:CA .... Main: **(714) 851-6352**
  TFree:(800) 366-7494 Fax:(714) 851-1314 Tech:(714) 851-2191
  $2.00 per minute:(900) 555-9366
Zeos International (Div of Micron):MN .... Main: **(612) 663-4591**
  TFree:(800) 423-5891 Fax:(612) 663-5224 Tech:(612) 633-7337
  Marketing:(208) 465-3434
Ziff-Davis Publishing (PC Week News): .... Main: **(212) 503-5446**
Ziff-Davis Publishing Co:NY .... Main: **(212) 503-5446**
Zilog Inc:CA .... Main: **(408) 370-8000**
  Fax:(408) 370-8056
Zoom Telephonics Inc:MA .... Main: **(617) 423-1072**
  TFree:(800) 666-6191 Fax:(617) 423-3923 Tech:(617) 423-1076
ZSoft Corp (see Softkey):
ZyLAB Corp:MD .... Main: **(301) 590-0900**
  TFree:(800) 544-6339 Fax:(301) 590-0903
ZyPCsom Inc:CA .... Main: **(510) 783-2501**
  Fax:(510) 783-2414   Tech:(510) 783-2501
ZyXEL USA:CA .... Main: **(714) 693-0808**
  TFree:(800) 255-4101 Fax:(714) 693-8811 Tech:(714) 693-0808

D

E

Index   **541**

Index   543

Notes

_____

_____

_____

_____

_____

_____

_____

_____

_____

_____

_____

_____

_____

_____

_____

_____

_____

_____

_____

_____

_____

_____

_____

_____

_____

_____